Lecture Notes in Computer Science 5416

Commenced Publication in 1973
Founding and Former Series Editors:
Gerhard Goos, Juris Hartmanis, and Jan van Leeuwen

Frank Nielsen (Ed.)

Emerging Trends in Visual Computing

LIX Fall Colloquium, ETVC 2008
Palaiseau, France, November 18-20, 2008
Revised Invited Papers

 Springer

Volume Editor

Frank Nielsen
Ecole Polytechnique, LIX
Route de Saclay, 91128 Palaiseau Cedex, France
E-mail: nielsen@lix.polytechnique.fr

Library of Congress Control Number: Applied for

CR Subject Classification (1998): I.4, I.5, I.2.10, I.3.3, I.3.5, I.3.7, I.2.6, F.2, G.1.2

LNCS Sublibrary: SL 6 – Image Processing, Computer Vision, Pattern Recognition, and Graphics

ISSN   0302-9743
ISBN-10   3-642-00825-9 Springer Berlin Heidelberg New York
ISBN-13   978-3-642-00825-2 Springer Berlin Heidelberg New York

springer.com

© Springer-Verlag Berlin Heidelberg 2009
Printed in Germany

Typesetting: Camera-ready by author, data conversion by Scientific Publishing Services, Chennai, India
Printed on acid-free paper   SPIN: 12612574   06/3180   5 4 3 2 1 0

Preface

ETVC 2008, the fall colloquium of the computer science department (LIX) of the École Polytechnique, held in Palaiseau, France, November 18-20, 2008, focused on the Emerging Trends in Visual Computing. The colloquium gave scientists the opportunity to sketch a state-of-the-art picture of the mathematical foundations of visual computing.

We were delighted to invite and welcome the following distinguished speakers to ETVC 2008 (listed in alphabetical order):

- Shun-ichi AMARI (Mathematical Neuroscience Laboratory, Brain Science Institute, RIKEN, Wako-Shi, Japan): *Information Geometry and Its Applications*

- Tetsuo ASANO (School of Information Science, Japan Advanced Institute of Science and Technology, JAIST, Japan): *Constant-Working-Space Algorithms for Image Processing*

- Francis BACH (INRIA/ENS, France): *Machine Learning and Kernel Methods for Computer Vision*

- Frédéric BARBARESCO (Thales Air Systems, France): *Applications of Information Geometry to Radar Signal Processing*

- Michel BARLAUD (I3S CNRS, University of Nice-Sophia-Antipolis, Polytech'Nice & Institut Universitaire de France, France): *Image Retrieval via Kullback Divergence of Patches of Wavelets Coefficients in the k-NN Framework*

- Jean-Daniel BOISSONNAT (GEOMETRICA, INRIA Sophia-Antipolis, France): *Certified Mesh Generation*

- Pascal FUA (EPFL, CVLAB, Switzerland): *Recovering Shape and Motion from Video Sequences*

- Markus GROSS (Department of Computer Science, Institute of Scientific Computing, Swiss Federal Institute of Technology Zurich, ETHZ, Switzerland): *3D Video: A Fusion of Graphics and Vision*

- Xianfeng David GU (State University of New York at Stony Brook, USA): *Discrete Curvature Flow for Surfaces and 3-Manifolds*

- Leonidas GUIBAS (Computer Science Department, Stanford University, USA): *Detection of Symmetries and Repeated Patterns in 3D Point Cloud Data*

- Sylvain LAZARD (VEGAS, INRIA LORIA Nancy, France): *3D Visibility and Lines in Space*

- Stéphane MALLAT (École Polytechnique, Centre de Mathématiques Appliquées (CMAP), France): *Sparse Geometric Super-Resolution*

- Hiroshi MATSUZOE (Department of Computer Science and Engineering, Graduate School of Engineering, Nagoya Institute of Technology, NITECH, Japan): *Computational Geometry from the Viewpoint of Affine Differential Geometry*

- Dimitris METAXAS (Computational Biomedicine Imaging and Modeling Center, CBMI, Rutgers University, USA): *Unifying Subspace and Distance Metric Learning with Bhattacharyya Coefficient for Image Classification*

- Frank NIELSEN (LIX, École Polytechnique, Paris, France & Sony Computer Science Laboratories Inc., Tokyo, Japan): *Computational Geometry in Dually Flat Spaces: Theory, Applications and Perspectives*

- Richard NOCK (CEREGMIA, University of Antilles-Guyane, France): *The Intrinsic Geometries of Learning*

- Nikos PARAGIOS (École Centrale de Paris, ECP, Paris, France): *Procedural Modeling of Architectures: Towards Large Scale Visual Reconstruction*

- Xavier PENNEC (ASCLEPIOS, INRIA Sophia-Antipolis, France): *Statistical Computing on Manifolds for Computational Anatomy*

- Ramesh RASKAR (MIT Media Lab, USA): *Computational Photography: Epsilon to Coded Imaging*

- Cordelia SCHMID (LEAR, INRIA Grenoble, France): *Large-Scale Object Recognition Systems*

- Gabriel TAUBIN (Division of Engineering, Brown University, USA): *Shape from Depth Discontinuities*

- Baba VEMURI (CISE Dept., University of Florida, USA): *Information-Theoretic Algorithms for Diffusion Tensor Imaging*

- Suresh VENKATASUBRAMANIAN (School of Computing, University of Utah, USA): *Non-standard Geometries and Data Analysis*

- Martin VETTERLI (School of Computer and Communication Sciences, EPFL, Switzerland): *Sparse Sampling: Variations on a Theme by Shannon*

- Jun ZHANG (Department of Psychology, University of Michigan, USA): *Information Geometry: Duality, Convexity and Divergences*

Invited speakers were encouraged to submit a state-of-the-art chapter on their research area. The review process was carried out by members of the Program Committee and other reviewers. We would like to sincerely thank the contributing authors and thank the reviewers for the careful feedback that helped the authors prepare their camera-ready papers.

Videos of the lectures synchronized with slides are available from

www.videolectures.net

We were very pleased to welcome all the 150+ participants to ETVC 2008. For those who did not attend, we hope the chapters of this publication provide a good snapshot of the current research status in visual computing.

December 2008   Frank Nielsen

Group picture of the participants at ETVC 2008 (November 19, 2008)

Organization

Frank Nielsen (Program Chair)

Evelyne Rayssac (Secretary)
Corinne Poulain (Secretary)

Philippe Baptiste (Financial Advisor)
Jean-Marc Steyaert (Scientific Advisor)

Luca Castelli Aleardi (Photographer)

Referees

S. Boltz	R. Keriven	S. Owada
F. Chazal	F. Nielsen	M. Pauly
B. Lévy	R. Nock	A. Vigneron
A. André	T. Nakamura	
F. Hetroy	S. Oudot	

Sponsoring Institutions

We gratefully acknowledge the following institutions for their generous support:

- CNRS
- DIGITEO
- École Polytechnique
- Groupe de Recherche Informatique & Mathématique (GdR IM)
- University of Antilles-Guyane, CEREGMIA Department

Table of Contents

Geometric Computing

Information Geometry and Applications

Computer Graphics and Vision

Information Retrieval

Medical Imaging and Computational Anatomy

Abstracts of the LIX Fall Colloquium 2008: Emerging Trends in Visual Computing

Frank Nielsen

Ecole Polytechnique, Palaiseau, France
Sony CSL, Tokyo, Japan

Abstract. We list the abstracts of the distinguished speakers that participated to the 2008 LIX fall colloquium.

Leonidas GUIBAS
Computer Science Department, Stanford University, USA

Detection of Symmetries and Repeated Patterns in 3D Point Cloud Data
Digital models of physical shapes are becoming ubiquitous in our economy and life. Such models are sometimes designed ab initio using CAD tools, but more and more often they are based on existing real objects whose shape is acquired using various 3D scanning technologies. In most instances, the original scanner data is just a set, but a very large set, of points sampled from the surface of the object. We are interested in tools for understanding the local and global structure of such large-scale scanned geometry for a variety of tasks, including model completion, reverse engineering, shape comparison and retrieval, shape editing, inclusion in virtual worlds and simulations, etc. This talk will present a number of point-based techniques for discovering global structure in 3D data sets, including partial and approximate symmetries, shared parts, repeated patterns, etc. It is also of interest to perform such structure discovery across multiple data sets distributed in a network, without actually ever bring them all to the same host.

Xianfeng David GU
State University of New York at Stony Brook, USA

Discrete Curvature Flow for Surfaces and 3-Manifolds
This talk introduce the concepts, theories and algorithms for discrete curvature flows for surfaces with arbitrary topologies. Discrete curvature flow for hyperbolic 3-manifolds with geodesic boundaries are also explained. Curvature flow method can be used to design Riemannian metrics by prescribed curvatures, and applied for parameterization in graphics, shape registration and comparison in vision and brain mapping in medical imaging, spline construction in computer aided geometric design, and many other engineering fields.

F. Nielsen (Ed.): ETVC 2008, LNCS 5416, pp. 1–12, 2009.

Jean-Daniel BOISSONNAT
GEOMETRICA, INRIA Sophia-Antipolis, France

Certified Mesh Generation
Given a domain D, the problem of mesh generation is to construct a simplicial complex that approximates D in both a topological and a geometrical sense and whose elements satisfy various constraints such as size, aspect ratio or anisotropy. The talk will cover some recent results on triangulating surfaces and volumes by Delaunay refinement, anisotropic mesh generation and surface reconstruction. Applications in medical images, computer vision and geology will be discussed.

Baba VEMURI
CISE Dept., University of Florida, USA

Information-Theoretic Algorithms for Diffusion Tensor Imaging
Concepts from Information Theory have been used quite widely in Image Processing, Computer Vision and Medical Image Analysis for several decades now. Most widely used concepts are that of KL-divergence, minimum description length (MDL), etc. These concepts have been popularly employed for image registration, segmentation, classification etc. In this chapter we review several methods, mostly developed by our group at the Center for Vision, Graphics & Medical Imaging in the University of Florida, that glean concepts from Information Theory and apply them to achieve analysis of Diffusion-Weighted Magnetic Resonance (DW-MRI) data. This relatively new MRI modality allows one to non-invasively infer axonal connectivity patterns in the central nervous system. The focus of this chapter is to review automated image analysis techniques that allow us to automatically segment the region of interest in the DWMRI image wherein one might want to track the axonal pathways and also methods to reconstruct complex local tissue geometries containing axonal fiber crossings. Implementation results illustrating the algorithm application to real DW-MRI data sets are depicted to demonstrate the effectiveness of the methods reviewed.

Xavier PENNEC
ASCLEPIOS, INRIA Sophia-Antipolis, France

Statistical Computing on Manifolds for Computational Anatomy
Computational anatomy is an emerging discipline that aims at analyzing and modeling the individual anatomy of organs and their biological variability across a population. The goal is not only to model the normal variations among a population, but also discover morphological differences between normal and pathological populations, and possibly to detect, model and classify the pathologies from structural abnormalities. Applications are very important both in neuroscience, to minimize the influence of the anatomical variability in functional group analysis, and in medical imaging, to better drive the adaptation of generic models of the anatomy (atlas) into patient-specific data (personalization). However, understanding and

modeling the shape of organs is made difficult by the absence of physical models for comparing different subjects, the complexity of shapes, and the high number of degrees of freedom implied. Moreover, the geometric nature of the anatomical features usually extracted raises the need for statistics and computational methods on objects that do not belong to standard Euclidean spaces. We investigate in this chapter the Riemannian metric as a basis for developing generic algorithms to compute on manifolds. We show that few computational tools derived from this structure can be used in practice as the atoms to build more complex generic algorithms such as mean computation, Mahalanobis distance, interpolation, filtering and anisotropic diffusion on fields of geometric features. This computational framework is illustrated with the joint estimation and anisotropic smoothing of diffusion tensor images and with the modeling of the brain variability from sulcal lines.

Cordelia SCHMID
LEAR, INRIA Grenoble, France

Large-Scale Object Recognition Systems
This paper introduces recent methods for large scale image search. State-of-the-art methods build on the bag-of-features image representation. We first analyze bag-of-features in the framework of approximate nearest neighbor search. This shows the sub-optimality of such a representation for matching descriptors and leads us to derive a more precise representation based on 1) Hamming embedding (HE) and 2) weak geometric consistency constraints (WGC). HE provides binary signatures that refine the matching based on visual words. WGC filters matching descriptors that are not consistent in terms of angle and scale. HE and WGC are integrated within the inverted file and are efficiently exploited for all images, even in the case of very large datasets. Experiments performed on a dataset of one million of images show a significant improvement due to the binary signature and the weak geometric consistency constraints, as well as their efficiency. Estimation of the full geometric transformation, i.e., a re-ranking step on a short list of images, is complementary to our weak geometric consistency constraints and allows to further improve the accuracy.

Pascal FUA
EPFL, CVLAB, Swiss

Recovering Shape and Motion from Video Sequences
In recent years, because cameras have become inexpensive and ever more prevalent, there has been increasing interest in video-based modeling of shape and motion. This has many potential applications in areas such as electronic publishing, entertainment, sports medicine and athletic training. It, however, is an inherently difficult task because the image-data is often incomplete, noisy, and ambiguous. In our work, we focus on the recovery of deformable and articulated 3D motion from single video sequences. In this talk, I will present the models we

have developed for this purpose and demonstrate the applicability of our technology for Augmented Reality and human body tracking purposes. Finally, I will present some open research issues and discuss our plans for future developments.

Ramesh RASKAR
MIT Media Lab, USA

Computational Photography: Epsilon to Coded Imaging
Computational photography combines plentiful computing, digital sensors, modern optics, actuators, and smart lights to escape the limitations of traditional cameras, enables novel imaging applications and simplifies many computer vision tasks. However, a majority of current Computational Photography methods involve taking multiple sequential photos by changing scene parameters and fusing the photos to create a richer representation. The goal of Coded Computational Photography is to modify the optics, illumination or sensors at the time of capture so that the scene properties are encoded in a single (or a few) photographs. We describe several applications of coding exposure, aperture, illumination and sensing and describe emerging techniques to recover scene parameters from coded photographs.

Dimitris METAXAS
Computational Biomedicine Imaging and Modeling Center, CBMI, Rutgers University, USA

Unifying Subspace and Distance Metric Learning with Bhattacharyya Coefficient for Image Classification
In this talk, we propose a unified scheme of subspace and distance metric learning under the Bayesian framework for image classification. According to the local distribution of data, we divide the k-nearest neighbors of each sample into the intra-class set and the inter-class set, and we aim to learn a distance metric in the embedding subspace, which can make the distances between the sample and its intra-class set smaller than the distances between it and its inter-class set. To reach this goal, we consider the intra-class distances and the inter-class distances to be from two different probability distributions respectively, and we model the goal with minimizing the overlap between two distributions. Inspired by the Bayesian classification error estimation, we formulate the objective function by minimizing the Bhattachyrra coefficient between two distributions. We further extend it with the kernel trick to learn nonlinear distance metric. The power and generality of the proposed approach are demonstrated by a series of experiments on the CMU-PIE face database, the extended YALE face database, and the COREL-5000 nature image database.

Nikos PARAGIOS
Ecole Centrale de Paris, ECP, Paris, France

Procedural Modeling of Architectures: Towards Large Scale Visual Reconstruction
Three-dimensional content is a novel modality used in numerous domains like
navigation, post production & cinematography, architectural modeling and urban planning. These domains have benefited from the enormous progress has
been made on 3D reconstruction from images. Such a problem consists of building geometric models of the observed environment. State of the art methods can
deliver excellent results in a small scale but suffer from being local and cannot be
considered in a large scale reconstruction process since the assumption of recovering images from multiple views for an important number of buildings is rather
unrealistic. On the other hand several efforts have been made in the graphics
community towards content creation with city engines. Such models are purely
graphics-based and given a set of rules (grammars) as well as dictionary of architectures (buildings) can produce virtual cities. Such engines could become far
more realistic through the use of actual city models as well as knowledge of building architectures. Developing 3D models/rules/grammars that are image-based
and coupling these models with actual observations is the greatest challenge of
urban modeling. Solving the large-scale geometric modeling problem from minimal content could create novel means of world representation as well as novel
markets and applications. In this talk, we will present some preliminary results
on large scale modeling and reconstruction through architectural grammars.

Gabriel TAUBIN
Division of Engineering, Brown University, USA

Shape from Depth Discontinuities
We propose a new primal-dual framework for representation, capture, processing,
and display of piecewise smooth surfaces, where the dual space is the space of
oriented 3D lines, or rays, as opposed to the traditional dual space of planes.
An image capture process detects points on a depth discontinuity sweep from a
camera moving with respect to an object, or from a static camera and a moving
object. A depth discontinuity sweep is a surface in dual space composed of the
time-dependent family of depth discontinuity curves span as the camera pose
describes a curved path in 3D space. Only part of this surface, which includes
silhouettes, is visible and measurable from the camera. Locally convex points
deep inside concavities can be estimated from the visible non-silhouette depth
discontinuity points. Locally concave point laying at the bottom of concavities,
which do not correspond to visible depth discontinuities, cannot be estimated,
resulting in holes in the reconstructed surface. A first variational approach to
fill the holes, based on fitting an implicit function to a reconstructed oriented
point cloud, produces watertight models.We describe a first complete end-to-end
system for acquiring models of shape and appearance.We use a single multi-flash
camera and turntable for the data acquisition and represent the scanned objects
as point clouds, with each point being described by a 3-D location, a surface
normal, and a Phong appearance model.

Shun-ichi AMARI
Mathematical Neuroscience Laboratory, Brain Science Institute, RIKEN, Wako-Shi, Japan

Information Geometry and Its Applications
Information geometry emerged from studies on invariant properties of a manifold of probability distributions. It includes convex analysis and its duality as a special but important part. Here, we begin with a convex function, and construct a dually flat manifold. The manifold possesses a Riemannian metric, two types of geodesics, and a divergence function. The generalized Pythagorean theorem and dual projections theorem are derived therefrom.We construct alpha-geometry, extending this convex analysis. In this review, geometry of a manifold of probability distributions is then given, and a plenty of applications are touched upon. Appendix presents an easily understable introduction to differential geometry and its duality.

Jun ZHANG
Department of Psychology, University of Michigan, USA

Information Geometry: Duality, Convexity and Divergences
In this talk, I explore the mathematical relationships between duality in information geometry, convex analysis, and divergence functions. First, from the fundamental inequality of a convex function, a family of divergence measures can be constructed, which specializes to the familiar Bregman divergence, Jenson difference, beta-divergence, and alpha-divergence, etc. Second, the mixture parameter turns out to correspond to the alpha ¡-¿ -alpha duality in information geometry (which I call "referential duality", since it is related to the choice of a reference point for computing divergence). Third, convex conjugate operation induces another kind of duality in information geometry, namely, that of biorthogonal coordinates and their transformation (which I call "representational duality", since it is related to the expression of geometric quantities, such as metric, affine connection, curvature, etc of the underlying manifold). Under this analysis, what is traditionally called "+1/-1 duality" and "e/m duality" in information geometry reflect two very different meanings of duality that are nevertheless intimately interwined for dually flat spaces.

Hiroshi MATSUZOE
Department of Computer Science and Engineering Graduate School of Engineering, Nagoya Institute of Technology, NITECH, Japan

Computational Geometry from the Viewpoint of Affine Differential Geometry
Incidence relations (configurations of vertexes, edges, etc.) are important in computational geometry. Incidence relations are invariant under the group of affine transformations. On the other hand, affine differential geometry is to study hypersurfaces in an affine space that are invariant under the group of

affine transformation. Therefore affine differential geometry gives a new sight in computational geometry. From the viewpoint of affine differential geometry, algorithms of geometric transformation and dual transformation are discussed. The Euclidean distance function is generalized by a divergence function in affine differential geometry. A divergence function is an asymmetric distance-like function on a manifold, and it is an important object in information geometry. For divergence functions, the upper envelope type theorems on statistical manifolds are given. Voronoi diagrams determined from divergence functions are also discussed.

Richard NOCK
CEREGMIA, University of Antilles-Guyane, France

The Intrinsic Geometries of Learning
In a seminal paper, Amari (1998) proved that learning can be made more efficient when one uses the intrinsic Riemanian structure of the algorithms' spaces of parameters to point the gradient towards better solutions. In this paper, we show that many learning algorithms, including various boosting algorithms for linear separators, the most popular top-down decision-tree induction algorithms, and some on-line learning algorithms, are spawns of a generalization of Amari's natural gradient to some particular non-Riemanian spaces. These algorithms exploit an intrinsic dual geometric structure of the space of parameters in relationship with particular integral losses that are to be minimized. We unite some of them, such as AdaBoost, additive regression with the square loss, the logistic loss, the top-down induction performed in CART and C4.5, as a single algorithm on which we show general convergence to the optimum and explicit convergence rates under very weak assumptions. As a consequence, many of the classification calibrated surrogates of Bartlett et al. (2006) admit efficient minimization algorithms.

Frédéric BARBARESCO
Thales Air Systems, France

Applications of Information Geometry to Radar Signal Processing
Main issue of High Resolution Doppler Imagery is related to robust statistical estimation of Toeplitz Hermitian positive definite covariance matrices of sensor data time series (e.g. in Doppler Echography, in Underwater acoustic, in Electromagnetic Radar, in Pulsed Lidar). We consider this problem jointly in the framework of Riemannian symmetric spaces and the framework of Information Geometry. Both approaches lead to the same metric, that has been initially considered in other mathematical domains (study of Bruhat-Tits complete metric Space & Upper-half Siegel Space in Symplectic Geometry). Based on Frechet-Karcher barycenter definition & geodesics in Bruhat-Tits space, we address problem of N Covariance matrices Mean estimation. Our main contribution lies in the development of this theory for Complex Autoregressive models (maximum

entropy solution of Doppler Spectral Analysis). Specific Blocks structure of the Toeplitz Hermitian covariance matrix is used to define an iterative & parallel algorithm for Siegel metric computation. Based on Affine Information Geometry theory, we introduce for Complex Autoregressive Model, Khler metric on reflection coefficients based on Khler potential function given by Doppler signal Entropy. The metric is closely related to Khler-Einstein manifold and complex Monge-Ampere Equation. Finally, we study geodesics in space of Khler potentials and action of Calabi & Khler-Ricci Geometric Flows for this Complex Autoregressive Metric. We conclude with different results obtained on real Doppler Radar Data in HF & X bands : X-band radar monitoring of wake vortex turbulences, detection for Coastal X-band & HF Surface Wave Radars.

Frank NIELSEN
LIX, Ecole Polytechnique, Paris, France & Sony Computer Science Laboratories Inc., Tokyo, Japan

Computational Geometry in Dually Flat Spaces: Theory, Applications and Perspectives
Computational information geometry emerged from the fruitful interactions of geometric computing with information geometry. In this talk, we survey the recent results obtained in that direction by first describing generalizations of core algorithms of computational geometry and machine learning to broad and versatile classes of distortion measures. Namely, we introduce the generic classes of Bregman, Csiszar and Burbea-Rao parametric divergences and explain their relationships and properties with respect to algorithmic design. We then present few applications of these meta-algorithms to the field of statistics and data analysis and conclude with perspectives.

Tetsuo ASANO
School of Information Science, Japan Advanced Institute of Science and Technology, JAIST, Japan

Constant-Working-Space Algorithms for Image Processing
This talk surveys recent progress in constant-working-space algorithms for problems related to image processing. An extreme case is when an input image is given as read-only memory in which reading an array element is allowed but writing any value at any array element is prohibited, and also the number of working storage cells available for algorithms is at most some constant. This chapter shows how a number of important fundamental problems can be solved in such a highly constrained situation.

Stéphane MALLAT
Ecole Polytechnique, Centre de Mathmatiques Appliques, CMAP, France

Sparse Geometric Super-Resolution

What is the maximum signal resolution that can be recovered from partial noisy or degraded data? This inverse problem is a central issue, from medical to satellite imaging, from geophysical seismic to HDTV visualization of Internet videos. Increasing an image resolution is possible by taking advantage of "geometric regularities", whatever it means. Super-resolution can indeed be achieved for signals having a sparse representation which is "incoherent" relatively to the measurement system. For images and videos, it requires to construct sparse representations in redundant dictionaries of waveforms, which are adapted to geometric image structures. Signal recovery in redundant dictionaries is discussed, and applications are shown in dictionaries of bandlets for image super-resolution.

Martin VETTERLI

School of Computer and Communication Sciences, EPFL, Switzerland

Sparse Sampling: Variations on a Theme by Shannon

Sampling is not only a beautiful topic in harmonic analysis, with an interesting history, but also a subject with high practical impact, at the heart of signal processing and communications and their applications. The question is very simple: when is there a one-to-one relationship between a continuous-time function and adequately acquired samples of this function? A cornerstone result is of course Shannon's sampling theorem, which gives a sufficient condition for reconstructing the projection of a signal onto the subspace of bandlimited functions, and this by taking inner products with a sinc function and its shifts. Many variations of this basic framework exist, and they are all related to a subspace structure of the classes of objects that can be sampled. Recently, this framework has been extended to classes of non-bandlimited sparse signals, which do not have a subspace structure. Perfect reconstruction is possible based on a suitable projection measurement. This gives a sharp result on the sampling and reconstruction of sparse continuous-time signals, namely that 2K measurements are necessary and sufficient to perfectly reconstruct a K-sparse continuous-time signal. In accordance with the principle of parsimony, we call this sampling at Occam's rate. We first review this result and show that it relies on structured Vandermonde measurement matrices, of which the Fourier matrix is a particular case. It also uses a separation into location and value estimation, the first being non-linear, while the second is linear. Because of this structure, fast, $O(K^3)$ methods exist, and are related to classic algorithms used in spectral estimation and error correction coding. We then generalize these results to a number of cases where sparsity is present, including piecewise polynomial signals, as well as to broad classes of sampling or measurement kernels, including Gaussians and splines. Of course, real cases always involve noise, and thus, retrieval of sparse signals in noise is considered. That is, is there a stable recovery mechanism, and robust practical algorithms to achieve it. Lower bounds by Cramer-Rao are given, which can also be used to derive uncertainty relations with respect to position and value of sparse signal estimation. Then, a concrete estimation method is given using an iterative algorithm due to Cadzow, and is shown to perform close to optimal over a wide range of signal to noise ratios. This indicates the robustness of such methods, as well as their practicality. Next, we consider the connection to compressed sensing and compressive sampling, a recent approach involving random measurement matrices, a discrete set up, and retrieval based on convex optimization. These methods have the advantage of unstructured measurement matrices (actually, typically random ones) and therefore a certain universality, at the cost of some redundancy. We compare the two approaches, highlighting differences, similarities, and respective advantages. Finally, we move to applications of these results, which cover wideband communications, noise removal, and superresolution imaging, to name a few. We conclude by indicating that sampling is alive and well, with new perspectives and many interesting recent results and developments. Joint work with Thierry Blu (CUHK), Lionel Coulot, Ali Hormati (EPFL), Pier-Luigi Dragotti (ICL) and Pina Marziliano (NTU).

Michel BARLAUD
I3S CNRS, University of Nice-Sophia-Antipolis, Polytech'Nice & Institut Universitaire de France, France

Image Retrieval via Kullback Divergence of Patches of Wavelets Coefficients in the k-NN Framework
This talk presents a framework to define an objective measure of the similarity (or dissimilarity) between two images for image processing. The problem is twofold: 1) define a set of features that capture the information contained in the image relevant for the given task and 2) define a similarity measure in this feature space. In this paper, we propose a feature space as well as a statistical measure on this space. Our feature space is based on a global description of the image in a multiscale transformed domain. After decomposition into a Laplacian pyramid, the coefficients are arranged in intrascale/ interscale/interchannel patches which reflect the dependencies of neighboring coefficients in presence of specific structures or textures. At each scale, the probability density function (pdf) of these patches is used as a description of the relevant information. Because of the sparsity of the multiscale transform, the most significant patches, called Sparse Multiscale Patches (SMP), describe efficiently these pdfs. We propose a statistical measure (the Kullback-Leibler divergence) based on the comparison of these probability density function. Interestingly, this measure is estimated via the nonparametric, k-th nearest neighbor framework without explicitly building the pdfs. This framework is applied to a query-by-example image retrieval method. Experiments on two publicly available databases showed the potential of our SMP approach for this task. In particular, it performed comparably to a SIFT-based retrieval method and two versions of a fuzzy segmentation-based method (the UFM and CLUE methods), and it exhibited some robustness to different geometric and radiometric deformations of the images.

Francis BACH
INRIA/ENS, France

Machine learning and kernel methods for computer vision
Kernel methods are a new theoretical and algorithmic framework for machine learning. By representing data through well defined dot-products, referred to as kernels, they allow to use classical linear supervised machine learning algorithms to non linear settings and to non vectorial data. A major issue when applying these methods to image processing or computer vision is the choice of the kernel. I will present recent advances in the design of kernels for images that take into account the natural structure of images.

Sylvain LAZARD
VEGAS, INRIA LORIA Nancy, France

3D Visibility and Lines in Space
Computing visibility information in a 3D environment is crucial to many applications such as computer graphics, vision and robotics. Typical visibility problems include computing the view from a given point, determining whether two objects partially see each other, and computing the umbra and penumbra cast by a light source. In a given scene, two points are visible if the segment joining them does not properly intersect any obstacle in the scene. The study of visibility is thus intimately related to the study of the set of free line segments in a scene. In this talk, I will review some recent combinatorial and algorithmic results related to non-occluded segments tangent to up to four objects in three dimensional scenes.

Suresh VENKATASUBRAMANIAN
School of Computing, University of Utah, USA

Non-standard Geometries and Data Analysis
Traditional data mining starts with the mapping from entities to points in a Euclidean space. The search for patterns and structure is then framed as a geometric search in this space. Concepts like principal component analysis, regression, clustering, and centrality estimation have natural geometric formulations, and we now understand a great deal about manipulating such (typically high dimensional) spaces. For many domains of interest however, the most natural space to embed data in is not Euclidean. Data might lie on curved manifolds, or even inhabit spaces endowed with different distance structures than l_p spaces. How does one do data analysis in such domains? In this talk, I'll discuss two specific domains of interest that pose challenges for traditional data mining and geometric methods. One space consists of collections of distributions, and the other is the space of shapes. In both cases, I'll present ongoing work that attempts to interpret and understand clustering in such spaces, driven by different applications.

Markus GROSS
Department of Computer Science, Institute of Scientific Computing, Swiss Federal Institute of Technology Zurich, ETHZ, Switzerland

3D Video: A Fusion of Graphics and Vision
In recent years 3-dimensional video has received a significant attention both in research and in industry. Applications range from special effects in feature films to the analysis of sports events. 3D video is concerned with the computation of virtual camera positions and fly-throughs of a scene given multiple, conventional 2D video streams. The high-quality synthesis of such view-independent video representations poses a variety of technical challenges including acquisition, reconstruction, processing, compression, and rendering. In this talk I will outline the research in this area carried out at ETH over the past years. I will discuss various concepts for passive and active acquisition of 3D video using combinations of multiple cameras and projectors. Furthermore, I will address topics related to the representation and processing of the massive amount data arising from such multiple video streams. I will highlight the underlying technical concepts and algorithms that draw upon knowledge both from graphics and from vision. Finally I will demonstrate some commercial applications targeting at virtual replays for sports broadcasts.

From Segmented Images to Good Quality Meshes Using Delaunay Refinement

Jean-Daniel Boissonnat[1], Jean-Philippe Pons[2], and Mariette Yvinec[1]

[1] INRIA Sophia-Antipolis, 2004 route des Lucioles, BP 93,
06902 Sophia-Antipolis Cedex, France
Jean-Daniel.Boissonnat@sophia.inria.fr
[2] CSTB, 290 route des Lucioles, BP 209, 06904 Sophia-Antipolis Cedex, France
Jean-Philippe.Pons@cstb.fr

Abstract. This paper surveys Delaunay-based meshing techniques for curved objects, and their application in medical imaging and in computer vision to the extraction of geometric models from segmented images. We show that the so-called Delaunay refinement technique allows to mesh surfaces and volumes bounded by surfaces, with theoretical guarantees on the quality of the approximation, from a geometrical and a topological point of view. Moreover, it offers extensive control over the size and shape of mesh elements, for instance through a (possibly non-uniform) sizing field. We show how this general paradigm can be adapted to produce anisotropic meshes, i.e. meshes elongated along prescribed directions. Lastly, we discuss extensions to higher dimensions, and especially to space-time for producing time-varying 3D models. This is also of interest when input images are transformed into data points in some higher dimensional space as is common practice in machine learning.

1 Introduction

Motivation. The ubiquity of digital imaging in scientific research and in industry calls for automated tools to extract high-level information from raster representations (2D, 3D, or higher-dimensional rectilinearly-sampled scalar/vector fields), the latter often being not directly suitable for analysis and interpretation. Notably, the computerized creation of *geometric* models from digital images plays a crucial role in many medical imaging applications.

A precondition for extracting geometry from images is usually to partition image pixels (voxels) into multiple regions of interest. This task, known as *image segmentation*, is a central long-standing problem in image processing and computer vision. Doing a review of this area is out of the scope of this paper. Let us only mention that it is a highly ill-posed problem due to various perturbing factors such as noise, occlusions, missing parts, cluttered data, etc. The interested reader may refer to e.g. [1] for a specific survey on segmentation of medical images.

This paper focuses on a step posterior to image segmentation: the automatic generation of discrete geometric representations from segmented images, such

F. Nielsen (Ed.): ETVC 2008, LNCS 5416, pp. 13–37, 2009.

as surface meshes representing boundaries between different regions of interest, or volume meshes of their interior. This step is determinant in numerous applications. For instance, in medicine, an increasing number of numerical simulations of physical or physiological processes call for geometric models of anatomical structures: electroencephalography (EEG) and magnetoencephalography (MEG), image-guided neurosurgery, electromagnetic modeling, blood flow simulation, etc.

However, this topic has attracted less interest than image segmentation so far. As a result, reliable fully-automated tools for the unstructured discretization of segmented images, and in particular of medical datasets, are still lacking. So that simplistic or low-quality geometric models are still of wide use in some applications. For example, in electromagnetic modeling, such as specific absorption rate studies, finite element methods (FEM) on unstructured grids conforming to anatomical structures would be desirable; but due to the difficulty of producing such models, most numerical simulations so far have been conducted using finite difference methods on rectilinear grids, although the poor definition of tissue boundaries (stair-casing effect) strongly limits their accuracy. Similarly, in the EEG/MEG source localization problem using the boundary element method (BEM), simplistic head models consisting of a few nested tissue layers remain more popular than realistic models featuring multiple junctions.

The generation of geometric models from segmented images presents many challenges. The output must fulfill many requirements in terms of geometric accuracy and topological correctness, smoothness, number, type, size and shape of mesh elements, in order to obtain acceptable results and make useful predictions, avoid instabilities in the simulations, or reduce the overall processing time. Notably, the conditioning of stiffness matrices in FEM directly depends on the sizes and shapes of the elements. Another example is image-guided neurosurgery, for which real-time constraints impose strong limitations on the complexity of the geometric brain model being dynamically registered onto the patient anatomy.

Grid-based methods. Commonly used techniques do not meet the aforementioned specifications. The most popular technique for producing surface meshes from raster data is undoubtedly the *marching cubes* algorithm, introduced by Lorensen and Cline [2]. Given a scalar field sampled on a rectilinear grid, the marching cubes algorithm efficiently generates a triangular mesh of an isosurface by tessellating each cubic cell of the domain according to a case table constructed off-line.

Unfortunately, this technique, as well as its many subsequent variants, typically produces unnecessarily large meshes (at least one triangle per boundary voxel) of very low quality (lots of skinny triangles). This may be acceptable for visualization purposes, but not for further numerical simulations. In order to obtain suitable representations, the resulting meshes often have to be regularized, optimized and decimated, while simultaneously controlling the approximation accuracy and preserving some topological properties, such as the absence of self-intersections. Sometimes, good tetrahedral meshes of the domains bounded by the marching cubes surfaces also have to be generated. Most of the time, these tasks are overconstrained.

Recently, the interest in grid-based techniques has been renewed by a few methods with theoretical guarantees. Plantiga and Vegter [3] propose an algorithm to mesh implicit surfaces with guaranteed topology, based on an adaptive octree subdivision controlled by interval arithmetic. But in its current form, this algorithm is relevant to closed-form expressions, not to sampled data.

The recent algorithm of Labelle and Shewchuck [4] fills an isosurface with a uniformly sized tetrahedral mesh whose dihedral angles are bounded between $10.7°$ and $164.8°$. The algorithm is very fast, numerically robust, and easy to implement because, like the marching cubes algorithm, it generates tetrahedra from a small set of precomputed stencils. Moreover, if the isosurface is a smooth 2-manifold with bounded curvature, and the tetrahedra are sufficiently small, then the boundary of the mesh is guaranteed to be a geometrically and topologically accurate approximation of the isosurface. However, this algorithm lacks flexibility: notably, it is limited to uniform surface meshes, and isotropic surface and volume meshes.

Delaunay-based methods. This paper surveys *Delaunay-based meshing* techniques for curved objects. It is recognized as one of the most powerful techniques for generating surface and volume meshes with theoretical guarantees on the quality of the approximation, from a geometrical and topological point of view. Moreover, it offers extensive control over the size and shape of mesh elements, for instance through a (possibly non-uniform) sizing field. It also allows to mesh several domains simultaneously. Recent extensions show that this general paradigm can be adapted to produce anisotropic meshes, i.e. meshes elongated along prescribed directions, as well as meshes in higher dimensions.

In this paper, we show how Delaunay-based meshing can be applied in medical imaging and in computer vision to the extraction of meshes from segmented images, with all the desired specifications. The rest of the paper is organized as follows. We first introduce the notion of *restricted Delaunay triangulation* in Section 2. We then show how to mesh surfaces (Section 3) and volumes bounded by surfaces (Section 4) using the so-called *Delaunay refinement* technique. Anisotropic meshes are discussed in Section 5. Lastly, we tackle extensions of Delaunay refinement to higher dimensions (Section 6), and especially to space-time for producing time-varying 3D models. This is also of interest when input images are transformed into data points in some higher dimensional space as is common practice in machine learning.

2   Restricted Delaunay Triangulations

In this section, we recall the definitions of Voronoi diagrams and Delaunay triangutions, and their generalization known as power (or Laguerre) diagrams and weighted Delaunay (or regular) triangulations. We then introduce the concept of restricted Delaunay triangulation which is central in this paper.

2.1   Voronoi Diagrams and Delaunay Triangulations

Voronoi diagrams are versatile structures which encode proximity relationships between objects. They are particularly relevant to perform nearest neighbor search and motion planning (e.g. in robotics), and to model growth processes (e.g. crystal growth in materials science). Delaunay triangulations, which are geometrically dual to Voronoi diagrams, are a classical tool in the field of mesh generation and mesh processing due to their optimality properties.

In the sequel, we call k-simplex the convex hull of $k + 1$ affinely independent points. For example, a 0-simplex is a point, a 1-simplex is a line segment, a 2-simplex is a triangle and a 3-simplex is a tetrahedron.

Let $E = \{p_1, \ldots, p_n\}$ be set of points in $\mathbb{R}^d$, called *sites*. Note that in this paper, we are mainly interested in $d = 3$, except in Section 6, where the case $d > 3$ is studied. The Voronoi region, or Voronoi cell, denoted by $V(p_i)$, associated to a point $p_i \in E$ is the region formed by points that are closer to p_i than to all other sites in E:

$$V(p_i) = \{x \in \mathbb{R}^d : \forall j, \|x - p_i\| \leq \|x - p_j\|\}.$$

$V(p_i)$ is the intersection of $n - 1$ half-spaces bounded by the bisector planes of segments $[p_i p_j]$, $j \neq i$. $V(p_i)$ is therefore a convex polyhedron, possibly unbounded. The Voronoi diagram of E, denoted by $\mathrm{Vor}(E)$, is the subdivision of space induced by the Voronoi cells $V(p_1), \ldots, V(p_n)$.

See Fig. 1 for a two-dimensional example of a Voronoi diagram. In two dimensions, the edges shared by two Voronoi cells are called Voronoi edges and the points shared by three Voronoi cells are called Voronoi vertices. Similarly, in three dimensions, we term Voronoi facets, edges and vertices the geometric objects shared by respectively two, three and four Voronoi cells, respectively. The Voronoi diagram is the collection of all these k-dimensional objects, with $0 \leq k \leq d$, which we call Voronoi faces. In particular, note that Voronoi cells $V(p_i)$ correspond to d-dimensional Voronoi faces.

To simplify the presentation and without real loss of generality, we will assume in the sequel that E does not contain any subset of $d + 2$ points that lie on a same hypersphere. We say that the points of E are then in *general position*.

The Delaunay triangulation of E, noted $\mathrm{Del}(E)$, is the *geometric dual* of $\mathrm{Vor}(E)$, and can be described as an embedding of the nerve[1] of $\mathrm{Vor}(E)$. The nerve of $\mathrm{Vor}(E)$ is the abstract simplicial complex that contains a simplex $\sigma = (p_{i_0}, \ldots, p_{i_k})$ iff $V(p_{i_0}) \cap \ldots \cap V(p_{i_k}) \neq \emptyset$. Specifically, if $k + 1$ Voronoi cells have a non-empty intersection, this intersection constitutes a $(d - k)$-dimensional face f of $\mathrm{Vor}(E)$. The convex hull of the associated $k + 1$ sites constitutes a k-dimensional simplex in the Delaunay triangulation and this simplex is the dual of face f. In 3D, the dual of a Delaunay tetrahedron is the Voronoi vertex that coincides with the circumcenter of the tetrahedron, the dual of a Delaunay facet is a Voronoi edge, the dual of a Delaunay edge is a Voronoi facet, and the dual of a Delaunay vertex p_i is the Voronoi cell $V(p_i)$. See Fig. 1.

---

[1] The notion of nerve of a covering is a basic concept in algebraic topology [5].

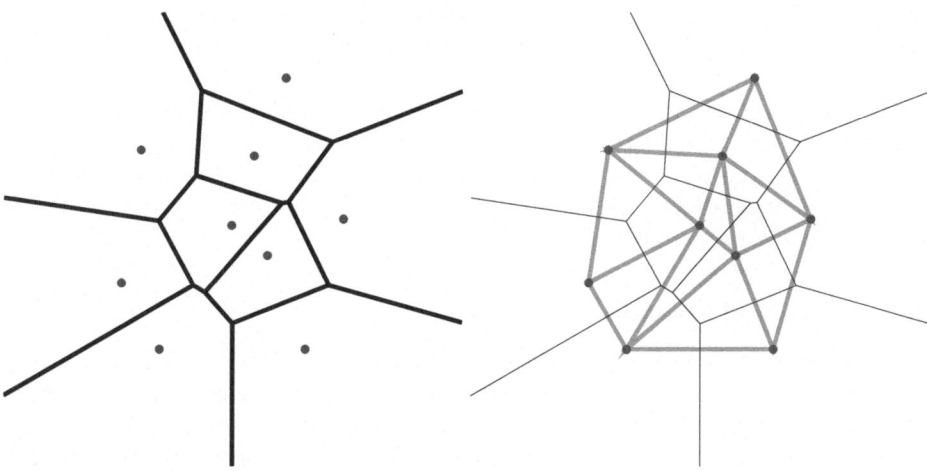

Fig. 1. The voronoi diagram of a set of points (left). Its dual Delaunay triangulation (right).

The Voronoi vertex v that is the dual of a d-dimensional simplex σ of $\mathrm{Del}(E)$ is the circumcenter of σ and, since v is closer to the vertices of σ than to all other points of E, the interior of the ball centered at v that circumscribes σ does not contain any point of E. We say that such a ball is *empty*. This property turns out to characterize Delaunay triangulations. Hence, $\mathrm{Del}(E)$ can be equivalently defined as the unique (under the general position assumption) triangulation of E such that each simplex in the triangulation can be circumscribed by an empty ball.

2.2   Power Diagrams Weighted Delaunay Triangulations

In this section, we introduce an extension of Voronoi diagrams that will be useful in the sequel. Point sites $p_1, \ldots, p_n$ are replaced by hyperspheres $\Sigma = \{\sigma_1, \ldots, \sigma_n\}$ and the Euclidean distance from a point x to a point site p_i is replaced by the power distance to hypersphere σ_i, i.e. the quantity $\sigma_i(x) = \|x - c_i\|^2 - r_i^2$ if c_i and r_i denote the center and radius of σ_i. One can then define the power cell of site σ_i as

$$V(\sigma_i) = \{x \in \mathbb{R}^d : \forall j, \sigma_i(x) \leq \sigma_j(x)\}.$$

Like Voronoi cells, power cells are convex polyhedra. The subdivision of space induced by the power cells $V(\sigma_1), \ldots, V(\sigma_n)$, constitutes the power diagram $V(\sigma)$ of Σ. As in the case of Voronoi diagrams, we define the geometric dual of the power diagram $V(\sigma)$ as an embedding of the nerve of $V(\sigma)$, where the dual of a face $f = \bigcap_{i=1,\ldots k} V(\sigma_i)$ is the convex hull of the centers $c_1, \ldots c_k$. If the spheres Σ are in general position, the geometric dual of the power diagram is a triangulation. This triangulation is called the *weighted Delaunay (or regular) triangulation* of Σ. Note that because some spheres of Σ may have an empty power cell, the set of vertices in the weighted Delaunay triangulation is only a subset of the centers of the σ_i.

It is a remarkable fact that weighted Delaunay triangulations can be computed almost as fast as non weighted Delaunay triangulations. An efficient implementation of both types of triangulations can be found in the CGAL library [6,7]. It is robust to degenerate configurations and floating-point errors through the use of exact geometric predicates.

2.3   Restricted Delaunay Triangulations

We introduce the concept of restricted Delaunay triangulation which, as the concept of Delaunay triangulation, is related to the notion of nerve. Given a subset $\Omega \subset \mathbb{R}^d$ and a set E of points, we call Delaunay triangulation of E restricted to Ω, and note $\mathrm{Del}_{|\Omega}(E)$, the subcomplex of $\mathrm{Del}(E)$ composed of the Delaunay simplices whose dual Voronoi faces intersect Ω. We refer to Fig. 2 to illustrate this concept in 2D. Fig. 2 (left) shows a Delaunay triangulation restricted to a curve C, which is composed of the Delaunay edges whose dual Voronoi edges intersect C. Fig. 2 (right) shows the Delaunay triangulation of the same set of points restricted to the region R bounded by the curve C. The restricted triangulation is composed of the Delaunay triangles whose circumcenters are contained in R. For an illustration in $\mathbb{R}^3$, consider a region $\mathcal{O}$ bounded by a surface $\mathcal{S}$ and a sample E, the Delaunay triangulation restricted to $\mathcal{S}$, $\mathrm{Del}_{|\mathcal{S}}(E)$, is composed of the Delaunay facets in $\mathrm{Del}(E)$ whose dual Voronoi edges intersect $\mathcal{S}$ while the Delaunay triangulation restricted to $\mathcal{O}$, $\mathrm{Del}_{|\mathcal{O}}(E)$, is made of those tetrahedra in $\mathrm{Del}(E)$ whose circumcenters belong to $\mathcal{O}$.

The attentive reader may have noticed that in both cases of Figure 2, the restricted Delaunay triangulation forms a good approximation of the object. Actually, this is a general property of the restricted Delaunay triangulation. It can be shown that, under some assumptions, and especially if E is a sufficiently dense sample of a smooth surface $\mathcal{S}$, $\mathrm{Del}_{|\mathcal{S}}(E)$ is a good approximation of $\mathcal{S}$, both in a topological and in a geometric sense. Specifically, $\mathrm{Del}_{|\mathcal{S}}(E)$ is a triangulated surface that is isotopic to $\mathcal{S}$; the isotopy moves the points by a quantity that becomes arbitrarily small when the density increases; in addition, normals of $\mathcal{S}$ of can be consistently approximated from $\mathrm{Del}_{|\mathcal{S}}(E)$.

Before stating precise results, we define what "sufficiently dense" means. The definition is based on the notion of medial axis. In the rest of the paper, $\mathcal{S}$ will denote a closed smooth surface of $\mathbb{R}^3$.

Definition 1 (Medial axis). *The* medial axis *of a surface $\mathcal{S}$ is the closure of the set of points with at least two closest points on $\mathcal{S}$.*

Definition 2 (lfs). *The* local feature size *at a point x on a surface $\mathcal{S}$, noted $\mathrm{lfs}(x)$, is the distance from x to the medial axis of $\mathcal{S}$. We write $\mathrm{lfs}(\mathcal{S}) = \inf_{x \in \mathcal{S}} \mathrm{lfs}(x)$.*

It can be shown that $\mathrm{lfs}(x)$ does not exceed the reach of $\mathcal{S}$ at x, denoted by $\mathrm{rch}(x)$. The reach at x is defined as the radius of the largest open ball tangent

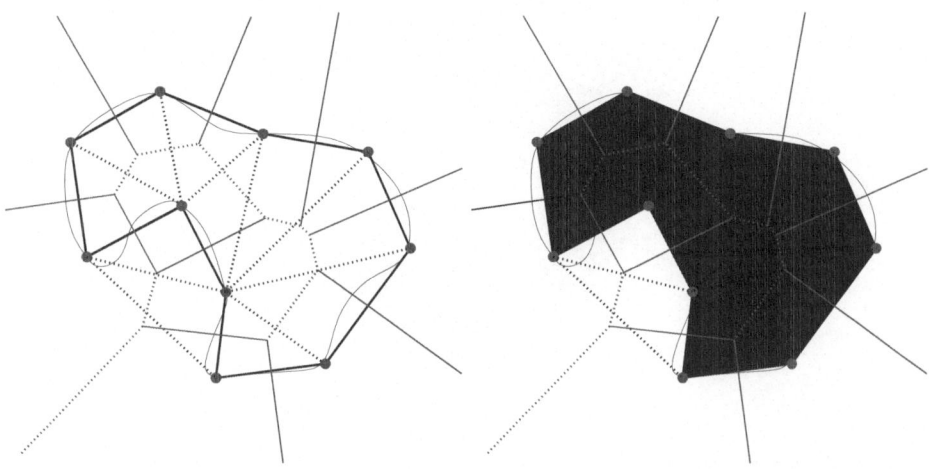

Fig. 2. The Voronoi diagram (in red) and the Delaunay triangulation (in blue) of a sample of red points on a planar closed curve C (in black). On the left: the edges of the Voronoi diagram and of the Delaunay triangulation that are restricted to the curve are in bold lines. On the right: the triangles belonging to the Delaunay triangulation of the sample restricted to the domain bounded by C are in blue.

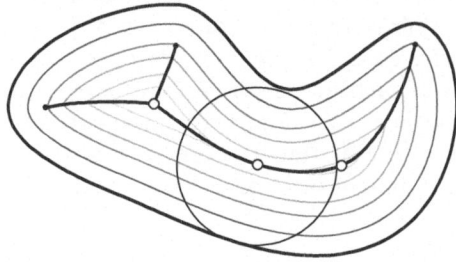

Fig. 3. The medial axis of a planar curve (only the portion inside the domain bounded by the curve is shown). The thin curves are parallel to the boundary of the domain.

to $\mathcal{S}$ at x whose interior does not contain any point of $\mathcal{S}$. Plainly, rch(x) cannot exceed the smallest radius of curvature at x and can be strictly less at points where the thickness of the object bounded by $\mathcal{S}$ is small. As shown by Federer [8], the local feature size of a smooth surface object is bounded away from 0.[2]

The following notion of ε-sample has been proposed by Amenta and Bern in their seminal paper on surface reconstruction [9].

---

[2] In fact, Federer proved the stronger result that the local feature size is bounded away from 0 as soon as $\mathcal{S}$ belongs to the class $C^{1,1}$ of surfaces that admit a normal at each point and whose normal field is Lipschitz. This class is larger than the class of C^2 surfaces and includes surfaces whose curvature may be discontinuous at some points. An example of a surface that is $C^{1,1}$ but not C^2 is the offset of a cube.

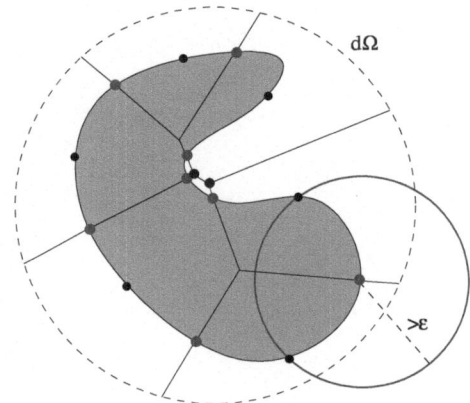

Fig. 4. A surface Delaunay ball whose center is a candidate for being inserted in E

Definition 3 (ε-sample). *Let $\varepsilon < 1$ and $\mathcal{S}$ be a smooth surface. We say that a finite point set $E \subset \mathcal{S}$ is an ε-sample of $\mathcal{S}$ if any point x of $\mathcal{S}$ is at distance at most $\varepsilon\,\mathrm{lfs}(x)$ from a point of E.*

The notion of ε-sample is not very handy since it requires that *any* point of the surface is close to a sample point. A more convenient notion of sample, called *loose ε-sample*, only requires a finite set of points of $\mathcal{S}$ to be close to the sample set [10]. More precisely, consider the Voronoi edges of $\mathrm{Vor}(E)$ that intersect $\mathcal{S}$. We require that each such intersection point is close to the sample set. By definition, these Voronoi edges are dual to the facets of $\mathrm{Del}_{|\mathcal{S}}(E)$. An intersection point of such an edge with $\mathcal{S}$ is thus the center of a so-called *surface Delaunay ball*, i.e. a ball circumscribing a facet of $\mathrm{Del}_{|\mathcal{S}}(E)$ and centered on the surface $\mathcal{S}$ (see Fig. 4).

Definition 4 (Loose ε-sample). *Let $\varepsilon < 1$ be a constant and $\mathcal{S}$ be a smooth surface. A point set $E \subset \mathcal{S}$ is a loose ε-sample of $\mathcal{S}$ if $\mathrm{Del}_{|\mathcal{S}}(E)$ has a vertex on each connected component of $\mathcal{S}$ and if, in addition, any surface Delaunay ball $B(c_f, r_f)$ circumscribing a facet f of $\mathrm{Del}_{|\mathcal{S}}(E)$ is such that $r_f < \varepsilon\mathrm{lfs}(c_f)$.*

The following theorem states that, for sufficiently dense samples, $\mathrm{Del}_{|\mathcal{S}}(E)$ is a good approximation of $\mathcal{S}$.

Theorem 1. *If E is a loose ε-sample of a smooth compact surface $\mathcal{S}$, with $\varepsilon < 0.12$, then the restriction of the orthogonal projection $\pi_S : \mathbb{R}^3 \setminus \mathcal{M}(\mathcal{S}) \to \mathcal{S}$, induces an isotopy that maps $\mathrm{Del}_{|\mathcal{S}}(E)$ to $\mathcal{S}$. The isotopy does not move the points of $\mathrm{Del}_{|\mathcal{S}}(E)$ by more than $O(\varepsilon^2)$. The angle between the normal to a facet f of $\mathrm{Del}_{|\mathcal{S}}(E)$ and the normals to $\mathcal{S}$ at the vertices of f is $O(\varepsilon)$.*

Weaker variants of this theorem have been proved by Amenta and Bern [9] and Boissonnat and Oudot [10]. Cohen-Steiner and Morvan have further shown that one can estimate the tensor of curvatures from $\mathrm{Del}_{|\mathcal{S}}(E)$ [11].

3   Surface Sampling and Meshing

In this section, we show how the concept of restricted Delaunay triangulation can be used to mesh smooth surfaces. The algorithm is proven to terminate and to construct good-quality meshes, while offering bounds on the accuracy of the original boundary approximation and on the size of the output mesh. The refinement process is controlled by highly customizable quality and size criteria on triangular facets. A notable feature of this algorithm is that the surface needs only to be known through an oracle that, given a line segment, detects whether the segment intersects the surface and, in the affirmative, returns an intersection point. This makes the algorithm useful in a wide variety of contexts and for a large class of surfaces.

The paradigm of Delaunay refinement has been first proposed by Ruppert for meshing planar domains [12]. The meshing algorithm presented in this section is due to Chew [13,14].

3.1   Delaunay Refinement for Meshing Surfaces

Let $\mathcal{S}$ be a surface of $\mathbb{R}^3$. If we know a loose ε-sample E of $\mathcal{S}$, with $\varepsilon < 0.12$, then, according to Theorem 1, the restricted Delaunay triangulation $\mathrm{Del}_{|\mathcal{S}}(E)$ is a good approximation of $\mathcal{S}$. In this section, we present an algorithm that can construct such a sample and the associated restricted Delaunay triangulation. We restrict the presentation to the case of smooth, compact and closed surfaces. Hence, $\mathrm{lfs}(\mathcal{S}) = \inf_{x \in \mathcal{S}} \mathrm{lfs}(x) > 0$.

The algorithm is greedy. It inserts points one by one and maintains the current set E, the Delaunay triangulation $\mathrm{Del}(E)$ and its restriction $\mathrm{Del}_{|\mathcal{S}}(E)$ to $\mathcal{S}$.

Let ψ be a function defined over $\mathcal{S}$ such that

$$\forall x \in \mathcal{S}, \ \ 0 < \psi_{\inf} \le \psi(x) \le \varepsilon \mathrm{lfs}(x).$$

where $\psi_{\min} = \inf_{x \in \mathcal{S}} \psi(x)$. Function ψ will control the sampling density and is called the *sizing field*.

The shape quality of the mesh facets is controlled through their *radius-edge* ratio, where the radius-edge ratio of a facet is the ratio between the circumradius of the facet and the length of its shortest edge. We define a *bad facet* as a facet f of $\mathrm{Del}_{|\mathcal{S}}(E)$ that:

- either has a too big surface Delaunay ball $B_f = B(c_f, r_f)$, meaning that $r_f > \psi(c_f)$,
- or is badly shaped, meaning that its radius-edge ratio ρ is such that $\rho > \beta$ for a constant $\beta \ge 1$.

Bad facets will be removed from the mesh by inserting the centers of their surface Delaunay balls, The algorithm is initialized with a (usually small) set of points $E_0 \subset \mathcal{S}$. Three points per connected component of $\mathcal{S}$ are sufficient. Then the algorithm maintains, in addition to $\mathrm{Del}(E)$ and $\mathrm{Del}_{|\mathcal{S}}(E)$, a list of bad facets and, as long as there remain bad facets, applies the following procedure

refine_facet(f)
    1. insert in E the center c_f of a surface Delaunay ball circumscribing f,
    2. update $\text{Del}(E)$, $\text{Del}_{|\mathcal{S}}(E)$ and the list of bad facets

An easy recurrence proves that the distance between any two points inserted in the sample is at least $\psi_{\text{inf}} > 0$. Since $\mathcal{S}$ is compact, the algorithm terminates after a finite number of steps. It can be shown that the number of inserted points is $O\left(\int_{\mathcal{S}} \frac{dx}{\psi^2(x)}\right)$.

Upon termination, any facet f of $\text{Del}_{|\mathcal{S}}(E)$ has a circumscribing surface Delaunay ball B_f of center c_f and radius $r_f < \psi(c_f)$. To be able to apply Theorem 1, we need to take $\psi \leq 0.12\,\text{lfs}$ and to ensure that $\text{Del}_{|\mathcal{S}}(E)$ has at least one vertex on each connected component of $\mathcal{S}$. This can be done by taking in E_0 three points per component of $\mathcal{S}$ that are sufficiently close.

We sum up the results in the following theorem.

Theorem 2. *Given a compact smooth and closed surface $\mathcal{S}$, and a positive Lipschitz function $\psi \leq \varepsilon\,\text{lfs}$ on $\mathcal{S}$, one can compute a loose ε-sample E of $\mathcal{S}$, of size $O\left(\int_{\mathcal{S}} \frac{dx}{\psi^2(x)}\right)$. If $\varepsilon \leq 0.12$, the restricted Delaunay triangulation is $\text{Del}_{|\mathcal{S}}(E)$ is a triangulated surface isotopic and close to $\mathcal{S}$.*

3.2   Implementation

Note that the surface is only queried through an *oracle* that, given a line segment f^* (to be the edge of $\text{Vor}(E)$ dual to a facet f of $\text{Del}_{|\mathcal{S}}(E)$), determines whether f^* intersects $\mathcal{S}$ and, in the affirmative, returns an intersection point and the value of ψ at this point.

Still, deciding whether a line segment intersects the surface may be a costly operation. However, a close examination of the proof of correctness of the algorithm shows that Theorems 1 and 2 still hold if we replace the previous oracle by a weaker one that checks if a given line segment s intersects $\mathcal{S}$ an *odd* number of times and, in the affirmative, computes an intersection point. Consider the case where $\mathcal{S}$ is an implicit surface $f(x) = 0$, e.g. an isosurface defined by interpolation in a 3D image. To know if s intersects $\mathcal{S}$ an odd number of times, we just have to evaluate the sign of f at the two endpoints of the segment. It is only in the case where the two signs are different that we will compute an intersection point (usually by binary search). This results in a dramatic reduction of the computing time.

Although the algorithm is quite simple, it is not easy in general to know lfs or even to bound lfs from below, which is required by the oracle. In practice, good results have been obtained using the following simple heuristics. We redefine bad facets to control the distance $\|c_f - c'_f\|$ between the center c_f of the surface Delaunay ball circumscribing a facet f of $\text{Del}_{|\mathcal{S}}(E)$ and the center c'_f of the smallest ball circumscribing f. This strategy nicely adapts the mesh density to the local curvature of $\mathcal{S}$. The local feature size $\text{lfs}(x)$ depends also on the thickness of $\mathcal{S}$

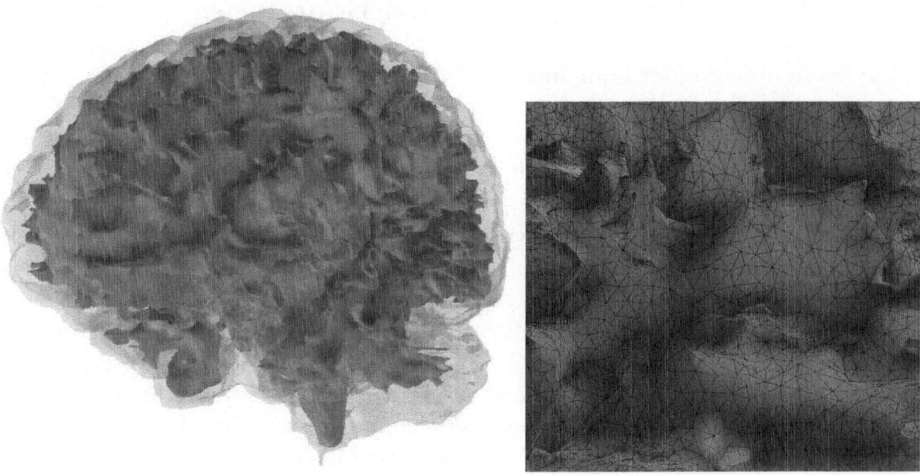

Fig. 5. Meshing an isosurface in a 3D image of the brain

at x, which is a global parameter and therefore difficult to estimate. However, if the sample is too sparse with respect to the object thickness, the restricted Delaunay triangulation is likely to be non manifold and/or to have boundaries. The algorithm can check on the fly that $\mathrm{Del}_{|\mathcal{S}}(E)$ is a triangulated surface with no boundary by checking that each edge in the restricted triangulation is incident to two facets, and that the link of each vertex (i.e. the boundary of the union of the facets incident to the vertex) is a simple polygon.

The issue of estimating lfs can also be circumvented by using a multiscale approach that has been first proposed in the context of manifold reconstruction [15,16]. We slightly modify the algorithm so as to insert at each step the candidate point that is furthest from the current sample. This will guarantee that the sample remains roughly uniform through the process. If we let the algorithm insert points, the topology of the triangulated surface maintained by the algorithm may well change. Consider, for instance, the case of an isosurface in a noisy image, say the brain in Fig. 5. Depending on the sampling density, the topology of the surface may be a topological sphere (which the brain is indeed) or a sphere with additional handles due to noise. Accordingly, the algorithm will produce intermediate meshes of different topologies approximating surfaces of various lfs. Since the changes of topology can be detected by computing at each step the Betti numbers of the current triangulated surface, we can output the various surfaces and the user can decide what is the best one.

The surface meshing algorithm is available in the open source library CGAL [7]. Fig. 5 shows a result on a medical image. A thorough discussion of the implementation of the algorithm and other experimental results can be found in [14].

4   Meshing Volumes with Curved Boundaries

Let $\mathcal{O}$ be an object of $\mathbb{R}^3$ bounded by a surface $\mathcal{S}$. The meshing algorithm of the previous section constructs the 3D Delaunay triangulation of the sample E and extracts from $\mathrm{Del}(E)$ the restricted Delaunay triangulation $\mathrm{Del}_{|\mathcal{S}}(E)$. Hence, the algorithm constructs a 3D triangulation T of $\mathcal{O}$ as well as a polyhedral surface approximating $\mathcal{S}$. However, since the algorithm does not insert points inside $\mathcal{O}$, the aspect ratio of the tetrahedra of T cannot be controlled. If further computations are to be performed, it is then mandatory to improve the shape of the tetrahedra by sampling also the interior of $\mathcal{O}$.

We present in this section a modification of the Delaunay-based surface mesher of the previous section due to Oudot et al. [17]. This algorithm samples the interior and the boundary of the object at the same time so as to obtain a Delaunay refinement volume mesher. Delaunay refinement removes all badly shaped tetrahedra except the so-called slivers. A special postprocessing is required to remove those slivers.

4.1   3D Mesh Refinement Algorithm

The algorithm is still a greedy algorithm that builds a sample E while maintaining the Delaunay triangulations $\mathrm{Del}(E)$ and its restrictions $\mathrm{Del}_{|\mathcal{O}}(E)$ and $\mathrm{Del}_{|\mathcal{S}}(E)$ to the object $\mathcal{O}$ and its bounding surface $\mathcal{S}$.

The sampling density is controlled by a function $\psi(x)$ defined over $\mathcal{O}$ called the *sizing field*. Using constant α, β and γ, we define two types of bad elements. As above, a facet f of $\mathrm{Del}_{|\mathcal{S}}(E)$ is considered as bad if

- either it has a too big surface Delaunay ball $B_f = B(c_f, r_f)$, i.e. $r_f > \alpha\psi(c_f)$,
- or it is badly shaped, meaning that its radius-edge ratio ρ_f is such that $\rho_f > \beta$.

A tetrahedron t of $\mathrm{Del}_{|\mathcal{O}}$ is considered as bad if

- either its circumradius r_t is too big, i.e. $r_t > \psi(c_t)$
- or it is badly shaped, meaning that its radius-edge ratio ρ_t is such that $\rho_t > \gamma$. The radius-edge ratio ρ_t of a tetrahedron t is the ratio between the circumradius and the length of the shortest edge.

The algorithm uses two basic procedures, `refine_facet`(f), which has been defined in Section 3 and the following procedure `refine_tet`(t).

`refine_tet`(t)
    1. insert in E the center c_t of the ball circumscribing t
    2. update $\mathrm{Del}(E)$, $\mathrm{Del}_{|\mathcal{S}}(E)$, $\mathrm{Del}_{|\mathcal{O}}(E)$ and the lists of bad elements.

The algorithm is initialized as the surface meshing algorithm. Then it applies the following refinement rules in order, Rule 2 being applied only when Rule 1 can no longer be applied.

Rule 1. If $\text{Del}_{|\mathcal{S}}(E)$ contains a facet f which has a vertex in $\mathcal{O} \setminus \mathcal{S}$ or is bad, $\texttt{refine\_facet}(f)$

Rule 2. If there is a bad tetrahedron $t \in \text{Del}_{|\mathcal{O}}(E)$
1. compute the center c_t of the circumscribing ball
2. if c_t is included in the surface Delaunay ball of some facet $f \in \text{Del}_{|\mathcal{S}}(E)$, $\texttt{refine\_facet}(f)$
3. else $\texttt{refine\_tet}(t)$.

It is proved in [17] that, for appropriate choices of parameters α, β and γ, the algorithm terminates. Upon termination, $\text{Del}_{|\mathcal{S}}(E) = \text{Del}_{|\mathcal{S}}(E \cap \mathcal{S})$ and $\text{Del}_{\mathcal{O}}(E)$ is a 3D-triangulation isotopic to $\mathcal{O}$.

4.2   Sliver Removal

While Delaunay refinement techniques can be proven to generate tetrahedra with a good radius-edge ratio, they may create flat tetrahedra of a special type called *slivers*. A sliver is a tetrahedron whose four vertices lie close to a plane and whose projection to that plane is a quadrilateral with no short edge. Slivers have a good radius-edge ratio but a poor radius-radius ratio (ratio between the circumradius and the radius of the largest contained sphere). Unfortunately, the latter measure typically influences the numerical conditioning of finite element methods. Slivers occur for example if one computes the Delaunay triangulation of points on a regular grid (slightly pertubed to avoid degeneracies). Each square in the grid can be circumscribed by an empty ball and is therefore a sliver of the triangulation.

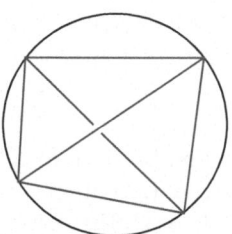

Fig. 6. A sliver

Two techniques are known to remove slivers from volume meshes. One consists of a post-processing step called sliver exudation [18]. This step does not include any new vertex in the mesh, nor does it move any of them. Each vertex is assigned a weight and the Delaunay triangulation is turned into a weighted Delaunay triangulation. The weights are carefully chosen so that no vertex disappear from the mesh, nor any change occurs in the boundary facets (i. e. the facets of $\text{Del}_{|\mathcal{S}}(E)$). Within these constraints, the weight of each vertex is optimized in turn to maximize the minimum dihedral angles of the tetrahedra incident to that vertex. Although the guaranteed theoretical bound on dihedral angles is known

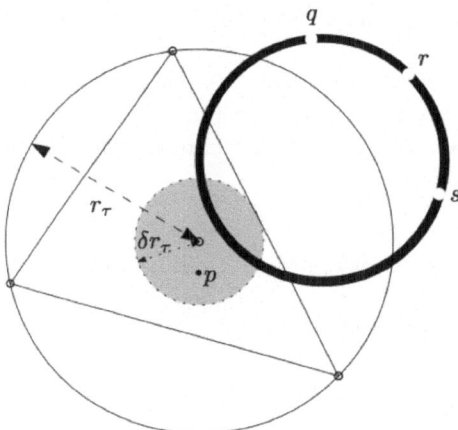

Fig. 7. The new point to be inserted is taken from the grey disk centered at the circumcenter of the bad element τ but not in the black annulus to prevent the creation of slivers

to be miserably low, this algorithm is quite efficient in practice at removing slivers.

Another technique, due to Li [19], avoids the appearance of small slivers in the mesh by relaxing the choice of the refinement points of a bad element (tetrahedron or boundary facet). The new points are no longer inserted at the circumcenters of Delaunay balls or surface Delaunay balls but in small *picking regions* around those circumcenters. Within such a picking region, we further avoid inserting points that would create slivers. (see Fig. 7).

4.3   Implementation

We present two results in Fig. 8 on both uniform and non uniform sizing fields. The uniform model is an approximation of an isosurface in a 3D medical image. The initial mesh of the surface had 33,012 vertices while the second step of the algorithm added 53,762 new vertices in the interior of the object and 2,471 new vertices on its boundary. The total CPU time was 20s on a Pentium IV (1.7 GHz). A thorough discussion of the implementation of the algorithm and other experimental results can be found in [17,20]. The algorithm will be soon available in the open source library CGAL [7].

4.4   Meshing of Multi-label Datasets

The above method seamlessly extends to the case of non-binary partitions, so that it can be applied to the generation of high quality geometric models with multiple junctions from multi-label datasets, frequently encountered in medical applications.

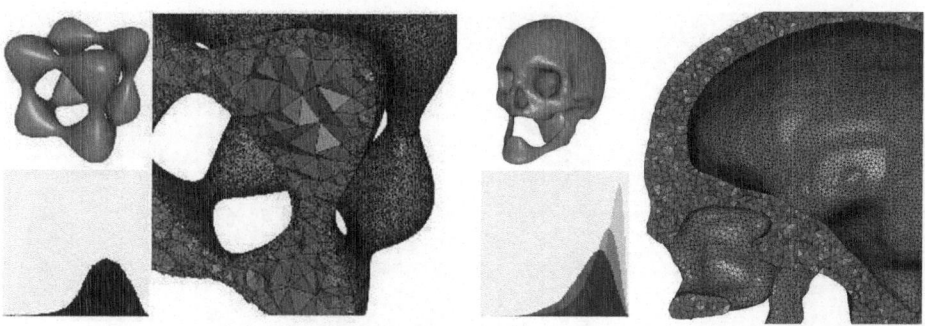

Fig. 8. Non uniform and uniform meshes obtained by the algorithm of Section 4. The lower left corners show histograms of the radius-radius ratios of tetrahedra in the mesh, where the radius-radius ratio of a tetrahedron is the ratio between the circumradius and the radius of the maximum inscribed ball.

To that end, we define a partition of Delaunay tetrahedra induced by a space subdivision. It is closely related to the concept of restricted Delaunay triangulation. Let us consider $\mathcal{P} = \{\Omega_0, \dots, \Omega_n\}$ a partition of space into the background 0 and n different regions, i.e.

$$\mathbb{R}^3 = \cup_{i \in \{0, \dots, n\}} \Omega_i$$

and let Γ denote the boundaries of the partition:

$$\Gamma = \cup_i \partial \Omega_i.$$

This continuous space subdivision is approximated by a discrete partition of a Delaunay triangulation: given a set of points E in $\mathbb{R}^3$, we define the partition of Delaunay tetrahedra induced by $\mathcal{P}$, denoted by $\mathrm{Del}_{|\mathcal{P}}(E)$, as the partition of the tetrahedra of $\mathrm{Del}(E)$ depending on the region containing their circumcenter. In other words, $\mathrm{Del}_{|\mathcal{P}}(E) = \{\mathrm{Del}_{|\Omega_0}(E), \dots, \mathrm{Del}_{|\Omega_n}(E)\}$, where $\mathrm{Del}_{|\Omega_i}(E)$ is the set of tetrahedra of $\mathrm{Del}(E)$ whose circumcenters are contained in Ω_i.

By construction, $\mathrm{Del}_{|\mathcal{P}}(E)$ induces watertight surface meshes free of self-intersections, and volume meshes associated to the different regions. All meshes are mutually consistent, including at multiple junctions. In particular, the surface meshes are composed of the triangular facets adjacent to two tetrahedra assigned to different regions (i.e. belonging to different parts of $\mathrm{Del}_{|\mathcal{P}}(E)$) and of the convex hull facets adjacent to non-background tetrahedra. These facets are called boundary facets in the sequel.

By the results of Sections 3 and 4, the surface and volume meshes form a good approximation of the original partition $\mathcal{P}$ as soon as E is a sufficiently dense sample. Hence, our meshing algorithm again consists in iteratively refining the point set until it forms a good sample of the boundaries between the different regions, and, if a quality volume mesh is desired, a good sample of their interior.

A notable feature of this approach is that the continuous partition need not be represented explicitly. It is known only through a labeling oracle that, given a

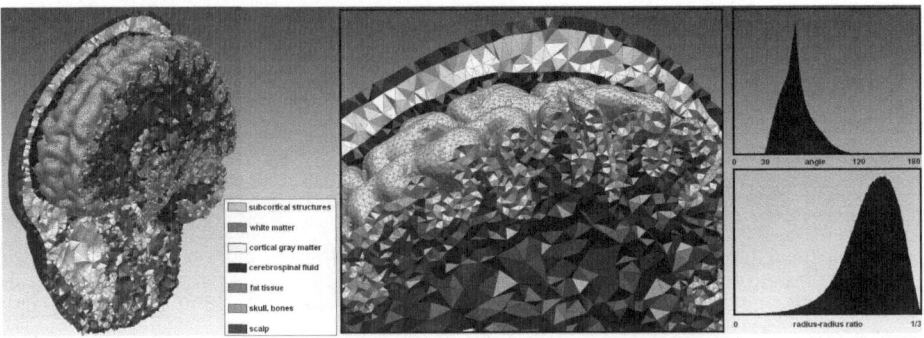

Fig. 9. *Left:* Surface and volume meshes of head tissues generated from a segmented magnetic resonance image. Cross-sections along different planes are displayed to make apparent the high quality of both boundary facets and tetrahedra. *Right:* Angle and radius-radius ratio distributions of surface meshes and volume meshes, respectively.

point in space, answers which region it belongs to. This oracle can be formulated as a labeling function $L_{\mathcal{P}} : \mathbb{R}^3 \to \{0, \ldots, n\}$ associated to the partition $\mathcal{P}$, such that $L_{\mathcal{P}}(p) = i$ if and only if $p \in \Omega_i$. Intersections of a segment or a line with Γ can be computed to the desired accuracy using a dichotomic search on $L_{\mathcal{P}}$.

This makes the approach applicable to virtually any combination of data sources, including segmented 3D images, polyhedral surfaces, unstructured volume meshes, fuzzy membership functions, possibly having different resolutions and different coordinate systems. The different data sources may even be inconsistent with each other due to noise or discretization artefacts. In this case, the labeling oracle has the responsibility of resolving the conflicts using some user defined rules. As a result, our meshing algorithm is not affected by the heterogeneity and possible inconsistency of the input datasets.

Another important source of flexibility of our approach is that the customizable quality criteria on boundary facets and/or on tetrahedra mentioned in Sections 3 and 4 can be tuned independently for the different regions. Thus, a boundary facet must be tested against the criteria of its two adjacent regions. It is classified as a good facet if it fulfills both criteria.

An experimental result on real medical data is shown in Fig. 9. For further discussion and experimental results, please refer to [21].

5   Anisotropic Meshes

Anisotropic meshes are triangulations of a given domain in the plane or in higher dimensions, with elements elongated along prescribed directions. Anisotropic triangulations have been shown to be particularly well suited for interpolation of functions or numerical modeling [22]. They allow minimizing the number of triangles in the mesh while retaining a good accuracy in computations. For such applications, the directions along which the elements should be elongated are usually given as quadratic forms at each point. These directions may be related to the curvature of the function to be interpolated, or to some specific directions taken into account in the equations to be solved.

Anisotropy represented in the form of metric tensors is widely used in image processing, in two main contexts. First, for a general scalar or vector-valued image, a structure tensor [23,24] which characterizes the local image structure can be defined. It is a classical tool for edge and corner detection. Second, a recent medical imaging modality called diffusion tensor magnetic resonance imaging (DT-MRI) produces a field of symmetric positive definite matrices which locally quantify the anisotropic diffusion of water molecules in the tissues. In both cases, these tensors induce Riemannian metrics on the image domain, which have frequently been embedded in segmentation and motion estimation algorithms, making the latter more faithful to image structure. Since intensity variations are typically correlated with the underlying geometry, these metrics can also enhance the extraction of geometric models from segmented images.

Various heuristic solutions for the generation of anisotropic meshes have been proposed. Li et al. [25] and Shimada et al. [26] use packing methods. Bossen and Heckbert [27] use a method consisting in centroidal smoothing, retriangulating and inserting or removing sites. Borouchaki et al. [28] adapt the classical Delaunay refinement algorithm to the case of an anisotropic metric. A related topic is anisotropic mesh adaptation, a popular technique used to improve numerical simulations. The mesh is iteratively improved by using a metric field computed from an error analysis until the mesh and the solution converge [29].

Recently, Labelle and Shewchuk [30] have settled the foundations for a rigorous approach for anisotropic mesh generation based on the so-called anisotropic Voronoi diagram. The framework is the following. We consider a domain $\Omega \subset \mathbb{R}^d$ and assume that each point $p \in \Omega$ is given a symmetric positive definite quadratic form represented by a $d \times d$ matrix M_p, called the metric at p. The distance between two points a and b, as measured by metric M_p is defined as

$$d_{M_p}(a,b) = \sqrt{(a-b)^t M_p(a-b)}.$$

In the sequel, $E = \{p_1, \ldots, p_n\}$ denotes a set of points. The points associated with their metrics, are called *sites*. We can associate to each point p_i of E its Voronoi cell

$$V(p_i) = \{x \in \mathbb{R}^d : \forall j, d_{M_{p_i}}(x) \le d_{M_{p_j}}(x)\}.$$

The subdivision induced by these Voronoi cells is called the *anisotropic diagram* of E (Fig. 10). In the special case where the metric is the same at each site, i.e. $M_{p_i} = M$ for $1 \le i \le n$, the anisotropic diagram is a power diagram. Indeed,

$$(x-p_i)^t M(x-p_i) < (x-p_j)^t M(x-p_j) \;\Leftrightarrow\; -2p_i^t Mx + p_i^t Mp_i < -2p_j^t Mx + p_j^t Mp_j.$$

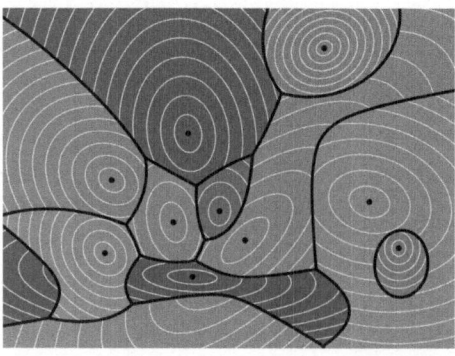

Fig. 10. An anisotropic diagram (from [30])

Write σ_i for the hypersphere of equation $x^2 - 2\,p_i^t M x + p_i^t M p_i = 0$. It follows from the inequality above that x belongs to $V(p_i)$ iff x belongs to the power cell of σ_i in the power diagram of $\sigma_1, \ldots, \sigma_n$. In addition, the anisotropic diagram has a dual triangulation, the regular triangulation dual to the power diagram of the σ_i.

Differently, in the general case where the M_{p_i} are distinct, the dual of the anisotropic diagram may not be a triangulation. Nevertheless, Labelle and Shewchuk have shown that, in the 2-dimensional case, the dual of the anisotropic diagram is an embedded triangulation when the density of the sample E is sufficiently high [30]. Based on this observation, they proposed a method to construct anisotropic triangulations of planar domains: the anisotropic diagram of a set of sample point is refined by insertion of new sites until the geometric dual diagram is an embedded triangulation. A simpler variant of the algorithm that provides a direct computation of the dual mesh without computing the anisotropic diagram can be found in [31].

The main limitation of Labelle and Shewchuk's approach is that it is restricted to the 2D case or the case of surfaces embedded in 3D [32]. The presence of slivers in higher dimensions, and especially in 3D, have prevented the extension of the method.

An alternative approach is presented in [33]. This approach, based on the notion of *locally uniform anisotropic triangulation*, still follows the Delaunay refinement paradigm. A locally uniform anisotropic triangulation of a set of points E is a triangulation T of E in which the star $T(v)$ of any vertex v coincides exactly with the star of this vertex in the Delaunay triangulation $\mathrm{Del}_v(E)$ of the set E computed for the metric M_v of v. Given a set of sites E and a site $v \in E$, computing the Delaunay triangulation $\mathrm{Del}_v(E)$ for the metric M_v is simple, since this triangulation is just the regular triangulation dual to a power diagram as explained above.

The algorithm maintains a sample E and a set of local triangulations, one for each site in E, where the local triangulation of site v is reduced to the star of v in $\mathrm{Del}_v(E)$. (An analog data structure was suggested by Shewchuk in [34]

Fig. 11. Anisotropic mesh of the surface of a torus

to handle triangulations of moving points.) At the beginning the local stars are inconsistent, meaning that a tetrahedron appearing in one local star may not appear in the local stars of its four vertices. The algorithm refines the sample E until there is no more inconsistencies. so that the local stars can be merged together to form a locally uniform anisotropic triangulation.

Inconsistencies among the local stars arise either because the metric is highly distorted on the domain covered by a single tetrahedron or in presence of *quasi-cospherical* configurations. The first situation is not problematic since introducing new points in the sample will reduce the distortion. The case of quasi-cospherical configurations is more serious and may prevent the refinement process to terminate. This problem is strongly related to the presence of slivers and can be solved by avoiding the creation of quasi-cocyclic configurations in a way similar to the way Li and Teng suggested to avoid slivers (see Section 4.2). New points are inserted in the so-called *picking region* which consists of a small ball around the circumcenter of a bad tetrahedron minus the locus of points yielding quasi-cospherical configurations.

This algorithm is simple and straightforward since it relies on the usual Delaunay predicates (applied to some stretched spaces). It may be extended to $\mathbb{R}^3$. In $\mathbb{R}^3$ the new points are inserted in picking regions so has to avoid both slivers and quasi-cospherical configurations. An anisotropic mesh of a surface torus, obtained with this method, is shown in Fig. 11.

6 Higher Dimensions

Remarkably, the framework described in the previous sections extends to Euclidean spaces of dimensions higher than three. In particular, it allows to address spatio-temporal problems frequently occurring in science and engineering. Let us mention temporal sequences of MR (magnetic resonance) images of the beating heart in medical imaging, and spatio-temporal reconstruction of moving scenes from videos in computer vision. The latter application is detailed in Section 6.2.

Spatio-temporal models are not the only motivation to construct meshes in higher dimensions. Although we will not discuss such applications in this paper, let us mention the study of physical dynamical systems which is naturally expressed in 6D phase-space. Also, many machine learning problems, notably in computer vision, are tackled by mapping input data into higher dimensional parametric spaces.

To extend our meshing algorithms, we first need to extend the construction of the Delaunay triangulation in higher dimensional spaces.

6.1 Computing Delaunay Triangulations in Spaces of Medium Dimensions

Very efficient and robust codes nowadays exist for constructing Delaunay triangulations in two and three dimensions [7], the situation is less satisfactory in higher dimensions: the few existing Delaunay codes in higher dimensions are either non robust, or very slow and space demanding, which make them of little use in practice. This situation is partially explained by the fact that the size of the Delaunay triangulation of points grows very fast (exponentially in the worst-case) with the dimension. However, a careful implementation can lead to dramatic improvement and quite big input sets can be triangulated in spaces of dimensions up to 6.

In [35], we propose a new C++ implementation of the well-known incremental construction. The algorithm maintains, at each step, the complete set of d-simplices together with their adjacency graph. Two main ingredients are used to speed up the algorithm. First, the input points are pre-sorted along a d-dimensional Hilbert curve to accelerate point location. In addition, the dimension of the embedding space is a C++ template parameter instanciated at compile time. We thus avoid a lot of memory management. The code is fully robust and computes the exact Delaunay triangulation of the input data set. Following the central philosophy of the CGAL library, predicates are evaluated exactly using arithmetic filters.

Fig. 12 presents a benchmark of the speed and memory usage of our implementation, with dimension ranging from 2 to 6 and input size ranging from $1K$ to $1024K$ points. We have run our code on input sets consisting of uniformly distributed random points in a unit cube with floating point (double) input coordinate type. In each case, the input points are provided at once, which permits the use of spatial sorting prior to inserting the points in the triangulation.

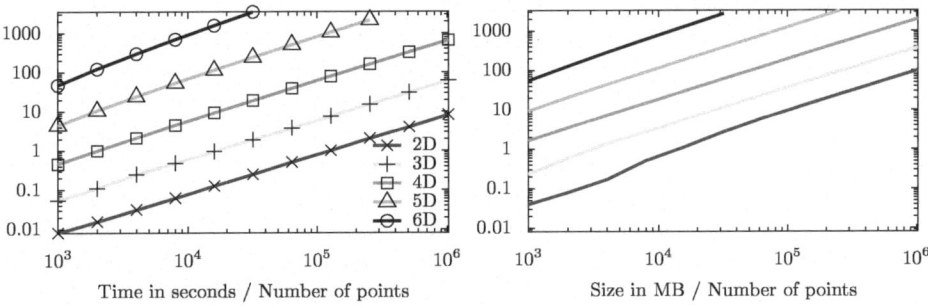

Fig. 12. Timings (left) and space usage (right) of our novel Delaunay triangulation implementation. All axes are logarithmic.

Similar results are observed when the points lie on a manifold of co-dimension 1, which is the case for points on a deforming surface. Further experiments are discussed in [35].

6.2 Application to Spatio-temporal Scene Modeling from Video Sequences

In [36], we have used a higher-dimensional extension of the meshing algorithm of Section 3 to compute 4D spatio-temporal representations of non-rigid dynamic scenes from multiple video sequences.

By considering time as an additional dimension, we could exploit seamlessly the time coherence between different video frames to produce a compact and high-quality 4D representation of the scene. The 3D model at a given time instant can easily be obtained by intersecting this 4D mesh with a temporal

Fig. 13. A few 3D slices of a 4D space-time reconstruction of a moving scene from real video data

plane. Compared to independent frame-by-frame computations, this point of view has several significant advantages. First, it exploits time redundancy to limit the size of the output representation. For example, parts of the scene that are immobile or have a uniform motion can be approximated by a piecewise-linear 4D mesh with few elements elongated in the time direction. In contrast, in the same configuration, a frame-by-frame approach would repeat 3D elements at each frame. Second, such an approach yields a temporally continuous representation, which is defined at any time, thus enabling interpolation of objects' shape between consecutive frames. This also makes a spatio-temporal smoothing possible, in order to recover from occasional outliers in the data. Third, a byproduct of the two first advantages is the reduction of flickering artefacts in synthesized views, as consecutive 3D slices have a similar geometry and connectivity by construction. At last, changes in 3D topology along time are handled naturally by our spatio-temporal embedding formulation.

A sample result is displayed in Fig. 13, in the form of several 3D slices of the output 4D mesh. More generally, this application demonstrates the feasibility of 4D hypersurface representations in image processing. It is likely to inspire progress in other applications, such as the spatio-temporal modeling of the beating heart from temporal sequences of MR images.

7   Conclusion

We have presented algorithms for mesh generation by Delaunay refinement and some of their applications in Computer Vision and Medical Imaging. As reported in this paper as well as in other recent survey papers [37,38], Delaunay-based meshing algorithms have advantages over grid-based algorithms like the marching cubes algorithm. Most notably, they offer theoretical guarantees on the quality of the approximation and also on the shape of the elements (facets or tetrahedra) of the mesh. Moreover, the paradigm of Delaunay refinement is quite flexible and can be adapted to mesh surfaces, 3D domains, or even higher dimensional manifolds, and to take into account anisotropic metric fields.

Due to limited space, we have assumed throughout the paper that the objects to be meshed were smooth. Extensions of the Delaunay refinement paradigm to non-smooth objects can be found in [10,20,39].

The algorithms discussed in this paper are based on the experience of the Geometrica group at INRIA Sophia-Antipolis[3]. The algorithms described in this paper are or will soon be available from the CGAL library [7]. They have been used for image segmentation [40], data assimilation for cardiac electrome-chanical modeling [41], surface reconstruction from unorganized data points [42,43]. We hope that they will find further applications in Computer Vision and Medical Imaging, Computer Aided Design, Computer Graphics and Numerical Simulation.

---

[3] http://www-sop.inria.fr/geometrica

Acknowledgments

Research reported in this paper has been conducted in collaboration with Steve Oudot, Laurent Rineau and Camille Wormser who are gratefully acknowledged.

References

1. Pham, D.L., Xu, C., Prince, J.L.: A survey of current methods in medical image segmentation. Annual Review of Biomedical Engineering 2, 315–338 (2000)
2. Lorensen, W.E., Cline, H.E.: Marching Cubes: A high resolution 3D surface construction algorithm. Computer Graphics 21(4), 163–169 (1987)
3. Plantinga, S., Vegter, G.: Isotopic meshing of implicit surfaces. The Visual Computer 23, 45–58 (2007)
4. Labelle, F., Shewchuk, J.: Isosurface stuffing: fast tetrahedral meshes with good dihedral angles. ACM Transactions on Graphics 26(3) (2007)
5. Edelsbrunner, E.: Geometry and Topology for Mesh Generation, Cambridge (2001)
6. Boissonnat, J.D., Devillers, O., Pion, S., Teillaud, M., Yvinec, M.: Triangulations in CGAL. Computational Geometry: Theory and Applications 22, 5–19 (2002)
7. CGAL, Computational Geometry Algorithms Library, http://www.cgal.org
8. Federer, H.: Curvature measures. Transactions of the American Mathematical Society 93(3), 418–491 (1959)
9. Amenta, N., Bern, M.: Surface reconstruction by Voronoi filtering. Discrete Comput. Geom. 22(4), 481–504 (1999)
10. Boissonnat, J.D., Oudot, S.: Provably good sampling and meshing of lipschitz surfaces. In: Proc. 22nd Annual ACM Symposium on Computational Geometry (2006)
11. Cohen-Steiner, D., Morvan, J.M.: Restricted Delaunay triangulations and normal cycle. In: Proc. 19th Annual ACM Symposium on Computational Geometry, pp. 237–246 (2003)
12. Ruppert, J.: A Delaunay refinement algorithm for quality 2-dimensional mesh generation. J. Algorithms 18, 548–585 (1995)
13. Chew, L.P.: Guaranteed-quality delaunay meshing in 3d (short version). In: SCG 1997: Proceedings of the thirteenth annual symposium on Computational geometry, pp. 391–393. ACM, New York (1997)
14. Boissonnat, J.D., Oudot, S.: Provably good sampling and meshing of surfaces. Graphical Models 67, 405–451 (2005)
15. Guibas, L.J., Oudot, S.Y.: Reconstruction using witness complexes. In: Proc. 18th ACM-SIAM Sympos. on Discrete Algorithms (SODA), pp. 1076–1085 (2007)
16. Boissonnat, J.D., Guibas, L., Oudot, S.: Learning smooth shapes by probing. Comput. Geom. Theory and Appl. 37, 38–58 (2007)
17. Oudot, S., Rineau, L., Yvinec, M.: Meshing volumes bounded by smooth surfaces. In: Proc. 14th International Meshing Roundtable, pp. 203–219 (2005)
18. Cheng, S.W., Dey, T.K., Edelsbrunner, H., Facello, M.A., Teng, S.H.: Silver exudation. J. ACM 47(5), 883–904 (2000)
19. Li, X.Y.: Sliver-free Three Dimensional Delaunay Mesh Generation. PhD thesis, University of Illinois at Urbana-Champaign (2000)
20. Rineau, L., Yvinec, M.: Meshing 3d domains bounded by piecewise smooth surfaces. In: Meshing Roundtable conference proceedings, pp. 443–460 (2007)

21. Pons, J.P., Ségonne, F., Boissonnat, J.D., Rineau, L., Yvinec, M., Keriven, R.: High-quality consistent meshing of multi-label datasets. In: Karssemeijer, N., Lelieveldt, B. (eds.) IPMI 2007. LNCS, vol. 4584, pp. 198–210. Springer, Heidelberg (2007)

22. Shewchuk, J.R.: What is a good linear finite element? Interpolation, conditioning, anisotropy, and quality measures (manuscript, 2002), http://www.cs.cmu.edu/ jrs/jrspapers.html

23. Bigun, J., Granlund, G.: Optimal orientation detection of linear symmetry. In: International Conference on Computer Vision, pp. 433–438 (1987)

24. Harris, C., Stephens, M.: A combined corner and edge detector. In: Proc. 4th Alvey Vision Conference, pp. 147–151 (1988)

25. Li, X.Y., Teng, S.H., Üngör, A.: Biting ellipses to generate anisotropic mesh. In: 8th International Meshing Roundtable (October 1999)

26. Shimada, K., Yamada, A., Itoh, T.: Anisotropic Triangulation of Parametric Surfaces via Close Packing of Ellipsoids. Int. J. Comput. Geometry Appl. 10(4), 417–440 (2000)

27. Bossen, F., Heckbert, P.: A pliant method for anisotropic mesh generation. In: 5th International Meshing Roundtable (October 1996)

28. Borouchaki, H., George, P.L., Hecht, F., Laug, P., Saltel, E.: Delaunay mesh generation governed by metric specifications. part I algorithms. Finite Elem. Anal. Des. 25(1-2), 61–83 (1997)

29. Dobrzynski, C., Frey, P.: Anisotropic delaunay mesh adaptation for unsteady simulations. In: Proc. 17th International Meshing Roundtable (2008)

30. Labelle, F., Shewchuk, J.R.: Anisotropic voronoi diagrams and guaranteed-quality anisotropic mesh generation. In: SCG 2003: Proceedings of the nineteenth annual symposium on Computational geometry, pp. 191–200. ACM Press, New York (2003)

31. Boissonnat, J.D., Wormser, C., Yvinec, M.: Anisotropic diagrams: Labelle shewchuk approach revisited. Theoretical Computer Science (to appear)

32. Cheng, S.W., Dey, T.K., Ramos, E.A., Wenger, R.: Anisotropic surface meshing. In: SODA 2006: Proceedings of the seventeenth annual ACM-SIAM symposium on Discrete algorithm, pp. 202–211. ACM, New York (2006)

33. Boissonnat, J.D., Wormser, C., Yvinec, M.: Locally uniform anisotropic meshing. In: Proceedings of the 24th Annu. ACM Sympos. Comput. Geom., pp. 270–277 (2008)

34. Shewchuk, R.: Star splaying: an algorithm for repairing delaunay triangulations and convex hulls. In: SCG 2005: Proceedings of the twenty-first annual symposium on Computational geometry, pp. 237–246. ACM, New York (2005)

35. Hornus, S., Boissonnat, J.D.: An efficient implementation of delaunay triangulations in medium dimensions. Technical report, INRIA (2008)

36. Aganj, E., Pons, J.P., Ségonne, F., Keriven, R.: Spatio-temporal shape from silhouette using four-dimensional delaunay meshing. In: IEEE International Conference on Computer Vision (2007)

37. Boissonnat, J.D., Cohen-Steiner, D., Mourrain, B., Rote, G., Vegter, G.: Meshing of surfaces. In: Boissonnat, J.D., Teillaud, M. (eds.) Effective Computational Geometry for Curves and Surfaces. Mathematics and Visualization, pp. 181–229. Springer, Heidelberg (2006)

38. Dey, T.: Delaunay mesh generation of three dimensional domains. Technical report, Ohio State University (2007)

39. Cheng, S.W., Dey, T.K., Levine, J.: A practical delaunay meshing algorithm for a large class of domains. In: Proc. 16th International Meshing Roundtable (2007)

40. Pons, J.P., Boissonnat, J.D.: Delaunay deformable models: Topology-adaptive meshes based on the restricted Delaunay triangulation. In: IEEE Conference on Computer Vision and Pattern Recognition CVPR 2007 (2007)
41. Moreau, P., Chapelle, D., Yvinec, M.: Cardiac motion extraction from images by filtering estimation based on a biomechanical model (to be submitted)
42. Boissonnat, J.D., Cazals, F.: Smooth surface reconstruction via natural neighbour interpolation of distance functions. Computational Geometry: Theory and Applications, 185–203 (2002)
43. Alliez, P., Cohen-Steiner, D., Tong, Y., Desbrun, M.: Voronoi-based variational reconstruction of unoriented point sets. In: EUROGRAPHICS Symposium on Geometry Processing, pp. 39–48 (2007)

Discrete Curvature Flows for Surfaces and 3-Manifolds

Xiaotian Yin[1], Miao Jin[2], Feng Luo[3], and Xianfeng David Gu[1],[*]

[1] Computer Science Department,
State University of New York at Stony Brook
{xyin,gu}@cs.sunysb.edu
[2] Center for Advanced Computer Studies,
University of Louisiana at Lafayette
mjin@cacs.louisiana.edu
[3] Department of Mathematics,
Rutgers University
fluo@math.rutgers.edu

Abstract. Intrinsic curvature flows can be used to design Riemannian metrics by prescribed curvatures. This chapter presents three discrete curvature flow methods that are recently introduced into the engineering fields: the discrete Ricci flow and discrete Yamabe flow for surfaces with various topology, and the discrete curvature flow for hyperbolic 3-manifolds with boundaries. For each flow, we introduce its theories in both the smooth setting and the discrete setting, plus the numerical algorithms to compute it. We also provide a brief survey on their history and their link to some of the engineering applications in computer graphics, computer vision, medical imaging, computer aided design and others.

Keywords: Curvature flow, the Ricci flow, Yamabe flow, discrete, surface, 3-manifold.

1 Introduction

Intrinsic curvature flows have been used in Riemannian geometry in the past 50 years with great successes. These flows deform a given Riemannian metric according to its curvature. Among the most famous ones are the *Ricci flow* and the *Yamabe flow*. Both of them can be used to design Riemannian metrics with special curvature properties.

The Ricci flow deforms the Riemannian metric according to its Ricci curvature. In particular, it can be used to find a metric with constant Ricci curvature. There is a simple physical intuition behind it. Given a compact manifold with a Riemannian metric, the metric induces the curvature function. If the metric is changed, the curvature will be changed accordingly. The metric can be deformed

---

[*] This work has been supported by NSF CCF-0448399, NSF DMS-0528363, NSF DMS-0626223, NSF IIS-0713145.

F. Nielsen (Ed.): ETVC 2008, LNCS 5416, pp. 38–74, 2009.
© Springer-Verlag Berlin Heidelberg 2009

in the following way: at each point, locally scale the metric, so that the scaling factor is proportional to the curvature at the point. After the deformation, the curvature will be changed. Repeating this deformation process, both the metric and the curvature will evolve like a heat diffusion. Eventually, the curvature function will become constant everywhere.

Another intrinsic curvature flow is called *Yamabe flow*. It has the same physical intuition with the Ricci flow, except for that it is driven by the scalar curvature instead of Ricci curvature. For 2-manifolds, the Yamabe flow is essentially equivalent to the Ricci flow. But for higher dimensional manifolds, Yamabe flow is much more flexible than the Ricci flow to reach constant-scalar-curvature metrics.

Due to the ability of intrinsic curvature flows on metric designs and their practical significance (see section 1.1), three special flows have been recently introduced into the engineering fields: a discrete Ricci flow on surfaces, a discrete Yamabe flow on surfaces and a discrete curvature flow on 3-manifolds. Through these work the power of curvature flows has been extended from the pure theoretical study to solving practical problems.

1.1 Motivations

Curvature flows have played critical roles in the study of differential geometry for a long time. One of the most recent examples appears in the proof of the Poincaré conjecture on 3-manifolds [Per02, Per03b, Per03a], where the Ricci flow is employed as a fundamental tool.

Besides that, intrinsic curvature flows also turn out to be able to help solve many practical problems in engineering fields, especially those that can be formulated as finding certain metrics with desired properties.

In graphics, a surface parametrization is commonly used, which refers to the process of mapping a given surface to a canonical domain. If the domain is planar, then it is equivalent to finding a Riemannian metric that induces zero Gaussian curvature everywhere. Such a metric is called a flat metric.

In digital geometry processing, if such a parameterization is known, any signal (e.g. texture) on the surface can be defined on the parametric domain. Complicated processing tasks on surfaces can be simplified to easier ones on the parametric domains, such as texturing [LPRM02] and re-meshing [AMD02].

In computer-aided geometric modeling, a flat metric is helpful for constructing manifold splines, whose parametric domains are manifolds with arbitrary topologies instead of planar domains. In order to build a manifold spline, a special atlas of the domain manifold is required, such that all local coordinate transition maps are affine. One way to construct such an atlas is to find a flat metric. Details of the manifold theory and the construction of an affine atlas can be found in [GHQ06].

In the medical imaging field, conformal brain mapping has been widely used, which maps the human brain cortical surfaces to the unit sphere to facilitate registration, fusion, and comparison. This is equivalent to finding a Riemannian metric on the brain cortical surface, such that the induced Gaussian curvature is a constant +1 everywhere.

For 3-manifolds, discrete curvature flow is also valuable, not only for the theoretical investigation of their topological structures and geometric properties, but also for many engineering applications over them, such as volumetric parameterization, registration, shape analysis and so on.

One should note that, in engineering fields manifolds are usually approximated using discrete constructions, such as piece-wise linear meshes; in order to employ curvature flow to solve practical problems, we need to extend the theories of curvature flows from the smooth setting to the corresponding discrete setting, and need to pay attention to the convergence of the later to the former. Based on the discrete theories and formula, one is allowed to design computer algorithms which can simulate and compute the flow.

1.2   A Brief History

The theory of intrinsic curvature flows originated from differential geometry, and were later introduced into the engineering fields. In this section, we give a brief overview of the literature that are directly related to the three flows mentioned above. For each flow, we would introduce some representative work on three aspects: theories in the smooth setting, theories in the discrete setting and computer algorithms to compute the flow.

The Ricci Flow on Surfaces. The Ricci flow was introduced by R. Hamilton in a seminal paper [Ham82] for Riemannian manifolds of any dimension. The Ricci flow has revolutionized the study of geometry of surfaces and 3-manifolds and has inspired huge research activities in geometry. In particular, it leads to a proof of the 3-dimensional Poincaré conjecture. In the paper [Ham88], Hamilton used the 2-dimensional Ricci flow to give a proof of the uniformization theorem for surfaces of positive genus. This leads a way for potential applications to computer graphics.

There are many ways to discretize smooth surfaces. The one which is particularly related to a discretization of conformality is the circle packing metric introduced by Thurston [Thu80]. The notion of circle packing has appeared in the work of Koebe [Koe36]. Thurston conjectured in [Thu85] that for a discretization of the Jordan domain in the plane, the sequence of circle packings converge to the Riemann mapping. This was proved by Rodin and Sullivan [RS87].

Colin de Verdiere [dVY91] established the first variational principle for circle packing and proved Thurston's existence of circle packing metrics. This paved a way for a fast algorithmic implementation of finding the circle packing metrics, such as the one by Collins and Stephenson [CS03]. In [CL03], Chow and Luo generalized Colin de Verdiere's work and introduced the discrete Ricci flow and discrete Ricci energy on surfaces. They proved a general existence and convergence theorem for the discrete Ricci flow and proved that the Ricci energy is convex. The algorithmic implementation of the discrete Ricci flow was carried out by Jin et al [JKLG08].

Another related discretization method is called circle pattern; it considers both the combinatorics and the geometry of the original mesh, and can be looked as a variant to circle packings. Circle pattern was proposed by Bowers and Hurdal

[BH03], and has been proven to be a minimizer of a convex energy by Bobenko and Springborn [BS04]. An efficient circle pattern algorithm was developed by Kharevych et al [KSS06].

The Yamabe Flow on Surfaces. The Yamabe problem aims at finding a conformal metric with constant scalar curvature for compact Riemannian manifolds. The first proof (with flaws) was given by Yamabe [Yam60], which was corrected and extended to a complete proof by several researchers including Trudinger [Tru68], Aubin [Aub76] and Schoen [Sch84]. A comprehensive survey on this topic was given by Lee and Parker in [LP87].

In [Luo04] Luo studied the discrete Yamabe flow on surfaces. He introduced a notion of discrete conformal change of polyhedral metric, which plays a key role in developing the discrete Yamabe flow and the associated variational principle in the field. Based on the discrete conformal class and geometric consideration, Luo gave the discrete Yamabe energy as an integration of a differential 1-form and proved that this energy is a locally convex function. He also deduced from it that the curvature evolution of the Yamabe flow is a heat equation.

In a very nice recent work of Springborn et al [SSP08] they were able to identify the Yamabe energy introduced by Luo with the Milnor-Lobachevsky function and the heat equation for the curvature evolution with the cotangent Laplace equation. They constructed an algorithm based on their explicit formula. Another recent work by Gu et al [CCG], which used the original discrete Yamabe energy from [Luo04], has produced an equally efficient algorithm in finding the discrete conformal metrics.

A Curvature Flow on 3-Manifolds. Due to the drastic difference between the geometry of 3-manifolds and that of 2-manifolds, it turns out that the study of curvature flows is much more complicated on the former than on the later. This is also reflected by the fact that it is harder and slower for the discrete curvature flow on 3-manifolds to be introduced into the engineering fields than that on 2-manifolds.

The very first work of the Ricci flow on 3-manifolds was given by Hamilton in his seminal paper [Ham82]. Following this line Perelman was able to apply the Ricci flow to prove the Poincaré conjecture and Thurston's geometrization conjecture in [Per02, Per03b, Per03a]. Inspired by the ideas from [Ham82], Luo introduced the discrete curvature flow on a special class of compact 3-manifolds whose boundary is consisting of surfaces of negative Euler characteristic. In a very recent work by Yin et al [YJLG08], they developed an algorithm to compute the discrete curvature flow and visualize the constant-curvature metrics on such 3-manifolds.

The rest of the chapter is organized as follows. We first introduce some basic concepts and theories of the surface Ricci flow in both the smooth setting (section 2) and the discrete setting (section 3), which is followed by the numerical algorithms to compute the flow (section 4). In section 5 we present the discrete algorithm of surface Yamabe flow. The discrete curvature flow on 3-manifolds with boundaries are introduced in section 6 and the numerical algorithm is presented in 7. Further details on discrete curvature flows and their variational principles can be found in [LGD07]. The details and source codes of the algorithms presented here can be found in [GY08] and [CCG].

2   Theories on the Smooth Surface Ricci Flow

In this section, we introduce the theory of the Ricci flow in the continuous setting, which will be extended to the discrete setting in 3.

2.1   Fundamental Group and Universal Covering Space

The closed loops on the surface can be classified by homotopy equivalence. If two closed curves on a surface M can deform to each other without leaving the surface, then they are *homotopic* to each other. Two closed curves sharing common points can be concatenated to form another loop. This operation defines the multiplication of homotopic classes. All the homotopy classes form the so called *first fundamental group* of M. A collection of curves on the surface is a *cut graph*, if their complement is a topological disk, which is called the *fundamental domain* of the surface.

For a genus g closed surface, the fundamental group has $2g$ generators. A set of fundamental group basis $\{a_1, b_1, a_2, b_2, \cdots, a_g, b_g\}$ is *canonical*, if a_i, b_i have only one geometric intersection, but neither a_i, a_j nor a_i, b_j have geometric intersections, where $i \neq j$. Figs. 8(a) and 6(a) show the sets of canonical fundamental group generators for the kitten model with zero Euler number and the amphora model with negative Euler number. If we slice M along the curves, we can get a disk-like domain with boundary $\{a_1 b_1 a_1^{-1} b_1^{-1} a_2 b_2 a_2^{-1} b_2^{-1} \cdots a_g b_g a_g^{-1} b_g^{-1}\}$, which is called the *canonical fundamental domain* of the surface M.

A covering space of M is a surface $\bar{M}$ together with a continuous surjective map $p : \bar{M} \to M$, such that for every $q \in M$ there exists an open neighborhood U of q such that $p^{-1}(U)$ (the inverse image of U under p) is a disjoint union of open sets in $\bar{M}$, each of which is mapped homeomorphically onto U by p. If $\bar{M}$ is simply connected, then $\bar{M}$ is called the *universal covering space* of M. Suppose $\phi : \bar{M} \to \bar{M}$, $p = \phi \circ p$, then ϕ is called a *deck transformation*. A deck transformation maps one fundamental domain to another fundamental domain. All the deck transformations form the so-called *deck transformation group*, which is isomorphic to the fundamental group. We use the algorithms in [CJGQ05] to compute the canonical fundamental group generators.

2.2   Riemannian Metric and Gaussian Curvature

All the differential geometric concepts and the detailed explanations can be found in [Gug77]. Suppose S is a C^2 smooth surface embedded in $\mathbb{R}^3$ with local parameter (u_1, u_2). Let $\mathbf{r}(u_1, u_2)$ be a point on S and $d\mathbf{r} = \mathbf{r}_1 du_1 + \mathbf{r}_2 du_2$ be the tangent vector defined at that point, where $\mathbf{r}_1, \mathbf{r}_2$ are the partial derivatives of

r with respect to u_1 and u_2, respectively. The *Riemannian metric* or the *first fundamental form* is:

$$< d\mathbf{r}, d\mathbf{r} >= \sum < \mathbf{r}_i, \mathbf{r}_j > du_i du_j, \quad i, j = 1, 2. \tag{1}$$

The Gauss map $G : S \to \mathbb{S}^2$ from the surface S to the unit sphere $\mathbb{S}^2$ maps each point p on the surface to its normal $\mathbf{n}(p)$ on the sphere. The *Gaussian curvature $K(p)$ is defined as the Jacobian of the Gauss map*. Intuitively, it is the ratio between the infinitesimal area of the Gauss image on the Gaussian sphere and the infinitesimal area on the surface.

Let ∂S be the boundary of the surface S, k_g the geodesic curvature, dA the area element, ds the line element, and $\chi(S)$ the Euler characteristic number of S. The total curvature is determined by the topology:

$$\int_S K dA + \int_{\partial S} k_g ds = 2\pi \chi(S). \tag{2}$$

2.3   Conformal Deformation

Let S be a surface embedded in $\mathbb{R}^3$. S has a Riemannian metric induced from the Euclidean metric of $\mathbb{R}^3$, denoted by **g**. Suppose $u : S \to \mathbb{R}$ is a scalar function defined on S. It can be verified that $\bar{\mathbf{g}} = e^{2u}\mathbf{g}$ is also a Riemannian metric on S. Furthermore, angles measured by **g** are equal to those measured by $\bar{\mathbf{g}}$. Therefore, we say $\bar{\mathbf{g}}$ is a *conformal deformation* from **g**.

A conformal deformation maps infinitesimal circles to infinitesimal circles and preserves the intersection angles among the infinitesimal circles. In Fig. 1, we illustrate this property by approximating infinitesimal circles by finite circles. We put a regular circle packing pattern on the texture and map the texture

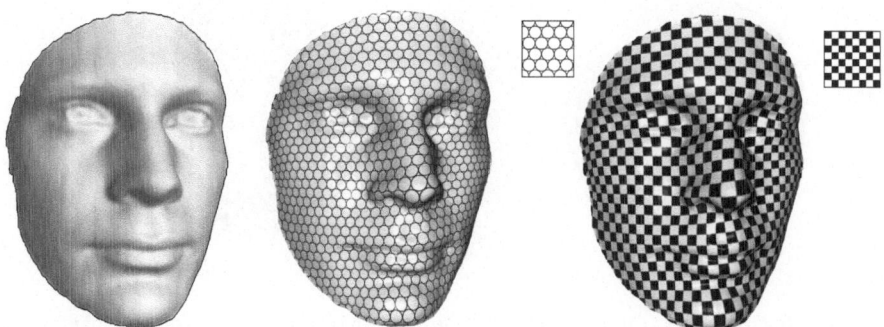

Fig. 1. Properties of Conformal Mapping: Conformal mappings transform infinitesimal circles to infinitesimal circles and preserve the intersection angles among the circles. Here, infinitesimal circles are approximated by finite ones. Notice that a circle in the texture appears in a scaled one in the texture mapping result. Also, the angles in the checkerboard pattern preserved in the texture mapping result.

to the surface using a conformal parameterization, where all the circles on the texture still look like circles on the surface, and all the tangency relations among the circles are preserved.

When the Riemannian metric is conformally deformed, curvatures will also be changed accordingly. Suppose $\mathbf{g}$ is changed to $\bar{\mathbf{g}} = e^{2u}\mathbf{g}$. Then, the Gaussian curvature will become

$$\bar{K} = e^{-2u}(-\Delta_{\mathbf{g}}u + K), \tag{3}$$

where $\Delta_{\mathbf{g}}$ is the Laplacian-Beltrami operator under the original metric $\mathbf{g}$. The geodesic curvature will become

$$\bar{k} = e^{-u}(\partial_{\mathbf{r}}u + k), \tag{4}$$

where $\mathbf{r}$ is the tangent vector orthogonal to the boundary. According to the Gauss-Bonnet theorem, the total curvature is still $2\pi\chi(S)$, where $\chi(S)$ is the Euler characteristic number of S.

2.4   Uniformization Theorem

Given a surface S with a Riemannian metric $\mathbf{g}$, there exists infinitely many metrics conformal to $\mathbf{g}$. The following uniformization theorem states that, among

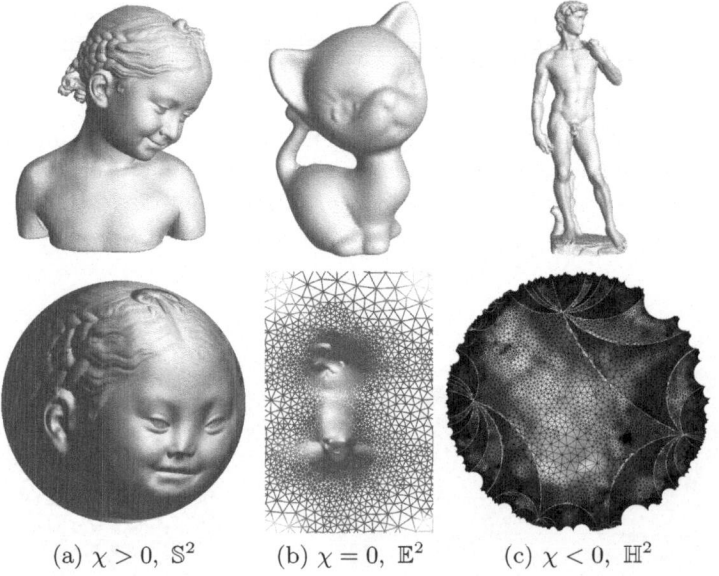

(a) $\chi > 0$, $\mathbb{S}^2$ (b) $\chi = 0$, $\mathbb{E}^2$ (c) $\chi < 0$, $\mathbb{H}^2$

Fig. 2. Uniformization Theorem: Each surface in $\mathbb{R}^3$ admits a uniformization metric, which is conformal to the original metric and induces constant Gaussian curvature; the constant is one of $\{+1, 0, -1\}$ depending on the Euler characteristic number χ of the surface. Its universal covering space with the uniformization metric can be isometrically embedded onto one of three canonical spaces: sphere, plane, or hyperbolic space. Here, we shows the parameterizations computed by using discrete spherical, Euclidean, and hyperbolic Ricci flows, respectively.

all of the conformal metrics, there exists a representative, which induces constant curvature. Moreover, the constant will be one of $\{+1, 0, -1\}$.

Theorem 1 (Uniformization Theorem). *Let $(S, \mathbf{g})$ be a compact 2-dimensional surface with a Riemannian metric $\mathbf{g}$, then there is a metric $\bar{\mathbf{g}}$ conformal to $\mathbf{g}$ with constant Gaussian curvature everywhere; the constant is one of $\{+1, 0, -1\}$. Furthermore, the constant -1 curvature metric is unique.*

We call such a metric the *uniformization metric* of S. According to the Gauss-Bonnet theorem (Eq. 2), the sign of the constant Gaussian curvature must match the sign of the Euler number of the surface: $+1$ for $\chi(S) > 0$, 0 for $\chi(S) = 0$, and -1 for $\chi(S) < 0$.

Therefore, we can embed the universal covering space of any closed surface using its uniformization metric onto one of the three canonical surfaces: the *sphere* $\mathbb{S}^2$ for genus zero surfaces with positive Euler numbers, the *plane* $\mathbb{E}^2$ for genus one surfaces with zero Euler number, and the *hyperbolic space* $\mathbb{H}^2$ for high genus surfaces with negative Euler numbers (see Fig. 2). Accordingly, we can say that surfaces with positive Euler number admit spherical geometry; surfaces with zero Euler number admit Euclidean geometry; and surfaces with negative Euler number admit hyperbolic geometry.

2.5 Spherical, Euclidean and Hyperbolic Geometry

The unit sphere is with Gaussian curvature $+1$ and admits the spherical geometry. The rigid motions in spherical geometry are rotations. The geodesics are great arcs. The Euclidean plane is with 0 curvature and admits the Euclidean geometry. Planar translations and rotations form the rigid motion group.

The hyperbolic space model we used in this paper is the Poincaré disk, which is a unit disk on the complex plane, with Riemannian metric

$$ds^2 = \frac{4dwd\bar{w}}{(1 - \bar{w}w)^2}, w \in \mathbb{C}.$$

In the Poincaré disk, rigid motion is a Möbius transformation,

$$z \to e^{i\theta} \frac{z - z_0}{1 - \bar{z}_0 z}, z_0 \in \mathbb{C}, \theta \in [0, 2\pi);$$

the geodesics are circular arcs which are orthogonal to the unit circle; the hyperbolic circle $(\mathbf{c}, r)$ ($\mathbf{c}$ represents the center, r the radius) coincides with an Euclidean circle $(\mathbf{C}, R)$ with

$$\mathbf{C} = \frac{2 - 2\mu^2}{1 - \mu^2 |\mathbf{c}|^2} \mathbf{c}, \quad R^2 = |\mathbf{C}|^2 - \frac{|\mathbf{c}|^2 - \mu^2}{1 - \mu^2 |\mathbf{c}|^2},$$

where $\mu = \frac{e^r - 1}{e^r + 1}$.

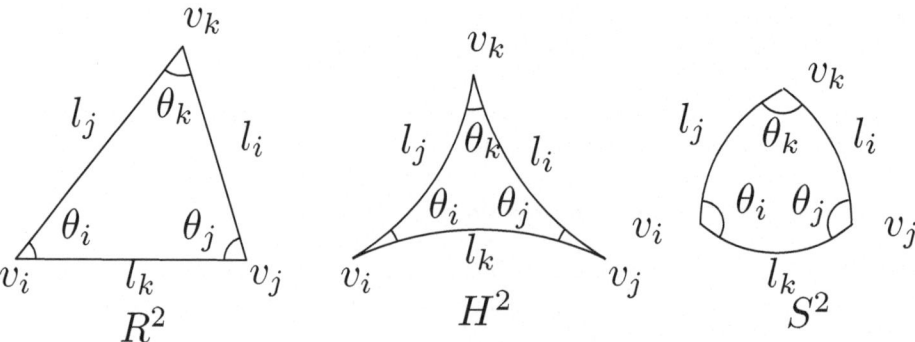

Fig. 3. Euclidean, hyperbolic and Spherical triangles

We also use the upper half plane model for hyperbolic space $\mathbb{H}^2$. $\mathbb{H}^2 = \{(x, y) \in \mathbb{R}^2 | y > 0\}$, with the Riemannian metric $ds^2 = \frac{dx^2 + dy^2}{y^2}$. In $\mathbb{H}^2$, hyperbolic lines are circular arcs and half lines orthogonal to the x-axis. The rigid motion is given by the so-called *Möbius transformation*

$$\frac{az + b}{cz + d}, ac - bd = 1, a, b, c, d \in \mathbb{R},$$

where $z = x + iy$ is the complex coordinates.

Similarly, the three dimensional hyperbolic space $\mathbb{H}^3$ can be represented using upper half space model, $\mathbb{H}^3 = \{(x, y, z) \in \mathbb{R}^3 | z > 0\}$, with Riemannian metric

$$ds^2 = \frac{dx^2 + dy^2 + dz^2}{z^2}.$$

In $\mathbb{H}^3$, the hyperbolic planes are hemispheres or vertical planes, whose equators are on the xy-plane. The xy-plane represents all the infinity points in $\mathbb{H}^3$. The rigid motion in H^3 is determined by its restriction on the xy-plane, which is a Möbius transformation on the plane, in the form

$$\frac{az + b}{cz + d}, ac - bd = 1, a, b, c, d \in \mathbb{C}.$$

Most of the computation is carried out on the xy-plane.

As shown in figure 4, triangles with spherical , Euclidean or hyperbolic background geometry (meaning triangles in $\mathbb{S}^2$, $\mathbb{E}^2$ and $\mathbb{H}^2$) satisfy different cosine laws:

$$(\mathbb{S}^2) \quad \cos l_i = \frac{\cos \theta_i + \cos \theta_j \cos \theta_k}{\sin \theta_j \sin \theta_k} \tag{5}$$

$$(\mathbb{H}^2) \quad \cosh l_i = \frac{\cos \theta_i + \cos \theta_j \cos \theta_k}{\sin \theta_j \sin \theta_k} \tag{6}$$

$$(\mathbb{E}^2) \quad 1 = \frac{\cos \theta_i + \cos \theta_j \cos \theta_k}{\sin \theta_j \sin \theta_k} \tag{7}$$

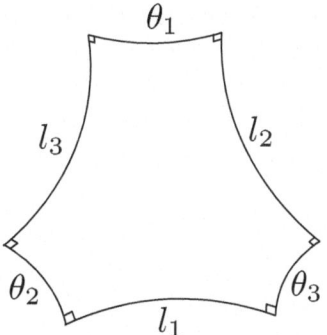

Fig. 4. Hyperbolic right-angled hexagon

We can interchange the role of edge and angle and get another three cosine laws:

$$(\mathbb{S}^2) \quad \cos\theta_i = \frac{\cos l_i - \cos l_j \cos l_k}{\sin l_j \sin l_k} \tag{8}$$

$$(\mathbb{H}^2) \quad \cos\theta_i = \frac{-\cosh l_i + \cosh l_j \cosh l_k}{\sinh l_j \sinh l_k} \tag{9}$$

$$(\mathbb{E}^2) \quad \cos\theta_i = \frac{-l_i^2 + l_j^2 + l_k^2}{2l_j l_k} \tag{10}$$

For the right-angled hyperbolic hexagon, let l_1, l_2, l_3 be three non-pairwise adjacent edges of the hexagon and the opposite edges $\theta_1, \theta_2, \theta_3$, the cosine law is

$$(\mathbb{H}^2) \quad \cosh l_i = \frac{\cosh\theta_i + \cosh\theta_j \cosh\theta_k}{\sinh\theta_i \sinh\theta_k}. \tag{11}$$

Based on the cosine laws, curvature flows on smooth surfaces can be generalized to discrete cases.

2.6   The Smooth Surface Ricci Flow

Suppose S is a smooth surface with a Riemannian metric **g**. The Ricci flow deforms the metric $\mathbf{g}(t)$ according to the Gaussian curvature $K(t)$ (induced by itself), where t is the time parameter

$$\frac{dg_{ij}(t)}{dt} = -2K(t)g_{ij}(t). \tag{12}$$

There is an analogy between the Ricci flow and the heat diffusion process. Suppose $T(t)$ is a temperature field on the surface. The heat diffusion equation is $dT(t)/dt = -\Delta_\mathbf{g}T(t)$, where $\Delta_\mathbf{g}$ is the Laplace-Beltrami operator induced by the surface metric. The temperature field becomes more and more uniform with the increase of t, and it will become constant eventually.

In a physical sense, the curvature evolution induced by the Ricci flow is exactly the same as heat diffusion on the surface, as follows:

$$\frac{dK(t)}{dt} = -\Delta_{\mathbf{g}(t)}K(t), \tag{13}$$

where $\Delta_{\mathbf{g}(t)}$ is the Laplace-Beltrami operator induced by the metric $\mathbf{g}(t)$. If we replace the metric in Eq. 12 with $g(t) = e^{2u(t)}g(0)$, then the Ricci flow can be simplified as

$$\frac{du(t)}{dt} = -2K(t), \tag{14}$$

which states that the metric should change according to the curvature.

The following theorems postulate that the Ricci flow defined in Eq. 12 is convergent and leads to a conformal uniformization metric. For surfaces with non-positive Euler numbers, Hamilton proved the convergence of the Ricci flow in [Ham88]:

Theorem 2 (Hamilton 1988). *For a closed surface of non-positive Euler characteristic, if the total area of the surface is preserved during the flow, the Ricci flow will converge to a metric such that the Gaussian curvature is constant everywhere.*

It is much more difficult to prove the convergence of the Ricci flow on surfaces with positive Euler numbers. The following result was proven by Chow in [Cho91]:

Theorem 3 (Chow 1991). *For a closed surface of positive Euler characteristic, if the total area of the surface is preserved during the flow, the Ricci flow will converge to a metric such that the Gaussian curvature is constant everywhere.*

The corresponding metric $\mathbf{g}(\infty)$ is the *uniformization metric*. Moreover, at any time t, the metric $\mathbf{g}(t)$ is conformal to the original metric $\mathbf{g}(0)$.

The Ricci flow can be easily modified to compute a metric with a *user-defined* curvature $\bar{K}$ as the following,

$$\frac{du(t)}{dt} = 2(\bar{K} - K). \tag{15}$$

With this modification, the solution metric $\mathbf{g}(\infty)$ can be computed, which induces the curvature $\bar{K}$.

3   Theories on the Discrete Surface Ricci Flow

In engineering fields, smooth surfaces are often approximated by simplicial complexes (triangle meshes). Major concepts, such as metric, curvature, and conformal deformation in the continuous setting can be generalized to the discrete setting. We denote a triangle mesh as Σ, a vertex set as V, an edge set as E, and a face set as F. e_{ij} represents the edge connecting vertices v_i and v_j, and f_{ijk} denotes the face formed by v_i, v_j, and v_k.

3.1 Background Geometry

In graphics, it is always assumed that a mesh Σ is embedded in the three dimensional Euclidean space $\mathbb{R}^3$, and therefore each face is Euclidean. In this case, we say the mesh is with Euclidean background geometry (see Fig. 2(a)). The angles and edge lengths of each face satisfy the Euclidean cosine law.

Similarly, if we assume that a mesh is embedded in the three dimensional sphere $\mathbb{S}^3$, then each face is a spherical triangle. We say the mesh is with spherical background geometry (see Fig. 2(b)). The angles and the edge lengths of each face satisfy the spherical cosine law.

Furthermore, if we assume that a mesh is embedded in the three dimensional hyperbolic space $\mathbb{H}^3$, then all faces are hyperbolic triangles. We say the mesh is with hyperbolic background geometry (see Fig. 2(c)). The angles and the edge lengths of each face satisfy the hyperbolic cosine law.

In the following discussion, we will explicitly specify the background geometry for a mesh when it is needed. Otherwise, the concept or the algorithm is appropriate for all kinds of background geometries.

3.2 Discrete Riemannian Metric

A discrete Riemannian metric on a mesh Σ is a piecewise constant metric with cone singularities. A metric on a mesh with Euclidean metric is a discrete Euclidean metric with cone singularities. Each vertex is a cone singularity. Similarly, a metric on a mesh with spherical background geometry is a discrete spherical metric with cone singularities; a metric on a mesh with hyperbolic background geometry is a discrete hyperbolic metric with cone singularities.

The edge lengths of a mesh Σ are sufficient to define a discrete Riemannian metric,

$$l : E \to \mathbb{R}^+, \tag{16}$$

as long as, for each face f_{ijk}, the edge lengths satisfy the triangle inequality: $l_{ij} + l_{jk} > l_{ki}$ for all the three background geometries, and another inequality: $l_{ij} + l_{jk} + l_{ki} < 2\pi$ for spherical geometry.

3.3 Discrete Gaussian Curvature

The discrete Gaussian curvature K_i on a vertex $v_i \in \Sigma$ can be computed from the angle deficit,

$$K_i = \begin{cases} 2\pi - \sum_{f_{ijk} \in F} \theta_i^{jk}, & v_i \notin \partial\Sigma \\ \pi - \sum_{f_{ijk} \in F} \theta_i^{jk}, & v_i \in \partial\Sigma \end{cases} \tag{17}$$

where θ_i^{jk} represents the corner angle attached to vertex v_i in the face f_{ijk}, and $\partial\Sigma$ represents the boundary of the mesh. The discrete Gaussian curvatures are determined by the discrete metrics.

3.4   Discrete Gauss-Bonnet Theorem

The Gauss-Bonnet theorem (Eq. 2) states that the total curvature is a topological invariant. It still holds on meshes as follows.

$$\sum_{v_i \in V} K_i + \lambda \sum_{f_i \in F} A_i = 2\pi\chi(M), \tag{18}$$

where A_i denotes the area of face f_i, and λ represents the constant curvature for the background geometry; $+1$ for the spherical geometry, 0 for the Euclidean geometry, and -1 for the hyperbolic geometry.

3.5   Discrete Conformal Deformation

Conformal metric deformations preserves infinitesimal circles and the intersection angles among them. The discrete conformal deformation of metrics uses circles with finite radii to approximate the infinitesimal circles.

The concept of the circle packing metric was introduced by Thurston in [Thu76] as shown in Fig. 5. Let Γ be a function defined on the vertices, $\Gamma : V \to \mathbb{R}^+$, which assigns a radius γ_i to the vertex v_i. Similarly, let Φ be a function defined on the edges, $\Phi : E \to [0, \frac{\pi}{2}]$, which assigns an acute angle $\Phi(e_{ij})$ to each edge e_{ij} and is called a *weight* function on the edges. Geometrically, $\Phi(e_{ij})$ is the intersection angle of two circles centered at v_i and v_j. The pair of vertex radius function and edge weight function on a mesh Σ, (Γ, Φ), is called a *circle packing metric* of Σ.

Fig. 5 illustrates the circle packing metrics. Each vertex v_i has a circle whose radius is γ_i. For each edge e_{ij}, the intersection angle ϕ_{ij} is defined by the two circles of v_i and v_j, which either intersect or are tangent.

Two circle packing metrics (Γ_1, Φ_1) and (Γ_2, Φ_2) on the same mesh are *conformally equivalent* if $\Phi_1 \equiv \Phi_2$. A *conformal deformation* of a circle packing metric only modifies the vertex radii and preserves the intersection angles Φ on the edges.

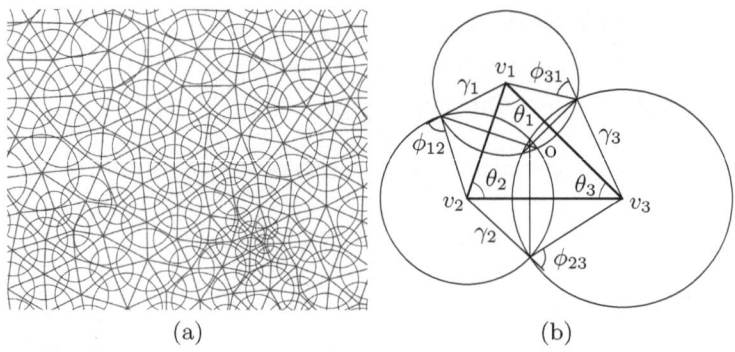

(a)   (b)

Fig. 5. Circle Packing Metric (a) Flat circle packing metric (b) Circle packing metric on a triangle

3.6 Admissible Curvature Space

A mesh Σ with edge weight Φ is called a *weighted mesh*, which is denoted as (Σ, Φ). In the following, we want to clarify the spaces of all possible circle packing metrics and all possible curvatures of a weighted mesh.

Let the vertex set be $V = \{v_1, v_2, \cdots, v_n\}$, and the radii be $\Gamma = \{\gamma_1, \gamma_2, \cdots, \gamma_n\}$. Let u_i be

$$u_i = \begin{cases} \log \gamma_i & \mathbb{E}^2 \\ \log \tanh \frac{\gamma_i}{2} & \mathbb{H}^2 \\ \log \tan \frac{\gamma_i}{2} & \mathbb{S}^2 \end{cases} \tag{19}$$

where $\mathbb{E}^2$, $\mathbb{H}^2$, and $\mathbb{S}^2$ indicate the background geometry of the mesh. We represent a circle packing metric on (Σ, Φ) by a vector $\mathbf{u} = (u_1, u_2, \cdots, u_n)^T$. Similarly, we represent the Gaussian curvatures at mesh vertices by the curvature vector $\mathbf{k} = (K_1, K_2, \cdots, K_n)^T$. All the possible $\mathbf{u}$'s form the *admissible metric space*, and all the possible $\mathbf{k}$'s form the *admissible curvature space*.

According to the Gauss-Bonnet theory (Eq. 18), the total curvature must be $2\pi\chi(\Sigma)$, and therefore the curvature space is $n - 1$ dimensional. We add one linear constraint to the metric vector $\mathbf{u}$, $\sum u_i = 0$, for the normalized metric. As a result, the metric space is also $n - 1$ dimensional. If all the intersection angles are acute, then the edge lengths induced by a circle packing satisfy the triangle inequality. There is no further constraint on $\mathbf{u}$. Therefore, the admissible metric space is simply $\mathbb{R}^{n-1}$.

A curvature vector $\mathbf{k}$ is *admissible* if there exists a metric vector $\mathbf{u}$, which induces $\mathbf{k}$. The admissible curvature space of a weighted mesh (Σ, Φ) is a convex polytope, specified by the following theorem. The detailed proof can be found in [CL03].

Theorem 4. *Suppose (Σ, Φ) is a weighted mesh with Euclidean background geometry, I is a proper subset of vertices, F_I is the set of faces whose vertices are in I and the link set $Lk(I)$ is formed by faces (e, v), where e is an edge and v is the third vertex in the face,*

$$Lk(I) = \{(e, v) | e \cap I = \emptyset, v \in I\},$$

then a curvature vector $\mathbf{k}$ is admissible if and only if

$$\sum_{v_i \in I} K_i > - \sum_{(e,v) \in Lk(I)} (\pi - \phi(e)) + 2\pi\chi(F_I). \tag{20}$$

The admissible curvature space for weighted meshes with hyperbolic or spherical background geometries is more complicated. We refer the readers to [LGD07] for detailed discussion.

3.7 The Discrete Surface Ricci Flow

Suppose (Σ, Φ) is a weighted mesh with an initial circle packing metric. The discrete Ricci flow is defined as follows.

$$\frac{du_i(t)}{dt} = (\bar{K}_i - K_i), \tag{21}$$

where $\bar{\mathbf{k}} = (\bar{K}_1, \bar{K}_2, \cdots, \bar{K}_n)^T$ is the user defined target curvature. The discrete Ricci flow has exactly the same form as the smooth Ricci flow (Eq. 15), which deforms the circle packing metric according to the Gaussian curvature, as in Eq. 21.

The discrete Ricci flow can be formulated in the variational setting, namely, it is a negative gradient flow of a special energy form. Let (Σ, Φ) be a weighted mesh with spherical (Euclidean or hyperbolic) background geometry. For two arbitrary vertices v_i and v_j, the following symmetric relation holds:

$$\frac{\partial K_i}{\partial u_j} = \frac{\partial K_j}{\partial u_i}.$$

Let $\omega = \sum_{i=1}^{n} K_i du_i$ be a differential one-form [Wei07]. The symmetric relation guarantees that the one-form is closed (curl free) in the metric space.

$$d\omega = \sum_{i,j} (\frac{\partial K_i}{\partial u_j} - \frac{\partial K_j}{\partial u_i}) du_i \wedge du_j = 0.$$

By Stokes theorem, the following integration is path independent,

$$f(\mathbf{u}) = \int_{\mathbf{u_0}}^{\mathbf{u}} \sum_{i=1}^{n} (\bar{K}_i - K_i) du_i, \tag{22}$$

where $\mathbf{u_0}$ is an arbitrary initial metric. Therefore, the above integration is well defined, and is called the *discrete Ricci energy*. The discrete Ricci flow is the negative gradient flow of the discrete Ricci energy. The discrete metric which induces $\bar{\mathbf{k}}$ is the minimizer of the energy.

Computing the desired metric with user-defined curvature $\bar{\mathbf{k}}$ is equivalent to minimizing the discrete Ricci energy.For Euclidean or hyperbolic cases, the discrete Ricci energy (see Eq. 22) was first proved to be strictly convex in the seminal work of Colin de Verdiere [dVY91] for the $\Phi = 0$ case, and was generalized to all cases of $\Phi \leq \pi/2$ in [CL03]. The global minimum uniquely exists, corresponding to the metric $\bar{\mathbf{u}}$, which induces $\bar{\mathbf{k}}$. The discrete Ricci flow converges to this global minimum.

Theorem 5 (Chow & Luo: Euclidean Ricci Energy). *The Euclidean Ricci energy $f(\mathbf{u})$ on the space of the normalized metric $\sum u_i = 0$ is strictly convex.*

Theorem 6 (Chow & Luo: Hyperbolic Ricci Energy). *The hyperbolic Ricci energy is strictly convex.*

Although the spherical Ricci energy is not strictly convex, the desired metric $\bar{\mathbf{u}}$ is still a critical point of the energy. In our experiments, the solution can be reached using Newton's method.

4   Algorithm of the Discrete Surface Ricci Flow

In this section, we explain the algorithm in detail. The unified pipeline for all kinds of the discrete Ricci flow algorithms is as follows:

1. Determine the target curvature and the background geometry;
2. Compute the initial circle packing metric;
3. Optimize the Ricci energy using either gradient descent or Newton's methods;
4. Compute the layout using the result metric.

Step 1. Determine the Target Curvature and the Background Geometry
The user is free to define the target curvatures for different applications, while obeying the Gauss-Bonnet theorem in Eq. 18 and admissible condition in Eq. 20.

For example, for constructing manifold splines (see [GHQ06] for details), it is desirable to obtain a flat metric with a minimal number of cone singularities. One can concentrate all the curvatures at a single vertex and make everywhere else flat. In this case, the background geometry of the mesh is chosen to be Euclidean and the curvature for the selected vertex is set to $2\pi\chi(\Sigma)$. The curvature at all other vertices is set to zero.

For the application of surface classification using conformal structures (see [JLYG07] for details), no cone singularities are allowed. All of the curvatures must be evenly distributed over the whole surface. In this case, the target curvature is zero for all vertices and the background geometry is hyperbolic for high genus meshes.

Step 2. Compute the Initial Circle Packing Metric
In this step, the initial circle packing metric (Γ, Φ) is computed. This metric should approximate the original Euclidean metric as much as possible. Suppose d_{ij} is the length of edge e_{ij} determined by the induced Euclidean metric in $\mathbb{R}^3$, l_{ij} is the edge length determined by the circle packing metric. Let ϕ_{ij} be the edge weight, γ_i and γ_j be the circle radii on vertices v_i and v_j, then l_{ij} can be computed according to the cosine law with different background geometries:

$$\begin{aligned}
l_{ij}^2 &= \gamma_i^2 + \gamma_j^2 + 2\gamma_i\gamma_j \cos\phi_{ij}, & \mathbb{E}^2 \\
\cosh l_{ij} &= \cosh\gamma_i \cosh\gamma_j + \sinh\gamma_i \sinh\gamma_j \cos\phi_{ij}, & \mathbb{H}^2 \\
\cos l_{ij} &= \cos\gamma_i \cos\gamma_j - \sin\gamma_i \sin\gamma_j \cos\phi_{ij}, & \mathbb{S}^2
\end{aligned} \qquad (23)$$

The initial circle packing metric can be obtained by minimizing the following energy

$$\min_{\gamma_i, \phi_{ij}} \sum_{e_{ij} \in \Sigma} |d_{ij} - l_{ij}|^2,$$

such that $\phi_{ij} \in (0, \frac{\Pi}{2}]$. If the initial mesh has too many obtuse angles and the requirement for the conformality is very high, we can use an extra re-meshing step to improve the triangulation quality.

Step 3. Optimize The Ricci Energy
In the following we introduce two methods to optimize the Ricci energy; one is the gradient descent method and the other is Newton's method.

Gradient Descent

The Ricci energy can be optimized using the gradient descent method, which is the direct analogy of the smooth Ricci flow. Note that during the computation the vertex radii Γ vary over time while the edge weights Φ are fixed. This reflects the fact that conformal metric deformation preserves angles.

1.Compute edge lengthes l_{ij} from the current vertices radii γ_i and γ_j and the fixed edge weight ϕ_{ij}, using the cosine law (Eq. 23) for the background geometry.
2.Compute the corner angles θ_i^{jk} in each face f_{ijk} from the current edge lengths by using the cosine law according to the background geometry.
3.Compute the discrete Gaussian curvature K_i of each vertex v_i by using Eq. 17.
4.Update u_i of each vertex v_i by using Eq. 22, as follows.

$$u_i = u_i + \epsilon(\bar{K}_i - K_i),$$

where $\bar{K}_i$ is the target Gaussian curvature. In our experiments, ϵ is no greater than 0.05.
5. Normalize the metrics. Let $s = \sum u_i$, then $u_i = u_i - \frac{s}{n}$, where n is the total number of vertices.
6. Update the radius γ_i of each vertex v_i, using u_i and Eq. 19.
7. Repeat the steps from 1 through 5, until the maximal curvature error falls below a threshold, $\max |\bar{K}_i - K_i| < \delta$, where δ is a user-specified error tolerance.

Newton's Method

As described in Section 3.6, the Ricci flow is the negative gradient flow of the discrete Ricci energy in Eq. 22. We can further improve the convergence speed by using Newton's method.

The key to Newton's method is to compute the Hessian matrix. Different Ricci flows have different Hessian matrices according to their background geometries. The Hessian matrix for the Euclidean Ricci energy is explained here. We refer readers to [JKLG08] for other cases.

As shown in figure 5, for each face, there are three circles centered at its vertices. Then there exists a unique circle, which is orthogonal to all three circles, whose center is called the center of the face. Two circles centered at the end vertices of an edge share a common chord. Three common chords intersect at the center o as shown in the figure. The center can be calculated explicitly. Let e_{ij} be an edge, attaching to two faces f_1 and f_2, whose centers are o_1 and o_2. The distance from o_k to e_{ij} is h_k, $k = 1, 2$. The edge coefficient w_{ij} is defined as

$$w_{ij} = h_1 + h_2.$$

If e_{ij} is on the boundary, f_2 does not exist, then $w_{ij} = h_1$.

The elements in the Hessian matrix are $\partial K_i / \partial u_j$, which has the following explicit formula

$$\frac{\partial K_i}{\partial u_j} = \begin{cases} -w_{ij} & i \neq j \\ \sum_k w_{ik} & i = j \end{cases}$$

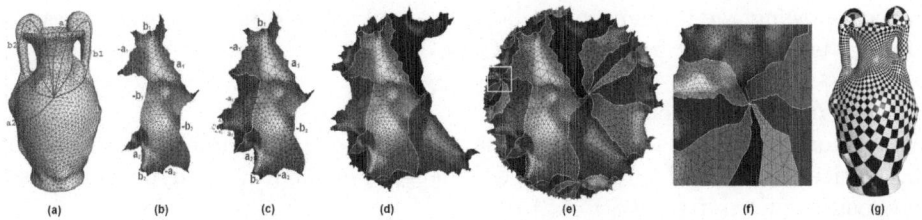

Fig. 6. The hyperbolic Ricci flow (a) Genus two vase model marked with a set of canonical fundamental group generators which cut the surface into a topological disk with eight sides: a_1, b_1, a_1^{-1}, b_1^{-1}, a_2, b_2, a_2^{-1}, b_2^{-1}. (b) The fundamental domain is conformally flattened onto the Poincaré disk with marked sides. (c) A Möbius transformation moves the side b_1 to b_1^{-1}. (d) Eight copies of the fundamental domain are glued coherently by eight Möbius transformations. (e) A finite portion of the universal covering space is flattened onto the Poincaré disk. (f) Zoom in on a region on the universal covering space, where eight fundamental domains join together. No seams or overlapping can be found. (g) Conformal parameterization induced by the hyperbolic flattening. The corners angle of checkers are well-preserved.

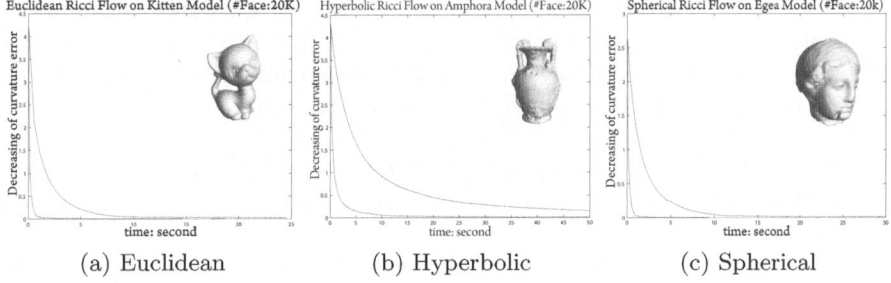

(a) Euclidean   (b) Hyperbolic   (c) Spherical

Fig. 7. Performance of the Ricci flow The horizontal axis represents time, and the vertical axis represents the maximal curvature error. The blue curves are for the Newton's method; the green curves are for the gradient descent method. The meshes have about $30k$ faces. The tests were carried out on a laptop with 1.7GHz CPU and 1G RAM. All the algorithms are written in C++ on a Windows platform without using any other numerical library.

Step 4. Compute the Layouts

In this step, we flatten the mesh with the target metric onto one of the canonical domains: the plane $\mathbb{E}^2$, the sphere $\mathbb{S}^2$, or the hyperbolic space $\mathbb{H}^2$. The algorithms in this step involve several topological concepts, such as fundamental domain, canonical fundamental group basis, universal covering space, etc. The following is the unified pipeline for computing the layout:

1. Flatten a seed face.
2. Flatten a fundamental domain.
3. Flatten the universal covering space.

In the following, we focus on hyperbolic case only. The other two cases are very similar, details can be found in [JKLG08].

1.Flatten a Seed Face

We randomly select a seed face f_{012}, and compute the parametric positions of the vertices v_0, v_1, and v_2 using the edge lengths of f_{012}. In the hyperbolic case, the positions are set as $\tau(v_0) = (0,0)$:

$$\tau(v_1) = \frac{e^{l_{01}} - 1}{e^{l_{01}} + 1}(1,0), \tau(v_2) = \frac{e^{l_{02}} - 1}{e^{l_{02}} + 1}(\cos \theta_0^{12}, \sin \theta_0^{12});$$

Then we put faces adjacent to the seed face into a queue.

2. Flatten a Fundamental Domain

In this step, we propagate the flattening to the rest of all faces, namely we want to embed a fundamental domain. We call the resulting layout a *fundamental polygon*.

To propagate the flattening, we put all unprocessed faces adjacent to the current face into the queue. We pop a face f_{ijk} from the queue and test whether all its vertices have been set to parametric positions. If so, we continue to pop the next one from the queue as long as the queue is nonempty. Otherwise, suppose that v_i and v_j have been embedded, then $\tau(v_k)$ can be computed as one of the two intersection points between the two circles, $c(\tau(v_i), l_{ki})$ and $c(\tau(v_j), l_{kj})$, satisfying $(\tau(v_j) - \tau(v_i)) \times (\tau(v_k) - \tau(v_i)) > 0$. computing the intersection points between hyperbolic circles boils down to finding intersections between Euclidean circles.

Different choices of the seed faces induce different layouts, which differ by a rigid motion. In the hyperbolic case, it is a Möbius transformation. Fig. 6 (b), (c) and (d) are the layouts for the same genus two model, shown in Fig. 6 (a), with different seed faces marked in red. The layouts in (c) and (d) are transformed to align with the layout in (b) by different Möbius transformations, as shown in Fig. 6(e).

3. Flatten the Universal Covering Space

For the purpose of texture mapping, it is enough to flatten a fundamental domain. For the purpose of constructing a manifold spline (see [GHQ06] for details) or surface classification by conformal equivalence (see [JLYG07] for details), we need to flatten a finite portion of the universal covering space.

The universal covering space of a mesh with a negative Euler number can be embedded onto the whole hyperbolic space $\mathbb{H}^2$. The algorithmic pipeline is as follows:

1. Embed a canonical fundamental domain.
2. Compute the deck transformation group generators.
3. Tile the whole canonical domain $\mathbb{R}^2$ or $\mathbb{H}^2$.

In the first step, we find a canonical fundamental group basis, then generate a canonical fundamental domain, then we flatten this canonical fundamental domain.

Figure 6(b) gives the embedding of the canonical fundamental domain for genus two amphora model on the Poincaré disk.

Compute Deck Transformation Group Generators
The embedding of a canonical fundamental domain for a closed genus g surface has $4g$ different sides, which induce $2g$ rigid transformations (as explained in below). These $2g$ rigid motions are the generators of the deck transformation group.

Fig. 6 illustrates the process for a mesh with a negative Euler number. Let $\{a_1, b_1, \cdots, a_g, b_g\}$ be a set of canonical fundamental group generators, where g is the genus. The embedding of its canonical fundamental domain in hyperbolic space has $4g$ sides, $\tau(a_1), \tau(b_1), \tau(a_1^{-1}), \tau(b_1^{-1}), ..., \tau(a_g), \tau(b_g), \tau(a_g^{-1}), \tau(b_g^{-1})$ (see Fig. 6(b) in Poincaré disk). There exists unique Möbius transformations α_k, β_k, which map the $\tau(a_k)$ and $\tau(b_k)$ to $\tau(a_k^{-1})$ and $\rho(b_k^{-1})$ respectively, as shown in Fig. 6(c) and (d). The Möbius transformations $\{\alpha_1, \beta_1, \alpha_2, \beta_2, \cdots, \alpha_g, \beta_g\}$ form a set of generators of the deck transformation group.

Tile the Canonical Domain
Any deck transformation can be produced by composing the generators $\{\alpha_k, \beta_k\}$. Then the whole canonical domain can be tiled by transforming a fundamental polygon by all deck transformations. This induces a flattening of the universal covering space of the mesh onto the canonical domain. Fig. 6(e) illustrates the layout of the universal covering space of a genus two amphora model onto the whole Poincaré disk.

The computation of the layout for a genus one surface is very similar, Fig. 8 shows the whole process for the kitten model.

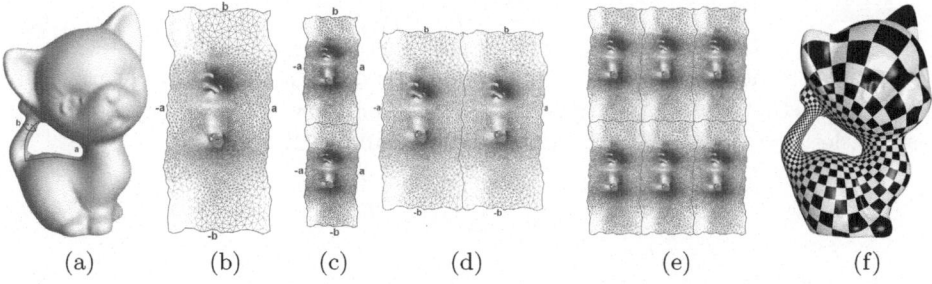

(a)   (b)   (c)   (d)   (e)   (f)

Fig. 8. The Euclidean Ricci flow (a) Genus one kitten model marked with a set of canonical fundamental group generators a and b. (b) A fundamental domain is conformally flattened onto the plane, marked with four sides $aba^{-1}b^{-1}$. (c) One translation moves the side b to b^{-1}. (d) The other translation moves the side a to a^{-1}. (e) The layout of the universal covering space of the kitten mesh on the plane, which tiles the plane. (f) The conformal parameterization is used for the texture mapping purpose. A checkerboard texture is placed over the parameterization in b). The conformality can be verified from the fact that all the corner angles of the checkers are preserved.

5   Discrete Surface Yamabe Flow

For smooth surfaces, the Ricci flow and Yamabe flow are equivalent. In discrete case, there is subtle difference, which is caused by a different notion of discrete conformal classes. The following summarizes the sharp distinctions:

1. The discrete Ricci flow requires circle packing, whereas discrete Yamabe flow is directly defined on triangulations. Therefore, Yamabe flow is more flexible.
2. Both the Ricci flow and the Yamabe flow are variational. The energy form for the Ricci flow and the Yamabe flow are convex. But the metric space (domain of $\mathbf{u}$) of the Ricci flow is convex, while the metric space of Yamabe flow is non-convex. Therefore, it is stable to use Newton's method for optimizing the Ricci energy. For Yamabe energy optimization, the algorithm takes more caution.
3. Yamabe flow can adapt the connectivity to the target curvature automatically, which makes it valuable for practical purposes. During Yamabe flow, if the algorithm detects a degenerate triangle, where one angle becomes π, then the algorithm swaps the edge against the angle and continue the flow. Unfortunately, this important technique of adapting connectivity to the target curvature during the flow can not be generalized to the Ricci flow directly.

Using the symbols in the previous discussion, let M be a triangle mesh embedded in $\mathbb{R}^3$. Let e_{ij} be an edge with end vertices v_i and v_j. d_{ij} is the edge length of e_{ij} induced by the Euclidean metric of $\mathbb{R}^3$. A function defined on the vertices $\mathbf{u} : V \to \mathbb{R}$ is the *discrete conformal factor*. The edge length l_{ij} is defined as

$$l_{ij} = e^{u_i+u_j} d_{ij}. \tag{24}$$

Let K_i and $\bar{K}_i$ denote the current vertex curvature and the target vertex curvature respectively. The discrete Yamabe flow is defined as

$$\frac{du_i(t)}{dt} = \bar{K}_i - K_i, \tag{25}$$

with initial condition $u_i(0) = 0$. The convergence of Yamabe flow is proven in [Luo04]. Furthermore, Yamabe flow is the gradient flow of the following Yamabe energy, let $\mathbf{u} = (u_1, u_2, \cdots, u_n)$, n is the total number of vertices,

$$f(\mathbf{u}) = \int_{\mathbf{u}_0}^{\mathbf{u}} \sum_i^n (\bar{K}_i - K_i) du_i. \tag{26}$$

Similar to the Ricci flow, one can show that

$$\frac{\partial K_i}{\partial u_j} = \frac{\partial K_j}{\partial u_i} \tag{27}$$

The Yamabe energy is well defined and convex. The Hessian matrix can be easily constructed as follows. Suppose faces f_{ijk} and f_{jil} are adjacent to the edge e_{ij}, define the *weight* of the edge e_{ij} as

$$w_{ij} = \cot \theta_k + \cot \theta_l, \tag{28}$$

where θ_k is the angle at v_k in f_{ijk}, θ_l is the angle at v_l in face f_{jil}. If the edge is on the boundary, and only attaches to f_{ijk}, then

$$w_{ij} = \cot \theta_k.$$

It can be shown by direct computation, the differential relation between the curvature and the conformal factor is

$$dK_i = \sum_j w_{ij}(du_i - du_j). \tag{29}$$

So the Hessian matrix of the yamabe energy is given by

$$\frac{\partial^2 f(\mathbf{u})}{\partial u_i \partial u_j} = -\frac{\partial K_i}{\partial u_j} = \begin{cases} w_{ij} & , i \neq j \\ -\sum_k w_{ik} & , i = j \end{cases} \tag{30}$$

The Hessian matrix is positive definite on the linear subspace $\sum_i u_i = 0$. By using the Hessian matrix formulate 30, the Yamabe energy 26 can be optimized effectively. But the major difficulty is that the *admissible metric space* $\Omega(\mathbf{u})$ for a mesh with fixed connectivity is not convex,

$$\Omega(\mathbf{u}) = \{\mathbf{u} | \forall f_{ijk} \in M, l_{ij} + l_{jl} > l_{li}\}$$

Therefore, during the optimization process using Newton's method, we need to ensure that the metric $\mathbf{u}$ is in the admissible metric space $\Omega(u)$ at each step. If a degenerated triangle f_{ijk} is detected, then we swap the longest edge of it. For example, if θ_k exceeds π, then we swap edge e_{ij} as shown in figure 9. The major difficulty for the discrete Ricci flow is to find a good initial circle packing with all acute edge intersection angles. This problem does not exist for discrete Yamabe flow. Therefore, yamabe flow in general produces better conformality in practice. Figure 10 shows the conformal parameterizations using Yamabe flow. In frames (a) and (b), the boundary target curvature is $\frac{2\pi}{m}$, where m is the total number of boundary vertices. In frames (c) and (d), the curvatures at the four corners are $\frac{\pi}{2}$'s, and are zeros everywhere else. The number of edge swaps depends on the initial connectivity, initial curvatures and the target curvatures.

There are many variations for discrete surface curvature flow. In the following, we discuss two of them: out-of-core mesh curvature flow, and curvature flow under mixed constraints.

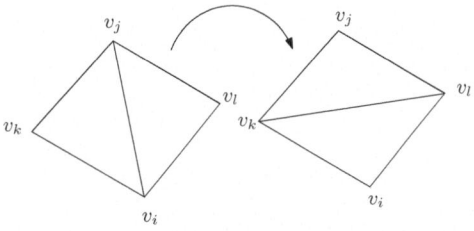

Fig. 9. Edge swap

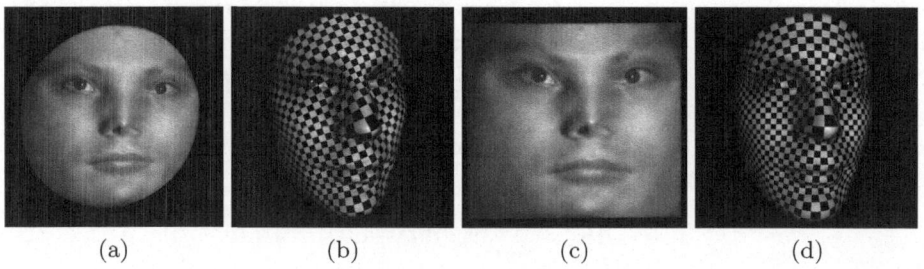

(a)	(b)	(c)	(d)

Fig. 10. Conformal parameterizations using Yamabe flow. (a) and (b), the boundary curvature is constant. (c) and (d), the curvatures at the four corners are $\frac{\pi}{2}$, and are zeros everywhere else.

Out-of-Core Curvature Flow. In practice, if the input mesh is too big to be contained in the memory of the computer, we call it a *out-of-core mesh*. The following method can be used to compute the desired metric for an out-of-core mesh based on either the Ricci flow or Yamabe flow. First, partition the vertex set V to $V_1, V_2, \cdots, V_k$, with each set being small enough to fit in the memory. We require that $V = \cup_{i=1}^{k} V_i$, and each vertex in V should be contained as inner vertex in at least one set V_l. Then the energy can be defined for each set

$$f_i(\mathbf{u}) = \int_{\mathbf{u}_0}^{\mathbf{u}} \sum_{v_j \in V_i} (\bar{K}_j - K_j) du_j.$$

Each $f_i(\mathbf{u})$ can be optimized separately and alternatively. Since the energy is convex, the alternating optimization converges to the global minima, which gives the desired metric.

Curvature Flow under Mixed Constraints. Rather than specifying the target curvature for each vertex, we can specify target curvatures $\bar{K}_i$ for some vertices, and specify conformal factor $\bar{u}_j$ for the rest. Let $V = V_k \cup V_u$, $V_k \cap V_u = \emptyset$, for each $v_i \in V_k$, the target curvature $\bar{K}_i$ is given, for each $v_j \in V_u$, the target conformal factor $\bar{u}_j$ is given. By optimizing the following energy

$$f(\mathbf{u}) = \int_{\mathbf{u}_0}^{\mathbf{u}} \sum_{v_i \in V_k} (\bar{K}_i - K_i) du_i,$$

under the constraints

$$u_j = \bar{u}_j, \forall v_j \in V_u$$

$$K_i = \bar{K}_i, \forall v_i \in V_k$$

we can still get the unique solution, as long as the target curvatures and the target conformal factors are compatible.

6   Theories on Discrete Curvature Flow for 3-Manifolds

All surfaces admit metrics with constant Gaussian curvature. This fact essentially holds for 3-manifolds. According to the Poincaré conjecture and the Thurston's geometrization conjecture, all 3-manifolds can be canonically decomposed to prime 3-manifolds. All prime 3-manifolds can be further decomposed by tori into pieces so that each piece has one of eight canonical geometries.

The study of topological and geometric structures of three dimensional manifolds has fundamental impacts in science and engineering. Computational algorithms for 3-manifolds can help topologist and geometers to investigate the complicated structures of 3-manifolds. They also have great potentials for a wide range of applications in the engineering world. The most direct applications include volumetric parameterizations, volumetric shape analysis, volumetric deformation, solid modeling and etc. Figure 11 shows a simple example of the volumetric parameterization for the volumetric Max Planck model, which is a topological ball.

Similar to the surface case, most 3-manifolds admit hyperbolic metric, which has constant sectional curvature. A hyperbolic 3-manifolds with boundaries is shown in Fig. 12, where the 3-manifold is the 3-ball with a knotted pipe removed, which is called *Thurston's knotted Y-shape*. Hyperbolic 3-manifolds with geodesic boundaries have the following topological properties:

1. The genus of boundary surfaces are greater than one.
2. For any closed curve on the boundary surface, if it can not shrink to a point on the boundary, then it can not shrink to a point inside the volume.

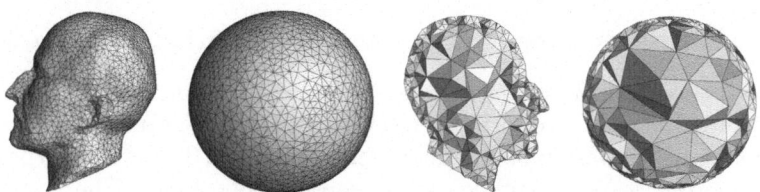

Fig. 11. Volumetric parameterization for a topological ball

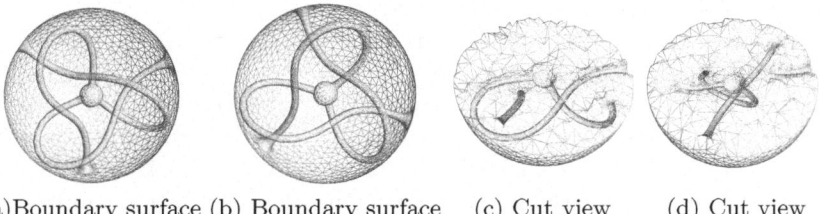

(a)Boundary surface (b) Boundary surface   (c) Cut view   (d) Cut view

Fig. 12. Thurston's Knotted Y-Shape

Table 1. Correspondence between surface and 3-manifold parameterizations

	Surface	3-Manifold
Manifold	with negative Euler number with boundaries Fig.13	Hyperbolic 3-manifold with geodesic boundaries Fig.12
Building Block	hyperbolic right-angled hexagons Fig.13	Truncated hyperbolic tetrahedra Fig.14
Curvature	Gaussian curvature Fig 15	Sectional curvature Fig.15, Fig.16
Algorithm	Discrete Ricci flow	Discrete curvature flow
Parameter domain	Upper half plane $\mathbb{H}^2$ Fig.13	Upper half space $\mathbb{H}^3$ Fig.25

Compared to the surface curvature flow, the discrete 3-dimensional curvature flow has some similar properties; meanwhile, it also owns some unique properties. Table 1 summaries the corresponding concepts involved in the curvature flow for surfaces and 3-manifolds respectively. For example, the primitive building blocks for surfaces are right-angled hyperbolic hexagons (Fig.13(c)); while for 3-manifolds, it is truncated hyperbolic tetrahedra (Fig.14). The discrete curvature used in the surface case is the vertex curvature (Fig.15), while for 3-manifolds it is the edge curvature (Fig. 16). The parameter domain for the surface case is the hyperbolic space $\mathbb{H}^2$ using the upper half plane model; the domain for 3-manifold case is the hyperbolic space $\mathbb{H}^3$ using the upper half space model. In the following part, we will address the similarities and differences in details respectively.

6.1 Similarities between Surface and Volumetric Curvature Flow

There are many intrinsic similarities between surface curvature flow and volumetric curvature flow. Discrete surface curvature flow can be naturally generalized to 3-manifold case. In particular, we have generalized the discrete hyperbolic Ricci flow from surfaces to 3-manifolds with geodesic boundaries. The 3-manifold is approximated by tetrahedra with hyperbolic background geometry, and the edge lengths determine the metric. During the curvature flow, the edge lengths are deformed according to the curvature. The resulting metric at the steady state will have the constant sectional curvature.

For the purpose of comparison, we first illustrate the discrete hyperbolic Ricci flow for surface case using figure 13. A surface with negative Euler number is parameterized and conformally embedded in the hyperbolic space $\mathbb{H}^2$. The three boundaries are mapped to geodesics. Given two arbitrary boundaries, there exists a unique geodesic orthogonal to both boundaries. Three such geodesics partition the whole surface into two right-angled hexagons, as shown in (c). A finite portion of the universal covering space is embedded in $\mathbb{H}^2$, as shown in(d).

For hyperbolic 3-manifolds with boundaries, things are quite similar. Given such a 3-manifold, such as the Thurston's knotted Y-shape in figure 12, discrete

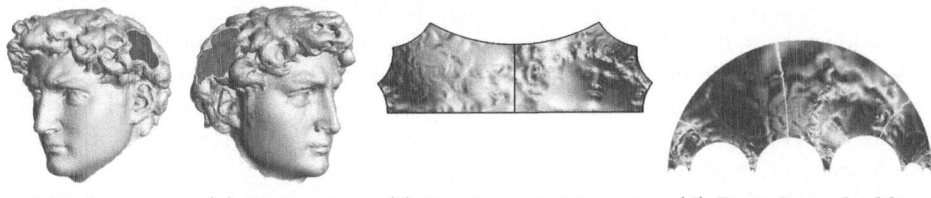

(a)Left view   (b) Right view   (c) Fundamental domain   (d) Periodic embedding

Fig. 13. Surface with boundaries with negative Euler number can be conformally periodically mapped to the hyperbolic space $\mathbb{H}^2$

curvature flow can lead to the canonical hyperbolic metric. The boundary surface become hyperbolic planes, which are geodesic submanifolds. By finding certain hyperbolic planes orthogonal to the boundary surfaces, we can decompose the 3-manifold into several hyperbolic truncated tetrahedra, as shown in Fig.14. Using the canonical hyperbolic metric, a finite portion of the universal covering space can be embedded in $\mathbb{H}^3$, as shown in Fig.25.

6.2 Differences between Surface and 3-Manifold Curvature Flow

Although curvature flow presents many similarities for the surface case and 3-manifold case, there are yet fundamental differences between them. One of the most prominent differences is the so called *Mostow rigidity* [Mos68]. Mostow rigidity states that the geometry of a finite volume hyperbolic manifold (for dimension greater than two) is determined by the fundamental group. Namely, for two complete finite volume hyperbolic n-manifolds ($n > 2$) M and N, if there exists a topological isomorphism $f : \pi_1(M) \to \pi_1(N)$, it will induce a unique isometry from M to N. For the surface case, however, the geometry cannot be determined by the fundamental group. Suppose M and N are two surfaces with hyperbolic metrics; even if M and N share the same topology (i.e. there exists an isomorphisms $f : \pi_1(M) \to \pi_1(N)$), there may not exist an isometry from M to N. In another word, fixing the fundamental group of the surface M, there are infinitely many pairwise non-isometric hyperbolic metrics on M; each of them corresponds to a certain conformal structure of M.

In a nutshell, surfaces have conformal geometry, while 3-manifolds do not. All the Riemannian metrics on a topological surface S can be classified by conformal equivalence, each equivalence class is a *conformal structure*. If the surface is with a negative Euler number, then there exists a unique hyperbolic metric in each conformal structure.

As a consequence of Mostow rigidity, the conformality for 3-manifold parameterization is quite different from surface parameterization. Conformal surface parameterization is equivalent to find a metric with constant Gaussian curvature conformal to the induced Euclidean metric; that is, it requires the original induced Euclidean metric. Namely, the vertex positions or the edge lengths are essential parts of the input. In contrast, for 3-manifolds, only topological

information is required. Different 3-manifolds have the same conformal parameterization if they have the same fundamental group. Consequently, the tessellation will affect the conformality of the surface parameterization, while it does not
affect the computational results of 3-manifolds parameterization. Utilizing this
special PROPERTY, we can reduce the computational complexity of 3-manifold
curvature flow by using the simplest triangulation for a given 3-manifold. For
example, Thurston's Knotted Y-Shape in Fig.12 can be either represented as a
high resolution tetrahedral mesh or a mesh with only 2 truncated tetrahedra,
and the resulting canonical metrics are identical.

Besides the Mostow rigidity, there are some other unique properties of 3-
manifold curvature flow, such as the representation of discrete curvature. On
discrete surfaces, there are only vertex curvatures, which is measured as the
angle deficient at each vertex. For discrete 3-manifolds (e.g. tetrahedral mesh),
however, there are both vertex curvatures and edge curvatures. The vertex curvature equals to 4π minus all the surrounding solid angles; the edge curvature
equals to 2π minus all the surrounding dihedral angles. And it turns out that
the vertex curvatures are totally determined by the edge curvatures. In our algorithm, we use the edge curvature to drive the flow.

6.3   Theories on Discrete Curvature Flow for Hyperbolic 3-Manifolds

In this section, we introduce the theoretical foundations of discrete curvature
flow for the class of 3-manifolds whose boundary is consisting of high genus
surfaces. In particular, we will cover the discrete approximation of 3-manifolds,
the representation of discrete curvature, and the principles of discrete curvature
flow.

Hyperbolic Tetrahedron and Truncated Hyperbolic Tetrahedron. 2-
manifolds (surfaces) can be approximated by triangular meshes with different
background geometries. Similarly, 3-manifolds can be approximated by tetrahedron meshes with different background geometry.

A closed 3-manifold can be triangulated using tetrahedra. The left frame in
Fig.14 shows a hyperbolic tetrahedron $[v_1 v_2 v_3 v_4]$. Each face f_i of a hyperbolic
tetrahedron is a hyperbolic plane, each edge e_{ij} is a hyperbolic line segment.

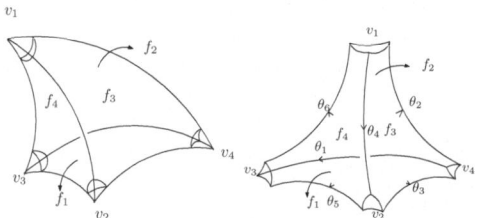

Fig. 14. Hyperbolic tetrahedron and truncated tetrahedron

A 3-manifold with boundary can be tessellated using truncated tetrahedra. The right frame in Fig.14 shows a truncated hyperbolic tetrahedron, where the four vertices are truncated by hyperbolic planes. The cutting plane at vertex v_i is perpendicular to the edges e_{ij}, e_{ik}, e_{il}. Therefore, each face of a truncated hyperbolic tetrahedron is a right-angled hyperbolic hexagon, each cutting section is a hyperbolic triangle. If the given manifold is tessellated by multiple tetrahedra, the face hexagons will be glued one another, while the cutting triangles form the boundary surface.

The geometry of the truncated tetrahedron is determined by dihedral angles, represented as $\{\theta_1, \theta_2, \cdots, \theta_6\}$ in Fig.14. For example, the hyperbolic triangle at v_2 has inner angles $\theta_3, \theta_4, \theta_5$, its edge lengths can be determined using formula 7. For face f_4, the edge length e_{12}, e_{23}, e_{31} are determined by the hyperbolic triangles at v_1, v_2, v_3 using the right-angled hyperbolic hexagon cosine law 11.

For another point of view, the geometry of a truncated tetrahedron is reflected by the length of edges $e_{12}, e_{13}, e_{14}, e_{23}, e_{34}, e_{42}$. Due to the fact that each face is a right angled hexagon, the above six edge lengths will determine the edge lengths of each vertex triangle, and therefore determines its three inner angles, which equal to the corresponding dihedral angles.

Discrete Curvature. For 3-manifolds, each tetrahedron $[v_i, v_j, v_k, v_l]$ (as shown in Fig.15) has four solid angles at their vertices, denoted as $\{\alpha_i^{jkl}, \alpha_j^{kli}, \alpha_k^{lij}, \alpha_l^{ijk}\}$. For an interior vertex, the vertex curvature is 4π minus the surrounding solid angles,

$$K(v_i) = 4\pi - \sum_{jkl} \alpha_i^{jkl}.$$

For a boundary vertex, the vertex curvature is 2π minus the surrounding solid angles.

Besides vertex curvature, the discrete approximation of a 3-manifold owns another type of curvature, *edge curvature*. Suppose $[v_i, v_j, v_k, v_l]$ is a tetrahedron, the dihedral angle on edge e_{ij} is denoted as β_{ij}^{kl}. If edge e_{ij} is an interior edge (i.e. not on the boundary surface), its edge curvature is defined as

$$K(e_{ij}) = 2\pi - \sum_{kl} \beta_{ij}^{kl}.$$

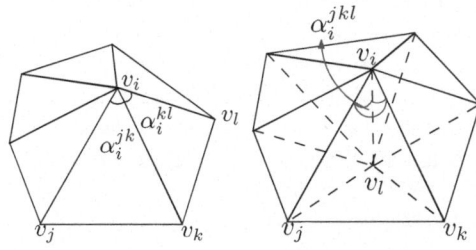

Fig. 15. Discrete vertex curvature for 2-manifold and 3-manifold

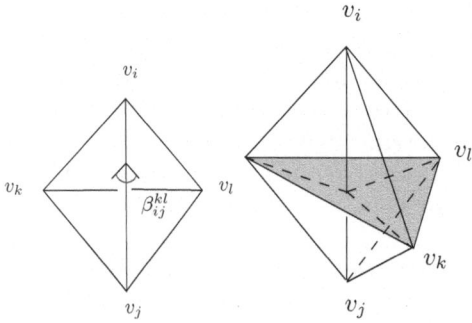

Fig. 16. Discrete edge curvature for a 3-manifold

If e_{ij} is on the boundary surface, its curvature is defined as

$$K(e_{ij}) = \pi - \sum_{kl} \beta_{ij}^{kl}.$$

It turns out that edge curvature is more essential for 3-manifolds than vertex curvature. The later is determined by the former.

Theorem Suppose M is a tetrahedron mesh, v_i is an interior vertex of M. Then

$$\sum_{j} K(e_{ij}) = K(v_i).$$

Discrete Curvature Flow. Given a hyperbolic tetrahedron in $\mathbb{H}^3$ with edge lengths x_{ij} and dihedral angles θ_{ij}, the *volume* of the tetrahedron V is a function of the dihedral angles $V = V(\theta_{12}, \theta_{13}, \theta_{14}, \theta_{23}, \theta_{24}, \theta_{34})$, and the Schlaefli formula can be expressed as

$$\frac{\partial V}{\partial \theta_{ij}} = \frac{-x_{ij}}{2}. \tag{31}$$

Namely, the differential 1-form dV is $\frac{-1}{2} \sum_{ij} x_{ij} d\theta_{ij}$. It can be further proved that the volume of a hyperbolic truncated tetrahedron is a strictly concave function of the dihedral angles.

If a 3-manifold is approximated by a set of truncated tetrahedra, we say that it is *ideally triangulated*. Given an ideally triangulated 3-manifold (M, T), let E be the set of edges in the triangulation. An assignment $x : E \to \mathbb{R}^+$ is called a *hyperbolic cone metric associated with the triangulation T* if for each tetrahedron t in T with edges $e_1, e_2, \cdots, e_6$, the $x(e_i)$ are the edge lengths of a hyperbolic truncated tetrahedron in $\mathbb{H}^3$. The set of all hyperbolic cone metrics associated with T is denoted as $L(M, T)$, which is an open set. The discrete curvature of a cone metric is a map $K(x) : L \to R$, mapping each edge e to its discrete curvature. The discrete curvature flow is then defined by

$$\frac{dx_{ij}}{dt} = K_{ij}, \tag{32}$$

where x_{ij} is the edge length of e_{ij}, K_{ij} is the edge curvature of e_{ij}. The curvature flow is the gradient flow of the function V over M,

$$V(\mathbf{x}) = \int_{\mathbf{x}_0}^{\mathbf{x}} \sum_{e_{ij}} K_{ij} dx_{ij}, \tag{33}$$

where $\mathbf{x}_0$ is the initial metric, which can be set to $(1, 1, \cdots, 1)$.

Theorem 7. *The equilibrium points of the discrete curvature flow Eqn.32 are the complete hyperbolic metric with totally geodesic boundary. Each equilibrium is a local attractor of the flow.*

Furthermore, a hyperbolic cone metric associated with an ideal triangulation is locally determined by its cone angles. For any ideal triangulated 3-manifold, under the discrete curvature flow, the discrete curvature $K_{ij}(t)$ evolves based on the discrete heat equation. Furthermore, the total curvature $\sum_{ij} K_{ij}^2$ is strictly decreasing until all edge curvatures (and hence all the vertex curvatures) are zeros. The theoretic proofs can be found in [Luo05].

7   Algorithm of Discrete Curvature Flow for Hyperbolic 3-Manifolds

The input to the algorithm is the boundary surface of a 3-manifold, represented as a triangular mesh. The output is a realization (i.e. fundamental domain) of the 3-manifold in the hyperbolic space $\mathbb{H}^3$. The algorithm pipeline is as the following; more details can be found in [YJLG08].

1. Compute a triangulation of the 3-manifold as a tetrahedral mesh. Simplify the triangulation such that the number of the tetrahedra is minimal.
2. Run discrete curvature flow on the tetrahedral mesh to obtain the hyperbolic metric.
3. Realize the mesh in the hyperbolic space $\mathbb{H}^3$ using the computed hyperbolic metric .

7.1   Triangulation and Simplification

Given the boundary surface of a 3-manifold, there are existing methods to tessellate the interior and construct the tetrahedral mesh. In this work, we use tetrahedral tessellation based on volumetric Delaunay triangulation.

The following algorithm will simplify the triangulation to a minimum number of truncated tetrahedra.

1. Denote the boundary of a 3-manifold M as $\partial M = \{S_1, S_2, \cdots, S_n\}$. For each boundary surface component S_i, create a cone vertex v_i; for each triangle face $f_j \in S_i$, create a new tetrahedron T_j^i whose vertex set consists of v_i and the vertices of f_j. In this way, M is augmented with a set of cone vertices and a set of new tetrahedra.

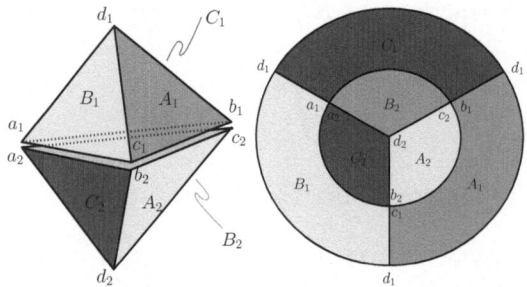

Fig. 17. Simplified triangulation and gluing pattern of Thurston's knotted-Y. The two faces with the same color are glued together.

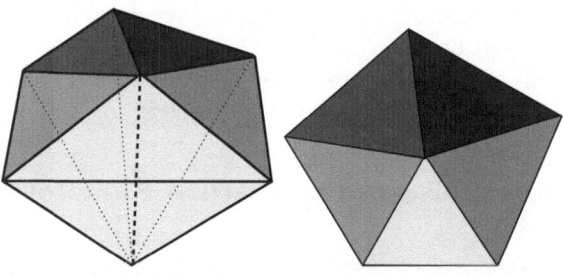

Fig. 18. Edge collapse in tetrahedron mesh

2. Use *edge collapse* as shown in Fig.18 to simplify the triangulation, such that all vertices are removed except for those cone vertices $\{v_1, v_2, \cdots, v_n\}$ inserted in the previous step. Denote the simplified tetrahedral mesh as $\tilde{M}$.
3. For each tetrahedron $\tilde{T}_i \in \tilde{M}$, cut it with the original boundary surface, remove the parts containing cone vertices, and thus make it a truncated tetrahedron (hyper ideal tetrahedron), denoted as T_i.

The simplified triangulation is represented as a collection of truncated tetrahedra and their gluing pattern. For the example in Fig.17, the simplified tetrahedral mesh consists of only two truncated tetrahedra T_1, T_2. Let A_i, B_i, C_i, D_i represent the four faces of the tetrahedron T_i; a_i, b_i, c_i, d_i represent the truncated vertices of T_i. The gluing pattern is given as follows:

$$A_1 \rightarrow B_2 \ \{b_1 \rightarrow c_2, d_1 \rightarrow a_2, c_1 \rightarrow d_2\}$$
$$B_1 \rightarrow A_2 \ \{c_1 \rightarrow b_2, d_1 \rightarrow c_2, a_1 \rightarrow d_2\}$$
$$C_1 \rightarrow C_2 \ \{a_1 \rightarrow a_2, d_1 \rightarrow b_2, b_1 \rightarrow d_2\}$$
$$D_1 \rightarrow D_2 \ \{a_1 \rightarrow a_2, b_1 \rightarrow c_2, c_1 \rightarrow b_2\}$$

The first row means that face $A_1 \in T_1$ is glued with $B_2 \in T_2$ by identifying b_1 with c_2, d_1 with a_2 and c_1 with d_2. Other rows can be interpreted in the same way.

7.2   Hyperbolic Embedding of 3-Manifolds

Once the edge lengths of the tetrahedral mesh are obtained, we can realize it in the hyperbolic space $\mathbb{H}^3$. First, we introduce how to construct a single truncated tetrahedron; then we explain how to glue multiple truncated tetrahedra by hyperbolic rigid motion.

Construction of a Truncated Hyperbolic Tetrahedron. The geometry of a truncated hyperbolic tetrahedron is determined by its dihedral angles. This section explains the algorithm to construct a truncated tetrahedron in the upper half space model of $\mathbb{H}^3$. The algorithm consists of two steps. First, construct a circle packing on the plane; second, compute a CSG (Constructive Solid Geometry) surface. The resulting surface is the boundary of the truncated tetrahedron.

Construct a Circle Packing. Suppose the dihedral angles of a truncated tetrahedron are given. The tetrahedron can be realized in $\mathbb{H}^3$ uniquely, up to rigid motion. The tetrahedron is the intersection of half spaces, the boundaries of these half spaces are the hyper planes on faces f_1, f_2, f_3, f_4 and the cutting planes at the vertices v_1, v_2, v_3, v_4. Each plane intersects the infinity plane at a hyperbolic line, which is a Euclidean circle on the xy-plane. By abusing the symbols, we use f_i to represent the intersection circle between the hyperbolic plane through the face f_i and the infinity plane. Similarly, we use v_j to represent the intersection circle between the cutting plane at v_j and the infinity plane. The goal of this step is to find planar circles (or lines) f_i's and v_j's, such that

1. f_i and circle f_j intersect at the given corresponding angle β_{ij}^{kl}.
2. circle v_i is orthogonal to circles f_j, f_k, f_l.

As shown in Fig.19, all the circles can be computed explicitly with two extra constraints, f_1 and f_2 are lines with two intersection points 0 and ∞, the radius of f_3 equals to one. The dihedral angle on edges $\{e_{34}, e_{14}, e_{24}, e_{12}, e_{23}, e_{13}\}$ are $\{\theta_1, \theta_2, \theta_3, \theta_4, \theta_5, \theta_6\}$ as shown in Fig.14.

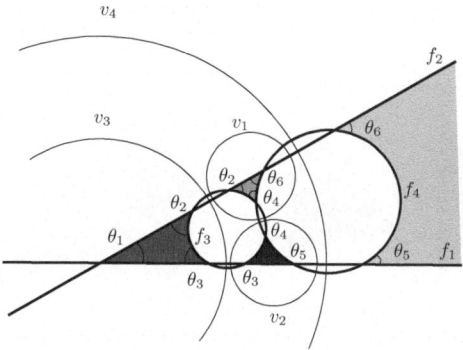

Fig. 19. Circle packing for the truncated tetrahedron

After finding v_1, v_2, v_3, v_4, we transform them back using ϕ. Let w_1, w_2, w_3 be points on the circle v_1, the $\phi(w_1), \phi(w_2), \phi(w_3)$ are the points on the circle $\phi(v_1)$.

CSG Modeling. After we obtain the circle packing, we can construct hemispheres whose equators are those circles. If the circle is a line, then we construct a half plane orthogonal to the xy-plane through the line. Computing CSG among these hemispheres and half-planes, we can get the truncated tetrahedron as shown in Fig.20.

Each hemisphere is a hyperbolic plane, and separates $\mathbb{H}^3$ to two half-spaces. For each hyperbolic plane, we select one half-space; the intersection of all such half-spaces is the desired truncated tetrahedron embedded in $\mathbb{H}^3$. We need to determine which half-space of the two is to be used. We use f_i to represent both the face circle and the hemisphere whose equator is the face circle f_i. Similarly, we use v_k to represent both the vertex circle and the hemisphere whose equator is the vertex circle. As shown in Fig.19, three face circles f_i, f_j, f_k bound a curved triangle Δ_{ijk}, which is color coded, one of them is infinite. If Δ_{ijk} is inside the circle f_i, then we choose the half space inside the hemisphere f_i; otherwise we choose the half-space outside the hemisphere f_i. Suppose vertex circle v_k is orthogonal to the face circles f_i, f_j, f_k; if Δ_{ijk} is inside the circle v_k, then we choose the half-space inside the hemisphere v_k; otherwise we choose the half-space outside the hemisphere v_k.

Fig.21 demonstrates a realization of a truncated hyperbolic tetrahedron in the upper half space model of $\mathbb{H}^3$, based on the circle packing in Fig.19.

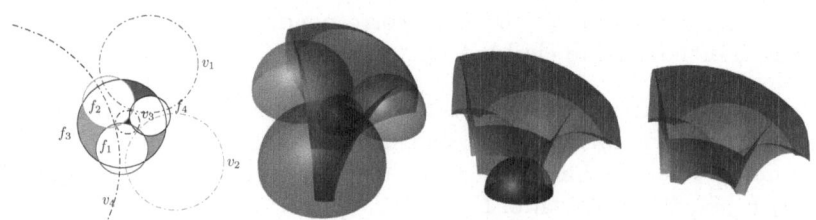

Fig. 20. Constructing an ideal hyperbolic tetrahedron from circle packing using CSG operators

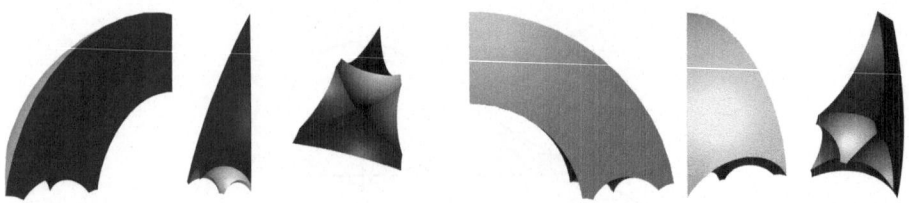

Fig. 21. Realization of a truncated hyperbolic tetrahedron in the upper half space model of $\mathbb{H}^3$, based on the circle packing in figure 19

Glue Two Truncated Hyperbolic Tetrahedra. Suppose we want to glue two truncated hyperbolic tetrahedra, T_1 and T_2, along their faces. We need to specify the correspondence between the vertices and faces between T_1 and T_2. As shown in Fig.22, suppose we want to glue $f_4 \in T_1$ to $f_l \in T_2$, such that $\{v_1, v_2, v_3\} \subset T_1$ are attached to $\{v_i, v_j, v_k\} \subset T_2$. Such a gluing pattern can be denoted as a permutation $\{1, 2, 3, 4\} \to \{i, j, k, l\}$. The right-angled hyperbolic hexagon of f_4 is congruent to the hexagon of f_l.

As shown in Fig.23, the gluing can be realized by a rigid motion in $\mathbb{H}^3$, which induces a Möbius transformation on the xy-plane. The Möbius transformation aligns the corresponding circles, $f_3 \to f_4$, $\{v_1, v_2, v_4\} \to \{v_1, v_2, v_3\}$. The Möbius transformation can be explicitly computed, and determines the rigid motion in $\mathbb{H}^3$.

Fig.24 shows the gluing between two truncated hyperbolic tetrahedra. By repeating the gluing process, we can embed the universal covering space of the hyperbolic 3-manifold in $\mathbb{H}^3$. Fig.25 shows different views of the embedding of the (finite portion) universal covering space of Thurston's knotted Y-Shape in $\mathbb{H}^3$ with the hyperbolic metric.

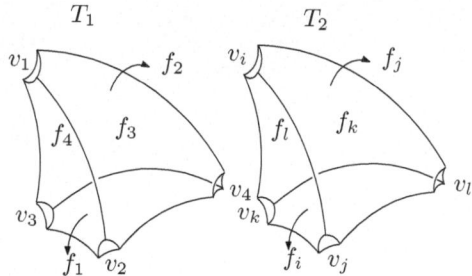

Fig. 22. Glue T_1 and T_2 along $f_4 \in T_1$ and $f_l \in T_2$, such that $\{v_1, v_2, v_3\} \subset T_1$ are attached to $\{v_i, v_j, v_k\} \subset T_2$

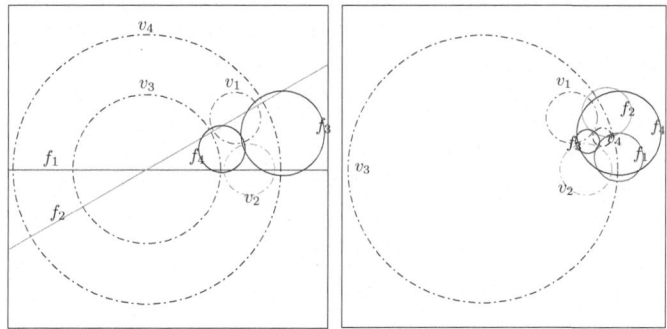

Fig. 23. Glue two tetrahedra by using a Möbius transformation to glue their circle packings, such that $f_3 \to f_4$, $v_1 \to v_1, v_2 \to v_2, v_4 \to v_3$

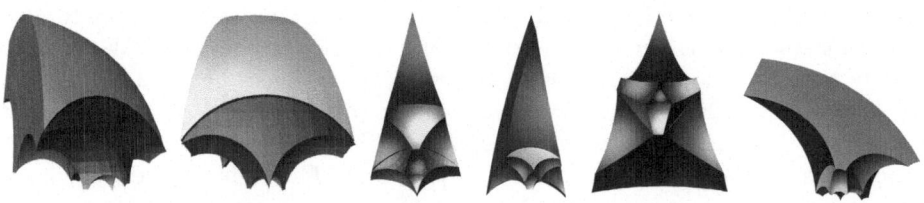

Fig. 24. Glue T_1 and T_2. Frames (a)(b)(c) show different views of the gluing $f_3 \to f_4$, $\{v_1, v_2, v_4\} \to \{v_1, v_2, v_3\}$. Frames (d) (e) (f) show different views of the gluing $f_4 \to f_3, \{v_1, v_2, v_3\} \to \{v_2, v_1, v_4\}$.

Fig. 25. Embed the 3-manifold periodically in the hyperbolic space $\mathbb{H}^3$

7.3   Future Work

Designing discrete curvature flow algorithms for general 3-manifolds is a challenging problem. The rigorous algorithms lead to a discrete version of a constructive proof of the Poincaré's conjecture and Thurston's geometrization conjecture. One of the approach is to study the property of the map from the edge length to the edge curvature. If the map is globally invertible, then one can design metrics by curvatures. If the map is locally invertible, then by carefully choosing a special path in the curvature space, one can design metrics by special curvatures. One of the major difficulties is to verify whether the prescribed curvature is admissible by the mesh. The degenerated tetrahedra will emerge in the process of the curvature flow. The understanding of the formation of the degeneracies will be the key to design the discrete 3-manifold curvature flow.

References

[AMD02]   Alliez, P., Meyer, M., Desbrun, M.: Interactive geometry remeshing. In: SIGGRAPH 2002, pp. 347–354 (2002)

[Aub76]   Aubin, T.: Équations diffréntielles non linéaires et problème de yamabe concernant la courbure scalaire. J. Math. Pures Appl. 55(3), 269–296 (1976)

[BH03]   Bowers, P.L., Hurdal, M.K.: Planar conformal mapping of piecewise flat
           surfaces. In: Visualization and Mathematics III, pp. 3–34. Springer, Berlin
           (2003)
[BS04]   Bobenko, A.I., Springborn, B.A.: Variational principles for circle patterns
           and koebe's theorem. Transactions of the American Mathematical Soci-
           ety 356, 659–689 (2004)
[CCG]   Computational conformal geometry library 1.1,
           http://www.cs.sunysb.edu/~manifold/CCGL1.1/
[Cho91]   Chow, B.: The Ricci flow on the 2-sphere. J. Differential Geom. 33(2),
           325–334 (1991)
[CJGQ05]   Carner, C., Jin, M., Gu, X., Qin, H.: Topology-driven surface mappings
           with robust feature alignment. In: IEEE Visualization 2005, pp. 543–550
           (2005)
[CL03]   Chow, B., Luo, F.: Combinatorial Ricci flows on surfaces. Journal Differ-
           ential Geometry 63(1), 97–129 (2003)
[CS03]   Collins, C., Stephenson, K.: A circle packing algorithm. Computational
           Geometry: Theory and Applications 25, 233–256 (2003)
[dVY91]   de Verdiere Yves, C.: Un principe variationnel pour les empilements de
           cercles. Invent. Math. 104(3), 655–669 (1991)
[GHQ06]   Gu, X., He, Y., Qin, H.: Manifold splines. Graphical Models 68(3), 237–254
           (2006)
[Gug77]   Guggenheimer, H.W.: Differential Geometry. Dover Publications (1977)
[GY08]   Gu, X.D., Yau, S.-T.: Computational Conformal Geometry. Advanced Lec-
           tures in Mathematics. High Education Press and International Press (2008)
[Ham82]   Hamilton, R.S.: Three manifolds with positive Ricci curvature. Journal of
           Differential Geometry 17, 255–306 (1982)
[Ham88]   Hamilton, R.S.: The Ricci flow on surfaces. Mathematics and general rel-
           ativity (Santa Cruz, CA, 1986). Contemp. Math. Amer.Math.Soc. Provi-
           dence, RI 71 (1988)
[JKLG08]   Jin, M., Kim, J., Luo, F., Gu, X.: Discrete surface ricci flow. IEEE Trans-
           action on Visualization and Computer Graphics (2008)
[JLYG07]   Jin, M., Luo, F., Yau, S.T., Gu, X.: Computing geodesic spectra of surfaces.
           In: Symposium on Solid and Physical Modeling, pp. 387–393 (2007)
[Koe36]   Koebe: Kontaktprobleme der Konformen Abbildung. Ber. Sächs. Akad.
           Wiss. Leipzig, Math.-Phys. Kl. 88, 141–164 (1936)
[KSS06]   Kharevych, L., Springborn, B., Schröder, P.: Discrete conformal mappings
           via circle patterns. ACM Trans. Graph. 25(2), 412–438 (2006)
[LGD07]   Luo, F., Gu, X., Dai, J.: Variational Principles for Discrete Surfaces. Ad-
           vanced Lectures in Mathematics. High Education Press and International
           Press (2007)
[LP87]   Lee, J.M., Parker, T.H.: The yamabe problem. Bulletin of the American
           Mathematical Society 17(1), 37–91 (1987)
[LPRM02]   Lévy, B., Petitjean, S., Ray, N., Maillot, J.: Least squares conformal maps
           for automatic texture atlas generation. In: SIGGRAPH 2002, pp. 362–371
           (2002)
[Luo04]   Luo, F.: Combinatorial yamabe flow on surfaces. Commun. Contemp.
           Math. 6(5), 765–780 (2004)
[Luo05]   Luo, F.: A combinatorial curvature flow for compact 3-manifolds with
           boundary. Electron. Res. Announc. Amer. Math. Soc. 11, 12–20 (2005)
[Mos68]   Mostow, G.D.: Quasi-conformal mappings in n-space and the rigidity of the
           hyperbolic space forms. Publ. Math. IHES 34, 53–104 (1968)

[Per02]   Perelman, G.: The entropy formula for the Ricci flow and its geometric applications. Technical Report arXiv.org (November 11, 2002)

[Per03a]   Perelman, G.: Finite extinction time for the solutions to the Ricci flow on certain three-manifolds. Technical Report arXiv.org (July 17, 2003)

[Per03b]   Perelman, G.: Ricci flow with surgery on three-manifolds. Technical Report arXiv.org (March 10, 2003)

[RS87]   Rodin, B., Sullivan, D.: The convergence of circle packings to the riemann mapping. Journal of Differential Geometry 26(2), 349–360 (1987)

[Sch84]   Schoen, R.: Conformal deformation of a riemannian metric to constant scalar curvature. J. Differential Geom. 20(2), 479–495 (1984)

[SSP08]   Springborn, B., Schröoder, P., Pinkall, U.: Conformal equivalence of triangle meshes. ACM Transactions on Graphics 27(3), 1–11 (2008)

[Thu76]   Thurston, W.P.: Geometry and Topology of Three-Manifolds. Princeton lecture notes (1976)

[Thu80]   Thurston, W.P.: Geometry and Topology of Three-Manifolds. Lecture notes at Princeton university (1980)

[Thu85]   Thurston, W.P.: The finite riemann mapping theorem (1985)

[Tru68]   Trudinger, N.S.: Remarks concerning the conformal deformation of riemannian structures on compact manifolds. Ann. Scuola Norm. Sup. Pisa 22(2), 265–274 (1968)

[Wei07]   Weitraub, S.H.: Differential Forms: A Complement to Vector Calculus. Academic Press, London (2007)

[Yam60]   Yamabe, H.: The yamabe problem. Osaka Math. J. 12(1), 21–37 (1960)

[YJLG08]   Yin, X., Jin, M., Luo, F., Gu, X.: Computing and visualizing constant-curvature metrics on hyperbolic 3-manifolds with boundaries. In: 4th International Symposium on Visual Computing (2008)

Information Geometry and Its Applications: Convex Function and Dually Flat Manifold

Shun-ichi Amari

RIKEN Brain Science Institute
Amari Research Unit for Mathematical Neuroscience
amari@brain.riken.jp

Abstract. Information geometry emerged from studies on invariant properties of a manifold of probability distributions. It includes convex analysis and its duality as a special but important part. Here, we begin with a convex function, and construct a dually flat manifold. The manifold possesses a Riemannian metric, two types of geodesics, and a divergence function. The generalized Pythagorean theorem and dual projections theorem are derived therefrom. We construct alpha-geometry, extending this convex analysis. In this review, geometry of a manifold of probability distributions is then given, and a plenty of applications are touched upon. Appendix presents an easily understable introduction to differential geometry and its duality.

Keywords: Information geometry, convex function, Riemannian geometry, dual affine connections, dually flat manifold, Legendre transformation, generalized Pythagorean theorem.

1 Introduction

Information geometry emerged from a study on the invariant geometrical structure of a family of probability distributions. We consider a family $S = \{p(x, \boldsymbol{\theta})\}$ of probability distributions, where x is a random variable and $\boldsymbol{\theta}$ is an n-dimensional vector parameter. This forms a geometrical manifold where $\boldsymbol{\theta}$ plays the role of a coordinate system.

We searched for the invariant structure to be introduced in S, and found a Riemannian structure together with a dual pair of affine connections (see Chentsov, 12; Amari and Nagaoka, 8). Such a structure has scarcely been studied in traditional differential geometry, and is still not familiar.

Typical families of probability distributions, e.g., exponential families and mixture families, are dually flat together with non-trivial Riemannian metrics. Some non-flat families are curved submanifolds of flat manifolds. For example, the family of Gaussian distributions

$$S = \left\{ p\left(x; \mu, \sigma^2\right) = \frac{1}{\sqrt{2\pi}} \exp\left\{ -\frac{(x-\mu)^2}{2\sigma^2} \right\} \right\}, \tag{1}$$

F. Nielsen (Ed.): ETVC 2008, LNCS 5416, pp. 75–102, 2009.

where μ is the mean and σ^2 is the variance, is a flat 2-dimensional manifold. However, when $\sigma^2 = \mu^2$ holds, the family of distributions

$$M = \left\{ p(x, \mu) = -\frac{1}{\sqrt{2\pi}} \exp\left\{ -\frac{(x - \mu)^2}{2\mu^2} \right\} \right\} \tag{2}$$

is a curved 1-dimensional submanifold (curve) embedded in S. Therefore, it is important to study the properties of a dually flat Riemannian space.

A dually flat Riemannian manifold possesses dual convex potential functions, and all the geometrical structure can be derived from them. In particular, a Riemannian metric, canonical divergence, generalized Pythagorean relation and projection theorem are their outcomes.

Conversely, given a convex function, we can construct a dually-flat Riemannian structure, which is an extension and foundation of the early approach by (Bregman, 10) and a geometrical foundation of the Legendre duality. The present paper focuses on a convex function, and reconstructs dually-flat Riemannian structure therefrom. See (Zhang, 28) for details.

Applications of information geometry are expanding, and we touch upon some of them. See Appendix for an understandable introduction to differential geometry.

2   Convex Function and Legendre Structure

A dually flat Riemannian manifold posseses a pair of convex functions. The set of all the discrete probability distributions gives a dually flat manifold. The geometrical structures are derived from the convex functions. Therefore, many useful results are derived from the analysis of a convex function. On the other hand, given a convex function together with its dual convex function, a dually flat Riemannian manifold is automatically derived. In the present section, we begin with a convex function and derive its fundamental properties from the dual geometry point of view. Convex analysis is important in many fields of science such as physics, optimization, information theory, signal processing and vision.

2.1   Metric Derived from Convex Function

Let us consider a smooth convex function $\psi(\boldsymbol{\theta})$ defined in an open set S of $\boldsymbol{R}^n$, where $\boldsymbol{\theta}$ plays the role of a coordinate system. Its second derivative, that is, the Hessian of ψ,

$$g_{ij}(\boldsymbol{\theta}) = \partial_i \partial_j \psi(\boldsymbol{\theta}) \tag{3}$$

is a positive definite matrix depending on position $\boldsymbol{\theta}$, where $\partial_i = \partial/\partial\theta^i$, and $\boldsymbol{\theta} = (\theta^1, \cdots, \theta^n)$.

Consider two infinitesimally nearby points $\boldsymbol{\theta}$ and $\boldsymbol{\theta} + d\boldsymbol{\theta}$, and define the square of their distance by

$$ds^2 = <d\boldsymbol{\theta}, d\boldsymbol{\theta}> = \sum g_{ij}(\boldsymbol{\theta}) d\theta^i d\theta^j, \tag{4}$$

where $< d\boldsymbol{\theta}, d\boldsymbol{\theta} >$ is the inner product defined in the above. This is the second-order term of the Taylor expansion of $\psi(\boldsymbol{\theta} + d\boldsymbol{\theta})$,

$$\psi(\boldsymbol{\theta} + d\boldsymbol{\theta}) = \psi(\boldsymbol{\theta}) + \sum \partial_i \psi d\theta^i + \frac{1}{2} \sum g_{ij} d\theta^i d\theta^j, \tag{5}$$

so that it is defined by the curvature of function ψ. A manifold in which an infinitesimal distance is defined by (4) is called a Riemannian manifold, where the matrix $g = (g_{ij})$ is called a Riemannian metric.

When

$$\psi(\boldsymbol{\theta}) = \frac{1}{2} \sum (\theta^i)^2, \tag{6}$$

we have

$$g_{ij} = \delta_{ij} = \begin{cases} 1, i = j, \\ 0, i \neq j, \end{cases} \tag{7}$$

and the space is Euclidean, because the squared distance is given by

$$ds^2 = \sum (d\theta^i)^2. \tag{8}$$

Hence our framework includes the Euclidean geometry as its special case.

We have fixed a coordinate system $\boldsymbol{\theta}$, and the metric is derived by using the convex function $\psi(\boldsymbol{\theta})$. In order to have a general geometrical structure, the geometry should be invariant under coordinate transformations. However, the convexity is not invariant under coordinate transformations. We define a geometrical structure by introducing a metric and affine connection in a manifold with respect to a specific coordinate system, that is $\boldsymbol{\theta}$ in our case, and then extend it invariantly to any coordinate systems.

The Riemannian metric is defined by (3). We define a geodesic in S such that a straight line connecting two points, $\boldsymbol{\theta}_1$ and $\boldsymbol{\theta}_2$,

$$\boldsymbol{\theta}(t) = (1 - t)\boldsymbol{\theta}_1 + t\boldsymbol{\theta}_2 \tag{9}$$

is a geodesic of S. The coordinates lines of θ^i of $\boldsymbol{\theta}$ are all geodesics. Mathematically speaking, a geodesic is defined by using an affine connection. In the present case, the covariant derivative reduces to the ordinary derivative in this coordinate system, implying the space is flat (that is, Riemann-Christoffel curvature vanishes and the coefficients of the connection are 0 in this coordinate system). See appendix.

The affine connection implicitly introduced here is not a metric connection, that is, it is not a Riemannian connection derived from the metric g_{ij}. Therefore, a geodesic is no more a minimal distance line connecting two points. In other words, the straightness and minimality of distance holding in a Euclidean space splits in a space of general affine connection. This looks ugly at first glance, but its deep structure becomes clear when we consider duality.

2.2   Legendre Transformation and Dual Coordinates

The gradient of $\psi(\boldsymbol{\theta})$ is given by partial derivatives

$$\boldsymbol{\eta} = \mathrm{Grad}\psi(\boldsymbol{\theta}), \quad \eta_i = \frac{\partial}{\partial\theta^i}\psi(\boldsymbol{\theta}). \tag{10}$$

It is remarkable that, given $\boldsymbol{\eta}$, its original $\boldsymbol{\theta}$ is uniquely determined, that is, the correspondence between $\boldsymbol{\theta}$ and $\boldsymbol{\eta}$ are one-to one. Hence we can use $\boldsymbol{\eta}$ as another coordinate system of S.

We use here lower indices like η_i to represent quantities related to the $\boldsymbol{\eta}$ coordinate system. This makes it clear that θ^i and η_i are mutually reciprocal.

The transformation from $\boldsymbol{\theta}$ to $\boldsymbol{\eta}$ is called the Legendre transformation. We can find a convex function of $\boldsymbol{\eta}$, defined by

$$\varphi(\boldsymbol{\eta}) = \max_{\boldsymbol{\theta}} \{\boldsymbol{\theta} \cdot \boldsymbol{\eta} - \psi(\boldsymbol{\theta})\}. \tag{11}$$

The two potential functions satisfy the relation

$$\psi(\boldsymbol{\theta}) + \varphi(\boldsymbol{\eta}) - \boldsymbol{\theta} \cdot \boldsymbol{\eta} = 0 \tag{12}$$

when $\boldsymbol{\theta}$ and $\boldsymbol{\eta}$ are respective coordinates of the same point, and the inverse transformation from $\boldsymbol{\eta}$ to $\boldsymbol{\theta}$ is given by the gradient

$$\boldsymbol{\theta} = \mathrm{Grad}\varphi(\boldsymbol{\eta}), \quad \theta^i = \frac{\partial}{\partial\eta_i}\varphi(\boldsymbol{\theta}). \tag{13}$$

Hence, they are dually coupled.

Since we have another coordinates $\boldsymbol{\eta}$ and another convex function $\varphi(\boldsymbol{\eta})$, we can define another geometric structure based on them in a similar manner. In this dual setting, η_i are dual geodesic coordinates, and any straight line connecting two points in the $\boldsymbol{\eta}$ coordinates is a dual geodesic. The Riemannian metric is given by

$$g^{ij} = \frac{\partial^2}{\partial\eta_i\partial\eta_j}\varphi(\boldsymbol{\eta}). \tag{14}$$

Since the Jacobian matrices of coordinate transformations are written as

$$g_{ij} = \frac{\partial\eta_i}{\partial\theta_j}, \quad g^{ij} = \frac{\partial\theta^i}{\partial\eta_j}, \tag{15}$$

we can prove the following theorem.

Theorem 1. The metric g^{ij} is the inverse matrix of the metric g_{ij}. Moreover, $\sum g_{ij}d\theta^i d\theta^j = \sum g^{ij}d\eta_i d\eta_j$ implying the two metrics defined in terms of $\boldsymbol{\theta}$ and $\boldsymbol{\eta}$ are the same.

Proof.   It is easy to see from (15) that $G = (g_{ij})$ and $G^{-1} = (g^{ij})$ are mutually inverse. We also see

$$d\boldsymbol{\eta} = G d\boldsymbol{\theta}, \quad d\boldsymbol{\theta} = G^{-1} d\boldsymbol{\eta}. \tag{16}$$

Hence

$$ds^2 = d\boldsymbol{\theta}^T G d\boldsymbol{\theta} = d\boldsymbol{\eta}^T G^{-1} d\boldsymbol{\eta}. \tag{17}$$

When we consider two points P and $P + dP$ whose coordinates are $\boldsymbol{\theta}$ and $\boldsymbol{\theta} + d\boldsymbol{\theta}$, and $\boldsymbol{\eta}$ and $\boldsymbol{\eta} + d\boldsymbol{\eta}$ in the respective coordinates, the above theorem shows that the squared distance between P and $P + dP$ is the same whichever coordinates we use. That is, the two Riemannian metrics are the same, and they are represented in different coordinate systems. This is because it is a tensor. However, the two types of geodesics are different.

2.3   Divergence

We introduce a divergence function between two points P and Q, of which coordinates are written as $\boldsymbol{\theta}_P$ and $\boldsymbol{\theta}_Q$, and also $\boldsymbol{\eta}_P$ and $\boldsymbol{\eta}_Q$ in the dual coordinates. The divergence is defined by

$$D(P : Q) = \psi(\boldsymbol{\theta}_P) + \varphi(\boldsymbol{\eta}_Q) - \boldsymbol{\theta}_P \cdot \boldsymbol{\eta}_Q, \tag{18}$$

where

$$\boldsymbol{\theta} \cdot \boldsymbol{\eta} = \sum \theta^i \eta_i. \tag{19}$$

It is easy to see

$$D(P : P) = 0, \tag{20}$$

and is positive otherwise. The divergence is not symmetric in general,

$$D(P : Q) \neq D(Q : P). \tag{21}$$

Changing the role of P and Q (or $\boldsymbol{\theta}$ and $\boldsymbol{\eta}$), we can define the dual divergence

$$D^*(P : Q) = \varphi(\boldsymbol{\eta}_P) + \psi(\boldsymbol{\theta}_Q) - \boldsymbol{\eta}_P \cdot \boldsymbol{\theta}_Q. \tag{22}$$

However, it is easy to see

$$D(P : Q) = D^*(Q : P). \tag{23}$$

Hence we need only one divergence. The other is obtained by changing the order of two points.

When Q is close to P, by putting $Q = P + dP$, we have

$$D(P : P + dP) = \frac{1}{2} \sum g_{ij} d\theta^i d\theta^j = \frac{1}{2} \sum g^{ij} d\eta_i d\eta_j \tag{24}$$

which is the squared Riemannian distance. Hence, the divergence is similar to the square of distance. Therefore, the triangle inequality does not hold. Instead, the Pythagoras-like theorem holds.

2.4   Generalized Pythagorean Theorem

We first define the orthogonality of two curves intersecting at a point. Let us consider two curves $\boldsymbol{\theta}(t)$ and $\boldsymbol{\theta}'(t)$ parameterized by scalar t and assume they intersect at $t = 0$, that is $\boldsymbol{\theta}(0) = \boldsymbol{\theta}'(0)$. The same curves can be represented by the dual coordinates as $\boldsymbol{\eta}(t)$ and $\boldsymbol{\eta}'(t)$. The tangent vector of a curve $\boldsymbol{\theta}(t)$ is a vector represented by $\dot{\boldsymbol{\theta}}(t) = \left(\dot{\theta}^1(t), \cdots, \dot{\theta}^n(t) \right)$ where $\dot{} = d/dt$ represents the derivative with respect to t.

The two curves are said to be orthogonal at the intersection point, when their inner product vanishes,

$$\left\langle \dot{\boldsymbol{\theta}}, \dot{\boldsymbol{\theta}}' \right\rangle = \sum g_{ij} \dot{\theta}^i \dot{\theta}'^j = 0. \tag{25}$$

This can be represented as

$$\sum g^{ij} \dot{\eta}_i \dot{\eta}'_2 = 0 \tag{26}$$

or

$$\dot{\boldsymbol{\theta}} \cdot \dot{\boldsymbol{\eta}}' = \sum \dot{\theta}^i \dot{\eta}'_i = 0 \tag{27}$$

by using the two coordinate systems.

Let us take three points P, Q and R in S.

Theorem 2. When the dual geodesic connecting P and Q is orthogonal to the geodesic connecting Q and R,

$$D(P : R) = D(P : Q) + D(Q : R). \tag{28}$$

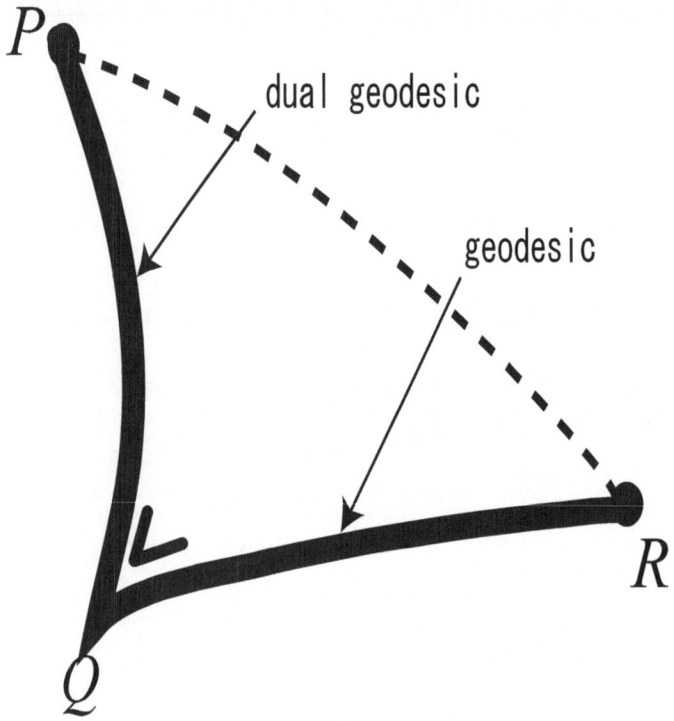

Fig. 1. Pythagorean theorem

Dually, when the geodesic connecting P and Q is orthogonal to the dual geodesic connecting Q and R,

$$D^*(P : R) = D^*(P : Q) + D^*(Q : R). \tag{29}$$

See Fig.1.

When the potential function $\psi(\boldsymbol{\theta})$ is quadratic,

$$\psi(\boldsymbol{\theta}) = \frac{1}{2} \sum \left(\theta^i\right)^2, \tag{30}$$

the metric reduces to the identity matrix $g_{ij} = \delta_{ij}$. The dual coordinates are the same as the primal ones, $\boldsymbol{\theta} = \boldsymbol{\eta}$, and two geodesics are the same. In this case, the above theorem is exactly the same as the Pythagorean theorem. Hence, our dually-flat manifold includes the Euclidean space as a special example.

2.5   Projection Theorem

Let us consider a closed region V included in S. Let P be a point in S not included in V. We search for the point in V which is closest to P in the sense of divergence. That is, we search for the point $P^\perp \in V$ that minimizes $D(P : Q)$, $Q \in V$. It is obvious that $P^\perp$ is on the boundary of V. This point $P^\perp$ is called the reverse I-projection or dual geodesic projection of P to V (Amari and Nagaoka, 2000; see also Csiszár, 1975).

Dually to the above, we may think about the point $P^{*\perp}$ in V that minimizes $D^*(P : Q) = D(Q : P)$, $Q \in V$. This is called the geodesic projection or the I-projection of P to V (Csiszár, 1975; Amari and Nagaoka, 2000).

We say V is convex, when the geodesic connecting two points R and R' are in V, that is,

$$(1 - t)\boldsymbol{\theta}_R + t\boldsymbol{\theta}_{R'} \in V. \tag{31}$$

We say that V is dual-convex, when the dual geodesic connecting R and R' is included in V, that is,

$$(1 - t)\boldsymbol{\eta}_R + t\boldsymbol{\eta}_{R'} \in V. \tag{32}$$

We have the following projection theorem.

Theorem 3. When $P^\perp$ is the dual projection of P to V, the dual geodesic connecting P and $P^\perp$ is orthogonal to the boundary surface of V. The dual projection is unique when V is convex. When $P^{*\perp}$ is the projection of P to V, the geodesic connecting P to $P^{*\perp}$ is orthogonal to the boundary surface of V. The projection is unique when V is dual convex. See Fig.2.

Corollary. The dual projection of P to a flat subspace is unique. The projection of P to a dual flat subspace is unique.

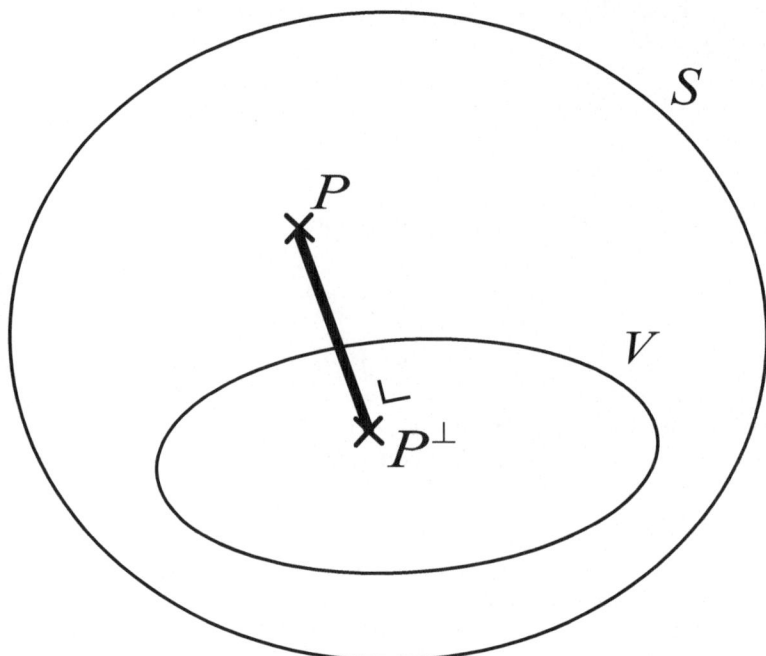

Fig. 2. Projection of P to V

Let V_1 and V_2 be two regions in S. Let us define the divergence (dual divergence) between V_1 and V_2 by

$$D\,(V_1 : V_2) = \min_{P \in V_1, Q \in V_2} D(P : Q) \tag{33}$$

$$D^*\,(V_2 : V_1) = \min_{P \in V_1, Q \in V_2} D^*(Q : P) \tag{34}$$

We search for the points $P^* \in V_1$ and $Q^* \in V_2$ such that

$$D\,(V_1 : V_2) = D^*\,(V_2 : V_1) = D\,(P^* : Q^*)\,, \tag{35}$$

Then, the two extremal points P^* and Q^* satisfy the following: The dual projection of P^* to V_2 is Q^*, and the projection of Q^* to V_1 is P^*.

There is an iterative algorithm to find P^* and Q^*:

1. Start from $R_1 = R$
2. For $i = 1, 2, \cdots$, dual-project R_i to V_2, and let it be Q_i
3. Then, project Q_i to V_1, and let it be R_{i+1}
4. End when $R_i = R_{i+1}$ (or equivalently $Q_i = Q_{i+1}$) is attained, or their divergence is sufficiently small.

This procedure is called the alternative minimization algorithm (Bregman, 1967). Csiszár and Tusnady (15) proposed this as an iterative procedure for the EM algorithm. The algorithm was studied in information geometry (Amari,3), see also (Amari, Kurata and Nagaoka, 7) and (Byrne, 11) for application to Boltzmann machine. There are many recent applications in relation to the EM algorithm and Bregman divergence.

2.6   Tangent Space and Foliation

The tangent space T_P of S at point P is a local linearization of S at P (see Appendix). Since S is flat, all the tangent spaces look equivalent. However, S is a Riemannian space, so its metric structure g_{ij} depends on P.

T_P is a vector space. Its basis is spanned by n vectors, $e_1, \cdots, e_n$ which represent the tangent vector of the coordinate curve $\theta^i, i = 1, \cdots, n$. Such a basis is called the natural basis induced by the coordinate system $\boldsymbol{\theta}$ (Fig. 3). The inner product of two basis vectors gives the Riemannian metric,

$$\langle e_i, e_j \rangle = g_{ij} \tag{36}$$

which in general depends on P.

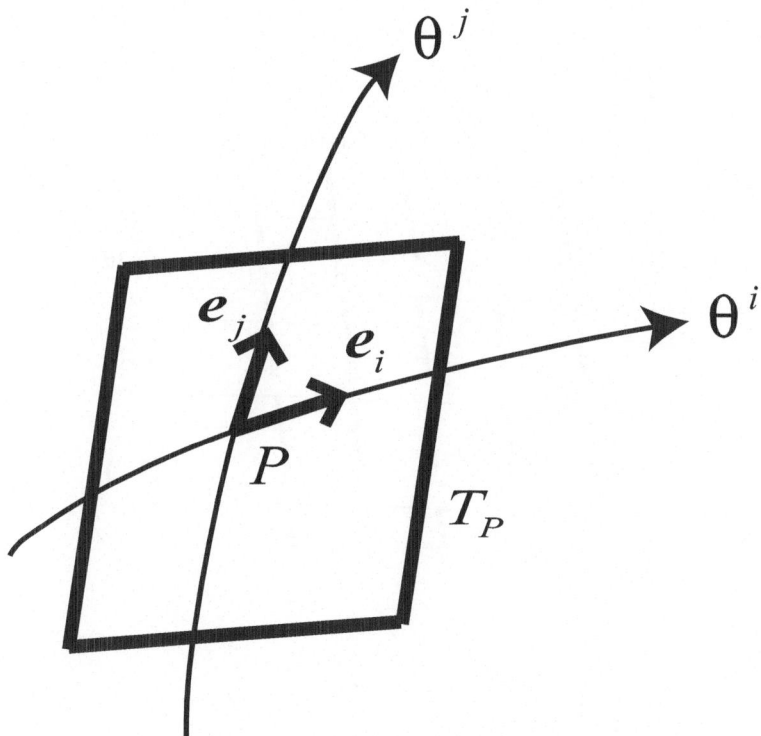

Fig. 3. Tangent space T_P and natural basis

Dually to the above, we have the natural basis with respect to the dual co-ordinate system, spanned by $e_1^*, \cdots, e_n^*$ which are the tangent vectors of the coordinate curves η_i. The inner product of two basis vectors gives

$$\langle e_i^*, e_j^* \rangle = g^{ij} \tag{37}$$

which is the Riemannian metric in the dual coordinate system.

The two bases of T_P are reciprocal in the following sense.

Theorem 4. The two sets of basis vectors, are mutually orthogonal,

$$\langle e_i, e_j^* \rangle = \delta_i^j \tag{38}$$

Proof. Since we have

$$e_j^* = \sum g^{ji} e_i \tag{39}$$

it is easy to derive (38).

Let us fix p dual coordinates $\boldsymbol{\eta}_p = (\eta_1, \cdots, \eta_p)$ in $\boldsymbol{\eta} = (\eta_1, \cdots, \eta_n)$, $p < n$, and consider the $(n-p)$-dimensional dually flat subspaces

$$M(\boldsymbol{\eta}_p) = \{P : \text{its first } p \ \boldsymbol{\eta}\text{-coordinates are } (\eta_1, \cdots, \eta_p)\}. \tag{40}$$

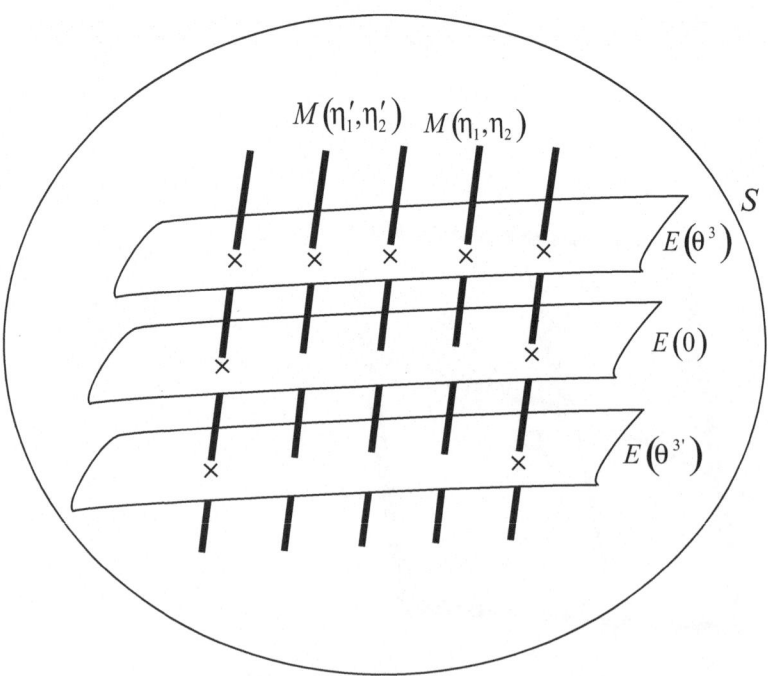

Fig. 4. Orthogonal foliation $(\eta_1, \eta_2; \theta^3)$

A family of subspaces $M\left(\boldsymbol{\eta}_p\right)$ for all $\boldsymbol{\eta}_p$, which do not overlap, and fills the entire space S. Such a family is called a foliation of S. Similarly, by fixing $n-p$ coordinates $\boldsymbol{\theta}_{n-p} = \left(\theta^{n-p+1}, \cdots, \theta^n\right)$, and consider p dimensional flat subspace

$$E\left(\boldsymbol{\theta}_{n-p}\right) = \{P : \text{its last } n - p \text{ coordinates are } \boldsymbol{\theta}_{n-p}\}. \tag{41}$$

Their family gives another foliation of S.

The two foliations are mutually orthogonal, in the sense that the tangent vectors of the respective subspaces at the intersection are orthogonal. The intersection of $M\left(\boldsymbol{\eta}_p\right)$ and $E\left(\boldsymbol{\theta}_{n-p}\right)$ is the point whose first p $\boldsymbol{\eta}$-coordinates are $\boldsymbol{\eta}_p$ and the last $n-p$ coordinates are $\boldsymbol{\theta}_{n-p}$ (Fig. 4). We may use a new coordinate system $\boldsymbol{\xi} = \left(\boldsymbol{\eta}_p, \boldsymbol{\theta}_{n-p}\right)$, which is very useful for applications.

The dual orthogonal geodesic foliation has lots of applications (Amari, 5).

2.7 α-Divergence and α-Geodesic

We have studied the dually flat structure of a manifold originated from a convex function, consisting of divergence function, Riemannian metric and dually flat affine connections. It is possible to extend this framework to the α-connections, where α is a real parameter (Zhang, 28). When $\alpha = 1$, it gives the original $\boldsymbol{\theta}$ structure and when $\alpha = -1$, it gives the dual $\boldsymbol{\eta}$ structure. We then have α-divergence and α-geodesic by extending our definition. Although the α-affine connection is not flat, but the α-connection and $-\alpha$-connection are dually coupled.

When $\alpha = 1$, we have a flat affine connection, and when $\alpha = -1$, we have a dual flat affine connection. Therefore, the α-divergence connects the primal and dual divergences continuously. Similarly, the α-geodesic connects the primal and dual geodesics continuously.

The α-divergence (Zhang, 28) between P and P' is defined by

$$D_\alpha\left(P : P'\right) = \frac{4}{1-\alpha^2}\left[1 - \exp\left\{\psi\left(\frac{1+\alpha}{2}\boldsymbol{\theta} + \frac{1-\alpha}{2}\boldsymbol{\theta}\right)\right.\right.$$
$$\left.\left. - \frac{1+\alpha}{2}\psi(\boldsymbol{\theta}) - \frac{1-\alpha}{2}\psi\left(\boldsymbol{\theta}'\right)\right\}\right]. \tag{42}$$

When $\alpha = \pm 1$, we take the limit $\alpha \to \pm 1$, and then have

$$D_{-1}\left(P : P'\right) = \psi(\boldsymbol{\theta}) + \varphi\left(\boldsymbol{\eta}'\right) - \sum \theta_i \eta_i', \tag{43}$$

$$D_1\left(P : P'\right) = \psi\left(\boldsymbol{\theta}'\right) + \varphi(\boldsymbol{\eta}) - \sum \theta_i' \eta_i. \tag{44}$$

The Riemannian metric derived from the α-divergence does not depend on α, giving the same metric.

The α-connection is derived from the α-divergence by calculating

$$\frac{\partial^3}{\partial\theta_i\partial\theta_j\partial\theta_k}D_\alpha\left(\boldsymbol{\theta} : \boldsymbol{\theta}'\right)_{|\boldsymbol{\theta}'=\boldsymbol{\theta}}. \tag{45}$$

This gives the α-connection in the primal coordinate system as

$$\overset{(\alpha)}{\Gamma}_{ijk} = \frac{1-\alpha}{2} T_{ijk}. \tag{46}$$

Here, T_{ijk} is a tensor defined by

$$T_{ijk} = \frac{\partial^3}{\partial\theta^i \partial\theta^j \partial\theta^k} \psi(\boldsymbol{\theta}) \tag{47}$$

and $\overset{(\alpha)}{\Gamma}$ is the coefficients of the α-connection.

The α-geodesic $\boldsymbol{\theta}(t)$ is given by the geodesic equation

$$\ddot{\theta}^i + \sum \overset{(\alpha)}{\Gamma}{}^i_{jk} \dot{\theta}^j \dot{\theta}^k = 0. \tag{48}$$

We do not discuss more details of the α-structure here, but it has wide applications. Sometimes, more robust results are obtained by using the α-projection instead of the primal or dual geodesic projections. See, for example, Matsushima (19).

3   Information Geometry of Probability Distributions

Let us consider a family of probability distributions $S = \{p(x, \boldsymbol{\xi})\}$, where x is a random variable and $\boldsymbol{\xi}$ is an n-dimensional vector parameter to specify a distribution. This is considered as an n-dimensional manifold, where $\boldsymbol{\xi}$ is coordinates, and a point $\boldsymbol{\xi}$ is regarded as a probability distribution $p(x, \boldsymbol{\xi})$.

In order to introduce an invariant geometrical structure to M, we require the following criterion:

Invariance Criterion: The geometry should be invariant under coordinate transformations of $\boldsymbol{\xi}$ and also under one-to-one transformations of random variable x.

When we transform x to y by

$$y = f(x), \quad x = f^{-1}(y), \tag{49}$$

the probability density function is changed from $p(x, \boldsymbol{\xi})$ to

$$\bar{p}(y, \boldsymbol{\xi}) = \frac{1}{\left|\frac{\partial y}{\partial x}\right|} p\left(f^{-1}(y), \boldsymbol{\xi}\right). \tag{50}$$

The above criterion requires that the geometrical structure is the same for $M = \{p(x, \boldsymbol{\xi})\}$ and $\bar{M} = \{\bar{p}(y, \boldsymbol{\xi})\}$.

Based on the criterion, we have the only invariant Riemannian metric, which is given by the Fisher information matrix (Chentsov, 12). We also have a one-parameter family of invariant affine connections.

Theorem 5. The invariant Riemannian metric is given by

$$g_{ij} = E\left[\frac{\partial}{\partial \xi_i} \log p(x, \boldsymbol{\xi}) \frac{\partial}{\partial \xi_j} \log p(x, \boldsymbol{\xi})\right] \tag{51}$$

and the invariant affine connection parameterized by α is

$$\overset{(\alpha)}{\Gamma}_{ijk} = [ij; k] - \alpha T_{ijk} \tag{52}$$

where $[ij; k]$ is the Christoffel symbol calculated from g_{ij} and

$$T_{ijk} = E\left[\frac{\partial}{\partial \xi_i} \log p(x, \boldsymbol{\xi}) \frac{\partial}{\partial \xi_j} \log p(x, \boldsymbol{\xi}) \frac{\partial}{\partial \xi_k} \log p(x, \boldsymbol{\xi})\right] \tag{53}$$

is an invariant tensor symmetric with respect to three indices.

The α-and $-\alpha$-affine connections are dual, in the sense that the two covariant derivatives ∇^α and $\nabla^{-\alpha}$ satisfy

$$X < Y, Z >= \langle \nabla_X^\alpha Y, Z \rangle + \langle \nabla_X^{-\alpha} Z, Y \rangle \tag{54}$$

for three vector fields X, Y and Z. We do not go into details here. See Appendix and (Amari and Nagaoka, 8).

It is also proved that, when the manifold is flat with respect to one affine connection, it is also flat with respect to the dual affine connection. Hence, we have a dually flat manifold. When a manifold is flat, we have a geodesic coordinate system $\boldsymbol{\theta}$ in which

$$\overset{(1)}{\Gamma}_{ijk}(\boldsymbol{\theta}) = 0. \tag{55}$$

Such a manifold has a convex potential function $\psi(\boldsymbol{\theta})$, by which two tensors are given by

$$g_{ij} = \frac{\partial^2}{\partial \theta^i \partial \theta^j} \psi(\boldsymbol{\theta}), \quad T_{ijk} = \frac{\partial^3}{\partial \theta^i \partial \theta^j \partial \theta^k} \psi(\boldsymbol{\theta}). \tag{56}$$

We also have a dual coordinate system, a dual potential function, and an invariant canonical divergence function $D(P : Q)$. An important family of probability distributions is the exponential family represented in the following form by taking an adequate dominating measure,

$$p(x, \boldsymbol{\theta}) = \exp\left\{\sum \theta^i x_i - \psi(\boldsymbol{\theta})\right\}. \tag{57}$$

In this case, the parameter $\boldsymbol{\theta}$ is called the canonical or natural parameter, and the function $\psi(\boldsymbol{\theta})$ is the cumulant generating function (in physics it is called the free energy), which is convex.

The manifold of an exponential family is dually flat, given by the convex function $\psi(\boldsymbol{\theta})$. The dual coordinates are the expectation parameters, $\boldsymbol{\eta}$

$$\eta_i = E[x_i]. \tag{58}$$

We have the dual structure explained in Section 2.

Another important dually flat manifold is a mixture family, which is written as

$$p(x, \boldsymbol{\xi}) = \sum \xi_i p_i(x), \quad \sum \xi_i = 1, \quad \xi_i \geq 0, \tag{59}$$

where $p_i(x)$ are fixed probability distributions.

There are many probability distributions which are submanifolds of an exponential family. They are called curved exponential families. Other families exist which are not embedded in an exponential family. They also have a dual structure.

When random variable x is discrete, taking a finite number of values, $x = 0, 1, 2, \cdots, n$, the set of all such distributions form an exponential family. This is because we have

$$p(x, \boldsymbol{\theta}) = \exp \left\{ \sum \theta^i \delta_i(x) - \psi(\boldsymbol{\theta}) \right\}, \tag{60}$$

where $\theta^i = \log p_i$ is the log probability of $x = i$ and $\delta_i(x)$ is the delta function

$$\delta_i(x) = \begin{cases} 1, \, x = i, \\ 0, \, \text{otherwise}. \end{cases} \tag{61}$$

This implies any parameterized family of probability distributions over discrete random variables is a curved exponential family, and is hence a submanifold in a dually flat manifold. This is the reason why a dually flat manifold is important.

Procedures of statistical inference, such as estimation and testing statistical hypothesis is well founded in the framework of information geometry.

Semiparametric statistical inference has been established in the fibre bundle theory of statistical inference (Amari and Kawanabe, 6).

4   Applications of Information Geometry

Plenty of applications of information geometry have been widely prevailing in many fields and are growing. Here, we mention only a simple list of applications.

1) Applications to statistical inference
Higher-order evaluation of statistical inference, including estimation and hypothesis testing, is the oldest applications (Amari, 1). Here, both of the primal e-curvature and dual m-curvature play a fundamental role. Other applications are given in the area of EM algorithm, semiparametric estimation and robust estimation.

2) Control theory and time series analysis
A linear system and a nonlinear system can be identified by the probability distribution of the system output when white noise is applied to its input. This gives one-to-one correspondence of a family of probability distributions and a

family of systems. Hence, the geometrical structure of the manifold of systems can be studied by information geometry (Amari, 2).

3) Applications to neural networks and systems

One application is found in multilayer perceptrons, where a set of perceptrons forms a Riemannian space. However, due to the symmetric structure of neurons in the hidden layer, the manifold is singular, and the Riemannian metric degenerates in symmetry regions (Amari, Park and Ozeki, 9). This causes serious difficulty in learning behaviors. We can overcome this difficulty by taking the Riemannian structure into account and modifying a learning algorithm to fit the Riemannian structure (the natural gradient method, Amari, 1998).

Another application is analysis of spike trains in a pool of neurons, where their firing is correlated. We can decompose correlated structure orthogonally in a sum of firing rates, pairwise correlations, third-order and higher-order correlations (Nakahara and Amari, 21). Dual geodesic foliations of information geometry plays a fundamental role in this decomposition.

4) Machine learning

Machine learning deals with stochastic situations and extracts necessary information from examples. In the case of a graphical model, the belief propagation algorithm uses e- and m-projections effectively (Ikeda, Tanaka and Amari, 16).

Another application is in the analysis of the boosting method of combining weak learners (Lebanon and Lafferty, 18; Murata et al., 20; Lebanon, 17). We can use the geometric idea of conformal transformation for improving the kernel function in the area of support vector machines (Wu and Amari, 27).

5) Convex programming

In the case of convex programming such as linear programming and semi-definite programming, the inner method can be used effectively. A convex potential function is given from the convex region as a barrier function from which the dual structure is introduced. The m-curvature plays a fundamental role in evaluating the complexity of the algorithm (Ohara, 23; Ohara and Tsuchiya, 24).

6) Signal processing and ICA (independent component analysis)

Independent component analysis is a technique to extract hidden signals from their mixtures. Here, the geometry of the manifold of mixing and unmixing matrices plays a fundamental role, together with the manifold of joint probability distributions which includes the submanifold of independent distributions in its inside (Cichocki and Amari, 13).

7) Other applications

We can find many applications in mathematics, physics and information theory.

4.1 Conclusions

Information geometry, I-projection, and alternative procedure of dual projections are important tools of frequent use. The present review paper constructs a dually flat manifold starting from a convex function. We have elucidated its dualistic differential-geometrical structure without going into details of differential geometry. This is possible because the manifold is dually flat. However, deeper mathematical framework would be required when we go further, and the present paper plays a role of introduction to information geometry.

It is also useful to point out the relation of information geometry to affine differential geometry (Nomizu and Sasaki, 22). A potential function $\psi(\boldsymbol{\theta})$ is regarded as an n-dimensional submanifold defined by $\theta^0 = \psi\left(\theta^1, \cdots, \theta^n\right)$ in the extended space $\left(\theta^0, \theta^1, \cdots, \theta^n\right)$. Then, affine differential geometry studies the geometry of this surface, where the space is regarded as an affine space. We may note that the Rényi entropy (Rényi, 25) and Tsallis entropy (Tsallis, 26) are closely related to the α-geometry.

Applications of information geometry are expanding. One can see some of them in the present monograph, e.g., applications to signal processing, vision analysis, shape analysis and others.

References

Amari, S.: Differential-Geometrical Methods in Statistics. Lecture Notes in Statistics, vol. 28. Springer, Heidelberg (1985)

Amari, S.: Differential geometry of a parametric family of invertible linear systems-Riemannian metric, dual affine connections and divergence. Mathematical Systems Theory 20, 53–82 (1987)

Amari, S.: Information geometry of the EM and em algorithms for neural networks. Neural Networks 8-9, 1379–1408 (1995)

Amari, S.: Natural gradient works efficiently in learning. Neural Computation 10, 251–276 (1998)

Amari, S.: Information geometry on hierarchy of probability distributions. IEEE Transactions on Information Theory 47, 1701–1711 (2001)

Amari, S., Kawanabe, M.: Information geometry of estimating functions in semi parametric statistical models. Bernoulli. 3(1), 29–54 (1997)

Amari, S., Kurata, K., Nagaoka, H.: Information geometry of Boltzmann machines. IEEE Transactions on Neural Networks 3, 260–271 (1992)

Amari, S., Nagaoka, H.: Methods of Information Geometry. Translations of Mathematical Monographs, vol. 191. AMS & Oxford University Press (2000)

Amari, S., Park, H., Ozeki, T.: Singularities affect dynamics of learning in neuromanifolds. Neural Computation 18, 1007–1065 (2006)

Bregman, L.M.: The relaxation method of finding the common point of convex sets and its application to the solution of problems in convex programming. USSR Computational Mathematics and Physics 7, 200–217 (1967)

Byrne, W.: Alternating minimization and Boltzmann machine learning. IEEE Transactions on Neural Networks 3, 612–620 (1992)

Chentsov (Čencov), N.N.: Statistical Decision Rules and Optimal Inference. American Mathematical Society, Rhode Islandm U.S.A. (1982); originally published in Russian, Nauka, Moscow (1972)

Cichocki, A., Amari, S.: Adaptive Blind Signal and Image Processing. John Wiley, Chichester (2002)

Csiszár, I.: I-divergence geometry of probability distributions and minimization problems. The Annals of Probability 3, 146–158 (1975)

Csiszár, I., Tusnády, G.: Information geometry and alternating minimization procedures. In: Dedewicz, E.F., et al. (eds.) Statistics and Decisions, vol. (1), pp. 205–237.
R. Oldenbourg Verlag, Munich (1984)

Ikeda, S., Tanaka, T., Amari, S.: Stochastic reasoning, free energy, and information
geometry. Neural Computation 16, 1779–1810 (2004)

Lebanon, G.: Riemannian Geometry and Statistical Machine Learning. CMU-LTI-05-
189, Carnegie-Mellon University (2005)

Lebanon, G., Lafferty, J.: Boosting and maximum likelihood for exponential models.
Advances in Neural Information Processing Systems, vol. 14, pp. 447–451. MIT
Press, Cambridge (2002)

Matsushima, Y.: The alpha EM algorithms: Surrogate likelihood maximization using
alpha-logarithmic information measures. IEEE Transactions on Information Theory 49, 692–706 (2003)

Murata, N., Takenouchi, T., Kanamori, T., Eguchi, S.: Information geometry of U-
boost and Bregman divergence. Neural Computation 16, 1437–1481 (2004)

Nakahara, H., Amari, S.: Information-geometric measure for neural spikes. Neural Computation 14, 2269–2316 (2002)

Nomizu, K., Sasaki, T.: Affine Differential Geometry. Cambridge University Press,
Cambridge (1994)

Ohara, A.: Geodesics for dual connections and means on symmetric cone. Interal Equation and Operator Theory 50, 537–548 (2004)

Ohara, A., Tsuchiya, T.: An information geometric approach to polynomial-time
interior-pint algorithms (submitted, 2008)

Rényi, A.: On measures of entropy and information. In: Proceedings of the 4th Berke-
ley Symposium on Mathematical Statistics and Probability, vol. 1, pp. 547–561.
University of California Press (1961)

Tsallis, C.: Possible generalization of Boltzmann-Gibbs statistics. Journal of Statistical
Physics 52, 479 (1988)

Wu, S., Amari, S.: Conformal transformation of kernel functions: A data-dependent
way to improve support vector machine classifiers. Neural Processing Letters 15,
59–67 (2002)

Zhang, J.: Divergence function, duality, and convex analysis. Neural Computation 16,
159–195 (2004)

Appendix

Introduction to Differential Geometry
— Intuitive Explanation

We give a brief and intuitively-understandable introduction to differential geometry with dual affine connections. We do not enter in mathematically rigorous
definitions and explanations but use intuitive ideas to understand the concepts.

For more rigorous treatments, refer to Boothby (2003), Kobayashi and Nomizu
(1969), and Amari and Nagaoka (2000).

A   Manifold and Coordinates

An n-dimensional manifold S is a space in which a neighborhood of each point
has an n-dimensional Euclidean-like structure. This means that S is a curved

version of a Euclidean space. In order to specify a point in S, we use a coordinate system

$$\boldsymbol{\xi} = \left(\xi^1, \cdots, \xi^n\right). \tag{62}$$

There are many coordinate systems, for example,

$$\boldsymbol{\zeta} = \left(\zeta^1, \cdots, \zeta^n\right) \tag{63}$$

in which $\zeta^i, i = 1, \cdots, n$, are smooth and invertible functions of $\boldsymbol{\xi}$. Any such coordinate system is eligible.

A manifold S may have global topological structure different from a Euclidean space. For example, a sphere or a torus is a two-dimensional manifold having a different topological structure from a Euclidean space, although a small neighborhood of each point looks like a two-dimensional Euclidean space. In such a case a single coordinate system might not cover the entire manifold. We use in such a case a number of coordinate systems to cover it. Global structure of a manifold is an important topic of geometry and topology. However, we study here only local structure of a manifold covered by a single coordinate system. We denote by $\{S, \boldsymbol{\xi}\}$ the manifold S with coordinate system $\boldsymbol{\xi}$.

B   Tangent Space

Let us consider an infinitesimally small neighborhood of point P in manifold S. Even when S is curved, we may regard a small neighborhood of P as a flat space. This is linear approximation of S in a small area around P. We show one example. The earth is a ball, and its surface is a sphere which is curved. However, we may regard its local area, say Tokyo area, as a flat surface approximately. This idea leads us to the concept of the tangent space T_P at P.

T_P is a linear space, which is locally an approximation of S around P. When one think of a curved surface in a 3-dimensional Euclidean space, we can easily think of a tangent space T_P at any point P. When S is curved, T_P depends on P and T_P and $T_{P'}$ are different in general, that is, having different two-dimensional orientations, when $P \neq P'$.

T_P is a vector space whose origin is at P. It is spanned by n vectors

$$\{e_1, e_2, \cdots, e_n\} \tag{64}$$

which form a basis. We may use any basis provided e_i are linearly independent. When we use a coordinate system $\boldsymbol{\xi}$, a convenient basis is to use n tangent vectors of the coordinate lines ξ^i. This is because n coordinate lines have different directions, and their tangent lines are linearly independent. Such a basis is called the natural basis associated with $\{S, \boldsymbol{\xi}\}$.

Mathematicians like to denote a natural basis vector e_i by the differential operators,

$$\partial_i = \frac{\partial}{\partial \xi^i}. \tag{65}$$

Given a function $f(\boldsymbol{\xi})$ on the manifold, $\partial_i f(\boldsymbol{\xi})$ denotes a rate of change of function f in the direction of the coordinate line ξ^i. Hence, they identify the direction $\boldsymbol{e}_i$ with its directional differentiation.

Any tangent vector $X \in T_P$ is written as

$$X = \sum X^i \boldsymbol{e}_i \tag{66}$$

by using a basis $\{\boldsymbol{e}_i\}$. The coefficients X^i are the components of X in this basis $\{\boldsymbol{e}_i\}$. By using different basis $\{\boldsymbol{e}_i'\}$, we have

$$X = \sum X'^i \boldsymbol{e}_i' \tag{67}$$

and components change, although the vector X is the same. So components depend on the basis.

From mathematician's point of view, a vector

$$X = \sum X^i \boldsymbol{e}_i \tag{68}$$

is a differential operator, where

$$X f = \sum X^i \partial_i f(\boldsymbol{\xi}) \tag{69}$$

gives a directional derivative of function $f(\boldsymbol{\xi})$.

Let us come back to the idea of local approximation. Let P be a point whose coordinates are $\boldsymbol{\xi}$, and let P' is a nearby point whose coordinates are $\boldsymbol{\xi} + d\boldsymbol{\xi}$. Then, the line element PP' is regarded as a tangent vector

$$PP' = dP = \sum d\xi^i \boldsymbol{e}_i \tag{70}$$

where we use the natural basis. Then, we have

$$dP f = \sum d\xi^i \partial_i f = df \tag{71}$$

giving the total differential of function in the direction of dP.

C   Riemannian Manifold

When the tangent space is Euclidean, we have the inner product of two tangent vectors. In particular, the square of its length is defined by the inner product of itself. When each tangent space is equipped with the inner product, the space is said to be Riemannian. A Euclidean space is a special case of the Riemannian manifold.

Let $G = (g_{ij})$ be a matrix defined by the inner product of basis vectors,

$$g_{ij} = \langle \boldsymbol{e}_i, \boldsymbol{e}_j \rangle . \tag{72}$$

It is a positive-definite symmetric matrix called the Riemannian metric tensor.

The inner product of two vectors

$$X = \sum X^i e_i, \quad Y = \sum Y^j e_j \tag{73}$$

is given in their component form by

$$< X, Y >= \sum X^i Y^j g_{ij}. \tag{74}$$

In particular, the square of the absolute length of a vector X is

$$\|X\|^2 =< X, X >= \sum X^i X^j g_{ij}. \tag{75}$$

Two vectors X and Y are said to be orthogonal, when their inner product vanishes,

$$< X, Y >= 0. \tag{76}$$

Let us consider two curves $\boldsymbol{\xi}(t)$ and $\boldsymbol{\xi}'(t)$ parameterized by t, such that they intersect at $t = 0$. Their tangent vectors are denoted by

$$\dot{\boldsymbol{\xi}}(t) = \sum \frac{d}{dt} \xi^i(t) e_i, \quad \dot{\boldsymbol{\xi}}' = \sum \frac{d}{dt} \xi'^i(t) e_i. \tag{77}$$

The two curves are said to be orthogonal when the inner product of the two tangent vectors vanishes,

$$\left\langle \dot{\boldsymbol{\xi}}(0), \dot{\boldsymbol{\xi}}'(0) \right\rangle = 0. \tag{78}$$

Let PP' be again a small line-element of S. The squared length of this line-element is given by

$$ds^2 = \langle d\boldsymbol{\xi}, d\boldsymbol{\xi} \rangle = \sum d\xi^i d\xi^j g_{ij}. \tag{79}$$

We now consider two points P and Q which are connected by a curve $\boldsymbol{\xi}(t)$, where P has coordinates $\boldsymbol{\xi}(1)$ and Q has coordinates $\boldsymbol{\xi}(0)$. Their length along the curve is given by the integral

$$s = \int_0^1 \sqrt{\sum \dot{\xi}^i(t) \dot{\xi}^j(t) g_{ij}} \, dt. \tag{80}$$

This obviously depends on the curve connecting them.

We sometimes consider a surface or m-dimensional submanifold M in $S(m < n)$. It is specified in a parametric form

$$\boldsymbol{\xi} = \boldsymbol{\xi}(u_1, \cdots, u_m). \tag{81}$$

Then, we consider the tangent space T_P^M of M at $P \in M$. This is a subspace of the tangent space of S at P,

$$T_P^M \subset T_P. \tag{82}$$

The tangent space T_P^M is spanned by m vectors

$$e_1^M = \frac{\partial \boldsymbol{\xi}}{\partial u_1}, \cdots, e_m^M = \frac{\partial \boldsymbol{\xi}}{\partial u_m}. \tag{83}$$

Let us consider a curve $\boldsymbol{\xi}(t)$ which transverses M at point P. Then, it is said to be orthogonal to M when the tangent vector $\boldsymbol{\xi}(t)$ is orthogonal to T_P^M at P,

$$\left\langle \dot{\boldsymbol{\xi}}, e_i^M \right\rangle = 0, \quad i = 1, \cdots, m. \tag{84}$$

D   Affine Connection

We have so far studied the metric structure of the tangent space of S at each point separately. This looks like cutting S into small local pieces, and study each piece separately. Since S is curved in general, tangent spaces of T_P and $T_{P'}$ are different. However, the manifold is smoothly connected, and when the point deviates from P slightly to P', the tangent space T_P changes slightly to $T_{P'}$. By studying how they change, we may recover the curved structure of S by connecting these neighboring tangent spaces.

Let us consider two tangent spaces T_P and $T_{P'}$, where $P' = P + dP$ is infinitesimally close to P. They are very similar, and become identical as P' approaches P. But $T_{P'}$ is different from T_P. So we map basis vector $\boldsymbol{e}_i$ of T_P to $T_{P'}$. The counterpart of $\boldsymbol{e}_i$ in $T_{P'}$ is given by this mapping. Since the manifold and its coordinates are smooth, we may consider $\boldsymbol{e}_i$ is very close to the basis vector $\boldsymbol{e}_i'$ of $T_{P'}$ at P'. So we assume that $\boldsymbol{e}_i$ is mapped to

$$\tilde{\boldsymbol{e}}_i = \boldsymbol{e}_i' + \delta \boldsymbol{e}_i \in T_{P'}, \tag{85}$$

where the deviation term $\delta \boldsymbol{e}_i$ is small (Fig. A1). When the manifold is flat like a Euclidean space, by using a linear coordinate system, $\boldsymbol{e}_i$ and $\boldsymbol{e}_i'$ are exactly the same. However, when the coordinate system is curved (e.g., a polar coordinate system), $\boldsymbol{e}_i$ and $\boldsymbol{e}_i'$ are not identical even in a Euclidean space. Hence, $\boldsymbol{e}_i$ is mapped to $T_{P'}$ in the above form even in the case of a Euclidean space.

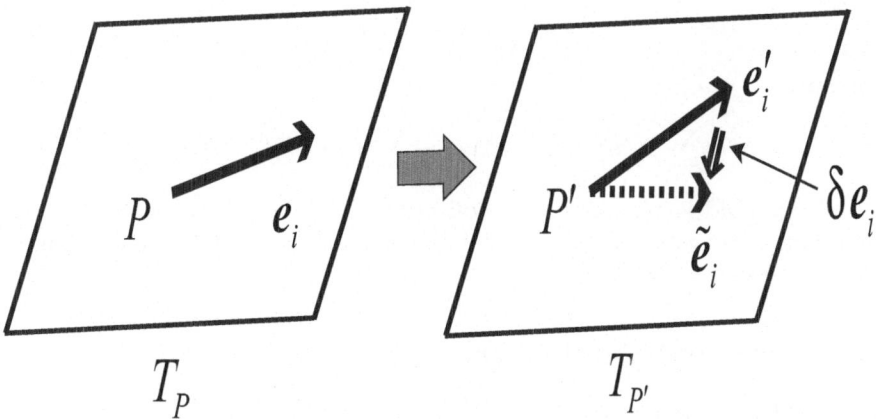

Fig. A1. Affine mapping of $e_i \in T_P$ to $T_{P'}$

Since δe_i is a vector in $T_{P'}$, we represent it in the component form,

$$\delta e_i = \sum_k \delta_i^k e_k'. \tag{86}$$

The components δ_i^k are small, and depend on the difference $d\xi$ of P and P', that is in which direction P' deviates from P. The correction term becomes 0 as $d\xi$ becomes 0. Hence, when $d\xi$ is infinitesimally small, the linear form in $d\xi$ suffices. So we express δe_i in the form

$$\delta e_i = -\sum_{i,k} \Gamma_{ji}^k d\xi^j e_k' \tag{87}$$

This mapping establishes the relation between two local linear approximations of S at P and P', because the relation between $e_i \in T_P$ and $e_i' \in T_{P'}$ are established. The relation is represented by a quantity Γ_{ij}^k having three indices i, j, k. This correspondence is called an affine connection, and the quantities Γ_{ji}^k are called the coefficients of affine connection. They are given by using the inner product as

$$\langle \delta e_i, e_k' \rangle = -\sum_{j,m} \Gamma_{ji}^m g_{mk} d\xi^j. \tag{88}$$

We put

$$\Gamma_{jik} = \sum_m \Gamma_{ji}^m g_{mk}. \tag{89}$$

We consider the case where

$$\Gamma_{jik} = \Gamma_{ijk} \tag{90}$$

holds. When this is not the case, S is said to have torsion. We do not treat the case with torsion in this appendix.

Once the mapping is established for the basis vectors, it is generalized to the mapping of any vector

$$X = \sum X^i e_i \in T_P. \tag{91}$$

It is mapped to $T_{P'}$ by

$$\tilde{X} = \sum X^i \tilde{e}_i = \sum X^i \left(e_i' - \sum \Gamma_{ji}^k e_k' d\xi^j \right) \in T_{P'}. \tag{92}$$

A curved manifold is regarded as a collection $\{T_P, P \in S\}$ of local linear approximations. They are connected by an affine connection, and the entire curved structure is recovered by it.

E   Geodesic and Parallel Transport

Let us consider a curve

$$\xi = \xi(t), \tag{93}$$

where $P = \boldsymbol{\xi}(t)$ and $P' = \boldsymbol{\xi}(t + dt)$. Its tangent vector at P and P' are

$$\dot{\boldsymbol{\xi}}(t) = \sum \dot{\xi}^i(t)\boldsymbol{e}_i, \quad \dot{\boldsymbol{\xi}}(t + dt) = \sum \dot{\xi}^i(t + dt)\boldsymbol{e}_i', \tag{94}$$

respectively. When the tangent vector $\dot{\boldsymbol{\xi}}(t)$ at P is mapped to $T_{P'}$, it is in general different from the tangent vector $\dot{\boldsymbol{\xi}}(t + dt)$ at P'. When they are the same, the curve does not change its tangent direction as t increases.

The tangent vector $\dot{\boldsymbol{\xi}}(t)$ at P is mapped to

$$\tilde{\dot{\boldsymbol{\xi}}}(t) = \sum \dot{\xi}^i(t)\boldsymbol{e}_i' - \sum \Gamma_{ji}^k d\xi^j \boldsymbol{e}_k' \dot{\xi}^i(t) \tag{95}$$

of $T_{P'}$. However, the tangent vector $\dot{\boldsymbol{\xi}}(t + dt)$ at $T_{P'}$ is

$$\dot{\boldsymbol{\xi}}(t + dt) = \sum \left(\dot{\xi}(t) + \ddot{\xi}^i(t)dt \right) \boldsymbol{e}_i'. \tag{96}$$

Hence, they are equal when

$$\ddot{\xi}^i + \sum \Gamma_{jk}^i \dot{\xi}^j \dot{\xi}^k = 0. \tag{97}$$

That is, when a curve $\boldsymbol{\xi}(t)$ satisfies the above equation, its tangent vectors are always the same by this affine correspondence.

Such a curve is called a geodesic. That is, a geodesic is a curve not changing its direction, so that it is an extension of a straight line.

Here, we assume that the tangent vector does not change its length, too. When we reparameterize t, this curve does not change its direction but its length may change. Here we consider only the case that both the direction and length do not change.

A vector

$$X = \sum X^i \boldsymbol{e}_i \tag{98}$$

at P is mapped to

$$\tilde{X} = \sum_k X^k \left(\boldsymbol{e}_k' - \sum_j \Gamma_{ji}^k d\xi^j \boldsymbol{e}_k' \right) \tag{99}$$

at P'. Let us consider a curve $\boldsymbol{\xi}(t)$ connecting two points P and Q, where P is denoted by $\boldsymbol{\xi}(0)$ and Q by $\boldsymbol{\xi}(1)$. Given vector $X(0)$ at P, we map it to a neighboring point P' along the curve. We may continue this process such that $X(t)$ is mapped to $X(t + dt)$

$$X(t + dt) = \tilde{X}(t) = \sum X^k(t)\boldsymbol{e}_k' - \sum_{i,k} \Gamma_{ji}^k \dot{\xi}^j X^i(t)\boldsymbol{e}_k' \tag{100}$$

along the curve. Since, we have

$$X^i(t + dt) = \sum X^i + \frac{\partial}{\partial \xi^j} X^i \dot{\xi}^j dt, \tag{101}$$

such a tangent vector $X(t)$ defined on the curve satisfies

$$\dot{X}^i(t) + \sum \Gamma^i_{jk}\dot{\xi}^j X^k = 0. \tag{102}$$

We say that $X(t)$ is a parallel transport of $X(0)$ along the curve (Fig. A2). A geodesic is the curve where $X(t) = \dot{\boldsymbol{\xi}}(t)$ is the tangent vector of the curve $\boldsymbol{\xi}(t)$.

Let $X(t)$ satisfy (102). This defines a mapping of $X(0)$ at P to $X(1)$ at Q along the curve $\boldsymbol{\xi}(t)$. We call $X(1)$ the parallel transport of $X(0)$ along the curve, and denote it as

$$X(1) = \prod_{\boldsymbol{\xi}(t)} X(0). \tag{103}$$

This obviously depends on which curve, connecting P and Q, is used to transport it. When the transport does not depend on the curve, the manifold is said to be flat. When S is flat, we have a coordinate system such that the coordinate curves are geodesics. Therefore, S is an affine space, except for the metric structure.

A manifold is flat when its Riemann-Christoffel curvature vanishes, where the curvature is calculated from the components of an affine connection.

F   Covariant Derivative

We can compare two vectors defined at different positions by using an affine connection, although the tangent spaces they belong to are different. Here we introduce the notion of the covariant derivative, which makes the differentiation or derivative of a vector function possible. This also makes it possible to have derivative of a tensor, but we do not mention it.

Let X be a vector field, that is a vector-valued function defined on S. It is represented as

$$X = \sum X^i(\boldsymbol{\xi})e_i(\boldsymbol{\xi}), \tag{104}$$

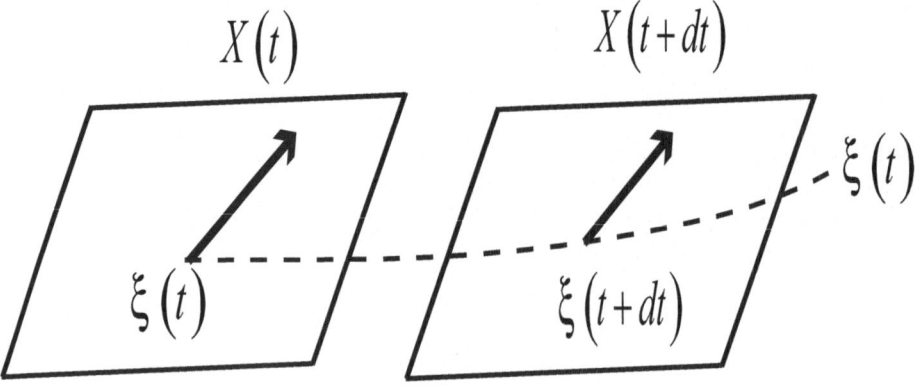

Fig. A2. Parallel transport $X(t)$

where $e_i(\boldsymbol{\xi})$ are the natural basis vectors at point $\boldsymbol{\xi}$. We want to know how $X(\boldsymbol{\xi})$ changes as the position P moves to P', where their coordinates are $\boldsymbol{\xi}$ and $\boldsymbol{\xi}+d\boldsymbol{\xi}$, respectively. This is given by the derivative of X in the direction of $d\boldsymbol{\xi}$. However, it is not mere derivatives of the components X, because the basis vectors changes from P to P'. Hence in order to have an intrinsic change of vector X, we need to subtract from $X(\boldsymbol{\xi}+d\boldsymbol{\xi})$ the map of $X(\boldsymbol{\xi})$. So the intrinsic change of vector X is given by

$$\delta X^i = X^i(\boldsymbol{\xi}+d\boldsymbol{\xi}) - \left(X^i(\boldsymbol{\xi}) - X^i\delta e_i\right) \tag{105}$$

Letting $d\boldsymbol{\xi}$ small, the derivative of X in the direction of the coordinate curve ξ^i is given by

$$\nabla_i X(\boldsymbol{\xi}) = \sum_k \left(\frac{\partial}{\partial \xi^i}X^k(\boldsymbol{\xi}) + \sum_j \Gamma_{ij}^k X^j\right) e_k \tag{106}$$

This is the covariant derivative of X in the direction of ξ^i. In general, the covariant derivative of X in the direction of vector Y is denoted by $\nabla_Y X$, and is

$$\nabla_Y X = \frac{\partial}{\partial \xi^i}X^k Y^i + \Gamma_{ij}^k Y^i X^j. \tag{107}$$

By using the covariant derivative, the equation of a geodesic is written as

$$\nabla_{\dot{\boldsymbol{\xi}}}\dot{\boldsymbol{\xi}} = 0. \tag{108}$$

Similarly, when vector $X(t)$ is parallelly transported along a curve $\boldsymbol{\xi}(t)$, we have

$$\nabla_{\dot{\boldsymbol{\xi}}}X = 0. \tag{109}$$

G   Riemannian Connection

We have defined an affine connection independently of the metric structure. An affine connection is related to the metric by the metric condition which we state now. We will see a more general idea of dual connections in the next section, which is also related to the metric.

Metric condition: The length of a vector X does not change by the parallel transport.

Under the metric condition, the affine connection is uniquely determined from the metric, provided S does not have torsion. This unique connection is called the Levi-Civita connection or Riemannian connection. It is a good exercise to derive the following theorem.

Theorem A1. The Riemannian connection is given by

$$\Gamma_{ijk} = [ij;k] = \frac{1}{2}\left(\frac{\partial}{\partial \xi_i}g_{jk} + \frac{\partial}{\partial \xi_j}g_{ik} - \frac{\partial}{\partial \xi_k}g_{ij}\right) \tag{110}$$

where $[ij; k]$ is called the Christoffel symbol.

A straight line connects two points P and Q by the shortest distance in a Euclidean space. The notions of straightness and minimality of distance coincide when we use the Riemannian connection.

Theorem A2. The minimal distance line connecting two points is given by the geodesic connecting them.

Proof is also an exercise, and is obtained by calculating the variational equation of (80).

This nice property connecting the straightness and minimal distance is valid only under the metric condition. When we use another affine connection, it does not hold. However, as we will see, there is nice dualistic extension of this.

H   Dual Connections

Let us consider a manifold having a Riemannian metric g_{ij} and two affine connections Γ_{ijk}, Γ_{ijk}^*. We denote the two connections by their covariant derivatives ∇, ∇^* or equivalently by the two parallel transport operators $\prod, \prod^*$. Each of the affine connections does not satisfy the metric condition in general. However, a pair of affine connections are said to be dual with respect to the metric, when they satisfy the following dual metric condition.

Dual metric condition: The inner product of two vectors X and Y does not change when X is parallelly transported from P to Q by one affine connection and Y by the other affine connection,

$$< X, Y >_P = \left\langle \prod_{\xi} X, \prod_{\xi_Y}^* \right\rangle_Q \tag{111}$$

When $X = Y$, we have

$$< X, X >_P = \left\langle \prod_{\xi} X, \prod_{\xi}^* X \right\rangle_Q \tag{112}$$

Hence, this is a generalization of the metric condition. When the affine connection happens to be self-dual, that is $\nabla = \nabla^*$, the dual metric condition reduces to the metric condition.

A space with dual affine connections is specified by its structure

$$\{S, \nabla, \nabla^*, g\}. \tag{113}$$

We have the differential version of the dual metric condition: Two affine connections ∇ and ∇^* are dual with respect to the metric, when the following equation holds for three vector fields:

$$X < Y, Z >= \langle \nabla_X Y, Z \rangle + \langle Y, \nabla_X^* Z \rangle, \tag{114}$$

where $< Y, Z >$ is the inner product of Y and Z,

$$< Y, Z >= \sum g_{ij} Y^i Z^j. \tag{115}$$

In terms of the coefficients of affine connections, the duality holds when

$$\frac{\partial}{\partial \xi^i} g_{jk} = \Gamma_{ijk} + \Gamma^*_{ikj}. \tag{116}$$

I   Dually Flat Manifold

When S is flat with respect to one affine connection, we can prove that it is automatically flat with respect to the dual affine connection. We call such a space a dually flat manifold.

A dually flat manifold plays a role of the Euclidean space in Riemannian geometry: Any n-dimensional Riemannian space is embedded in $n(n + 1)/2$-dimensional Euclidean space as its curved submanifold. Similarly, a manifold with dual affine connections can be embed in a dually flat manifold of high dimensions, possibly of infinite dimensions.

The following is a fundamental theorem on the dually flat manifold.

Theorem A3. A dually flat manifold S has two special coordinate systems denoted by $\boldsymbol{\theta} = \left(\theta^1, \cdots, \theta^n\right)$ and $\boldsymbol{\eta} = (\eta_1, \cdots, \eta_n)$ such that $\boldsymbol{\theta}$ is an affine coordinate system of ∇-connection and $\boldsymbol{\eta}$ is an affine coordinate system of ∇^*-connection. There exist two potential functions $\psi(\boldsymbol{\theta})$ and $\varphi(\boldsymbol{\eta})$ which are strictly convex, and are connected by the Legendre transformation such that

$$\psi(\boldsymbol{\theta}) + \varphi(\boldsymbol{\eta}) - \sum \theta^i \eta_i = 0, \tag{117}$$

where $\boldsymbol{\theta}$ and $\boldsymbol{\eta}$ are the respective coordinates of the same point. S has a canonical divergence between two points P and Q defined by

$$D[P : Q] = \psi\left(\boldsymbol{\theta}_P\right) + \varphi\left(\boldsymbol{\eta}_Q\right) - \sum \theta^i_P \eta_{Qi} \tag{118}$$

where $\boldsymbol{\theta}_P$ and $\boldsymbol{\eta}_Q$ are respective coordinates of points P and Q.

Theorem A4. The canonical divergence function of a dually flat manifold satisfies the Pythagorean relation,

$$D = [P : R] = D[P : Q] + D[Q : R] \tag{119}$$

when ∇^*-geodesic connection P and Q is orthogonal at Q to ∇-geodesic connecting Q and R.

J α-Connections

Given a dual manifold $\{S, \nabla, \nabla^*, g_{ij}\}$, we can construct the α-connection by

$$\nabla^{(\alpha)} = \frac{1+\alpha}{2} \nabla + \frac{1-\alpha}{2} \nabla^*. \tag{120}$$

A family of the α-connections connect ∇-and ∇^*-connections by one-parameter family. Even when ∇-and ∇^*-connections are flat, the intermediate $\nabla^{(\alpha)}$ connections are not necessarily flat.

It is remarkable that $\alpha = 0$ connection is the Riemannian connection. Hence starting with a Riemannian space with 0-connection, straightness is split into two pairs of dual straight concepts by the α-connections, which satisfy the dual metric condition. This is possible when and only when we have symmetric tensor T_{ijk}. Then, we can define the induced connection ∇, which satisfies

$$T_{ijk} = \nabla_i g_{jk}, \tag{121}$$

and is symmetric with respect to three indices i, j, k.

Given the metric g_{ij} and affine connection ∇, we define its derivative

$$T_{ijk} = \nabla_i g_{ik}. \tag{122}$$

When this vanishes, ∇ is the Riemannian connection satisfying the metric condition. When T_{ijk} is symmetric with respect to the three indices, we have a torsion-less dual connection

$$\Gamma^*_{ijk} = \Gamma_{ijk} - T_{ijk}, \tag{123}$$

and manifold $\{S, \nabla, \nabla^*, g_{ij}\}$ has dual structure. We construct the α-connection by

$$\Gamma^{(\alpha)}_{ijk} = \Gamma^{(0)}_{ijk} + \frac{\alpha}{2} T_{ijk}, \tag{124}$$

where $\Gamma^{(0)}_{ijk}$ with $\alpha = 0$ is the Riemannian connection.

The α-connection sometimes plays an interesting role in applications.

Computational Geometry from the Viewpoint of Affine Differential Geometry

Hiroshi Matsuzoe*

Department of Computer Science and Engineering
Graduate School of Engineering
Nagoya Institute of Technology
Gokiso-cho, Showa-ku, Nagoya, 466-8555, Japan
matsuzoe@nitech.ac.jp
http://venus.kyy.nitech.ac.jp/~matsuzoe/

Abstract. In this paper, we consider Voronoi diagrams from the view point of affine differential geometry. A main object of affine differential geometry is to study hypersurfaces in an affine space that are invariant under the action of the group of affine transformations. Since incidence relations (configurations of vertexes, edges, etc.) in computational geometry are invariant under affine transformations, we may say that affine differential geometry gives a new sight in computational geometry.

The Euclidean distance function can be generalized by a divergence function in affine differential geometry. For such divergence functions, we show that Voronoi diagrams on statistical manifolds are invariant under (-1)-conformal transformations. We then give some typical figures of Voronoi diagrams on a manifold. These figures may give good intuition for Voronoi diagrams on a manifold because the figures or constructing algorithms on a manifold strongly depend on the realization or on the choice of local coordinate systems. We also consider the upper envelope type theorems on statistical manifolds, and give a constructing algorithm of Voronoi diagrams on (-1)-conformally flat statistical manifolds.

Keywords: information geometry, affine differential geometry, dually flat space, statistical manifold, divergence, contrast function, Voronoi diagram, geometric transformation.

1 Introduction

The purpose of this paper is to study computational geometry from the viewpoint of affine differential geometry. In particular, we study geometric properties of Voronoi diagrams on statistical manifolds, and the geometric transformation algorithms.

---

* This research was partially supported by the Ministry of Education, Science, Sports and Culture, Grant-in-Aid for Young Scientists (B), No. 19740033, and by the NSF Grant No. 0631541.

F. Nielsen (Ed.): ETVC 2008, LNCS 5416, pp. 103–123, 2009.

In computational geometry, incidence relations which represent configurations of vertexes, edges, etc., are important (cf. [3]). From a result of elementary geometry, an order of points on a straight line is invariant under affine transformations. This implies that incidence relations are also invariant under affine transformations.

On the other hand, the main object of affine differential geometry is to study properties of hypersurfaces in an affine space that are invariant under the action of the group of affine transformations (cf. [17]). Hence it is natural to formulate computational geometry from the viewpoint of affine differential geometry.

In addition, duality of affine connections arises naturally in affine differential geometry. Hence this geometry is also related to information geometry, which gives geometrical methods for mathematical sciences. For example, a parametric statistical model has a *statistical structure*. This structure is a pair of a torsion-free affine connection and a Riemannian metric on a manifold M which satisfies a symmetric condition (see Section 2, [2] and [9]). Some kind of affine hypersurfaces also have such geometric structures (Appendix B, see also [6], [10], etc.).

In information geometry, an asymmetric distance-like function on $M \times M$ called a *canonical divergence* or a *contrast function* is an essential tool, and a divergence function can be regarded as an asymmetric generalization of the Euclidean distance function (cf. [2] and [4]). We can discuss such divergence functions in affine differential geometry. In fact, the Euclidean distance function or the canonical divergences can be generalized by a geometric divergence or an affine support function [6], [11].

In this paper, we consider Voronoi diagrams determined from divergence functions based on [13]. At first, we give some basic remarks of Voronoi diagrams on a manifold. Figures of Voronoi diagrams strongly depend on the realization of a manifold or on the choice of local coordinate systems, even if Voronoi diagrams give a same tessellation. We then show that Voronoi diagrams on statistical manifolds are invariant under (-1)-conformal transformation. Next, we consider the upper envelope type theorems for divergence functions on conformally-projectively flat statistical manifolds. We show that a (-1)-conformally flat statistical manifold has a Voronoi diagram. Though the upper envelope type theorems for a dually flat space or the hyperbolic space have been studied previously (cf. [19] and [21]), our theorems can be regarded as a generalization of such theorems.

In this paper, we need notions and basic facts of geometry of statistical manifolds and affine differential geometry. We give brief summaries in Appendixes.

2   Preliminaries

In this section, we summarize geometry of statistical manifolds and geometry of contrast functions. For more details about statistical manifolds, see [7], [9], [10] and [14], for example. For more details about contrast functions, see [4], [6], [10], [11] and [12]. Basic notions of differential geometry are summarized in [2]. Short tutorials of geometry of manifolds and of affine differential geometry are given in [25].

We assume that all objects, functions, vector fields, tensor fields, etc., are smooth (infinity times differentiable) throughout this paper. In addition, we may assume that a manifold is simply connected because we do not discuss topological properties on a manifold in this paper.

2.1 Statistical Manifolds and Dual Connections

Let M be a manifold, and h a semi-Riemannian metric on M, that is, $h = (h_{ij})$ is a non-degenerate symmetric tensor field of order two. For geometry of statistical manifolds, the assumption "positive definiteness" is not necessary in general. Let ∇ be a torsion-free affine connection on M. That is, ∇ is an affine connection and the torsion tensor of ∇,

$$T^{\nabla}(X, Y) := \nabla_X Y - \nabla_Y X - [X, Y],$$

where X and Y are arbitrary vector fields on M, vanishes everywhere on M.

Definition 1. *We call the triplet (M, ∇, h) a statistical manifold if the covariant derivative of h is totally symmetric:*

$$(\nabla_X h)(Y, Z) = (\nabla_Y h)(X, Z),$$

where X, Y and Z are arbitrary vector fields on M. We also call the pair (∇, h) a statistical structure on M.

A statistical structure is called a *Codazzi structure*, and the symmetric $(0, 3)$-tensor field $C(X, Y, Z) := (\nabla_X h)(Y, Z)$ is called a *cubic form* in differential geometry [23].

For a given statistical manifold (M, ∇, h), we can define another affine connection ∇^* by

$$Xh(Y, Z) = h(\nabla_X Y, Z) + h(Y, \nabla_X^* Z).$$

In a local coordinate expression, the above formula is written as

$$\frac{\partial h_{jk}}{\partial x^i} = \Gamma_{ij,k} + \Gamma_{ik,j}^*,$$

where

$$\nabla_{\frac{\partial}{\partial x^i}} \frac{\partial}{\partial x^j} = \sum_{k=1}^{n} \Gamma_{ij}^k \frac{\partial}{\partial x^k},$$

$$\Gamma_{ij,k} = h\left(\nabla_{\frac{\partial}{\partial x^i}} \frac{\partial}{\partial x^j}, \frac{\partial}{\partial x^k}\right) = \sum_{l=1}^{n} h_{kl} \Gamma_{ij}^l.$$

We call ∇^* the *dual connection* (or *conjugate connection*) of ∇ with respect to h. It is easy to check that ∇^* is torsion-free, $\nabla^* h$ is totally symmetric, and $(\nabla^*)^* = \nabla$. Hence the triplet (M, ∇^*, h) is also a statistical manifold. We say that (M, ∇^*, h) is the *dual statistical manifold* of (M, ∇, h).

We remark that a parametric statistical model has a statistical structure (cf.[2] and [9]). Let (Ω, β) be a measurable space. Suppose that $\mathcal{M}$ is a set of probability distributions on (Ω, β) parametrized by $\theta = (\theta^1, \ldots, \theta^n) \in \Theta \subset \boldsymbol{R}^n$:

$$\mathcal{M} = \left\{ p(x, \theta) \,\middle|\, p(x, \theta) > 0, \int_\Omega p(x, \theta) dx = 1 \right\}.$$

For an arbitrary constant $\alpha \in \boldsymbol{R}$, set

$$g_{ij}(\theta) := \int_\Omega \left(\frac{\partial \log p}{\partial \theta^i}(x; \theta) \right) \left(\frac{\partial \log p}{\partial \theta^j}(x; \theta) \right) p(x; \theta) dx,$$

$$\Gamma_{ij,k}^{(\alpha)}(\theta) := \int_\Omega \left\{ \frac{\partial \log p}{\partial \theta^i \partial \theta^j}(x; \theta) + \frac{1-\alpha}{2} \left(\frac{\partial \log p}{\partial \theta^i}(x; \theta) \right) \left(\frac{\partial \log p}{\partial \theta^j}(x; \theta) \right) \right\}$$
$$\times \left(\frac{\partial \log p}{\partial \theta^k}(x; \theta) \right) p(x; \theta) dx.$$

Under suitable conditions,

1. $\mathcal{M}$ is regarded as a manifold with local coordinates $(\theta^1, \ldots, \theta^n)$.
2. $\{g_{ij}(\theta)\}$ determines a Riemannian metric on $\mathcal{M}$, which is called the *Fisher metric*, and (g_{ij}) is its component matrix.
3. $\{\Gamma_{ij,k}^{(\alpha)}\}$ determines a torsion-free affine connection $\nabla^{(\alpha)}$ on $\mathcal{M}$, which is called the α-*connection*.

We can check that $\nabla^{(\alpha)}$ and $\nabla^{(-\alpha)}$ are mutually dual with respect to g, and $\nabla^{(\alpha)} g$ is totally symmetric for arbitrary α. Therefore, $(\mathcal{M}, \nabla^{(\alpha)}, g)$ is a statistical manifold, and its dual statistical manifold is $(\mathcal{M}, \nabla^{(-\alpha)}, g)$.

2.2 Contrast Functions

Let M be a manifold, and ρ a function on $M \times M$. We define a function on M by

$$\rho[X_1, \ldots, X_i | Y_1, \ldots, Y_j](p) = (X_1)_p \cdots (X_i)_p (Y_1)_q \cdots (Y_j)_q \rho(p, q)|_{p=q}.$$

We say that ρ is a *contrast function* on M if the following conditions hold:

$$\rho(p, p) = 0 \quad (p \in M),$$
$$\rho[X|] = \rho[|Y] = 0, \tag{1}$$
$$h(X, Y) = -\rho[X|Y], \tag{2}$$

where h is a semi-Riemannian metric on M. We remark that divergence functions in information geometry, (Kullback-Leibler divergences on exponential families or Bregman divergences, etc.) are typical examples of contrast functions. We also remark that the condition (1) is not necessary if h is positive definite.

For a given contrast function ρ, we define torsion-free affine connections by

$$h(\nabla_X Y, Z) = -\rho[XY|Z], \tag{3}$$
$$h(Y, \nabla_X^* Z) = -\rho[Y|XZ]. \tag{4}$$

Proposition 1. *Let ρ be a contrast function on M. Suppose that h, ∇ and ∇^* are the induced metric and the induced affine connections from Equations (2), (3) and (4), respectively. Then (M, ∇, h) and (M, ∇^*, h) are statistical manifolds, and mutually dual with respect to h.*

We say that the statistical manifold (M, ∇, h) is *induced* from ρ. That is, an arbitrary contrast function induces a statistical structure on M. On the other hand, it is known that an arbitrary statistical manifold has a contrast function [15]. Contrast functions can be defined from the Hooke's law in classical mechanics [5].

The following proposition gives conformal relations of contrast functions. See also Appendix A.2 about conformal equivalence relations for statistical manifolds.

Proposition 2. *Let ρ and $\tilde{\rho}$ be contrast functions on M, and let ϕ and ψ be functions on M. Suppose that (M, ∇, h) and $(M, \tilde{\nabla}, \tilde{h})$ are statistical manifold induced from ρ and $\tilde{\rho}$, respectively. Then the followings hold.*

1. *If $\tilde{\rho}(p, q) = e^{\phi(p)} \rho(p, q)$, then (M, ∇, h) and $(M, \tilde{\nabla}, \tilde{h})$ are (−1)-conformally equivalent.*
2. *If $\tilde{\rho}(p, q) = e^{\psi(q)} \rho(p, q)$, then (M, ∇, h) and $(M, \tilde{\nabla}, \tilde{h})$ are 1-conformally equivalent.*
3. *If $\tilde{\rho}(p, q) = e^{\psi(p) + \phi(q)} \rho(p, q)$, then (M, ∇, h) and $(M, \tilde{\nabla}, \tilde{h})$ are conformally-projectively equivalent.*

Proof. Suppose that $\tilde{\rho}(p, q) = e^{\psi(p) + \phi(q)} \rho(p, q)$. Then the induced objects satisfy

$$\tilde{h}(X, Y) = e^{\psi + \phi} h(X, Y),$$
$$\tilde{h}(\tilde{\nabla}_X Y, Z) = e^{\psi + \phi} h(\nabla_X Y, Z) - d\psi(Z) e^{\psi + \phi} h(X, Y)$$
$$+ d\phi(Y) e^{\psi + \phi} h(X, Z) + d\phi(X) e^{\psi + \phi} h(Y, Z).$$

These equations imply that (M, ∇, h) and $(M, \tilde{\nabla}, \tilde{h})$ are conformally-projectively equivalent. Setting ψ or ϕ are constant, the statements 1 or 2 also hold. □

3 Voronoi Diagrams on a Manifold

In this section, we consider Voronoi diagrams on a manifold.

At first, we consider Voronoi diagrams on the unit sphere as an example.

Let S^2 be the unit sphere. Figures 1 give a same Voronoi diagram on the unit sphere with respect to the standard arc length. These Voronoi diagrams are drawn with respect to inclusion into $\mathbf{R}^3$, the stereographic projection, and the Mercator projection. (See Appendix C.) Therefore, we have to remark that the figures of Voronoi diagrams on a manifold depend on the realization or on the choice of local coordinate systems, even though these give a same tessellation.

Next, we give the definition of Voronoi diagram determined from a contrast function.

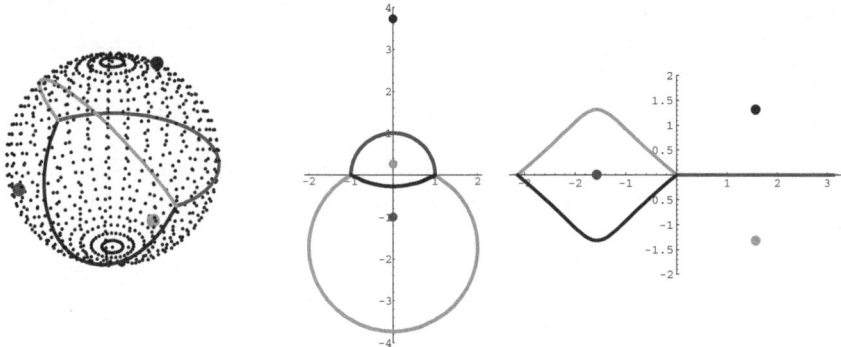

Fig. 1. Figures of Voronoi diagrams on the unit sphere with respect to the standard arc length. The left figure is a Voronoi diagram with respect to inclusion. The center one is a Voronoi diagram with respect to the stereographic projection. The right one is a Voronoi diagram with respect to the Mercator projection.

Definition 2. *Let ρ be a contrast function on M, and let $P = \{p_1, p_2, \cdots, p_m\}$ be a set of m points on M. For a point $p_i \in P$,*

$$V(p_i) = \bigcap_{i \neq j} \{x \in M | \rho(x, p_i) < \rho(x, p_j)\}$$

is called the (contrast) *Voronoi region for p_i.*

For the set of points P, Voronoi regions partition M into m regions, denoted Vor(P) *and called the* (contrast) *Voronoi diagram of P.*

We remark that a contrast function is not symmetric in general. We have to pay attention to the positions of the arguments.

The definition of the contrast Voronoi diagram is independent of the choice of local coordinate systems. However, figures or algorithms for construction of Voronoi diagrams may depend on the choice of local coordinate systems. Several authors have studied about Voronoi diagrams on statistical manifolds. These results are mainly obtained under some fixed local coordinates. (See [16], [19] and [21], for example.) On the other hand, [20] studied mathematical properties of Voronoi diagrams on a manifold.

The following theorem gives a coordinate free mathematical property of Voronoi diagrams on statistical manifolds. To state the theorem, we need the notions of conformal equivalence relations and geometric divergences on statistical manifolds. Readers who are not familiar with affine differential geometry, see also Appendix A and Appendix B.

Theorem 1. *Suppose that (M, ∇, h) and $(M, \tilde{\nabla}, \tilde{h})$ are conformally-projectively flat statistical manifolds with geometric divergences ρ and $\tilde{\rho}$, respectively. If two statistical manifolds (M, ∇, h) and $(M, \tilde{\nabla}, \tilde{h})$ are (-1)-conformally equivalent, then they have same Voronoi diagrams.*

Proof. From Proposition 7 in Appendix B, there exists a function ϕ on M such that geometric divergences ρ and $\tilde{\rho}$ are related as $\tilde{\rho}(p, q) = e^{\phi(p)}\rho(p, q)$ since (M, ∇, h) and $(M, \tilde{\nabla}, \tilde{h})$ are (-1)-conformally equivalent. Therefore, from the definition of Voronoi diagram (Definition 2), the Voronoi diagrams are invariant under (-1)-conformal change.   □

In Figures 2, we give an example of Theorem 1.

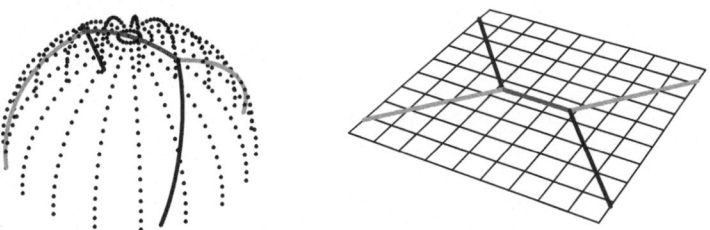

Fig. 2. Figures of Voronoi diagrams on a hemisphere with respect to the standard arc length. The right figure is a Voronoi diagram with respect to the central azimuthal projection. The image coincides with a Voronoi diagram on the standard Euclidean space.

Remark 1. Recall that contrast functions are asymmetric. If the Voronoi region for $p_i \in P$ is defined as follows,

$$V(p_i) = \bigcap_{i \neq j}\{x \in M | \rho(p_i, x) < \rho(p_j, x)\},$$

that is, the positions of arguments are converted, then the statement of the theorem above is changed. In this case, 1-conformal changes preserve Voronoi regions.

4   The Algorithm of Geometric Transformations

In this section, we consider the algorithm of geometric transformations, and the construction of Voronoi diagrams in terms of affine differential geometry. Further arguments have given in [13].

In this section, we need the notion of flatness or conformal equivalence relations for statistical manifolds, and the notion of affine immersions. These summaries are given in Appendix A and Appendix B.

For the geometric transformation algorithm on dually flat spaces, the following theorem is known. (See also Appendix A about dually flat spaces.)

Theorem 2 ([19]). *Let (M, h, ∇, ∇^*) be a simply connected dually flat space with a global ∇-affine coordinate system $\{\theta^i\}$. Let ψ be the θ-potential function on M, and ρ the canonical divergence on M. Denote by l_q the tangent hyperplane* of ψ at $\psi(q)$. Then the canonical divergence $\rho(p,q)$ is equivalent to the difference between $\psi(p)$ and $l(p)$, i.e., the following equation holds:

$$\rho(p,q) = \psi(p) - l_q(p).$$

Proof. The key idea of the proof is nothing but a Legendre transformation. The tangent hyperplane at $\psi(q)$ is given as

$$l_q(p) = \sum_{i=1}^{n} \frac{\partial \psi}{\partial \theta^i}(q)(\theta^i(p) - \theta^i(q)) + \psi(q)$$

$$= -\phi(q) - \sum_{i=1}^{n} \eta_i(q)\theta^i(p).$$

Therefore, the canonical divergence $\rho(p,q)$ is equivalent to $\psi(p) - l_q(p)$. $\qquad\square$

Since Legendre transformations are generalized by conormal transformations or dual maps, we can state the following theorems. (See also Appendix B about geometry of affine immersions.)

Theorem 3. *Let (M, ∇, h) be a 1-conformally flat statistical manifold which is realized into the affine space $\mathbf{R}^{n+1}$ by a non-degenerate equiaffine immersion $\{f, \xi\}$. Denote by l_q the tangent hyperplane of f at $f(q)$. Suppose that an open set U_p is a neighborhood at $p \in M$, and $q \in U_p$. Then the geometric divergence $\rho(p,q)$ is equivalent to the difference between $f(p)$ and the projection of $f(p)$ to l_q in the direction of ξ_q.*

Theorem 4. *Let (M, ∇, h) be a conformally-projectively flat statistical manifold which is realized into the affine space $\mathbf{R}^{n+2}$ by a non-degenerate equiaffine centroaffine immersion of codimension two $\{f, \xi\}$. Denote by l_q the tangent hyperplane at $f(q)$ spanned by f_*T_qM and $\mathrm{Span}\{f(q)\}$. Suppose that an open set U_p is a neighborhood at $p \in M$, and $q \in U_p$. Then the geometric divergence $\rho(p,q)$ is equivalent to the difference between $f(p)$ and the projection of $f(p)$ to l_q in the direction of ξ_q.*

Proof. Suppose that $\{f, \xi\}$ is a non-generate equiaffine immersion (of codimension one). We can define the conormal map v of $\{f, \xi\}$. Set $f(p) = f(q) + f_*X_q + a\xi_p$. Then we have

$$\rho(p,q) = \langle v(q), f(p) - f(q) \rangle$$
$$= \langle v(q), f_*X_q + a\xi_q \rangle$$
$$= a.$$

In the case of centroaffine immersion of codimension two, Set $f(p) = f(q) + f_*X_q + a\xi_p + bf(p)$. From similar calculations, the statement holds. $\qquad\square$

Let us consider algorithms for constructing Voronoi diagrams.

Let (M, ∇, g) be a flat statistical manifold with a positive definite Riemannian metric g and a global ∇-affine coordinate system $\{\theta^i\}$. Then (M, ∇, g) is realized in $\boldsymbol{R}^{n+1}$ as a graph immersion $\{f, \xi\}$ with θ-potential function ψ. In this case, we can take a transversal vector field $\xi = (0, \ldots, 0, 1)^T$.

Let P be a set of m points $\{p_1, \ldots, p_m\}$. Denote by l_i the tangent hyperplane at $f(p_i)$. We define a polyhedron l_P determined by the maximum of all tangent hyperplanes in the direction of ξ:

$$l_P(q) = \max\{l_i(q) | q \in M, 1 \le i \le m\}.$$

We call l_P the *upper envelope* of $\{l_i\}$. Since the divergence $\rho(p, q)$ is equivalent to the difference $f(p)$ and $l_q(p)$, we can obtain the Voronoi diagram $\mathrm{Vor}(P)$ with respect to θ-coordinate by the projection of intersections of l_P.

In general, we cannot apply the upper envelope theorem for affine immersions though the difference between $f(p)$ and $l_q(p)$ is equivalent to the divergence $\rho(p, q)$. Since the transversal vector field is not parallel, we cannot determine the direction of projection. Let us consider a sufficient condition that a statistical manifold (M, ∇, h) has a Voronoi diagram.

We say that a statistical manifold (M, ∇, h) is *globally (-1)-conformally flat* if there exists a flat statistical manifold $(M, \tilde{\nabla}, \tilde{h})$ with a global affine coordinate system such that (M, ∇, h) is globally (-1)-conformally equivalent to $(M, \tilde{\nabla}, \tilde{h})$. That is, there exist a flat statistical manifold $(M, \tilde{\nabla}, \tilde{h})$ and a function ϕ such that

$$\tilde{h}(X, Y) = e^\phi h(X, Y),$$
$$h(\tilde{\nabla}_X Y, Z) = h(\nabla_X Y, Z) + d\phi(Y)\, h(X, Z) + d\phi(X)\, h(Y, Z).$$

Since a (-1)-conformally flat statistical manifold is conformally-projectively flat, it can be realized in $\boldsymbol{R}^{n+2}$. In addition, the (-1)-conformally flatness is characterized as follows (cf.[11]).

Lemma 1. *Let (M, ∇, h) be a globally (-1)-conformally flat statistical manifold of dimension n (≥ 3). Then there exists a centroaffine immersion of codimension two $\{f, \xi\}$ such that it realizes (M, ∇, h) in $\boldsymbol{R}^{n+2}$ and ξ is a parallel vector field.*

We show the upper envelope theorem for globally (-1)-conformally flat statistical manifolds

Let (M, ∇, g) be a globally (-1)-conformally flat statistical manifold with a positive definite Riemannian metric g. Suppose that (M, ∇, g) is realized in $\boldsymbol{R}^{n+2}$ by a centroaffine immersion of codimension two $\{f, \xi\}$. For each point $p \in M$, denote by l_p the tangent hyperplane spanned by $f_*(T_p M)$ and $\mathrm{Span}\{f(p)\}$ at $f(p) \in \boldsymbol{R}^{n+2}$. Since h is positive definite, for each point $p \in M$, $f(M)$ is supported by the tangent hyperplane l_p. We denote by $l^{pos}(p)$ the half space in which $f(M)$ exists. For a set of points $P = \{p_1, \ldots, p_m\}$ on M, a polyhedron $\mathrm{Poly}(P)$ is defined by

$$\mathrm{Poly}(P) = \left\{ x \in \boldsymbol{R}^{n+2} \; \middle| \; \bigcap_{i=1}^{m} l^{pos}(p_i) \right\}.$$

We say that the boundary $\partial\text{Poly}(P)$ is the *upper envelope* for P. From Theorem 4 and Lemma 1, we obtain the following theorem.

Theorem 5. *Let (M, ∇, h) be a simply connected globally (-1)-conformally flat statistical manifold of dimension $n(\geq 3)$. Suppose that $P = \{p_1, \ldots, p_m\}$ is a set of points on M. Then the contrast Voronoi diagram $\text{Vor}(P)$ with respect to the realization of a centroaffine immersion of codimension two can be obtained by the projection of the upper envelope in the direction of ξ.*

5   Conclusions

In this paper, we considered Voronoi diagrams on manifolds. Then we showed that Voronoi diagrams with respect to the geometric divergence are invariant under (-1)-conformal change (or 1-conformal change, which depends on the definition of Voronoi region). We also gave the algorithm of geometric transformations in terms of affine differential geometry. Though given manifolds can be realized in an affine space of dimension at least 5, our results have applications in the fields of likelihood ratio statistics, etc.

References

1. Abe, N.: Affine immersions and conjugate connections. Tensor 55, 276–280 (1994)
2. Amari, S., Nagaoka, H.: Method of information geometry. Amer. Math. Soc., Providence. Oxford University Press, Oxford (2000)
3. Edelsbrunner, H.: Algorithms in combinatorial geometry. Springer, Berlin (1987)
4. Eguchi, S.: Geometry of minimum contrast. Hiroshima Math. J. 22, 631–647 (1992)
5. Henmi, M., Kobayashi, R.: Hooke's law in statistical manifolds and divergences. Nagoya Math. J. 159, 1–24 (2000)
6. Kurose, T.: On the divergences of 1-conformally flat statistical manifolds. Tôhoku Math. J. 46, 427–433 (1994)
7. Kurose, T.: Conformal-projective geometry of statistical manifolds. Interdiscip. Inform. Sci. 8, 89–100 (2002)
8. Kurose, T.: Manifold structures and geometric structures on maximal exponential models. Lecture note for Osaka City University Advanced Mathematical Institute Mini-School on Introduction to Information Geometry and Its Applications II (in Japanese) (2007)
9. Lauritzen, S.L.: Statistical manifolds. In: Differential Geometry in Statistical Inferences. IMS Lecture Notes Monograph Series, vol. 10, pp. 96–163. Institute of Mathematical Statistics, Hayward California (1987)
10. Matsuzoe, H.: On realization of conformally-projectively flat statistical manifolds and the divergences. Hokkaido Math. J. 27, 409–421 (1998)
11. Matsuzoe, H.: Geometry of contrast functions and conformal geometry. Hiroshima Math. J. 29, 175–191 (1999)
12. Matsuzoe, H.: Contrast functions on statistical manifolds with Norden metric. JP J. Geom. Topol. 2, 97–116 (2002)
13. Matsuzoe, H.: Voronoi diagrams on (-1)-conformally flat statistical manifolds. Far East J. Math. Sci. 4, 235–249 (2002)

14. Matsuzoe, H.: Geometry of statistical manifolds and its generalization. In: Proceedings of the 8th International Workshop on Complex Structures and Vector Fields, pp. 244–251. World Scientific, Singapore (2007)
15. Matumoto, T.: Any statistical manifold has a contrast function – On the C^3-function taking the minimum at the diagonal of the product manifold. Hiroshima Math. J. 23, 327–332 (1993)
16. Nielsen, F., Boissonnat, J.D., Nock, R.: On Bregman Voronoi diagrams. In: Proceedings of the eighteenth annual ACM-SIAM symposium on Discrete algorithms, pp. 746–755 (2007)
17. Nomizu, K., Sasaki, T.: Affine differential geometry – Geometry of Affine Immersions. Cambridge University Press, Cambridge (1994)
18. Nomizu, K., Sasaki, T.: Centroaffine immersions of codimension two and projective hypersurface theory. Nagoya Math. J. 132, 63–90 (1993)
19. Onishi, K., Imai, H.: Voronoi diagrams for an exponential family of probability distributions in information geometry. In: Japan-Korea joint workshop on algorithms and computation, pp. 1–8 (1997)
20. Onishi, K., Itoh, J.: Voronoi diagrams in simply connected complete manifolds. IEICE Transactions E85-A, 944–948 (2002)
21. Onishi, K., Takayama, N.: Construction of Voronoi diagram on the upper half-plane. IEICE Transactions 79-A, 533–539 (1996)
22. Shima, H.: The Geometry of Hessian Structures. World Scientific, Singapore (2007)
23. Simon, U., Schwenk-Schellschmidt, A., Viesel, H.: Introduction to the affine differential geometry of hypersurfaces. Lecture notes of the Science, University of Tokyo (1991)
24. Zhang, J.: A note on curvature of a-connections of a statistical manifold. Ann. Inst. Stat. Math. 59, 161–170 (2007)
25. Zhang, J., Matsuzoe, H.: Dualistic Riemannian manifold structure induced from convex function. Advances in Mechanics and Mathematics (to appear)

A   Flatness and Conformal Flatness on Statistical Manifolds

In this section, we summarize curvature properties and conformal properties of statistical manifolds.

Denote by R^∇ the curvature tensor of ∇, that is,

$$R^\nabla(X,Y)Z = \nabla_X \nabla_Y Z - \nabla_Y \nabla_X Z - \nabla_{[X,Y]}Z.$$

Denote by ∇^* the dual connection of ∇ with respect to h. From straightforward calculations,

$$h(R^\nabla(X,Y)Z,W) = h(Z, R^{\nabla^*}(X,Y)W) \tag{5}$$

holds.

We say that ∇ (or a statistical manifold (M, ∇, h)) is *flat* if ∇ is torsion-free and the curvature R^∇ vanishes. We say that ∇ (or (M, ∇, h)) is of *constant curvature* K if there exists a constant K such that

$$R^\nabla(X,Y)Z = K\{h(Y,Z)X - h(X,Z)Y\}.$$

If (M, ∇, h) is of constant curvature, then the dual statistical manifold (M, ∇^*, h) is also a space of constant curvature.

We remark that some formulae for curvature tensors on statistical manifolds have given in [24].

A.1   Dually Flat Spaces

Let (M, ∇, h) be a statistical manifold. If the connection ∇ is flat, there exists a coordinate system such that all the connection coefficients $\{\Gamma^{\nabla}_{ij}{}^k\}$ $(i, j, k = 1, \ldots, n)$ vanish everywhere on the coordinates. We call such a coordinate system an *affine coordinate system* of ∇. In addition, if ∇ is flat, then the dual connection ∇^* is also flat because of (5). In this case, we say that the tetrad (M, h, ∇, ∇^*) is a *dually flat space*.

Suppose that (M, h, ∇, ∇^*) is a dually flat space, and $\{\theta^i\}$ is a ∇-affine coordinate system. Then there exists a ∇^*-affine coordinate system $\{\eta_i\}$ such that $h(\partial/\partial\theta^i, \partial/\partial\eta_j) = \delta_i^j$. We call the coordinate system $\{\eta_i\}$ the *dual coordinate system* of $\{\theta^i\}$.

Proposition 3. *Let (M, h, ∇, ∇^*) be a dually flat space with a global ∇-affine coordinate system $\{\theta^i\}$. Denote by $\{\eta_i\}$ the dual coordinate system of $\{\theta^i\}$. Then there exist functions ψ and ϕ on M such that*

$$\frac{\partial\psi}{\partial\theta^i} = \eta_i, \quad \frac{\partial\phi}{\partial\eta_i} = \theta^i, \quad \psi(p) + \phi(p) - \sum_{i=1}^{n}\theta^i(p)\eta_i(p) = 0 \ (p \in M). \tag{6}$$

In addition, the following formulae hold:

$$h_{ij} = \frac{\partial^2\psi}{\partial\theta^i\partial\theta^j}, \quad h^{ij} = \frac{\partial^2\phi}{\partial\eta_i\partial\eta_j}, \tag{7}$$

where h_{ij} is the (i, j)-component of h and h^{ij} is the (i, j)-component of the inverse matrix of (h_{ij}).

Formula (6) implies that the dually flat space (M, h, ∇, ∇^*) has a *Legendre transformation*.

Formula (7) implies that (M, h, ∇, ∇^*) has a *Hessian structure*. Thus, the function ψ is called the *θ-potential*, and ϕ the *η-potential*. For this reason, a dually flat space (or a flat statistical manifold) is called a *Hessian manifold* in differential geometry [22].

From the functions ψ and ϕ, we can define a function on $M \times M$ by

$$\rho(p, q) := \psi(p) + \phi(q) - \sum_{i=1}^{n}\theta^i(p)\eta_i(q) \quad (p, q \in M). \tag{8}$$

We call the function ρ the *(∇-canonical) divergence* of (M, h, ∇, ∇^*). From the Legendre transformation, the canonical divergence coincides with the Bregman divergence. Further arguments of divergence functions have given in Chapter 3 in [2].

Example 1. Suppose that $(\boldsymbol{R}^n, D, g_E)$ is the Euclidean statistical manifold, that is, $(\boldsymbol{R}^n, D, g_E)$ is the Euclidean space with the standard inner product g_E and the standard flat affine connection D. Of course, $(\boldsymbol{R}^n, g_E, D, D)$ is a dually flat space.

Suppose that $(x^1, \ldots, x^n)$ is the standard affine coordinate system. In this case, the graph of the potential function is the hyperparaboloid, that is,

$$\psi(p) = \phi(p) = \frac{1}{2}\left((x^1(p))^2 + \cdots + (x^n(p))^2\right).$$

The canonical divergence (8) is a half of the Euclidean distance:

$$\rho(p, q) = \frac{1}{2}\|p - q\|^2.$$

A.2   Conformal Equivalence Relations

In this section, we summarize conformal equivalence relations on manifolds. For more details, see [7], [10] and [11].

Projective equivalence: Let M be an n-dimensional manifold. We say that two affine connections ∇ and $\tilde{\nabla}$ on M are *projectively equivalent* if there exists a 1-form τ on M such that

$$\tilde{\nabla}_X Y = \nabla_X Y + \tau(Y)X + \tau(X)Y. \tag{9}$$

We say that an affine connection ∇ is *projectively flat* if ∇ is projectively equivalent, at least locally, to some flat affine connection in a neighbourhood of an arbitrary point of M.

Dual-projective equivalence: Suppose that (M, ∇, h) and $(M, \tilde{\nabla}, \tilde{h})$ are statistical manifolds. We say that two affine connections ∇ and $\tilde{\nabla}$ on M are *dual-projectively equivalent* if there exists a 1-form τ on M such that

$$\tilde{\nabla}_X Y = \nabla_X Y - h(X, Y)\tau^{\#}, \tag{10}$$

where $\tau^{\#}$ is the metrical dual vector field defined by $h(\tau^{\#}, X) := \tau(X)$.

We say that an affine connection ∇ is *dual-projectively flat* if ∇ is dual-projectively equivalent, at least locally, to some flat affine connection in a neighbourhood of an arbitrary point of M.

Conformal equivalence: Suppose that g and $\tilde{g}$ are Riemannian metrics on M. We say that g and $\tilde{g}$ are *conformally equivalent* if there exists a function ϕ on M such that

$$\tilde{g}(X, Y) = e^{2\phi} g(X, Y).$$

We say that a Riemannian metric g is *flat* if its Levi-Civita connection is flat. We say that g is *conformally flat* if g is conformally equivalent, at least locally, to a flat Riemannian metric in a neighbourhood of an arbitrary point of M.

If Riemannian metrics g and $\tilde{g}$ are conformally equivalent, then their Levi-Civita connections ∇^g and $\nabla^{\tilde{g}}$ satisfy

$$h(\nabla^{\tilde{g}}_X Y, Z) = h(\nabla^g_X Y, Z) - d\phi(Z)h(X,Y)$$
$$+d\phi(Y)\,h(X,Z) + d\phi(X)\,h(Y,Z).$$

Conformal-projective equivalence: Suppose that (M, ∇, h) and $(M, \tilde{\nabla}, \tilde{h})$ are statistical manifolds. We say that (M, ∇, h) and $(M, \tilde{\nabla}, \tilde{h})$ are *conformally-projectively equivalent* (or *generalized conformally equivalent*) if there exist two functions ϕ and ψ on M such that

$$\tilde{h}(X,Y) = e^{\psi+\phi}h(X,Y), \tag{11}$$
$$h(\tilde{\nabla}_X Y, Z) = h(\nabla_X Y, Z) - d\psi(Z)h(X,Y)$$
$$+d\phi(Y)\,h(X,Z) + d\phi(X)\,h(Y,Z). \tag{12}$$

We say that a statistical manifold (M, ∇, h) is *conformally-projectively flat* if (M, ∇, h) is conformally-projectively equivalent to a flat statistical manifold in a neighbourhood of an arbitrary point of M.

Suppose that (M, ∇, h) and $(M, \tilde{\nabla}, \tilde{h})$ are conformally-projectively equivalent, that is, we suppose Equations (11) and (12) hold.

1. If ϕ is constant, we say that (M, ∇, h) and $(M, \tilde{\nabla}, \tilde{h})$ are *1-conformally equivalent*. In this case, from Equations (9) and (12), ∇ and $\tilde{\nabla}$ are projectively equivalent.
2. If ψ is constant, we say that (M, ∇, h) and $(M, \tilde{\nabla}, \tilde{h})$ are *(-1)-conformally equivalent*. In this case, from Equations (10) and (12), ∇ and $\tilde{\nabla}$ are dual-projectively equivalent.

B   Affine Immersions

In this section, we summarize the definitions and basic results of affine differential geometry. For more details, see [17].

B.1   Affine Immersions

Let M be an n-dimensional manifold. Let f be an immersion from M to $\mathbf{R}^{n+1}$, that is, $f = (f^1, \ldots, f^{n+1})^T$ is a map from M to $\mathbf{R}^{n+1}$ and its differential $(f_*)_p = (df)_p : T_p M \to T_{f(p)}\mathbf{R}^{n+1} \cong \mathbf{R}^{n+1}$ is an injective linear map. In local coordinate expression, the vectors

$$f_*\left(\frac{\partial}{\partial x^1}\right) = \begin{pmatrix} \frac{\partial f^1}{\partial x^1} \\ \vdots \\ \frac{\partial f^{n+1}}{\partial x^1} \end{pmatrix}, \quad \cdots, \quad f_*\left(\frac{\partial}{\partial x^n}\right) = \begin{pmatrix} \frac{\partial f^1}{\partial x^n} \\ \vdots \\ \frac{\partial f^{n+1}}{\partial x^n} \end{pmatrix}$$

in $\mathbf{R}^{n+1}$ are linearly independent.

Let ξ be a vector field along f, that is, ξ is a vector field defined on the image $f(M)$.

Definition 3. *We say that the pair $\{f, \xi\}$ is an* affine immersion *from M to $\mathbf{R}^{n+1}$ if, for each point $p \in M$, the tangent space $T_{f(p)}\mathbf{R}^{n+1}$ decomposed as follows:*

$$T_{f(p)}\mathbf{R}^{n+1} = f_*(T_pM) \oplus \operatorname{Span}\{\xi_p\}. \tag{13}$$

We call ξ a transverse vector field.

In local coordinate expression, Equation (13) implies that

$$\left\{ f_*\left(\frac{\partial}{\partial x^1}\right), \ldots, f_*\left(\frac{\partial}{\partial x^n}\right), \xi \right\}$$

spans the affine space $\mathbf{R}^{n+1} \cong T_{f(p)}\mathbf{R}^{n+1}$.

We denote by D the standard flat affine connection on $\mathbf{R}^{n+1}$. Identifying the covariant derivative along f with D, we have the following decompositions:

$$D_X f_* Y = f_* \nabla_X Y + h(X, Y)\xi, \tag{14}$$
$$D_X \xi = -f_* SX + \tau(X)\xi. \tag{15}$$

In local coordinate expression, above equations are

$$\frac{\partial^2 f^a}{\partial x^i \partial x^j} = \sum_{k=1}^n \Gamma_{ij}^k \frac{\partial f^a}{\partial x^k} + h_{ij}\xi^a, \tag{16}$$

$$\frac{\partial \xi^a}{\partial x^i} = -\sum_{k=1}^n S_i^k \frac{\partial f^a}{\partial x^k} + \tau_i \xi^a, \tag{17}$$

where $a = 1, \ldots, n+1$. Equations (14) or (16) are called the *Gauss equation*, and Equations (15) or (17) are called the *Weingarten equation*.

Since the connection D is torsion-free, ∇ is a torsion-free affine connection, h is a symmetric $(0, 2)$-tensor field, S is a $(1, 1)$-tensor field, and τ is 1-form on M, respectively. The induced objects ∇, h, S and τ are said to be the *induced connection*, the *affine fundamental form*, the *affine shape operator* and the *transversal connection form*, respectively.

If the affine fundamental form h is positive definite everywhere on M, the immersion f is called *strictly convex*. If h is non-degenerate, f is called *non-degenerate*. If $\tau \equiv 0$, the affine immersion $\{f, \xi\}$ is called *equiaffine*.

Since the affine connection D is flat, induced objects satisfy the following equations. These equations are called *fundamental structural equations* for affine immersions.

The Gauss equation:

$$R(X, Y)Z = h(Y, Z)SX - h(X, Z)SY. \tag{18}$$

The Codazzi equations:

$$(\nabla_X h)(Y, Z) + \tau(X)h(Y, Z) = (\nabla_Y h)(X, Z) + \tau(Y)h(X, Z), \tag{19}$$
$$(\nabla_X S)(Y) - \tau(X)SY = (\nabla_Y S)(X) - \tau(Y)SX. \tag{20}$$

The Ricci equation:

$$h(X, SY) - h(Y, SX) = (\nabla_X \tau)(Y) - (\nabla_Y \tau)(X) \quad (= d\tau(X, Y)). \qquad (21)$$

Equations (18)–(21) are the $f_*(T_pM)$ component of $R^D(X, Y)f_*Z$, the ξ_p component of $R^D(X, Y)f_*Z$, the $f_*(T_pM)$ component of $R^D(X, Y)\xi$, and the ξ_p component of $R^D(X, Y)\xi$, respectively.

If an affine immersion $\{f, \xi\}$ is non-degenerate and equiaffine, the induced objects (M, ∇, h) form a statistical manifold from the Codazzi equation for h.

Moreover, the following result is obtained in [6].

Theorem 6. *Suppose that $\{f, \xi\}$ is a non-degenerate equiaffine immersion from M to $\mathbf{R}^{n+1}$. Denote by ∇ the induced connection and by h the affine fundamental form. Then (M, ∇, h) is a 1-conformally flat statistical manifold.*

Conversely, if (M, ∇, h) is a simply connected 1-conformally flat statistical manifold of dimension $n(\geq 2)$, then there exists an affine immersion $\{f, \xi\}$ which realizes (M, ∇, h) in $\mathbf{R}^{n+1}$.

Now we consider geometry of flat statistical manifolds in affine differential geometry.

Example 2. Let Θ be a domain of $\mathbf{R}^n$, and ψ be a function on Θ. We say that an affine immersion $\{f, \xi\} : \Theta \to \mathbf{R}^{n+1}$ is a *graph immersion* if the hypersurface is a graph of ψ, i.e., $\{f, \xi\}$ is given by

$$f : \begin{pmatrix} \theta^1 \\ \vdots \\ \theta^n \end{pmatrix} \mapsto \begin{pmatrix} \theta^1 \\ \vdots \\ \theta^n \\ \psi \end{pmatrix}, \quad \xi = \begin{pmatrix} 0 \\ \vdots \\ 0 \\ 1 \end{pmatrix}.$$

Then we have

$$\frac{\partial^2 f}{\partial \theta^i \partial \theta^j} = \psi_{ij} \xi.$$

This implies that $\Gamma_{ij}^k = 0$. Then the induced connection ∇ is flat, and $\{\theta^i\}$ is a ∇-affine coordinate system.

Conversely, as a corollary of Theorem 6, we have the following.

Corollary 1. *Let (M, h, ∇, ∇^*) be a simply connected dually flat space. Suppose that $\{\theta^i\}$ is a global affine coordinate system of ∇, and $\{\eta_i\}$ is its dual affine coordinate system. Suppose that ψ is the θ-potential function, and ϕ is the η-potential function. Then (M, ∇, h) is realized in $\mathbf{R}^{n+1}$ by a graph immersion with potential ψ and (M, ∇^*, h) is realized by a graph immersion with ϕ.*

Let $\{f, \xi\}$ be an affine immersion. If $\xi = -f$, where we identify f with the position vector of $\mathbf{R}^{n+1}$, we say that the pair $\{f, -f\}$ is a *centroaffine immersion*.

Proposition 4. *Suppose that $\{f, -f\}$ is a non-degenerate centroaffine immersion. Then $\{f, -f\}$ is equiaffine and the induced statistical manifold is of constant curvature $R = 1$.*

Proof. From Weingarten equation (15), the affine shape operator $S = id$ and the affine transversal connection form $\tau = 0$. From Gauss equation (18) and Codazzi equation (19), (M, ∇, h) is a space of constant curvature 1. $\qquad\square$

We define contrast functions determined from affine immersions.

Let $\boldsymbol{R}_{n+1}$ be the dual space of $\boldsymbol{R}^{n+1}$. Denote by $\langle\ ,\ \rangle$ the pairing of $\boldsymbol{R}_{n+1}$ and $\boldsymbol{R}^{n+1}$. Suppose that $\{f, \xi\}$ is a non-degenerate equiaffine immersion, then an immersion $v : M \to \boldsymbol{R}_{n+1}$ can be defined by

$$\langle v(p), \xi_p \rangle = 1, \tag{22}$$

$$\langle v(p), f_* X_p \rangle = 0. \tag{23}$$

We call v the *conormal map* of $\{f, \xi\}$, and the correspondence $f(p) \mapsto v(p)$ the *conormal transformation*.

In local coordinate expression, above equations are

$$\sum_{\alpha=1}^{n+1} v_\alpha(p) \xi_p^\alpha = 1,$$

$$\sum_{\alpha=1}^{n+1} v_\alpha(p) \frac{\partial f^\alpha}{\partial x^i}(p) = 0, \quad (i = 1, \ldots, n).$$

Solving simultaneous linear equations, we obtain the conormal map v.

Remark 2. We remark that the conormal map $v(p)$ is the "normal" vector of the tangent hyperplane at $f(p)$. (Strictly speaking, we cannot consider orthogonality in the target space $\boldsymbol{R}^{n+1}$, because we do not assume a metric on $\boldsymbol{R}^{n+1}$. This is for this reason, v is called the "conormal" vector.)

In particular, if we consider the standard Euclidean space $(\boldsymbol{R}^n, g_E, D, D)$, the conormal transformation is essentially equivalent to the dual transformation in computational geometry.

Then we define a function ρ on $M \times M$ by

$$\rho(p, q) = \langle v(q), f(p) - f(q) \rangle.$$

We call the function ρ a *geometric divergence* (see [6] and [10]).

Proposition 5. *The geometric divergence ρ is a contrast function on M.*

Proof. From Equations (14), (22) and (23), we have

$$\begin{aligned} X\langle v, f_* Y \rangle &= \langle v_* X, f_* Y \rangle + \langle v, D_X f_* Y \rangle \\ &= \langle v_* X, f_* Y \rangle + h(X, Y) \\ &= 0. \end{aligned} \tag{24}$$

From Equations (23) and (24), we obtain

$$\rho[X\|](p) = \langle v(q), f_* X_p \rangle_{p=q} = 0,$$
$$\rho[\|Y](p) = \langle v_* X_q, f(p) - f(q) \rangle_{p=q} + \langle v(q), -f_* X_q \rangle_{p=q} = 0,$$
$$\rho[X|Y](p) = \langle v_* X_q, f_* X_p \rangle_{p=q} = -h_p(X, Y).$$

This implies that ρ is a contrast function on M.   □

We remark that the geometric divergence is independent of the realization of (M, ∇, h) into $\mathbf{R}^{m+1}$.

Proposition 6. *Suppose that (M, h, ∇, ∇^*) is a simply connected dually flat space. Then the canonical divergence and the geometric divergence on (M, ∇, h) coincide.*

Proof. Suppose that $\{\theta^i\}$ is a ∇-affine coordinate system, and η is its dual coordinate system. Denote by ψ the $\{\theta^i\}$-potential function, and by ϕ the η-potential function. The the canonical divergence $\rho^C(p, q)$ is given as

$$\rho^C(p, q) = \psi(p) + \phi(q) - \sum_{i=1}^{n} \theta^i(p) \eta_i(q).$$

On the other hand, the statistical manifold (M, ∇, h) is realized in $\mathbf{R}^{n+1}$ as a graph immersion

$$f : \begin{pmatrix} \theta^1 \\ \vdots \\ \theta^n \end{pmatrix} \mapsto \begin{pmatrix} \theta^1 \\ \vdots \\ \theta^n \\ \psi \end{pmatrix}, \quad \xi = \begin{pmatrix} 0 \\ \vdots \\ 0 \\ 1 \end{pmatrix}.$$

In this case, from the definitions of conormal map (22) and (23) and the Legendre transformation (6), the conormal map is calculated as

$$v : (\eta_1, \ldots, \eta_n) \mapsto (-\eta_1, \ldots, -\eta_n, 1).$$

Using the Legendre transformation (6), the geometric divergence ρ^G is given by

$$\rho^G(p, q) = \langle v(q), f(p) - f(q) \rangle$$
$$= \psi(p) - \sum_{i=1}^{n} v_i(q) \theta^i(p) - \psi(q) + \sum_{i=1}^{n} v_i(q) \theta^i(q)$$
$$= \psi(p) + \phi(q) - \sum_{i=1}^{n} v_i(q) \theta^i(p).$$

This implies $\rho^G(p, q) = \rho^C(p, q)$.   □

We remark that similar arguments hold even if M is an infinite dimensional functional space [8].

B.2   Centroaffine Immersions of Codimension Two

Let M be an n-dimensional manifold, and f an immersion from M to $\boldsymbol{R}^{n+2}$. Denote by ξ a vector field along f, and we identify f with the position vector of $\boldsymbol{R}^{n+2}$.

Definition 4. *We say that the pair $\{f, \xi\}$ is a* centroaffine immersion of codimension two *from M to $\boldsymbol{R}^{n+2}$ if, for each point p in M, $T_{f(p)}\boldsymbol{R}^{n+2}$ is decomposed as follows:*

$$T_{f(p)}\boldsymbol{R}^{n+2} = f_*(T_pM) \oplus \mathrm{Span}\{\xi_p\} \oplus \mathrm{Span}\{f(p)\}.$$

We call ξ a transverse vector field.

The induced objects can be defined by the following formulae:

$$D_X f_* Y = f_* \nabla_X Y + h(X,Y)\xi + k(X,Y)f,$$
$$D_X \xi = -f_* S X + \tau(X)\xi + \mu(X)f.$$

If the affine fundamental form h is positive definite everywhere on M, the immersion f is called *strictly convex*. If f is non-degenerate, f is called *non-degenerate*. If $\tau \equiv 0$, the centroaffine immersion $\{f, \xi\}$ is called *equiaffine*.

In the same way as affine immersions (of codimension one), a non-degenerate equiaffine centroaffine immersion of codimension two induces a statistical manifold. Moreover, the following theorem has been obtained in [10].

Theorem 7. *Suppose that $\{f, \xi\}$ is a non-degenerate equiaffine centroaffine immersion of codimension two from M to $\boldsymbol{R}^{n+2}$. Denote by ∇ the induced connection and by h the affine fundamental form. Then (M, ∇, h) is a conformally-projectively flat statistical manifold.*

Conversely, if (M, ∇, h) is a simply connected conformally-projectively flat statistical manifold, then there exists a centroaffine immersion of codimension two $\{f, \xi\}$ which realizes (M, ∇, h) in $\boldsymbol{R}^{n+2}$.

We define the dual map of a centroaffine immersion of codimension two.

Let $\boldsymbol{R}_{n+2}$ be the dual space of $\boldsymbol{R}^{n+2}$. Denote by $\langle\ ,\ \rangle$ the pairing of $\boldsymbol{R}_{n+2}$ and $\boldsymbol{R}^{n+2}$. Suppose that $\{f, \xi\}$ is a non-degenerate equiaffine centroaffine immersion of codimension two, then a centroaffine immersion of codimension two $\{v, w\}$: $M \to \boldsymbol{R}_{n+2}$ can be defined by

$$
\begin{aligned}
\langle v(p), \xi_p \rangle &= 1, \\
\langle v(p), f(p) \rangle &= 0, \\
\langle v(p), f_* X_p \rangle &= 0, \\
\langle w(p), \xi_p \rangle &= 0, \\
\langle w(p), f(p) \rangle &= 1, \\
\langle w(p), f_* X_p \rangle &= 0.
\end{aligned}
$$

(25)

(26)

We call $\{v, w\}$ the *dual map* of $\{f, \xi\}$. We remark that the dual map is a generalization of the Legendre transformation. In fact, suppose that (M, h, ∇, ∇^*) is a dually flat space. Then (M, h, ∇) is realized in $\boldsymbol{R}^{n+2}$ by

$$
f : \begin{pmatrix} \theta^1 \\ \vdots \\ \theta^n \end{pmatrix} \mapsto \begin{pmatrix} \theta^1 \\ \vdots \\ \theta^n \\ \psi \\ 1 \end{pmatrix}, \quad \xi = \begin{pmatrix} 0 \\ \vdots \\ 0 \\ 1 \\ 0 \end{pmatrix}.
$$

The dual map is calculated as

$$
\begin{aligned}
v &: (\eta_1, \ldots, \eta_n,) \mapsto (\eta_1, \ldots, \eta_n, 1, \phi), \\
w &= (0, \ldots, 0, 0, 1).
\end{aligned}
$$

Substituting $f(p)$ and $v(p)$ into (25), we have

$$
\sum_{i=1}^{n} \eta_i(p) \theta^i(p) + \psi(p) + \phi(p) = 0.
$$

The differentials of f and v are given as

$$
\begin{aligned}
\frac{\partial f}{\partial \theta^i} &= \left(0, \ldots, 1, \ldots, 0, \frac{\partial \psi}{\partial \theta^i}, 0 \right)^T, \\
\frac{\partial v}{\partial \eta_i} &= \left(0, \ldots, 1, \ldots, 0, 0, \frac{\partial \phi}{\partial \eta_i} \right).
\end{aligned}
$$

From Equations (26) and (25), we have

$$
\langle v_* X_p, f(p) \rangle = 0. \tag{27}
$$

Equations (26) and (27) imply

$$
\frac{\partial \psi}{\partial \theta^i} = \eta_i, \quad \frac{\partial \phi}{\partial \eta_i} = \theta^i.
$$

Therefore, the definition of the dual map coincides with the Legendre transformation if (M, h, ∇, ∇^*) is dually flat.

We define a function ρ on $M \times M$ by

$$
\rho(p, q) = \langle v(q), f(p) - f(q) \rangle.
$$

We call ρ the *geometric divergence* on M. We remark that the geometric divergence is a contrast function on M, and the geometric divergence is independent of the realization of (M, ∇, h) into $\boldsymbol{R}^{n+1}$.

Proposition 7. *Suppose that ρ and $\tilde{\rho}$ are geometric divergences of (M, ∇, h) and $(M, \tilde{\nabla}, \tilde{h})$, respectively. If (M, ∇, h) and $(M, \tilde{\nabla}, \tilde{h})$ are (-1)-conformally equivalent, there exists a function ϕ such that $\tilde{\rho}(p, q) = e^{\phi(p)} \rho(p, q)$ holds.*

Proof. Suppose that (M, ∇, h) and $(M, \tilde{\nabla}, \tilde{h})$ are realized in the affine space $\mathbf{R}^{n+2}$ by $\{f, \xi\}$ and $\{\tilde{f}, \xi\}$, respectively. Since these statistical manifolds are (-1)-conformally equivalent, from the uniqueness of centroaffine immersions, there exists a function ϕ such that $\tilde{f} = e^{\phi}f$. (cf. Section 2 in [18]) From the definition of dual maps, $\{f, \xi\}$ and $\{\tilde{f}, \xi\}$ have same conormal map v. This implies that $\tilde{\rho}(p, q) = e^{\phi(p)}\rho(p, q)$ holds. $\qquad\square$

Our formulations are followed from the textbook [17]. We can see quite another formulation in [1], which is also useful in information geometry.

C   Local Coordinates on a Sphere

Let S^2 be the *unit sphere* in $\mathbf{R}^2$. That is,

$$S^2 = \left\{ (x, y, z)^T \mid x^2 + y^2 + z^2 = 1 \right\} \tag{28}$$

$$= \left\{ (\cos u \cos v, \sin u \cos v, \sin v)^T \ \Big| \ -\pi \le u \le \pi, -\frac{\pi}{2} \le v \le \frac{\pi}{2} \right\}, \tag{29}$$

where (28) is the inclusive representation, and (29) is the parametrization with respect to the spherical polar coordinates.

Since S^2 is a manifold, S^2 has local coordinate systems.

The *stereographic projection* (from the north pole $(0, 0, 1)^T$ to the plane $z = 0$) is a local coordinate system defined by

$$S^2 \backslash \left\{ \begin{pmatrix} 0 \\ 0 \\ 1 \end{pmatrix} \right\} \to \mathbf{R}^2, \quad \begin{pmatrix} x \\ y \\ z \end{pmatrix} \mapsto \begin{pmatrix} \dfrac{x}{1 - z} \\ \dfrac{y}{1 - z} \end{pmatrix}.$$

In this projection, circles on the sphere are mapped to the circles on the local coordinates. For each points, angles are also preserved.

The *Mercator projection* is defined by

$$S^2 \backslash \left\{ \begin{pmatrix} 1 \\ 0 \\ 0 \end{pmatrix}, \begin{pmatrix} 0 \\ 0 \\ 1 \end{pmatrix} \right\} \to [-\pi, \pi] \times \mathbf{R}, \quad \begin{pmatrix} u \\ v \end{pmatrix} \mapsto \begin{pmatrix} u \\ \log\left(\tan\left(\dfrac{v}{2} + \dfrac{\pi}{4}\right)\right) \end{pmatrix}.$$

In this projection, parallels and meridians are straight and perpendicular to each other, and angles are preserved between the sphere and the local coordinates.

Denote by S_+^2 the (upper) hemisphere, that is,

$$S_+^2 = \left\{ (x, y, z)^T \mid x^2 + y^2 + z^2 = 1, z > 0 \right\}.$$

The *central azimuthal projection* is defined by

$$S_+^2 \to \mathbf{R}^2, \quad \begin{pmatrix} x \\ y \\ z \end{pmatrix} \mapsto \begin{pmatrix} x/z \\ y/z \end{pmatrix}.$$

In this projection, great-circles (geodesics) on the sphere are mapped to the straight lines on the local coordinates.

Interactions between Symmetric Cone and Information Geometries: Bruhat-Tits and Siegel Spaces Models for High Resolution Autoregressive Doppler Imagery

Frederic Barbaresco

Thales Air Systems, Strategy Technology & Innovation Department,
Hameau de Roussigny, F-91470 Limours, France
frederic.barbaresco@thalesgroup.com

Abstract. Main issue of High Resolution Doppler Imagery is related to robust statistical estimation of Toeplitz Hermitian positive definite covariance matrices of sensor data time series (e.g. in Doppler Echography, in Underwater acoustic, in Electromagnetic Radar, in Pulsed Lidar...). We consider this problem jointly in the framework of Riemannian symmetric spaces and the framework of Information Geometry. Both approaches lead to the same metric, that has been initially considered in other mathematical domains (study of Bruhat-Tits complete metric Space and Upper-half Siegel Space in Symplectic Geometry). Based on Frechet-Karcher barycenter definition and geodesics in Bruhat-Tits space, we address problem of N Covariance matrices Mean estimation. Our main contribution lies in the development of this theory for Complex Autoregressive models (maximum entropy solution of Doppler Spectral Analysis). Specific Blocks structure of the Toeplitz Hermitian covariance matrix is used to define an iterative and parallel algorithm for Siegel metric computation. Based on Affine Information Geometry theory, we introduce for Complex Autoregressive Model, Kähler metric on reflection coefficients based on Kähler potential function given by Doppler signal Entropy. The metric is closely related to Kähler-Einstein manifold and complex Monge-Ampere Equation. Finally, we study geodesics in space of Kähler potentials and action of Calabi and Kähler-Ricci Geometric Flows for this Complex Autoregressive Metric. We conclude with different results obtained on real Doppler Radar Data in HF and X bands : X-band radar monitoring of wake vortex turbulences, detection for Coastal X-band and HF Surface Wave Radars.

Keywords: Information Geometry, Symmetric Cone Geometry, Kähler Geometry, Bruhat-Tits Space, Siegel Space, von Mangoldt-Cartan-Hadamard Manifold, Mazur-Ulam Theorem, Bregman Kernel, Kähler-Ricci Flow, Calabi Flow, Complex Monge-Ampere Equation, Complex Autoregressive Model, Matrices Mean, Doppler Imagery.

1 Introduction

Symmetric Space and Kähler Manifold are two miracles in Riemannian Geometry, as explained by Marcel Berger in a recent Book. We will describe some interactions between Symmetric Cone and Kähler Geometries with Rao's Information Geometry.

F. Nielsen (Ed.): ETVC 2008, LNCS 5416, pp. 124–163, 2009.
© Springer-Verlag Berlin Heidelberg 2009

"La théorie des espaces symétriques peut être considérée comme le premier miracle de la géométrie riemannienne, en fait comme un nœud de forte densité dans l'arbre de toutes les mathématiques. ... On doit à Elie Cartan dans les années 1926 d'avoir découvert que ces géométries sont , dans une dimension donnée, en nombre fini, et en outre toutes classées. ... .
[second miracle] Entre les variétés localement symétriques et les variétés riemanniennes générales, il existe une catégorie intermédiaire, celle des variétés kählériennes. ... On a alors affaire pour décrire le panorama des métriques kählériennes sur notre variété, non pas à un espace de formes différentielles quadratiques, très lourd, mais à un espace vectoriel de fonctions numériques. ... La richesse Kählérienne fait dire à certains que la géométrie kählérienne est plus importante que la géométrie riemannienne. ... .
Ne cherchez pas d'autres miracles du genre des espaces (localement) symétriques et des variétés kählériennes. En effet, c'est un fait depuis 1953 que les seules variétés riemanniennes irréductibles qui admettent un invariant par transport parallèle autre que g elle-même (et sa forme volume) sont les espaces localement symétriques, les variétés kählériennes, les variétés kählérienne de Calabi-Yau, et les variétés hyperkählériennes."

Marcel Berger (IHES), « 150 ans de Géométrie Riemannienne », [25]
Géométrie au 20ième siècle, Histoire et horizons, Hermann Éditeur, 2005

In the following, we will use notations : A^T for transpose of matrix A, A^* for conjugate of matrix A, and A^+ for trans-conjugate of matrix A. "." Will indicate classical multiplication.

In signal and image processing domains, many algorithms manipulate covariance matrices. For Electromagnetic or Acoustic sensors, and more especially for Radar, Lidar or Echography, we have to process spatial complex data for array processing or time complex data for Doppler processing : $Z_n = [z_1 \quad z_2 \quad \cdots \quad z_n]^T$

Covariance matrices of these complex data $R_n = E[Z_n Z_n^+]$ are Toeplitz Hermitian Positive Definite matrices :

$$R_n = \begin{bmatrix} r_0 & r_1^* & \cdots & r_{n-1}^* \\ r_1 & r_0 & \ddots & \vdots \\ \vdots & \ddots & \ddots & r_1^* \\ r_{n-1} & \cdots & r_1 & r_0 \end{bmatrix} \text{ with } r_k = E[z_n z_{n-k}^*] \text{ and } \begin{cases} \forall Z \in C^n \ , \ Z^+ R_n Z > 0 \\ R_n^+ = R_n \end{cases}$$

For time series of Electromagnetic pulsed lidar or acoustic sensors, Doppler information, related to measured radial speed V_r of observed reflectors in the range cell, is captured by this covariance matrix estimation and by mean of the following equations :

$$f_{Doppler} = 2 \frac{V_r/c}{1-V_r/c} f_0 \underset{V_r/c \ll 1}{\approx} 2.\frac{V_r}{\lambda}$$

with Transmitted signal: $s(t) = u(t).e^{2\pi f_0 t}$ and Received signal: $z(t) \approx A.u\left(t - \frac{2R}{c}\right)e^{i(2\pi f_0 + 2\pi f_{Doppler})t}e^{i\varphi}$

By Doppler-Fizeau effect, the original waveform frequency f_0 is shifted by Doppler frequency $f_{Doppler}$. This shift is proportional to radial speeds of observed reflectors V_r. Fourier Transform is then a classical tool used for Doppler Power Spectral Density estimation : $S_Z(f) = \sum_{k=-n}^{+n} r_k.e^{-i2\pi f k}$

Classically, Fourier Analysis is used for Doppler Processing and Doppler Imagery. Our new approach is purely geometric and will use specific Geometry of Hermitian Positive Definite Matrices Space. For short waveforms (short time series of Data), Classical FFT (Fast Fourier Transform) or Doppler Filter Banks are not efficient, and suffer of the following drawbacks compared to our geometric approach :

- Poor Doppler Resolution
- If signal Doppler frequency is in between two Doppler filters, its energy is spread over adjacent filters and Doppler imagery is non-longer optimal
- High intensity of coloured noise is not limited to one Doppler filter but pollution is spread over all filters due to poor Filter-Banks Resolution and Doppler Filter side lobes.

Our geometric approach don't use any decomposition of signal on orthogonal filter banks, as Fourrier transform does. Our method estimate robust distance between covairnces matrices of signal taken into acount their own statistics (covariance matrix variance, that is the main drawback in case of short time serie analysis).

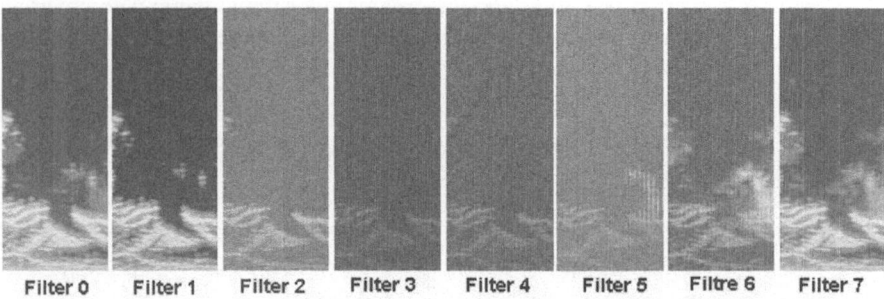

| Filter 0 | Filter 1 | Filter 2 | Filter 3 | Filter 4 | Filter 5 | Filtre 6 | Filter 7 |

Fig. 1. Pollution of all Doppler Filters by "strong" coloured noise in zero Doppler hit (energy of zero Doppler coloured noise has contribution on other filters outputs due to their poor side lobes)

To solve this geometric problem, use of classical flat metric and normed space for Symmetric Positive Definite covariance matrices is non optimal. Classically, signal processing community used flat metric:

$$\|A - B\|_F = \langle A - B, A - B \rangle = Tr\left[(A-B)(A-B)^T\right]$$
$$A \circ B = \frac{A+B}{2} \quad , \quad \gamma(t) = A + t(B-A)$$

We will explain in the paper that there are many reasons to prefer the information geometry metric on the symmetric cone given by :

$$\left\|\log\left(A^{-1/2}BA^{-1/2}\right)\right\|_F \quad \text{with} \quad \|X\|_F = \langle X, X \rangle = Tr\left(XX^T\right)$$

$$A \circ B = A^{1/2}\left(A^{-1/2}BA^{-1/2}\right)^{1/2}A^{1/2} \quad , \quad \gamma(t) = A^{1/2}\left(A^{-1/2}BA^{-1/2}\right)^t A^{1/2}$$

The symmetric cone is not a vector space (metric space is different of normed space). The flat metric can still be used because the set of SPD matrices is convex but vector space assumption can to degrade algorithms. Since the geodesic A+t(B-A) is not a positive metric for all t, the set of SPD matrices with flat metric is not a geodesically complete space. With Information Geometry metric, it is geodesically complete. Information metric coincides with the metric defined for the homogeneous barrier – logdetA on the symmetric cone (which is a convex set) in optimization. Information Geometry metric, defined by Fisher Information matrix, takes into account statistics of matrices. Finally, Invariance to the group action (transitive action of GL(n) via congruence and inversion), that could needed for some applications.

We will introduce new tools, to replace Classical Fourier Transform, and to improve Doppler imagery performances. More especially, we will use different concepts from fundamental and applied mathematics. Our tools will be based on :

1.   **Information Geometry**, that has been introduced by C.R.Rao [2], and axiomatized by N. Chentsov [13], (with same roots that the well-known Cramer-Rao bound), allows to build a distance between statistical distributions that is invariant to non-singular parameterization transformations.

2.   **Symplectic Geometry**, used by C.L. Siegel [1][11] to define distance between complex symmetric matrix whose the imaginary part is Positive Definite. This is an extension for matrix of the upper half space of Poincare. The associate metric and distance is invariant under generalized Möbius transform.

3.   **Geometry on Symmetric Cones** [17][19], where Symmetric Hermitian Space is equivalent to a tube domain, where we can define a "geodesic between matrices" by mean of Semi-Simple Lie Group Theory [14] and Jordan Algebra [15][16]. In case of Symmetric matrix, this space is called Bruhat-Tits [9] space or Cartan-Hadamard Manifold.

Firstly, we will develop links between concepts used in Figure 2. We consider our problem jointly in the framework of Riemannian symmetric spaces and the framework of Information Geometry. Both approaches lead to the same metric, that has been initially considered in other mathematical domains (study of Bruhat-Tits complete metric space and Upper-half Siegel Space in Symplectic Geometry). Based on Frechet-Karcher barycenter definition and geodesics in Bruhat-Tits space, we address problem of N Covariance matrices Mean estimation.

Secondary, we will develop applications for Doppler Processing based on Complex Autoregressive Models. Specific Blocks structure of the Toeplitz Hermitian covariance matrix is used to define an iterative and parallel algorithm for Siegel metric computation. Based on Affine Information Geometry theory, we introduce for Complex Autoregressive Model, Kähler metric on reflection coefficients based on Kähler potential function given by Doppler signal Entropy. The metric is closely related to

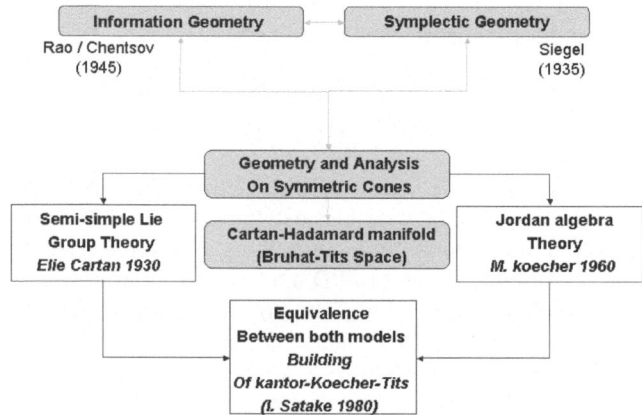

Fig. 2. Panoramic View of links between different Mathematic concept

Kähler-Einstein manifold and complex Monge-Ampere Equation. Finally, we study geodesics in space of Kähler potentials and action of Calabi and Kähler-Ricci Geometric Flows for this Complex Autoregressive Metric. We conclude with different results obtained on real Doppler Radar Data in HF and X bands : X-band radar monitoring of wake vortex turbulences, detection for Coastal X-band and HF Surface Wave Radars.

2   Information Geometry

In his seminal paper of 1945, C.R.Rao [2] has introduced two concepts: Cramer-Rao bound and Information Geometry. The tool of Cramer-Rao bound is largely used in Signal Processing and Radar communities, but Information Geometry is less popular. The Cramer-Rao bound is given by the inverse of the Fisher Information Matrix $I(\theta)$:

$$E\left[\left(\theta-\hat{\theta}\right)\left(\theta-\hat{\theta}\right)^{T}\right] \geq I(\theta)^{-1} \tag{1}$$

In following section, we will introduce Information Geometry that help us to define robust distance between our covariance matrices.

2.1   Rao and Chentsov's Information Geometry

Chentsov [13] was the first to introduce the Fisher information matrix as a Riemannian metric on the parameter space, considered as a differentiable manifold. Chentsov was led by decision theory when he considered a category whose objects are probability spaces and whose morphisms are Markov Kernels. Chentsov's great achievement was that up to a constant factor the Fisher information yields the only monotone family of Riemannian metrics on the class of finite probability simplexes.

In parallel, Burbea and Rao [2] have introduced a family of distance measures, based on the so-called α-order entropy metric, generalizing the Fisher Information metric that corresponds to the Shannon entropy. Such a choice of the matrix for the quadratic differential metric was shown to have attractive properties through the concepts of discrimination and divergence measures between probability distribution. As is well known from differential geometry, the Fisher information matrix is a covariant symmetric tensor of the second order, and hence, the associate metric is invariant under the admissible transformations of the parameters. The information geometry considers probability distributions as differentiable manifolds, while the random variables and their expectation appear as vectors and inner products in tangent spaces to these manifolds.

Chentsov [13] has introduced a distance between parametric families of probability distributions $G_\Theta = \{p(./\theta) : \theta \in \Theta\}$ with Θ the space of parameters, by considering, to the first order, the difference between the log-density functions. Its variance defines a positive definite quadratic differential form based on the elements of the Fisher matrix. If we note traditional Fisher information matrix:

$$I(\theta) = E\left[s(x,\theta).s(x,\theta)^+\right] \quad \text{where} \quad s(x,\theta) = \frac{\partial \ln p(x/\theta)}{\partial \theta} \tag{2}$$

$$d \ln p(x/\theta) = \sum_i \frac{\partial \ln p(x/\theta)}{\partial \theta_i}.d\theta_i \tag{3}$$

Its variance defines a positive definite quadratic differential form based on the elements of the Fisher matrix and a Taylor expansion to the 2nd order of the Kullback divergence gives a Riemannian metric:

$$K(\theta,\tilde{\theta})\Big|_{\tilde{\theta}=\theta+d\theta} \cong K(\theta,\theta) + \left(\frac{\partial K(\theta,\tilde{\theta})}{\partial \tilde{\theta}}\right)^+_{\tilde{\theta}=\theta} (\tilde{\theta}-\theta) + \frac{1}{2}(\tilde{\theta}-\theta)^+ \left(\frac{\partial^2 K(\theta,\tilde{\theta})}{\partial \tilde{\theta}\partial \tilde{\theta}^*}\right)(\tilde{\theta}-\theta) \cong \frac{1}{2}\sum_{i,j} g_{ij}(\theta)d\theta_i.d\theta_j^*$$

$$K[p(./\theta), p(./\theta+d\theta)] = \frac{1}{2!}\sum_{i,j} g_{ij}(\theta).d\theta_i.d\theta_j^* + O\left(|d\theta|^3\right) \tag{4}$$

$$\text{where} \quad I(\theta) = [g_{ij}(\theta)] \quad \text{and} \quad g_{ij}(\theta) = E\left[\frac{\partial \ln p(x/\theta)}{\partial \theta_i} \cdot \frac{\partial \ln p(x/\theta)}{\partial \theta_j^*}\right]$$

2.2 Information Geometry for Doppler Data Model Based on Complex Circular Multivariate Gaussian Distribution

Previous theory of information geometry can be developed for multivariate law. In this section, we will illustrate information geometry on complex circular multivariate Gaussian distribution of zero mean that classically models Radar data and given by :

$$p(X_n / R_n) = (\pi)^{-n}.|R_n|^{-1}.e^{-Tr[\hat{R}_n.R_n^{-1}]} \tag{5}$$

$$\text{with} \quad \hat{R}_n = (X_n - m_n).(X_n - m_n)^+ \quad \text{and} \quad E[\hat{R}_n] = R_n$$

Fisher matrix elements are provided by derivatives of first moments:

$$g_{ij}(\theta) = -E\left[\frac{\partial \ln p(X_n/\theta_n)}{\partial \theta_i.\partial \theta_j}\right] = -Tr[\partial_i R_n.\partial_j R_n^{-1}] + \partial_i m_n^+.R_n^{-1}.\partial_j m_n \tag{6}$$

If we assume zero-mean process $m_n = 0$, we deduce from :

$$R_n.R_n^{-1} = I_n \Rightarrow \partial R_n = -R_n.\partial R_n^{-1}.R_n \tag{7}$$

that :

$$g_{ij}(\theta) = Tr\left[\left(R_n.\partial_i R_n^{-1}\right)\left(R_n.\partial_j R_n^{-1}\right)\right] \tag{8}$$

Then, we obtain an extended expression of the metric :

$$ds^2(\theta) = Tr\left[R_n.\left(\sum_i \partial_i R_n^{-1}.d\theta_i\right).R_n.\left(\sum_j \partial_j R_n^{-1}.d\theta_j\right)\right] \tag{9}$$

that can be simplified by using that $dR_n^{-1} = \sum_i \partial_i R_n^{-1} d\theta_i$

We conclude that Information metric can be written:

$$ds^2 = Tr\left[\left(R_n dR_n^{-1}\right)^2\right] = Tr\left[\left(d\ln R_n\right)^2\right] \tag{10}$$

This metric is a $GL(g,R)$-invariant Riemannian metric and its Laplacian is given by :

$$\Delta = Tr\left(\left(R_n \frac{\partial}{\partial R_n}\right)^2\right)$$

We write this metric synthetically by mean of Frobenius Norm :

$$ds^2 = \left\|R_n^{-1/2} dR_n R_n^{-1/2}\right\|^2 \tag{11}$$

$$\text{with } \|A\|^2 = \langle A, A \rangle \text{ and } \langle A, B \rangle = Tr\left(AB^T\right)$$

This metric is invariant under the action of the Linear matrix group $(GL_n(C),.)$:
$R_n \to W_n.R_n.W_n^+$, $W_n \in GL_n(C)$

We can observe that this metric is also invariant by inversion :

As $R^{-1}R = I \Rightarrow dR^{-1}R = -R^{-1}dR \Rightarrow ds_R^2 = ds_{R^{-1}}^2$, then $D(R_1, R_2) = D(R_1^{-1}, R_2^{-1})$

Geodesic equation for the metric given by (11) is :

$$\begin{cases} \frac{d}{dt}(R^{-1}\dot{R}) = 0 \\ tr\left[(R^{-1}\dot{R})^2\right] = 1 \end{cases} \text{ with } \dot{R} = \frac{dR}{dt} \Rightarrow \begin{cases} R^{-1}\dot{R} = A^{-1}BA \text{ with } R(t) = A^+ e^{tB} A \\ tr\left[A^{-1}B^2 A\right] = tr\left[B^2\right] = 1 \end{cases}$$

then

$$\begin{cases} R(0) = R_1 \\ R(s) = R_2 \end{cases} \Rightarrow \begin{cases} A^+A = R_1 \\ e^{sB} = (A^{-1})^+ R_2 A^{-1} \end{cases} \Rightarrow \begin{cases} A = R_1^{1/2} \\ sB = \log\left((A^{-1})^+ R_2 A^{-1}\right)_{\|B\|_F = tr(B^2) = 1} \end{cases} \Rightarrow d^2(R_1, R_2) = \left\|\log\left(R_1^{-1/2}.R_2.R_1^{-1/2}\right)\right\|^2$$

By integration, the distance between 2 Radar Hermitian SPD (Symmetric Positive Definite) matrices, R_1 and R_2, is deduced from their extended eigen-values $\{\lambda_k\}_{k=1}^n$ [19]:

$$d^2(R_1, R_2) = \left\| \log\left(R_1^{-1/2}.R_2.R_1^{-1/2}\right) \right\|^2 = \sum_{k=1}^{n} \log^2(\lambda_k) \tag{12}$$

$$\text{with} \quad \det\left(R_1^{-1/2}.R_2.R_1^{-1/2} - \lambda.I\right) = \det(R_2 - \lambda R_1) = 0$$

We have considered the case of zero mean $m = 0$, but for general case, we have :
$ds^2 = dm^+ R^{-1} dm + Tr\left(\left(R^{-1} dR\right)^2\right)$ associated with the following isometries :

$$(m, R) \rightarrow (m', R') = \left(A^+ m + a, A^+ RA\right) \tag{13}$$

$$ds^2 \mapsto ds'^2 = ds^2 \quad \text{with} \quad (a, A) \in C^n \mathrm{x} GL(n, C)$$

2.3 Information Geometry for Complex Autoregressive Model

Information geometry metric (12) that has been deduced for complex circular multi-variate Gaussian model of zero mean in section 2.2, can be developed more deeply by introducing complex autoregressive model. It has been demonstrated by Burg that autoregressive model can be naturally introduced by Maximum Entropy Approach. Then, we consider the following complex autoregressive model :

$$z_n = -\sum_{k=1}^{N} a_k^{(N)} z_{n-k} + b_n \quad \text{with} \quad E\left[b_n b_{n-k}^*\right] = \delta_{k,0} \sigma^2 \quad \text{and} \quad A_N = \left[a_1^{(N)}...a_N^{(N)}\right]^T \tag{14}$$

For this model, covariance and inverse covariance matrices can be expressed by the following blocks structure :

$$R_n^{-1} = \begin{bmatrix} \alpha_{n-1} & \alpha_{n-1}.A_{n-1}^+ \\ \alpha_{n-1}.A_{n-1} & R_{n-1}^{-1} + \alpha_{n-1}.A_{n-1}.A_{n-1}^+ \end{bmatrix} \quad \text{and} \quad R_n = \begin{bmatrix} \alpha_{n-1}^{-1} + A_{n-1}^+.R_{n-1}.A_{n-1} & -A_{n-1}^+.R_{n-1} \\ -R_{n-1}.A_{n-1} & R_{n-1} \end{bmatrix} \tag{15}$$

$$\text{with} \quad \alpha_n^{-1} = \left[1 - |\mu_n|^2\right] \alpha_{n-1}^{-1} \quad \text{and} \quad A_n = \begin{bmatrix} A_{n-1} \\ 0 \end{bmatrix} + \mu_n. \begin{bmatrix} A_{n-1}^{(-)} \\ 1 \end{bmatrix} \tag{16}$$

we note $V^{(-)} = J.V^*$ where $J = \begin{bmatrix} 0 & \cdots & 0 & 1 \\ \vdots & & \cdot^{\cdot^{\cdot}} & 0 \\ 0 & 1 & \cdot^{\cdot^{\cdot}} & \vdots \\ 1 & 0 & \cdots & 0 \end{bmatrix}$

μ_n called reflection coefficient, is computed by Regularized Burg algorithm [24] and is defined in the unit disk $|\mu_k| < 1, \forall k = 1,...,n$.

The Blocks structures of covariance matrix and its inverse will allow to develop an iterative and parallel procedure to compute the previous trace metric (12).

If we consider two matrices indexed '1' and '2', we can exploit Cholesky factorization to obtain a new expression of the symmetric hermitian matrix of metric (12) :

$$R_n^{(1)} = \begin{bmatrix} \alpha_{n-1}^{(1)-1} + A_{n-1}^{(1)+}.R_{n-1}^{(1)}.A_{n-1}^{(1)} & -A_{n-1}^{(1)+}.R_{n-1}^{(1)} \\ -R_{n-1}^{(1)}.A_{n-1}^{(1)} & R_{n-1}^{(1)} \end{bmatrix} = R_n^{(1)1/2}.R_n^{(1)1/2+} \quad \text{with} \quad R_n^{(1)1/2} = \begin{bmatrix} \dfrac{1}{\sqrt{\alpha_{n-1}^{(1)}}} & -A_{n-1}^{(1)+}.R_{n-1}^{(1)1/2} \\ 0 & R_{n-1}^{(1)1/2} \end{bmatrix}$$

$$\text{and} \quad R_n^{(2)-1} = \begin{bmatrix} \alpha_{n-1}^{(2)} & \alpha_{n-1}^{(2)}.A_{n-1}^{(2)+} \\ \alpha_{n-1}^{(2)}.A_{n-1}^{(2)+} & R_{n-1}^{(2)} + \alpha_{n-1}^{(2)}.A_{n-1}^{(2)}.A_{n-1}^{(2)+} \end{bmatrix}$$

Composition of both expressions leads to :

$$\Omega_n = R_n^{(1)1/2+}.R_n^{(2)-1}.R_n^{(1)1/2} = \begin{bmatrix} \beta_{n-1} & \beta_{n-1}.W_{n-1}^+ \\ \beta_{n-1}.W_{n-1} & \Omega_{n-1} + \beta_{n-1}.W_{n-1}.W_{n-1}^+ \end{bmatrix} \tag{17}$$

with $\quad W_{n-1} = \sqrt{\alpha_{n-1}^{(1)}}.R_{n-1}^{(1)1/2+}.\left[A_{n-1}^{(2)} - A_{n-1}^{(1)}\right]$ and $\quad \beta_{n-1} = \dfrac{\alpha_{n-1}^{(2)}}{\alpha_{n-1}^{(1)}}$

We can observe that the Autoregressive blocks structure is the same in (15) and (17). Previous trace metric (12) can then be easily computed recursively by using this following equations giving interleaving eigenvalues $\Lambda_n = diag\left\{\cdots\lambda_i^{(n)}\cdots\right\}$ of $\Omega_n = R_n^{(1)1/2+}.R_n^{(2)-1}.R_n^{(1)1/2}$ at each order n, and their eigenvectors $\left\{X_{k1}^{(n)}\right\}_{k=1}^n$ and associate matrix $U_n = \left[X_1^{(n)}\cdots X_n^{(n)}\right]$:

$$\begin{cases} F^{(n)}\left(\lambda_k^{(n)}\right) = \lambda_k^{(n)} - \beta_{n-1} + \beta_{n-1}.\lambda_k^{(n)}.\sum_{i=1}^{n-1}\dfrac{\left|W_{n-1}^+.X_i^{(n-1)}\right|^2}{\left(\lambda_i^{(n-1)} - \lambda_k^{(n)}\right)} = 0 \\ \dfrac{X_k^{(n)}}{X_{k,1}^{(n)}} = \left[-\lambda_k^{(n)}.U_{n-1}.\left(\Lambda_{n-1} - \lambda_k^{(n)}.I_{n-1}\right)^{-1}.U_{n-1}^+.W_{n-1} \right] \end{cases} \tag{18}$$

At each order n, eigen vectors are normalized :

$$\dfrac{X_k^{(n)}}{X_{k,1}^{(n)}} \rightarrow \rho_k^{(n)}.\dfrac{X_k^{(n)}}{X_{k,1}^{(n)}} \quad \text{with} \quad \rho_k^{(n)} = \left(1 + \lambda_k^{(n)2}.\sum_{i=1}^{n-1}\dfrac{\left|W_{n-1}^+.X_i^{(n-1)}\right|^2}{\left(\lambda_i^{(n-1)} - \lambda_k^{(n)}\right)^2}\right)^{-1/2} \tag{19}$$

The extended Autoregressive vector $\begin{bmatrix} 1 & W_{n-1} \end{bmatrix}^T$ can be decomposed on this basis of the eigen-vectors:

$$\sum_{k=1}^n\left(\dfrac{\partial F^{(n)}\left(\lambda_k^{(n)}\right)}{\partial \lambda}\right)^{-1} = 1 \quad \text{and} \quad \begin{bmatrix} 1 \\ W_{n-1} \end{bmatrix} = \sum_{k=1}^n\left(\dfrac{\partial F^{(n)}\left(\lambda_k^{(n)}\right)}{\partial \lambda}\right)^{-1}.\dfrac{X_k^{(n)}}{X_{k,1}^{(n)}} \tag{20}$$

As given by Wilkinson Theorem, for interlaced matrices, their eigen-values are interlaced. We recover this theorem for our block structure:

$$0 < \lambda_n^{(n)} < \lambda_{n-1}^{(n-1)} < \lambda_{n-1}^{(n)} < \ldots < \lambda_2^{(n)} < \lambda_1^{(n-1)} < \lambda_1^{(n)} < Tr\left[\Omega_n\right] \tag{21}$$

The trace $Tr\left[\Omega_n\right]$ is an higher bound of these eigen-values, because matrices are positive definite (positive eigen-values) and can be computed recursively :

$$Tr\left[\Omega_n\right] = Tr\left[\Omega_{n-1}\right] + \beta_{n-1}\begin{bmatrix} 1 \\ W_{n-1} \end{bmatrix}^+\begin{bmatrix} 1 \\ W_{n-1} \end{bmatrix} \tag{22}$$

Zeros of $F^{(n)}(\lambda)$ provide eigenvalues at order n, using property that $F^{(n)}(\lambda)$ is strictly monotone on each interval $\left]\lambda_{k-1}^{(n-1)}, \lambda_k^{(n-1)}\right[$:

$$\dfrac{\partial F^{(n)}(\lambda)}{\partial \lambda} = \dfrac{\beta_{n-1}}{\lambda_k^{(n)}\left|X_{k,1}^{(n)}\right|^2} = 1 + \beta_{n-1}.\sum_{k=1}^{n-1}\dfrac{\lambda_k^{(n-1)}\left|W_{n-1}^+.X_k^{(n-1)}\right|^2}{\left(\lambda_k^{(n-1)} - \lambda\right)^2} > 1 \tag{23}$$

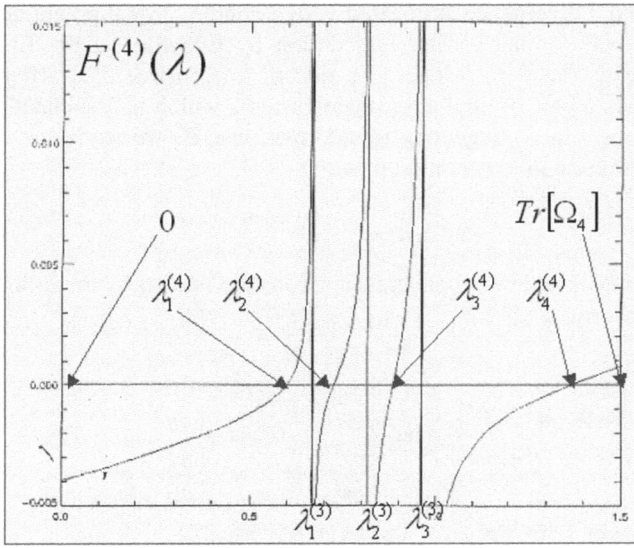

Fig. 3. Example of Curve $F^{(n)}\left(\lambda_i^{(n)}\right)$ for n=4

Then, eigen-values can be computed, recursively at each order n, and in parallel by dichotomy on each interval by computing zero of the function $F^{(n)}\left(\lambda_i^{(n)}\right)$.

This Blocks structure of covariance matrix for complex autoregressive model is closely related Siegel Group (Siegel Approach will be developed hereafter) and this link can be established by mean of Choleski decomposition of this matrix:

$$\Omega_n = (\alpha_n . R_n)^{-1} = W_n . W_n^+ = \left(1 - |\mu_n|^2\right) \begin{bmatrix} 1 & A_{n-1}^+ \\ A_{n-1} & \Omega_{n-1} + A_{n-1}.A_{n-1}^+ \end{bmatrix} \tag{24}$$

with $W_n = \sqrt{1 - |\mu_n|^2} \begin{bmatrix} 1 & 0 \\ A_{n-1} & \Omega_{n-1}^{1/2} \end{bmatrix}$ and $\Omega_{n-1} = \Omega_{n-1}^{1/2}.\Omega_{n-1}^{1/2+}$

All distribution of n-dimensional variable is naturally associated to Affine Group : it is the element such that its action on vector $Z \sim N_n(0, I_n)$ transforms it to the other

vector $X \sim N_n(A_n, \Omega_n)$: $\begin{bmatrix} 1 & 0 \\ A_{n-1} & \Omega_{n-1}^{1/2} \end{bmatrix} \begin{bmatrix} 1 \\ Z \end{bmatrix} = \begin{bmatrix} 1 \\ \Omega_{n-1}^{1/2}.Z + A_{n-1} \end{bmatrix} = \begin{bmatrix} 1 \\ X \end{bmatrix}$ (25)

We can consider this definition of Affine Group elements as non-symmetric squared-root of one element of Siegel Group : $\begin{bmatrix} 1 & A_{n-1}^+ \\ A_{n-1} & \Omega_{n-1} + A_{n-1}.A_{n-1}^+ \end{bmatrix}$ (26)

2.4 Dual Differential Information Geometry

In this section, we present information geometry in a more general framework of affine geometry. More precisely , the geometry of a family of probability distribution is also characterized by a dual differential geometry determined by a couple of affine connections and a divergence associated with a couple of dual potential functions [3]. This kind of dual geometry was studied first by Eugenio Calabi. If a Riemannian manifold *(M,g)* is flat with respect to a pair of torsion-free dual affine connections, then there exists a pair of dual coordinate systems which is associated with dual potential functions via a Legendre transformations. If we consider a multivariate Gaussian distribution in exponential form:

$$p(X/m,R) = e^{-\frac{1}{2}X^T R^{-1} X + X^T R^{-1} m - \psi(m,R)} \tag{27}$$

Dual coordinates and dual potential functions are related by the following Fenchel-Legendre transform: $\tilde{\Phi} \equiv \langle \tilde{\Theta}, \tilde{H} \rangle - \tilde{\Psi}$ where $\langle \tilde{\Theta}, \tilde{H} \rangle = Tr(\Theta \eta^T + \Theta H^T)$ $\tag{28}$

$$\begin{cases} \tilde{\Theta} = (\theta,\Theta) = (R^{-1}m, (2R)^{-1}) \\ \tilde{H} = (\eta,H) = (m, -R + mm^T) \end{cases} \text{ and } \begin{cases} \dfrac{\partial \tilde{\Psi}}{\partial \theta} = \eta \\ \dfrac{\partial \tilde{\Psi}}{\partial \Theta} = H \end{cases} \text{ and } \begin{cases} \dfrac{\partial \tilde{\Phi}}{\partial \eta} = \theta \\ \dfrac{\partial \tilde{\Phi}}{\partial H} = \Theta \end{cases} \tag{29}$$

$$\Rightarrow \begin{cases} \tilde{\Psi}(\tilde{\Theta}) = 2^{-2} Tr(\Theta^{-1}\theta\theta^T) - 2^{-1}\log(\det\Theta) + 2^{-1}n\log(\pi) \\ \tilde{\Phi}(\tilde{H}) = -2^{-1}\log(1 + \eta^T H^{-1}\eta) - 2^{-1}\log(\det(-H)) - 2^{-1}n\log(2\pi e) \end{cases}$$

This relation between dual potential function is closely related to variational approach introduced by S. Varadhan [34] in the framework of large deviation theory, where logarithm of cumulant generating function is Fenchel-Legendre transform of rate function (Kullback divergence).

We can observe that one of the potential function is the Entropy of the process X : $\tilde{\Phi}(\tilde{H}) = E[\log p]$. These dual potential functions and coordinates are related to Kullback divergence:

$$\int p(X/m_1, R_1)\log \frac{p(X/m_1,R_1)}{p(X/m_2,R_2)}dX = \tilde{\Psi}(\tilde{\Theta}_2) + \tilde{\Phi}(\tilde{H}_1) - \langle \tilde{\Theta}_2, \tilde{H}_1 \rangle = \tilde{\Psi}(\tilde{\Theta}_1) + \tilde{\Phi}(\tilde{H}_2) - \langle \tilde{\Theta}_1, \tilde{H}_2 \rangle \tag{30}$$

As these potential function are convex, their Hessian $g_{ij} = \dfrac{\partial^2 \tilde{\Psi}}{\partial \Theta_i \partial \Theta_j}$ and $g_{ij}^* \equiv \dfrac{\partial^2 \tilde{\Phi}}{\partial H_i \partial H_j}$

with $g_{ij}(\Theta)g_{jk}^*(H) = \delta_k^i$ define Riemannian metrics, as previously explained for Information Geometry:

$$ds^2 = \frac{1}{2}g_{ij}d\Theta_i d\Theta_j + O(|d\Theta_i|^3) = \frac{1}{2}g^{ij}dH_i dH_j + O(|dH_i|^3) \tag{31}$$

2.5 Dual Information Geometry for Complex Autoregressive Model and Its Kähler Metric

Dual differential geometry introduced in previous 2.4 section can be applied to complex autoregressive models by mean of Kähler geometry, which is a natural extension of classical Riemannian geometry for complex variables. If we apply Dual Information geometry as developed in the previous section, on Doppler data modeled by a complex autoregressive process [6], we can define the metric as the Hessian of Entropy given by reflection coefficients (or Schur coefficients) $\{\mu_k \,/|\mu_k|<1\}_{k=1}^{n-1}$:

$$g_{ij} \equiv \frac{\partial^2 \tilde{\Phi}}{\partial H_i \partial H_j} \quad \text{with} \quad \tilde{\Phi}(R) = -\log(\det R) - n\log(\pi e) \tag{32}$$

If we use blocks structure : $R_n^{-1} = \begin{bmatrix} \alpha_{n-1} & \alpha_{n-1}.A_{n-1}^+ \\ \alpha_{n-1}.A_{n-1} & R_{n-1}^{-1} + \alpha_{n-1}.A_{n-1}.A_{n-1}^+ \end{bmatrix}$ with $\alpha_n^{-1} = \left[1-|\mu_n|^2\right]\alpha_{n-1}^{-1}$

We know that if $G = \begin{bmatrix} a & V^+ \\ W & B \end{bmatrix}$ then $\det(G) = \det(a).\det\left(B - a^{-1}.W.V^+\right)$ \tag{33}

The Entropy of the process can then be expressed according to reflection coefficients :

$$\tilde{\Phi}(R_n) = \sum_{k=1}^{n-1}(n-k).\ln\left[1-|\mu_k|^2\right] + n.\ln[\pi.e.P_0] \quad \text{with} \quad \begin{cases} \alpha_0^{-1} = P_0 = \frac{1}{n}\sum_{k=1}^{n}|z_k|^2 \\ Z_n = \begin{bmatrix} z_1 & \cdots & z_n \end{bmatrix}^T \end{cases} \tag{34}$$

A seminal paper of Erich Kähler [5] has introduced natural extension of Riemannian geometry to Complex Manifold during 30th 's of last century. We can easily apply this geometric framework for information metric definition. Let a complex Manifold M^n of dimension n, we can associate a Kählerian metric, which can be locally defined by its definite positive Riemannian form: $ds^2 = 2\sum_{i,j=1}^{n} g_{i\bar{j}}.dz^i d\bar{z}^j$. Kähler assumption sets that we can define a Kähler potential Φ , such that $g_{i\bar{j}} = \frac{\partial^2 \Phi}{\partial z^i \partial \bar{z}^j}$. Fundamental relation, given by Erich Kähler, is that Ricci tensor can be expressed by :

$$R_{i\bar{j}} = -\frac{\partial^2 \log(\det g_{k\bar{l}})}{\partial z_i \partial \bar{z}_j} \tag{35}$$

with the associated scalar curvature : $R = \sum_{k,l=1}^{n} g^{k\bar{l}} R_{k\bar{l}}$ \tag{36}

In case of Complex Auto-Regressive (CAR) models, if we choose as Kähler potential Φ the Entropy of the process expressed according to reflection coefficients in the unit Polydisk $\{Z = (z_1,...,z_n)/|z_k|<1 \;\forall k = 1,...n\}$, Kähler potential is given by:

$$\Phi = \sum_{k=1}^{n-1} \rho_k \ln\left[1-|z_k|^2\right] = \ln K_D(z,z) \tag{37}$$

from Bergman kernel $K_D(z,z) = \prod_{k=1}^{n-1}\left(1-|z_k|^2\right)^{\rho_k}$ \tag{38}

Very surprisingly, this case was the first example of potential studied by Erich Kähler in his seminal paper, named by Erich Kähler *"Hyper-Abelian case"* [5], relatively to the other case studied by him as Hyper-Fuchsian Case $\Phi = \rho.\ln\left(1-\sum_{k=1}^{n}|z_k|^2\right)$ in

unit hyper-ball $\left\{Z = (z_1,...,z_n)/\sum_{k=1}^{n}|z_k|^2 <1\right\}$.

If we compute the Hessian of Entropy with the following system of coordinates [7]:

$$\theta^{(n)} = \begin{bmatrix} P_0 & \mu_1 & \cdots & \mu_{n-1} \end{bmatrix}^T = \begin{bmatrix} \theta_1^{(n)} & \cdots & \theta_n^{(n)} \end{bmatrix}^T \tag{39}$$

we can deduce expression of Information metric :

$$g_{11} = n\alpha_0^2 = nP_0^{-2} \quad \text{and} \quad g_{ij} = \frac{(n-i).\delta_{ij}}{\left(1 - |\mu_i|^2\right)^2} \tag{40}$$

Affine Information geometry with potential function given by process Entropy is :

$$ds_n^2 = n.\left(\frac{dP_0}{P_0}\right)^2 + \sum_{i=1}^{n-1} (n-i)\frac{|d\mu_i|^2}{\left(1 - |\mu_i|^2\right)^2} \tag{41}$$

Ricci tensor is directly computed by Kähler formula (35) :

$$R_{k\bar{l}} = -2\delta_{kl}\left(1 - |\mu_k|^2\right)^{-2} \quad \text{for} \quad k = 2,...,n-1 \quad \text{and} \quad R_{11} = -2P_0^{-2} \tag{42}$$

Identically, we can deduce scalar curvature by relation (36) :

$$R = -2\left[n^{-1} + \sum_{j=1}^{n-1}(n-j)^{-1}\right] = -2\left[\sum_{j=0}^{n-1}(n-j)^{-1}\right] \tag{43}$$

This curvature diverges when n tends to infinity, that is to say when the correlation of the process is increasing. We can observe that we have not a Kähler-Einstein metric ($R_{i\bar{j}} = k_0 g_{i\bar{j}}$) but a more general relation defined by :

$$\left[R_{i\bar{j}}\right] = B^{(n)}\left[g_{i\bar{j}}\right] \quad \text{with} \quad R = Tr\left[B^{(n)}\right] \quad \text{where} \quad B^{(n)} = -2diag\left\{.,(n-i)^{-1},..\right\} \tag{44}$$

3 Symplectic Geometry and Siegel Upper-Half Space

In this chapter, we will see that the metric introduced by Information Geometry is a particular case of metric introduced by Carl Ludwig Siegel in the framework of Symplectic geometry.

Symplectic Group $Sp_{2n}R$ is one possible generalization of the group $SL_2R = Sp_2R$ (group of invertible matrices with determinant 1) to higher dimensions. This generalization goes further, since they act on a symmetric homogeneous space, the Siegel upper half plane, and this action has quite a few similarities with the action of SL_2R on the hyperbolic plane. Carl Ludwig Siegel did a study of this action in 1935 in his book "Symplectic Geometry" [1].

Let F be either the real or the complex field, the symplectic Group is the group of all matrices $M \in GL_{2n}F$ satisfying :

$$Sp(n, F) \equiv \left\{M \in GL(2n, F) / M^T JM = J\right\}, J = \begin{pmatrix} 0 & I_n \\ -I_n & 0 \end{pmatrix} \in SL(2n, R) \tag{45}$$

$$\text{or } M = \begin{pmatrix} A & B \\ C & D \end{pmatrix} \in Sp(n, F) \Leftrightarrow A^T C \text{ et } B^T D \quad \text{symmetric} \quad \text{and} \quad A^T D - C^T D = I_n$$

The Siegel upper half plane is the set of all complex symmetric (n x n) matrices with positive definite imaginary part. We denote it by :

$$SH_n = \{Z = X + iY \in Sym(n, C) / \operatorname{Im}(Z) = Y > 0\} \tag{46}$$

The action of the Symplectic Group on the Siegel upper half plane is transitive. The group $PSp(n, R) \equiv Sp(n, R) / \{\pm I_{2n}\}$ is group of SH_n biholomorphisms via generalized Möbius transformations: $M = \begin{pmatrix} A & B \\ C & D \end{pmatrix} \Rightarrow M(Z) = (AZ + B)(CZ + D)^{-1}$ (47)

We can observe that $M(Z) \in SH_n$:

If we set $M \begin{bmatrix} Z \\ I \end{bmatrix} = \begin{bmatrix} E \\ F \end{bmatrix} = \begin{bmatrix} AZ + B \\ CZ + D \end{bmatrix}$

$$\begin{cases} M^T JM = J \\ Z \in SH_n \ (Z^T = Z, \operatorname{Im}(Z) > 0) \end{cases} \Rightarrow \begin{cases} F \text{ invertible} \Rightarrow M(Z) = EF^{-1} \\ EF^{-1} \text{ symmetric} \\ \operatorname{Im}(EF^{-1}) > 0 \end{cases} \tag{48}$$

The proof is given by the following arguments :

$$\text{if } Z \in SH_n \text{ then } Z^T = Z, \operatorname{Im}(Z) = \frac{1}{2i}(Z - \bar{Z}) > 0 \tag{49}$$

$$\begin{cases} \begin{bmatrix} E \\ F \end{bmatrix}^T J \begin{bmatrix} E \\ F \end{bmatrix} = J \Rightarrow [Z^T \ I] J \begin{bmatrix} Z \\ I \end{bmatrix} = 0 \text{ because } Z^T = Z \\ -\frac{1}{2i}[\bar{E} \ \bar{F}] J \begin{bmatrix} E \\ F \end{bmatrix} = -\frac{1}{2i}[\bar{Z} \ I] J \begin{bmatrix} Z \\ I \end{bmatrix} > 0 \text{ because } \operatorname{Im}(Z) > 0 \end{cases} \tag{50}$$

$$\begin{cases} E^T F = F^T E & (*) \\ -\frac{1}{2i}(\bar{E} F - \bar{F} E) > 0 & (**) \end{cases}$$

If $Fv = 0 \Rightarrow \bar{v}\bar{F} = 0 \Rightarrow \bar{v}(\bar{E}F - \bar{F}E)v = 0 \Rightarrow v = 0 \Rightarrow F \text{ invertible}$ (51)

$(*) \Rightarrow EF^{-1}$ symmetric and $(**) \Rightarrow \operatorname{Im}(EF^{-1}) > 0$

We have also to remark that symplectic group action on SH_n is transitive :

$$\phi_1(Z) \equiv \begin{pmatrix} I_n & X \\ 0 & I_n \end{pmatrix} \begin{pmatrix} Y^{1/2} & 0 \\ 0 & Y^{-1/2} \end{pmatrix} = \begin{pmatrix} Y^{1/2} & XY^{-1/2} \\ 0 & Y^{-1/2} \end{pmatrix} \Bigg\} \Rightarrow \phi_1(iI) = X + iY \tag{52}$$
$$Z \mapsto Y^{1/2} Z Y^{1/2} \text{ and } Z \mapsto Z + X$$

$PSp(n, R)$ acts as a sub-group of isometries. Siegel has proved that Symplectic transformations are isometries for the Siegel metric in SH_n. It can be defined on SH_n using the distance element at the point $Z = X + iY$, as defined by [12][18] :

$$ds_{Siegel}^2 = Tr(Y^{-1}(dZ)Y^{-1}(d\bar{Z})) \text{ with } Z = X + iY \tag{53}$$

This metric is a $Sp(n,F)$-invariant Kähler metric on SH_n and Maass has proved that its Laplacian is given by [11] : $\Delta = 4.Tr\left(Y'\left(Y\dfrac{\partial}{\partial \overline{Z}}\right)\dfrac{\partial}{\partial Z}\right)$ (54)

This invariance can be proved by given following arguments :

We are looking for metric that is invariant by : $Z' = (AZ + B)(CZ + D)^{-1}$ (55)

So, we can write: $\left.\begin{array}{l} dZ' = (CZ + D)^{-1t}(dZ)(CZ + D)^{-1} \\ Im(Z') = (C\overline{Z} + D)^{-1t} Im(Z)(CZ + D)^{-1} \end{array}\right\}$ because $A'D - C'B = I_n$ (56)

Let's $Z = X + iY$, most general matrices that transform Z into $i.I_n$ are the following :

$$\begin{bmatrix} A & B \\ C & D \end{bmatrix} = \begin{bmatrix} \alpha & \beta \\ -\beta & \alpha \end{bmatrix}\begin{bmatrix} Y^{-1/2} & -Y^{-1/2}X \\ 0 & Y^{1/2} \end{bmatrix} = \begin{bmatrix} \alpha Y^{-1/2} & \beta Y^{1/2} - \alpha Y^{-1/2}X \\ -\beta Y^{1/2} & \beta Y^{-1/2}X + \alpha Y^{1/2} \end{bmatrix}$$ (57)

$(\alpha - i\beta)$ unit , $CZ + D = (\alpha - i\beta)Y^{1/2}$ and $C\overline{Z} + D = (\alpha + i\beta)Y^{1/2}$ (58)

We then directly deduced that :

$$dZ' = (\alpha - i\beta)^{-1t}Y^{-1/2}(dZ)Y^{-1/2}(\alpha - i\beta)^{-1}$$

$$Im(Z') = Y' = (\alpha + i\beta)^{-1t}Y^{-1/2} Im(Z)Y^{-1/2}(\alpha - i\beta)^{-1} = Y^{-1/2} Im(Z)Y^{-1/2} = I_n$$ (59)

From which, we deduce the invariance of the Siegel metric according to general Möbius transform (55) :

$$Tr\left(Y'^{-1} dZ'Y'^{-1} d\overline{Z}'\right) = Tr\left(dZ' d\overline{Z}'\right) = Tr\left(Y^{1/2}(dZ)Y^{-1}(d\overline{Z})Y^{-1/2}\right) = Tr\left(Y^{-1}dZY^{-1}d\overline{Z}\right)$$ (60)

The Siegel metric can be also closely related to classical metric given by :

$$d_p(A,B) = \left(\sum_{i=1}^{n}\left|\log\sigma_j\left(A^{-1}B\right)\right|^p\right)^{1/p} \xrightarrow[p\to\infty]{} Max\left\{\left|\log\sigma_1\left(A^{-1}B\right)\right|, \left|\log\sigma_1\left(A^{-1}B\right)\right|\right\}$$ (61)

Both metrics are related by : $ds_{Siegel}(Z,W) = \sqrt{2}d_2(\phi_1(Z), \phi_1(W)) \quad \forall Z, W \in SH_n$ (62)

by mean of the following bijection

$$\begin{array}{l} \Phi_1 : SH_n \to Sp(n,R)/K_n \\ Z \mapsto \phi_1(Z)K_n \\ \text{with } \phi_1 : SH_n \to Sp(n,R) \end{array} \quad \text{where} \quad \left\{\begin{array}{l} O \in K_n = Stab(iI_n) \text{ and } O = \begin{pmatrix} A & B \\ -B & A \end{pmatrix} \\ \text{with } -A^T = A \text{ et } B^T = B \end{array}\right.$$ (63)

This transform can be written : $\phi_1(Z) \equiv \begin{pmatrix} I_n & X \\ 0 & I_n \end{pmatrix}\begin{pmatrix} Y^{1/2} & 0 \\ 0 & Y^{-1/2} \end{pmatrix} = \begin{pmatrix} Y^{1/2} & XY^{-1/2} \\ 0 & Y^{-1/2} \end{pmatrix}$ (64)

we can observe that is a more general case that previous one studied in framework of Information Geometry. If we set $X = 0$ and $Y = R$, such that $Z = iR$, in Siegel metric (53) then we recover previous metric (10) : $ds^2 = Tr\left((R^{-1}(dR))^2\right)$.

The distance induced in SH_n by this Riemannian metric can be found in Siegel work and is given after integration by [19] :

$$d_{Siegel}(Z_1, Z_2) = \left(\sum_{k=1}^{n}\log^2\left(\dfrac{1+\sqrt{r_k}}{1-\sqrt{r_k}}\right)\right)^{1/2} \quad \text{with } Z_1, Z_2 \in SH_n$$ (65)

where the r_k's are the eigenvalues of the cross-ratio :

$$R(Z_1, Z_2) = (Z_1 - Z_2)(Z_1 - \overline{Z}_2)^{-1}(\overline{Z}_1 - \overline{Z}_2)(\overline{Z}_1 - Z_2)^{-1} \qquad (66)$$

This metric can be used for multivariate Gaussian model with non zero mean. We set as matrix variable Z: $Z = mm^T + iR$ $\qquad (67)$

For complex Autoregessive model, we can develop the Rao (10) or Siegel (53) metric, using blocks structure (15) and (16) :

$$ds_n^2 = Tr\left[(R_n.dR_n^{-1})^2\right] = ds_{n-1}^2 + \left(\frac{d\alpha_{n-1}}{\alpha_{n-1}}\right)^2 + \alpha_{n-1}.dA_{n-1}^+.R_{n-1}.dA_{n-1} \qquad (68)$$

The second term can be written :

$$\left(\frac{d\alpha_{n-1}}{\alpha_{n-1}}\right)^2 + \alpha_{n-1}.dA_{n-1}^+.R_{n-1}.dA_{n-1} = d\begin{bmatrix} \log\alpha_{n-1} \\ A_{n-1} \end{bmatrix}^+ . \begin{bmatrix} 1 & 0 \\ 0 & \alpha_{n-1}R_{n-1} \end{bmatrix} d\begin{bmatrix} \log\alpha_{n-1} \\ A_{n-1} \end{bmatrix} \qquad (69)$$

From which, we can deduce the covariance matrix of Autogressive vector A, as inverse of Fisher Information matrix : $\begin{cases} R_{\hat{A}_n}^{-1} = I[A_{n-1}] = \alpha_{n-1}R_{n-1} \\ \log\alpha_{n-1} \perp A_{n-1} \end{cases}$ $\qquad (70)$

Then, distance between complex autoregressive models can be deduced from previous formula based on bi-ratio eigen-values expressed by mean of the following matrix variable :

$$Z = \begin{bmatrix} \log\alpha_{n-1} \\ A_{n-1} \end{bmatrix}\begin{bmatrix} \log\alpha_{n-1} \\ A_{n-1} \end{bmatrix}^+ + i\begin{bmatrix} 1 & 0 \\ 0 & (\alpha_{n-1}R_{n-1})^{-1} \end{bmatrix} \qquad (71)$$

For our applicative case, $Z = iR$, and the distance is given by the eigenvalues of the cross-ratio : $R(Z_1, Z_2) = (R_1 - R_2)(R_1 + R_2)^{-1}(R_1 - R_2)(R_1 + R_2)^{-1}$ $\qquad (72)$

As we previously observed for AR, this metric is Kählerian [12] :

$$\Omega = \frac{1}{2i}Tr\left(Y^{-1}dZ \wedge Y^{-1}d\overline{Z}\right) = Tr\left(dX \wedge d\left(Y^{-1}\right)\right) \Rightarrow d\Omega = 0 \qquad (73)$$

For instance, for Siegel Upper-half space, we can find Bergman Kernel of Kähler metric by mean of Siegel Unit Disk :

$$SD_n = \left\{Z \in Sym(n,C)/\|Z\|_2 < I\right\} \text{ with } \|Z\|_2 = Z\overline{Z} \qquad (74)$$

The Siegel Unit Disk is obtained by Generalized Cayley Transform of Siegel Upperhalf space : $\Psi:SH_n \rightarrow SD_n$ $\qquad (75)$

$$Z \mapsto (Z - iI_n)(Z + iI_n)^{-1}$$

We will then consider the following Kähler Potential : $\Phi = -\ln K_B(Z,Z)$ $\qquad (76)$

and its associated Bergman Kernel : $K_B(Z,W) = (I - Z\overline{W})$ with $Z \in SD_n$ $\qquad (77)$

We can then deduced Kähler metric given by :

$$ds^2 = \frac{\partial^2\Phi}{\partial Z\partial\overline{Z}}dZd\overline{Z} = Tr\left((I - Z\overline{Z})^{-1}dZ(I - Z\overline{Z})^{-1}d\overline{Z}\right) \qquad (78)$$

To conclude on seminal work of Siegel, we can observe that in his book "Symplectic Geometry", he has also introduced an other expression of what we call Siegel distance. If we consider $R = T_{12}^2 = T_{12}^+ . T_{12}$ with $T_{12} = \left(\Sigma_1^{-1} - \Sigma_2^{-1}\right)\left(\Sigma_1^{-1} + \Sigma_2^{-1}\right)^{-1}$ (79)

Eigenvalues of this matrix are closely related to previous extended eigenvalues for initial Siegel distance by : $r_k = \left(\dfrac{1 - \lambda_k}{1 + \lambda_k}\right)^2$ with $r_k = \sigma(R)$ and $\lambda_k = \sigma\left(\Sigma_1^{-1/2}\Sigma_2\Sigma_1^{-1/2}\right)$ (80)

Then, the new distance introduced by Siegel is given by :

$$D^2(\Sigma_1, \Sigma_2) = \frac{1}{2}Tr\left[\log^2\left(\frac{I + R^{1/2}}{I - R^{1/2}}\right)\right] = \frac{1}{2}\sum_{k=1}^{n}\log^2\left(\frac{1 + r_k^{1/2}}{1 - r_k^{1/2}}\right) \tag{81}$$

where $\log^2\left(\dfrac{I + R^{1/2}}{I - R^{1/2}}\right) = 4.\left[\tanh^{-1}R^{1/2}\right]^2 = 4.R.\left(\displaystyle\sum_{k=0}^{\infty}\frac{R^k}{2.k+1}\right)^2$ and $Tr\left[R^j\right] = \displaystyle\sum_{k=1}^{n}r_k^j$ (82)

4 Geometry of Symmetric Cones

As introduced in introductive section, in parallel of information geometry branch, Geometry of Symmetric Cones has been studied in the framework of Semi-Lie Group theory by Elie Cartan in 1930 an in the framework of Euclidean Algebra theory by M. Koecher in 1960. These theories have close links to the information geometry.

Euclidean Jordan Algebra is an Euclidean Vectors Space equipped with following bilinear product :

$$G(\Omega) = \left\{g \in GL(V)/g\Omega = \Omega\right\} \text{ and } \begin{vmatrix} xy = yx \ , \ x\left(x^2 y\right) = x^2(xy) \\ \langle xy, z\rangle = \langle y, xz\rangle \end{vmatrix} \tag{83}$$

$$L \text{ and } P \text{ auto-adjoint} : L(x)y = xy \text{ and } P(x) = 2L^2(x) - L\left(x^2\right)$$

An example of Euclidean Jordan Algebra is given by :

$V = Sym(n, R)$ with $x \circ y = \dfrac{1}{2}(xy + yx)$ and $\langle x, y\rangle = Tr(xy)$

$\left.\begin{array}{l} \Omega_{sym} : \text{set of symmetric positive definite matrices} \\ G\left(\Omega_{sym}\right) : \text{Linear Group} \end{array}\right\} \Rightarrow P(x)y = xyx$

$g_x(u, v) = \left\langle P(x)^{-1}u, v\right\rangle$, $x \in \Omega$, $u, v \in V$ define a structure of Riemannian Symmetric space on Ω isomorphic to $G(\Omega)_0/K(\Omega)_0$ where $G(\Omega)_0$ is the identity component of $G(\Omega)$, and $K(\Omega)_0 = \left\{g \in G(\Omega)_0/ge = e\right\}$ with e identity component of V

In this theory, it can be proved existence and unicity of geodesics given by :

$$\delta(x, y) = \left(\sum_{k=1}^{r}\log^2 \lambda_k(x, y)\right)^{1/2} \tag{84}$$

$\left\{\lambda_k(x, y)\right\}_{k=1}^{r}$ eigen-values of $P(y)^{-1/2}x$

with $\begin{cases} P : \text{quadratic form of Jordan Algebra } V \\ \log^2 \lambda_k(x, y) : \text{angles (contracted by semi-group } S_\Omega) \end{cases}$

Let Ω be an open convex cone in a Euclidean vector space V of dimension n, T_Ω is the tube domain : $T_\Omega = V + i\Omega = \{z = x + iy \,/\, x \in V, y \in \Omega\}$. It is a Hermitian symmetric space isomorphic to G/K where G is the group of holomorphic automorphisms of T_Ω and K is the stabilizer of $i.e$ in G. In the case of $V = Sym(n, R)$, the tube domain is the Siegel upper half plane $T_{\Omega Sym}$, the group G is the Symplectic group $Sp_n R$ and K is the unitary group $U(n)$.

5 Bruhat-Tits Space and Mangoldt-Cartan-Hadamard Manifold

Cases studied in chapters 2, 3 & 4 can be encapsulated in a more general theory of Mangoldt-Cartan-Hadamard Manifold and more precisely Bruhat-Tits space. We will develop in this chapter this theory to underline interactions with previous ones.

With respect to the distance metric δ (arising from the previously defined Riemannian trace metric) on space of symmetric positive definite matrices, the space is a Bruhat-Tits space [9][16], and the unique midpoint of any two points is given by their geometric mean $A \circ B$.

$$\delta(A, B) = \left(\sum_{i=1}^{n} \log^2 \lambda_i \right) \text{ with } \det\!\left(AB^{-1} - \lambda I\right) = 0$$

$$\delta(A, B) = 2\delta(A, A \circ B) = 2\delta(B, A \circ B) \tag{85}$$

$$\delta\!\left(C^T AC, C^T BC\right) = \delta(A, B) = \delta(A^{-1}, B^{-1})$$

A Bruhat-Tits space is a space with complete metric that satisfies the semi-parallelogram law: $\begin{cases} \forall x_1, x_2 \in X \quad \exists z \in X \text{ such that:} \\ \delta(x_1, x_2)^2 + 4\delta(x, z)^2 \le 2\delta(x, x_1)^2 + 2\delta(x, x_2)^2 \quad \forall x \in X \end{cases}$ $\qquad$ (86)

This inequality is motivated by the parallelogram law, in planar geometry which states that, using the Euclidean distance d^2, the sum of the squared lengths of the diagonals equals the sum of the squared lengths of the sides of the parallelogram :

$$d_2(x_1, x_2)^2 + d_2(x, x_3)^2 = 2d_2(x, x_1)^2 + 2d_2(x, x_2)^2 \tag{87}$$

Let z the midpoint between x_1 and x_2. Since $2.d_2(x, z) = d_2(x, x_3)$, substitution in the parallelogram law yields:

$$d_2(x_1, x_2)^2 + 4d_2(x, z)^2 = 2d_2(x, x_1)^2 + 2d_2(x, x_2)^2 \tag{88}$$

Generalizing this to Bruhat-Tits space (X, δ) and allowing for a weak inequality, (X, δ) is said to satisfy the semi-parallelogram law given by (35). It is a theorem of P. Jordan and J. von Neumann that each normed space satisfying parallelogram law is Euclidean. In fact, $\langle a, b \rangle = \dfrac{\|a + b\|^2 - \|a - b\|^2}{4}$ is a positive definite symmetric bilinear form with $\|a\| = \sqrt{\langle a, a \rangle}$. Therefore, the Euclidean spaces are the normed spaces satisfying the semi-parallelogram law.

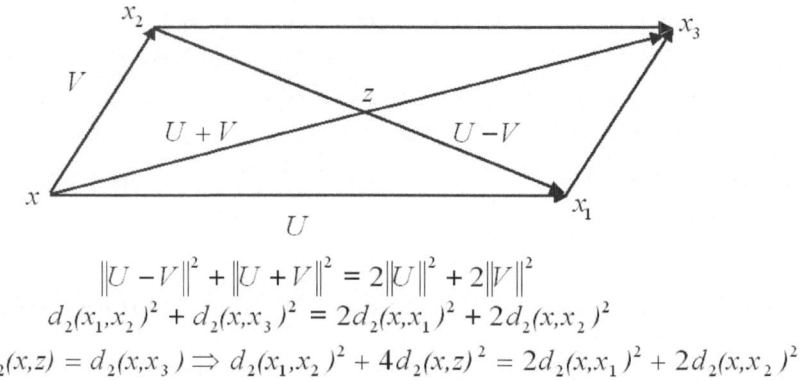

$$\|U - V\|^2 + \|U + V\|^2 = 2\|U\|^2 + 2\|V\|^2$$
$$d_2(x_1,x_2)^2 + d_2(x,x_3)^2 = 2d_2(x,x_1)^2 + 2d_2(x,x_2)^2$$
$$2.d_2(x,z) = d_2(x,x_3) \Rightarrow d_2(x_1,x_2)^2 + 4d_2(x,z)^2 = 2d_2(x,x_1)^2 + 2d_2(x,x_2)^2$$

Fig. 4. Parallelogram Law

Bruhat-Tits spaces arise from a much larger class of Riemannian manifolds, the Cartan-Hadamard manifolds, which are complete simply connected Riemannian manifold with semi-negative curvature [10]. A Cartan-Hadamard Manifold is contractible (it has the homotopy type of a single point) and, ***between two points, there is a unique geodesic segment.*** For closed surfaces of non-positive curvature, Von Mangoldt and Hadamard proved the the exponential map at a point is a covering map, so that the universal covering space of the manifold is R^2. This result was generalized by Elie Cartan and is usually referred to in this form as the Mangoldt-Cartan-Hadamard theorem.

The midpoint property of the geometric mean can be established independently of the theory of Bruhat-Tits spaces. Geometric mean can be defined as solution of the Riccati Equation: $XA^{-1}X = B$ or by Frechet definition [22] :

$$\arg \underset{R}{Min} H(R) \text{ with } H(R) = \left\|\log\left(A^{-1/2}.R..A^{-1/2}\right)\right\|^2 + \left\|\log\left(B^{-1/2}.R..B^{-1/2}\right)\right\|^2 \quad (89)$$
$$\Rightarrow \nabla H(R) = R\left[\log\left(A^{-1/2}.R..A^{-1/2}\right) + \log\left(B^{-1/2}.R..B^{-1/2}\right)\right] = 0$$

The Geometric mean is then given by:

$$A \circ B = A^{1/2}\left(A^{-1/2}BA^{-1/2}\right)^{1/2}A^{1/2} \text{ with } A^{1/2} = e^{\frac{1}{2}\log A} \text{ and } e^A = \sum_{n=0}^{\infty}\frac{A^n}{n!} \quad (90)$$

We can also recover this geometric mean from Riccati equation. In scalar case, geometric mean of a,b>0 satisfies for x>=0 : $x = \sqrt{ab} \Leftrightarrow x^2 = ab \Leftrightarrow xa^{-1}x = b$ (91)

The last « symmetrized » version is suitable for generalization to noncommutative settings : the geometric mean is the unique solution of $xa^{-1}x = b$, if the unique solution exists. We define a group equipped with the operation $x \bullet y = xy^{-1}x$:

$$xa^{-1}x = b \Leftrightarrow x \bullet a = b \Leftrightarrow x = a \circ b \quad (92)$$

To solve $x \bullet e = a$, we need $xex = x^2 = e$ to have a unique solution. Every element must have a unique square root : $e \circ a = a^{1/2}$ (93)

We can extend this approach for Matrix Geometric Mean between two matrices :

$$XA^{-1}X = B \Rightarrow A^{-1/2}(XA^{-1/2}A^{-1/2}X)A^{-1/2} = A^{-1/2}BA^{-1/2}$$
$$\Rightarrow (A^{-1/2}XA^{-1/2})(A^{-1/2}XA^{-1/2}) = A^{-1/2}BA^{-1/2} \tag{94}$$
$$\Rightarrow A^{-1/2}XA^{-1/2} = \left(A^{-1/2}BA^{-1/2}\right)^{1/2}$$
$$\Rightarrow X = A^{1/2}\left(A^{-1/2}BA^{-1/2}\right)^{1/2}A^{1/2} = A \circ B$$

This definition satisfy the following properties:

$$\begin{cases} A \circ A = A \text{ Idempotence}, (A \circ B)^{-1} = A^{-1} \circ B^{-1} \text{ Inversion} \\ A \circ B = B \circ A \text{ Commutativity} \\ \Gamma_C(A) \circ \Gamma_C(B) = \Gamma_C(A \circ B) \text{ with } \Gamma_C(A) = C^T A C \\ 2\left(A^{-1} + B^{-1}\right)^{-1} \le A \circ B \le (A+B)/2 \end{cases} \tag{95}$$

We can also defined the unique geodesic in this space joining the two matrices A and B. If $t \to \gamma(t)$ is the geodesic between A and B , where $t \in [0,1]$ is such that $\delta(A, \gamma(t)) = t.\delta(A, B)$, then the mean of A and B is the matrix $A \circ B = \gamma(1/2)$. The geodesic parameterized by the length as previously is given by::

$$\gamma(t) = A^{1/2}\left(A^{-1/2}BA^{-1/2}\right)^t A^{1/2} \text{ with } 0 \le t \le 1 \tag{96}$$
$$\gamma(0) = A \ , \ \gamma(1) = B \text{ and } \gamma(1/2) = A \circ B$$

We have seen that for SPD matrices, we have to consider the geometric mean. To convince reader by intuition , that $(R_1 + R_2)/2$ is not a well adapted mean of two SPD matrices R_1 and R_2, consider Multivariate Gaussian model case. We have seen that variance of R is proportional to R, that means to take into account variance of $(R_1 + R_2)/2$, we should consider the inverse matrix that depends on $\det[(R_1 + R_2)/2]^{-1}$ that could have a bad behavior. Inversely, metric proposed by Rao $ds^2 = Tr\left(\left(R^{-1}(dR)\right)^2\right)$ takes into account variance of R to build a robust metric invariant by non singular parameters transformation : $w = \Theta(\theta) \Rightarrow ds_w^2 = ds_\theta^2$ \tag{97}

We have seen that we have to compute the geometric mean $A \circ B = A^{1/2}\left(A^{-1/2}BA^{-1/2}\right)^{1/2}A^{1/2}$. Then, we have to compute square root of positive definite matrix. A first approach could be to use the Denman-Beabers iteration for the square root of a matrix A with no negative eigen-values :

$$X_{k+1} = \begin{bmatrix} 0 & Y_{k+1} \\ Z_{k+1} & 0 \end{bmatrix} = \frac{1}{2}\left(\begin{bmatrix} 0 & Y_k \\ Z_k & 0 \end{bmatrix} + \begin{bmatrix} 0 & Z_k^{-1} \\ Y_k^{-1} & 0 \end{bmatrix} \right) \text{with } X_0 = \begin{bmatrix} 0 & A \\ I & 0 \end{bmatrix} \tag{98}$$

The iteration has the properties that : $\underset{k \to \infty}{Lim} X_k = \begin{bmatrix} 0 & A^{1/2} \\ A^{-1/2} & 0 \end{bmatrix}$ \tag{99}

To avoid matrix inversion, Schulz iteration can be used :

$$X_{k+1} = \begin{bmatrix} 0 & Y_{k+1} \\ Z_{k+1} & 0 \end{bmatrix} = \frac{1}{2}X_k(3I - X_k^2) \tag{100}$$

We can also used Schur Method for Matrix Square root introduced by Björk [20]. Based on Schur decomposition of A, $Q^+AQ = T$ (T upper triangular), uses a recurrence to obtain an upper triangular U such that $U^2 = T$. A square root of A is given by:

$$X = QUQ^+ \tag{101}$$

For matrix logarithm, when matrix A is near the identity matrix several methods can be used to approximate $\log A$, that is, without any nontrivial transformation of A. For example, we can truncate the Taylor series :

$$\log(I + W) = -W - W^2/2 - W^3/3 - ... \text{ where } W = I - A \tag{102}$$

Alternatively, we can use Padé approximations. Unfortunately, if A is not near the identity then these methods either do not converge or converge so slowly that they are not practical to use. The standard way of dealing with the problem is to use the square root operator repeatedly to bring A near the identity : $\log A = 2^k \log A^{1/2^k}$ (103) where square root function for matrices is given in previous section. As k increases, $A^{1/2^k} \to I$, so for sufficiently large k, we can apply a direct method to $A^{1/2^k}$. This procedure for the logarithm was introduced by Kenney and Laub.

We have mainly considered Bruhat-Tits space for metric space, but recently, Constantin C. Niculescu [23] has extended Mazur-Ulam Theorem, previously defined for normed linear space, in the framework of metric spaces and has defined Mazur-Ulam space. The Mazur-Ulam Theorem is based on property that a bijective isometry to T to preserve midpoints of line segments.

Mazur-Ulam Theorem:
Every bijective isometry $T : E \to E$ acting on a real normed linear space is an affine map : $T(\lambda x + (1 - \lambda)y) = \lambda T(x) + (1 - \lambda)T(y)$ (104)

As generalization, Mazur-Ulam space for metric space can be defined by :
Mazur-Ulam Space Definition :
A Mazur-Ulam space is any metric space $M = (M,d)$ *on which there is a given pairing* $\bullet : M \times M \to M$ *with the following properties*
$A \bullet A = A$ *(idempotence)*
$A \bullet B = B \bullet A$ *(commutativity)*
$d(A,B) = 2d(A, A \bullet B) = 2d(B, A \bullet B)$ *(midpoint property)*
$T(A \bullet B) = T(A) \bullet T(B)$ *for all bijective isometries T (transformation property)*

Suppose that $M = (M,d)$ is a metric space such that for every pair (A,B) of points of M there exists a bijective isometry $G_{(A,B)}$ from M to itself with following properties :

$$G_{(A,B)}A = B \text{ and } G_{(A,B)}B = A \tag{105}$$

$G_{(A,B)}$ has a unique fixed point Z (denoted $A \bullet B$) and $d(G_{(A,B)}X, X) = 2d(X,Z)$ (106)

For space of symmetric definite positive matrices, bijective isometry is given by :

$$G_{(A,B)}X = (A \bullet B)X^{-1}(A \bullet B) \text{ with } A \bullet B = A^{1/2}\left(A^{-1/2}BA^{-1/2}\right)^{1/2}A^{1/2} \tag{107}$$

This is a generalization of isometry for metric space $\left(R_+^*, \delta(x,y) = \left| \log \dfrac{x}{y} \right|, a \bullet b = \sqrt{ab} \right)$

with $\quad G_{(a,b)}x = \sqrt{ab}\ x^{-1}\sqrt{ab}$ \hfill (108)

We can also compare with normed vector space $\left(R, \delta(x,y) = |x-y|, a \bullet b = \dfrac{a+b}{2} \right)$

where the reflection is given by : $G_{(a,b)}x = \left(\dfrac{a+b}{2} \right) \cdot x + \left(\dfrac{a+b}{2} \right)$ \hfill (109)

Obviously, $A^{1/2}\left(A^{-1/2}BA^{-1/2}\right)^{1/2}A^{1/2}$ is the only fixed point because :

$$CX^{-1}C = X \Rightarrow \left(X^{-1/2}CX^{-1/2}\right)\left(X^{-1/2}CX^{-1/2}\right) = I \underset{\text{unicity of square root}}{\Rightarrow} X^{-1/2}CX^{-1/2} = I \Rightarrow X = C \quad (110)$$

and $\quad d\left((A\bullet B)X^{-1}(A\bullet B), X\right) = d\left((A\bullet B)X^{-1}(A\bullet B)X^{-1}, I\right) = 2d\left(X,(A\bullet B)\right)$ \hfill (111)

due to trace property of :

$$d(X,(A\bullet B)) = \left(\sum_{k=1}^{n} \log^2 \lambda_i \right) \quad \text{with } \{\lambda_i\}_{i=1}^{n} \text{ eigenvalues of } (A\bullet B)X^{-1} \quad (112)$$

For space of Symmetric Positive Definite matrices, the analogue of $\lambda x + (1-\lambda)y$ is :

$$A \bullet_\lambda B = A^{1/2}\left(A^{-1/2}BA^{-1/2}\right)^\lambda A^{1/2} \quad (113)$$

the Mazur-Ulam spaces constitute a natural framework for a generalized theory of convexity, where the role of arithmetic mean is played by a midpoint pairing : f is called $(\bullet_1, \bullet_2)$-convex if $f(X \bullet_1 Y) \leq f(X) \bullet_2 f(Y)$ \hfill (114)

For space of symmetric positive definite matrices, an affine function is given by:

$$f = \log \det \quad (115)$$

and is closely related to entropy : $Entropy = -\log\det(R) + cste$

6 Mean of N Hermitian Positive Definite Matrices

In previous chapter 5, we have defined geometric mean of 2 symmetric positive define matrices. We would like to extend this definition to N matrices by defining a barycenter on this space.

Different authors have tried to extend this notion of Geometric means for a set of N Symmetric Positive definite matrices.

For 3 matrices, D. Petz has proposed a symmetrization procedures by a Cauchy sequences with respect to the geodesic distance δ. The space is complete with respect to this metric and the three sequences (of interleaved triangles) have a common limit points :

$$
\begin{aligned}
&A \circ B = A^{1/2}\left(A^{-1/2}BA^{-1/2}\right)^{1/2}A^{1/2} \\
&\begin{cases} A_1 = A,\ B_1 = B,\ C_1 = C \\ A_{n+1} = A_n \circ B_n,\ B_{n+1} = A_n \circ C_n,\ C_{n+1} = B_n \circ C_n \end{cases} \\
&G(A,B,C) = \underset{n\to\infty}{Lim}\, A_n = \underset{n\to\infty}{Lim}\, B_n = \underset{n\to\infty}{Lim}\, C_n
\end{aligned}
\quad (116)
$$

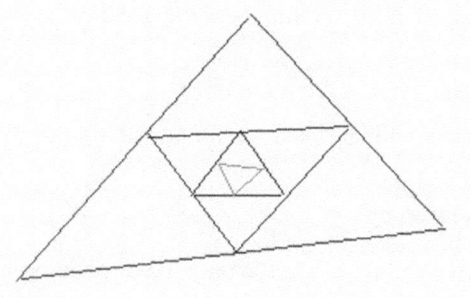

Fig. 5. Symmetrization procedures with Cauchy sequences

For the extension to N matrices of geometric means, we can observe that naïve extension cannot be applied due to the following limitations:

1) $(A_1 A_2 ... A_N)^{1/N}$ is not positive definite if A_i don't commute

2) $e^{(\log A_1 + \log A_2)/2}$ is not monotone

because $A \geq B \Rightarrow e^A \geq e^B$ is not true

$$(117)$$

T. Ando has proposed that the Geometric Mean of 3 matrices should verify the following properties from P1 to P9 :

P1: If A, B and C commute then $G(A, B, C) = (ABC)^{1/3}$ and $G(A, A, A) = A$

P2: $G(\alpha A, \beta B, \gamma C) = (\alpha \beta \gamma)^{1/3} G(A, B, C)$ with $\alpha, \beta, \gamma > 0$

P3: $\forall \pi(A, B, C)$ permutation of (A, B, C)
then $G(A, B, C) = G(\pi(A, B, C))$

P4: If $A \geq A_0, B \geq B_0, C \geq C_0 \Rightarrow G(A, B, C) \geq G(A_0, B_0, C_0)$

P5: $\{A_n\}, \{B_n\}, \{C_n\}$ monotone decreasing sequences $\Rightarrow \{G(A_n, B_n, C_n)\} \underset{n \to \infty}{\to} G(A, B, C)$

P6: $\forall S$ inversible, $G(S^* A S, S^* B S, S^* C S) = S^* G(A, B, C) S$

P7: $G(\lambda A_1 + (1 - \lambda) A_2, \lambda B_1 + (1 - \lambda) B_2, \lambda C_1 + (1 - \lambda) C_2) \geq$
$\lambda G(A_1, B_1, C_1) + (1 - \lambda) G(A_2, B_2, C_2)$ with $0 < \lambda < 1$

P8: $G(A, B, C) = G(A^{-1}, B^{-1}, C^{-1})^{-1}$

P9: $\det G(A, B, C) = (\det A. \det B. \det C)^{1/3}$

$$(118)$$

T. Ando [4] has proposed a definition for geometric mean of N positive definite matrices by mean of an iterative sequence that converges to same limit for all components :

$$G(A_1, A_2) = A_1^{1/2} (A_1^{-1/2} A_2 A_1^{-1/2})^{1/2} A_1^{1/2}$$

for k = 3,..., N do
$\left\{ \begin{array}{l} \{G((A_i)_{i \neq l})\}_{l=1}^{k+1} \text{ have been iteratively defined} \\ \begin{cases} A^{(1)} = (A_1, ..., A_{k+1}) \\ A^{(r+1)} = T(A^{(r)}) = (G((A_i^{(r)})_{i \neq 1}), ..., G((A_i^{(r)})_{i \neq k+1})) \end{cases}, r = 1, 2, ... \\ G(A_1, ..., A_k, A_{k+1}) = \tilde{A} \text{ with } \underset{r \to \infty}{Lim} A^{(r)} = (\tilde{A}, ..., \tilde{A}) \end{array} \right.$

$$(119)$$

In parallel, H. Kosaki has also proposed a new definition of geometric mean for N matrices based on the following definition of Geometric Mean for 2 matrices :

$$G(A,B) = \frac{1}{\pi} \int_0^1 \left(\lambda B^{-1} + (1-\lambda)A^{-1}\right)^{-1} \left(\lambda^{-1/2}.(1-\lambda)^{-1/2}\right) d\lambda \Rightarrow G(A,B) = A \circ B = A^{1/2}\left(A^{-1/2}BA^{-1/2}\right)^{1/2} A^{1/2}$$

because $\displaystyle\int_0^1 \frac{\lambda^{\alpha-1}(1-\lambda)^{\beta-1}}{\left(\lambda a^{-1} + (1-\lambda)b^{-1}\right)^{\alpha+\beta}} d\lambda = \frac{\Gamma(\alpha)\Gamma(\beta)}{\Gamma(\alpha+\beta)} a^\alpha b^\beta$ (for $\alpha = \beta = 1/2$)

Then, he has extended this definition for N matrices :

$$G_K^+(A_1,...,A_k) = \frac{1}{\Gamma(1/k)^k} \int_{\Delta_k} \left(\sum_{j=1}^k \lambda_j A_j^{-1}\right)^{-1} \left(\prod_{j=1}^k \lambda_j^{1/k-1}\right) d\lambda_1...d\lambda_k \text{ with } \Delta_k = \left\{(\lambda_1,...,\lambda_k)/\lambda_k \geq 0, \sum_{j=1}^k \lambda_j = 1\right\}$$

But this definition does not verify properties P8 and P9 that have been proposed by T. Ando.

Alternatively, we propose an iterative "gradient" algorithm based on Jacobi Field and Exponential Map. For Karcher Barycenter, the Jacobi Field is equal to zero (see M. Arnaudon works [27]). The Jacobi Field for Barycenter is equal to the sum of tangent vectors to all geodesics (from barycentre to each point). We have already seen that Geodesic between 2 points A and B is given by:

$$\begin{cases} \gamma(t) = A^{1/2}\left(A^{-1/2}BA^{-1/2}\right)^t A^{1/2} \\ \gamma(0) = A \ , \ \gamma(1) = B \text{ and } \gamma(1/2) = A \circ B \end{cases} \tag{120}$$

We can then compute Jacobi Field for point A (at $t=0$) to N points B_k :

$$\gamma_k(t) = A^{1/2}\left(A^{-1/2}B_kA^{-1/2}\right)^t A^{1/2} = A^{1/2}e^{t\log\left(A^{-1/2}B_kA^{-1/2}\right)}A^{1/2}$$
$$\left.\frac{d\gamma_k(t)}{dt}\right|_{t=0} = A^{1/2}\log\left(A^{-1/2}B_kA^{-1/2}\right)A^{1/2} \tag{121}$$

The summation of all these vectors should be equal to zero:

$$G_A = \sum_{k=1}^N \frac{d\gamma_k(t)}{dt}\Big|_{t=0} = 0 \Rightarrow G_A = A^{1/2}\left(\sum_{k=1}^N \log\left(A^{-1/2}B_kA^{-1/2}\right)\right)A^{1/2} = 0 \tag{122}$$

Then, the barycentre A of the N matrices B_k should verify :

$$\sum_{k=1}^N \log\left(A^{-1/2}B_kA^{-1/2}\right) = 0 \tag{123}$$

We can deduce an iterative "gradient" algorithm to compute the barycentre with exponential map:

$$A_{t+1} = \Gamma_{A_t,G_{A_t}}(-\varepsilon) = \exp_{A_t}(-\varepsilon G_{A_t}) = A_t^{1/2}e^{-\varepsilon\left(A_t^{-1/2}G_{A_t}A_t^{-1/2}\right)}A_t^{1/2} \tag{124}$$

Finally, Karcher Barycenter is given by following gradient algorithm:

$$A_{t+1} = A_t^{1/2}e^{-\varepsilon\left(\sum_{k=1}^N \log\left(A_t^{-1/2}B_kA_t^{-1/2}\right)\right)}A_t^{1/2} \tag{125}$$

In the following figure, the property on Jacobi field is illustrated for Barycenter:

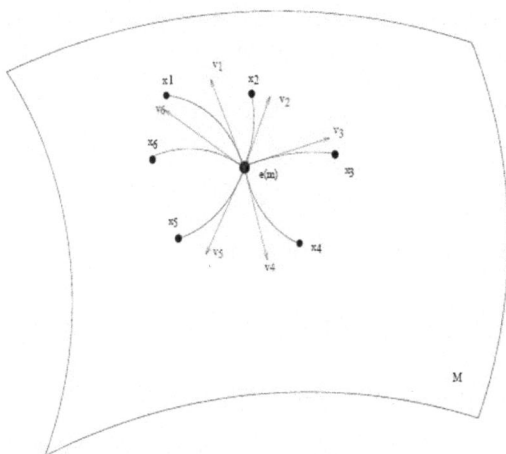

Fig. 6. Jacobi Field (tangent vectors for each Geodesic) for Karcher Barycenter of N points on a manifold is equal to zero (see work of Marc Arnaudon [27])

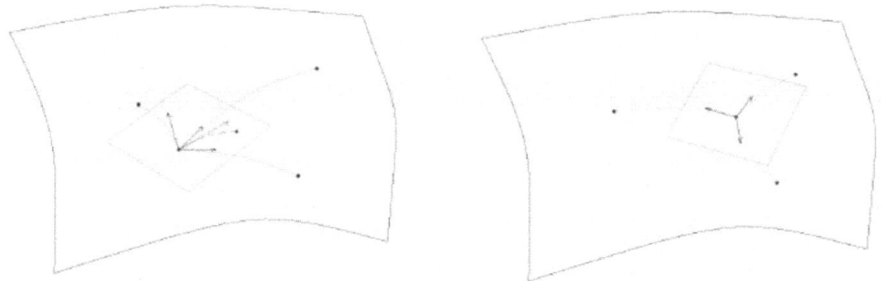

Fig. 7. (at left) Initiation, (at right) convergence of gradient flow (127) to the karcher barycentre

Recently, K.T. Sturm has developed an other approach based on iterative barycentre method. A natural way to define the « expectation » E(Y) of a random variable Y is to use generalizations of the law of large numbers.

Given any sequence $\{B_k\}_{k=1}^n$ of points, he defines a new sequence $\{S_k\}_{k=1}^n$ of points by induction on n as follow (inductive mean) :

$$S_1 = B_1 \quad \text{and} \quad S_n = S_{n-1} \bullet_{1/n} B_n = S_{n-1}^{1/2} \left(S_{n-1}^{-1/2} B_n S_{n-1}^{-1/2} \right)^{1/n} S_{n-1}^{1/2}$$

that strongly depend on permutations but $E\left(\delta^2 (E(B_1), S_n) \right) \le \frac{1}{n} V(B_1)$

This approach is a natural extension of scalar case :

$$s_1 = b_1 \quad \text{and} \quad s_n = s_{n-1} \bullet_{1/n} b_n = \left(1 - \frac{1}{n} \right) s_{n-1} + \frac{1}{n} b_n$$

7 Information Geometry and Calabi Flow: Geodesics in the Space of Kähler Potentials

It could be also interesting to define geodesics in space of Kähler potentials. This kind of approach has been studied by Donaldson that has conjectured that the space of Kähler potentials is a metric space which is path connected with respect to the Weil-Peterson metric that has been defined by Mabuchi. The Weil-Peterson metric is defined in the space of Kähler potential :

$$H = \left\{ \phi / g_{\alpha\bar\beta}^{\phi} = g_{\alpha\bar\beta}^{0} + \frac{\partial^2 \phi}{\partial z_\alpha \partial z_{\bar\beta}} > 0 \right\} \tag{126}$$

For any tangent vector $\psi \in T_\phi H$ (real valued function), its length is defined by :

$$\|\psi\|^2 = \int \psi^2 d\mu_\phi \tag{127}$$

The geodesic equation for this metric is given by : $\ddot\phi(t) - g_\phi^{\alpha\bar\beta} \dfrac{\partial \dot\phi}{\partial z_\alpha} \dfrac{\partial \dot\phi}{\partial z_{\bar\beta}} = 0 \tag{128}$

Semmes has first observed that one can complexified the $t = z_{n+1}$ variable, and reduce the geodesic equation to an homogeneous complex Monge-Ampere equation :

$$\det\left(g_{i\bar j}^0 + \frac{\partial^2 \phi}{\partial z_i \partial z_{\bar j}} \right)_{(n+1)\times(n+1)} = 0 \tag{129}$$

This has been considered by Sturm for $\overline{M} = X \times Q$, where X is a compact Kähler manifold of dimension n, and $Q = \left\{ w \in C / 1 \le |w| \le e \right\}$. Let $\phi : [0,1] \to \phi(t) \in H$ be a smooth path joining $\phi(0)$ to $\phi(1)$, we can define : $\Phi : M \to R$

$$\phi(z,w) = \phi(t)(z) \text{ with } t = \log|w|$$

and the corresponding metric : $g_{i\bar j}^\Phi = g_{i\bar j}^0 + \dfrac{\partial^2 \Phi}{\partial z_i \partial \overline{z}_j} \tag{130}$

In local coordinates $\{z_i\}_{1,\dots,n}$ for X and $v = \log w$ for Q, we can write [26] :

$$\left[g_{i\bar j}^\Phi \right]_{i,j=1}^{n+1} = \begin{bmatrix} \left[g_{i\bar j}^0 + \dfrac{\partial^2 \phi}{\partial z_i \partial \overline{z}_j} \right]_{i,j=1}^n & \dfrac{1}{2} B \\ \dfrac{1}{2} B^+ & \dfrac{1}{4} \ddot\phi \end{bmatrix} \text{ with } B = \begin{bmatrix} \dfrac{\partial \dot\phi}{\partial z_1} \\ \vdots \\ \dfrac{\partial \dot\phi}{\partial z_n} \end{bmatrix} \tag{131}$$

This condition on volume $\Omega_\Phi^{n+1} = 0$ is equivalent to geodesic equation (128) and leads to volume equation:

$$\int_{X \times Q} \Omega_\Phi^{n+1} = \int_0^1 \int_X \left(\ddot\phi - |\partial\dot\phi|^2 \right) \omega_\phi^n dt = \int_0^1 \frac{d}{dt} \left(\int_X \dot\phi \omega_\phi^n \right) dt = \int_X \dot\phi(1) \omega_{\phi(1)}^n - \int_X \dot\phi(0) \omega_{\phi(0)}^n \tag{132}$$

with $\Omega_\Phi^{n+1} = \dfrac{1}{4} \left(\ddot\phi - |\partial\dot\phi|^2 \right) \omega_\phi^n \wedge \left(\dfrac{i}{2} dv \wedge d\overline{v} \right)$

This Donaldson conjecture has been verified by Calabi and Chen, who have proved that the space is a path length space of non-positive curvature and it is geodesically convex in the sense that any two points are joined by a unique path, which is always length minimizing and of class $C^{1,1}$. Suppose ϕ_A, ϕ_B and ϕ_C are 3 points in the space of Kähler potentials and P_λ is a geodesic interpolation point of ϕ_B and ϕ_C for $0 \le \lambda \le 1$, the following inequality holds :

$$d(\phi_A, P_\lambda)^2 \le (1 - \lambda)d(\phi_A, \phi_B)^2 + \lambda d(\phi_A, \phi_C)^2 - \lambda(1 - \lambda)d(\phi_B, \phi_C)^2 \tag{133}$$

In this framework, Calabi has proposed to used a fourth order heat equation to prove the existence of extremal Kähler metrics. This Intrinsic Geometric Flow is called Calabi Flow and is deduced from a functional minimization that depends on the square of the scalar curvature :

$$\Theta(g) = \int_M R^2(g)dV(g) \tag{134}$$

Solution is defined as steady state of the PDE equation : $\dfrac{\partial \phi}{\partial t} = R_\phi - \overline{R}$ $\qquad$ (135)

with ϕ Kähler potential associated to the Kähler metric $g_{i\bar{j}} = \dfrac{\partial^2 \phi}{\partial z^i \partial z^{\bar{j}}}$, R_ϕ scalar curvature and $\overline{R}$ its mean value on the Manifold : $\overline{R} = \dfrac{\displaystyle\int_M R(g)dV(g)}{\displaystyle\int_M dV(g)}$ $\qquad$ (136)

This flow preserves the volume and the Kähler class of the metric. Critical points of the flow are called extremal metrics. The functional (134) decreases monotonically along the Calabi Flow. Calabi has proved that, given any two Kähler potentials ϕ_1 and ϕ_2 in H and a smooth curve $C(t)$ in H connecting them, the length of this curve strictly decreases under Calabi flow (135) unless this curve in H represents a path of holomorphic transformations. More specifically, if $\phi(t)$ $(0 \le t < 1)$ is a curve in H, and L is the length of this curve, and suppose $\phi(s,t)$ is the family of curves under the Calabi Flow (135), then: $L(s) = \displaystyle\int_0^1 \left(\int_V \left(\frac{\partial \phi(s,t)}{\partial t} \right)^2 .dg(s,t) \right)^{\frac{1}{2}} .dt$ $\qquad$ (137)

where $g(s,t)$ is the Kähler metric corresponding to the Kähler potential $\phi(s,t)$ and D is the Lichernowicz operator.

$$\frac{dL(s)}{ds} = -\int_0^1 \left(\int_V \left| D\frac{\partial\phi}{\partial t} \right|^2_{\phi(s,t)} .dg(s,t) \right) \left(\int_V \left| \frac{\partial\phi}{\partial t} \right|^2 dg(s,t) \right)^{-\frac{1}{2}} .dt$$

$$\text{with } Df = \sum_{\alpha,\beta=1}^n \left(\sum_{\lambda,\mu=1}^n g_{\lambda\bar{\mu}} \frac{\partial}{\partial\bar{z}_\beta} \left(g^{\lambda\bar{\mu}} \frac{\partial f}{\partial\bar{z}_\mu} \right) \right) dz^\alpha \otimes dz^\beta$$

If all geodesics are smooth, then the extremal Kähler metric is unique up to some holomorphic automorphisms.

We will illustrate Calabi flow action for Complex Autoregressive Model where the gradient flow (135) will act on Entropy defined as Kähler potential. Calabi Flow is given by :

$$\sum_{i=1}^{n-1}(n-i).\frac{\partial \ln\left|1-\left|\mu_i\right|^2\right|}{\partial t}+n.\frac{\partial \ln\left[\pi.e.P_0\right]}{\partial t}=-2.\left[\sum_{i=1}^{n}\frac{1}{n-i}+\frac{1}{n}\right] \qquad (138)$$

We then deduce the asymptotic behaviour of coordinates submitted to Calabi Flow :

$$\frac{\partial \ln\left(1-\left|\mu_k\right|^2\right)}{\partial t}=-\frac{2}{(n-k)^2} \text{ and } \frac{\partial \ln P_0}{\partial t}=-\frac{2}{n^2} \qquad (139)$$

From which, we obtain the behaviour of each term of Information metric :

$$1-\left|\mu_i(t)\right|^2=\left(1-\left|\mu_i(0)\right|^2\right)e^{-\frac{2t}{(n-i)^2}} \text{ and } P_0(t)=P_0(0)e^{-\frac{2t}{n^2}} \qquad (140)$$

$$ds_n^2(t)=n.\left(\frac{dP_0}{P_0(t)}\right)^2+\sum_{i=1}^{n-1}(n-i)\frac{\left|d\mu_i\right|^2}{\left(1-\left|\mu_i(t)\right|^2\right)^2}=n\left(\frac{dP_0}{P_0(0)}\right)^2 e^{\frac{4t}{n^2}}+\sum_{i=1}^{n-1}(n-i)\frac{\left|d\mu_i\right|^2}{\left(1-\left|\mu_i(0)\right|^2\right)^2}e^{\frac{4t}{(n-i)^2}} \qquad (141)$$

Before Calabi Flow, first of Intrinsic Geometric Flow that has been studied is Ricci Flow. Historical Root of Ricci flow can be found in Hilbert work on General Relativity, where the Minimal Action Principal is defined with tool of Calculus of variations. Einstein Equation was derived by Hilbert from Functional Minimisation, where the "Hilbert Action" S is defined as the integral of scalar Curvature R on the Manifold M^n:

$$S(g)=\int_{M^n}R.\sqrt{\det(g)}.d^n x=\int_{M^n}R.dV(g) \qquad (142)$$

with volume $:V(g)=\int_{M^n}dV(g)$ and $R=\sum_{\mu}\sum_{\nu}g^{\mu\nu}.R_{\mu\nu}$ \qquad (143)

the scalar curvature defined by mean of Ricci Tensor $R_{\mu\nu}$ and the metric tensor $g^{-1}=\left[g^{ij}\right]$. Fundamental theorem of Hilbert said that for $n\geq 3$, $S(g)$ is minimal with $V(g)=cste$ if $R(g)$ is constant and g is an Einstein metric : $R_{ij}=\frac{1}{n}R.g_{ij}$ \qquad (144)

So the more natural geometric flow that converges to Einstein metric is given by :
$\frac{\partial g_{ij}}{\partial t}=2\left[-R_{ij}+\frac{1}{n}Rg_{ij}\right]$, but unfortunately this flow exhibits some convergence problems in finite time. That the main raison why R. Hamilton has introduced the following Ricci flow : $\frac{\partial g_{ij}}{\partial t}=2\left[-R_{ij}+\frac{1}{n}r.g_{ij}\right]$ with $r=\left(\int_{M^n}Rd\eta\right)/\left(\int_{M^n}d\eta\right)$ \qquad (145)

where R has been replaced by r the mean scalar curvature on the Manifold or equivalently this one after coordinate change : $\frac{\partial g_{ij}}{\partial t}=-2.R_{ij}$ $\forall i,j$ \qquad (146)

This flow can be interpreted as Fourier Heat Operator acting on metric g, by using isothermal coordinates introduced by G. Darmois. In such local isothermal coordinates system $\{x^i\}_{i=1,2}$, following relations are cancelled : $F^k = \Delta_g x^i = -\sum_{\lambda,\mu} g^{\lambda\mu} \Gamma^k_{\lambda\mu}$

With Laplace-Beltrami operator. : $\Delta_g f = \sum_{\lambda,\mu} g^{\lambda\mu}\left(\partial^2_{\lambda\mu} f - \sum_k \Gamma^k_{\lambda\mu}\partial_k f\right)$ \hfill (147)

More specifically A. Lichnerowicz has proved that we can expressed Ricci tensor as

$R_{ij} = -G_{ij} - L_{ij}$ with $G_{ij} = \frac{1}{2}\sum_{\lambda\mu} g^{\lambda\mu}\partial^2_{\lambda\mu} g_{ij} + H_{ij}$ and $L_{ij} = \frac{1}{2}\left(\sum_\mu g_{i\mu}\partial_j F^\mu + \sum_\mu g_{j\mu}\partial_i F^\mu\right)$

Then in isothermal coordinates, we have : $-2.R_{ij} = \sum_k \sum_l g^{kl} \cdot \frac{\partial^2 g_{ij}}{\partial x^k \partial x^l} + Q_{ij}\left(g^{-1},\partial g\right)\cdot$

So, Ricci Flow can be interpreted as a Diffusion Equation action on metric g :

$$\frac{\partial g_{ij}}{\partial t} = \Delta_g g_{ij} \tag{148}$$

This geometric flow has been extended in the framework of Kähler Geometry with the Kähler-Ricci Flow : $\frac{\partial g_{ij}}{\partial t} = -R_{ij} \quad \forall i,j$ \hfill (149)

If we illustrate Kähler-Ricci flow action on metric g derived from Entropy/Kähler potential in case of a Complex Autoregressive models, then we can express Kähler-Ricci flow :

$$\frac{\partial \ln\left(1-|\mu_i|^2\right)}{\partial t} = -\frac{1}{(n-i)} \text{ and } \frac{\partial \ln P_0}{\partial t} = -\frac{1}{n} \tag{150}$$

From which, we obtain the behaviour of each term of Information metric :

$$1-|\mu_i(t)|^2 = \left(1-|\mu_i(0)|^2\right)e^{-\frac{t}{(n-i)}} \text{ and } P_0(t) = P_0(0)e^{-\frac{t}{n}} \tag{151}$$

$$ds_n^2(t) = n\left(\frac{dP_0}{P_0(t)}\right)^2 + \sum_{i=1}^{n-1}(n-i)\frac{|d\mu_i|^2}{\left(1-|\mu_i(t)|^2\right)^2} = n\left(\frac{dP_0}{P_0(0)}\right)^2 e^{\frac{2t}{n}} + \sum_{i=1}^{n-1}(n-i)\frac{|d\mu_i|^2}{\left(1-|\mu_i(0)|^2\right)^2}e^{\frac{2t}{(n-i)}} \tag{152}$$

This flow has same kind of action than Calabi flow on autoregressive Kähler metric. Bakas [6] has recently proved that there is a relation between the Kähler-Ricci and Calabi Flows on Kähler manifolds of arbitrary dimension that manifests by squaring the time evolution operator. The proof is given by taking time derivative of the Kähler-Ricci Flow :

$$\frac{\partial g_{ij}}{\partial t} = -R_{ij} \Rightarrow \begin{cases} \frac{\partial^2 g_{ij}}{\partial t^2} = -\frac{\partial R_{ij}}{\partial t} \\ R_{ij} = -\frac{\partial^2 \log(\det(g))}{\partial z_i \partial z_j^*} \end{cases} \Rightarrow \begin{cases} \frac{\partial^2 g_{ij}}{\partial t^2} = -\frac{\partial^2}{\partial z_i \partial z_j^*}\left(\frac{\partial \log(\det(g))}{\partial t}\right) \\ \frac{\partial \log(\det(g))}{\partial t} = -\sum_{i,j} g^{ij} R_{ij} = -R \end{cases} \Rightarrow \frac{\partial^2 g_{ij}}{\partial t^2} = -\frac{\partial^2 R}{\partial z_i \partial z_j^*}$$

If the second derivative of the metric with respect to the Ricci time is identified with minus its first derivative to the Calabi time, the two flows are formally the same:

$\frac{\partial^2}{\partial t_R^2} = -\frac{\partial t}{\partial t_C}$. Considering the two dimensions case, and a system of conformally flat (Kähler) coordinates : $ds^2 = 2e^{\Phi(z,z^*,t)}dz.dz^*$. The only non-vanishing components of the Ricci curvature tensor is :

$$R_{zz^*} = -\frac{\partial^2 \Phi}{\partial z \partial z^*} \text{ because } \begin{cases} R_{zz^*} = -\frac{\partial^2 \log(\det(g))}{\partial z \partial z^*} \\ g_{zz^*} = e^{\Phi} \end{cases} \tag{153}$$

For the Kähler-Ricci flow :

$$\frac{\partial g_{ij}}{\partial t} = -R_{ij} \Rightarrow \frac{\partial e^{\Phi}}{\partial t} = \frac{\partial^2 \Phi}{\partial z \partial z^*} \Rightarrow e^{\Phi}\frac{\partial \Phi}{\partial t} = \frac{\partial^2 \Phi}{\partial z \partial z^*} \Rightarrow \frac{\partial \Phi}{\partial t} = \Delta\Phi \text{ with } \Delta. = e^{-\Phi}\frac{\partial^2.}{\partial z \partial z^*} \tag{154}$$

For the Calabi flow :

$$\begin{cases} \frac{\partial g_{ij}}{\partial t} = \frac{\partial^2 R}{\partial z \partial z^*} \\ R = \sum_{i,j} g^{ij} R_{ij} = -e^{-\Phi}\frac{\partial^2 \Phi}{\partial z \partial z^*} = -\Delta\Phi \end{cases} \Rightarrow \frac{\partial e^{\Phi}}{\partial t} = -\frac{\partial^2 \Delta\Phi}{\partial z \partial z^*} \Rightarrow \frac{\partial \Phi}{\partial t} - \Delta\Delta\Phi \tag{155}$$

We can observe that Kähler-Ricci and Calabi Flows (respectively of 2nd and 4th oder) are Fourier Heat Flow on Kähler potential function.

8 Conclusion and Perspectives

We have developed new tools for computation of Geometric mean of N Symmetric Positive Definite matrices for complex autoregressive models based on information geometry and Bruhat-tits metric spaces, introduced by Jacques Tits (Abel Prize 2008). Performances of associated algorithms for Doppler Imagery and Doppler detection is illustrated in the following chapter 9. This approach is new in signal processing that mainly used flat metric and normed space for the same kind of problems. Use of metric space and negative curvature space in place of normed & flat space to manipulate Symmetric Positive Definite covariance matrices could drastically improve performances of classical signal processing algorithms.

We can extend this approach by observing that intense research activity on "Metric Measure Space" theory has emerged, with works done by J.Lott, C.Villani and K.T. Sturm. Metric space is a prominent concept in many field of mathematics, with close links with optimal transport theory based on seminal Monge's papers. Metric measure space is a dense knot of high intensity between different branches of mathematics : analysis, geometry and probability. Doppler imagery problems that have been developed in our paper could be considered in the more general framework of metric measure space [33]. We have also seen that theory of large deviation, introduced by S. Varadhan (Abal Prize 2007) [34], could be explored in this context by mean of Fenchel-Legendre Transform (logarithm of cumulant generating function is Fenchel-Legendre transform of rate function related to Kullback divergence).

9 Application for High Resolution Doppler Imagery

We conclude with different results obtained on real Doppler Radar Data in HF and X bands using barycenter computation defined in previous chapters. Algorithms are tested on the following cases :

1. X-band radar monitoring of wake vortex turbulences,
2. Target detection for Coastal X-band and HF Surface Wave Radars.

These cases have previously revealed that Fourier Transform has low performances, especially for rotating radar antenna where only few complex samples are available for each radar cell (8 pulses are classically used) for Doppler Analysis.

We will use previously defined theory to apply results for complex autoregressive model to compute :

1. Rao-Siegel Distance between Toeplitz Hermitian Positive Definite Covariance matrices to estimate proximity between 2 covariance matrices
2. Karcher Barycenter by gradient flow of N Toeplitz Hermitian Positive Definite Covariance matrices to estimate Doppler ambiance in the neighbourhood.

9.1 Turbulence Monitoring for Airport Wake Vortex Hazards Mitigation

The Wake Vortices shed by an aircraft are a natural consequence of its lift. The wake flow behind an aircraft can be described by near field and far field characteristics. In the near field small vortices emerge from that vortex sheet at the wing tips and at the edges of the landing flaps. After roll-up the wake generally consists of two coherent counter-rotating swirling flows, like horizontal tornadoes, of about equal strength: the aircraft wake vortices.

When the forces which act on the aircraft are in balance, the aircraft lift and the flux of wake vertical momentum are also equal to the weight of the aircraft. We can then observe that Wake Vortex Circulation Strength (in $m^{2/}s$) is proportional to Aircraft mass and inversely proportional to Wingspan and Aircraft speed :

$$\Gamma_0 = \frac{M.g}{(\rho.V.s.B)} \begin{cases} M: Aircraft\ mass \\ V: Aircraft\ Speed \\ B: Wingspan \end{cases} \begin{cases} g: Gravitational \\ \quad acceleration \\ \rho: Air\ density \\ \Gamma_0: Root\ Circulation \\ s = \pi/4 \end{cases} \tag{156}$$

THALES radar trials have revealed radar echoes from aircraft wakes in clear air. Two mechanisms causing refractive index gradients are considered : radial density gradient in the Vortex Cores, transport of atmospheric fluid in the oval surrounding the vortices. Radar trials took place at Paris ORLY and CDG Airports. Wake Vortices have been monitored in the glide slope of landing at ILS Interception Area for Orly, perpendicular to Landing runways for CDG .

Wake Vortex tangential velocities in each roll-up generate a specific Doppler Radar signature, where turbulences is measured through different Time/Doppler slopes in Power Spectral Density, as illustrated in figure 9 .

Fig. 8. Wake Vortex Hazards shed by an aircraft

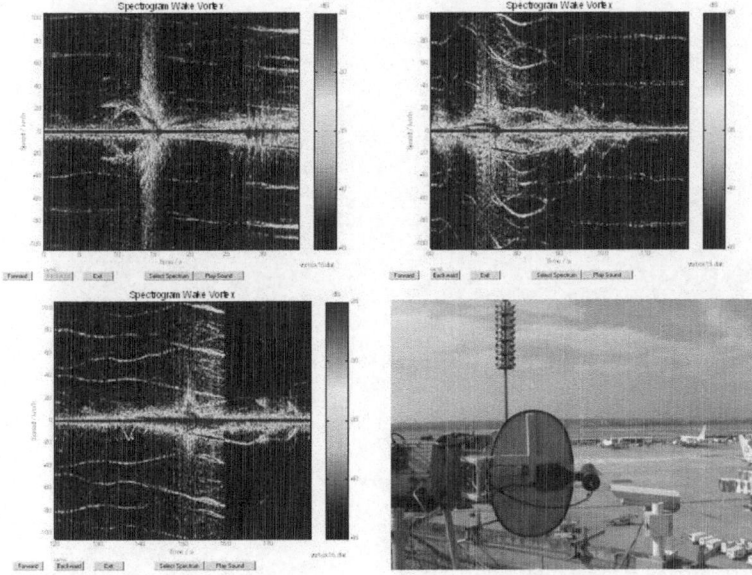

Fig. 9. Doppler/Time Wake Vortex signature (upper left and right, and lower left) with X-band Radar in antenna staring mode (lower right)

Wake vortex detection is based on Regularized High Resolution Doppler analysis : Quadratic Regularization of Burg's Autoregressive Algorithm. We have previously seen that the Information metric for complex autoregressive model can be given according to reflection coefficients :

$$ds_n^2 = n\left(\frac{dP_0}{P_0}\right)^2 + \sum_{i=1}^{n-1}(n-i)\frac{|d\mu_i|^2}{\left(1-|\mu_i|^2\right)^2} \tag{157}$$

As we have to differentiate Doppler Wake Vortex signature from intense ground clutter (signal of zero Doppler) and/or turbulent Rain Clutter (non zero mean Doppler and Doppler width from atmospheric turbulence), we don't take into account signal intensity given by P_0 but only "Doppler Shape Information" given by reflection coefficients $\{\mu_k\}_{k=1}^{n-1}$. Distance is deduce by integration :

$$M_{turn} = \sum_{k=2}^{n-1}(n-k)\left(\frac{1}{2}\ln\left(\frac{1+|\mu_k|}{1-|\mu_k|}\right)\right)^2 \qquad (158)$$

We can observe that we begin summation at index k=2 to avoid detection of atmospheric turbulence.

The value (158) is illustrated in figures 10,11 & 12. This value is representative of "richness of speed" in the radar cell compared to mono Doppler frequency spectrum (e.g. ground clutter Doppler spectrum).

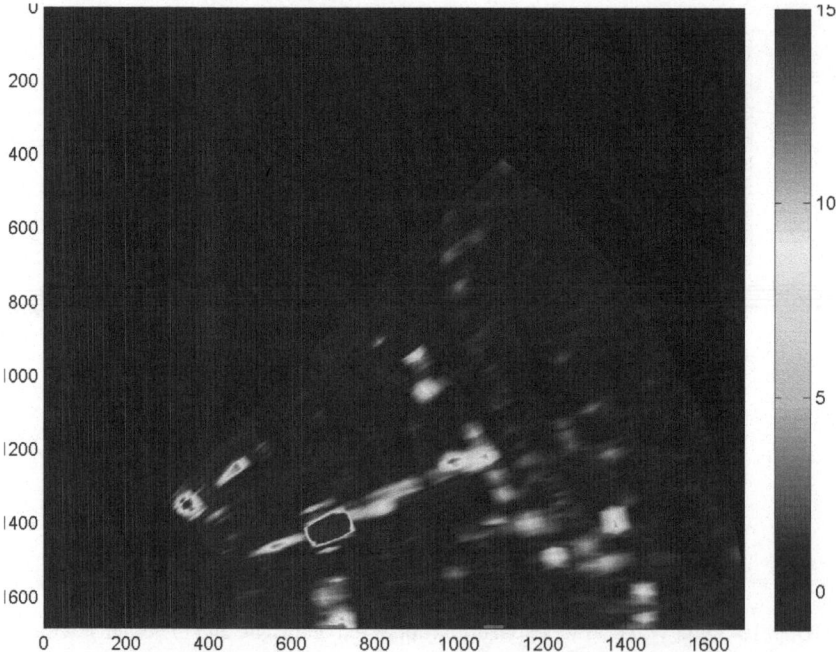

Fig. 10. Wake Vortex Monitoring based on Information Geometry, distance (158) on reflection coefficients in Horizontal scanning mode (CDG Airport on runways)

9.2 High Resolution Doppler Detection of Small/Stealth Targets in Inhomogeneous Sea Clutter for Coastal Radars Applications

Detection of small and stealth targets in inhomogeneous clutter is a main issue in Coastal radar domain. THALES has developed new High Resolution Doppler detectors based on information geometry. These new detectors have been validated on real radar from Coastal X-band radar and HF Surface Wave Radar (HFSWR). X-band radar has a range resolution of few meters and HF radar one of few cents of meters but has longer range coverage due to Surface Wave propagation effect in low frequency band.

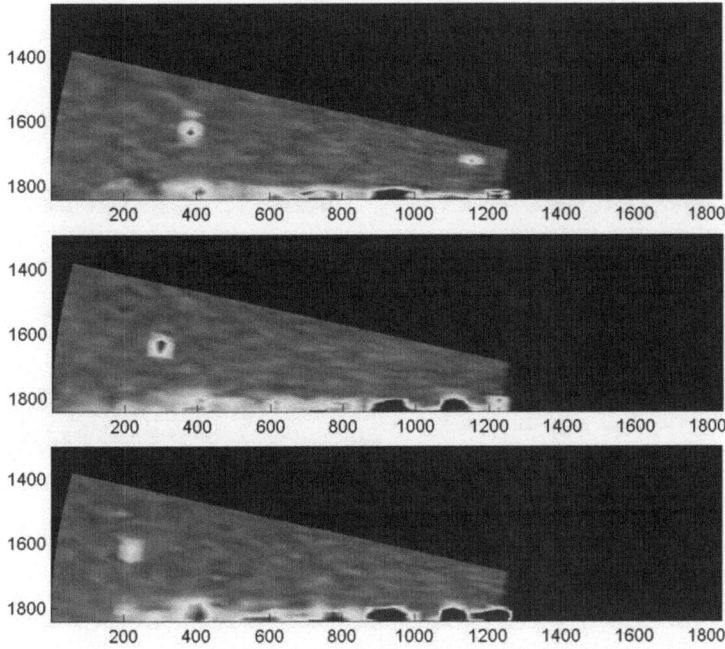

Fig. 11. Wake Vortex Monitoring based on Information Geometry, distance (158) on reflection coefficients in Vertical scanning mode (CDG Airport along runways)

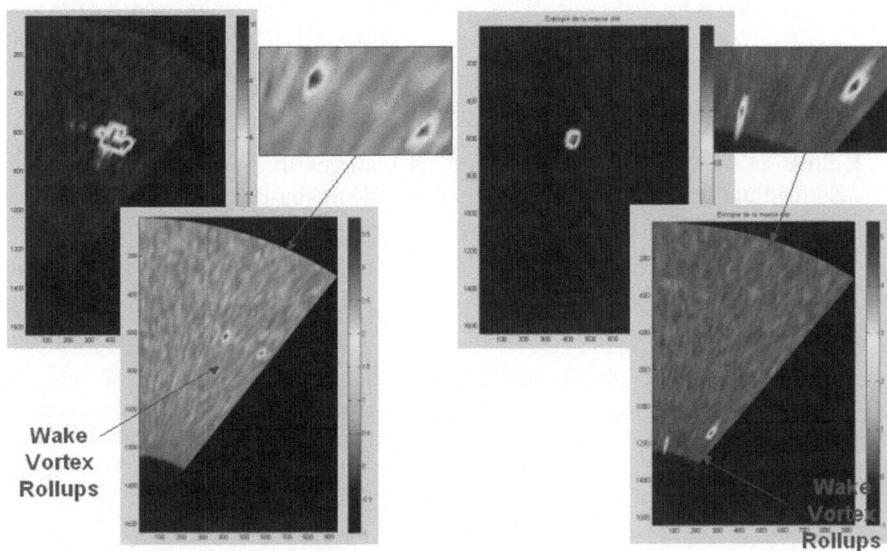

Fig. 12. Wake Vortex Monitoring based on Information Geometry, distance (158) on reflection coefficients in Vertical scanning mode (ORLY Airport in ILS)

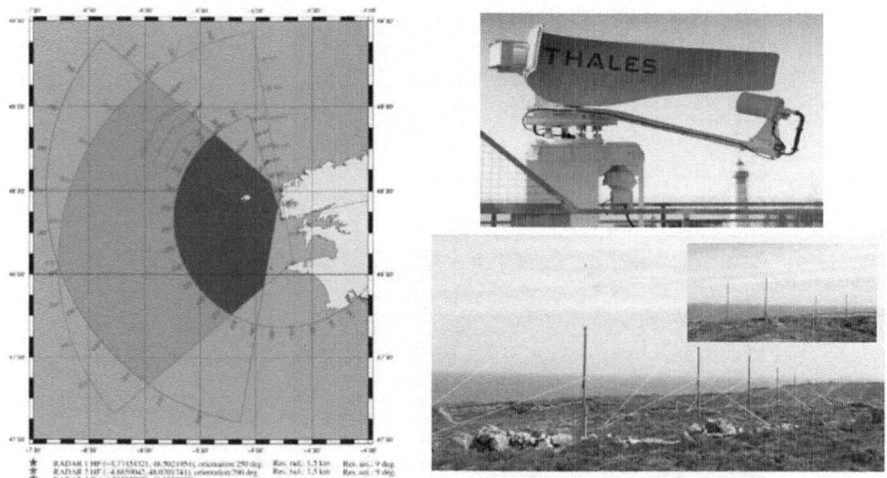

Fig. 13. THALES X-band Radar (upper right) and Actimar's HFSWR Radar (lower right) used for coastal trials

The Doppler detector based on Information geometry is built in 3 steps :

3. Estimation of inverse covariance matrix for each radar cell based on Trench Algorithm (Cholesky Decomposition) according to Regularized Autoregressive parameters

$$\Omega_n = (\alpha_n . R_n)^{-1} = W_n . W_n^+ = (1 - |\mu_n|^2) \begin{bmatrix} 1 & A_{n-1}^+ \\ A_{n-1} & \Omega_{n-1} + A_{n-1} . A_{n-1}^+ \end{bmatrix} \tag{159}$$

with $W_n = \sqrt{1 - |\mu_n|^2} \begin{bmatrix} 1 & 0 \\ A_{n-1} & \Omega_{n-1}^{1/2} \end{bmatrix}$ and $\Omega_{n-1} = \Omega_{n-1}^{1/2} . \Omega_{n-1}^{1/2+}$

4. Estimation of the Mean/Barycenter of N matrices in the neighbourhood of the radar cell under test by iterative method introduced based on Geometric Mean extension through Karcher/Frechet Barycenter :

$$A_{t+1} = A_t^{1/2} e^{-\varepsilon \left(A_t^{-1/2} G_{A_t} A_t^{-1/2} \right)} A_t^{1/2} \quad \text{with} \quad G_{A_t} = A_t^{1/2} \left(\sum_{k=1}^{N} \log \left(A_t^{-1/2} B_k A_t^{-1/2} \right) \right) A_t^{1/2} \tag{160}$$

5. Computation of Siegel distance between the covariance matrix of radar cell under test and Matrices Mean in the neighbourhood using blocks structure of complex autoregressive model (iterative and parallel computation of extended eigenvalues):

$$d^2(R_1, R_2) = \left\| \log \left(R_1^{-1/2} . R_2 . R_1^{-1/2} \right) \right\|^2 = \sum_{k=1}^{n} \log^2(\lambda_k) \tag{161}$$

with $\det \left(R_1^{-1/2} . R_2 . R_1^{-1/2} - \lambda . I \right) = \det(R_2 - \lambda R_1) = 0$

using Blocks structure :

$$\Omega_n = R_n^{(1)1/2+}.R_n^{(2)-1}.R_n^{(1)1/2} = \begin{bmatrix} \beta_{n-1} & \beta_{n-1}.W_{n-1}^+ \\ \beta_{n-1}.W_{n-1} & \Omega_{n-1} + \beta_{n-1}.W_{n-1}.W_{n-1}^+ \end{bmatrix} \quad (162)$$

with $W_{n-1} = \sqrt{\alpha_{n-1}^{(1)}}.R_{n-1}^{(1)1/2+}.\left[A_{n-1}^{(2)} - A_{n-1}^{(1)}\right]$ and $\beta_{n-1} = \dfrac{\alpha_{n-1}^{(2)}}{\alpha_{n-1}^{(1)}}$

with eigenvalues estimation iteratively and in parallel by zeros computation of this function :

$$\begin{cases} F^{(n)}\left(\lambda_k^{(n)}\right) = \lambda_k^{(n)} - \beta_{n-1} + \beta_{n-1}.\lambda_k^{(n)}.\sum_{i=1}^{n-1} \dfrac{\left|W_{n-1}^+.X_i^{(n-1)}\right|^2}{\left(\lambda_i^{(n-1)} - \lambda_k^{(n)}\right)} = 0 \\ \dfrac{X_k^{(n)}}{X_{k,1}^{(n)}} = \begin{bmatrix} 1 \\ -\lambda_k^{(n)}.U_{n-1}.\left(\Lambda_{n-1} - \lambda_k^{(n)}.I_{n-1}\right)^{-1}.U_{n-1}^+.W_{n-1} \end{bmatrix} \end{cases} \quad (163)$$

We give in the following results of this detector on coastal X-band and HFSWR radars Data. We compare classical Doppler processing based on Fourier transform on the left and new geometric method on the right.

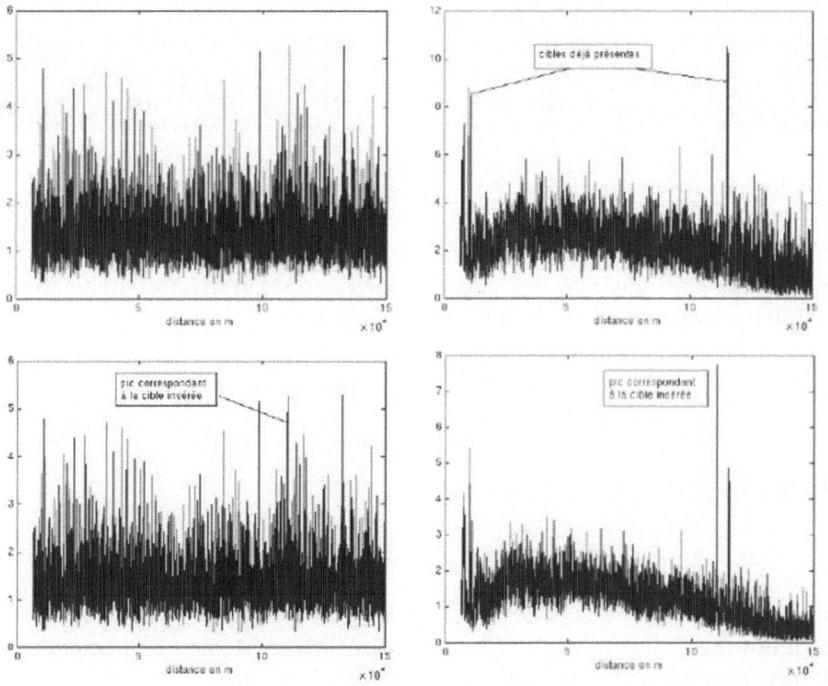

Fig. 14. Doppler detection on X-band Coastal Radar data (x axis : range) for one azimuth. (at left) classical method based on Fourier transform with false alarm and non detection, (at right) new detector with small target detection and no false alarm

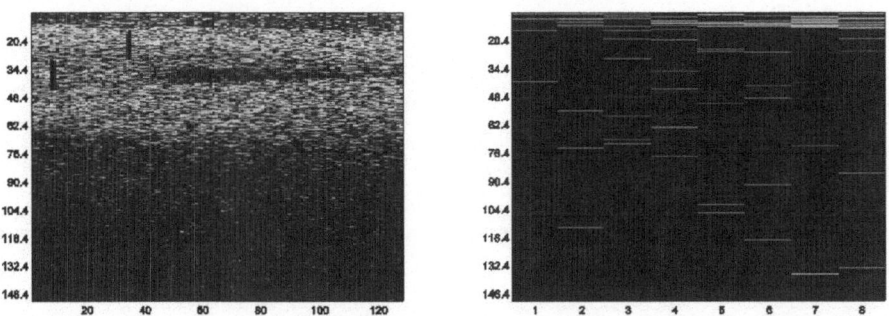

Fig. 15. Doppler detection on X-band Coastal Radar, (at left) raw data on reflectivity in range/azimuth plane, (at right) output of Doppler detector with low noise level

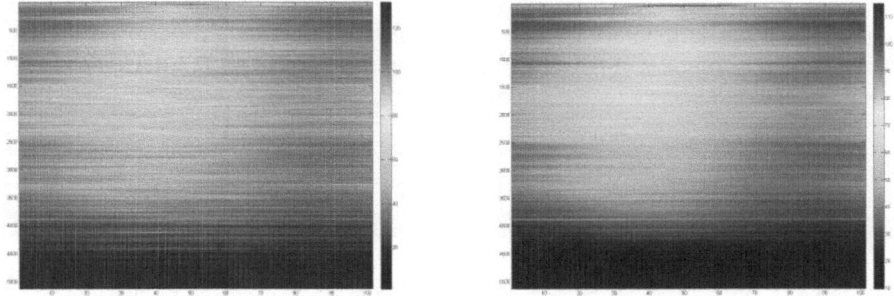

Fig. 16. Doppler/Range Capon Spectrum of (at left) Raw Covariance matrix, (at right) Mean covariance matrix (barycentre of 8 matrices in the range neighbourhood)

In the following figure 16, we illustrate Matrices Mean Method by iterative equation (160) by computation of Capon Doppler Spectrum :

$$S_{Capo,}(f) = \frac{1}{\sum_{k=1}^{n} \frac{1}{\lambda_k} \left| X_k^+ E(f) \right|^2} \text{ with } R^{(n)} X_k = \lambda_k X_k \text{ and } E(f) = \begin{bmatrix} 1 & e^{-j2\pi f} & \cdots & e^{-j2\pi(n-1)f} \end{bmatrix}$$

and by Autoregressive Doppler Spectrum :

$$S_{Capo,}(f) = \frac{\alpha_n^{-1}}{\left| A^{(n)}(f) \right|^2} \text{ with } A^{(n)}(f) = \sum_{k=0}^{n} a_k^{(n)} e^{-i2\pi f k}$$

In the following figure 17, we illustrate Matrices Mean Method by iterative equation (159) by computation of Autoregressive Doppler Spectrum :

$$S_{Capo,}(f) = \frac{\alpha_n^{-1}}{\left| A^{(n)}(f) \right|^2} \text{ with } A^{(n)}(f) = \sum_{k=0}^{n} a_k^{(n)} e^{-i2\pi f k}$$

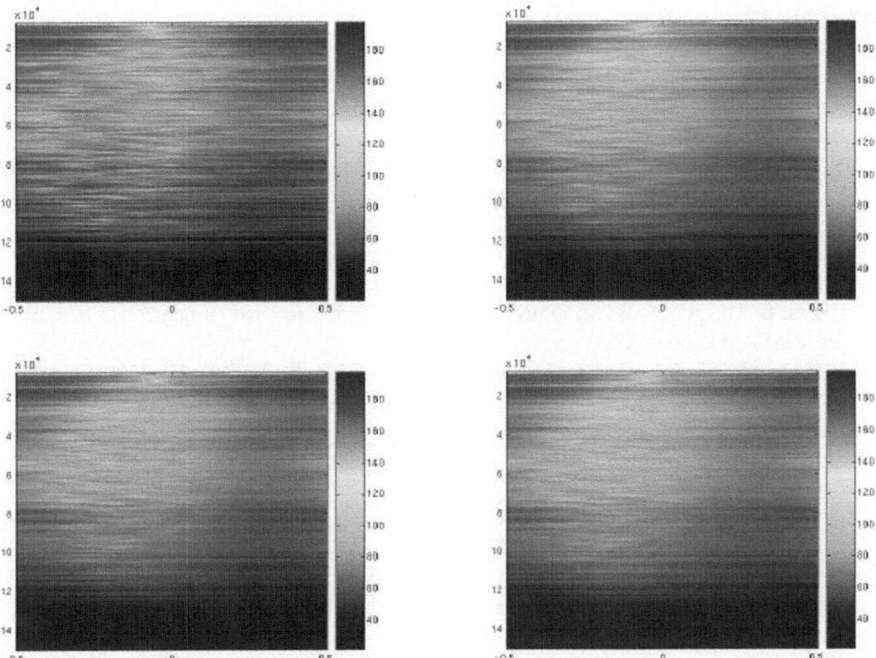

Fig. 17. Doppler/Range Autoregressive Spectrum of (upper left) Raw Covariance matrix, Mean covariance matrix (barycentre of N matrices in the range neighbourhood) with different values of iterations

In the following figure 18, we give detection results on HFSWR Radar data. We apply first a statistical segmentation of data based on Doppler information (reflection coefficients and their Kähler metric). Based on this map of homogeneous clutter area, detector is the same as in X-band but neighbourhood windows are limited to homogeneous area provided by statistical segmentation. We compare the new detector on a small target with classical detector based on Fourier transform.

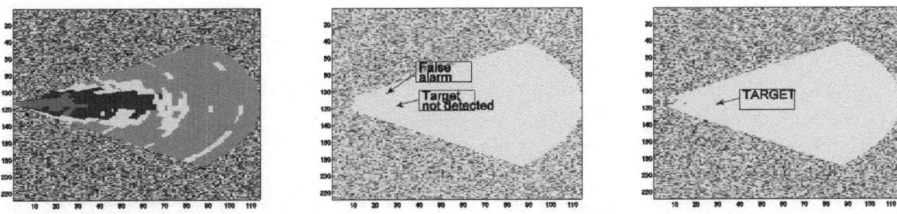

Fig. 18. Doppler detection on HF-band Coastal Radar, (at upper left) Statistical Doppler segmentation in homogeneous Doppler area based on information geometry on reflection coefficients, (at upper right) detection with classical Fourier Transform, (at lower left)new Doppler detector based on Information geometry

References

1. Siegel, C.L.: Symplectic Geometry. Academic Press, New York (1964)
2. Rao, C.R.: Information and Accuracy attainable in the estimation of statistical parameters. Bull. Calcutta Math. Soc. 37, 81–91 (1945)
3. Yoshizawa, S., Tanabe, K.: Dual Differential Geometry associated with the Kullback-Leibler Information on the Gaussian Distributions and its 2-parameter Deformations. SUT Journal of Mathematics 35(1), 113–137 (1999)
4. Ando, T., et al.: Geometric Means. Linear Algebra Appl. 385, 305–334 (2004)
5. Erich, K.: Mathematical Works, Berlin, Walter de Gruyter, ix (2003)
6. Bakas, I.: The Algebraic Structure of Geometric Flows in Two Dimensions., Inst. of Physics, SISSA (October 2005)
7. Barbaresco, F.: Information Intrinsic Geometric Flows. In: MaxEnt 2006 Conference, Paris, vol. 872, pp. 211–218 (June 2006) (published in American Institute of Physics, AIP)
8. Barbaresco, F.: Innovative Tools for Radar Signal Processing Based on Cartan's Geometry of SPD Matrices and Information Geometry. In: IEEE International Radar Conference, Rome (May 2008)
9. Bruhat, F., Tits, J.: Groupes réductifs sur un corps local. IHES 41, 5–251 (1972)
10. Gromov, M.: Hyperbolic Groups. Essays in Group Theory, Math. Sci. Res. Inst. Publ. 8, New york, pp. 75–263 (1987)
11. Maass, H.: Siegel Modular Forms and Derichlet Series. Lecture Notes in Math., vol. 216. Springer, Berlin (1971)
12. Cartan, H.: Ouverts fondamentaux pour le groupe modulaire. Séminaire Henri Cartan, tome 10(1), exp. n°3, p. 1–12 (1957)
13. Chentsov, N.N.: Statistical Decision Rules and Optimal Inferences. Trans. of Math. Monog, vol. 53. Amer. Math. Society, Providence (1982)
14. Cartan, E.: Sur les domaines bornés homogènes de l'espace de n variables complexes. Abh. Math. Semin. hamb. Univ. 11, 116–162 (1935)
15. Koecher, M.: Jordan Algebras and their Applications, Univ. of Minnesota, Minneapolis. Lect. Notes (1962)
16. Satake, I.: Algebraic Structures of Symmetric Domains. Kano memorial Lectures, vol. 4. Princeton University Press, Princeton (1980)
17. Faraut, J., Koranyi, A.: Analysis on Symmetric Cones. Oxford University Press, Oxford (1994)
18. Bougerol, P.: Kalman Filtering with Random Coefficients and Contractions. SIAM J. Control and Optimization 31(4), 942–959 (1993)
19. Koufany, K.: Analyse et Géométrie des domaines bornés symétriques. HDR, Institut de Mathematiques Elie Cartan, Nancy (November 2006)
20. Björk, A., Hammarling, S.: A Schur method for the square root of a matrix. Linear Algebra and Appl. 52/53, 127–140 (1983)
21. Karcher, H.: Riemannian center of mass and mollifier smoothing. Comm. Pure Applied Math. 30, 509–541 (1977)
22. Fefferman, C.: Monge-Ampère Equations, the Bergman Kernel, and geometry of pseudoconvexs domains. Ann. Of Math. 103, 395–416 (1976)
23. Niculescu, C.P.: An Extension of the Mazur-Ulam Theorem. American Institute of Physics Proc. 729, 248–256 (2004)
24. Barbaresco, F.: Calculus of Variations and Regularized Spectral Estimation. In: MaxEnt 2000 Conf., American Institute of Physics, AIP, vol. 568, pp. 361–374 (2000)
25. Berger, M.: Panoramic View of Riemannian Geometry. Springer, Heidelberg (2004)

26. Phong, D.H., Sturm, J.: The Monge-Ampère Equation and geodesics in the space of Kähler Potentials, arXiv:math/0504157v2 [math DG] (May 1, 2005)
27. Arnaudon, M., Li, X.: Barycentres of measures transported by stochastic flows. Ann. Probab. 33(4), 1509–1543 (2005)
28. Charon, N.: Une nouvelle approche pour la detection de cibles dans les images radar. Technical Report Thales/ENS-Cachan, Master MVA report (September 2008)
29. Lapuyade-Lahorgue, J.: Evolutions des radars de surveillance côtière, revue REE, vol. 8 (September 2008)
30. Lapuyade-Lahorgue, J.: Détection de cibles furtives par segmentation statistique et TFAC Doppler, PhD report (French MoD, DGA), ch. 6 (December 2008)
31. Bonnabel, S., Sepulchre, R.: Geometric distance and mean for positive semi-definite matrices of fixed rank, arXiv:0807.4462v1, 28 (July 2008)
32. Dhillon, L.S., Tropp, J.A.: Matrix nearness problems with bregman divergences. SIAM J. matrix anal. Appl. 29, 1120–1146 (2007)
33. Ledoux, M.: Géométrie des espaces métriques mesurés: les travaux de Lott, Villani, Sturm. séminaire Bourbaki, 60ème année, vol. 990, pp. 1–21 (March 2008)
34. Varadhan, S.: Large Deviations. The Annals of Probability 36(2), 397–419 (2008)

Clustering Multivariate Normal Distributions

Frank Nielsen[1,2] and Richard Nock[3]

[1] LIX — Ecole Polytechnique, Palaiseau, France
nielsen@lix.polytechnique.fr
[2] Sony Computer Science Laboratories Inc., Tokyo, Japan
nielsen@csl.sony.co.jp
[3] CEREGMIA — Université Antilles-Guyane, Schoelcher, France
rnock@martinique.univ-ag.fr

Abstract. In this paper, we consider the task of clustering multivariate normal distributions with respect to the relative entropy into a prescribed number, k, of clusters using a generalization of Lloyd's k-means algorithm [1]. We revisit this information-theoretic clustering problem under the auspices of mixed-type Bregman divergences, and show that the approach of Davis and Dhillon [2] (NIPS*06) can also be derived directly, by applying the Bregman k-means algorithm, once the proper vector/matrix Legendre transformations are defined. We further explain the dualistic structure of the sided k-means clustering, and present a novel k-means algorithm for clustering with respect to the symmetrical relative entropy, the J-divergence. Our approach extends to differential entropic clustering of arbitrary members of the same exponential families in statistics.

1 Introduction

In this paper, we consider the problem of clustering multivariate normal distributions into a given number of clusters. This clustering problem occurs in many real-world settings where each datum point is naturally represented by multiple observation samples defining a mean and a variance-covariance matrix modeling the underlying distribution: Namely, a multivariate normal (Gaussian) distribution. This setting allows one to conveniently deal with anisotropic noisy data sets, where each point is characterized by an individual Gaussian distribution representing locally the amount of noise. Clustering "raw" normal data sets is also an important algorithmic issue in computer vision and sound processing. For example, Myrvoll and Soong [3] consider this task for adapting hidden Markov model (HMM) parameters in a structured maximum a posteriori linear regression (SMAPLR), and obtained improved speech recognition rate. In computer vision, Gaussian mixture models (GMMs) abound from statistical image modeling learnt by the expectation-maximization (EM) soft clustering technique [4], and therefore represent a versatile source of raw Gaussian data sets to manipulate efficiently. The closest prior work to this paper is the differential entropic clustering of multivariate Gaussians of Davis and Dhillon [2], that can be derived from our framework as a special case.

F. Nielsen (Ed.): ETVC 2008, LNCS 5416, pp. 164–174, 2009.

A central question for clustering is to define the appropriate information-theoretic measure between any pair of multivariate normal distribution objects as the Euclidean distance falls short in that context. Let $N(m, S)$ denote[1] the d-variate normal distribution with mean m and variance-covariance matrix S. Its probability density function (pdf.) is given as follows [5]:

$$p(x; m, S) = \frac{1}{(2\pi)^{\frac{d}{2}}\sqrt{\det S}} \exp\left(-\frac{(x-m)^T S^{-1}(x-m)}{2}\right), \qquad (1)$$

where $m \in \mathbb{R}^d$ is called the mean, and $S \succ 0$ is a positive semi-definite matrix called the variance-covariance matrix, satisfying $x^T S x \geq 0 \; \forall x \in \mathbb{R}^d$. The variance-covariance matrix $S = [S_{i,j}]_{i,j}$ with $S_{i,j} = E[(X^{(i)} - m^{(i)})(X^{(j)} - m^{(j)})]$ and $m_i = E[X^{(i)}] \; \forall i \in \{1, ..., d\}$, is an invertible symmetric matrix with positive determinant: $\det S > 0$. A normal distribution "statistical object" can thus be interpreted as a "compound point" $\tilde{\Lambda} = (m, S)$ in $D = \frac{d(d+3)}{2}$ dimensions by stacking the mean vector m with the $\frac{d(d+1)}{2}$ coefficients of the symmetric variance-covariance matrix S. This encoding may be interpreted as a serialization or linearization operation. A fundamental distance between statistical distributions that finds deep roots in information theory [6] is the *relative entropy*, also called the Kullback-Leibler divergence or information discrimination measure. The oriented distance is asymmetric (ie., $\text{KL}(p||q) \neq \text{KL}(q||p)$) and defined as:

$$\text{KL}(p(x; m_i, S_i)||p(x; m_j, S_j)) = \int_{x \in \mathbb{R}^d} p(x; m_i, S_i) \log \frac{p(x; m_i, S_i)}{p(x; m_j, S_j)} dx. \qquad (2)$$

The Kullback-Leibler divergence expresses the *differential relative entropy* with the *cross-entropy* as follows:

$$\text{KL}(p(x; m_i, S_i)p(x; m_j, S_j)) = -H(p(x; m_i, S_i)) - \int_{x \in \mathbb{R}^d} p(x; m_i, S_i) \log p(x; m_j, S_j) dx, \qquad (3)$$

where the Shannon' differential entropy is

$$H(p(x; m_i, S_i)) = -\int_{x \in \mathbb{R}^d} p(x; m_i, S_i) \log p(x; m_i, S_i) dx, \qquad (4)$$

independent of the mean vector:

$$H(p(x; m_i, S_i)) = \frac{d}{2} + \frac{1}{2} \log(2\pi)^d \det S_i. \qquad (5)$$

Fastidious integral computations yield the well-known Kullback-Leibler divergence formula for multivariate normal distributions:

---

[1] We do not use the conventional (μ, Σ) notations to avoid misleading formula later on, such as $\sum_{i=1}^{n} \Sigma_i$, etc.

$$KL(p(x; m_i, S_i) || p(x; m_j, S_j)) = \frac{1}{2} \log |S_i^{-1} S_j| +$$

$$\frac{1}{2} \text{tr} \left((S_i^{-1} S_j)^{-1} \right) - \frac{d}{2} + \frac{1}{2} (m_i - m_j)^T S_j^{-1} (m_i - m_j), \tag{6}$$

where $\text{tr}(S)$ is the trace of square matrix S, the sum of its diagonal elements: $\text{tr}(S) = \sum_{i=1}^{d} S_{i,i}$. In particular, the Kullback-Leibler divergence of normal distributions reduces to the quadratic distance for unit spherical Gaussians: $KL(p(x; m_i, I) || p(x; m_j, I)) = \frac{1}{2} ||m_i - m_j||^2$, where I denotes the $d \times d$ identity matrix.

2 Viewing Kullback-Leibler Divergence as a Mixed-Type Bregman Divergence

It turns out that a neat generalization of both statistical distributions and information-theoretic divergences brings a *simple way* to find out the same result of Eq. 6 by *bypassing* the integral computation. Indeed, the well-known normal density function can be expressed into the canonical form of *exponential families* in statistics [7]. Exponential families include many familiar distributions such as Poisson, Bernoulli, Beta, Gamma, and normal distributions. Yet exponential families do not cover the full spectrum of usual distributions either, as they do not contain the uniform nor Cauchy distributions.

Let us first consider univariate normal distributions $N(m, s^2)$ with associated probability density function:

$$p(x; m, s^2) = \frac{1}{s\sqrt{2\pi}} \exp - \left(\frac{(x - m)^2}{2s^2} \right). \tag{7}$$

The pdf can be mathematically rewritten to fit the *canonical decomposition* of distributions belonging to the exponential families [7], as follows:

$$p(x; m, s^2) = p(x; \theta = (\theta_1, \theta_2)) = \exp \left\{ < \theta, t(x) > -F(\theta) + C(x) \right\}, \tag{8}$$

where $\theta = (\theta_1 = \frac{\mu}{\sigma^2}, \theta_2 = -\frac{1}{2\sigma^2})$ are the *natural parameters* associated with the *sufficient statistics* $t(x) = (x, x^2)$. The *log normalizer* $F(\theta) = -\frac{\theta_1^2}{4\theta_2} + \frac{1}{2} \log \frac{-\pi}{\theta_2}$ is a strictly convex and differentiable function that specifies uniquely the exponential family, and the function $C(x)$ is the carrier measure. See [7,8] for more details and plenty of examples. Once this canonical decomposition is figured out, we can simply apply the generic *equivalence theorem* [9] [8] Kullback-Leibler↔Bregman divergence [10]:

$$KL(p(x; m_i, S_i) || p(x; m_j, S_j)) = D_F(\theta_j || \theta_i), \tag{9}$$

to get the closed-form formula easily. In other words, this theorem (see [8] for a proof) states that the Kullback-Leibler divergence of two distributions of the *same* exponential family is equivalent to the Bregman divergence for the log normalizer generator by *swapping* arguments. The Bregman divergence [10] D_F is defined as the tail of a Taylor expansion for a strictly convex and differentiable function F as:

$$D_F(\theta_j || \theta_i) = F(\theta_j) - F(\theta_i) - < \theta_j - \theta_i, \nabla F(\theta_i) >, \tag{10}$$

where $< \cdot, \cdot >$ denote the vector inner product ($< p, q >= p^T q$) and ∇F is the gradient operator. For multivariate normals, the same kind of decomposition exists but on *mixed-type* vector/matrix parameters, as we shall describe next.

3   Clustering with Respect to the Kullback-Leibler Divergence

3.1   Bregman/Kullback-Leibler Hard k-Means

Banerjee et al. [9] generalized Lloyd's k-means hard clustering technique [1] to the broad family of Bregman divergences D_F. The Bregman hard k-means clustering of a point set $\mathcal{P} = \{p_1, ..., p_n\}$ works as follows:

1. **Initialization.** Let $C_1, ..., C_k$ be the initial k cluster centers called the seeds. Seeds can be initialized in many various ways and is an important step to consider in practice, as explained in [11]. The simplest technique, called Forgy's initialization [12], is to allocate *at random* seeds from the source points.
2. **Repeat until converge or stopping criterion is met**
   (a) **Assignment.** Associate to each "point" p_i its closest center with respect to divergence D_F: $p_i \rightarrow \arg\min_{C_j \in \{C_1, ..., C_k\}} D_F(p_i || C_j)$. Let $\mathcal{C}_l$ denote the lth cluster, the set of points closer to center C_l than to any other cluster center. The clusters form a partition of the point set $\mathcal{P}$. This partition may be geometrically interpreted as the underlying partition emanating from the Bregman Voronoi diagram of the cluster centers $C_1, ..., C_k$ themselves, see [8].
   (b) **Center re-estimation.** Choose the new cluster centers $C_i \, \forall i \in \{1, ..., k\}$ as the cluster respective centroids: $C_i = \frac{1}{|\mathcal{C}_i|} \sum_{p_j \in \mathcal{C}_i} p_j$. A key property emphasized in [9] is that the Bregman centroid defined as the minimizer of the right-side intracluster average $\arg\min_{c \in \mathbb{R}^d} \sum_{p_i \in \mathcal{C}_l} D_F(p_i || c)$ is *independent* of the considered Bregman generator F, and always coincide with the center of mass.

The Bregman hard clustering enjoys the same convergence property as the traditional k-means. That is, the *Bregman loss* function $\sum_{l=1}^{k} \sum_{p_i \in \mathcal{C}_l} D_F(p_i || C_l)$ monotonically decreases until convergence is reached. Thus a stopping criterion can also be choosen to terminate the loop as soon as the difference between the Bregman losses of two successive iterations goes below a prescribed threshold. In fact, Lloyd's algorithm [1] is a Bregman hard clustering for the quadratic Bregman divergence ($F(x) = \sum_{i=1}^{d} x_i^2$) with associated (Bregman) quadratic loss. As mentioned above, the centers of clusters are found as right-type sum average minimization problems. For a n-point set $\mathcal{P} = \{p_1, ..., p_n\}$, the center is defined as

$$\arg\min_{c \in \mathbb{R}^d} D_F(p_i || c) = \frac{1}{n} \sum_{i=1}^{n} p_i. \tag{11}$$

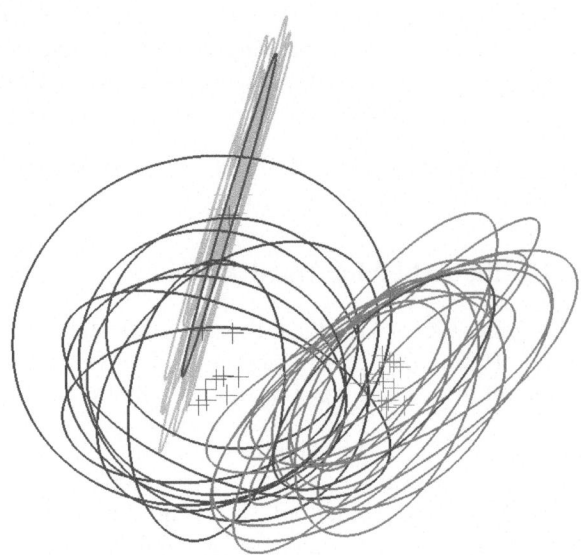

Fig. 1. Bivariate normal k-means clustering ($k = 3$, $d = 2$, $D = 5$) with respect to the right-type Bregman centroid (the center of mass of natural parameters, equivalent to the left-type Kullback-Leibler centroid) of 32 bivariate normals. Each cluster is displayed with its own color, and the centroids are rasterized as red variance-covariance ellipses centered on their means.

That is, the Bregman right-centroid is surprisingly invariant to the considered Bregman divergence [9] and always equal to the center of mass. Note that although the squared Euclidean distance is a Bregman (symmetric) divergence, it is not the case for the single Euclidean distance for which the minimum average distance optimization problem yields the Fermat-Weber point [13] that *does not admit closed-form* solution.

Thus for clustering normals with respect to the Kullback-Leibler divergence using this Bregman hard clustering, we need to consider the oriented distance $D_F(\theta_i||\omega_l)$ for the log normalizer of the normal distributions interpreted as members of a given exponential family, where ω_l denote the cluster centroid in the natural parameter space. Since $D_F(\theta_i||\omega_l) = \mathrm{KL}(c_l||p_i)$ it turns out that the hard Bregman clustering minimizes the Kullback-Leibler loss $\sum_{l=1}^{k} \sum_{p_i \in \mathcal{C}_l} \mathrm{KL}(c_l||p_i)$. We now describe the primitives required to apply the Bregman k-means clustering to the case of the Kullback-Leibler clustering of multivariate normal distributions.

3.2   Mixed-Type Parameters of Multivariate Normals

The density function of multivariate normals of Eq. 1 can be rewritten into the canonical decomposition of Eq. 8 to yield an exponential family of order $D = \frac{d(d+3)}{2}$ (the mean vector and the positive definite matrix S^{-1} accounting respectively for d and $\frac{d(d+1)}{2}$ parameters). The sufficient statistics is *stacked* onto a two-part D-dimensional vector/matrix entity

$$\tilde{x} = (x, -\frac{1}{2}xx^T) \tag{12}$$

associated with the natural parameter

$$\tilde{\Theta} = (\theta, \Theta) = (S^{-1}m, \frac{1}{2}S^{-1}). \tag{13}$$

Accordingly, the source parameter are denoted by $\tilde{\Lambda} = (m, S)$. The log normalizer specifying the exponential family is (see [14]):

$$F(\tilde{\Theta}) = \frac{1}{4}\mathrm{Tr}(\Theta^{-1}\theta\theta^T) - \frac{1}{2}\log\det\Theta + \frac{d}{2}\log 2\pi. \tag{14}$$

To compute the Kullback-Leibler divergence of two normal distributions $N_p = \mathcal{N}(\mu_p, \Sigma_p)$ and $N_q = \mathcal{N}(\mu_q, \Sigma_q)$, we use the Bregman divergence as follows:

$$\mathrm{KL}(N_p||N_q) = D_F(\tilde{\Theta}_q||\tilde{\Theta}_p) \tag{15}$$

$$= F(\tilde{\Theta}_q) - F(\tilde{\Theta}_p) - <(\tilde{\Theta}_q - \tilde{\Theta}_p), \nabla F(\tilde{\Theta}_p)>. \tag{16}$$

The inner product $<\tilde{\Theta}_p, \tilde{\Theta}_q>$ is a *composite* inner product obtained as the sum of two inner products of vectors and matrices:

$$<\tilde{\Theta}_p, \tilde{\Theta}_q> = <\Theta_p, \Theta_q> + <\theta_p, \theta_q>. \tag{17}$$

For matrices, the inner product $<\Theta_p, \Theta_q>$ is defined by the trace of the matrix product $\Theta_p\Theta_q^T$:

$$<\Theta_p, \Theta_q> = \mathrm{Tr}(\Theta_p\Theta_q^T). \tag{18}$$

Figure 1 displays the Bregman k-means clustering result on a set of 32 bivariate normals.

4   Dual Bregman Divergence

We introduce the Legendre transformation to interpret *dually* the former k-means Bregman clustering. We refer to [8] for detailed explanations that we concisely summarize here as follows: Any Bregman generator function F admits a *dual* Bregman generator function $G = F^*$ via the Legendre transformation

$$G(y) = \sup_{x \in \mathcal{X}}\{<y, x> -F(x)\}. \tag{19}$$

The supremum is reached at the *unique* point where the gradient of $G(x) = <y, x> -F(x)$ vanishes, that is when $y = \nabla F(x)$. Writing $\mathcal{X}_F'$ for the *gradient space* $\{x' = \nabla F(x)|x \in \mathcal{X}\}$, the convex conjugate $G = F^*$ of F is the function $\mathcal{X}_F' \subset \mathbb{R}^d \to \mathbb{R}$ defined by

$$F^*(x') = <x, x'> -F(x). \tag{20}$$

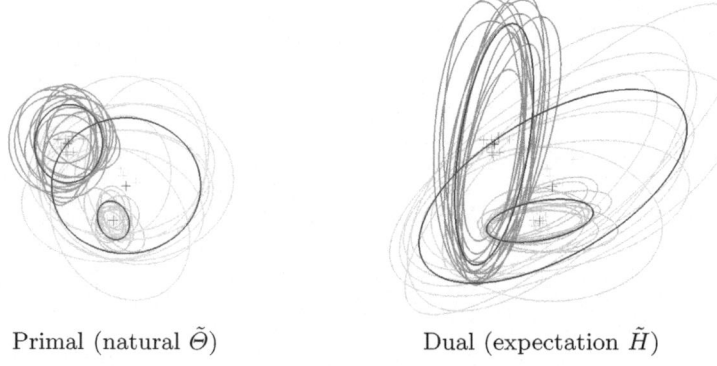

Primal (natural $\tilde{\Theta}$)   Dual (expectation $\tilde{H}$)

Fig. 2. Clustering in the primal (natural) space $\tilde{\Theta}$ is dually equivalent to clustering in the dual (expectation) space $\tilde{H}$. The transformations are reversible. Both normal data sets are visualized in the source parameter space $\tilde{\Lambda}$.

It follows from Legendre transformation that *any* Bregman divergence D_F admits a *dual* Bregman divergence D_{F^*} related to D_F as follows:

$$D_F(p\|q) = F(p) + F^*(\nabla F(q)) - <p, \nabla F(q)>, \qquad (21)$$
$$= F(p) + F^*(q') - <p, q'>, \qquad (22)$$
$$= D_{F^*}(q'\|p'). \qquad (23)$$

Yoshizawa and Tanabe [14] carried out non-trivial computations that yield the dual natural/expectation coordinate systems arising from the canonical decomposition of the density function $p(x; m, S)$:

$$\tilde{H} = \begin{pmatrix} \eta = \mu \\ H = -(\Sigma + \mu\mu^T) \end{pmatrix} \Longleftrightarrow \tilde{\Lambda} = \begin{pmatrix} \lambda = \mu \\ \Lambda = \Sigma \end{pmatrix}, \qquad (24)$$

$$\tilde{\Lambda} = \begin{pmatrix} \lambda = \mu \\ \Lambda = \Sigma \end{pmatrix} \Longleftrightarrow \tilde{\Theta} = \begin{pmatrix} \theta = \Sigma^{-1}\mu \\ \Theta = \frac{1}{2}\Sigma^{-1} \end{pmatrix} \qquad (25)$$

The strictly convex and differentiable dual Bregman generator functions (ie., potential functions in information geometry) are $F(\tilde{\Theta}) = \frac{1}{4}\text{Tr}(\Theta^{-1}\theta\theta^T) - \frac{1}{2}\log \det\Theta + \frac{d}{2}\log\pi$, and $F^*(\tilde{H}) = -\frac{1}{2}\log(1 + \eta^T H^{-1}\eta) - \frac{1}{2}\log\det(-H) - \frac{d}{2}\log(2\pi e)$ defined respectively both on the topologically open space $\mathbb{R}^d \times \mathcal{C}_d^-$, where $\mathcal{C}_d$ denote the d-dimensional cone of symmetric positive definite matrices. The $\tilde{H} \Leftrightarrow \tilde{\Theta}$ coordinate transformations obtained from the Legendre transformation are given by

$$\tilde{H} = \nabla_{\tilde{\Theta}} F(\tilde{\Theta}) = \begin{pmatrix} \nabla_{\tilde{\Theta}} F(\theta) \\ \nabla_{\tilde{\Theta}} F(\Theta) \end{pmatrix} = \begin{pmatrix} \frac{1}{2}\Theta^{-1}\theta \\ -\frac{1}{2}\Theta^{-1} - \frac{1}{4}(\Theta^{-1}\theta)(\Theta^{-1}\theta)^T \end{pmatrix} \qquad (26)$$

$$= \begin{pmatrix} \mu \\ -(\Sigma + \mu\mu^T) \end{pmatrix} \qquad (27)$$

and

$$\tilde{\Theta} = \nabla_{\tilde{H}} F^*(\tilde{H}) = \begin{pmatrix} \nabla_{\tilde{H}} F^*(\eta) \\ \nabla_{\tilde{H}} F^*(H) \end{pmatrix} = \begin{pmatrix} -(H + \eta\eta^T)^{-1}\eta \\ -\frac{1}{2}(H + \eta\eta^T)^{-1} \end{pmatrix} = \begin{pmatrix} \Sigma^{-1}\mu \\ \frac{1}{2}\Sigma^{-1} \end{pmatrix}. \quad (28)$$

These formula simplify significantly when we restrict ourselves to diagonal-only variance-covariance matrices S_i, spherical Gaussians $S_i = s_i I$, or univariate normals $\mathcal{N}(m_i, s_i^2)$.

5 Left-Sided and Right-Sided Clusterings

The former Bregman k-means clustering makes use of the *right-side* of the divergence for clustering. It is therefore equivalent to the *left-side* clustering for the dual Bregman divergence on the gradient point set (see Figure 2). The left-side Kullback-Leibler clustering of members of the same exponential family is a right-side Bregman clustering for the log normalizer. Similarly, the right-side Kullback-Leibler clustering of members of the same exponential family is a *left-side* Bregman clustering for the log normalizer, that is itself equivalent to a right-side Bregman clustering for the dual convex conjugate $F*$ obtained from Legendre transformation.

We find that the left-side Bregman clustering (ie., right-side Kullback-Leibler) is *exactly* the clustering algorithm reported in [2]. In particular, the cluster centers for the right-side Kullback-Leibler divergence are left-side Bregman centroids that have been shown to be generalized means [15], given as (for $(\nabla \tilde{F})^{-1} = \nabla \tilde{F}^*$):

$$\tilde{\Theta} = (\nabla \tilde{F})^{-1} \left(\sum_{i=1}^{n} \nabla \tilde{F}(\tilde{\Theta}_i) \right). \quad (29)$$

After calculus, it follows in accordance with [2] that

$$S^* = \left(\frac{1}{n} \sum_i S_i^{-1} \right)^{-1}, \quad (30)$$

$$m^* = S^* (\sum_{i=1}^{n} \frac{1}{n} S_i^{-1} m_i). \quad (31)$$

6 Inferring Multivariate Normal Distributions

As mentioned in the introduction, in many real-world settings each datum point can be sampled several times yielding multiple observations assumed to be drawn from an underlying distribution. This modeling is convenient for considering individual noise characteristics. In many cases, we may also assume Gaussian sampling or Gaussian noise, see [2] for concrete examples in sensor data network and statistical debugging applications. The problem is then to infer from observations $x_1, ..., x_s$ the parameters m and S. It turns out that the maximum likelihood estimator (MLE) of exponential families is the centroid of the sufficient statistics evaluated on the observations [7]. Since multivariate normal distributions belongs to the exponential families with statistics $(x, -\frac{1}{2}xx^T)$, it follows from the maximum likelihood estimator that

$$\hat{\mu} = \frac{1}{s}\sum_{i=1}^{s} x_i, \tag{32}$$

and

$$\hat{S} = \left(\frac{1}{2s}\sum_{i=1}^{s} x_i x_i^T\right) - \hat{\mu}\hat{\mu}^T. \tag{33}$$

This estimator may be *biased* [5].

7   Symmetric Clustering with the J-Divergence

The symmetrical Kullback-Leibler divergence $\frac{1}{2}(\text{KL}(p||q)+\text{KL}(q||p))$ is called the J-divergence. Although centroids for the left-side and right-side Kullback-Leibler divergence admit elegant closed-form solutions as *generalized means* [15], it is also known that the symmetrized Kullback-Leibler centroid of discrete distributions does not admit such a closed-form solution [16]. Nevertheless, the centroid of symmetrized Bregman divergence has been *exactly* geometrically characterized as the intersection of the geodesic linking the left- and right-sided centroids (say, c_L^F and c_R^F respectively) with the mixed-type bisector: $M_F(c_R^F, c_L^F) = \{x \in \mathcal{X} \mid D_F(c_R^F||x) = D_F(x||c_L^F)\}$. We summarize the geodesic-walk approximation heuristic of [15] as follows: We initially consider $\lambda \in [\lambda_m = 0, \lambda_M = 1]$ and repeat the following steps until $\lambda_M - \lambda_m \leq \epsilon$, for $\epsilon > 0$ a *prescribed* precision threshold:

1. **Geodesic walk.** Compute interval midpoint $\lambda_h = \frac{\lambda_m + \lambda_M}{2}$ and corresponding geodesic point

$$q_h = (\nabla F)^{-1}((1 - \lambda_h)\nabla F(c_R^F) + \lambda_h \nabla F(c_L^F)), \tag{34}$$

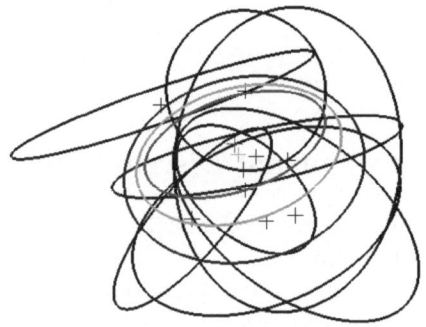

Fig. 3. The left-(red) and right-sided (blue) Kullback-Leibler centroids, and the symmetrized Kullback-Leibler J-divergence centroid (green) for a set of eight bivariate normals

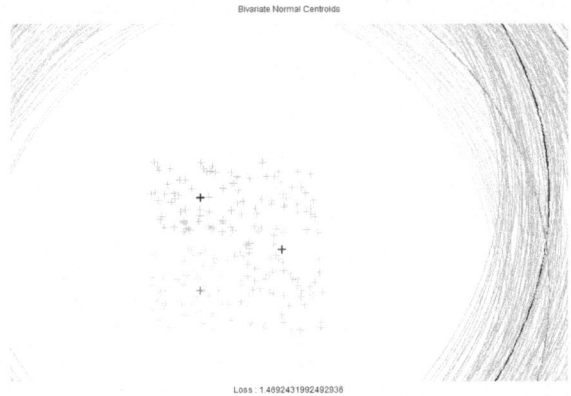

Fig. 4. Clustering sided or symmetrized multivariate normals. For identical variance-covariance matrices, this Bregman clustering amounts to the regular k-means. Indeed, in this case the Kullback-Leibler becomes proportional to the squared Euclidean distance. See demo applet at http://www.sonycsl.co.jp/person/nielsen/KMj/

2. **Mixed-type bisector side.** Evaluate the sign of $D_F(c_R^F||q_h) - D_F(q_h||c_L^R)$, and
3. **Dichotomy.** Branch on $[\lambda_h, \lambda_M]$ if the sign is negative, or on $[\lambda_m, \lambda_h]$ otherwise.

Figure 3 shows the two sided left- and right-sided centroids, and the symmetrized centroid for the case of bivariate normals (handled as points in 5D). We can then apply the classical k-means algorithm on these symmetrized centroids. Figure 4 displays that the multivariate clustering applet, which shows the property that it becomes the regular k-means if we fix all variance-covariance matrices to identity. See also the recent work of Teboulle [17] that further generalizes center-based clustering to Bregman and Csiszár f-divergences.

8   Concluding Remarks

We have presented the k-means hard clustering techniques [1] for clustering multivariate normals in arbitrary dimensions with respect to the Kullback-Leibler divergence. Our approach relies on instantiating the generic Bregman hard clustering of Banerjee et al. [9] by using the fact that the relative entropy between any two normal distributions can be derived from the corresponding mixed-type Bregman divergence obtained by setting the Bregman generator as the log normalizer function of the normal exponential family. This in turn yields a dual interpretation of the right-sided k-means clustering as a left-sided k-means clustering that was formerly studied by Davis and Dhillon [2] using an *ad-hoc* optimization technique. Furthermore, based on the very recent work on symmetrical Bregman centroids [15], we showed how to cluster multivariate normals with respect to the symmetrical Kullback-Leibler divergence, called the J-divergence.

This is all the more important for applications that require to handle symmetric information-theoretic measures [3].

References

1. Lloyd, S.P.: Least squares quantization in PCM. IEEE Transactions on Information Theory 28(2), 129–136 (1982); first published in 1957 in a Technical Note of Bell Laboratories
2. Davis, J.V., Dhillon, I.S.: Differential entropic clustering of multivariate gaussians. In: Scholkopf, B., Platt, J., Hoffman, T. (eds.) Neural Information Processing Systems (NIPS), pp. 337–344. MIT Press, Cambridge (2006)
3. Myrvoll, T.A., Soong, F.K.: On divergence-based clustering of normal distributions and its application to HMM adaptation. In: Proceedings of EuroSpeech, Geneva, Switzerland, vol. 2, pp. 1517–1520 (2003)
4. Dempster, A.P., Laird, N.M., Rubin, D.B.: Maximum likelihood from incomplete data via the em algorithm. Journal of the Royal Statistical Society. Series B (Methodological) 39(1), 1–38 (1977)
5. Amari, S.I., Nagaoka, N.: Methods of Information Geometry. Oxford University Press, Oxford (2000)
6. Cover, T.M., Thomas, J.A.: Elements of Information Theory. Wiley Series in Telecommunications and Signal Processing. Wiley-Interscience, Hoboken (2006)
7. Barndorff-Nielsen, O.E.: Parametric statistical models and likelihood. Lecture Notes in Statistics, vol. 50. Springer, New York (1988)
8. Nielsen, F., Boissonnat, J.D., Nock, R.: Bregman Voronoi diagrams: Properties, algorithms and applications, Extended abstract appeared in ACM-SIAM Symposium on Discrete Algorithms 2007. INRIA Technical Report RR-6154 (September 2007)
9. Banerjee, A., Merugu, S., Dhillon, I.S., Ghosh, J.: Clustering with Bregman divergences. Journal of Machine Learning Research (JMLR) 6, 1705–1749 (2005)
10. Bregman, L.M.: The relaxation method of finding the common point of convex sets and its application to the solution of problems in convex programming. USSR Computational Mathematics and Mathematical Physics 7, 200–217 (1967)
11. Redmond, S.J., Heneghan, C.: A method for initialising the k-means clustering algorithm using kd-trees. Pattern Recognition Letters 28(8), 965–973 (2007)
12. Forgy, E.W.: Cluster analysis of multivariate data: efficiency vs interpretability of classifications. Biometrics 21, 768–769 (1965)
13. Carmi, P., Har-Peled, S., Katz, M.J.: On the Fermat-Weber center of a convex object. Computational Geometry 32(3), 188–195 (2005)
14. Yoshizawa, S., Tanabe, K.: Dual differential geometry associated with Kullback-Leibler information on the Gaussian distributions and its 2-parameter deformations. SUT Journal of Mathematics 35(1), 113–137 (1999)
15. Nielsen, F., Nock, R.: On the symmetrized Bregman centroids, Sony CSL Technical Report (submitted) (November 2007)
16. Veldhuis, R.N.J.: The centroid of the symmetrical Kullback-Leibler distance. IEEE Signal Processing Letters 9(3), 96–99 (2002)
17. Teboulle, M.: A unified continuous optimization framework for center-based clustering methods. Journal of Machine Learning Research 8, 65–102 (2007)

Intrinsic Geometries in Learning

Richard Nock[1] and Frank Nielsen[2,3]

[1] CEREGMIA — Université Antilles-Guyane, Schoelcher, France
rnock@martinique.univ-ag.fr
[2] LIX — Ecole Polytechnique, Palaiseau, France
nielsen@lix.polytechnique.fr
[3] Sony Computer Science Laboratories Inc., Tokyo, Japan
nielsen@csl.sony.co.jp

Abstract. In a seminal paper, Amari (1998) proved that learning can be made more efficient when one uses the intrinsic Riemannian structure of the algorithms' spaces of parameters to point the gradient towards better solutions. In this paper, we show that many learning algorithms, including various boosting algorithms for linear separators, the most popular top-down decision-tree induction algorithms, and some on-line learning algorithms, are spawns of a generalization of Amari's natural gradient to some particular non-Riemannian spaces. These algorithms exploit an intrinsic dual geometric structure of the space of parameters in relationship with particular integral losses that are to be minimized. We unite some of them, such as AdaBoost, additive regression with the square loss, the logistic loss, the top-down induction performed in CART and C4.5, as a single algorithm on which we show general convergence to the optimum and explicit convergence rates under very weak assumptions. As a consequence, many of the classification calibrated surrogates of Bartlett *et al.* (2006) admit efficient minimization algorithms.

1 Introduction

This paper is an attempt to unite some supervised learning algorithms that have led the last decade on iterative learning algorithms, and bring some novel performance- or structural-related results. Among the algorithms concerned, there are AdaBoost and related boosting algorithms, top-down decision tree induction algorithms (including those of CART, C4.5), and some on-line learning algorithms.

Our starting point is a result of [1], which states that gradient-based learning leads to better results if one takes into account in the gradient the Riemannian structure of the space of parameters. During the last decade, most of the successes in supervised learning algorithms have been obtained when minimizing functions that serve as primers for the minimization of the empirical risk — functions called surrogates. This is the case for AdaBoost, additive logistic regression, decision tree induction, Support Vector Machines, on-line learning algorithms [14,23,25,36,38], and many others. These surrogates work on spaces of parameters, on which they define singular geometries — generally, they are

F. Nielsen (Ed.): ETVC 2008, LNCS 5416, pp. 175–215, 2009.
© Springer-Verlag Berlin Heidelberg 2009

not symmetric and do not obey the triangular inequality. A significant amount of work has recently been devoted to set in order the huge set of candidate surrogates. For example, statistical consistency properties have been shown for a wide set containing most of the surrogates relevant to learning, *classification calibrated surrogates* [5]; other important properties, like the algorithmic questions about minimization, have been explicitly left as important problems to settle [5]. A relevant contribution on this side came earlier from [29], who proved mild convergence results on an algorithm inducing linear separators and working on a large class of convex surrogates, not necessarily classification calibrated; [29] also left as an important problem the necessity to fully solve this algorithmic question, such as by providing convergence rates.

In this paper, we show that our algorithms of interest can be seen as particular geodesic walks on the space of parameters, and these geodesic walk take benefit of the non Riemannian geometric structure of this space to progress towards better or optimal solutions, thus generalizing the Riemannian approach of [1]. Informally, the update of parameters is located on iso-Bregman divergence surfaces, progressing towards the minimization of various functions — edges in boosting, Bregman divergences in on-line learning. This progression scheme is very efficient: we show that a very large subset of classification calibrated losses may be minimized by a single boosting algorithm, with guaranteed rates of convergence under weak assumptions. We also show that this algorithm unifies various boosting algorithms, ranging from the top-down induction for decision trees performed in CART [9], C4.5 [34] to AdaBoost [36] and other boosting algorithms for linear separators. Thus, this geometric approach and its performances do not pertain to a specific kind of formalism for classifiers.

Our contribution is also structural: we show that a particular subset of classification calibrated surrogates has analytical, statistical and classification rationales, and strong ties with the maximum likelihood estimation for a subset of the exponential families of distributions. Finally, we provide experimental results on various surrogates, using a single surrogate to learn, or making attempts to tune the surrogate at hand for a more efficient optimization.

In Section 2, we present the learning settings; Section 3 presents the losses and surrogates, and their properties. Section 4 presents the related geometric problems. Section 5 presents our applications on linear separators, and Section 6 does the same for other classifiers. Section 7 presents our experimental results.

2   Learning Settings

2.1   General Considerations on Supervised Learning

Bold faced variables such as w and x, represent vectors whose dimension shall be clear from context. Unless otherwise stated, sets are represented by calligraphic upper-case alphabets, *e.g.* $\mathcal{X}$, and enumerated following their lower-case, such as $\{x_i : i = 1, 2, ...\}$ for vector sets, and $\{x_i : i = 1, 2, ...\}$ for other sets. Blackboard faces such as $\mathbb{S}$ denote subsets of (powers of) $\mathbb{R}$, the set of real numbers.

Machine learning refers in general to the possibility, for a computer, to improve its performances based on its experience. This definition may be formalized as the automatized construction of models to minimize losses based on training data. At the risk of oversimplifying, a major trend focuses on *supervised learning* (that we sometimes call *classification* for short) with *batch* or *on-line* algorithms.

The key input of supervised learning is the notion of *example*. An example is an ordered pair (o, c). The *observation* o belongs to a domain $\mathcal{O}$ of dimension n (such as $\{0, 1\}^n$, $\mathbb{R}^n$, the set of all patient descriptions, etc.), and the *class* c belongs to a set

$$\mathcal{C} = \{c^+, c^-\} \tag{1}$$

of *two* classes or labels (such as "ill/not ill" if the observations describe patients). We adopt the common convention that c^+ is called the positive class, and c^- the negative class.

The common problem to batch and on-line learning is the *efficient* and *accurate* automated construction of *classifiers*. Without entering into unnecessary details, in both settings, "efficiency" essentially means for the learning algorithms to be polynomial in relevant parameters. A classifier is a function $H : \mathcal{O} \to \mathcal{C}$, which belongs to a set defined by a particular formalism, whose choice is generally made by the user. This choice defines an absolute *bias*: a bias since it influences learning, and absolute since it is not questioned once it is done [28,32]. The freedom in the choice of the classifier is of primary importance, as users sometimes feel uncomfortable with some formalisms, in particular when it comes to interpreting the classifiers themselves [26,32]. Learning algorithms for any formalism should thus be appreciated in the light of their portability, their scalability to other formalisms.

There are many formalisms available, two of which are of primary importance, as they are the most frequently used in supervised learning: linear separators (LS) and decision trees (DT).

A LS is a weighted linear vote:

$$H(o) \doteq \sum_t \alpha_t h_t(o) \; , \tag{2}$$

with real leveraging coefficients, α_t, and votes, sometimes called features, that can be themselves classifiers $h_t(.) : \mathcal{O} \to \mathbb{O} \subseteq \mathbb{R}$. The output of these classifiers is not necessarily $\mathbb{R}$: the simplest case is $\mathbb{O} = \{-1, 1\}$; sometimes, one also uses features that *abstain*, with $\mathbb{O} = \{-1, 0, 1\}$, and so on until $\mathbb{R}$ itself [32,36]. In general, $\mathbb{O}$ is centered around the origin (hereafter, this property shall be assumed when using notation $\mathbb{O}$). Regarding such real votes, the notation of the classes in (1) is not convenient anymore. It is more convenient to carry out a first abstraction of the classes by a bijective mapping:

$$c \in \{c^-, c^+\} \rightleftharpoons y^* \in \{-1, +1\} \; .$$

The convention is $c^+ \rightleftharpoons +1$ and $c^- \rightleftharpoons -1$. We thus have two distinct notations for an example: (o, c), (o, y^*), that shall be used without ambiguity. Let us define

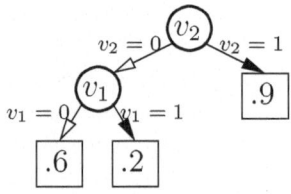

Fig. 1. A DT with 3 leaves and 2 internal nodes

threshold function $\sigma : \mathbb{R} \to \{-1, +1\}$, $+1$ iff $x \geq 0$ and -1 otherwise. Then the class assigned by a LS H is $\sigma \circ H$.

An ordinary, 2-ary DT, is a rooted directed acyclic tree whose internal nodes have outdegree two (see Figure 1). Each internal node is labeled by a description variable, and each of its outgoing arcs is labeled by a Boolean test over this variable, in such a way that the two outgoing arcs of an internal nodes have complementary tests over the variable. Assume for example that $\mathcal{O} = \{0, 1\}^n$, that is, observations are represented with Boolean variables. In Figure 1, arcs with a black arrow symbolize the test that the related Boolean variable is 1 (**true**), while arcs with a white arrow symbolize the test that the related Boolean variable is 0 (**false**). Starting from the root, an observation $o \in \mathcal{O}$ follows the path whose tests it satisfies, until it reaches a leaf used to predict its class. The fundamental difference between DT and LS is that DT makes a partition of $\mathcal{O}$ in cells (convex for ordinary decision trees) of constant values, and this partition is made in a recursive fashion, which is not the case for LS[1]. It is thus very convenient to put, at each leaf, a constant value representing the class assigned to all observations that reach the leaf. In addition to the two first already exposed, a third convention is used, which consists in putting a value in $[0, 1]$ being an "estimator" for the positive class membership probability for leaf k:

$$H(o) = \hat{\mathbf{Pr}}[c = c^+ | o \text{ reaches leaf } k] \ . \tag{3}$$

A second abstraction of the classes in (1) becomes convenient in this case:

$$c \in \{c^-, c^+\} \rightleftharpoons y \in \{0, 1\} \ .$$

The convention is $c^+ \rightleftharpoons 1$ and $c^- \rightleftharpoons 0$. We have one more notation for an example, that shall be used without ambiguity with the two others: (o, y). We define a second threshold function $\tau : [0, 1] \to \{0, 1\}$, 1 iff $x \geq 1/2$ and 0 otherwise. Then, the class assigned by a DT H is $\tau \circ H$.

The quality of a classifier H on example (o, c) is obtained by comparing the prediction $H(o)$ to the true class c of the example, via a *loss* function ℓ. Intuitively, ℓ is an increasing function of the discrepancy between c and the output of H. The simplest and most natural loss, which historically served as

---

[1] Modulo some technical assumptions on the votes h_t that virtually systematically hold, any LS also defines a partition of $\mathcal{O}$ in regions of constant values, but this partition is not recursive.

the basis for supervised learning models [37], is the *0/1 loss*, $\ell^{0/1}(c, H)$, which may be defined in two equivalent ways depending on $\text{im}(H)$:

$$\ell_{\mathbb{R}}^{0/1}(y^*, H) \doteq 1_{y^* \neq \sigma \circ H} \text{ if } \text{im}(H) = \mathbb{O} \ , \tag{4}$$

$$\ell_{[0,1]}^{0/1}(y, H) \doteq 1_{y \neq \tau \circ H} \text{ if } \text{im}(H) = [0, 1] \ . \tag{5}$$

Here, 1_π is the indicator variable that takes value 1 iff predicate π is **true**, and 0 otherwise. In the general loss case, wherever needed for a clear distinction of the output of H, we put in index to ℓ an indication of its image ($\mathbb{R}$, meaning it is actually some $\mathbb{O} \subseteq \mathbb{R}$, or $[0, 1]$). Sometimes, we also put in exponent an indication of the loss name, as we have done in (4) and (5) for the 0/1 loss. Both losses $\ell_{\mathbb{R}}$ and $\ell_{[0,1]}$ are defined simultaneously via popular *transfer* functions, such as the *logit* transform [14]:

$$\text{logit}(p) \doteq \log \frac{p}{1 - p} \ , \forall p \in [0, 1]. \tag{6}$$

The following examples on the 0/1 loss are easy to check:

$$\ell_{[0,1]}^{0/1}(y, H) = \ell_{\mathbb{R}}^{0/1}(y^*, \text{logit}(H)) \ ,$$

$$\ell_{\mathbb{R}}^{0/1}(y^*, H) = \ell_{[0,1]}^{0/1}(y, \text{logit}^{-1}(H)) \ .$$

We have implicitly closed the domain of the logit, adding two symbols $\pm\infty$ to ensure that the eventual infinite values for H can be scaled back to $[0, 1]$. Hereafter, functions on which the closure of both the domain and the image is assumed are called *admissible*. The loss is then used in a general *risk* which aggregates the losses over a particular set of examples. The way this risk is computed is different in batch and on-line learning.

2.2   Our Batch Setting

The most important model of batch learning is the so-called *PAC* (for Probably Approximately Correct) learning model of Valiant [37]. In this model, learning has two requirements, one which is computational, and the other, which is statistical. The input is a sample $\mathcal{S} = \{(o_1, c_1), (o_2, c_2), ..., (o_m, c_m)\}$ of training examples, supposed sampled i.i.d. from a subset of $\mathcal{O} \times \mathcal{C}$. The sampling distribution is unknown, but fixed. Thus, we cannot require that the classifier built on $\mathcal{S}$ be a perfect match for the class of any example of the whole domain, as for example it may be the case that we sample the same example m times. Rather, the statistical constraint is a slightly weaker form of generalization constraint, as we want that H represents a good approximation, with high probability, of the true labeling of the examples. It turns out that modulo some structural conditions on the formalism of H, a sufficient condition to learn is to build classifiers with a small overall loss over $\mathcal{S}$, that is, a small *empirical risk* (we follow a convention of [10]):

$$\varepsilon^{0/1}(\mathcal{S}, H) \doteq \sum_i \ell^{0/1}(c_i, H(o_i)) \ . \tag{7}$$

The 0/1 loss has a significant drawback: is not differentiable and not continuous (see Figure 4). Thus, while it is the criterion used to evaluate classifiers, it precludes important candidate machineries for its minimization, and calls in fact for other risks to optimize. For this objective, we define out of a general loss ℓ a general *risk* ε:

$$\varepsilon(\mathcal{S}, H) \doteq \sum_i \ell(c_i, H(\boldsymbol{o}_i)) \ . \tag{8}$$

To finish up with batch learning, we focus on a particular batch process for learning which is iterative by nature. In *boosting* [13,22,24,33], we suppose that H is built in a iterative, greedy fashion: at each main step t of the algorithm, we request for a *weak classifier* h_t to a *weak learner*, and H is built by repeatedly folding in all the weak classifiers obtained so far. This growing process for H must ensure that the current classifier keeps the desired formalism: when H is a LS, weak classifiers are simply summed up in the overall vote. When H is a DT, each weak classifier is a decision tree with a single internal node (a *stump*) which replaces a leaf in the current DT H. With respect to on-line learning (see below), boosting is dual in the sense that the stream of examples of on-line learning becomes a "stream" of weak classifiers in boosting.

2.3   Our On-Line Setting

The setting of on-line learning is inherently iterative but quite different from batch learning [15,25]. In particular, we are not given set $\mathcal{S}$. Rather, we receive examples one by one, out of an infinite stream of examples. The endless nature of the stream is important: should the stream be supposed to end at some moment, the difference with batch learning would be superficial; in particular, efficient learning would essentially boil down to waiting for the stream to end, and then batch learn on the examples seen so far.

In this endless supply of examples, a convenient thing to do is to repeatedly update the current classifier H each time an example is received, to stay close to some *reference* classifier. We start with an initial "guess" classifier H_0 which can be a constant prediction, and we repeat infinitely many times (i) the receipt of example $(\boldsymbol{o}_t, c_t)$, (ii) the update of classifier H_{t-1} to classifier H_t, for $t = 1, 2, \dots$. At iteration t, if we denote $\mathcal{S}_t$ the set of current examples received so far, a natural objective for learning is to ensure that the set of classifiers that have been built so far has achieved over the stream of examples a 0/1 loss which stays close to that of a *reference* classifier taken from the same set of classifiers as ours. More formally, this objective may be formalized as requiring, for any $T > 0$ and any reference classifier H_r:

$$\sum_{t=1}^{T} \ell^{0/1}(c_t, H_{t-1}(\boldsymbol{o}_t)) \leq \sum_{t=1}^{T} \ell^{0/1}(c_t, H_r(\boldsymbol{o}_t)) + \text{penalty} \ , \tag{9}$$

or, from a more general standpoint,

$$\sum_{t=1}^{T} \ell(c_t, H_{t-1}(o_t)) \leq \sum_{t=1}^{T} \ell(c_t, H_r(o_t)) + \text{ penalty } ; \qquad (10)$$

this objective becomes perhaps more meaningful from the goodness-of-fit stand-point, if we think of H_r as achieving a convenient minimization of the right-hand side of (9). This, however, may require for H_r a bit more than simply minimizing the risk of the right-hand side, as the penalty can depend upon H_r as well. The role of complexity is naturally pregnant in on-line learning, as the stream may provide us with examples at extremely fast pace. To finish up with on-line learning, we extend the general risk definition in (8) to its relevant twin in on-line learning:

$$\varepsilon\left(\mathcal{S}_T, \{H_t\}_{t=0}^{T-1}\right) \doteq \sum_{t=1}^{T} \ell(c_t, H_{t-1}(o_t)) \, , \forall T > 0 \, , \qquad (11)$$

so that (10) may be written: $\varepsilon\left(\mathcal{S}_T, \{H_t\}_{t=0}^{T-1}\right) \leq \varepsilon(\mathcal{S}_T, H_r) + \text{ penalty}$.

3   Bregman Loss Functions

We now present alternative losses that may be used in both batch and on-line learning. Most interestingly, the same alternatives emerge almost independently out of analytical, classification or statistical rationales.

3.1   Integral Losses

Linear separators, decision trees, and many other classifiers, are naturally "more powerful" than what is required since they encode a much greater number of values than the set of two classes. These values typically belong to two kinds of sets. The first contains signed intervals $\mathbb{O}$ typically centered on 0. In the case of LS, it would be $\mathbb{R}$ itself. The second can be reduced to the interval $[0, 1]$ or positive intervals centered on $1/2$.

Suppose that there exists an admissible *transfer function* [25] between these two kinds of sets: a strictly increasing (thus invertible) continuous function $\varrho : \mathbb{O} \rightarrow [0, 1]$. Figure 2 presents an example of a transfer function. Monotonicity provides a convenient mapping of the classes between the two kinds of possible outputs of a classifier, as the more "probable" the membership probability to the positive class and the larger (and positive) the real value, and reciprocally. For this reason, we use the transfer function to compute a discrepancy between two predictions, as the area depicted in Figure 2. This discrepancy is called an *integral loss*.

Definition 1. *The integral loss with parameter ϱ between two predictions y and y' in $[0, 1]$ is:*

$$\ell_{\mathbb{R}}^{\varrho}(H, H') \doteq \int_{H}^{H'} (\varrho(x) - y)\mathrm{d}x \, , \qquad (12)$$

with $H \doteq \varrho^{-1}(y)$ and $H' \doteq \varrho^{-1}(y')$.

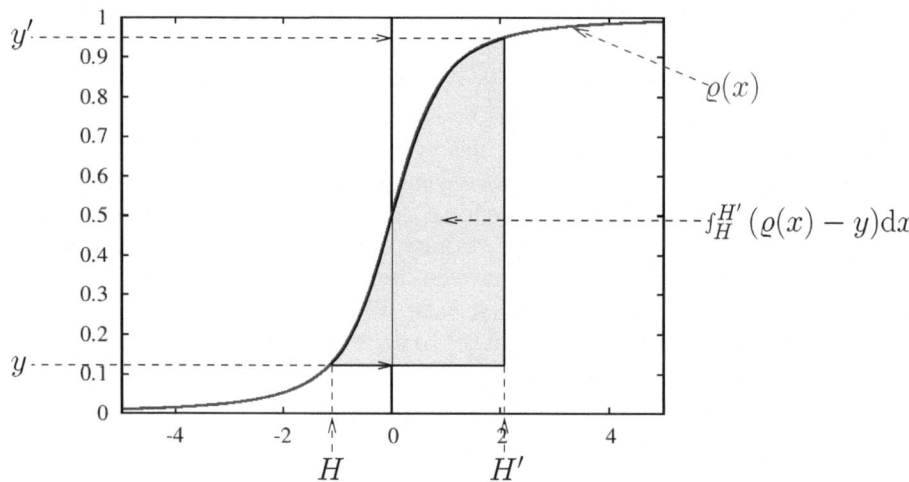

Fig. 2. The loss as computed in (12) for transfer function ϱ

logit^{-1} is an example of a transfer function (6). The rightmost column of Table 2 presents other examples of transfer functions. Figure 3 shows that the 0/1 loss is not an integral loss, but a limit case, considering that the integrals can be computed from limit histograms and the 0/1 loss is the simplest non-trivial case of histogram. Figure 2 displays an invariance of the integral loss which is particularly convenient for classification. Indeed, because ϱ is invertible, we have:

$$\ell_{\mathbb{R}}^{\varrho}(H, H') = \int_{y'}^{y} (\varrho^{-1}(x) - H')\mathrm{d}x = \ell_{\mathbb{R}}^{(\varrho^{-1})}(y', y) \ . \tag{13}$$

Both integrals in eq. (12) and (13) can be rephrased as follows, if we denote $\psi \doteq \int \varrho$ and $\psi^{\star} \doteq \int \varrho^{-1}$:

$$\begin{aligned}
\ell_{\mathbb{R}}^{\varrho}(H, H') &= \psi(H') - \psi(H) - (H' - H)\varrho(H) \\
&= \psi^{\star}(y) - \psi^{\star}(y') - (y - y')\varrho^{-1}(y') \\
&= \ell_{\mathbb{R}}^{(\varrho^{-1})}(y', y) \ .
\end{aligned}$$

Integral losses coincide with a particular kind of distortion measure: Bregman Loss Functions [3].

Definition 2. *For any strictly convex function $\psi : \mathbb{X} \to \mathbb{R}$ defined over a closed interval $\mathbb{X}$ of $\mathbb{R}$, differentiable over the opened interval, the Bregman Loss Function (BLF, [3]) D_{ψ} with generator ψ is:*

$$D_{\psi}(x || x') \doteq \psi(x) - \psi(x) - (x - x')\nabla_{\psi}(x') \ , \tag{14}$$

where ∇_{ψ} denotes the first derivative of ψ.

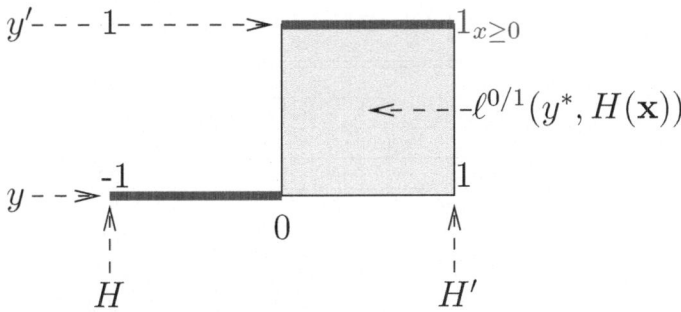

Fig. 3. The 0/1 loss is a limit case of integral loss for function $1_{x \geq 0}$, and real-valued classifiers that can only take on values in $\{-1, 1\}$

The parameter ϱ in the integral loss is thus the derivative of the BLF generator. We also make use of a vector-based notation for BLFs, and it shall mean a component-wise sum of BLFs, such as:

$$D_\psi(\boldsymbol{a}||\boldsymbol{b}) = \sum_i D_\psi(a_i||b_i) \ . \tag{15}$$

BLFs define a subset of a set of distortion measures with interesting geometric features: Bregman divergences [8].

Definition 3. *For any strictly convex function* $\psi : \mathbb{X} \to \mathbb{R}$ *defined over a closed convex set* $\mathbb{X}$ *of* $\mathbb{R}^m$, *and continuously differentiable over its relative interior, the Bregman divergence* D_ψ *with generator* ψ *is:*

$$D_\psi(\boldsymbol{x}||\boldsymbol{x}') \doteq \psi(\boldsymbol{x}) - \psi(\boldsymbol{x}) - (\boldsymbol{x} - \boldsymbol{x}')^\top \boldsymbol{\nabla}_\psi(\boldsymbol{x}') \ , \tag{16}$$

where $\boldsymbol{\nabla}_\psi$ *denotes the gradient of* ψ.

Table 1 gives some examples of Bregman divergences. The first three are *separable* as they satisfy (15) [12]. Kullback-Leibler is convex in its both parameters, while Itakura-Saito is not; the Squared Euclidean distance is symmetric — in fact, Mahalanobis distortion is the only symmetric Bregman divergence [31].

In our context, it shall be useful to think the gradients as being admissible, thus making it possible to extend the corrresponding Bregman divergences to $\mathbb{X}^2$, and not simply $\mathbb{X}$ times its relative interior. The invariance described in (13) is captured with the following important notion.

Definition 4. *For any strictly convex function* $\psi : \mathbb{X} \to \mathbb{R}$ *defined over a closed convex set* $\mathbb{X}$ *of* $\mathbb{R}^m$, *the Legendre transform* $\psi^\star$ *of* ψ *is:*

$$\psi^\star(\boldsymbol{x}) \doteq \sup_{\boldsymbol{x}'}\{\boldsymbol{x}^\top \boldsymbol{x}' - \psi(\boldsymbol{x}')\} \ , \tag{17}$$

where $\boldsymbol{x}$ *belongs to the relative interior of* $\mathbb{X}$.

Table 1. Examples of Bregman divergences (spd = symmetric positive definite)

$\psi(\boldsymbol{x})$	$D_\psi(\boldsymbol{x}\|\boldsymbol{x}')$	Name
$\sum_i x_i \log x_i - x_i$	$\sum_i \{x_i \log(x_i/x_i') - x_i + x_i'\}$	Kullback-Leibler
$\sum_i -\log x_i$	$\sum_i \{(x_i/x_i') - \log(x_i/x_i') - 1\}$	Itakura-Saito
$\sum_i x_i^2$	$\sum_i (x_i - x_i')^2$	Squared Eucl. dist.
$\boldsymbol{x}^\top \Sigma \boldsymbol{x}$	$(\boldsymbol{x} - \boldsymbol{x}')^\top \Sigma (\boldsymbol{x} - \boldsymbol{x}')$	Mahalanobis (Σ spd)
$(1/2)\|\boldsymbol{x}\|_q^2$ $= \frac{1}{2}\left[\left(\sum_i |x_i|^q\right)^{1/q}\right]^2$	$(1/2)\|\boldsymbol{x}\|_q^2 - (1/2)\|\boldsymbol{x}'\|_q^2 - (\boldsymbol{x} - \boldsymbol{x}')^\top \nabla_\psi(\boldsymbol{x}')$ $\nabla_\psi(\boldsymbol{x})_i = \sigma(x_i)|x_i|^{q-1}/\|\boldsymbol{x}\|_q^{q-2}$	q-norm ($q > 1$)

Because of the strict convexity of ψ, the analytic expression of the Legendre transform becomes:

$$\psi^\star(\boldsymbol{x}) \doteq \boldsymbol{x}^\top \nabla_\psi^{-1}(\boldsymbol{x}) - \psi(\nabla_\psi^{-1}(\boldsymbol{x})) \ . \tag{18}$$

$\psi^\star$ is also strictly convex and differentiable. There are two important results to note, that easily follow from the identity $\nabla_\psi = \nabla_{\psi^\star}^{-1}$:

$$\psi^{\star\star} = \psi \ ,$$
$$D_\psi(\boldsymbol{x}\|\boldsymbol{x}') = D_{\psi^\star}(\nabla_\psi(\boldsymbol{x}')\|\nabla_\psi(\boldsymbol{x})) \ ,$$

and that latter equality is just a generalization of (13). To summarize, BLFs have a strong analytical rationale to compute the losses of classifiers with dense outputs like LS and DT. The 0/1 loss is a limit case of BLF.

3.2   Surrogate Losses and Classification Calibrated Losses

We now introduce a popular formalization for losses over real-valued classifiers. A serious alternative to directly minimizing (7) is to rather focus on the minimization of a *surrogate risk* [5] (surrogate, for short). This is a function $\varepsilon(\mathcal{S}, H)$ as in (8) whose *surrogate loss* $\ell(c, H(\boldsymbol{o}))$ satisfies

$$\ell^{0/1}(c, H(\boldsymbol{o})) \leq \ell(c, H(\boldsymbol{o})) \ .$$

Four surrogate losses are particularly important in supervised learning:

$$\ell_\mathbb{R}^{\exp}(y^*, H) \doteq \exp(-y^* H) \ , \tag{19}$$
$$\ell_\mathbb{R}^{\log}(y^*, H) \doteq \log(1 + \exp(-y^* H)) \ , \tag{20}$$
$$\ell_\mathbb{R}^{\mathrm{sqr}}(y^*, H) \doteq (1 - y^* H)^2 \ , \tag{21}$$
$$\ell_\mathbb{R}^{\mathrm{hinge}}(y^*, H) \doteq \max\{0, 1 - y^* H\} \ . \tag{22}$$

(19) is the exponential loss, (20) is the logistic loss, (21) is the squared loss and (22) is hinge loss. The first three are examples of *strictly convex losses*; all are plotted in Figure 4.

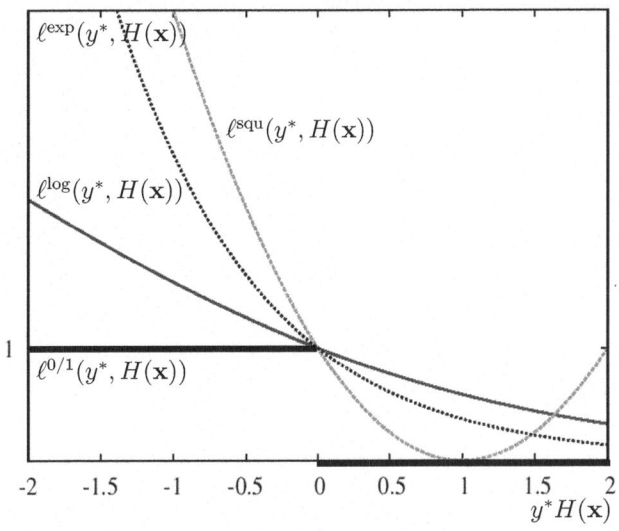

Fig. 4. The surrogate losses in (19), (20), (21) versus the 0/1 loss

Definition 5. *A Strictly Convex Loss (SCL) is a strictly convex function ψ :
$\mathbb{X} \to \mathbb{R}_+$ differentiable on the opened interval and such that $\nabla_\psi(0) < 0$, with $\mathbb{X}$
centered on zero.*

Once again, it shall be useful to think of the derivative as being admissible.
There is an immediate link between the 0/1 loss and any SCL, as dividing the
SCL by $\psi(0) > 0$ immediately yields an upperbound of the 0/1 loss. Thus, any
efficient machinery to minimize the surrogate yields an indirect minimization of
the empirical risk.

We now explain the rationale of SCL, and in particular its importance for
classification. Following [5], we first define classification calibrated losses (CCL).
Suppose that all examples in $\mathcal{S}$ have the same observation, o, and the two classes
are in proportion η for the positive class, and $1 - \eta$ for the negative class. Any
general surrogate $\varepsilon_\mathbb{R}$ with surrogate loss $\ell_\mathbb{R}$ simplifies over this sample and can
be written:

$$\varepsilon_\mathbb{R}(\eta, H) \doteq \eta \ell_\mathbb{R}(H) + (1 - \eta)\ell_\mathbb{R}(-H) \ , \tag{23}$$

where H is a real constant prediction. Classification calibration requires that,
for any $\eta \neq 1/2$, the minimal risk is smaller than the minimal risk in which we
require H to be of a different sign than $2\eta - 1$. More precisely, $\ell_\mathbb{R}$ belongs to
classification calibrated losses (CCL) iff:

$$\varepsilon_\mathbb{R}^+(\eta) < \varepsilon_\mathbb{R}^-(\eta) \ , \forall \eta \neq 1/2 \ , \tag{24}$$

$$\varepsilon_\mathbb{R}^+(\eta) \doteq \inf_H \varepsilon_\mathbb{R}(\eta, H) \ ,$$

$$\varepsilon_\mathbb{R}^-(\eta) \doteq \inf_{H:H(2\eta-1)\leq 0} \varepsilon_\mathbb{R}(\eta, H) \ . \tag{25}$$

Table 2. Correspondence between permissible functions, the corresponding BCLs and the transfer functions

$\phi(x)$	a_ϕ	$\mathrm{im}(\nabla_\phi)$ $\supseteq \mathrm{im}(H)$	$F_\phi(y^*H)$ $= (\phi^\star(-y^*H) - a_\phi)/b_\phi$	$\hat{\mathbf{Pr}}_\phi[c = c^+\|H; o]$ $= \nabla_\phi^{-1}(H)$
(27)	μ	$\mathbb{R}$	$\frac{1}{1-\mu}\left(-y^*H + \sqrt{(1-\mu)^2 + (y^*H)^2}\right)$	$\frac{1}{2}\left(1 + H/\sqrt{(1-\mu)^2 + H^2}\right)$
(28)	0	$\mathbb{R}$	$-y^*H + \sqrt{1 + (y^*H)^2}$	$\frac{1}{2}\left(1 + H/\sqrt{1 + H^2}\right)$
(29)	0	$\mathbb{R}$	$\log(1 + \exp(-y^*H))$	$\exp(H)/(1 + \exp(H))$
(26)	0	$[-1, 1]$	$(1 - y^*H)^2$	$\frac{1}{2}(1 + H)$

In our setting, quantity $2\eta - 1 \in [-1, 1]$ is the inverse of the transfer function for the following convex function:

$$\psi = \phi_\mathrm{B}(x) \doteq -x(1 - x) \ . \tag{26}$$

We could have replaced this transfer function by many other examples, like for example logit in (6). We use this particular case because (25) is the original definition of classification calibrated losses of [5]. Furthermore, (26) is to play an important role later.

To summarize, condition $H(2\eta - 1) \leq 0$ in (25) imposes H to be an overall wrong real prediction on $\mathcal{S}$. Thus, condition (24) states that from the efficient minimization of the surrogate necessarily follows the most accurate prediction of the classes, for every observation. Failing to meet this weak condition would make the surrogate meaningless for classification purposes. It follows from [5], Theorem 4, that SCL⊂CCL, spanning all strictly convex differentiable and classification calibrated losses, such as (19), (20), (21).

So far, we have defined two main classes of losses, integral losses with some analytical rationale, and strictly convex losses with some classification rationale. There seems to be a visual difference between these two classes of losses, as the former distinguish class y and prediction H as different parameters, while the latter aggregate y^* and H in a single parameter, y^*H which can be called an *edge* (see *e.g.* (19) — (22)). The following section shows that this difference is essentially superficial.

3.3   Balanced Convex Losses

Let us adopt a principled approach on what should be a "good" loss function for classification. Ne need to import the main three assumptions that underlie classification losses in a majority of works in supervised learning. These assumptions, stated for $\mathrm{im}(H) \subseteq [0, 1]$ without loss of generality, are:

(**A1**) *The loss is lower-bounded* by 0. We have:

$$\ell_{[0,1]}(.,.) \geq 0 \ .$$

(**A2**) *The loss is a proper scoring rule.* Consider a singleton domain $\mathcal{O} = \{o\}$. Then, the best (constant) prediction is:

$$\arg\min_{H \in [0,1]} \varepsilon_{[0,1]}(\mathcal{S}, H) = \eta \doteq \hat{\mathbf{Pr}}[c = c^+ | o] \in [0,1] \ ,$$

where p is the proportion of positive examples with observation o.

(**A3**) *The loss is symmetric* in the following sense:

$$\ell_{[0,1]}(y, H) = \ell_{[0,1]}(1 - y, 1 - H), \forall y \in \{0,1\}, \forall H \in [0,1] \ .$$

Lower-boundedness in **A1** is standard. For **A2**, we can equivalently write an analogue of (23) for $[0,1]$ classifiers:

$$\varepsilon_{[0,1]}(\mathcal{S}, H) = \varepsilon_{[0,1]}(\eta, H) = \eta\ell_{[0,1]}(1, H) + (1 - \eta)\ell_{[0,1]}(0, H) \ ,$$

which is just the expected loss of zero-sum games used in [18] (eq. (8)) with Nature states reduced to the class labels. The fact that the minimum is achieved at $H = \eta$ makes the loss a proper scoring rule. η also defines *Bayes classifier, i.e.* the one which minimizes the 0/1 loss [2]. **A3** scales to $H \in [0,1]$ a well-known symmetry in the *cost matrix* that holds for domains without class dependent misclassification costs. This 2×2 matrix, L, gives

$$l_{ij} \doteq \ell(i - 1, j - 1)$$

for any values $(i, j) \in \{1, 2\}^2$. Usually, it is admitted that $\ell(1, 1) = \ell(0, 0)$, *i.e.* right classification incurs the same loss regardless of the class. Generally, this loss is zero. Problems *without* class-dependent misclassification costs, on which focus the vast majority of theoretical studies, also make the assumption that $\ell(1, 0) = \ell(0, 1)$. Assumption **A3** scales theses two properties to $H \in [0,1]$. We now extend a terminology due to [23]

Definition 6. *A function $\phi : [0,1] \to \mathbb{R}_+$ is permissible iff $-\phi$ is differentiable on $(0,1)$, strictly concave, symmetric about $x = 1/2$, and with $-\phi(0) = -\phi(1) \doteq a_\phi \geq 0$.*

Hereafter, ϕ refers to a permissible function. Once again, it shall be useful to think of the derivative of ϕ as being admissible (assuming the logit closure we make in Subsection 2.1, all permissible functions are admissible). Definition 6 relies on $-\phi$ rather than ϕ because $-\phi$ is the function generally used, as it spans *e.g.* a subset of the generalized entropies [18], or it represents the function actually used for the induction of some classifiers including DT (see Section 6) [19,23]. For all popular permissible ϕ, we have $a_\phi = 0$ [23]. We let $b_\phi \doteq -\phi(1/2) - a_\phi > 0$. In addition to (26), below are more examples of permissible functions ϕ, that have been arranged from the bottom-most to the topmost function (when scaled so that $\phi(1/2) = -1$).

$$\phi_\mu(x) \doteq -(\mu + (1 - \mu)\sqrt{x(1 - x)}) \ , \forall \mu \in (0, 1) \ . \tag{27}$$

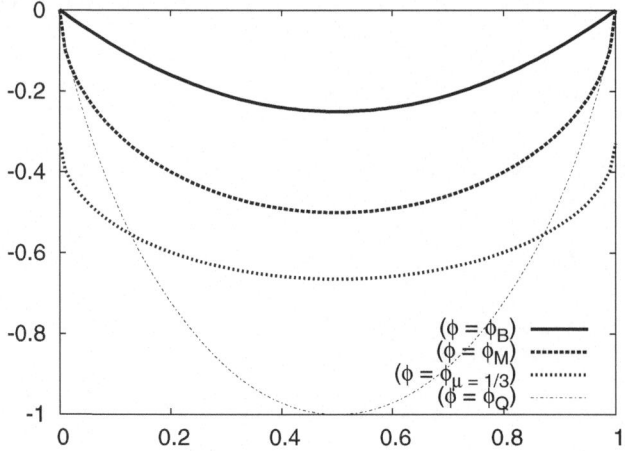

Fig. 5. The permissible functions in (26), (27), (28), (29)

$$\phi_M(x) \doteq -\sqrt{x(1-x)} \ , \tag{28}$$

$$\phi_Q(x) \doteq x \log x + (1-x) \log(1-x) \ , \ . \tag{29}$$

When scaled so that $\phi(1/2) = -1$, most confound with the opposite of popular choices: Gini index for (26) [9], Bit-entropy for (29) [34], and Matsushita's error for (28) [23,27]. Figure 5 plots these permissible functions. Finally, we say that loss $\ell_{[0,1]}$ is *properly defined* iff $\mathrm{dom}(\ell_{[0,1]}) = [0,1]^2$ and it is twice differentiable on $(0,1)^2$. This last definition is only a technical convenience: even the 0/1 loss coincides on $\{0,1\}$ with properly defined losses. In addition, the differentiability condition would be satisfied by many popular surrogates. Hinge loss (22) is a notable exception, yet it plays a key role in the properties of *balanced convex surrogates*, for which the following Lemma is central.

Lemma 1. *Any loss $\ell_{[0,1]}(.,.)$ is properly defined and satisfies assumptions **A1**, **A2** and **A3** if and only if*

$$\ell_{[0,1]}(y,H) = D_\phi(y\|H) \ ,$$

for some permissible function ϕ.

Proof: ($\Leftarrow$) Assumption **A3** follows from the strict concavity and symmetry of $-\phi$. Assumptions **A1** and **A2** follow from usual properties of BLFs [3]. ($\Rightarrow$) Without assumption **A3**, $\ell_{[0,1]}(y,H)$ is a BLF [3], $D_\phi(y\|H)$ for some strictly convex function ϕ, differentiable on $(0,1)$. Modulo rearrangements in assumption **A3**, we obtain

$$\nabla_{\tilde{\phi}}(H) = (\tilde{\phi}(H) - \tilde{\phi}(y))/(H - y), \forall y, H \in [0,1] \ ,$$

with $\tilde{\phi}(x) = -\phi(1-x) + \phi(x)$. It comes that $\tilde{\phi}(x) = ax + b$ for some $a, b \in \mathbb{R}$. Since $\tilde{\phi}(1-x) = -\tilde{\phi}(x)$, we easily obtain $a = b = 0$, *i.e.* $\phi(x) = \phi(1-x)$.

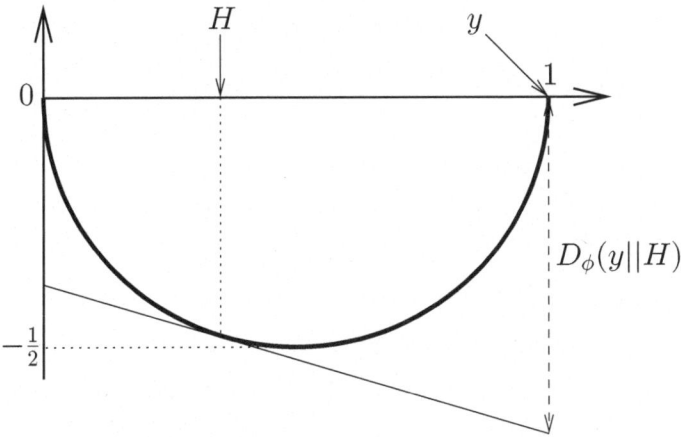

Fig. 6. Plot of $\ell(y, H) = D_\phi(y||H)$ (Lemma 1) for $\phi = \phi_M(x)$ in (28) and $y, H \in [0, 1]$

Ultimately, since a BLF $D_\phi(y||H)$ does not change by adding a constant term to ϕ, we can suppose without loss of generality that $\phi(0) = \phi(1) = -a_\phi \leq 0$, which makes that ϕ is permissible.   □

ϕ is thus the "signature" of the loss. We insist on the fact that we could have replaced **A1** by a simple lower-boundedness condition without reference to zero, in which case from Lemma 1 the loss would be a BLF plus a constant factor, without impact on the structural or minimization properties that are to come. Using Lemma 1, Figure 6 depicts an example of $\ell(y, H)$ for ϕ as in (28). Permissible functions are useful to define the following subclass of SCL, of particular interest

Definition 7. *Let ϕ permissible. The Balanced Convex Loss (BCL) with signature ϕ, F_ϕ, is:*

$$F_\phi(x) \doteq (\phi^\star(-x) - a_\phi)/b_\phi \ . \tag{30}$$

Balanced Convex Surrogates (BCS) are defined accordingly as sums of BCL:

$$\varepsilon_\mathbb{R}^\phi(\mathcal{S}, H) \doteq \sum_i F_\phi(y_i^* H(\boldsymbol{o}_i)) \ . \tag{31}$$

All BCL share a common shape. Indeed, $\phi^\star(x)$ satisfies the following relationships:

$$\phi^\star(x) = \phi^\star(-x) + x \ , \tag{32}$$

$$\lim_{x \to \text{infim}(\nabla_\phi)} \phi^\star(x) = a_\phi \ . \tag{33}$$

Noting that $F_\phi(0) = 1$ and $\nabla_{F_\phi}(0) = -(1/b_\phi)\nabla_\phi^{-1}(0) < 0$, it follows that BCS $\subset$ SCS, where the strict inequality comes from the fact that (19) is a SCL but not a BCL. It also follows

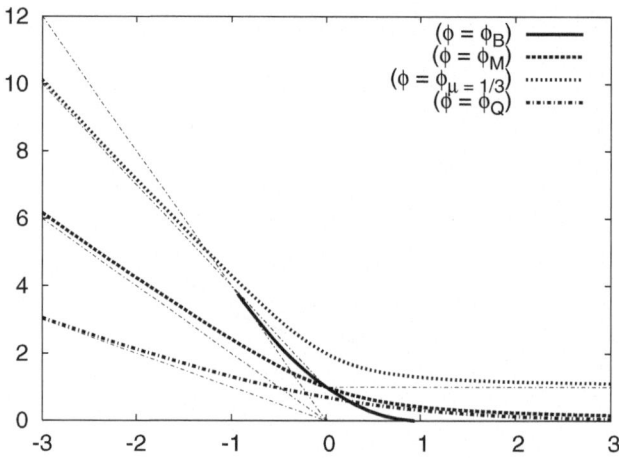

Fig. 7. Bold curves depict plots of $\phi^*(-x)$ for the ϕ in (26), (27), (28), (29); thin dotted half-lines display parts of its asymptotes

$$\lim_{x \to \mathrm{supim}(\nabla_\phi)} F_\phi(x) = 0 \text{ from (33)} ,$$

$$\lim_{x \to \mathrm{infim}(\nabla_\phi)} F_\phi(x) = -x/b_\phi \text{ from (32)} .$$

We get that the asymptotes of any BCL can be summarized as

$$\underline{\ell}(x) \doteq x(\sigma(x) - 1)/(2b_\phi) . \tag{34}$$

When $b_\phi = 1$, this is the linear hinge loss [16], a generalization of (22) for which $x \doteq y^* H - 1$. Thus, while hinge loss is not a BCL, it is the limit behavior of any BCL. Figure 7 presents examples of BCL. Figure 8 presents the inverse of the transfer functions for the same ϕ as in Figure 7. The additional sigmoid curve indexed by variable ζ, is for a permissible ϕ_ζ as follows ($\forall \zeta \in \mathbb{R}_{-,*}$):

$$\phi_\zeta(x) \doteq -\frac{2}{\zeta} \log \cosh \left(\frac{\zeta}{2} \left(x - \frac{1}{2} \right) \right) . \tag{35}$$

When properly scaled, this permissible function is located in between $2\phi_B$ in (26) and $-\min\{x, 1-x\}$ (and strictly in between for $x \neq 0, 1/2, 1$) — in this last case, the corresponding transfer function converges to the 0/1 loss. Tuning $\zeta \in \mathbb{R}_{-,*}$ makes the function span all the available area. It was chosen to show that there can be different concave/convex regimes for ∇_ϕ. Since $\mathrm{dom}(F_\phi) = \mathrm{im}(\nabla_\phi)$, there are also much different domains for the BCLs.

The following Lemma states some relationships that are easy to check using $\psi^{\star\star} = \psi$. They are particularly interesting when $\mathrm{im}(H) = \mathbb{O} \subseteq \mathbb{R}$.

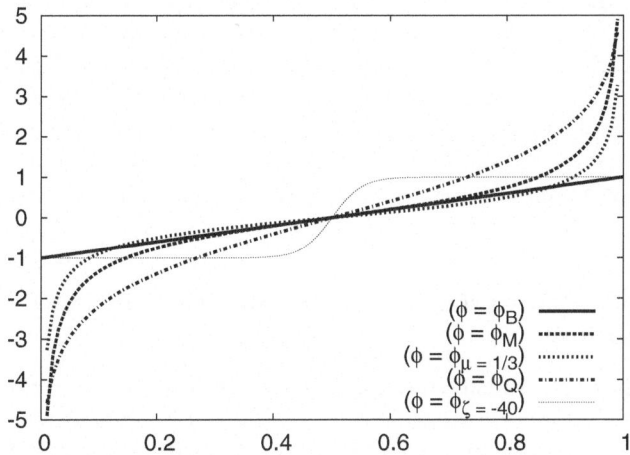

Fig. 8. Plots of ∇_ϕ for the same ϕ as in Figure 7, plus an additional one that displays a particular regime (see text for details)

Lemma 2. *For any* SCL ψ,

$$\psi(y^*H) = D_{\psi^\star}(0||\nabla_{\psi^\star}^{-1}(y^*H)) - \psi^\star(0) \ . \tag{36}$$

Furthermore, for any BCL F_ϕ,

$$D_\phi(y||\nabla_\phi^{-1}(H)) = b_\phi F_\phi(y^*H) \ , \tag{37}$$

$$= D_\phi(1||\nabla_\phi^{-1}(y^*H)) \ . \tag{38}$$

Finally, for any SCL ψ, *there exists a functions* φ *such that*

$$D_\varphi(y||\nabla_\varphi^{-1}(H)) = \psi(y^*H) \tag{39}$$

iff the restriction of $\psi^\star(-x)$ *to the interval* $\nabla_\psi^{-1}([-1, 0])$ *is permissible.*

Proof: The equalities are straightforward to check, so we concentrate on the last property, that we only have to check for the implication $\Rightarrow$. We note that:

$$D_\varphi(y||\nabla_\varphi^{-1}(H)) = \varphi(y) + \varphi^\star(H) - yH \ . \tag{40}$$

Making the difference of (39) for $y = 0$ and $y = 1$ yields $\psi(H) = \psi(-H) - H + (\varphi(1) - \varphi(0))$, *i.e.* $\varphi(0) = \varphi(1)$ (obtained with $H = 0$). Differentiating (39) = (40) in H for $y = 0$ yields $\nabla_{\varphi^\star}(x) = -\nabla_\psi(-x)$, *i.e.* $\varphi(x) = \psi^\star(-x) + K$. We easily obtain $\nabla_\varphi(1/2) = 0$ and $\nabla_\varphi(x) = -\nabla_\varphi(1 - x)$, *i.e.* φ is permissible. $\quad\square$

To summarize, up to additive constants that play no role in their minimization, integral losses and strictly convex losses coincide; they are just different writings of the same losses, that can be used as an efficient primer for the minimization of the 0/1 loss. Both match a wide subset of classification calibrated losses, and contain a set called balanced convex losses. In addition to the analytical and classification rationales of its supersets, BCL coincides with losses that match **A1 — A3**. The transfer function defines the signature of the loss, a crucial part of the loss. The following Subsection shows that BCL has another rationale which ties its minimization to maximum likelihood estimation for popular families of densities, whose members are precisely parameterized by the signature of the loss.

3.4   Balanced Convex Losses and Exponential Families of Distributions

(37) tells us that the transfer function as used in Figure 2 is in fact the inverse of the permissible function's gradient (∇_ϕ^{-1}) in a BCL. This provides us with an estimator of the membership probability to the positive class, if H is such that $\mathrm{im}(H) = \mathbb{O}$:

$$\hat{\mathbf{Pr}}_\phi[c = c^+|H; \boldsymbol{o}] \doteq \nabla_\phi^{-1}(H(\boldsymbol{o})) \ . \tag{41}$$

We can shed some statistical light in the estimation given in (41), illustrated in Table 2 (rightmost column). This exploits famous distributions known as the exponential families of distributions [30]. Prominent members include Bernoulli (multinomial), normal, Poisson, Laplacian, negative binomial, Rayleigh, Wishart, Dirichlet, and Gamma distributions, but we shall only need a subset which turns out to be in bijection with the set of all BCLs. More precisely, using the general bijection between BLFs and the exponential families of distributions of [4], there exists through eq. (36) a bijection between the set of BCL and a subset of these exponential families whose members' pdfs may be written:

$$\mathbf{Pr}_\phi[y|\theta] = \exp(-D_\phi(y||\nabla_\phi^{-1}(\theta)) + \phi(y) - \nu(y)) \ ,$$

where $\theta \in \mathbb{R}$ denotes the natural parameter of the pdf, and $\nu(.)$ is used for normalization. Plugging $\theta = H(\boldsymbol{o})$, using (36) and (41), we obtain that any BCS (31) can be rewritten as:

$$\varepsilon_\mathbb{R}^\phi(\mathcal{S}, H) = u + \sum_i -\log \hat{\mathbf{Pr}}_\phi[y_i|H(\boldsymbol{o}_i)] \ ,$$

where u does not play a role in the minimization of the BCS with H. We obtain the following Lemma, in which we suppose again $\mathrm{im}(H) = \mathbb{O}$.

Lemma 3. *Minimizing any BCS with classifier H yields a maximum likelihood estimation, for each observation $\boldsymbol{o}$, of the natural parameter $\theta = H(\boldsymbol{o})$ of an exponential family defined by signature ϕ.*

Real-valued hypotheses like linear separators may thus be viewed as estimating the natural parameters; by duality, classifiers that are able to fit $[0, 1]$ values, like decision trees, would rather be considered estimating the expectation parameters of the corresponding exponential families, *i.e.* obtained via the transfer function, $\nabla_\phi^{-1}(\theta)$ (Subsection 3.1).

To end up, only one exponential family is in fact concerned in our setting. Assuming $y \in \{0, 1\}$, the pdf simplifies and we end up with

$$\mathbf{Pr}_\phi[y|\theta] = \frac{1}{1 + \exp(-\theta)} \ ,$$

the logistic prediction for a Bernoulli prior. To summarize, minimizing any surrogate whose loss meets **A1**, **A2** and **A3** (*i.e.* any BCS) amounts to the same ultimate goal. The crux of the choice of the BCS mainly relies on algorithmic and data-dependent considerations for its efficient minimization.

3.5   Margins

It has been soon remarked in machine learning that the output of classifiers returning real values is useful beyond its thresholding via functions σ or τ (Subsection 2.1). In fact, we can also retrieve a measure of its "confidence" [36]. For example, when $\mathrm{im}(H) = \mathbb{O}$, it can be its absolute value [36]. Intuitively, learning should aim at providing classifiers that decide right classes with large confidences. Integrating both notions of class and confidence in criteria to optimize was done via margins [33,35]. Informally, the (normalized) margin of H on example (o, y^*), $\mu_H((o, y^*))$, takes value in $[-1, 1]$; it is positive only when the class assigned by H is the right one, and its absolute value quantifies the confidence in the classification. Different definitions of margins coexist, each of which tailored to a particular kind of classifier, with a particular kind of outputs: for example, in the case of linear separators, we may have [36,35]:

$$\mu_H((o, y^*)) \doteq \frac{y^* \sum_t \alpha_t h_t(o)}{\sum_t \alpha_t} \ .$$

Lemma 2 suggests a general and simple margin definition that we state for $\mathrm{im}(H) = \mathbb{O}$ and any permissible ϕ. Fix:

$$\mu_H((o, y^*)) \doteq 2\nabla_\phi^{-1}(y^* H(o)) - 1 \ . \tag{42}$$

Eq. (42) is just a scaling of the transfer function to interval $[-1, 1]$. When ϕ is chosen as in (29), (42) simplifies to the margin adopted in [33] for linear separators. The link between the maximization of margins as in (42) and loss minimization comes from Lemma 2. Indeed, (38) states that the minimization of any loss that meet **A1**, **A2**, **A3** is equivalent to margin maximization. Finally, since ϕ is permissible, (41) yields:

$$\mu_H((o, y^*)) = y^*(2\hat{\mathbf{Pr}}_\phi[c = c^+|H; o] - 1) \ \in [-1, 1] \ . \tag{43}$$

(43) shows that the margin simplifies to a quantity homogeneous to an edge as defined in Subsection 3.2, for any permissible ϕ. This is convenient for experiments, as we can make fair comparisons between margins for different ϕ.

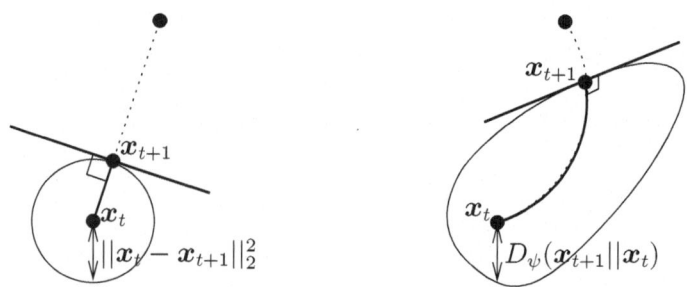

Fig. 9. The ordinary gradient (left), Amari's natural gradient and our geodesic walk (right) make that $\boldsymbol{x}_t$ is moved along a curve orthogonal to the Bregman ball defined by the constraint in (44) for the corresponding Bregman divergence (see text)

4 Bregman Geometric Problems

In this Section, our iterative settings for learning shifts to a geometric problem in which we move along a particular path in the closed convex set $\mathbb{X}$ of Definitions 2 and 3.

4.1 A Geodesic Walk

We are going to build in an iterative fashion elements $\boldsymbol{x}_t$, $t = 1, 2, ...T$, and seek them so as to progressively minimize a function $\vartheta(\boldsymbol{x})$, under the constraint that the step length $\kappa_t > 0$ is of fixed size, and this size is measured with a Bregman divergence D_ψ. More formally, we want:

$$\boldsymbol{x}_{t+1} = \arg\min_{\boldsymbol{x}\in\mathbb{X}} \vartheta(\boldsymbol{x}) \text{ s.t. } D_\psi(\boldsymbol{x}||\boldsymbol{x}_t) = \kappa_t \text{ , } \forall t = 1, 2, ... \tag{44}$$

Lemma 4. *The solution to (44) is*

$$\boldsymbol{x}_{t+1} = \boldsymbol{\nabla}_\psi^{-1}\left(\boldsymbol{\nabla}_\psi(\boldsymbol{x}_t) - \frac{1}{\lambda(\kappa_t)}\boldsymbol{\nabla}_\vartheta(\boldsymbol{x}_t)\right) \text{ ,} \tag{45}$$

for some $\lambda(\kappa_t) \in \mathbb{R}_*$.

Proof: Write $\boldsymbol{x} \doteq \boldsymbol{x}_t + \epsilon\boldsymbol{a}$ for some sufficiently small constant ϵ. Then we search for the $\boldsymbol{a}$ which minimizes:

$$\vartheta(\boldsymbol{x}) = \vartheta(\boldsymbol{x}_t) + \epsilon\boldsymbol{\nabla}_\vartheta^\top(\boldsymbol{x}_t)\boldsymbol{a} \text{ ,} \tag{46}$$

and the constraint becomes:

$$D_\psi(\boldsymbol{x}_t + \epsilon\boldsymbol{a}||\boldsymbol{x}_t) = \psi(\boldsymbol{x}_t + \epsilon\boldsymbol{a}) - \psi(\boldsymbol{x}_t) - \epsilon\boldsymbol{\nabla}_\psi^\top(\boldsymbol{x}_t)\boldsymbol{a} = \kappa_t \text{ .} \tag{47}$$

The stationarity conditions of the Lagrangian give us after differentiating by $\boldsymbol{a}$ $\boldsymbol{\nabla}_\psi(\boldsymbol{x}_t+\epsilon\boldsymbol{a}) = \boldsymbol{\nabla}_\psi(\boldsymbol{x}_t) - (1/\lambda)\boldsymbol{\nabla}_\vartheta(\boldsymbol{x}_t)$ (λ is the constraint's Lagrange multiplier), *i.e.* the statement of the Lemma. $\square$

Lemma 4 provides us with a geodesic walk to the minimization of function $\vartheta(\boldsymbol{x})$ [31,30], namely:

$$\boldsymbol{x}_{t+1} = \boldsymbol{\nabla}_\psi^{-1} \left(\boldsymbol{\nabla}_\psi(\boldsymbol{x}_t) - \eta_t \boldsymbol{\nabla}_\vartheta(\boldsymbol{x}_t) \right) \ , \tag{48}$$

where η_t is a learning rate [1,25]. This geodesic walk works only if the domains of ϑ and ψ are compatible, which shall be the case in what follows. Lemma 4 brings a generalization of Amari's *natural gradient* [1]. To see this, take D_ψ as Mahalanobis distortion (Table 1). Then (48) simplifies and we obtain that the steepest descent direction $\boldsymbol{a}$ satisfies :

$$\boldsymbol{a} = \Sigma^{-1} \boldsymbol{\nabla}_\vartheta(\boldsymbol{x}_t) \ .$$

This is a general form of Amari's natural gradient defined on Riemannian spaces. Lemma 4 tells that Amari's seminal notion may be generalized to a non-metric space embedded with a general Bregman divergence. The solution to (44) moves along a curve orthogonal to the ball defined by the constraint, where the orthogonality uses the Bregman-Pythagoras Theorem of Subsection 4.2 [30,31] (see Figure 9). For the sake of simplicity, we write

$$\boldsymbol{u} \diamond \boldsymbol{p} \doteq \boldsymbol{\nabla}_\psi^{-1} \left(\boldsymbol{\nabla}_\psi(\boldsymbol{p}) + \boldsymbol{u} \right) \ ,$$

where ψ becomes implicit and clear from context; also, we call $\boldsymbol{u} \diamond \boldsymbol{p}$ the *Legendre dual* of the ordered pair $(\boldsymbol{u}, \boldsymbol{p})$. The Legendre dual satisfies:

$$\boldsymbol{\nabla}_\psi(\boldsymbol{u} \diamond \boldsymbol{p}) = \boldsymbol{\nabla}_\psi(\boldsymbol{p}) + \boldsymbol{u} \ , \tag{49}$$

$$\boldsymbol{u} \diamond (\boldsymbol{u}' \diamond \boldsymbol{p}) = (\boldsymbol{u} + \boldsymbol{u}') \diamond \boldsymbol{p} \ , \forall \boldsymbol{u}, \boldsymbol{u}' \in \boldsymbol{\nabla}_\psi(\mathbb{X}), \forall \boldsymbol{p} \in \mathbb{X} \ . \tag{50}$$

The construction of the Legendre dual can be explained in a simple way, as depicted in Figure 10 when $\psi = \phi$ is a permissible function (Definition 6).

Here is how we use the geodesic walk of Lemma 4. $\boldsymbol{x}_t$ refers to an object that we update to learn. This object, which has historically been called $\boldsymbol{w}$ rather than $\boldsymbol{x}$ since it refers to "weights", belongs to a set that we should denote $\mathbb{W}$ rather than $\mathbb{X}$. This object is different in boosting and on-line learning: in on-line learning, it refers to the classifiers H_t ($t = 0, 1, ...$), while in boosting, it refers to the learning sample $\mathcal{S}$, and more precisely, weights $\boldsymbol{w}_t$ that are put on the examples. For the boosting part, we define $m \times T$ matrix M with

$$m_{it} \doteq -y_i^* h_t(\boldsymbol{o}_i) \ . \tag{51}$$

Given leveraging coefficients vector $\boldsymbol{\alpha} \in \mathbb{R}^T$ for classifier H, we thus get:

$$- y_i^* H(\boldsymbol{o}_i) = (\mathrm{M}\boldsymbol{\alpha})_i \ . \tag{52}$$

In this case, $\vartheta(\boldsymbol{w}_t)$ is the *edge* of the classifier (a generalization of the notion previously defined in Subsection 3.2):

$$\vartheta(\boldsymbol{w}_t) \doteq -\boldsymbol{w}_t^\top \mathrm{M}\boldsymbol{\alpha} \ , \tag{53}$$

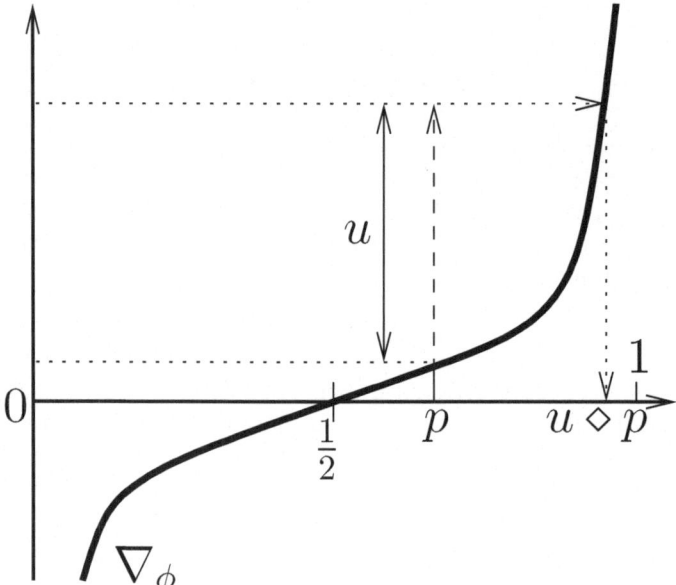

Fig. 10. Construction of the Legendre dual $u\diamond p$ for some permissible ϕ. ∇_ϕ is symmetric around point $(1/2, 0)$, for any permissible ϕ.

and we get

$$\nabla_\vartheta(\boldsymbol{w}_t) = \nabla_\vartheta(\boldsymbol{\alpha}) = -\mathrm{M}\boldsymbol{\alpha} \ . \tag{54}$$

In on-line learning, we shall consider for the sake of simplicity only linear separators as classifiers. Thus, we let $H_t(\boldsymbol{o}) \doteq \boldsymbol{w}_t^\top \boldsymbol{o}, t = 0, 1, ...,$ and consider a general BCL as in (37); in our on-line learning context (10), ϑ refers to the BCL over the current example, and we get:

$$\vartheta(\boldsymbol{w}_{t-1}) \doteq D_\phi(y_t || \nabla_\phi^{-1}(\boldsymbol{w}_{t-1}^\top \boldsymbol{o}_t)) \ . \tag{55}$$

We obtain:

$$\nabla_\vartheta(\boldsymbol{w}_{t-1}) = \nabla_\vartheta(\boldsymbol{w}_{t-1}, \boldsymbol{o}_t, y_t) = (\nabla_\phi^{-1}(\boldsymbol{w}_{t-1}^\top \boldsymbol{o}_t) - y_t)\boldsymbol{o}_t \ . \tag{56}$$

4.2   A Bregman-Pythagoras Theorem

The following Lemma states a fundamental property on Bregman divergences.

Lemma 5. *For any elements $\boldsymbol{u}, \boldsymbol{x}, \boldsymbol{x}'$ such that $(\boldsymbol{x}'-\boldsymbol{u})^\top(\nabla_\psi(\boldsymbol{x})-\nabla_\psi(\boldsymbol{x}')) = 0$, we have:*

$$D_\psi(\boldsymbol{u}||\boldsymbol{x}) = D_\psi(\boldsymbol{u}||\boldsymbol{x}') + D_\psi(\boldsymbol{x}'||\boldsymbol{x}) \ . \tag{57}$$

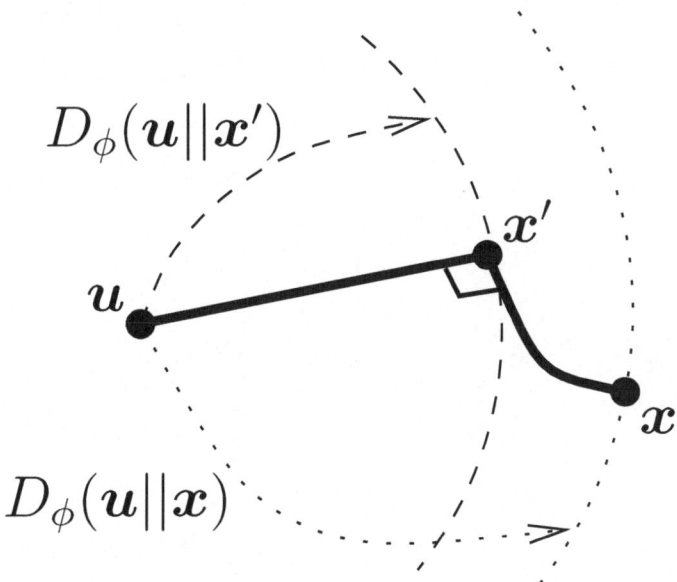

Fig. 11. An illustration of Bregman-Pythagoras theorem

The proof of this Lemma is immediate once we remark the three-points property:

$$D_\psi(\boldsymbol{u}||\boldsymbol{x}) = D_\psi(\boldsymbol{u}||\boldsymbol{x}') + D_\psi(\boldsymbol{x}'||\boldsymbol{x}) + (\boldsymbol{x}' - \boldsymbol{u})^\top(\boldsymbol{\nabla}_\psi(\boldsymbol{x}) - \boldsymbol{\nabla}_\psi(\boldsymbol{x})) \ . \quad (58)$$

Lemma 5 gives us a generalization of Pythagoras theorem, that we retrieve with the squared Euclidean distance (Table 1). In the literature, some more sophisticated generalizations of Pythagoras theorem have been published [20,30]. The one we propose in Lemma 5 is sufficient for our purpose. Figure 11 gives a schematic view of Bregman-Pythagoras theorem.

4.3   An Optimisation Problem Associated to the Geodesic Walk

There is an interesting problem related to the geodesic walk, which relies on a point $\boldsymbol{x}_0$ of $\mathbb{X}$ and the subset of $\mathbb{X}$ which may be reached through geodesic walks starting from $\boldsymbol{x}_0$. As this problem is particularly interesting for boosting, we use the boosting formulation for $\boldsymbol{\nabla}_\varepsilon$ in (54). The set is:

$$\mathbb{X}_0 \doteq \{\mathrm{M}\boldsymbol{\alpha} \diamond \boldsymbol{x}_0 : \boldsymbol{\alpha} \in \mathbb{R}^m\} \ . \quad (59)$$

The problem we want to solve is:

$$\boldsymbol{x}_\star = \arg\min_{\boldsymbol{x} \in \overline{\mathbb{X}}_0} D_\psi(\boldsymbol{x}_1||\boldsymbol{x}) \ , \quad (60)$$

for some $\boldsymbol{x}_1 \in \mathbb{X}$. Here, $\overline{\mathbb{X}}_0$ is the closure of $\mathbb{X}_0$. There is a dual and "orthogonal" optimization problem of interest, namely:

$$\boldsymbol{x}_\star = \arg\min_{\boldsymbol{x} \in \mathbb{X}_1} D_\psi(\boldsymbol{x}||\boldsymbol{x}_0) \ , \quad (61)$$

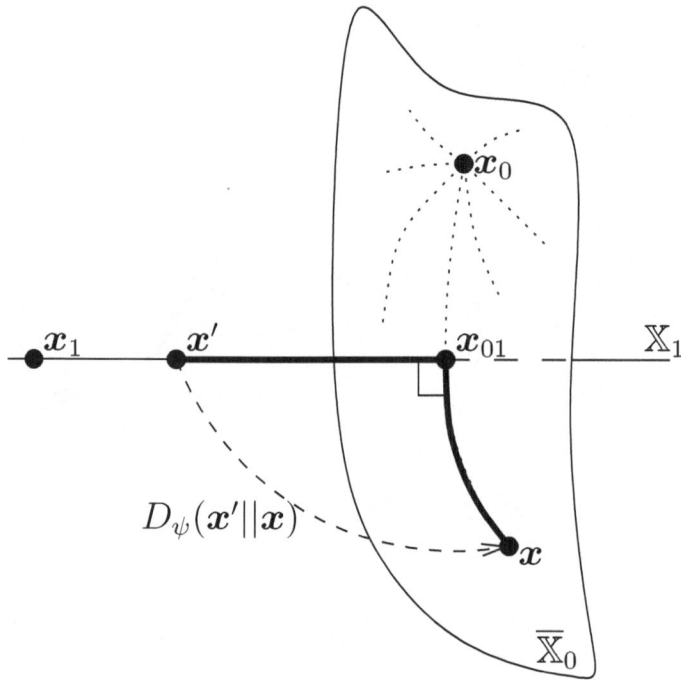

Fig. 12. Illustration of Lemma 6: the solutions of (60) and (61) naturally emerge as a consequence as the Bregman-Pythagoras orthogonality of $\overline{\mathbb{X}}_0$ and $\mathbb{X}_1$.

where

$$\mathbb{X}_1 \doteq \{ \boldsymbol{x} \in \mathbb{X} : \mathbf{M}\boldsymbol{x} = \mathbf{M}\boldsymbol{x}_1 \} \ . \tag{62}$$

What is particularly interesting is when $\overline{\mathbb{X}}_0 \cap \mathbb{X}_1 \neq \emptyset$, a condition which would not necessarily hold without the closure of $\mathbb{X}_0$ (for the technical reasons, we refer to [10]). Provided the intersection is not empty, we let:

$$\boldsymbol{x}_{01} \in \overline{\mathbb{X}}_0 \cap \mathbb{X}_1 \ . \tag{63}$$

We have an interesting four-points property met by any Bregman divergence:

$$D_\psi(\boldsymbol{x}_a'||\boldsymbol{x}_a) - D_\psi(\boldsymbol{x}_a'||\boldsymbol{x}_b) - D_\psi(\boldsymbol{x}_b'||\boldsymbol{x}_a) + D_\psi(\boldsymbol{x}_b'||\boldsymbol{x}_b)$$
$$= (\boldsymbol{x}_a' - \boldsymbol{x}_b')^\top (\boldsymbol{\nabla}\psi(\boldsymbol{x}_b) - \boldsymbol{\nabla}\psi(\boldsymbol{x}_a)) \ , \forall \boldsymbol{x}_a, \boldsymbol{x}_b, \boldsymbol{x}_a', \boldsymbol{x}_b' \in \mathbb{X} \ . \tag{64}$$

Take $\boldsymbol{x}_a, \boldsymbol{x}_b \in \mathbb{X}_0$. We obtain:

$$(\boldsymbol{x}_a' - \boldsymbol{x}_b')^\top (\boldsymbol{\nabla}\psi(\boldsymbol{x}_b) - \boldsymbol{\nabla}\psi(\boldsymbol{x}_a)) \overset{(59)}{=} (\boldsymbol{x}_a' - \boldsymbol{x}_b')^\top (\mathbf{M}\boldsymbol{\alpha}_b - \mathbf{M}\boldsymbol{\alpha}_a)$$
$$= (\boldsymbol{\alpha}_b - \boldsymbol{\alpha}_a)^\top (\mathbf{M}\boldsymbol{x}_a' - \mathbf{M}\boldsymbol{x}_b') \ , \tag{65}$$

and if we make the additional assumption that $\boldsymbol{x}_a', \boldsymbol{x}_b' \in \mathbb{X}_1$ (62), then (65) is zero. If we take $\boldsymbol{x}_a = \boldsymbol{x}_a' = \boldsymbol{x}_{01}$, then we obtain the following Lemma.

Lemma 6. $D_\psi(x'||x) = D_\psi(x'||x_{01}) + D_\psi(x_{01}||x), \forall x \in \mathbb{X}_0, \forall x' \in \mathbb{X}_1$.

This Lemma, illustrated in Figure 12, gives us the solutions of both (60) and (61).

Lemma 7. $x_{01} = x_\star$, the solution of (60) and (61).

Proof: Take any $x \in \overline{\mathbb{X}}_0$ and $x' = x_1$ in Lemma 6: we obtain $D_\psi(x_1||x) = D_\psi(x_{01}||x) + D_\psi(x_1||x_{01}) \geq D_\psi(x_1||x_{01})$, with equality iff $x = x_{01}$. Hence, x_{01} is the solution to (60). The same reasoning with $x' \in \mathbb{X}_1$ and $x = x_0$ in Lemma 6 yields the same result for (61). □

Thus, the optimization problems in (60) ad (61) reduce to finding an element in the intersection of $\overline{\mathbb{X}}_0$ and $\mathbb{X}_1$. Figure 12 provides us with a graphical interpretation of Lemma 7.

5   Applications on Linear Separators

5.1   Boosting

Here is the way we assemble the geometric pieces of Section 4 to devise a general boosting algorithm for LS. We keep our notations in (51) for matrix M, and show how to minimize any SCS

$$\varepsilon_\mathbb{R}^\psi(\mathcal{S}, H) \doteq \sum_i \psi(y_i^* H(o_i)) , \qquad (66)$$

for any SCL ψ with $\mathrm{dom}(\psi) = \mathbb{R}$. This assumption on the domain of ψ is not restrictive for LS, as otherwise it would make it necessary to truncate the outputs of the LS to remain within the domain, and it is known that such procedures present significant masking problems [14]. For some BCL, we may be forced to give up with the BCL regime to make the fitting, at the expense of the lost of the direct relationships with the maximum likelihood fitting explained in Subsection 3.4. For example, we can use (21), *but* it is necessary to get out of the BCL regime and work in $\mathbb{R}$ instead of $[-1, 1]$.

To simplify notations, we let:

$$\tilde{\psi}(x) \doteq \psi^\star(-x) . \qquad (67)$$

With this notation, (36) becomes:

$$\psi(y^* H) = D_{\tilde{\psi}}(0||\nabla_{\tilde{\psi}}^{-1}(-y^* H)) - \tilde{\psi}(0) . \qquad (68)$$

We let $\mathbb{W} \doteq \mathrm{dom}(\nabla_{\tilde{\psi}}) = -\mathrm{im}(\nabla_\psi)$, where this latter equality comes from $\nabla_{\tilde{\psi}}(x) = -\nabla_{\psi^\star}(-x) = -\nabla_\psi^{-1}(-x)$. It also comes $\mathrm{im}(\nabla_{\tilde{\psi}}) = \mathbb{R}$. Algorithm ULS provides us with a general induction scheme for LS, whose properties hold regardless of the SCL at hand. The step which is not explained in the algorithm

---

Algorithm 1: Algorithm ULS(M, ψ)

Input: $M \in \mathbb{R}^{m \times T}$, SCL ψ with $\text{dom}(\psi) = \mathbb{R}$;

Let $\boldsymbol{\alpha}_1 \leftarrow \mathbf{0}$;

Let $\boldsymbol{w}_0 \leftarrow \nabla_{\tilde{\psi}}^{-1}(0)\mathbf{1}$;

for $j = 1, 2, \ldots J$ **do**

  //Weight Update: make a geodesic walk on $D_{\tilde{\psi}}$ to minimize $\vartheta = $ edge (53)

$$\boldsymbol{w}_j \leftarrow (M\boldsymbol{\alpha}_j) \diamond \boldsymbol{w}_0 \; ; \tag{69}$$

  Let $\mathcal{T}_j \subseteq \{1, 2, \ldots, T\}$;

  Let $\boldsymbol{\delta}_j \leftarrow \mathbf{0}$;

  //Leveraging Coefficients: ensure Bregman-Pythagoras Theorem on weights

$$\forall t \in \mathcal{T}_j, \text{ pick } \delta_{j,t} \text{ such that } : \sum_{i=1}^{m} m_{it}((M\boldsymbol{\delta}_j) \diamond \boldsymbol{w}_j)_i = 0 \; ; \tag{70}$$

  Let $\boldsymbol{\alpha}_{j+1} \leftarrow \boldsymbol{\alpha}_j + \boldsymbol{\delta}_j$;

Output: $H(\boldsymbol{o}) \doteq \sum_{t=1}^{T} \alpha_{J+1,t} h_t(\boldsymbol{o}) \in \text{LS}$

---

is the choice of the set of indices $\mathcal{T}_j$ on which we compute the leveraging coefficients of the features. In fact, this step does not really belong to ULS: ever since the seminal works on boosting [21], this step has mostly been the retrieval, by a weak learner, of a single weak classifier — called feature here because everything is like if it were mapping each observation to a new real variable which is used to build the final LS. Thus, we can suppose for the moment that this choice is assumed by the weak learner, and we shall discuss it later. Through the more recent works on boosting, the choice of $\mathcal{T}_j$ has come with various flavors: in classical boosting, at step j, we would fit a single α_t [10]; in totally corrective boosting, we would rather fit $\{\alpha_t, 1 \leq t \leq j\}$ [39]. Intermediate schemes may be used as well for $\mathcal{T}_j$, provided they ensure that, at each step j of the algorithm and for any feature h_t, it may be chosen at some $j' > j$. ULS is displayed in Algorithm 1. In Algorithm 1, $\mathcal{T}_j$ may be chosen according to whichever scheme underlined above.

The following Theorem provides a first general convergence property for ULS.

Theorem 1. *The output of ULS(M, ψ) converges to a classifier $H_\star$ realizing:*

$$H_\star = \arg \min_{H \in \text{LS}} \varepsilon_{\mathbb{R}}^{\psi}(\mathcal{S}, H) \; . \tag{71}$$

Proof: In (69), (50) brings $\boldsymbol{w}_{j+1} = (M\boldsymbol{\alpha}_{j+1}) \diamond \boldsymbol{w}_0 = (M\boldsymbol{\delta}_j) \diamond \boldsymbol{w}_j$. We thus have:

$$D_{\tilde{\psi}}(\mathbf{0}\|\boldsymbol{w}_{j+1}) - D_{\tilde{\psi}}(\mathbf{0}\|\boldsymbol{w}_j) = -[\tilde{\psi}((M\boldsymbol{\delta}_j) \diamond \boldsymbol{w}_j) - \tilde{\psi}(\boldsymbol{w}_j) + \boldsymbol{w}_j^\top \nabla_{\tilde{\psi}}(\boldsymbol{w}_j)]$$
$$+ ((M\boldsymbol{\delta}_j) \diamond \boldsymbol{w}_j)^\top \nabla_{\tilde{\psi}}((M\boldsymbol{\delta}_j) \diamond \boldsymbol{w}_j) \; . \tag{72}$$

Because of (49), (72) is just (for short, $r \doteq ((M\boldsymbol{\delta}_j) \diamond \boldsymbol{w}_j)^\top \nabla_{\tilde{\psi}}(\boldsymbol{w}_j)$):

$$((M\boldsymbol{\delta}_j) \diamond \boldsymbol{w}_j)^\top \nabla_{\tilde{\psi}}((M\boldsymbol{\delta}_j) \diamond \boldsymbol{w}_j) = r + ((M\boldsymbol{\delta}_j) \diamond \boldsymbol{w}_j)^\top M\boldsymbol{\delta}_j$$

$$= r - \sum_{i=1}^{m} y_i^* \sum_{t=1}^{T} \delta_{j,t} h_t(\boldsymbol{o}_i)((M\boldsymbol{\delta}_j) \diamond \boldsymbol{w}_j)_i$$

$$= r - \sum_{t=1}^{T} \delta_{j,t} \sum_{i=1}^{m} y_i^* h_t(\boldsymbol{o}_i)((M\boldsymbol{\delta}_j) \diamond \boldsymbol{w}_j)_i$$

$$= r + \sum_{t=1}^{T} \delta_{j,t} \underbrace{\sum_{i=1}^{m} m_{it}((M\boldsymbol{\delta}_j) \diamond \boldsymbol{w}_j)_i}_{b_t}$$

$$= r \; . \tag{73}$$

(73) holds because $\delta_{j,t} = 0$, or $b_t = 0$ from the choice of $\delta_{j,t}$ in (70). We obtain:

$$D_{\tilde{\psi}}(\boldsymbol{0}||\boldsymbol{w}_{j+1}) - D_{\tilde{\psi}}(\boldsymbol{0}||\boldsymbol{w}_j) = -D_{\tilde{\psi}}(\boldsymbol{w}_{j+1}||\boldsymbol{w}_j) \; . \tag{74}$$

This is Bregman-Pythagoras Theorem on weights (Lemma 5). This relationship is fundamental for the proof. Indeed, it comes from (68) and (69) that:

$$\varepsilon_{\mathbb{R}}^{\psi}(\mathcal{S}, H_j) = D_{\tilde{\psi}}(\boldsymbol{0}||\boldsymbol{w}_j) - m\tilde{\psi}(0) = D_{\tilde{\psi}}(\boldsymbol{0}||\boldsymbol{w}_j) + \text{ const } . \tag{75}$$

Thus, (74) is the difference between two successive SCS, a measure of the progress to the limit classifier. Since any SCS is lowerbounded and the right-hand side of (74) cannot be strictly positive, ULS must converge, and so there remains to characterize the classifier obtained after convergence, i.e. when $\boldsymbol{w}_j = \boldsymbol{w}_{j+1}$. Take

$$\boldsymbol{x}_0 \doteq \nabla_{\tilde{\psi}}^{-1}(0)\boldsymbol{1} \text{ in (61) } , \tag{76}$$

$$\mathbb{X}_0 \doteq \mathbb{W} \text{ in (59) } . \tag{77}$$

$$\boldsymbol{x}_1 \doteq \boldsymbol{0} \text{ in (60) } , \tag{78}$$

$$\mathbb{X}_1 \doteq \{\boldsymbol{\alpha} \in \mathbb{R}^m : M^\top \boldsymbol{\alpha} = M^\top \boldsymbol{x}_1 = \boldsymbol{0}\} = \text{Ker} M^\top \text{ in (62) } , \tag{79}$$

Problem (60) can thus be rewritten as $\boldsymbol{w}_\star = \arg\min_{\boldsymbol{w} \in \overline{\mathbb{W}}} D_{\tilde{\psi}}(\boldsymbol{0}||\boldsymbol{w})$, or equivalently, with (75), as:

$$H_\star = \arg\min_{H \in \text{LS}} \varepsilon_{\mathbb{R}}^{\psi}(\mathcal{S}, H) \; . \tag{80}$$

The geodesic walk in (69) and (70) ensures:

$$\boldsymbol{1}_{\mathcal{T}_j}^\top M^\top \boldsymbol{w}_{j+1} = 0 \; , \tag{81}$$

where $\boldsymbol{1}_{\mathcal{T}_j}$ is the Boolean vector with ones on the indexes of $\mathcal{T}_j$. After convergence, $M\boldsymbol{\delta}_j = \boldsymbol{0}$ for any $\mathcal{T}_j$, and hence the corresponding vector $\boldsymbol{w}_{j+1}$ is such that (81)

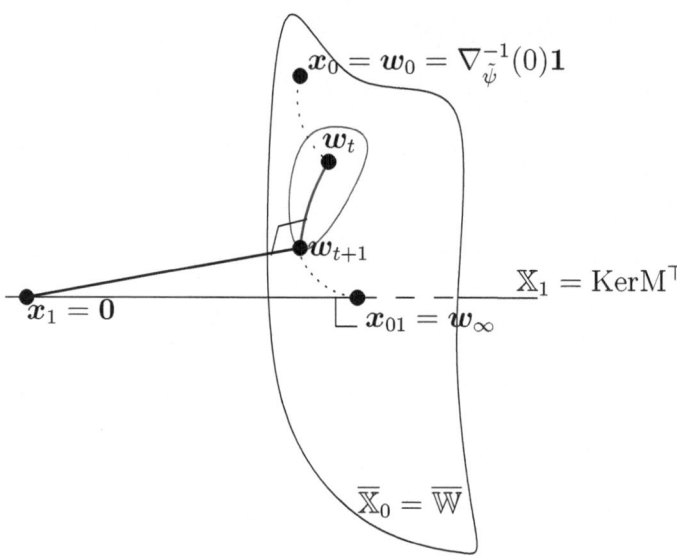

Fig. 13. A schematic view of how ULS behaves: iterating geodesic walks make the weight vector converge to the null space of $\mathrm{M}^\top$, and the classifier H converges to the optimum of the surrogate risk $\varepsilon_\mathbb{R}^\psi(\mathcal{S}, H)$ (see text)

holds regardless of the choice of $\mathbf{1}_{\mathcal{T}_j}$. Taking (81) for each possible singleton index in $\mathcal{T}_j$, we obtain that, after convergence:

$$\mathrm{M}^\top \boldsymbol{w}_{j+1} = \mathbf{0} \;\Rightarrow\; \boldsymbol{w}_{j+1} \in \mathrm{KerM}^\top \;. \tag{82}$$

Hence, $\boldsymbol{w}_{j+1} = \boldsymbol{w}_\star$, the optimal solution to (60), and the corresponding classifier we end up with is $H_\star$, the solution to (80). $\qquad\square$

We emphasize the fact that Theorem 1 proves the convergence towards the global optimum of $\varepsilon_\mathbb{R}^\psi$, regardless of ψ. The optimum is defined by the LS with features in M that realizes the smallest $\varepsilon_\mathbb{R}^\psi$. Figure 13 displays the way ULS behaves. The Bregman ball around $\boldsymbol{w}_j$ shows the geodesic walk made in step (69) to compute $\boldsymbol{w}_{j+1}$ by nullifying the current edge of the features selected in $\mathcal{T}_j$. Notice that in practice, it may be a tedious task to satisfy exactly (74), in particular for totally corrective boosting [39]. ULS has the flavor of boosting algorithms repeatedly modifying a set of weights $\boldsymbol{w}$ over the examples, the most popular algorithm being AdaBoost [13].

In fact, this similarity is more than syntactical, as ULS satisfies two first popular algorithmic boosting properties, the first of which being (70) which implies (81): after the computation of the leveraging coefficients, the next weights are somehow decorrelated with the classes, if we refer to the zero edge. One may wonder under which conditions (70) admits a solution. The following Lemma shows that it always admit a finite solution when no "trivial" solution exist for the minimization of the SCS at hand.

Lemma 8. *Suppose that there does not exist some h_t with all m_{it} of the same sign, $\forall i = 1, 2, ..., m$. Then, for any choice of $\mathcal{T}_j$ in ULS, (70) has always a finite solution.*

Proof: Let:

$$Z \doteq D_{\tilde{\psi}}(\mathbf{0}\|(M\boldsymbol{\alpha}_{j+1}) \diamond \boldsymbol{w}_0) \ . \tag{83}$$

We have

$$Z = m\tilde{\psi}(0) + \sum_{i=1}^{m} \tilde{\psi}((M(\boldsymbol{\delta}_j + \boldsymbol{\alpha}_j))_i)$$

from (68), a function convex in all leveraging coefficients. Define $|\mathcal{T}_j| \times |\mathcal{T}_j|$ matrix E with:

$$e_{uv} \doteq \frac{\partial^2 Z}{\partial \delta_{j,u} \partial \delta_{j,v}}$$

(for the sake of simplicity, $\mathcal{T}_j = \{1, 2, ..., |\mathcal{T}_j|\}$, where $|.|$ denotes the cardinal). We have:

$$e_{uv} = \sum_{i=1}^{m} \frac{m_{iu} m_{iv}}{\varphi(((M\boldsymbol{\delta}_j) \diamond \boldsymbol{w}_j)_i)} \ ,$$

with:

$$\varphi(x) \doteq \frac{\mathrm{d}^2 \tilde{\psi}(x)}{\mathrm{d}x^2} \ , \tag{84}$$

a function strictly positive in the relative interior of $\mathbb{W}$ since $\tilde{\psi}$ is strictly convex. Let $q_{i,j} \doteq 1/\varphi(((M\boldsymbol{\delta}_j) \diamond \boldsymbol{w}_j)_i) > 0$. It is easy to show that:

$$\boldsymbol{x}^\top E \boldsymbol{x} = \sum_{i=1}^{m} q_{i,j} (\boldsymbol{x}^\top \tilde{\boldsymbol{m}}_i)^2 \geq 0 \ , \forall \boldsymbol{x} \in \mathbb{R}^{|\mathcal{T}_j|} \ , \tag{85}$$

with $\tilde{\boldsymbol{m}}_i \in \mathbb{R}^{|\mathcal{T}_j|}$ the vector containing the entries m_{it} with $t \in \mathcal{T}_j$. Thus, E is positive semidefinite; as such, (70), which is the same as solving $\partial Z / \partial \delta_{j,u} = 0$, $\forall u \in \mathcal{T}_j$ (*i.e.* minimizing Z) has always a solution. □

The condition for the Lemma to work is absolutely not restrictive, as if such an h_t were to exist, we would not need to run ULS: indeed, we would have either $\varepsilon^{0/1}(\mathcal{S}, h_t) = 0$, or $\varepsilon^{0/1}(\mathcal{S}, -h_t) = 0$.

We give three examples of specializations of ULS:

- take for example $\psi(x) = \exp(-x)$ (19). In this case, $\mathbb{W} = \mathbb{R}_+$, $\boldsymbol{w}_0 = \mathbf{1}$ and it is not hard to see that ULS matches real AdaBoost with unnormalized weights [36]. The difference is syntactical: the LS output by ULS and real AdaBoost are the same;

– now, take any BCL. In this case, $\tilde{\psi} = \phi$, $\mathbb{W} = [0, 1]$ (recall that we close $\mathbb{W}$ in the same way as we did for the logit in Section 2.1), and $\boldsymbol{w}_0 = 1/2\mathbf{1}$. In all these cases, where $\mathbb{W} \subseteq \mathbb{R}_+$, $\boldsymbol{w}_j$ is always a distribution up to a normalization factor, and this would also be the case for any strictly decreasing SCS ψ. The BCL case brings an interesting display of how the weights behave through the geodesic walk.

Figure 10 displays a typical Legendre dual for a BCL. Consider example $(\boldsymbol{o}_i, y_i)$, and its weight update, $w_{j,i} \leftarrow (M\boldsymbol{\alpha}_j)_i \diamond w_{0,i} = (-y_i^* H(\boldsymbol{o}_i)) \diamond w_{0,i}$ for the current classifier H. Fix $p = w_{0,i}$ and $u = -y_i^* H(\boldsymbol{o}_i)$ in Figure 10. We see that the new weight of the example gets larger iff $u > 0$, *i.e.* iff the example is given the *wrong* class by H, which is the second boosting property met by ULS;

– as a last example, take $\psi(x) = (1 - x)^2$ in (21). In this case, as argued at the beginning of Subsection 5.1, we leave the BCL regime to work with the function defined over $\mathbb{R}$ instead of $[-1, 1]$. Since $\nabla_{\tilde{\psi}}^{-1}(x) = 2(1 - x)$, weights actually span $\mathbb{R}$ itself, and the negative regime appears for $x \geq 1$. This is not surprising as the SCL is increasing when $x \geq 1$, and so minimizing it in this region "reverses" the polarity of search with respect to the BCL regime.

ULS turns out to meet a third boosting property, and the most important as it contributes to root the algorithm in the seminal boosting theory of the early nineties: we have guarantees on its convergence rate under a generalization of the well-known "Weak Learning Assumption" (WLA) [36]. To state the WLA, we plug the iteration in the index of the distribution normalization coefficient in (83), and define $Z_j \doteq ||\boldsymbol{w}_j||_1$ ($||.||_k$ is the L_k norm). The WLA is:

$$\textbf{(WLA)}\forall j, \exists \gamma_j > 0 : \left| \frac{1}{|\mathcal{T}_j|} \sum_{t \in \mathcal{T}_j} \frac{1}{Z_j} \sum_{i=1}^m m_{it} w_{j,i} \right| \geq \gamma_j . \tag{86}$$

This is indeed a generalization of the usual WLA for boosting algorithms, that we obtain taking $|\mathcal{T}_j| = 1$, $h_t \in \{-1, +1\}$ [33]. Few algorithms are known that formally boost WLA in the sense that requiring only WLA implies guaranteed rates for the minimization of $\varepsilon_{\mathbb{R}}^\psi$. We show that ULS meets this property $\forall \psi \in$ SCL. To state this, we need few more definitions. Let $\boldsymbol{m}_t$ denote the tth column vector of M, $a_{\boldsymbol{m}} \doteq \max_t ||\boldsymbol{m}_t||_2$ and $a_Z \doteq \min_j Z_j$. Let a_γ denote the average of γ_j ($\forall j$), and $a_\varphi \doteq \min_{x \in \text{int}(\mathbb{W})} \varphi(x)$ (φ defined in (84)).

Theorem 2. *Under the WLA, ULS reaches the minimum of the surrogate risk* $\varepsilon_{\mathbb{R}}^\psi(\mathcal{S}, H)$ *in*

$$J = \mathcal{O}\left(\frac{m a_{\boldsymbol{m}}^2}{a_\varphi a_Z^2 a_\gamma^2} \right) \tag{87}$$

iterations.

Proof: We use Taylor expansions with Lagrange remainder for $\tilde{\psi}$, and then the mean-value theorem, and obtain that $\forall w, w + \Delta \in \mathbb{W}, \exists w^\star \in [\min\{w + \Delta, w\}, \max\{w + \Delta, w\}]$ such that:

$$D_{\tilde{\psi}}(w + \Delta || w) = \Delta^2 \varphi(w^*)/2 \geq (\Delta^2/2)a_\varphi \geq 0 \ . \tag{88}$$

We use m times this inequality with $w = w_{j,i}$ and $\Delta = (w_{j+1,i} - w_{j,i})$, sum the inequalities, combine with Cauchy - Schwartz and Jensen's inequalities, and obtain:

$$D_{\tilde{\psi}}(\boldsymbol{w}_{j+1} || \boldsymbol{w}_j) \geq a_\varphi \left(\frac{a_Z \gamma_j}{2a_m} \right)^2 \ . \tag{89}$$

Using (74), we obtain that $D_{\tilde{\psi}}(\mathbf{0} || \boldsymbol{w}_{J+1}) - m\tilde{\psi}(0)$ equals:

$$-m\tilde{\psi}(0) + D_{\tilde{\psi}}(\mathbf{0} || \boldsymbol{w}_1) + \sum_{j=1}^{J} (D_{\tilde{\psi}}(\mathbf{0} || \boldsymbol{w}_{j+1}) - D_{\tilde{\psi}}(\mathbf{0} || \boldsymbol{w}_j))$$

$$= m\psi(0) - \sum_{j=1}^{J} D_{\tilde{\psi}}(\boldsymbol{w}_{j+1} || \boldsymbol{w}_j) \ . \tag{90}$$

But, (68) together with the definition of $\boldsymbol{w}_j$ in (69) yields

$$D_{\tilde{\psi}}(\mathbf{0} || w_{J+1,i}) = \tilde{\psi}(0) + \psi(y_i^* H(\boldsymbol{o}_i)), \forall i = 1, 2, ..., m \ , \tag{91}$$

which ties up the SCS to (90); the guaranteed decrease in the right-hand side of (90) by (89) makes that there remains to check when the right-hand side becomes negative to conclude that ULS has reached the optimum. This gives the bound of the Theorem. $\qquad\square$

The bound in Theorem 2 is mainly useful to prove that the WLA guarantees a convergence rate of order $\mathcal{O}(m/a_\gamma^2)$ for ULS, but not the best possible as it is in some cases far from being optimal.

To finish up with ULS, if we update a single leveraging coefficient for h_t at step j, then the WLA can be simplified as (using the same notation as in (81)):

$$\left| \mathbf{1}_{\{t\}}^\top \mathrm{M}^\top \boldsymbol{w}_j \right| \geq \gamma_j Z_j \ . \tag{92}$$

Without loss of generality, we can suppose that the edge of h_t on $\boldsymbol{w}_t$ is always strictly positive, since otherwise we can consider $-h_t$. Suppose that h_t is retrieved by a weak learner, distinct from ULS: the role of the weak learner is to obtain a bottomline weak classifier h_t with strictly positive edge, while ULS systematically reduces the edge of this weak classifier to zero by a geodesic walk in (69), yielding $\mathbf{1}_{\{t\}}^\top \mathrm{M}^\top \boldsymbol{w}_{j+1} = 0$ in (81), and forcing the weak learner to find a different weak classifier for the next step. Most of ULS thus reduces to an edge game parametrized by M, the weak learner picking $\mathbf{1}_{\{t\}}^\top$ while ULS picks $\boldsymbol{w}_{j+1}$. The game ends when the weak learner has no more possibility to ensure the WLA, in which case ULS has converged to the optimal classifier H_*.

5.2   On-Line Learning

To keep this Section short, we refer the reader to *e.g.* [17,25] for more details. The principle of the learning algorithm is simpler than for ULS, as we only make the geodesic walk each time an example is received from the stream. The geodesic walk is parametrized by (55) and (56), from which we obtain Algorithm 2 [25].

We recall that function ϑ is a general BCL $D_\phi(y_t||\nabla_\phi^{-1}(\boldsymbol{w}_{t-1}^\top\boldsymbol{o}_t))$, and that our objective is to obtain an upperbound of the kind $\varepsilon\left(\mathcal{S}_T, \{H_t\}_{t=0}^{T-1}\right) \leq \varepsilon(\mathcal{S}_T, H_r) +$ penalty (10), where H_r is a reference LS characterized by weight (leveraging) vector $\boldsymbol{r}$.

There is a particularly interesting Bregman divergence to compute a convenient penalty, the q-norm divergence D_{ψ_q} [15,25] (Table 1). There is an interesting result regarding D_{ψ_q} for OLS, namely that if we perform the geodesic walk on D_{ψ_q}, it is necessarily bounded. Its proof follows [25].

Lemma 9. *Assume $1 < q \leq 2 \leq p < \infty$, and $1/p + 1/q = 1$. Then:*

$$D_{\psi_q}(\boldsymbol{w}_{t-1}||\boldsymbol{w}_t) \leq \frac{\eta^2(p-1)}{2}(\nabla_\phi^{-1}(\boldsymbol{w}_{t-1}^\top\boldsymbol{o}_t) - y_t)^2||\boldsymbol{o}_t||_p^2 . \tag{94}$$

Furthermore, it can be noticed that we have:

$$D_\phi(y_t||\nabla_\phi^{-1}(\boldsymbol{w}_{t-1}^\top\boldsymbol{o}_t)) = \frac{\varphi(x_t)}{2}(\nabla_\phi^{-1}(\boldsymbol{w}_{t-1}^\top\boldsymbol{o}_t) - y_t)^2 , \tag{95}$$

for some x_t in the interior of the interval defined by $\nabla_\phi^{-1}(\boldsymbol{w}_{t-1}^\top\boldsymbol{o}_t)$ and y_t, where φ is as defined in (84) with $\tilde{\psi} = \phi$. There are two reasonable assumptions to make about Algorithm 2. The first states that the p-norm of any observation of the stream is upperbounded:

$$\sup_t ||\boldsymbol{o}_t||_p \leq \lambda_p . \tag{96}$$

The second states that $\varphi(x_t)$ is lowerbounded in (95), which is also reasonable given that the main quantity which could be responsible of extreme deviations in the geodesic walk is itself bounded (96):

$$\inf_t \varphi(x_t) \geq \lambda . \tag{97}$$

Algorithm 2: Algorithm OLS($\mathcal{S}$)

Input: Stream $\mathcal{S}$ of examples $(\boldsymbol{o}_t, c_t), t = 1, 2, ...$, with $\boldsymbol{o}_t \in \mathbb{R}^m$;

Let $\boldsymbol{w}_0 \leftarrow \boldsymbol{0}$;

for $t = 1, 2, ...$ **do**

> //Classifier Update: make a geodesic walk on D_{ψ_q} to minimize $\vartheta =$BCL (55)
>
> $$\boldsymbol{w}_t \leftarrow (-\eta(\nabla_\phi^{-1}(\boldsymbol{w}_{t-1}^\top\boldsymbol{o}_t) - y_t)\boldsymbol{o}_t) \diamond \boldsymbol{w}_{t-1} ; \tag{93}$$

Output: $H_t(\boldsymbol{o}) \doteq \boldsymbol{w}_t^\top\boldsymbol{o} \in$ LS

The following Theorem, whose proof follows [25], gives us a desired bound on the deviation of H_t with respect to the reference LS H_r. To interpret this bound, one can take as reference the optimal vector $r_\star$ of the optimal LS $H_\star$ in term of BCL, and suppose that $r_\star$ has few non-zero entries. In this case, Algorithm 2 manages to stay quite close to the optimum.

Theorem 3. *Assume* $1 < q \le 2 \le p < \infty$, $1/p + 1/q = 1$, *and*

$$\eta \doteq \frac{\lambda}{(p-1)\lambda_p^2} \tag{98}$$

in Algorithm 2 (parameters defined in (96) and (97)). Then the following holds for any $T > 0$:

$$\sum_{t=1}^{T} D_\phi(\nabla_\phi^{-1}(w_{t-1}^\top o_t)\|\nabla_\phi^{-1}(r^\top o_t)) \le \sum_{t=1}^{T} D_\phi(y_t\|\nabla_\phi^{-1}(r^\top o_t)) + \frac{(p-1)\lambda_p^2\|r\|_q^2}{2\lambda} .$$

Proof: In the same way as we do for (74), we can measure a progress to reference d_t as:

$$d_t \doteq D_{\psi_q}(r\|w_{t-1}) - D_{\psi_q}(r\|w_t) . \tag{99}$$

$$\overset{(58)}{=} (w_{t-1} - r)^\top (\nabla_{\psi_q}(w_{t-1}) - \nabla_{\psi_q}(w_t)) - D_{\psi_q}(w_{t-1}\|w_t)$$

$$\overset{(93)}{=} \eta(\nabla_\phi^{-1}(w_{t-1}^\top o_t) - y_t)(w_{t-1}^\top o_t - r^\top o_t) - D_{\psi_q}(w_{t-1}\|w_t) . \tag{100}$$

From the three-points property in (58), we obtain for any BLF D_ϕ:

$$D_\phi(y_t\|\nabla_\phi^{-1}(w_{t-1}^\top o_t)) + D_\phi(\nabla_\phi^{-1}(w_{t-1}^\top o_t)\|\nabla_\phi^{-1}(r^\top o_t))$$
$$- D_\phi(y_t\|\nabla_\phi^{-1}(r^\top o_t))$$
$$= (\nabla_\phi^{-1}(w_{t-1}^\top o_t) - y_t)(w_{t-1}^\top o_t - r^\top o_t) . \tag{101}$$

Combining (100) and (101), we get:

$$d_t \quad = \quad \eta\left\{ D_\phi(\nabla_\phi^{-1}(w_{t-1}^\top o_t)\|\nabla_\phi^{-1}(r^\top o_t)) - D_\phi(y_t\|\nabla_\phi^{-1}(r^\top o_t)) \right\}$$
$$+ \eta D_\phi(y_t\|\nabla_\phi^{-1}(w_{t-1}^\top o_t)) - D_{\psi_q}(w_{t-1}\|w_t)$$

$$\overset{(94),(96),(97)}{\ge} \eta\left\{ D_\phi(\nabla_\phi^{-1}(w_{t-1}^\top o_t)\|\nabla_\phi^{-1}(r^\top o_t)) - D_\phi(y_t\|\nabla_\phi^{-1}(r^\top o_t)) \right\}$$
$$+ \frac{\eta}{2}(\nabla_\phi^{-1}(w_{t-1}^\top o_t) - y_t)^2 (\lambda - \eta(p-1)\lambda_p^2)$$

$$\overset{(98)}{=} \eta\left\{ D_\phi(\nabla_\phi^{-1}(w_{t-1}^\top o_t)\|\nabla_\phi^{-1}(r^\top o_t)) - D_\phi(y_t\|\nabla_\phi^{-1}(r^\top o_t)) \right\} .$$

We sum this inequality for $t = 1, 2, ..., T$, rearrange, and get:

$$\sum_{t=1}^{T} D_\phi(\nabla_\phi^{-1}(w_{t-1}^\top o_t)\|\nabla_\phi^{-1}(r^\top o_t))$$

$$\le \frac{(p-1)\lambda_p^2}{\lambda} \sum_{t=1}^{T} d_t + \sum_{t=1}^{T} D_\phi(y_t\|\nabla_\phi^{-1}(r^\top o_t)) . \tag{102}$$

Now, we sum (99) for $t = 1, 2, ..., T$, and get:

$$\sum_{t=1}^{T} d_t = D_{\psi_q}(\boldsymbol{r}||\boldsymbol{w}_0) - D_{\psi_q}(\boldsymbol{r}||\boldsymbol{w}_T)$$

$$= \frac{1}{2}||\boldsymbol{r}||_q^2 - D_{\psi_q}(\boldsymbol{r}||\boldsymbol{w}_T)$$

$$\leq \frac{1}{2}||\boldsymbol{r}||_q^2 . \tag{103}$$

We combine (103) and (102), and get the statement of the Theorem.   □

6   Applications to More Classifiers

In Subsection 2.1, we have presented the importance of the choice of the classifier for the user. In the preceding Section, all algorithms rely on linear separators. While the choice seems natural for on-line learning — it is easy to update a LS, while it may be much harder to cope with on-line modifications of DT —, the boosting setting calls for more applications to other formalisms. Apart from LS, the main formalisms on which boosting algorithms have been developed are decision trees [23,21]. We now show that ULS is scalable to DT as well. More precisely, one can naturally induce a DT with ULS, and it turns out that this algorithm, which immediately captures the theoretical properties of ULS, is a generalization of the most popular DT induction algorithms [9,23,34].

We refer to Subsection 2.1 for a presentation of DT. Recall that the structure of a DT makes it possible to label the leaves with $[0, 1]$ or arbitrary real values. In Figure 1, the tree uses the former convention. In Figure 14 (left), we provide a tree which is equivalent from the empirical risk standpoint, but uses signed values at the leaves. We make use some new notations that we now present.

A DT H induces a partition of $\mathcal{S}$ according to subsets $\mathcal{S}_k$, where $k \in \mathcal{L}(H) \subset \mathbb{N}_*$, and $\mathcal{L}(H)$ is a subset of natural integers in bijection with the set of leaves of

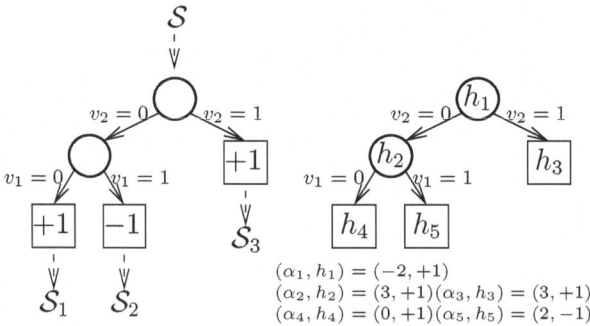

Fig. 14. Left: a decision tree with 3 leaves (squares) and 2 internal nodes (circles), with real-valued leaves, equivalent from the empirical risk standpoint to the DT in Figure 1; right: an equivalent linearized decision tree, for the proof of Theorem 4

Algorithm 3: Algorithm UDT$(\mathcal{S}, \phi)$

Input: Learning sample $\mathcal{S}$, permissible function ϕ;

Let $H \leftarrow$ single leaf;

for $j = 1, 2, ...J$ **do**

Pick some leaf $k' \in \mathcal{L}(H)$, and some observation variable v such that:

$$A_\phi(H, H_{|k' \rightarrow v}) \doteq \sum_{k \in \mathcal{L}(H_{|k' \rightarrow v})} \frac{|\mathcal{S}_k|}{b_\phi} \left(-\phi\left(\frac{|S_k^+|}{|S_k|}\right)\right)$$

$$- \sum_{k \in \mathcal{L}(H)} \frac{|\mathcal{S}_k|}{b_\phi} \left(-\phi\left(\frac{|S_k^+|}{|S_k|}\right)\right)$$

$$< 0 ; \tag{104}$$

Let $H \leftarrow H_{|k' \rightarrow v}$;

Output: $H \in$ DT

---

the DT (see Figure 14). We let $S_k^+ \doteq \{(\boldsymbol{o}, c^+) \in \mathcal{S}_k\}$ denote the subset of positive examples that fall on leaf k. To decide a class, we can label leaves using real values to make predictions, following the convention of linear separators (used in Figure 14), or use $[0, 1]$ values. In fact, using assumption **A2** on balanced convex losses, the estimator for the class membership probabilities in (3) naturally becomes for leaf k:

$$\hat{\mathbf{Pr}}[c = c^+ | H; \boldsymbol{o} \text{ reaches leaf } k] = \frac{|S_k^+|}{|S_k|} \in [0, 1] \ .$$

The most popular DT induction algorithms integrate a stage in which a large DT is induced in a top-down fashion, the so-called TDIDT scheme (Top-Down Induction of DT). This scheme consists, after having initialized the DT to a single leaf, in repeatedly replacing a leaf by a sub-tree with two leaves (a stump) [9,23,34]. For this reason, it is convenient to define, for any $k \in \mathcal{L}(H)$ and any Boolean description variable v, $H_{|k \rightarrow v}$ to be the DT built from H after having replaced leaf k by the subtree of two leaves rooted at v. The TDIDT scheme can be conveniently abstracted as displayed in Algorithm 3. In UDT, ϕ is the free parameter which is instantiated with different choices to yield all popular schemes: (26) is chosen in [9], (29) is chosen in [34] and (28) is chosen in [23]. In fact, it is the *opposite* of the permissible function which is used (we would have $\phi = \tilde{\psi}$ in ULS), but we keep ϕ in order not to laden our notations. All popular TDIDT schemes would also also normalize A_ϕ (division by m), but this does not change the choices made for k' and v, as after having picked k', they all pick the best stump, *i.e.* the one which minimizes (104).

Because all ϕ considered in existing algorithms are permissible, we also restrict ourselves to balanced convex surrogates, and so we seek the minimization of the BCS in (31). In the following Theorem, we not only show that UDT achieves the minimization of any BCS with signature ϕ: while bitterly different from each other on paper, we show that UDT and ULS are offshoots of the same algorithm, thereby generalizing an observation of [19] to the whole family of losses that meet assumptions **A1**, **A2** and **A3**.

Theorem 4. *The output of UDT($\mathcal{S}$, ϕ) converges to a classifier $H_\star$ realizing:*

$$H_\star = \arg \min_{H \in \mathrm{DT}} \varepsilon_{\mathbb{R}}^{\phi}(\mathcal{S}, H) \ . \tag{105}$$

Proof: The proof makes use of linearized decision trees (LDT) of [19]. A LDT has the same graph shape as a DT, but real values are put on every node (not just on leaves). The classification of some observation sums these real values over the whole path that it follows, from the root to a leaf. To each path from the root to a leaf can thus be associated a constant LS, that sums these real values. The right part of Figure 14 presents how to generate the equivalent LDT from the DT given on the left. We can indeed check that $\alpha_1 h_1 + \alpha_2 h_2 + \alpha_4 h_4 = +1$, and so on for the other leaves.

Thus, we can use ULS to build each of these LS: each feature h_t is constant and put on some tree node, ULS is run on the subset of $\mathcal{S}$ that reaches the node, in order to compute the leveraging coefficient α_t. The splits are computed after a further minimization of the given BCS.

Suppose that the current LDT H has T nodes, and we wish to compute α_k for some h_k located at leaf node index k. To do so, we number the internal nodes using natural integers, excluding from the choices the integers chosen for the leaves. Let $\wp(k)$ be the set of indices corresponding to the path from the root to leaf k. The solution of (70) can be computed exactly, and yields:

$$\alpha_k = \frac{1}{h_k} \left(\nabla_\phi \left(\frac{|S_k^+|}{|S_k|} \right) - \sum_{t \in \wp(k) \setminus \{k\}} \alpha_t h_t \right) \ .$$

Thus, for any observation o that reaches leaf k, we get:

$$H(o) = \nabla_\phi \left(\frac{|S_k^+|}{|S_k|} \right) \ , \tag{106}$$

naturally the inverse of (105). Finally, the BCS of H simplifies as:

$$\varepsilon_{\mathbb{R}}^{\phi}(\mathcal{S}, H) \doteq \sum_i F_\phi(y_i^* H(o_i)) = \frac{1}{b_\phi} \sum_i D_\phi(y_i \| \nabla_\phi^{-1}(H(o_i)))$$

$$= \frac{1}{b_\phi} \sum_{k \in \mathcal{L}(H)} \sum_{(o,y) \in \mathcal{S}_k} D_\phi \left(y \left\| \frac{|S_k^+|}{|S_k|} \right. \right)$$

$$= \frac{1}{b_\phi} \sum_{k \in \mathcal{L}(H)} |S_k| \times \left\{ \frac{|S_k^+|}{|S_k|} D_\phi \left(1 \left\| \frac{|S_k^+|}{|S_k|} \right. \right) + \left(1 - \frac{|S_k^+|}{|S_k|} \right) D_\phi \left(0 \left\| \frac{|S_k^+|}{|S_k|} \right. \right) \right\}$$

$$= -\frac{m a_\phi}{b_\phi} + \sum_{k \in \mathcal{L}(H)} \frac{|S_k|}{b_\phi} \left(-\phi \left(\frac{|S_k^+|}{|S_k|} \right) \right) \ .$$

It is straightforward to check from this last equality and Lemma 2 that the progress to optimum in (74) ULS becomes exactly (104) in UDT. The LDT obtained is equivalent [19] (see also Figure 14) to a twin DT in which we put at leaf k either:

$$\frac{|S_k^+|}{|S_k|} \in [0, 1] \; ,$$

or:

$$\nabla_\phi \left(\frac{|S_k^+|}{|S_k|} \right) \in \mathrm{im}(\nabla_\phi) \subseteq \mathbb{R} \; ,$$

eventually closing once again the domain of the gradient of ϕ to ensure proper scalability in $[0, 1]$. We finally end up with UDT. □

From (106), it comes that the $[0, 1]$ value put at leaf k satisfies:

$$\frac{|S_k^+|}{|S_k|} = \nabla_\phi^{-1}(H(o)) \; ,$$

with o any observation that reaches leaf k. From Subsection 3.4 and Lemma 3, it comes that the leaf value is also $\nabla_\phi^{-1}(\theta)$, and so fitting a DT to the minimization of a BCS yields local (leaves-based) maximum likelihood estimators of the expectation parameter of the exponential family defined by signature ϕ.

7 Experiments

This section is an attempt to summarize some interesting experimental properties that seem to emerge out of the numerous surrogates and classifiers considered. To remain concise, we have chosen to focus only on ULS. We have compared against each other 11 flavors of ULS, including AdaBoost [36], on a benchmark of 52 domains (49 from the UCI repository [7]), with $32 \leq m \leq 14500$. True risks are estimated via stratified 10-fold cross validation; ULS is ran for r (fixed) features h_t, each of which is a boolean rule: **If** Monomial **then** Class$= \pm 1$ **else** Class $= \mp 1$, with at most l (fixed) literals, induced following the greedy minimization of the SCS at hand. Leveraging coefficients (70) are approximated up to 10^{-10} precision. Figure 15 summarizes the results.

Out of the 11 flavors, only one picks ψ in SCS\BCS (AdaBoost); the ten others exclusively rely on BCS. Out of these ten, the first four flavors pick ϕ in (26), (27), (28) and (29). The fifth uses another generalization of (28):

$$\phi_v(x) \doteq (x(1 - x))^v \; , \forall v \in (0, 1) \; . \tag{107}$$

Recent works have demonstrated the interest in fitting a metric (Mahalanobis) to the domain at hand, *prior* to using an instanced-based (*non inductive*) classification algorithm [11]. The wide range of SCS available for ULS inspired us to

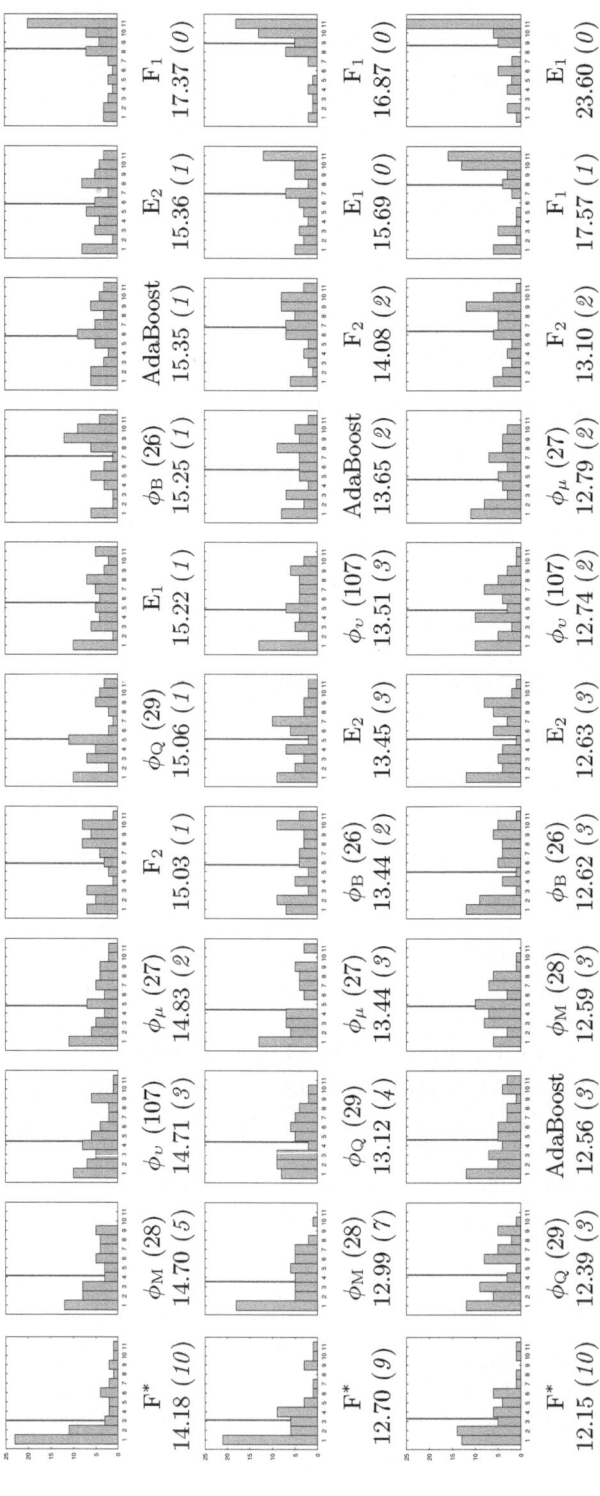

Fig. 15. Summary of our results over the 52 domains for the 11 algorithms. Rows are respectively for $l = 2, r = 10$ (top), $l = 10, r = 20$ (middle), $l = 3, r = 100$ (bottom). In each row, ranking histograms (wrt true risks) are given for each algorithm; vertical (red) bars show the average rank over all domains. Histograms are ordered from left to right in increasing average true risk over all domains (shown below histograms). The *italic* numbers give, for each algorithm, the number of algorithms it *beats* according to a Student paired t-test over all domains with .1 threshold probability.

kill two birds in one shot: mix the *adaptive tuning* of a SCS to the domain at hand with the *inductive learning* of a LS with ULS on this domain. We relate experiments on the adaptive tuning of a BCS out-of-a-bag of BCS. This gives the five last flavors of ULS with BCS. The first four fit the BCS at *each stage* of the inner loop (**for** j ...) of ULS. Two (noted "$F_.$") pick the BCS which minimizes the empirical risk in the bag; two others (noted "$E_.$") pick the BCS which maximizes the current edge. There are two different bags corresponding to four permissible functions each: the first (index "1") contains (26), (27), (28) and (29); the second (index "2") contains (27), (28), (29) and (107). We wanted to evaluate (26) because it forces to renormalize the leveraging coefficients in H each time it is selected, to ensure that the output of H lies in $[-1,1]$. The last adaptive flavor, F^*, "externalizes" the choice of the BCS: it selects for each fold the BCS which yields the smallest empirical risk in a bag corresponding to five ϕ: (26), (27), (28), (29) and (107). It was suggested by the fact that, if ULS resists overfitting as AdaBoost does, we might hope for good performances at least for small classifiers. We selected small bags not only for time considerations: if there were to be some particular interest in a fine selection of the BCS, it would ideally already happen for small bags.

All results in Figure 15 advocate for the superiority of F^* against all other approaches. For example, when $l = 2, r = 10$, F^* tops all algorithms for almost half the domains. Even when we replace the .1 threshold probability by a .01 threshold probability (see Figure 15), F^* still beats 7 algorithms. An interesting phenomenon happens for small classifiers: permissible functions with stronger concave regimes (e.g. (28)) tend to improve performances. While it was previously remarked for decision tree induction in [23], it is actually predicted up to some extent by Theorem 2, as the bound on J is inversely proportional to the minimum of the second derivative of $\tilde{\psi}$. This phenomenon becomes (predictibly) dampened as classifiers become large, but we ultimately cannot conclude that (29) beats (28) and / or AdaBoost, according to Student paired t-test ($l = 3, r = 100$).

This makes the SCL derived from (28) a very interesting alternative to the logistic loss and AdaBoost, which might be useful in other supervised learning schemes as well. Finally, mixing permissible functions with different gradient images (E_1, F_1) is clearly a bad choice, but F^* and E_2 are advocacies for further works on mixed fittings of SCS and classifiers. This is confirmed by a close look at the domains: for almost each algorithm and each choice of (l, r), there exists a domain on which it ranks first, and one on which it ranks last. This is all the more important as previous works highlight the role of early stopping in consistency for convex surrogates [6].

Acknowledgments

Support is acknowledged by ANR *Blanc* project ANR-07-BLAN-0328-01 "Computational Information Geometry and Applications". The second author acknowledge support from DIGITEO GAS: Geometric Algorithms for Statistics.

References

1. Amari, S.-I.: Natural Gradient works efficiently in Learning. Neural Computation 10, 251–276 (1998)
2. Azran, A., Meir, R.: Data dependent risk bounds for hierarchical mixture of experts classifiers. In: Shawe-Taylor, J., Singer, Y. (eds.) COLT 2004. LNCS, vol. 3120, pp. 427–441. Springer, Heidelberg (2004)
3. Banerjee, A., Guo, X., Wang, H.: On the optimality of conditional expectation as a bregman predictor. IEEE Trans. on Information Theory 51, 2664–2669 (2005)
4. Banerjee, A., Merugu, S., Dhillon, I., Ghosh, J.: Clustering with Bregman divergences. Journal of Machine Learning Research 6, 1705–1749 (2005)
5. Bartlett, P., Jordan, M., McAuliffe, J.D.: Convexity, classification, and risk bounds. Journal of the Am. Stat. Assoc. 101, 138–156 (2006)
6. Bartlett, P., Traskin, M.: Adaboost is consistent. In: NIPS*19 (2006)
7. Blake, C.L., Keogh, E., Merz, C.J.: UCI repository of machine learning databases (1998), http://www.ics.uci.edu/~mlearn/MLRepository.html
8. Bregman, L.M.: The relaxation method of finding the common point of convex sets and its application to the solution of problems in convex programming. USSR Comp. Math. and Math. Phys. 7, 200–217 (1967)
9. Breiman, L., Freidman, J.H., Olshen, R.A., Stone, C.J.: Classification and regression trees. Wadsworth (1984)
10. Collins, M., Schapire, R., Singer, Y.: Logistic regression, adaboost and Bregman distances. In: COLT 2000, pp. 158–169 (2000)
11. Davis, J., Kulis, B., Jain, P., Sra, S., Dhillon, I.: Information-theoretic metric learning. In: ICML 2007 (2007)
12. Dhillon, I., Sra, S.: Generalized non-negative matrix approximations with Bregman divergences. In: Advances in Neural Information Processing Systems, vol. 18 (2005)
13. Freund, Y., Schapire, R.E.: A Decision-Theoretic generalization of on-line learning and an application to Boosting. Journal of Comp. Syst. Sci. 55, 119–139 (1997)
14. Friedman, J., Hastie, T., Tibshirani, R.: Additive Logistic Regression: a Statistical View of Boosting. Ann. of Stat. 28, 337–374 (2000)
15. Gates, G.W.: The Reduced Nearest Neighbor rule. IEEE Trans. on Information Theory 18, 431–433 (1972)
16. Gentile, C., Warmuth, M.: Linear hinge loss and average margin. In: NIPS*11, pp. 225–231 (1998)
17. Gentile, C., Warmuth, M.: Proving relative loss bounds for on-line learning algorithms using Bregman divergences. In: Tutorials of the 13 th International Conference on Computational Learning Theory (2000)
18. Grünwald, P., Dawid, P.: Game theory, maximum entropy, minimum discrepancy and robust Bayesian decision theory. Ann. of Statistics 32, 1367–1433 (2004)
19. Henry, C., Nock, R., Nielsen, F.: Real boosting a la Carte with an application to boosting Oblique Decision Trees. In: Proc. of the 21 st International Joint Conference on Artificial Intelligence, pp. 842–847 (2007)
20. Herbster, M., Warmuth, M.: Tracking the best regressor. In: COLT 1998, pp. 24–31 (1998)
21. Kearns, M.J., Vazirani, U.V.: An Introduction to Computational Learning Theory. MIT Press, Cambridge (1994)
22. Kearns, M.J.: Thoughts on hypothesis boosting, ML class project (1988)
23. Kearns, M.J., Mansour, Y.: On the boosting ability of top-down decision tree learning algorithms. Journal of Comp. Syst. Sci. 58, 109–128 (1999)

24. Kearns, M.J., Valiant, L.: Cryptographic limitations on learning boolean formulae and finite automata. In: Proc. of the 21 th ACM Symposium on the Theory of Computing, pp. 433–444 (1989)
25. Kivinen, J., Warmuth, M., Hassibi, B.: The p-norm generalization of the LMS algorithm for adaptive filtering. IEEE Trans. on Signal Processing 54, 1782–1793 (2006)
26. Kohavi, R.: The power of Decision Tables. In: Proc. of the 10 th European Conference on Machine Learning, pp. 174–189 (1995)
27. Matsushita, K.: Decision rule, based on distance, for the classification problem. Ann. of the Inst. for Stat. Math. 8, 67–77 (1956)
28. Mitchell, T.M.: The need for biases in learning generalization. Technical Report CBM-TR-117, Rutgers University (1980)
29. Murata, N., Takenouchi, T., Kanamori, T., Eguchi, S.: Information geometry of $\mathcal{U}$-Boost and Bregman divergence. Neural Computation, 1437–1481 (2004)
30. Nielsen, F., Boissonnat, J.-D., Nock, R.: On Bregman Voronoi diagrams. In: Proc. of the 19 th ACM-SIAM Symposium on Discrete Algorithms, pp. 746–755 (2007)
31. Nielsen, F., Boissonnat, J.-D., Nock, R.: Bregman Voronoi Diagrams: properties, algorithms and applications, 45 p. (submission, 2008)
32. Nock, R.: Inducing interpretable Voting classifiers without trading accuracy for simplicity: theoretical results, approximation algorithms, and experiments. Journal of Artificial Intelligence Research 17, 137–170 (2002)
33. Nock, R., Nielsen, F.: A Real Generalization of discrete AdaBoost. Artif. Intell. 171, 25–41 (2007)
34. Quinlan, J.R.: C4.5: programs for machine learning. Morgan Kaufmann, San Francisco (1993)
35. Schapire, R.E., Freund, Y., Bartlett, P., Lee, W.S.: Boosting the margin: a new explanation for the effectiveness of voting methods. Annals of statistics 26, 1651–1686 (1998)
36. Schapire, R.E., Singer, Y.: Improved boosting algorithms using confidence-rated predictions. Machine Learning Journal 37, 297–336 (1999)
37. Valiant, L.G.: A theory of the learnable. Communications of the ACM 27, 1134–1142 (1984)
38. Vapnik, V.: Statistical Learning Theory. John Wiley, Chichester (1998)
39. Warmuth, M., Liao, J., Rätsch, G.: Totally corrective boosting algorithms that maximize the margin. In: ICML 2006, pp. 1001–1008 (2006)

Shape from Depth Discontinuities

Gabriel Taubin, Daniel Crispell, Douglas Lanman, Peter Sibley, and Yong Zhao

Division of Engineering, Brown University
Box D, Providence, RI 02912, USA
taubin@brown.edu
http://mesh.brown.edu

Abstract. We propose a new primal-dual framework for representation, capture, processing, and display of piecewise smooth surfaces, where the dual space is the space of oriented 3D lines, or *rays*, as opposed to the traditional dual space of planes. An image capture process detects points on a depth discontinuity sweep from a camera moving with respect to an object, or from a static camera and a moving object. A depth discontinuity sweep is a surface in dual space composed of the time-dependent family of depth discontinuity curves span as the camera pose describes a curved path in 3D space. Only part of this surface, which includes silhouettes, is visible and measurable from the camera. Locally convex points deep inside concavities can be estimated from the visible non-silhouette depth discontinuity points. Locally concave point laying at the bottom of concavities, which do not correspond to visible depth discontinuities, cannot be estimated, resulting in holes in the reconstructed surface. A first variational approach to fill the holes, based on fitting an implicit function to a reconstructed oriented point cloud, produces watertight models. We describe a first complete end-to-end system for acquiring models of shape and appearance. We use a single multi-flash camera and turntable for the data acquisition and represent the scanned objects as point clouds, with each point being described by a 3-D location, a surface normal, and a Phong appearance model.

Keywords: Multi-view reconstruction, appearance modeling, multi-flash, shape-from-silhouette.

1 Introduction

Because of the relative ease and robustness (particularly in controlled environments) of capturing object silhouettes, there exists a large body of work focused on reconstructing 3-D object shape based on silhouettes imaged from multiple viewpoints. All methods based purely on object silhouettes, however, face an inherent limitation: surface points which do not appear as part of the object silhouette from any viewpoint cannot be reconstructed. This limitation often leads to unsatisfactory results when the imaged objects contain details located within concavities that "protect" them from the occluding contour. Our method addresses this limitation by supplementing the silhouette information with additional depth discontinuity contours located on the object interior, providing a more complete and detailed reconstruction.

F. Nielsen (Ed.): ETVC 2008, LNCS 5416, pp. 216–237, 2009.

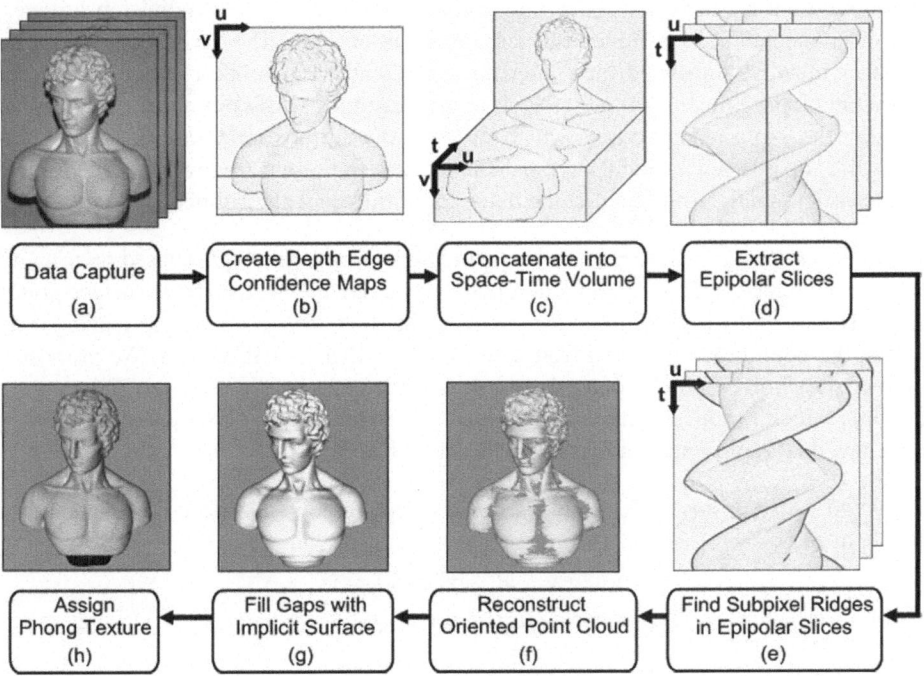

Fig. 1. The multi-flash 3-D photography pipeline. Data capture involves acquiring four images (using illumination from the top, left, bottom, and right) for each of 670 viewpoints of the object. Following data capture, a *depth edge confidence map* is estimated for each viewpoint. The confidence maps are concatenated to form a space-time volume. Each volume "slice" corresponding to an image scanline through all time is processed independently. After extracting subpixel ridges in the slices, differential reconstruction is applied to estimate an oriented point cloud. In order to fill sampling gaps, an implicit surface is fitted. Finally, for each point a Phong reflectance model (i.e., diffuse and specular colors) is estimated using 67 viewpoints.

We propose a new primal-dual framework for representation, capture, geometry processing, and display of piecewise smooth surfaces, with particular emphasis on implementing efficient digital data processing operations in dual space, and we describe our preliminary work based on multi-flash 3D photography [1,2] and vector field isosurface (VFIso) fitting to oriented point clouds [3].

Piecewise Smooth Surfaces: Piecewise smooth surfaces are a very popular way to describe the shape of solid objects, such as those that can be fabricated with machine tools. They are composed of smooth surface patches which meet along piecewise smooth patch boundary curves called feature lines. Across feature lines the vector field of surface normals can be discontinuous.

Surface Representations and Sampling: The family of piecewise smooth surfaces has infinite dimensionality. *Surface representations* with finite numbers of parameters must be used to operate on these surfaces in computers. Several popular surface representations are in use: irregular polygon meshes, semi-regular subdivision surfaces, and disconnected point-sampled surfaces are some of them. The desired operations on surfaces must be translated into algorithms applicable on the corresponding surface representations. Since information such as surface normal discontinuities can be lost through the sampling processes which produce the surface representations for computer use, or just not explicitly representable, it is important to develop a theoretical framework to analyze and predict the behavior of different algorithms.

Depth Discontinuities: Current 3D shape measurement technologies based on triangulation capture points on smooth surface patches, but are unable to sample surface points along feature lines [4,5,6,7]. Several prior-art methods try to detect the feature lines lost in the point cloud obtained from one of these off-the-shelf sensors. We propose a new shape capture modality potentially able to directly detect feature lines. This capture process, which produces data complementary to triangulation based devices, is based on a new dual representation for piecewise smooth surfaces.

The Dual Space of Rays: The dual space considered here is the space of oriented lines in 3D, or *rays*

$$\{(q,v) : q,v \in \mathbb{R}^3, \|v\| = 1\} = \mathbb{R}^3 \times S^2$$

Points in this space correspond to rays defined in parametric form:

$$R_{qv} = \{p(\lambda) = q + \lambda v : \lambda \geq 0\} \,.$$

This space has been popularized by the image-based rendering literature: a light field [8] or lumigraph [9] is a function from the space of rays into the RGB color space. Image pixels correspond to points in $\mathbb{R}^3$ through the intrinsic equations of image formation which depend on the camera type, and the extrinsic camera pose. For an orthographic camera (which corresponds to a physical camera with a telecentric lens), the pixels correspond to a regular array of parallel rays; for a perspective (pinhole) camera, all the rays share a common origin: the optical center of the lens; catadioptric cameras may not have an optical center, and the mapping from pixels to rays may be more complex, as has been shown by many authors, including [10,11].

Representation of Surfaces in Dual Space: A smooth surface is represented as the set of all its tangent rays. This representation can be extended to piecewise smooth surfaces by considering the set of all its supporting rays (in the sense of convexity theory). We call this set the set of *depth discontinuities* of the surface. Note that locally concave points of the surface, deep inside concavities, do not correspond to visible depth discontinuities as seen from a camera located outside of the object bounded by the surface (Figure 2).

For example, let $S_F = \{p : f(p) = 0\} \subseteq \mathbb{R}^3$ be an implicit surface, with $f : \mathbb{R}^3 \to \mathbb{R}$ a smooth function which belongs to a family parameterized by a finite dimensional vector F (e.g. a polynomial of degree $\leq D$), and let $q \in \mathbb{R}^3$ be a point external to S_F. For every unit vector v we have a ray $R_{qv} = \{q + \lambda v : \lambda > 0\}$. The necessary and sufficient condition for the ray R_{qv} to be tangent to the surface S_F at some point is that:

$$\exists \lambda > 0 : \begin{cases} f(q + \lambda v) & = 0 \\ v^t \nabla f(q + \lambda v) = 0 \end{cases} \tag{1}$$

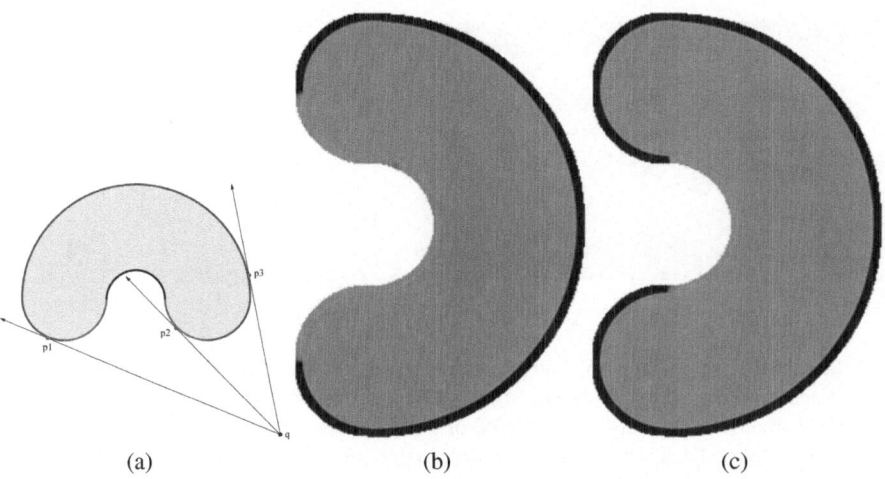

Fig. 2. (a) An object with concave surface points and the regions captured by: both depth discontinuity and silhouette-based reconstructions (blue), depth discontinuity-based reconstructions only (green), and neither (black). Points $p1$ and $p3$ are captured by both methods from camera position q, while $p2$ is only captured by depth discontinuity-based methods. (b) Visible silhouette points. (c) Visible depth discontinuity points.

Eliminating the variable λ from these two equations we obtain a single *resultant* equation

$$\phi_F(q,v) = 0 \tag{2}$$

which provides a necessary condition for tangency: in general if $\phi_F(q,v) = 0$ then the straight line supporting the ray is tangent to S at a point $p = q + \lambda v$, where the λ here is not necessarily positive (in which case the opposite ray satisfies the equation for positive λ because $q + \lambda v = q + (-\lambda)(-v)$). An expression for λ as a function of (F,q,v) is usually obtained as a byproduct of the elimination process, and can be used to determine the correct orientation for the ray. The set of depth discontinuities of the surface S_F is the set

$$\Phi_F = \{(q,v) : \phi_F(q,v) = 0\} \subseteq \mathbb{R}^3 \times S^2 \tag{3}$$

Most previous works based on duality (e.g. [12,13]) represent a smooth surface as the set of all its tangent planes.

Depth Discontinuity Sweeps: A *depth discontinuity sweep* is the time-dependent family of depth discontinuity curves span as the pose describes a curved path in 3D. This is a 2-surface in dual space, which typically includes self-intersections and cusps. For example, for a pinhole camera whose center of projection moves along a trajectory $q(\theta)$, corresponding to the points along a curve

$$C = \{q(\theta) : \theta \in \Theta \subseteq \mathbb{R}\}, \tag{4}$$

the corresponding depth discontinuity sweep is the set

$$\Phi_F^C = \{(q(\theta),v) : \theta \in \Theta, \ v \in S^2, \ \phi_F(q(\theta),v) = 0\}. \tag{5}$$

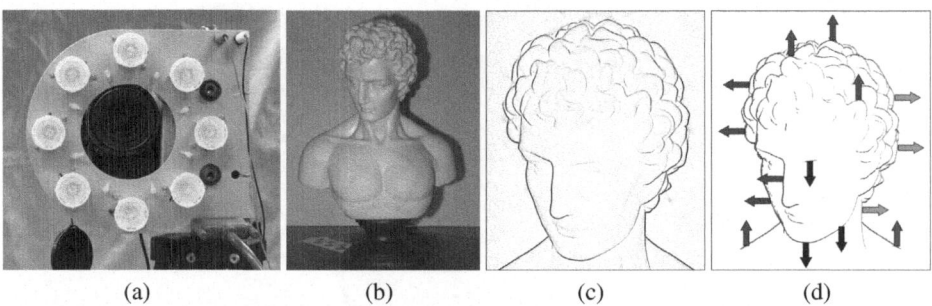

(a)   (b)   (c)   (d)

Fig. 3. (a) Multi-flash camera. (b) Sample image acquired with flash located to the left of the camera's center of projection. (c) Depth edge confidence image produced by method in [14], with darker pixels representing a higher likelihood of a depth edge. (d) Approximate edge orientation corresponding to the flash with a maximum depth edge response. Up, down, left, and right edge orientations are shown in red, blue, purple, and green, respectively.

For a turntable sequence, the curve C is a circle of radius $r > 0$ in $\mathbb{R}^3$. As shown in figure 2, only part of depth discontinuity sweep is visible and measurable from a moving camera. Depth discontinuity pixels correspond to samples of the dual surface. The depth discontinuities visible from a particular camera pose are curves which include the silhouette visible from that pose, but convex points deep inside concavities can be estimated from the additional information, which is impossible just from silhouettes. Surface points laying at the bottom of concavities, however, do not correspond to depth discontinuities and cannot be measured, resulting in holes in the reconstructed surface. One of our future goals is to develop very efficient methods to fill these holes directly in dual space based on extrapolating the depth discontinuity curves to include the non-visible depth discontinuities. One method to fill these holes in primal space is described in section 4.5.

2   Multi-flash 3D Photography

We proceed to describe a first 3-D scanning system which exploits the depth discontinuity information captured by a multi-flash camera as an object being scanned is rotated on a turntable. Our method extends traditional shape-from-silhouette algorithms by utilizing the full set of visible depth discontinuities on the object surface. The resulting 3-D representation is an oriented point cloud which is, in general, unevenly sampled in primal space. We fit an implicit surface to the point cloud in order to generate additional points on the surface of the object in regions where sampling is sparse. Alternatively, the implicit surface can be regarded as the output of the reconstruction process. Finally, the appearance of each surface point is modeled by fitting a Phong reflectance model to the BRDF samples using the visibility information provided by the implicit surface. We present an overview of each step in the capture process and experimental results for a variety of scanned objects. The remainder of the article is structured as follows. In Section 3 we describe previous work related to both our reconstruction and appearance modeling procedures. In Section 4 we describe in detail each stage of the reconstruction procedure, and discuss its inherent advantages and limitations in Section 5. In Section 6 we present results for a variety of scanned objects to demonstrate the accuracy and versatility of the proposed system. Finally, we conclude in Section 7.

3   Related Work

Our system draws upon several important works in both the surface reconstruction and appearance modeling fields of computer vision. We describe these works, their strengths and limitations, and how we extend and integrate them into our modeling system.

3.1   Surface Reconstruction

Surface reconstruction based on observing an object's silhouette as it undergoes motion has been extensively studied and is known broadly as *shape-from-silhouette* [15]. In general, shape-from-silhouette algorithms can be classified into two groups: those with volumetric, or global, approaches, and those which utilize differential, or local, information. Although our system falls under the category of the differential approach, we describe both here for completeness.

Space carving and visual hull algorithms [16] follow a global volumetric approach. A 3-D volume which completely encloses the object is defined, and the object is imaged from multiple viewpoints. The object silhouette is extracted in each of the images, and portions of the volume which project to locations outside of an object silhouette in any of the images are removed from the representation. Although robust, the quality of the results is somewhat limited, especially for complex objects containing concavities and curved surfaces.

An alternative differential approach uses the local deformation of the silhouettes as the camera moves relative to the object to estimate the depth of the points [17]. Related methods use a dual-space approach, where tangent planes to the object surface are represented as points in dual space, and surface estimates can be obtained by examining neighboring points in this space [18,19]. These systems provide a direct method for estimating depth based solely on a local region of camera motion, but are subject to singularities in degenerate cases. They also are not capable of modeling surface contours that do not appear as part of the object silhouette for any view, e.g. structures protected by concavities. Our method is similar in principle to these methods, but supplements the input silhouette information with all visible depth discontinuities. This extra information allows us to reconstruct structures protected by concavities that do not appear as part of the object silhouette in any view.

3.2   Multi-view Stereo Algorithms

In addition to purely silhouette-based approaches, multi-view stereo algorithms [20] are a class of hybrid approaches which combine image texture and color information with silhouette information [21,22,23]. These methods are capable of producing very accurate results, even recovering shape in areas protected by concavities. In most of

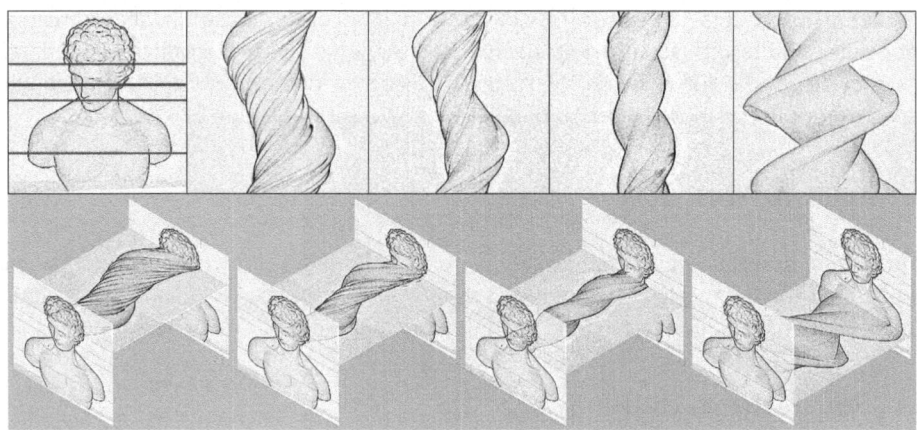

Fig. 4. In our multi-flash 3D photography system, depth edge confidence maps estimated for each viewpoint are concatenated to form a space-time volume, which is then sliced parallel to the image scan lines to produce *epipolar slices*

these algorithms the silhouette data is only used to construct an initial estimate of the visual hull surface represented as a polygon mesh, which is then iteratively deformed to minimize a properly formulated photo-consistency energy function. We look at these algorithms as operating mainly in primal space. Our system uses depth discontinuity information alone in order to produce the surface reconstruction. There is great potential to obtain more accurate surface reconstruction algorithms by combining multi-view stereo and depth discontinuities. We plan to follow this path in the near future. Again, what our multi-flash 3D photography algorithm shows is the 3D information contained only in the visible depth discontinuities.

3.3 Appearance Modeling

Appearance modeling has become an increasingly active area of research in both the computer vision and graphics communities. In [24], Lensch et al. introduced the notion of a *lumitexel*: a data structure composed of all available geometric and photometric information for a point on an object's surface. In addition, Lensch advocated lumitexel clustering to group similar surface components together and effectively increase the diversity of BRDF measurements. These methods were recently applied by Sadlo et al. to acquire point-based models using a structured light scanning system [25]. We apply a similar approach to assign a per-point reflectance model to the oriented point clouds obtained using our system.

4   System Architecture

The modeling system consists of a complete pipeline from data capture to appearance modeling (Figure 1). Here we describe the operation at each stage of the pipeline.

4.1 Data Capture

We use a turntable and stationary 8 megapixel digital camera to acquire data from up to 670 viewpoints in a circular path around the object (Figure 1(a)). We have constructed a camera rig similar to those used by Raskar et al. [14] consisting of eight 120 lumen LEDs positioned around the camera lens (Figure 3(a)) which are used as flashes. For each turntable position, we capture four images using illumination from the top, left, right, and bottom flashes, respectively. We have found that the four flashes positioned on the diagonals do not add a significant amount of extra information and are therefore not used in our experiments. The camera is intrinsically calibrated using Bouguet's camera calibration toolbox [26], and its position and orientation with respect to the turntable are determined using a calibration grid placed on the table. Once the data has been captured, we rectify each of the images to remove any radial distortion, and to align the camera's u axis with the direction of camera motion (i.e. perpendicular to the turntable axis of rotation and with zero translation in the u direction as shown in Figure 1(b)).

4.2 Depth Edge Estimation

Using the four images captured with different illumination at each turntable position, we are able to robustly compute depth edges in the images (Figure 1(b)) using the algorithms introduced by Raskar et al. [14] for non-photorealistic rendering. The distances between the camera center and the four flashes are small compared with the distance to the scene, so a narrow shadow can be observed adjacent to each depth discontinuity (Figure 3(b)) in at least one of the four images. As presented in [14], a simple method exists to extract both the position and orientation of the depth edges using the information encoded in these shadows. First, a *maximum composite* is formed by taking the largest intensity observed in each pixel over the multi-flash sequence. In general, this composite should be free of shadows created by the flashes. In order to amplify the shadowed pixels in each flash image (and attenuate texture edges), a *ratio image* is formed by dividing (per pixel) each flash image by the maximum composite. Afterwards, the depth edges can be detected by searching for negative transitions along the direction from the flash to the camera center (projected into the image plane) in each ratio image. With a sufficient distribution of flash positions and under some limiting assumptions on the baseline and material properties of the surface [14], this procedure will estimate a considerable subset of all depth discontinuities in the scene. A *depth edge confidence image* corresponding to the likelihood of a pixel being located near a depth discontinuity (see Figure 3(c)) is produced for each of the 670 turntable positions. Images encoding the flash positions which generated the greatest per-pixel responses are also stored in order to facilitate surface normal estimation in the reconstruction stage. By dividing the high resolution images between a cluster of 15 processors, we are able to complete the depth edge estimation for all 670 positions in under one hour.

4.3 Extracting Curves in Epipolar Slices

The *epipolar parameterization* for curved surfaces has been extensively studied in the past [27,17]. For two cameras with centers q_1 and q_2, an epipolar plane is defined as the

Fig. 5. Simulated orthographic epipolar slices showing invisible depth discontinuities

plane containing q_1, q_2, and a world point X being imaged. The epipolar planes slice the image planes, forming a pencil of *epipolar lines* in each image, and each point in one image corresponds to an epipolar line in another. A point x_1 along an apparent contour in one image is therefore matched to a point x_2 in the second image by intersecting the epipolar line defined by q_1,q_2, and x_1 with the corresponding apparent contour in the second image. For a continuous path of camera centers, $q(t)$, an epipolar plane at time t is spanned by the tangent vector $\dot{q}(t)$ to $q(t)$ and a viewing ray $r(t)$ from $q(t)$ to a world point p. So called *frontier points* occur when the epipolar plane is identical to the tangent plane of the surface.

Because we have rectified each input image so that the camera motion is parallel to the image u axis (Section 4.1), the depth edge confidence images exhibit the same property. By stacking the sequence of confidence images (Figure 1(c)) and "slicing" across a single scanline, we have an approximation to the epipolar constraint in local regions. We refer to these images containing a particular scanline from each image as *epipolar slices* (Figures 1(d) and 4). By tracking the motion of apparent contours in the slices, we are in effect implicitly utilizing the epipolar constraint for curve matching. The tracking problem can be solved using a form of edge following optimized to take advantage of properties of the slice images. The curve extraction stage is decomposed into three sub-stages: subpixel edge detection, edge linking, and polynomial curve fitting. Although nearby slice images are strongly correlated, we treat them as independent in order to facilitate parallel processing. However, the inherent correlation between epipolar slices is exploited in the extraction of surface normals as described in section 4.4. So in fact, each estimated 3D point is a function of a 3D neighborhood of the corresponding depth discontinuity point in dual space.

Edge Detection. We begin by detecting the pixel-level position of the depth discontinuities by applying a two-level hysteresis threshold. Afterward, we estimate the subpixel position of each depth discontinuity by fitting a sixth order polynomial to the neighboring confidence values. Non-maximum suppression is applied to ensure that a single subpixel position is assigned to each depth edge.

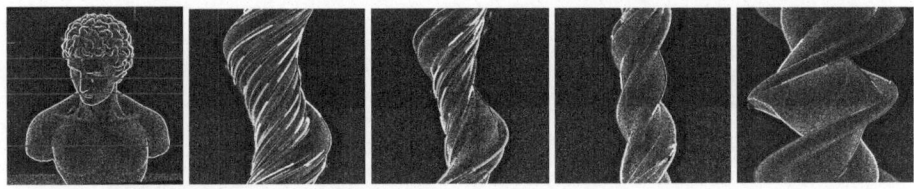

Fig. 6. Epipolar slice curve tracking and fitting

Edge Linking. As shown in Figures 1(d) and 5, the epipolar slices are complex and typically contain many junctions, indicating points of bi-tangency. These junctions emerge for a variety of reasons, including when external silhouettes becomes internal contours (and vice versa). Our edge linking algorithm follows edges through such transitions. We initialize the tracking process by finding the first detection to the left of the axis of rotation in an epipolar slice. Next, we search for the closest detection in the neighboring views within a small window. If any match is found, then we initiate a track using a linear prediction based on these two observations. We proceed to search for new detections within a neighborhood of the predicted edge position. The closest detection (if any) to the prediction is added to the track and neighboring detections are removed from future consideration. Once three or more detections have been linked, we predict the next position using a quadratic model. If a track ends, a new edge chain is initiated using the first available detection either to the left or right of the axis of rotation. This process continues until all detections have been considered. While simple, this tracking method consistently and accurately links depth discontinuities through junctions.

Curve Fitting. Once the subpixel detections have been linked, a sixth order polynomial is fit to each chain – providing an analytic model for the motion of depth discontinuities as a function of viewpoint. Sixth order polynomials were chosen because of their tendency to fit the chain points with low error, and no over-fitting in practice. RMS errors for the polynomial fits vary depending on the length and curvature of the chain, but are generally on the order of one pixel. Typical results achieved using this method are shown in Figure 1(e) and 6.

4.4 Point Cloud Generation

Once curves in the epipolar slice domain have been extracted, we can directly estimate the depth of the points on these curves and produce a point cloud representation of the object (Figure 1(f)).

The properties of surface shapes based on the apparent motion of their contours in images are well-studied [27,17]. In general, we represent a surface point p on a depth discontinuity edge as

$$p = q + \lambda r \tag{6}$$

where q is the camera center, r is the camera ray vector corresponding to a pixel $[u, v]$, and λ is the scaling factor that determines the depth. Cipolla and Giblin [17] showed that the parameter λ can be obtained from the following equation

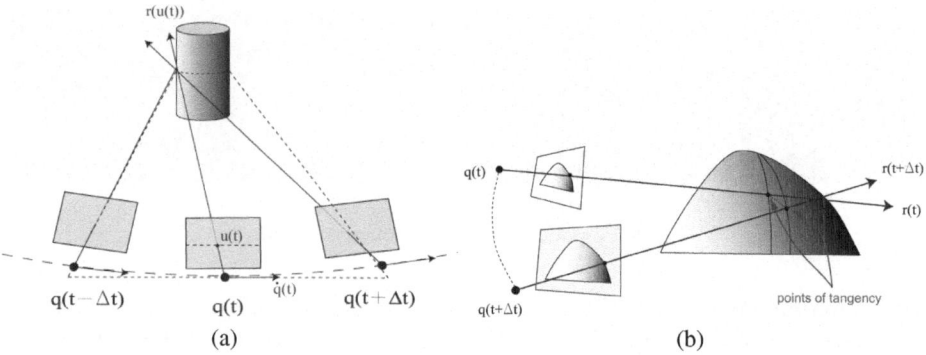

Fig. 7. (a) The epipolar plane (dotted line) used for curve parametrization is spanned by the viewing ray, r, and the camera's velocity vector, $\dot{q}$. The images are rectified such that the epipolar lines correspond to scan lines in the image. Unless the camera motion is linear, this plane is only an approximation for finite Δt, since the neighboring camera centers are, in general, not contained in the plane. (b) The tangent ray from the camera to the object slides over the surface as the camera moves. Depth can be estimated based on the apparent motion of the contour in the image plane relative to the camera motion in space.

$$\lambda = -\frac{n^t \dot{q}}{n^t \dot{r}} \tag{7}$$

where n is the normal vector to the surface at the point p, and $\dot{r}, \dot{q}$ are derivatives in time as the the camera moves with respect to the object and the camera ray r "slides over" the object (Figure 7-(b)). This method assumes that the functions $q(t)$, $r(t)$, and $n(t)$, as well as their derivatives with respect to t are known. The epipolar parametrization is then used to construct these curves from multiple silhouettes. Because the camera motion $q(t)$ is known from calibration, we effectively recover the function $r(t)$ by fitting analytic models to the curves in the epipolar slice images. For a given epipolar slice image, we have constant $v = v_s$ and image axes corresponding to u and t, where, for a given contour, u is function of t. We therefore express Equation 6 as:

$$p(u(t),t) = q(t) + \lambda\, r(u(t),t) \tag{8}$$

and Equation 7 as

$$\lambda = -\frac{n(u(t),t)^t\, \dot{q}(t)}{n(u(t),t)^t\, \frac{d}{dt}\{r(u(t),t)\}} \tag{9}$$

where

$$\frac{d}{dt}\{r(u(t),t)\} = \frac{\partial r}{\partial u}(u(t),t)\,\dot{u}(t)\,. \tag{10}$$

We use the standard pinhole camera model with projection matrix

$$P = K\,[I\,0]\begin{bmatrix} R & T \\ 0 & 1 \end{bmatrix} \tag{11}$$

where R is a 3x3 rotation matrix and T is a 3x1 translation vector relating the world coordinate frame to that of the camera. K is a 3x3 matrix containing the camera's intrinsic projection parameters. We recover these parameters along with 5 radial and tangential distortion coefficients using Bouguet's camera calibration toolbox [26]. We project image points in homogeneous coordinates to vectors in world space using the "inverse" projection matrix, $\hat{P}$.

$$\hat{P} = \begin{bmatrix} R^t & -R^t T \\ 0 & 1 \end{bmatrix} \begin{bmatrix} I \\ 0 \end{bmatrix} K^{-1} \tag{12}$$

The function $\frac{\partial r}{\partial u}(u(t),t)$ can then be calculated from the inverse projection matrix (Equation 12) associated with camera position $q(t)$:

$$\frac{\partial r}{\partial u}(u(t)) = \begin{bmatrix} \hat{P}_{1,1}(t) \\ \hat{P}_{2,1}(t) \\ \hat{P}_{3,1}(t) \end{bmatrix} \tag{13}$$

The contour path's motion in the u direction, $\dot{u}(t)$, can be obtained directly from the coefficients of the curve fit to the contour path (Section 4.3) in the slice image. We estimate the image normal $m(u(t),t)$ by performing principal component analysis (PCA) on a local region about the point $(u(t),v_s)$ in the original depth edge image corresponding to time t. There exists a sign ambiguity in this normal computation, so we compare m with the coarse normal information given by the flash with the maximum depth edge response (Section 4.2) and flip its direction as needed. The surface normal $n(u(t),t)$ in 3-D must then be perpendicular to the viewing ray $r(u(t),t)$, and contained in the plane spanned by $r(u(t),t)$ and the projection of $n(u(t),t)$ onto the image plane, $m(u(t),t)$.

$$n(u(t),t) = (\hat{P}(t) \begin{bmatrix} m(u(t),t) \\ 0 \end{bmatrix} \times r(u(t),t)) \times r(u(t),t) \tag{14}$$

Substituting back in to Equation 9, we can now recover the depth of any point on the contour path, assuming known camera motion $\dot{q}(t)$. In our experiments, we dealt with the simple case of circular motion, so $\dot{q}(t)$ is well defined for all t.

Again dividing the computations between 15 processors, the curve extraction and depth estimation procedures take on the order of 20 minutes for our data sets.

4.5   Hole Filling

Each curve in each slice is processed independently, and sampled uniformly in t. This sampling in t causes the reconstructed points to be sampled very densely in areas of high curvature (since the viewing ray moves slowly over these regions) and conversely, very sparsely in areas of very low curvature, e.g. planes. The effects of this non-uniform sampling can be seen in Figure 1(f) in the form of gaps in the point cloud. Several approaches have been developed for resampling and filling holes in point clouds. Moving Least Square surfaces [28] provide resampling and filtering operations in terms of local projection operations, however these methods are not well-suited for filling large holes. Diffusion-based methods for meshes [29] and point clouds [30] have also been developed. As an alternative to these advanced methods, a standard approach is to fit an implicit surface or polygonal mesh to the point cloud and subsequently display this representation using the conventional graphics modeling and rendering pipeline.

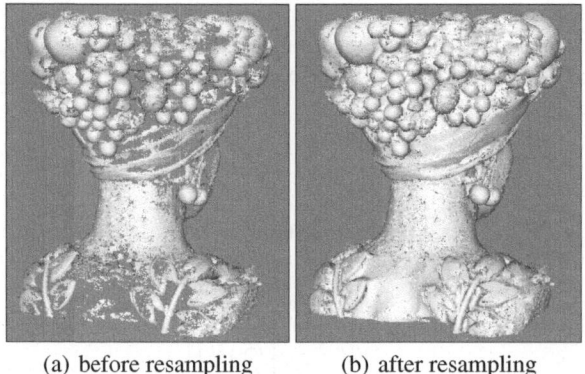

(a) before resampling   (b) after resampling

Fig. 8. Example of filling sampling gaps using the implicit surface as described in Section 4.5

We use a variant of this approach proposed by Sibley and Taubin [31] since we require both an intermediate surface for visibility computations as well as a method for introducing samples in regions that were not acquired using the multi-flash reconstruction (e.g., those shown in Figures 1(g) and 8). The surface fitting reduces to solving a linear least squares problem, and proceeds as follows: Given an oriented point cloud $\mathscr{D} = \{(p_1, n_1), \ldots, (p_m, n_m)\}$ sampled from a surface M, the method computes an implicit surface $M' = \{p \mid f(p) = 0\}$ where $f : \mathbb{R}^3 \to \mathbb{R}$ is a scalar function, such that ideally $\nabla f(p_i) = n_i$, and $f(p_i) = 0$. If p_α denotes the position of a grid node, the problem reduces to the minimization of the following quadratic energy

$$E = \sum_i f(p_i)^2 + \mu \sum_i \|\nabla f(p_i) - n_i\|^2 + \lambda \sum_{(\alpha, \beta)} \|\nabla f(p_\alpha) - \nabla f(p_\beta)\|^2 \qquad (15)$$

where (α, β) are edges of the grid, and $\mu, \lambda > 0$ are a regularization constant. The scalar field f is represented as a linear combination of basis functions (e.g., trilinear) defined on a uniform Cartesian grid, $f(p) = \sum_\alpha f_\alpha \phi_\alpha(p)$, where $f_\alpha = f(p_\alpha)$. The gradient is approximated with finite differences.

Afterwards, we extract a triangular mesh with Marching Cubes (as shown in Figure 1(g)), and use it to resample the surface in regions where the original sampling was sparse.

Of course, since no information is captured from the invisible depth discontinuity points, the locally concave points at the bottom of concave areas are only hallucinated by this algorithm. Figure 9 is a simple illustration of some of the variability encountered in practice. The five shapes in this figure have identical visible depth discontinuities. The reconstruction produced by our algorithm is most probably close to the fourth example because the third terms in our energy function tends to minimize the variation of the function gradient, i.e., of the surface normal. So, holes tend to be filled with patches of relatively constant curvature. Additional primal space information, such as from triangulation-based sensors or multi-view stereo photometric information, is needed to differentiate amongst these shapes and to produce a more accurate reconstruction. In our view, the multi-view stereo approach, which is based on a similar variational formulation, seems to be the simplest to integrate with our system, as we already capture

Fig. 9. Different shapes that produce the same visible depth discontinuity epipolar slices. Note the variability in the shape and location of the curves corresponding to invisible depth discontinuity points.

the necessary photometric information (currently ignored). As we mentioned before, we plan to explore these ideas.

4.6 Appearance Modeling

As shown in Figures 1(g) and 8(b), the output of the gap-filling stage is a dense oriented point cloud. Given this representation of the surface shape, we assign a per-point appearance model using a subset of 67 images acquired from the turntable sequence. Note that, despite the relatively large number of available viewpoints, the BRDF remains sparsely-sampled since the illumination sources and camera are nearly coincident. As a result, we simply fit a Phong reflection model to the set of reflectance observations at each point. For simplicity, we assume that the surface does not exhibit significant subsurface scattering or transparency and can be represented by a linear combination of a diffuse term and a specular reflection lobe as described in the Phong model.

We begin the appearance modeling process by extracting a set of color observations for each point by back-projecting into each image. In order to determine the visibility of a point $p = q + \lambda r$, where q is the camera's center of projection, we perform a ray-mesh intersection test with the triangulated implicit surface. The first point of intersection is given by $p' = q + \lambda' r$. If p is outside some displacement ε from p' or if the point is facing away from the camera, then we mark the point as invisible, otherwise the color of the corresponding pixel is assigned to the observation table. Note that, unlike similar texture assignment methods such as [25], we can detect (or remove) shadows automatically using the *maximum composite* of the four images (described in Section 4.2) before assigning a color to the observation table. As a result, the combination of the implicit surface visibility test and the shadow removal afforded by the multi-flash system minimizes the set of erroneous color observations.

As described by Lensch et al. [24], we obtain a *lumitexel* representation for each point (i.e., a set color observations). We apply the Phong reflection model given by

$$I_\lambda = k_{a\lambda} + k_{d\lambda}\mathbf{n} \cdot \mathbf{l} + k_{s\lambda}(\mathbf{r} \cdot \mathbf{v})^n \qquad (16)$$

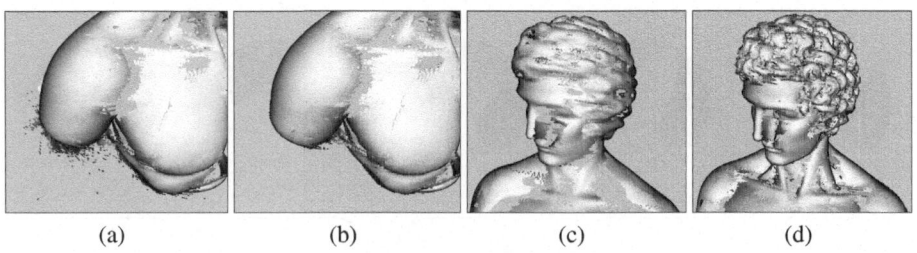

Fig. 10. (a) A portion of the bust point cloud, generated with no outlier rejection. An area of instability can be seen under the arm, where the surface is nearly perpendicular with the axis of rotation. (b) Outliers removed by back-projection validation using a small set of segmented images. (c) The generated point cloud using our algorithm with silhouette information only. (d) Reconstruction using all depth discontinuities. Notice increased detail in the eyes, hair, and neck concavities.

where I_λ is the wavelength-dependent irrandiance and $\{k_{a\lambda}, k_{d\lambda}, k_{s\lambda}, n\}$ are the ambient, diffuse, and specular coefficients, and the specular exponent, respectively. In this equation, the directions to the light source and camera are given by $\mathbf{l}$ and $\mathbf{v}$, whereas the direction of the peak of the specular reflection lobe is given by $\mathbf{r}$ and the surface normal is $\mathbf{n}$. Given the small baseline between the camera's center of projection and the flashes, we make the simplifying assumption that the flashes are coincident with the camera center (such that $\mathbf{l} = \mathbf{v}$).

We fit the per-point Phong reflectance model independently in each color channel. Following a similar approach as [25], we estimate the model parameters by applying Levenberg-Marquart nonlinear optimization. When insufficient data is available to fit the specular reflection component, we only estimate the diffuse albedo. Typical appearance modeling results are shown in Figure 12, where (c) and (d) illustrate typical diffuse and specular reconstructions, respectively. Note that, experimentally, we found that the *median diffuse albedo* (given by the median of the *lumitexel* values) was a computationally-efficient and visually-plausible substitute for the diffuse component of the Phong model. For applications in which only the diffuse albedo is required, the median diffuse albedo eliminates the need for applying a costly nonlinear estimation routine.

5   Analysis of Reconstruction Algorithm

5.1   Stability

One drawback to using Equation 7 to estimate depth is its dependence on usually noisy derivatives. In fact, in a previous implementation we used first order difference operators to estimate the derivatives and observed noisy and unstable depth estimates. By fitting polynomial curves to the contour samples in the epipolar slices, we essentially average out the noise and obtain accurate and stable derivative measurements as shown in our results.

A second drawback of our reconstruction algorithm is its ill-conditioning close to frontier points, where $n(t)^t \dot{r}(t) \approx 0$. In these cases, the denominator of Equation 7 approaches zero, causing unreliable depth estimates. Giblin and Weiss [27] have presented an alternate expression for depth that avoids this mathematical instability, but in our experiments the depth estimates remained unstable at frontier points. This is most likely due to the imprecision of matching when the epipolar lines are tangent to the surface contours. We combat this ill-conditioning in two ways. First, we reject reconstructed points with an infinitesimally small $n(t)^t \dot{r}(t)$ value (i.e. frontier points) outright, since they rarely provide meaningful reconstructions. Second, we deal with instability in the regions near these frontier points by performing the simple validation proposed by Liang and Wong [19]. We segment the object from the background in a small subset (15 views) of the original input images. We then back-project the reconstructed points into the images, making sure that each point lies within the image foreground. For the bust data set, 3.7% of points were removed in this way (Figure 10-(a,b)). One drawback of this approach is that points which are incorrectly reconstructed "inside" of the surface are not removed.

5.2 Surface Coverage

One key contribution of our reconstruction system is the use of the additional information provided by the full set of observable depth discontinuities. A typical example of the additional surface information that can be extracted can be seen in Figure 10-(c,d). Structure located in the concavities of the hair, eyes, and neck is successfully captured, while lacking in the silhouette-based reconstruction. Although a significant improvement in surface coverage can be seen, locally concave regions which do not produce visible depth discontinuities are not captured. Figure 2 demonstrates the theoretical limit of surface regions that can and cannot be captured with the two approaches.

6 Experimental Results

As presented, the multi-flash 3-D photography system represents a new, self-contained method for acquiring point-based models of both shape and appearance. In this section, we first present the reconstruction results for a 3-D test object with known dimensions in order to assess the system's accuracy. We then discuss (qualitatively) the reconstructions obtained for a variety of other physical objects in order to explore the system's versatility.

6.1 System Accuracy

In order to experimentally verify the accuracy of the system, we designed and manufactured a test object using the SolidWorks 3-D modeling program and a rapid prototyping machine. The rapid prototyping machine specifications indicate that it is accurate to within 0.1 mm. We designed an object roughly in the shape of a half-torus, with varying curvature at different points on the surface (Figure 11-(a)). We then reconstructed a point cloud of the the model using the algorithm described in Sections 4.1 through 4.4, and aligned it with a rigid transformation to the original SolidWorks mesh using ICP. No segmentation-based outlier detection or surface fitting were used. Figure 11-(b,c) shows the aligned reconstructed point cloud, with points color-coded according

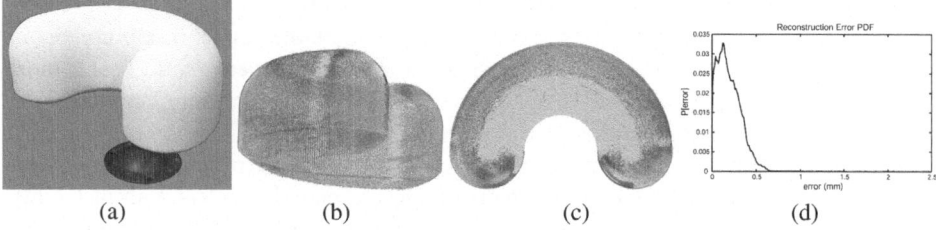

Fig. 11. (a) The manufactured test object. (b) Reconstructed point cloud overlayed on original mesh. (c) The reconstructed points are color-coded according to their absolute reconstruction error in mm. (d) The probability distribution of the point cloud reconstruction errors.

to their absolute distance from the original mesh. As expected, concave surface points are not reconstructed, nor are regions close to frontier points. Scanning the object using multiple camera paths and merging the reconstructions could alleviate this deficiency. Figure 11-(d) shows the distribution of the reconstruction errors. Roughly 9% of the points had error greater than 2.5 mm and were considered outliers. These points were mainly due to reconstruction of surfaces not part of the CAD model, such as the base

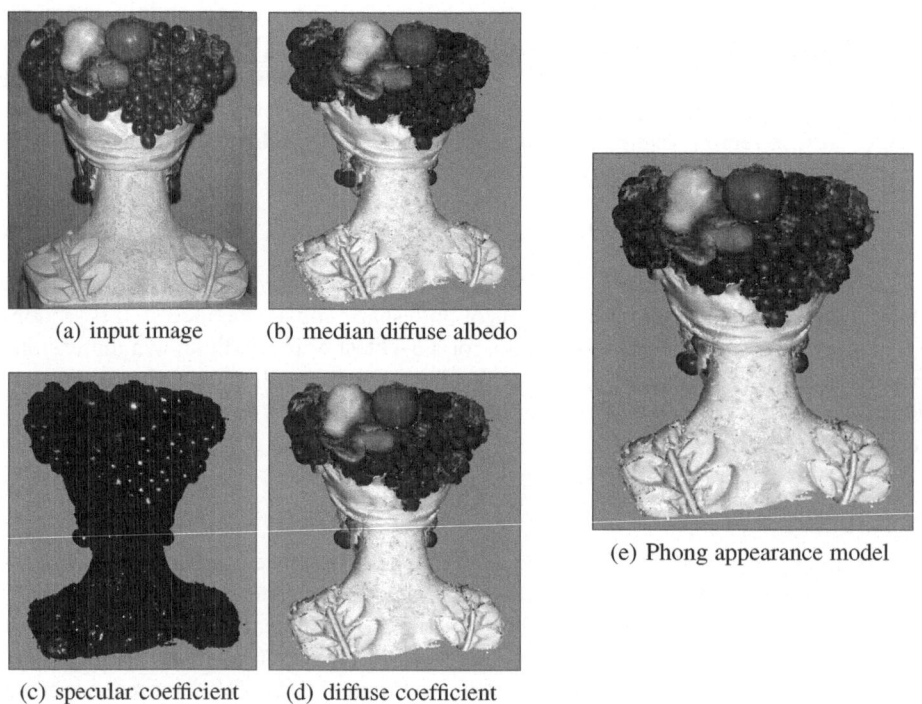

(a) input image   (b) median diffuse albedo

(c) specular coefficient   (d) diffuse coefficient

(e) Phong appearance model

Fig. 12. Estimated appearance for "woman with fruit basket" using 67 images. Note how the *median diffuse albedo* provides a computationally-efficient and visually-plausible substitute for the diffuse component of the Phong model.

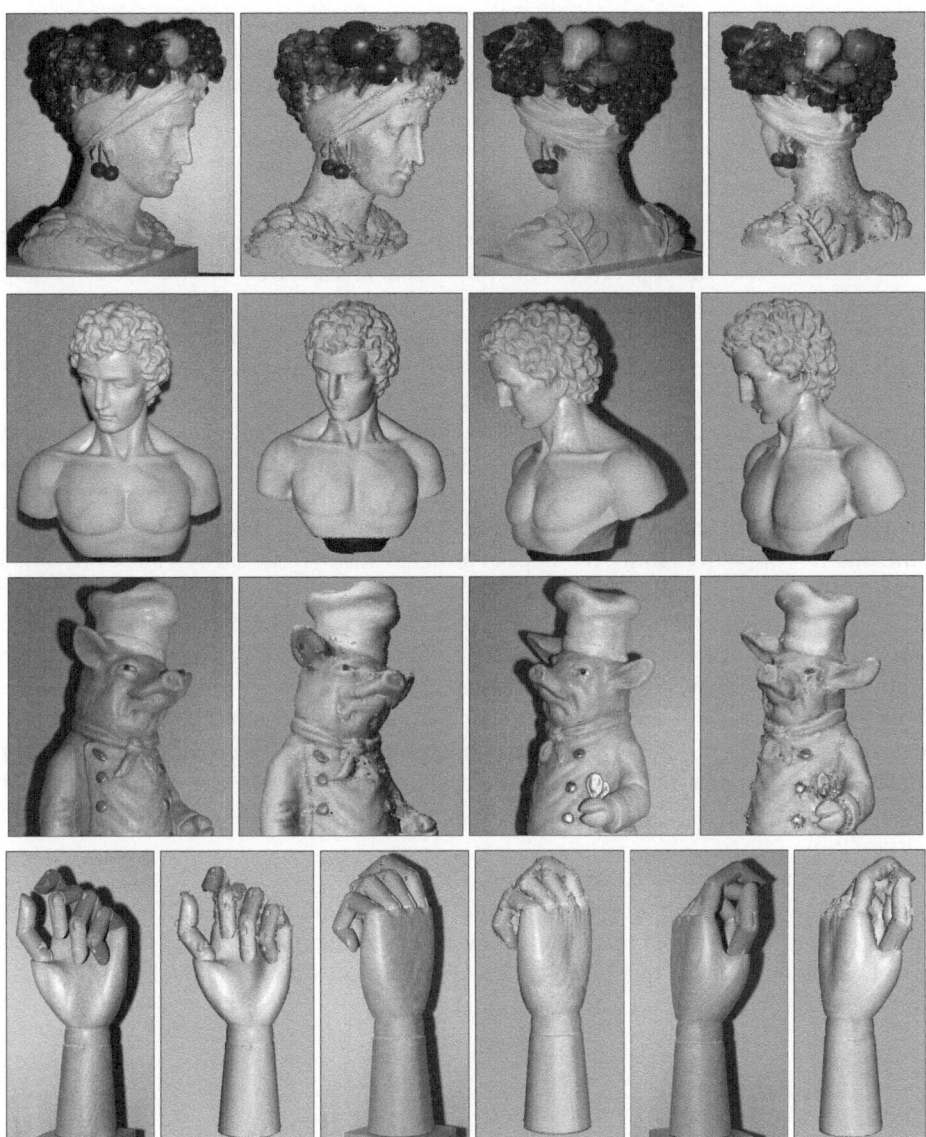

Fig. 13. Summary of reconstruction results. From left to right on each row: an input image, the reconstruction viewed under similar illumination conditions, another input image, and a corresponding view of the model. The first through fourth rows show the "woman with fruit basket", "bust", "pig chef", and "hand" models, respectively. Each model is represented by approximately $1,000,000$ points and was processed using a polygonal implicit surface with about $250,000$ faces. Note that, for the hand model, both the diffuse wood grain and highlights were reliably reconstructed. Similarly, the detailed geometric and color structure of the "women with fruit basket" were also captured.

used to hold the object. Disregarding the outliers, the mean reconstruction error was 0.20 mm, with a standard deviation of 0.16 mm. These results are very promising and suggest that the accuracy of the system is on par with commercially available scanning systems.

6.2 System Versatility

As shown in Figure 13, four objects were acquired with varying geometric and material complexities (from the top to bottom row: "woman with fruit basket", "bust", "pig chef", and "hand" models).

The "pig chef" model (shown on the third row of Figure 13) demonstrates low geometric complexity (i.e. its surface is nearly cylindrical with few self-occlusions). Similarly, its material properties are fairly benign – most of the surface is composed of a diffuse material and specularities are isolated to the jacket buttons and the spoon in the left arm). As with laser scanners or other active illumination systems, we find that highly specular surfaces cannot be reconstructed reliably. For example, consider the geometric and material modeling errors produced by the highly specular spoon in the left arm. Future work will examine methods to mitigate these errors, such as those presented in [32].

The "hand" model (shown on the last row of Figure 13) is challenging due to multiple self-occlusions and the moderately specular wood grain. For this example, we find the multi-flash approach has successfully reconstructed the fingers – regions that could not be reconstructed reliably using existing shape-from-silhouette or visual hull algorithms. In addition, the specular appearance was modeled in a visually-acceptable manner using the Phong appearance model. Note the "bust" model (shown on the second row of Figure 13) demonstrates similar self-occlusions in the hair and was also reconstructed successfully.

The "woman with fruit basket" model (shown on the first row of Figure 13) represents both material and geometric complexity with multiple self-occlusions and regions of greatly-varying material properties. As with other examples, we find the multi-flash approach has achieved a qualitatively acceptable model which accurately captures the surface shape and appearance of the original object.

7 Conclusions

We have presented in this article a fully self-contained system for acquiring point-based models of both shape and appearance using multi-flash photography. As demonstrated by the experimental results in Section 6, the proposed method accurately reconstructs points on objects with complex features, including those located within concavities. The geometric reconstruction algorithm is direct and does not require solving any non-linear optimization problems. In addition, the implicit surface fitted to the oriented point cloud provides an efficient proxy for filling holes in the surface, as well as determining the visibility of points. Finally, recent work in appearance modeling has been extended to the specific problem of texturing multi-flash image sequences.

While current results demonstrate the significant potential of this approach, we believe that the greatest benefit of multi-flash 3-D photography will be achieved by combining it with existing methods for shape recovery (e.g. laser scanners and structured light systems). These systems provide an efficient means to reconstruct regions of low-curvature, whereas the multi-flash reconstruction accurately models high-curvature regions and points of bi-tangency where these approaches have difficulties. Future work will explore the synergistic combination with existing approaches, especially with regard to planning optimal viewpoints for 3-D scanning.

7.1 Future Work

While sampling is regular for triangulation-based systems in primal space, in the proposed approach samples are highly concentrated in the vicinity of high curvature points. Feature line points, which are highly localized in primal space, are easy to estimate in dual space because they correspond to extended and smooth curve segments. We will implement hybrid systems combining depth discontinuities with triangulation-based systems, as well as multi-view photometric stereo, to achieve more accurate reconstructions of solid objects bound by piecewise smooth surfaces with accuracy guarantees for metrology applications. Applications to be explored range from reverse engineering to real-time 3D cinematography. Variational algorithms to fit watertight piecewise smooth implicit surfaces to the capture data, as well as isosurface algorithms to triangulate these implicit surfaces preserving feature lines will be developed as well.

References

1. Crispell, D., Lanman, D., Sibley, P., Zhao, Y., Taubin, G.: Beyond Silhouettes: Surface Reconstruction using Multi-Flash Photography. In: 3rd International Symposium on 3D Data Processing, Visualization and Transmission (3DPVT 2006), UNC, Chapel Hill, USA (June 2006)
2. Lanman, D., Crispell, D., Sibley, P., Zhao, Y., Taubin, G.: Multi-flash 3d photography: Capturing shape and appearance. In: Siggraph 2006, Poster session, Boston, MA (July 2006)
3. Sibley, P.G., Taubin, G.: Vectorfield Isosurface-based Reconstruction from Oriented points. In: Siggraph 2005, Sketch (2005)
4. Chen, F., Brown, G.M., Song, M.: Overview of three-dimensional shape measurement using optical methods. Optical Engineering 39(1), 10–22 (2000)
5. Mada, S., Smith, M., Smith, L., Midha, S.: An overview of passive and active vision techniques for hand-held 3d data acquisition. In: Opto Ireland 2003: Optical Metrology, Imaging, and Machine Vision (2003)
6. Wu, H., Chen, Y., Wu, M., Guan, C., Yu, X.: 3d measurement technology by structured light using stripe-edge-based gray code. In: International Symposium on Instrumentation Science and Technology. Journal of Physics: Conference Series, vol. 48, pp. 537–541 (2006)
7. Zhang, L., Curless, B., Seitz, S.M.: Spacetime stereo: Shape recovery for dynamic scenes. In: IEEE Conference on Computer Vision and Pattern Recognition, pp. 367–374 (June 2003)
8. Levoy, M.: Light Field Rendering. In: Siggraph 1996, Conference Proceedings, pp. 31–42 (1996)

9. Gortler, S., Grzeszczuk, R., Szeliski, R., Cohen, M.: The Lumigraph. In: Siggraph 1996, Conference Proceedings, pp. 43–54 (1996)
10. Lanman, D., Crispell, D., Wachs, M., Taubin, G.: Spherical Catadioptric Arrays: Construction, Geometry, and Calibration. In: 3rd International Symposium on 3D Data Processing, Visualization and Transmission (3DPVT 2006), UNC, Chapel Hill, USA (June 2006)
11. Lanman, M., Wachs, D., Taubin, G., Cukierman, F.: Reconstructing a 3D Line from a Single Catadioptric Image. In: 3rd International Symposium on 3D Data Processing, Visualization and Transmission (3DPVT 2006), UNC, Chapel Hill, USA (June 2006)
12. Kang, K., Tarel, J.-P., Fishman, R., Cooper, D.: A linear dual-space approach to 3d surface reconstruction from occluding contours using algebraic surfaces. In: IEEE International Conference on Computer Vision (ICCV 2001), vol. I, pp. 198–204 (2001)
13. Liang, C., Wong, K.-Y.K.: Complex 3d shape recovery using a dual-space approach. In: IEEE Conference on Computer Vision and Pattern Recognition (CVPR 2005) (2005)
14. Raskar, R., Tan, K.-H., Feris, R., Yu, J., Turk, M.: Non-photorealistic camera: depth edge detection and stylized rendering using multi-flash imaging. ACM Trans. Graph. 23(3), 679–688 (2004)
15. Annotated computer vision bibliography on surface and shape from contours or silhouettes, http://www.visionbib.com/bibliography/shapefrom408.html
16. Matusik, W., Buehler, C., Raskar, R., Gortler, S., McMillan, L.: Image-based visual hulls. In: SIGGRAPH 2000 (2000)
17. Cipolla, R., Giblin, P.: Visual Motion of Curves and Surfaces. Cambridge University Press, Cambridge (2000)
18. Cross, G., Zisserman, A.: Quadric surface reconstruction from dual-space geometry. In: IEEE International Conference on Computer Vision (1998)
19. Liang, C., Wong, K.-Y.K.: Complex 3d shape recovery using a dual-space approach. In: IEEE Conference on Computer Vision and Pattern Recognition (2005)
20. Seitz, S., Curless, B., Diebel, J., Scarstein, D., Szeliski, R.: A comparison and evaluation of multi-view stereo reconstruction algorithms. In: IEEE Conference on Computer Vision and Pattern Recognition (2006)
21. Esteban, C.H., Schmitt, F.: Silhouette and stereo fusion for 3d object modeling. Comput. Vis. Image Underst. 96(3), 367–392 (2004)
22. Furukawa, Y., Ponce, J.: Carved visual hulls for image-based modeling. In: European Conference on Computer vision 2006 (2006)
23. Goesele, M., Seitz, S., Curless, B.: Multi-view stereo revisited. In: IEEE Conference on Computer Vision and Pattern Recognition (2006)
24. Lensch, H.P.A., Kautz, J., Goesele, M., Heidrich, W., Seidel, H.-P.: Image-based reconstruction of spatially varying materials. In: Proceedings of Eurographics Rendering Workshop (2001)
25. Sadlo, F., Weyrich, T., Peikert, R., Gross, M.: A practical structured light acquisition system for point-based geometry and texture. In: Eurographics Symposium on Point-Based Graphics, pp. 89–98 (June 2005)
26. Bouguet, J.-Y.: Complete camera calibration toolbox for matlab, http://www.vision.caltech.edu/bouguetj/calib_doc
27. Giblin, P.J., Weiss, R.S.: Epipolar curves on surfaces. Image and Vision Computing 13(1), 33–34 (1995)
28. Alexa, M., Behr, J., Cohen-Or, D., Fleishman, S., Levin, D., Silva, C.T.: Computing and rendering point set surfaces. IEEE Trans. on Visualization and Computer Graphics 9(1), 3–15 (2003)

29. Davis, J., Marschner, S., Garr, M., Levoy, M.: Filling holes in complex surfaces using volumetric diffusion. In: 3DPVT 2002 (2002)
30. Park, S., Guo, X., Shin, H., Qin, H.: Shape and appearance repair for incomplete point surfaces. In: IEEE International Conference on Computer Vision, vol. 2 (2005)
31. Sibley, P.G., Taubin, G.: Vectorfield Isosurface-based Reconstruction from Oriented Points. In: SIGGRAPH 2005, Sketch (2005)
32. Feris, R., Raskar, R., Tan, K.-H., Turk, M.: Specular reflection reduction with multi-flash imaging. In: 17th Brazilian Symposium on Computer Graphics and Image Processing (October 2004)

Computational Photography: Epsilon to Coded Photography

Ramesh Raskar

Media Laboratory
Massachusetts Institute of Technology
Cambridge, MA 02139, USA
raskar@media.mit.edu
http://web.media.mit.edu/~raskar/

Abstract. Computational photography combines plentiful computing, digital sensors, modern optics, actuators, and smart lights to escape the limitations of traditional cameras, enables novel imaging applications and simplifies many computer vision tasks. However, a majority of current Computational photography methods involves taking multiple sequential photos by changing scene parameters and fusing the photos to create a richer representation. Epsilon photography is concerned with synthesizing omnipictures and proceeds by multiple capture single image paradigm (MCSI).The goal of Coded computational photography is to modify the optics, illumination or sensors at the time of capture so that the scene properties are encoded in a single (or a few) photographs. We describe several applications of coding exposure, aperture, illumination and sensing and describe emerging techniques to recover scene parameters from coded photographs.

Keywords: Digital photography, Fourier transform, Fourier optics, Optical heterodyning, Coded aperture imaging, digital refocusing, plenoptic camera.

1 Introduction

Computational photography combines plentiful computing, digital sensors, modern optics, actuators, and smart lights to escape the limitations of traditional cameras, enables novel imaging applications and simplifies many computer vision tasks. Unbounded dynamic range, variable focus, resolution, and depth of field, hints about shape, reflectance, and lighting, and new interactive forms of photos that are partly snapshots and partly videos are just some of the new applications found in Computational photography.

In this paper, we discuss Coded photography which involves encoding of the photographic signal and post-capture decoding for improved scene analysis. With film-like photography, the captured image is a 2D projection of the scene. Due to limited capabilities of the camera, the recorded image is a partial representation of the view. Nevertheless, the captured image is ready for human consumption: what you see is what you almost get in the photo.

F. Nielsen (Ed.): ETVC 2008, LNCS 5416, pp. 238–253, 2009.
© Springer-Verlag Berlin Heidelberg 2009

In Coded photography, the goal is to achieve a potentially richer representation of the scene during the encoding process. In some cases, Computational photography reduces to *Epsilon photography*, where the scene is recorded via multiple images, each captured by epsilon variation of the camera parameters. For example, successive images (or neighboring pixels) may have a different exposure, focus, aperture, view, illumination, or instant of capture. Each setting allows recording of partial information about the scene and the final image is reconstructed from these multiple observations. In Coded computational photography, the recorded image may appear distorted or random to a human observer. But the corresponding decoding recovers valuable information about the scene. *Less is more* in Coded photography. By blocking light over time or space, we can preserve more details about the scene in the recorded single photograph. In this paper we look at four specific examples:

1. **Coded exposure:** By blocking light in time, by fluttering the shutter open and closed in a carefully chosen binary sequence, we can preserve high spatial frequencies of fast moving objects to support high quality motion deblurring.
2. **Coded aperture optical heterodyning:** By blocking light near the sensor with a sinusoidal grating mask, we can record 4D light field on a 2D sensor. And by blocking light with a mask at the aperture, we can extend the depth of field and achieve full resolution digital refocussing.
3. **Coded illumination:** By observing blocked light at silhouettes, a multi-flash camera can locate depth discontinuities in challenging scenes without depth recovery.
4. **Coded sensing:** By sensing intensities with lateral inhibition, a gradient sensing camera can record large as well as subtle changes in intensity to recover a high-dynamic range image.

We describe several applications of Coding exposure, aperture, illumination and sensing and describe emerging techniques to recover scene parameters from coded photographs. But first, we give a introductory overview of the concepts involved in light fields.

1.1   What is a Light Field?

The light field is a function that describes the amount of light traveling in every direction through every point in space [17]. In geometric optics, the fundamental carrier of light is a ray. The measure for the amount of light traveling along a ray is radiance. The radiance along all such rays in a region of three-dimensional space illuminated by an unchanging arrangement of lights is called the *plenoptic* function. The plenoptic illumination function is an idealized function used in computer vision and computer graphics to express the image of a scene from any possible viewing position at any viewing angle at any point in time. Since rays in space can be parameterized by three spatial coordinates, x, y and z and two angles θ and ϕ it is a five-dimensional function [17].

The 4D Light Field. Radiance along a ray remains constant if there are no blockers. If we restrict ourselves to locations outside the convex hull of an

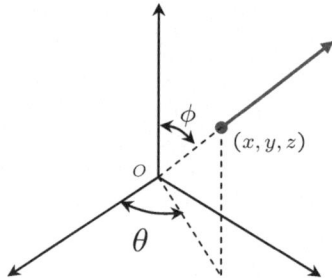

Fig. 1. A ray in 3D space is specified by its position (x, y, z) and direction (θ, ϕ)

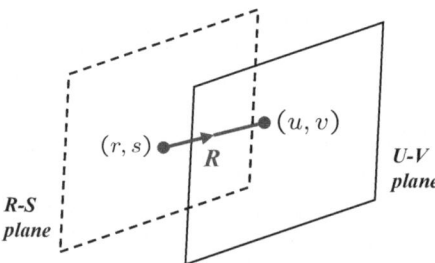

Fig. 2. The two plane parametrization of the 4D light field: using pairs of points on two planes in any general position to represent the flow of light through an empty region of three-dimensional space [17]

object, then we can measure the plenoptic function easily using a digital camera. Moreover, in this case the function contains redundant information, because the radiance along a ray remains constant from point to point along its length. In fact, the redundant information is exactly one dimension, leaving us with a four-dimensional function. Parry Moon dubbed this function the photic field, while researchers in computer graphics call it the 4D light field or *Lumigraph* [12], [13]. Formally, the 4D light field is defined as radiance along rays in empty space.

Most commonly, the set of rays in a light field can be parameterized using the two-plane parametrization. While this parametrization cannot represent all rays, for example rays parallel to the two planes if the planes are parallel to each other, it has the advantage of relating closely to the analytic geometry of perspective imaging. A light field parameterized this way is sometimes called a light slab [17].

4D Reflectance Field. The bidirectional reflectance distribution function (BRDF) is a 4-dimensional function that defines how light is reflected at an opaque surface [18]. The function takes an incoming light direction, and outgoing direction, both defined with respect to the surface normal and returns the ratio of reflected radiance exiting along the outgoing direction to the irradiance incident on the surface from incoming direction. Note that each direction is itself

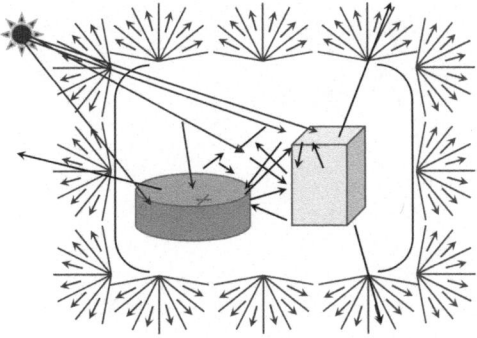

Fig. 3. When we measure all the light rays going out of the enclosure, it comprises of the 4D light field (figure from [16])

parameterized by azimuth angle and elevation, therefore the BRDF as a whole is 4-dimensional. As a further intuitive illustration [16] of 4D light fields imagine a convex enclosure of a 3D scene and an inward-facing ray camera at every surface point. Pick the *outgoing* rays you need for *any* camera outside the convex enclosure. The 2D surface of cameras and the 2D ray set for each camera gives rise to the 4D set of rays (4D light field of Lumigraph). When the similar idea is applied to the 4D set of *incoming* rays it comprises the 4D illumination field. Together, they give rise to the 8D reflectance field.

1.2   Film-Like Photography

Photography is the process of making pictures by, literally, *drawing with light* or recording the visually meaningful changes in the light leaving a scene. This goal was established for film photography about 150 years ago.

Currently, *digital photography* is electronically implemented film photography, refined and polished to achieve the goals of the classic film camera which were

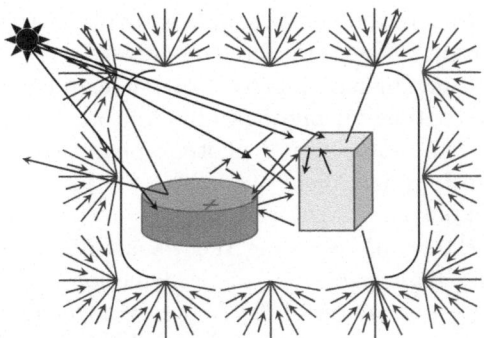

Fig. 4. When we measure all the light rays coming into the enclosure, it comprises of the 4D illumination field (figure from [16])

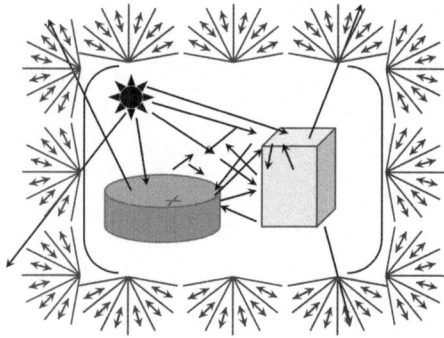

Fig. 5. Taken together, the 4D light field and the 4D illumination field give rise to the 8D reflectance field (Figure from [16]). Also define ratio R_{ij} = Outgoing ray$_i$/Incoming ray$_j$.

governed by chemistry, optics, mechanical shutters. Film-like photography presumes (and often requires) artful human judgment, intervention, and interpretation at every stage to choose viewpoint, framing, timing, lenses, film properties, lighting, developing, printing, display, search, index, and labelling.

In this article we plan to explore a progression away from film and film-like methods to something more comprehensive that exploits plentiful low-cost computing and memory with sensors, optics, probes, smart lighting and communication.

1.3   What Is Computational Photography?

Computational photography (CP) is an emerging field. We don't know where it will end up, we can't yet set its precise, complete definition, nor make a reliably comprehensive classification. But here is the scope of what researchers are currently exploring in this field.

– Computational photography attempts to record a richer visual experience, captures information beyond just a simple set of pixels and makes the recorded scene representation far more machine readable.
– It exploits computing, memory, interaction and communications to overcome long-standing limitations of photographic film and camera mechanics that have persisted in film-style digital photography, such as constraints on dynamic range, depth of field, field of view, resolution and the extent of scene motion during exposure.
– It enables new classes of recording the visual signal such as the *moment*, shape boundaries for non-photorealistic depiction [1], foreground versus background mattes, estimates of 3D structure, *relightable* photos and interactive displays that permit users to change lighting, viewpoint, focus, and more, capturing some useful, meaningful fraction of the *light field* of a scene, a 4-D set of viewing rays.

- It enables synthesis of impossible photos that could not have been captured at a single instant with a single camera, such as wrap-around views (*multiple-center-of-projection* images), fusion of time-lapsed events [1], the motion-microscope (motion magnification), video textures and panoramas. They also support impossible physical camera movements such as the *freeze effect* (in the movie Matrix) sequence recorded with multiple cameras with staggered exposure times.
- It encompass previously exotic forms of scientific imaging and data gathering techniques e.g. from astronomy, microscopy, and tomography.

1.4 Elements of Computational Photography

Traditional film-like photography involves a lens, a 2D planar sensor and a processor that converts sensed values into an image. In addition, the photography may involve external illumination from point sources (e.g. flash units) and area sources (e.g. studio lights). Computational photography generalizes the following four elements.

1. **Generalized optics:** Each optical element is treated as a 4D ray-bender that modifies a light field. The incident 4D light field for a given wavelength is transformed into a new 4D light field. The optics may involve more than one optical axis [15]. In some cases the perspective foreshortening of objects based on distance may be modified using wavefront coded optics [14]. In recent *lens-less* imaging methods and Coded aperture imaging used for gamma-ray and X-ray astronomy, the traditional lens is missing entirely. In some cases optical elements such as mirrors outside the camera adjust the linear combinations of ray bundles that reach the sensor pixel to adapt the sensor to the viewed scene.

2. **Generalized sensors:** All light sensors measure some combined fraction of the 4D light field impinging on it, but traditional sensors capture only a 2D projection of this light field. Computational photography attempts to capture more; a 3D or 4D ray representation using planar, non-planar or even volumetric sensor assemblies. For example, a traditional out-of-focus 2D image is the result of a capture-time decision: each detector pixel gathers light from its own bundle of rays that do not converge on the focused object. But a plenoptic Camera [9], [10] subdivides these bundles into separate measurements. Computing a weighted sum of rays that converge on the objects in the scene creates a digitally refocused image, and even permits multiple focusing distances within a single computed image. Generalizing sensors can extend their dynamic range [2] and wavelength selectivity as well. While traditional sensors trade spatial resolution for color measurement (wavelengths) using a Bayer grid or red, green or blue filters on individual pixels, some modern sensor designs determine photon wavelength by sensor penetration, permitting several spectral estimates at a single pixel location.

3. **Generalized reconstruction:** Conversion of raw sensor outputs into picture values can be much more sophisticated. While existing digital cameras perform *de-mosaicking*, (interpolate the Bayer grid), remove fixed-pattern noise, and hide *dead* pixel sensors, recent work in computational photography can do more. Reconstruction might combine disparate measurements in novel ways by considering the camera intrinsic parameters used during capture. For example, the processing might construct a high dynamic range scene from multiple photographs from coaxial lenses, from sensed gradients, [2] or compute sharp images of a fast moving object from a single image taken by a camera with a *fluttering* shutter [3]. Closed-loop control during photography itself can also be extended, exploiting traditional cameras' exposure control, image stabilizing, and focus, as new opportunities for modulating the scene's optical signal for later decoding.

4. **Computational illumination:** Photographic lighting has changed very little since the 1950's: with digital video projectors, servos, and device-to-device communication, we have new opportunities to control the sources of light with as much sophistication as we use to control our digital sensors. What sorts of spatio-temporal modulations for light might better reveal the visually important contents of a scene? Harold Edgerton showed high-speed strobes offered tremendous new appearance-capturing capabilities; how many new advantages can we realize by replacing the *dumb* flash units, static spot lights and reflectors with actively controlled spatio-temporal modulators and optics? Already we can capture occluding edges with multiple flashes [1], exchange cameras and projectors by Helmholz reciprocity, gather relightable actor's performances with light stages and see through muddy water with coded-mask illumination. In every case, better lighting control during capture allows one to build richer representations of photographed scenes.

2   Sampling Dimensions of Imaging

2.1   Epsilon Photography for Optimizing Film-Like Cameras

Think of film cameras at their best as defining a *box* in the multi-dimensional space of imaging parameters. The first, most obvious thing we can do to improve digital cameras is to expand this box in every conceivable dimension. This effort reduces Computational photography to *Epsilon photography*, where the scene is recorded via multiple images, each captured by epsilon variation of the camera parameters. For example, successive images (or neighboring pixels) may have different settings for parameters such as exposure, focus, aperture, view, illumination, or the instant of capture. Each setting allows recording of partial information about the scene and the final image is reconstructed from these multiple observations. Epsilon photography is thus concatenation of many such boxes in parameter space; multiple film-style photos computationally merged to make a more complete photo or scene description. While the merged photo is superior, each of the individual photos is still useful and comprehensible on its

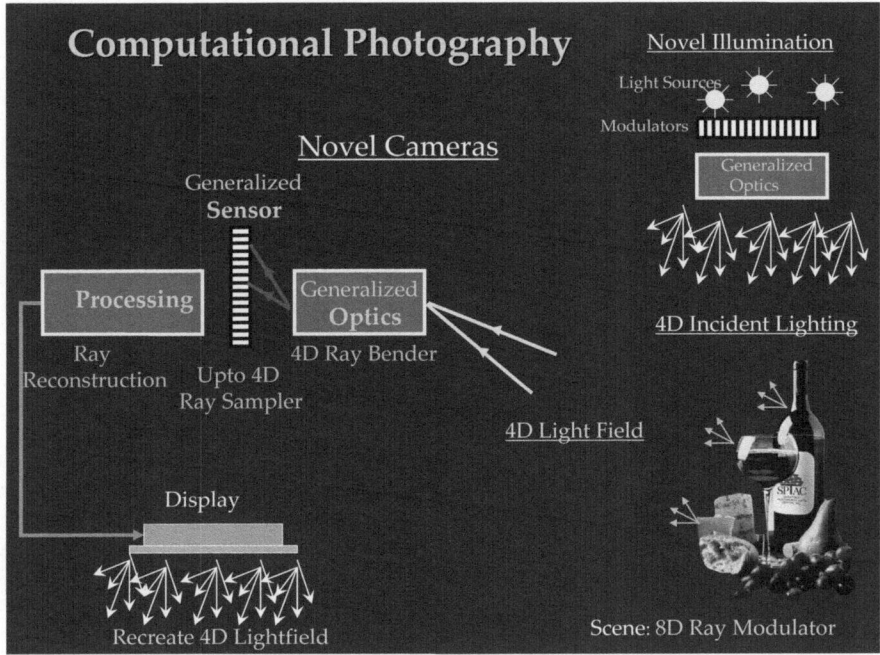

Fig. 6. Elements of Computational photography

own, without any of the others. The merged photo contains the best features from all of them.

1. **Field of view:** A wide field of view panorama is achieved by stitching and mosaicking pictures taken by panning a camera around a common center of projection or by translating a camera over a near-planar scene.
2. **Dynamic range:** A high dynamic range image is captured by merging photos at a series of exposure values [6]
3. **Depth of field:** All-in-focus image is reconstructed from images taken by successively changing the plane of focus.
4. **Spatial resolution:** Higher resolution is achieved by tiling multiple cameras (and mosaicking individual images) or by jittering a single camera.
5. **Wavelength resolution:** Traditional cameras sample only 3 basis colors. But multi-spectral (multiple colors in the visible spectrum) or hyper-spectral (wavelengths beyond the visible spectrum) imaging is accomplished by taking pictures while successively changing color filters in front of the camera, using tunable wavelength filters or using diffraction gratings.
6. **Temporal resolution:** High speed imaging is achieved by staggering the exposure time of multiple low-frame rate cameras. The exposure durations of individual cameras can be non-overlapping or overlapping.

Taking multiple images under varying camera parameters can be achieved in several ways. The images can be taken with a single camera over time. The

Coded Exposure   **Coded Aperture**

Temporal 1-D   Spatial 2-D
broadband code   broadband code

Fig. 7. Blocking light to achieve Coded photography. (Left) Using a 1-D code in time to block and unblock light over time, a coded exposure photo can reversibly encode motion blur ([3]). (Right) Using a 2-D code in space to block parts of the light via a masked aperture, a coded aperture photo can reversibly encode defocus blur ([4]).

images can be captured simultaneously using *assorted pixels* where each pixel is a tuned to a different value for a given parameter [5]. Simultaneous capture of multiple samples can also be recorded using multiple cameras, each camera having different values for a given parameter. Two designs are currently being used for multi-camera solutions: a camera array and single-axis multiple parameter (co-axial) cameras [8].

2.2   Coded Photography

There is much more beyond the *best possible film camera*. We can virtualize the notion of the camera itself if we consider it as a device that collects bundles of rays, each ray with its own wavelength spectrum and exposure duration.

Coded photography is a notion of an *out-of-the-box* photographic method, in which individual (ray) samples or data sets may or may not be comprehensible as *images* without further decoding, re-binning or reconstruction. Coded aperture techniques, inspired by work in astronomical imaging, try to preserve high spatial frequencies so that out of focus blurred images can be digitally re-focused [4]. By coding illumination, it is possible to decompose radiance in a scene into direct and global components. Using a Coded exposure technique, one can rapidly flutter open and close the shutter of a camera in a carefully chosen binary sequence, to capture a single photo. The fluttered shutter encoded the motion in the scene in the observed blur in a reversible way. Other examples include confocal images and techniques to recover glare in the images.

We may be converging on a new, much more capable *box* of parameters in computational photography that we don't yet recognize; there is still quite a bit

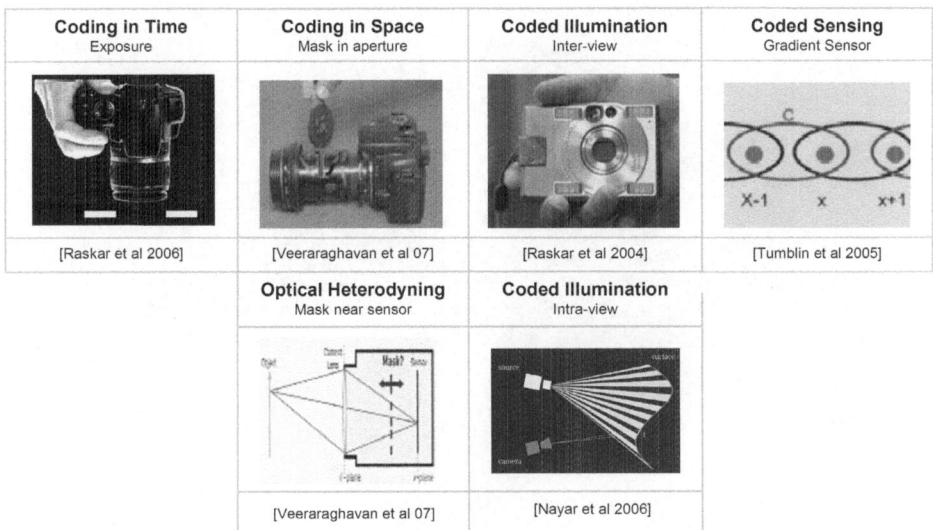

Fig. 8. An overview of projects. Coding in time or space, coding the incident active illumination and coding the sensing pattern.

of innovation to come! In the rest of the article, we survey recent techniques that exploit exposure, focus, active illumination and sensors.

3   Coded Exposure

In a conventional single-exposure photograph, moving objects or moving cameras cause motion blur. The exposure time defines a temporal box filter that smears the moving object across the image by convolution. This box filter destroys important high-frequency spatial details so that deblurring via deconvolution becomes an ill-posed problem. We have proposed to flutter the camera's shutter open and closed during the chosen exposure time with a binary pseudo-random sequence, instead of leaving it open as in a traditional camera [3]. The flutter changes the box filter to a broad-band filter that preserves high-frequency spatial details in the blurred image and the corresponding deconvolution becomes a well-posed problem.

Results on several challenging cases of motion-blur removal including outdoor scenes, extremely large motions, textured backgrounds and partial occluders were presented. However, the authors assume that PSF (Point spread function) is given or is obtained by simple user interaction. Since changing the integration time of conventional CCD cameras is not feasible, an external ferro-electric shutter is placed in front of the lens to code the exposure. The shutter is driven opaque and transparent according to the binary signals generated from PIC [20] using the pseudo-random binary sequence.

Fig. 9. The flutter shutter camera. The Coded exposure is achieved by fluttering the shutter open and closed. Instead of a mechanical movement of the shutter, we used a ferro-electric LCD in front of the lens. It is driven opaque and transparent according to the desired binary sequence.

4   Coded Aperture and Optical Heterodyning

Can we capture additional information about a scene by inserting a patterned mask inside a conventional camera? We use a patterned attenuating mask to encode the light field entering the camera. Depending on where we put the mask, we can effect desired frequency domain modulation of the light field. If we put the mask near the lens aperture, we can achieve full resolution digital refocussing. If we put the mask near the sensor, we can recover a 4D light field without any additional lenslet array.

Coded aperture imaging has been historically used in radar (SAR) [19]. Ren Ng et. al. have developed a camera that can capture the 4D light field incident on the image sensor in a single photographic exposure [10]. This is achieved by inserting a microlens array between the sensor and main lens, creating a plenoptic camera. Each microlens measures not just the total amount of light deposited at that location, but how much light arrives along each ray. By re-sorting the measured rays of light to where they would have terminated in slightly different, synthetic cameras, one can compute sharp photographs focused at different depths. A linear increase in the resolution of images under each microlens results in a linear increase in the sharpness of the refocused photographs. This property allows one to extend the depth of field of the camera without reducing the aperture, enabling shorter exposures and lower image noise.

Digital Refocusing

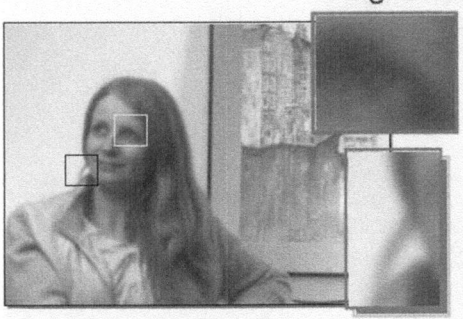

Fig. 10. Encoded blur camera, i.e. with mask in the aperture, can preserve high spatial images frequencies in the defocus blur. Notice the glint in the eye. In the misfocused photo, on the left, the bright spot appears blurred with the bokeh [21] of the chosen aperture (shown in the inset). In the deblurred result, on the right, the details on the eye are correctly recovered.

Our group has shown that it is also possible to create a plenoptic camera using a patterned mask instead of a lenslet array. The geometric configurations remains nearly identical [4]. The method is known as *spatial optical heterodyning*. Instead of remapping rays in 4D using microlens array so that they can be captured on a 2D sensor, spatial optical heterodyning remaps frequency components of the 4D light field so that the frequency components can be recovered from Fourier transform of the captured 2D image. In microlens array based design, each pixel effectively records light along a single ray bundle. With patterned masks, each pixel records a linear combination multiple ray-bundles. By carefully coding the linear combination, the coded heterodyning method can reconstruct the values of individual ray-bundles.

This is reversible modulation of 4D light field by inserting a patterned planar mask in the optical path of a lens based camera. We can reconstruct the 4D light field from a 2D camera image. The patterned mask attenuates light rays inside the camera instead of bending them, and the attenuation recoverably encodes the ray on the 2D sensor. Our mask-equipped camera focuses just as a traditional camera might to capture conventional 2D photos at full sensor resolution, but the raw pixel values also hold a modulated 4D light field. The light field can be recovered by rearranging the tiles of the 2D Fourier transform of sensor values into 4D planes, and computing the inverse Fourier transform.

5   Coded Illumination

By observing blocked light at silhouettes, a multi-flash camera can locate depth discontinuities in challenging scenes without depth recovery. We used a multi-flash camera to find the silhouettes in a scene [1]. We take four photos of an object with four different light positions (above, below, left and right of the

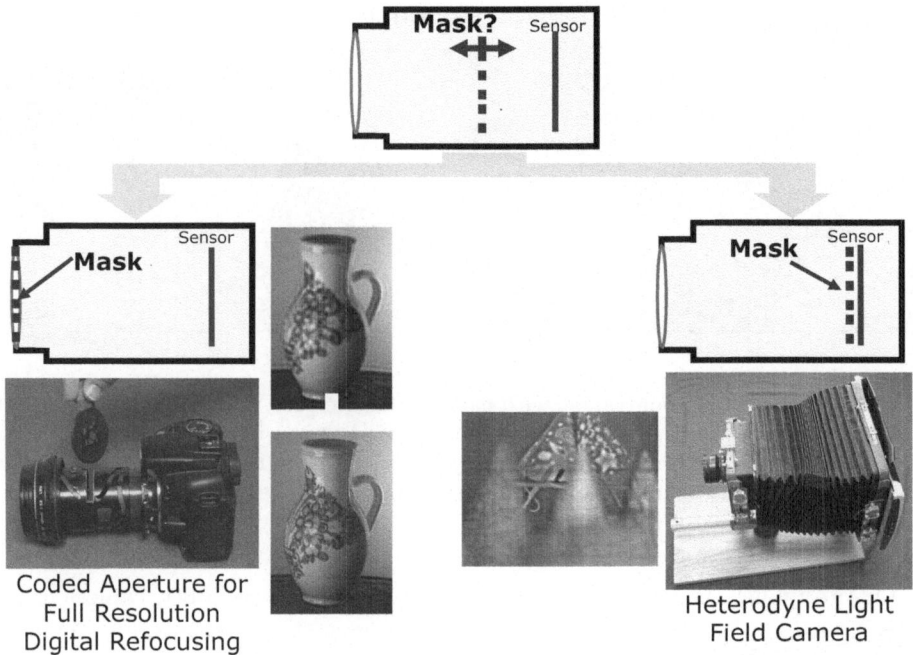

Fig. 11. Coding Light Field entering a camera via a mask

lens). We detect shadows cast along the depth discontinuities and use them to detect depth discontinuities in the scene. The detected silhouettes are then used for stylizing the photograph and highlighting important features. We also demonstrate silhouette detection in a video using a repeated fast sequence of flashes.

6   High Dynamic Range Using a Gradient Camera

A camera sensor is limited in the range of highest and lowest intensities it can measure. To capture the high dynamic range, one can adaptively set the exposure the sensor so that the signal to noise ratio is high over the entire image, including in the the dark and brightly lit regions. One approach for faithfully recording the intensities in a high dynamic range scenes is to capture multiple images using different exposures, and then to merge these images. The basic idea is that when longer exposures are used, dark regions are well exposed but bright regions are saturated. On the other hand, when short exposures are used, dark regions are too dark but bright regions are well imaged. If exposure varies and multiple pictures are taken of the same scene, value of a pixel can be taken from those images where it's neither too dark nor saturated. This type of approach is often referred to as exposure bracketing.

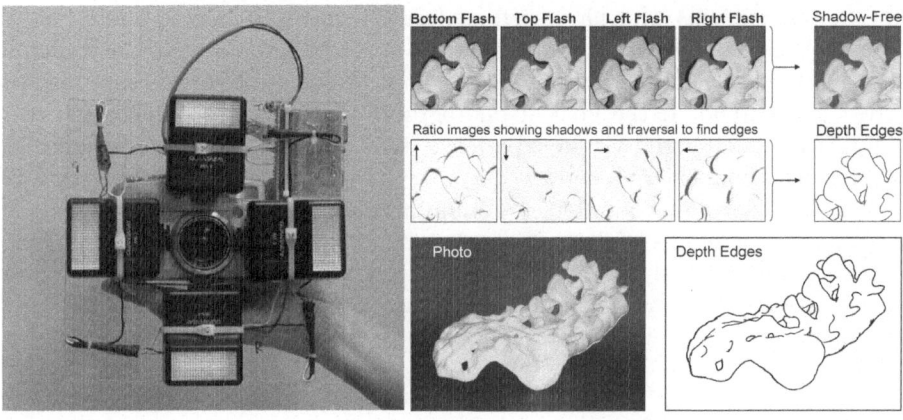

Fig. 12. Multi-flash Camera for Depth Edge Detection. (Left) A camera with four flashes. (Right) Photos due to individual flashes, highlighted shadows and epipolar traversal to compute the single pixel depth edges.

At the sensor level, various approaches have also been proposed for high dynamic range imaging. One type of approach is to use multiple sensing elements with different sensitivities within each cell. Multiple measurements are made from the sensing elements, and they are combined on-chip before a high dynamic range image is read out from the chip. Spatial sampling rate is lowered in these sensing devices, and spatial resolution is sacrificed. Another type of approach is to adjust the well capacity of the sensing elements during photocurrent integration but this gives higher noise.

By sensing intensities with lateral inhibition, a gradient sensing camera can record large as well as subtle changes in intensity to recover a high-dynamic range image. By sensing difference between neighboring pixels instead of actual intensities, our group has shown that a *Gradient Camera* can record large global variations in intensity [2]. Rather than measure absolute intensity values at each pixel, this proposed sensor measures only forward differences between them, which remain small even for extremely high-dynamic range scenes, and reconstructs the sensed image from these differences using Poisson solver methods. This approach offers several advantages: the sensor is nearly impossible to over- or under-expose, yet offers extremely fine quantization, even with very modest A/D convertors (e.g. 8 bits). The thermal and quantization noise occurs in the gradient domain, and appears as low frequency *cloudy* noise in the reconstruction, rather than uncorrelated high-frequency noise that might obscure the exact position of scene edges.

7   Conclusion

As these examples indicate, we have scarcely begun to explore the possibilities offered by combining computation, 4D modeling of light transport, and novel optical systems. Nor have such explorations been limited to photography and computer graphics or computer vision. Microscopy, tomography, astronomy and other optically driven fields already contain some ready-to-use solutions to borrow and extend. If the goal of photography is to capture, reproduce, and manipulate a meaningful visual experience, then the camera is not sufficient to capture even the most rudimentary birthday party. The human experience and our personal viewpoint is missing. Computational Photography can supply us with visual experiences, but can't decide which one's matter most to humans. Beyond coding the first order parameters like exposure, focus, illumination and sensing, maybe the ultimate goal of Computational Photography is to encode the human experience in the captured single photo.

Acknowledgements

We wish to thank Jack Tumblin and Amit Agrawal for contributing several ideas for this paper. We also thank co-authors and collaborators Ashok Veeraraghavan, Ankit Mohan, Yuanzen Li, Karhan Tan, Rogerio Feris, Jingyi Yu, Matthew Turk. We thank Shree Nayar and Marc Levoy for useful comments and discussions and Ahmed Kirmani for a thorough rewrite and editing of this final draft.

References

1. Raskar, R., Tan, K., Feris, R., Yu, J., Turk, M.: Non-photorealistic Camera: Depth Edge Detection and Stylized Rendering Using a Multi-Flash Camera. In: Proc. ACM SIGGRAPH (2004)
2. Tumblin, J., Agrawal, A., Raskar, R.: Why I want a Gradient Camera. IEEE Computer Vision and Pattern Recognition (2005)
3. Raskar, R., Agrawal, A., Tumblin, J.: Coded exposure photography: motion deblurring using fluttered shutter. ACM Transactions on Graphics 25(3), 795–804 (2006)
4. Veeraraghavan, A., Raskar, R., Agrawal, A., Mohan, A., Tumblin, J.: Dappled Photography: Mask-Enhanced Cameras for Heterodyned Light Fields and Coded Aperture Refocusing. In: Proc. ACM SIGGRAPH (2007)
5. Nayar, S.K., Narasimhan, S.G.: Assorted Pixels: Multi-Sampled Imaging With Structural Models. In: Heyden, A., Sparr, G., Nielsen, M., Johansen, P. (eds.) ECCV 2002. LNCS, vol. 2353, pp. 636–652. Springer, Heidelberg (2002)
6. Debevec, M.: Recovering high dynamic range radiance maps from photographs. In: Proc. ACM SIGGRAPH (1997)
7. Mann, P.: Being 'undigital' with digital cameras: Extending dynamic range by combining differently exposed pictures. In: Proc. Imaging Science and Technology 46th ann. conference (1995)
8. Morgan, M., Matusik, P., Hughes, D.: Defocus Video Matting. ACM Transactions on Graphics 24(3) (July 2005) (Proceedings of ACM SIGGRAPH 2005)
9. Adelson, E.H., Wang, J.Y.A.: Single Lens Stereo with a Plenoptic Camera. IEEE Transactions on Pattern Analysis and Machine Intelligence 14(2) (February 1992)
10. Ren, N.: Fourier Slice Photography. In: ACM SIGGRAPH (2005)

11. Morimura: Imaging method for a wide dynamic range and an imaging device for a wide dynamic range. U.S. Patent 5455621 (October 1993)
12. Levoy, M., Hanrahan, P.: Light field rendering. In: ACM SIGGRAPH, pp. 31–42 (1996)
13. Gortler, S.J., Grzeszczuk, R., Szeliski, R., Cohen, M.F.: The Lumigraph. In: ACM SIGGRAPH, pp. 43–54 (1996)
14. Dowski Jr., E.R., Cathey, W.T.: Extended depth of field through wave-front coding. Applied Optics 34(11), 1859–1866 (1995)
15. Georgiev, T., Zheng, C., Nayar, S., Salesin, D., Curless, B., Intwala, C.: Spatio-angular Resolution Trade-Offs in Integral Photography. In: Proceedings of Eurographics Symposium on Rendering (2006)
16. Tumblin, J.: Slides on the Photographic Signal and Film-like Photography. In: Course 3: Computational Photography, ACM SIGGRAPH (2005), www.merl.com/people/raskar/photo/Slides/01BasicJTJuly31.ppt
17. Light fields, http://en.wikipedia.org/wiki/Light_field
18. Bidirectional reflectance distribution function, http://en.wikipedia.org/wiki/BRDF
19. Synthetic Aperture Radar, http://en.wikipedia.org/wiki/Synthetic_aperture_radar
20. Programmable Interface Controller, http://en.wikipedia.org/wiki/PIC_microcontroller
21. Bokeh, http://en.wikipedia.org/wiki/Bokeh

Unifying Subspace and Distance Metric Learning with Bhattacharyya Coefficient for Image Classification

Qingshan Liu and Dimitris N. Metaxas

Department of Computer Sciences, Rutgers, the State University of New Jersey,
110 Frelinghuysen Road, Piscataway, NJ 08854-8019
{qsliu,dnm}@cs.rutgers.edu

Abstract. In this paper, we propose a unified scheme of subspace and distance metric learning under the Bayesian framework for image classification. According to the local distribution of data, we divide the k-nearest neighbors of each sample into the intra-class set and the inter-class set, and we aim to learn a distance metric in the embedding subspace, which can make the distances between the sample and its intra-class set smaller than the distances between it and its inter-class set. To reach this goal, we consider the intra-class distances and the inter-class distances to be from two different probability distributions respectively, and we model the goal with minimizing the overlap between two distributions. Inspired by the Bayesian classification error estimation, we formulate the objective function by minimizing the Bhattachyrra coefficient between two distributions. We further extend it with the kernel trick to learn nonlinear distance metric. The power and generality of the proposed approach are demonstrated by a series of experiments on the CMU-PIE face database, the extended YALE face database, and the COREL-5000 nature image database.

1 Introduction

It is well-known that subspace learning methods are widely used in the communities of computer vision and pattern recognition. The general goal of subspace learning is to find some transformation to project high-dimensional data into a low-dimensional subspace. A lot of subspace learning methods have been proposed according to different objective functions. We will review some popular subspace methods in Section 2. However, for any practical application, similarity measurement or classification scheme is needed to further analyze the relationship of the data or to predict their labels based on the extracted features. Distance metric learning is a technique to learn a distance based similarity measurement and classification scheme, and has attracted much attention in machine learning and computer vision in recent years. Its original goal is to directly learn the distance metric from the available training data, in order to improve the performance of distance-based classifiers. Due to the encouraging effectiveness of the simple nearest neighbor rule, most studies focused on learning the similarity matrix of the Mahalanobis distance to improve the performance of the nearest neighbor classification. A common strategy is to minimize various separation criteria between the classes assuming equivalent relations over all the data or the k-nearest neighbors.

F. Nielsen (Ed.): ETVC 2008, LNCS 5416, pp. 254–267, 2009.

A brief review will be given in Section 2. However, for high dimensional data, such as image data (the dimension of an image with the size of 100×100 is up to 10^4), learning the metric matrix directly in such a high dimensional space, not only results in high computational cost, but also is sensitive to noise.

In this paper, we propose a unified scheme of subspace and distance metric learning for image classification under the Bayesian framework. In order to learn a local distance metric with subspace dimensionality reduction, we divide the k-nearest neighbors of each sample into the intra-class set and the inter-class set according to the local distribution of the data, and we aim to make the distances between the sample and its intra-class set smaller than the distances between it and its inter-class set in the embedding subspace, so as to handle the high-dimensional data well. We define the intra-class distances and the inter-class distances in the subspace to be from two different probability distributions. Thus, the problem can be converted to minimize the overlap between two distributions. Inspired by the Bayesian classification error estimation, we formulate it by minimizing the Bhattachyrra coefficient measurement between two distributions, and the solution can be obtained by the gradient descent optimization. We further extend it with the kernel trick to learn nonlinear distance metric. The proposed work has some characteristics: 1) It is based on local neighbors, so it does not make assumption on the global distribution of the data. 2) It can be directly used for multi-class problems without any modification or extension. 3) It links to Bayesian classification error and has an intuitionistic geometric property due to adoption of the Bhattachyrra coefficient measurement. We conduct the experiments on three benchmarks, CMU-PIE face database [1], extended YALE face database [2],and the COREL-5000 nature image database [3]. The experimental results show the promising performance of the proposed work compared to the state-of-the-arts.

The rest of paper is organized as follows: The related subspace and distance learning works are briefly reviewed in Section 2. We present a unified framework of subspace and distance metric learning in Section 3, and we report the experiments in Section 4. We discuss the kernel extension of our method in Section 5. Finally conclusions are drawn.

2   Related Work

Subspace learning is a popular approach for high dimensional data analysis, which maps the high dimensional data into a low dimensional subspace based on some criteria. Principal Component Analysis (PCA) [4] and Linear Discriminant Analysis (LDA) [5] [6]are two classical and popular subspace methods. PCA seeks to maximize the covariance over all the data, which is optimal for data reconstruction, but it is not optimal for classification. The idea of LDA is to find a linear subspace projection that maximizes the between-class scatter and minimizes the within-class scatter. However, LDA assumes that the within-class distributions of samples are similar. Kernel PCA (KPCA) and Kernel LDA (KDA) combine the nonlinear kernel trick with PCA and LDA to get nonlinear principal component and discriminant subspaces [7] [8]. However, for the kernel methods, the kernel function design is still an open problem, and different kernels will give different performances. Manifold based subspace methods, such as LLE [9] and ISOMAP [10], aim to preserve the local geometric relations of the data in both the original high dimensional space and the transformed low dimensional space, while they often have a problem of "out of sample". Local Preserving Projection (LPP) gives a linear approximation of manifold structure to deal with this problem [11]. In [12], the idea of LDA is integrated into LPP to enhance the discriminating performance of LPP. In [13], M. Sugiyama proposed to compute the within-class scatter and between-class scatter in LDA with a weighting scheme inspired by LPP. A generalized interpretation for these methods based on graph analysis is discussed in [14]. From the view of subspace dimensionality reduction, our work is similar to LDA, which aims to find a transformation of separating one class from the others, and it can be also extended with the kernel trick. However, our work is different from LDA as follows: 1) it imposes no constraints on the global distribution of the data, because it is based on the local neighbors' distribution of the data; 2) it preserves the neighborhood relationship of the data during the dimension reduction as in manifold learning.

Subspace learning can be thought as a method of feature representation, while distance metric learning is related to constructing a data classification scheme. The nearest neighbor rule is simple and surprisingly effective. However, its performance crucially depends on the distance metric. For different distance metrics, it will produce different nearest neighbor relationships. Most previous studies aim to improve the performance of the nearest neighbor classification by learning a distance metric based on the Mahalanobis distance from the labeled samples. E. Xing et al [15] tried to find an optimal Mahalanobis metric from contextual constrains in combination with a constrained K-means algorithm. B. Hilled et al [16] [17] proposed a much simpler approach called Relevance Component Analysis (RCA), which identities and downscales global unwanted variability within data. However, it does not consider the between class pairwise information, which will influence its performance on classification [18]. K. Q. Weinberger et al [19] proposed to learn the distance metric by penalizing large distances between each input and its neighbors and by penalizing small distances between each input and all other inputs that do not share the same label. Its solution is based on complex quadratic programming. Torresani and Lee [20] extended this method with dimensional reduction, but its objective function is non-convex. Neighborhood Component Analysis (NCA) aimed at directly maximizing a stochastic variant of the leave one out *K-NN* score on the training set [21]. Later, A. Globerson et al [22] converted the formula of NCA to a convex optimization problem with a strong assumption that all the samples in the same class were mapped to a single point and infinitely far from points in different classes. Actually, this assumption is unreasonable for practical data. In [23], the bound optimization algorithm [24] was adopted to search a local distance metric for the non-convex function. Most of the above methods do not consider the dimensionality reduction for high dimensional data except for RCA [16] [17], NCA [21], and [20]. However, the proposed method is different from them in that it links to Bayesian classification error and has an intuitionistic geometric property due to adoption of the Bhattachyrra coefficient measurement.

3   Our Work

In this section, we propose a new unified framework of subspace and distance metric learning, which is inspired by the Bayesian classification error estimation. We first present our purpose and then give a Bhattacharyya coefficient based solution.

3.1   The Purpose

Let $X = \{x_1, x_2, \cdots, x_n\} \in R^D$ denote the training set of n labeled samples in C classes. Let $l(x_i)$ be the label of sample x_i, i.e., $l(x_i) \in \{1, 2, \ldots, C\}$. Most distance metric learning methods seek to directly find a similarity matrix Q based on the Mahalanobis distance to maximize the performance of the nearest neighbor classification. The Mahalanobis distance between samples x_i and x_j is defined as

$$P_{i,j} = (x_i - x_j)^T Q(x_i - x_j). \tag{1}$$

However, learning Q directly in a high dimensional space, such as the image space, will be sensitive to noise to some extent, besides being computationally expensive. Since Q is a $D \times D$ semi-definite matrix, it can be rewritten as: $Q = AA^T$. If the dimension of A is $D \times d$, $d < D$, (1) is equivalent to calculating the Euclidean distance in the transformed subspace with A as

$$P_{i,j} = \|A^T x_i - A^T x_j\|^2 = (x_i - x_j)^T AA^T(x_i - x_j). \tag{2}$$

Thus, the distance metric Q for high dimensional data can be computed by an explicit embedding transformation A. In this paper, we will focus on how to first learn this transformation A, and then compute Q. Actually the transformation A is corresponding to subspace dimension reduction, so this idea is equivalent to integrating the subspace and distance metric learning together.

Before presenting the details of our approach, we first give some definitions. The set $N_r(x_i)$ is the k-nearest neighbors of sample . Same as in [19] [20], the neighbors are computed by the Euclidean distance in the original data space. We divide $N_r(x_i)$ into two sets using the labels of the samples, $N_r(x_i) = S_i \bigcup D_i$, where the labels of the set S_i are same as the label of x_i, $x_s \in S_i, l(x_s) = l(x_i)$, and the samples in D_i have different labels from the sample x_i, $x_d \in D_i, l(x_d) \neq l(x_i)$,. We call them the intra-class set and inter-class set respectively.

Intuitively, a good distance metric should make each sample close to the samples in the same class and far from the samples in the different classes. Based on the nearest neighbor classification scheme, we can compare each sample against its k-nearest neighbors. We aim to find a distance metric that makes each sample far from the samples in its inter-class set and close to the samples in its intra-class set. Thus, our goal can be described as follows:

Given any samples x_i and its two kinds of neighbors $x_s \in S_i$ and $x_d \in D_i$, the intra-class distance $P_{is}(A)$ between x_i and x_s should be smaller than the inter-class distance $P_{id}(A)$ between x_i and x_d:

$$P_{is}(A) = \|A^T(x_i - x_s)\|^2, x_s \in S_i, \tag{3}$$

$$P_{id}(A) = \|A^T(x_i - x_d)\|^2, x_d \in D_i, \tag{4}$$

$$P_{is}(A) < P_{id}(A), for \forall i, s, d. \tag{5}$$

3.2   Bhattacharyya Coefficient Based Solution

For convenience, we define the variable $P_s(A)$ to represent all the intra-class distances, and the variable $P_d(A)$ to represent all the inter-class distances. Assuming that $P_s(A)$ and $P_d(A)$ are from two distributions respectively, $P_s(A) \sim \rho_s(P(A))$ and $P_d(A) \sim \rho_d(P(A))$, we can achieve our goal to find a transformation A that minimizes the overlap between these two distributions. Figure 1 gives an illustration. It can be found that minimizing the overlap means to separate the intra-class distances $P_s(A)$ from the inter-class distances $P_d(A)$ as much as possible, and it is also equivalent to minimizing the up-boundary of the classification error as much as possible under the Bayesian framework.

The Bhattacharyya coefficient is a divergence-type measure which has an has an intuitionistic geometric interpretation [25]. Moreover, it is a popular technique to estimate the boundary of the classification error, i.e., the overlap between two distributions [26]. Given two distributions, $\rho_1(x)$ and $\rho_2(x)$, their Bhattacharyya coefficient is $\int \sqrt{\rho_1(x)\rho_2(x)}dx$. A small Bhattacharyya coefficient means a small overlap between two distributions which may lead to a small classification error in a sense. Let the Bhattacharyya distance between $\rho_1(x)$ and $\rho_2(x)$ as follows:

$$J_B(x) = -\ln \int \sqrt{\rho_1(x)\rho_2(x)}dx. \tag{6}$$

Thus, we can find an optimal A by maximizing the Bhattacharyya distance between $\rho_s(P(A))$ and $\rho_d(P(A))$. In this paper, we use two different Gaussian distribution to model the distribution of the variables of the intra-class distance and inter-class distance

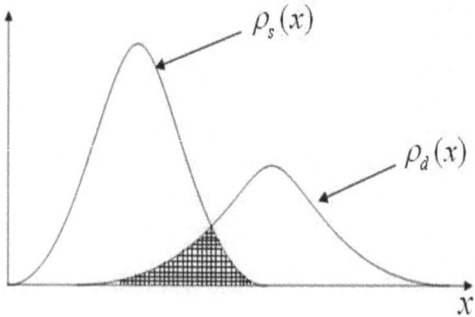

Fig. 1. An illustration of minimizing the overlap

respectively. We define the mean and variance of $P_s(A)$ as $\mu_s(A)$ and $\Sigma_s(A)$, and the mean and covariance of $P_d(A)$ as $\mu_d(A)$ and $\Sigma_d(A)$ i.e.,

$$\rho_s(P(A)) = N(\mu_s(A), \Sigma_s(A)), \tag{7}$$

$$\rho_d(P(A)) = N(\mu_d(A), \Sigma_d(A)), \tag{8}$$

where $N(\mu, \Sigma)$ represents a Gaussian distribution with mean μ and covariance Σ. Now the objection function (6) can be written as [26]:

$$J_B(A) = \max \left\{ \frac{1}{4} \frac{(\mu_s(A) - \mu_d(A))^2}{\Sigma_s(A) + \Sigma_d(A)} + \frac{1}{2} \ln \frac{\Sigma_s(A) + \Sigma_d(A)}{2\sqrt{\Sigma_s(A)\Sigma_d(A)}} \right\}. \tag{9}$$

Denote $E(\cdot)$ represents the expectation operation, and $Tr(X)$ is the trace of the matrix X. Since any $\|A^T x_{ij}\|^2 = Tr(A^T x_{ij} x_{ij}^T A)$, where $x_{ij} = x_i - x_j$, we have

$$\mu_s(A) = E(P_s(A)) = Tr(A^T E(x_{is} x_{is}^T) A), \tag{10}$$

$$\mu_d(A) = E(P_d(A)) = Tr(A^T E(x_{id} x_{id}^T) A), \tag{11}$$

$$\Sigma_s(A) = E(P_s(A) - \mu_s(A))^2 = E(P_s(A))^2 - \mu_s^2(A), \tag{12}$$

$$\Sigma_d(A) = E(P_d(A) - \mu_d(A))^2 = E(P_d(A))^2 - \mu_d^2(A). \tag{13}$$

The solution of (9) can be obtained by the gradient descent algorithms, such as the conjugate gradient method. For simplicity, we ignore (A) in all the $J_B(A)$, $\mu_s(A)$, $\Sigma_s(A)$, $\mu_d(A)$, and $\Sigma_d(A)$. Denote $E(x_{is} x_{is}^T) = M_s$, and $E(x_{id} x_{id}^T) = M_d$. The differentiation of J_B with respect to A is as follows:

$$\frac{\partial J_B}{A} = \frac{(\mu_s - \mu_d)(\frac{\partial \mu_s}{\partial A} - \frac{\partial \mu_d}{\partial A}) + (\frac{\partial \Sigma_s}{\partial A} + \frac{\partial \Sigma_d}{\partial A})}{2(\Sigma_s + \Sigma_d)}$$

$$- \frac{(\mu_s - \mu_d)^2(\frac{\partial \Sigma_s}{\partial A} + \frac{\partial \Sigma_d}{\partial A})}{4(\Sigma_s + \Sigma_d)^2} - \frac{\frac{\partial \Sigma_s}{\partial A}}{2\Sigma_s} - \frac{\frac{\partial \Sigma_d}{\partial A}}{2\Sigma_d} \tag{14}$$

where

$$\frac{\partial \mu_s}{\partial A} = 2M_s A, \tag{15}$$

$$\frac{\partial \Sigma_s}{\partial A} = 4E(Tr(A^T x_{is} x_{is}^T A) x_{is} x_{is}^T A) - 4\mu_s M_s A, \tag{16}$$

$$\frac{\partial \Sigma_d}{\partial A} = 4E(Tr(A^T x_{id} x_{id}^T A) x_{id} x_{id}^T A) - 4\mu_d M_d A, \tag{17}$$

$$\frac{\partial \mu_d}{\partial A} = 2M_d A. \tag{18}$$

From the above description, we can see that the proposed method tries to find the embedding subspace during learning the distance metric inspired by the Bayesian classification error estimation. The transformation A does not change the k-nearest neighborhood relationship of the data, which is similar to the local preserving property of manifold learning, but it is different from popular manifold learning methods in that it aims to make each sample far from its inter-class set and close to its intra-class set. Although we use the Gaussian distribution to model the the variables of the intra-class distances and inter-class distances in the subspace, they are based on the local neighbors, so we do not make assumption on the global distribution of the data compared to LDA. Compared with most distance metric learning methods, the proposed method uses the Bhattacharyya coefficient measurement, which has intuitionistic geometric interpretation and links to Bayesian classification error. The proposed method can handle high dimensional data well.

4   Experiments

We test the proposed method on the three benchmarks, i.e., the CMU-PIE face database [1], the extended YALE face database [2], and the Corel-5000 image database [3]. The data of the first two face databases are download directly from [27]. In our experiments, we take the PCA as the baseline, where we keep 98% energy of eigenvalues. We also compare the proposed method with LDA and RCA. The codes of RCA is downloaded from [28]. For RCA, we use the prior label information to form the chunklets. On the two face databases, we also compare the proposed method with the Bayesian face subspace [29]. In the Bayesian face subspace, the face images are modeled by the intra-face and the inter-face subspaces, which are represented by PCA directly in the input data space. For the Bayesian face subspace, we construct the principal subspace with the 90% energy of the eigenvalues, and the complemental subspace with the rest of 10% energy. In the experiments, we set the number of neighbors k as the training numbers of each class minus 1. For simplicity, we denote the Bayesian face subspace and the proposed method as BFS and MBC respectively.

4.1   CMU-PIE Face Database

The CMU PIE face database contains 68 subjects and 41368 images [25]. Each subject has 13 different poses, 43 different illuminations, and 4 different expressions. In this paper, our dataset is composed of all the images from five near frontal poses $(C05, C07, C09, C27, C29)$ including all the illumination and expression variations as in [30] [27]. There are 170 face images for each subject in our dataset. The images are cropped by fixing two eyes, and the cropped image size is 32×32. No image preprocessing is performed except normalizing the image into unit vector as in [30] [27]. Figure 2 shows some samples.

We randomly select 30 images from each subject for training, and the other 140 images of each subject for testing. The experiments are randomly run 50 times, and all the results reported in Figure 3 are the average of 50 times experiments. Because there are 68 classes, the maximum feature dimension of LDA is 68-1 = 67. From Figure 3, we can see that MBC is better than PCA, LDA, RCA, and BFC. The minimum classification error of MBC is 5.46%, while those of PCA, LDA, RCA, and BSF are 29.4%, 7.84%, 14.62%, and 6.76% respectively. The performance of MBC is still better than the modified LPP [30]. In [30] [27], the modified LPP obtained the minimum average

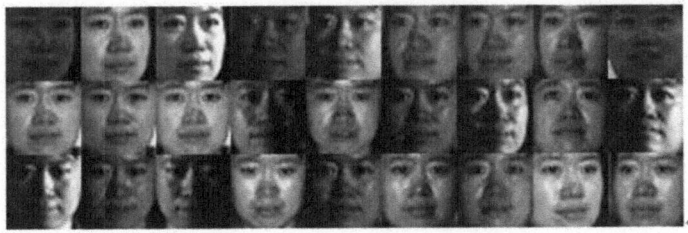

Fig. 2. Samples of the CMU-PIE database

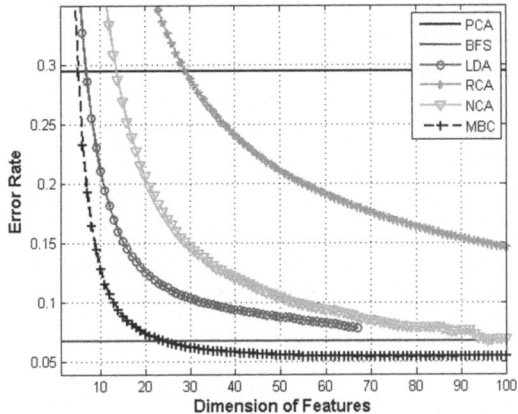

Fig. 3. Testing error rate on the CMU-PIE database

classification error of 7.5% over 50 times experiments under the same testing protocol, i.e., 30 images are randomly selected from each subject, and the rest images of each subject are used for testing.

4.2 Extended YALE Face Database

The extended YALE face database has 38 subjects, each subjects has 64 near frontal view images under different illuminations [27] [2]. The images are cropped to 32×32, and images are normalized into unit vectors as in [30] [27]. Figure 4 shows some samples.

Same as the experiments on the CMU-PIE database, we randomly select 30 images from each individual for training, and the rest 34 images per subject are used for testing. The experiments are run 50 times, and Figure 5 reports their average results. Because the training data has 38 classes, the maximum feature dimensions of LDA is 38-1 = 37. The minimum classification error of MBC is 2.5%, while those of PCA, LDA, RCA, and BSF are 25.59%, 13.34%, 10.88%, and 3.93% respectively. The performance of MBC is still better than the modified LPP [30], for the minimum classification error of the latter reported is 7.5% under a similar testing in [30] [27].

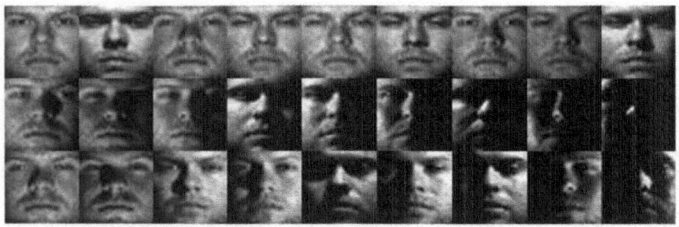

Fig. 4. Samples of the extended YALE database

4.3   Corel-5000 Image Database

The Corel-5000 database is widely used for evaluating image retrieval methods [3]. It consists of 5000 nature images of 50 categories, each represented by 100 images. Such common categories exhibit high intra-class variability. The images are of size 384×256. Figure 6 shows some samples. Four kinds of visual features are used to represent the images [31]: color histogram, color moments, wavelet based texture and directionality. Color histogram is taken in HSV space with quantization of $8 \times 4 = 32$ bins on H and S channels; the first three moments from each of the three color channels are used for color moment; an 24-dimensional PWT based wavelet texture features and an 8-dimensional directionality features are contained to construct an 73-dimensional feature vector for each image.

We randomly select 30 images from each class for training, and the rest 70 images are used for testing. The experiments are run 50 times too, and the results reported in Figure 7 are their average. Since there are 50 classes, the maximum feature dimension

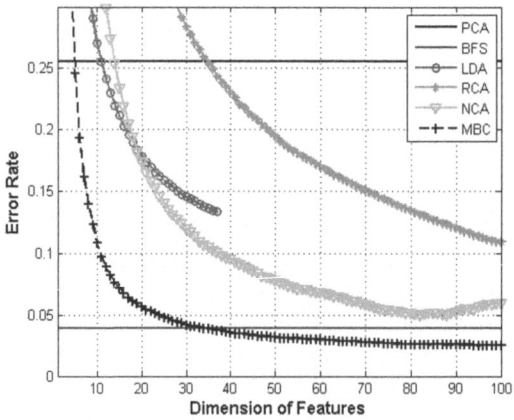

Fig. 5. Results on the extended YALE database

Fig. 6. Samples of the Corel's database

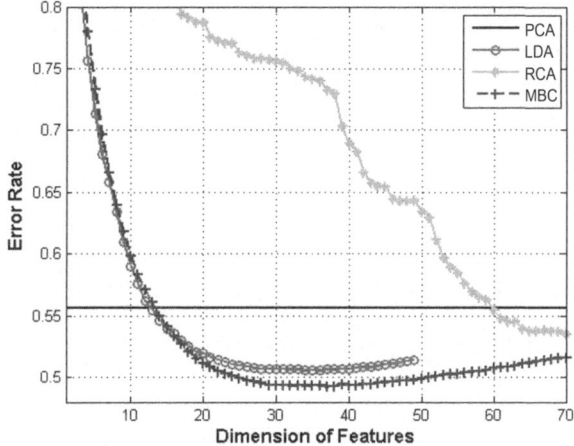

Fig. 7. Results on the Corel-5000 image database

of LDA is 50-1 = 49. We can see that the proposed method outperforms the others as well as the results on the CMU-PIE and extended YALE face databases. The minimum classification errors of MBC is 49.25%, while those of PCA, LDA, and RCA are 55.61%, 50.55%, and 53.51% respectively.

5   Extension with the Kernel Trick

Since the kernel trick achieved a great success in SVM [32], it has been given much attention. The idea of the kernel based methods is first to map the input data into an implicit feature space F with a nonlinear mapping, $x \to \phi(x)$, and then the data is analyzed in F. In the implementation, we do not need to know the feature vector ϕ explicitly. We just need to know the dot product between implicit features with a dot kernel, such as the Gaussian kernel, $k(x_i, x_j) = (\phi(x_i) \cdot \phi(x_j)) = \exp(-\gamma \|x_i - x_j\|^2)$. In this section, we extend our work with the kernel trick to obtain a nonlinear transformation for the subspace and distance metric learning.

Our idea is to first project the data into F, and then we aim to find a nonlinear transformation A^ϕ to satisfy the following rules for each sample x_i:

$$P_i s(A^\phi) = \left\|(A^\phi)^T(\phi(x_i) - \phi(x_s))\right\|^2, x_s \in S_i, \tag{19}$$

$$P_i d(A^\phi) = \left\|(A^\phi)^T(\phi(x_i) - \phi(x_d))\right\|^2, x_d \in D_i, \tag{20}$$

$$P_i s(A^\phi) < P_i d(A^\phi), for \forall i, s, d. \tag{21}$$

Here, the neighbor relationship is computed in F by:

$$\|\phi(x_i) - \phi(x_j)\|^2 = k(x_i, x_i) + k(x_j, x_j) - 2k(x_i, x_j). \tag{22}$$

Because A^ϕ is a linear transformation in F, so it can be represented by linear combinations of all the $\phi(x_i)$. We define the matrix $\Phi(X) = [\phi(x_1), \phi(x_2), ..., \phi(x_n)]$. Then A^ϕ can be rewritten as:

$$A^\phi = \Phi(X)G, \tag{23}$$

where G represents the matrix of coefficients. Thus, we can convert the above $P_{is}(A^\phi)$ and $P_{id}(A^\phi)$ into:

$$P_{is}(A^\phi) = P_{is}(G) = \left\|G^T(K(x_i) - K(x_s))\right\|^2, \tag{24}$$

$$P_{id}(A^\phi) = P_{id}(G) = \left\|G^T(K(x_i) - K(x_d))\right\|^2, \tag{25}$$

where $K(x)$ means a vector composed of the products between x and all the training samples, $K(x) = (k(x_1, x), k(x_2, x), ..., k(x_n, x))^T$. Regarding $K(x)$ as the kernel feature of x, the problem is equivalent to finding a transformation G make all the intra-class distances smaller than all the inter-class distances based on the kernel features.

Similarly, we can define two variables: $P_s(G)$ and $P_d(G)$ to represent all the local distances $P_{is}(G)$ and $P_{id}(G)$ respectively, and assume that they are from two Gaussian distributions, $\rho_s(P(G)) = N(\mu_s(G), \Sigma_s(G))$ and $\rho_d(P(G)) = N(\mu_d(G), \Sigma_d(G))$.

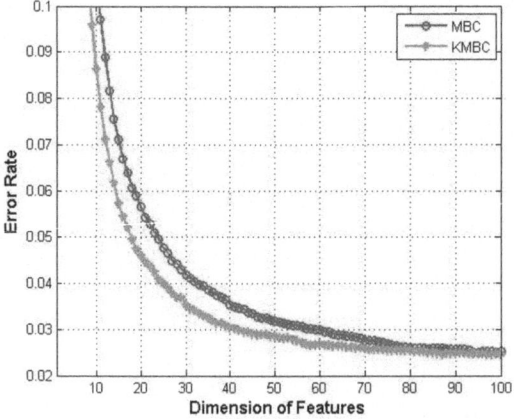

Fig. 8. Results on the extended YaleB database

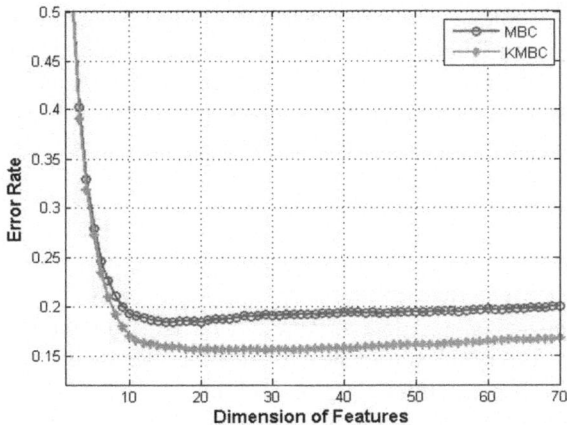

Fig. 9. Results on the subset of the Corel-5000 database

As in (6), the problem is converted to maximize the following Bhattacharyya distance between $\rho_s(P(G))$ and $\rho_d(P(G))$:

$$
\begin{aligned}
J_B(G) &= \max\{-\ln \int \sqrt{\rho_s(P(G))\rho_d(P(G))}dP(G)\} \\
&= \max\left\{\frac{1}{4}\frac{(\mu_s(G)-\mu_d(G))^2}{\Sigma_s(G)+\Sigma_d(G)} + \frac{1}{2}\ln\frac{\Sigma_s(G)+\Sigma_d(G)}{2\sqrt{\Sigma_s(G)\Sigma_d(G)}}\right\}
\end{aligned}
\tag{26}
$$

Denote $K_{ij} = K(x_i) - K(x_j)$. Based on the kernel features, $K(x_i), i = 1, 2, ..., n$, the $\mu_s(G)$, $\mu_d(G)$, $\Sigma_s(G)$, and $\Sigma_d(G)$) are computed as follows:

$$
\mu_s(G) = E(P_s(G)) = Tr(G^T E(K_{is}K_{is}^T)G),
\tag{27}
$$

$$
\mu_d(G) = E(P_d(G)) = Tr(G^T E(x_{id}x_{id}^T)G),
\tag{28}
$$

$$
\Sigma_s(G) = E(P_s(G) - \mu_s(G))^2 = E(P_s(G))^2 - \mu_s^2(G),
\tag{29}
$$

$$
\Sigma_d(G) = E(P_d(G) - \mu_d(G))^2 = E(P_d(G))^2 - \mu_d^2(G).
\tag{30}
$$

Its solution can be obtained by the gradient descent as well as in Section 3.2. The distance of two samples x_i and x_j is computed with the nonlinear distance metric as follows:

$$
P_{i,j} = (K(x_i) - K(x_j))^T GG^T (K(x_i) - K(x_j)).
\tag{31}
$$

As we know, some issues are still open in the kernel methods, especially the kernel function and its parameter selection, for different kernel function will construct different implicit feature space and produce different performance. Additionally the computational cost of the kernel methods will be increased rapidly with the increase of the training samples, for the Grammar matrix, $K = [K(x_1), K(x_2), ..., K(x_n)]$, needs to be computed and saved during the learning. Due to the above issues, here we just investigate the performance of our kernel extension (we denoted it as KMBC against MBC). The experiments are conducted on the extended YaleB database and a subset of the Corel-5000 database. We select the 10 categories from the Corel-5000 database: African people and villages, beach, buildings, buses, dinosaurs, elephants, flowers, horses, mountain and glaciers, and food, which is called the Wang's nature image database [33]. The Gaussian kernel is used, and its parameter is set as $\gamma = 0.05$. Figure 8 and 9 show the results on the extended YaleB and the subset of the Corel-5000 database respectively. It is illustrated that KMBC can achieve better performances than MBC in these two datasets.

6   Conclusions

In this paper, we presented a unified scheme of subspace and distance metric learning under the Bayesian framework for image classification. We divided the k-nearest neighbors of each sample into the intra-class set and the inter-class set according the local distribution of the data, and we attempted to learn a distance metric in the embedding subspace, which made the distances between the sample and its intra-class set smaller than the distances between it and its inter-class set in the embedding subspace. To reach this goal, we modeled the intra-class distances and the inter-class distances with two Gaussian distributions respectively. Inspired by Bayesian classification error estimation, we formulate our goal with minimizing the Bhattachyrra coefficient measurement between these two distributions. We further discussed its kernel extension with the kernel trick to learn nonlinear distance metric. The proposed framework made no assumption on the global distribution of the data. It could be used directly for multi-class classification problems without any modification or extension. Moreover, it has an intuitionistic geometric interpretation and links to Bayesian classification error. We proved the power and generality of the proposed approach on the CMU-PIE face database, the extended YALE face database, and the Corel-5000 image database.

References

1. Sim, T., Baker, S., Bsat, M.: The cmu pose, illumination, and expression database. IEEE Trans. on PAMI 25(12), 1615–1618 (2003)
2. Lee, K.C., Ho, J., Kriegman, D.: Acquiring linear subspaces for face recognition under variable lighting. IEEE Trans. Pattern Analysis and Machine Intelligence 27(5), 1–15 (2005)
3. Tong, H., He, J., Li, M., Zhang, C., Ma, W.: Graph based multi-modality learning. In: Proc. ACM Multimedia (2005)
4. Turk, M., Pentland, A.: Eigenfaces for recognition. Journal of Cognitive Neuroscience 3(1), 72–86 (1991)
5. Zhao, W., Chellappa, R., Phillips, P.J.: Subspace linear discriminant analysis for face recognition. Tech. Report CAR-TR-914, University of Maryland (1999)
6. Belhumeur, P.N., Hespanha, J.P., Kriegman, D.J.: Eigenfaces vs. fisherfaces: Recognition using class specific linear projection. IEEE Trans. Pattern Analysis and Machine Intelligence 19(7), 711–720 (1997)
7. Scholkopf, B., Smola, A., Muller, K.R.: Nonlinear component analysis as a kernel eigenvalue problem. Neural Computation 10(5), 1299–1319 (1998)
8. Mika, S., Ratsch, G., Weston, J.: Fisher discriminant analysis with kernels. In: Proc. of Neural Networks for Signal Processing Workshop (1999)

9. Roweis, S.T., Saul, L.K.: Nonlinear dimensionality reduction by locally linear embedding. Sciences 290(5500), 2323–2326 (2000)
10. Tenenbaum, J.B., de Silva, V., Langford, J.C.: A global geometric framework for nonlinear dimensionality reduction. Sciences 290(5500), 2319–2323 (2000)
11. He, X.F., Niyogi, P.: Locality preserving projections. In: Advances in Neural Information Processing Systems (NIPS) (2003)
12. Chen, H.T., Chang, H.W., Liu, T.L.: Local discriminant embedding and its variants. In: Proc. of Int. Conf. Computer Vision and Pattern Recognition (CVPR) (2005)
13. Sugiyama, M.: Local fisher discriminant analysis for supervised dimensionality reduction. In: Proc. of Int. Conf. Machine Learning (ICML) (2006)
14. Yan, S.C., Xu, D., Zhang, B.Y., Zhang, H.J.: Graph embedding: A general framework for dimensionality reduction. In: Proc. of Int. Conf. Computer Vision and Pattern Recognition (CVPR) (2005)
15. Xing, E., Ng, A., Jordan, M., Russell, S.: Distance metric learning, with application to clustering with side-information. In: Advances in Neural Information Processing Systems (NIPS) (2004)
16. Bar-Hillel, A., Hertz, T., Shental, N., Weinshall, D.: Learning a mahalanobis metric from equivalence constrains. Journal of Machine Learning Research (2005)
17. Shental, N., Hertz, T., Weinshall, D., Pavel, M.: Adjustment learning and relevant component analysis. In: Europen Conf. on Computer Vision (ECCV) (2003)
18. Hoi, S.C., Liu, W., Lyu, M.R., Ma, W.Y.: Learning distance metrics with contextual constraints for image retrieval. In: Proc. of Int. Conf. Computer Vision and Pattern Recognition (CVPR) (2006)
19. Weinberger, K.Q., Blitzer, J., Saul, L.K.: Metric learning for large margin nearest neighbor classification. In: Advances in Neural Information Processing Systems (NIPS) (2005)
20. Torresani, L., Lee, K.C.: Large margin component analysis. In: Advances in Neural Information Processing Systems (NIPS) (2006)
21. Goldberger, J., Roweis, S., Hinton, G., Salakhutdinov, R.: Neighborhood component analysis. In: Advances in Neural Information Processing Systems (NIPS) (2004)
22. Globerson, A., Roweis, S.: Metric learning by collapsing classes. In: Advances in Neural Information Processing Systems (NIPS) (2005)
23. Yang, L., Jin, R., Sukthankar, R., Liu, Y.: An efficient algorithm for local distance metric learning. In: AAAI (2006)
24. Salakhutdinov, R., Roweis, S.T.: Adaptive over- relaxed bound optimization methods. In: Proc. of Int. Conf. Machine Learning (ICML) (2003)
25. Comaniciu, D., Ramesh, V., Meer, P.: Kernel-based object tracking. IEEE Trans. on Pattern Analysis and Machine Intelligence 25(5), 564–577 (2003)
26. Fukunaga, K.: Introduction to statistical pattern recognition. Academic Press, New York (1990)
27. http://ews.uiuc.edu/~dengcai2/data/data.html
28. http://www.cs.huji.ac.il/~aharonbh/
29. Moghaddam, B., Jebara, T., Pentland, A.: Bayesian face recognition. Pattern Recognition 33(11), 1771–1782 (2000)
30. Cai, D., He, X., Han, J.: Using graph model for face analysis. Tech Report UIUCDCS-R-2636, University of UIUC (2005)
31. Wu, H., Lu, H.Q., Ma, S.D.: A practical svm-based algorithm for ordinal regression in image retrieval. In: Proc. ACM Multimedia (2003)
32. Osuna, E., Freund, R., Girosi, F.: Support vector machines: Training and applications. Tech Report, AI Lab, MIT (1997)
33. Chen, Y., Wang, J.Z.: Image categorization by learning and reasoning with regions. Journal of Machine Learning Research (2004)

Constant-Working-Space Algorithms for Image Processing

Tetsuo Asano

School of Information Science, JAIST,
Japan Advanced Institute of Science and Technology,
Nomi, 923-1292, Japan
t-asano@jaist.ac.jp

Abstract. This chapter surveys recent progress in constant-working-space algorithms for problems related to image processing. An extreme case is when an input image is given as read-only memory in which reading an array element is allowed but writing any value at any array element is prohibited, and also the number of working storage cells available for algorithms is at most some constant. This chapter shows how a number of important fundamental problems can be solved in such a highly constrained situation.

1 Introduction

Recent progress in image related technologies is remarkable. High-resolution digital camera and digital movie camera are now widely used. The image size is monotonically increasing and it is time now to restart the design of various image-processing algorithms from a view point of memory consumption. In this chapter we propose a new model of computation in this direction and survey some new attempts to reduce working space, especially, how to design constant-working space algorithms in image processing.

Another requirement of limited working storage comes from applications to built-in or embedded software in intelligent hardwares. Digital cameras and scanners are good examples of intelligent hardware. We measure the space efficiency of an algorithm by the number of working storage cells (or the amount of working space) used by the algorithm. Ultimate efficiency is achieved when only constant number of variables are used in addition to input array(s). We call such an algorithm *a constant working space algorithm*. Strictly speaking, there are two types of such algorithms. One should be rather referred to as an *in-place* algorithm. In this type of algorithms, input data are given by some constant number of arrays. Those arrays can be used as working space although there must be some upper limit on values to be stored in those arrays. Heapsort is a typical in-place algorithm. Ordinary implementation of mergesort requires a working array of the same size as the input array and thus it is not in-place. Recently there are some attempts to design in-place versions of the mergesort [17,18,20,22,25]. Quicksort does not require any array, but it is not in-place since its recursion

F. Nielsen (Ed.): ETVC 2008, LNCS 5416, pp. 268–283, 2009.

depth depends on input size ($O(\log n)$ in average) which should be included in the working storage.

The other type of constant-working-space algorithm satisfies that condition in a more strict sense. That is, it should not use any working space of size dependent on input size and an array storing input data is given as read-only memory so that no value in the array can be changed. Constant-working-space algorithms for image processing in [1,3,4] are in-place algorithms in this sense. The algorithm for image scan with arbitrary angle [2] is a constant-working-space algorithm with input in read-only memory. The same framework has been studied in complexity theory. A typical problem is a so-called "st-connectivity" problem: given an undirected graph G with n vertices in read-only memory, and two vertices s and t in G, determine whether they are connected or not using only a constant number of variables of $O(\log n)$ bits. Reingold [38] succeeded for the first time in proving that the problem can be solved in polynomial time. It is a great break-through in this direction.

One of the most fundamental problems in image processing is *Connected Components Labeling* in which we are requested to label each pixel in a given binary image by a component number (index) to which the pixel belongs [5,13,29,30,36,39,41]. Its simplified version is *Connected Components Counting*, which just requires to count the number of connected components in an input binary image. These problems are well studied in the image processing literature (see [27,40] for survey). Figure 1 shows an example of connected components labeling. An input binary image shown in the left contains four connected components. Each white pixel is replaced by its component number (index), which is shown in the right.

In Connected Components Labeling each white pixel(one of value 1) is labeled by some positive integer assigned to a component to which the pixel belongs. Thus, it seems impossible to have a constant-working-space algorithm with input image in read-only memory. If we could put some information on the input array, we could label each pixel without using any extra array. More formally, there is an in-place algorithm for the problem [4] which runs in linear time. The same algorithm can be extended to Connected Components Counting on

```
000000000000000000000000        000000000000000000000000
011110000000000111000110        011110000000000222000330
001110000000000011100110        001110000000000022200330
000111011110000000111000        000111011110000000222000
000001110110000000000000        000001110110000000000000
000001100010000000000000        000001100010000000000000
000001100010000000000000        000001100010000000000000
000011111111111111000000        000011111111111111000000
000000000000000011000000        000000000000000011000000
011111111110000000000000        044444444440000000000000
001110000011111100000000        004440000004444400000000
000011111111100000000000        000044444444400000000000
000000000000000000000000        000000000000000000000000
```

Fig. 1. Connected Components Labeling. An input binary image (left) and a result of connected components labeling.

read-only memory. An unpublished algorithm by the author finds the number of components in $O(N \log N)$ time where N is the total number of pixels in the binary image.

Space-efficient algorithms have been rigorously investigated in computational geometry [8,10,14,11,15]. The read-only memory model is not so popular in the community, but the author believes that there is a considerable number of interesting problems in this direction.

2   New Computation Models

In this section we describe our computation model. Our model is based on a popular RAM (Random Access Machine) Model:

(Polynomially-bounded) RAM model

Input size: Input size is denoted by n.

Storage Size: The total size of working storage (or the total number of working storage cells) available must be bounded by some polynomial in n. Each cell or element (variable or array element) in the working space used in an algorithm has $O(\log n)$ bits.

Recursive Call: Implicit storage consumption required by recursive calls is also considered as a part of working space. In other words, if the maximum depth of recursive calls is k, then they contribute to the working space by $O(k)$.

Memory Access: Any memory cell can be accessed in constant time independently of n. Further, any basic arithmetic operation is done in constant time.

Basic Assumption on Image Array

Image Size: We assume an intensity image (without color, for simplicity). The total number of pixels in an input image is denoted by N. An image is given as a rectangular array of size $h \times w$, where h and w are the numbers of rows and columns, respectively, and hence we have $N = h \times w$. We assume that both of h and w are $O(\sqrt{N})$.

Intensity Levels: Each pixel has some nonnegative intensity level, which is assumed to be an integer between 0 and L. That is, an intensity level is expressed in $\log_2 L$ bits. We implicitly assume $L < N$.

Our goal here is to develop space-efficient algorithms for image processing, which require only small amount of working storage in addition to an input image array. An extreme situation is to allow only constant number of variables in algorithms. Throughout this chapter we implicitly assume that each variable in any algorithm has $O(\log N)$ bits, sometimes, exactly $\log_2 N$ bits. Such an algorithm is commonly referred to as an log-*space algorithm* in the complexity theory since the total number of bits in working space is bounded by $O(\log n)$

for an algorithm with input of size n. In this chapter we use the term "constant-working-space algorithm" instead of log-space algorithm since it is more intuitive for image processing.

Here is a classification of algorithms from space efficiency. Algorithms for image processing are usually allowed to use a constant number of arrays of the same size as that of an input image array. We are sometimes allowed to use only a one-dimensional array to keep some rows or columns in an image. In an extreme case we are allowed to use only constant number of variables in addition to the image array.

Variation on Space-Efficiency

Linear Working Space: A constant number of arrays of the same size as that of an input image array are allowed as working storage cells.

$O(\sqrt{N})$ **Working Space:** A constant number of one-dimensional arrays of size $O(\sqrt{N})$ are allowed as working storage cells. Each such array is as large as a row or a column of the input image.

Constant Working Space: Only a constant number of variables are allowed as working storage cells.

Our polynomially-bounded RAM model assumes that every memory element can be accessed in constant time. More precisely, given an index in an array, we can read and write the element of the index in constant time. Note that the content of the element is of $O(\log N)$ bits. We could also consider a model in which an image array can be accessed in a read-only manner. That is, we can read any pixel value in constant time, but we are not allowed to modify any pixel value. In this chapter we distinguish the two models by read-write and read-only models.

Accessibility to Image Array

Random-Access Model: Any pixel value can be altered to any value of $O(\log N)$ bits.

Read-Only Model: We can read any pixel value in constant time, but we are not allowed to alter any pixel value.

3 Hardware Assistance

Suppose we have a range sensor which can measure its distance from the sensor to the closest obstacle in any direction. Whenever a direction is specified, we can measure the corresponding distance in constant time. In this situation there is no need to store distance values at all possible directions in a two-dimensional array. Whenever we need a distance in some direction, we can measure it at constant time.

We have a similar situation for *object embedding*. Suppose a set of n objects is given and for each pair of objects (i, j) their dissimilarity is denoted by $\delta_{i,j}$.

Using the dissimilarity information, we want to map objects into points in a low dimensional space while dissimilarities are preserved as the distances between the corresponding points. We often encounter this situation in practice. Converting distance information into coordinate information is helpful for human perception because we can see how close two objects are. Because of its practical importance, this topic has been widely studied under the name of dimension reduction [7].

Multi-Dimensional Scaling (MDS) [16] is a generic name for a family of algorithms for dimensionality reduction. Although MDS is powerful, it has a serious drawback for practical use, that is, its high space complexity. The input to MDS is an $n \times n$ matrix specifying pairwise dissimilarities (or distances). Asano et. [6] proposes an approach for dimensionality reduction that avoids this high space complexity if the dissimilarity information is given by a function that can be evaluated in constant time.

A key idea in this linear-space algorithm for the distance preserving graph embedding problem is to use *clustering*. They propose a simple algorithm for finding a size-constrained clustering and show that their solution achieves the largest inter-cluster distance, or maximizes the smallest distance between objects from different clusters. That is, given a set of n objects, with a function evaluating dissimilarities for pairs of objects, we embed those objects into points in a low-dimensional space so that pairwise distances are as close to their dissimilarities as possible. Then, the point set is partitioned into $O(\sqrt{n})$ disjoint subsets, called *clusters*, where each cluster contains $O(\sqrt{n})$ points (objects). Formally, using a positive integer c the set is partitioned into k subsets $C_1, C_2, \ldots, C_k$ in such a way that each cluster contains at most $2c$ objects except possibly one cluster which has at most c elements. For $c = O(\sqrt{n})$ the number k of clusters and also the largest cluster size bounded by $2c$ are both $O(\sqrt{n})$. Since, each cluster has a relatively small number of objects, and thus performing MDS with a distance matrix for each cluster separately requires only $O(n)$ working space. Using this they devise linear space algorithms for embedding all the objects in the plane.

4   Thresholding Intensity Images

Thresholding an intensity image into a binary image is one of the most important and fundamental problems in image processing and a number of algorithms have been proposed (see [27,34,36]). A simple algorithm is to use a histogram which expresses frequencies of intensity levels. If there are two obvious peaks, then any level separating them may work as a good threshold. Ohtsu's thresholding algorithm [34] is mathematically beautiful in the sense that the problem is defined as a combinatorial optimization problem based on discriminant analysis. That is, it computes a threshold that maximizes the inter-cluster distance between two clusters defined by the threshold. Once we have a histogram, we can find an optimal threshold in linear time in the number of intensity levels, i.e., $O(L)$ time. To implement the algorithm we need $O(L)$ working space for the histogram. What happens if we have only constant working space?

Thresholding technique is applied in a wide range of applications. One of them is fingerprint identification. Given a fingerprint image, the first step is to convert it into a binary image. Our experience tells us that a threshold is good for succeeding the fingerprint identification if ridges and valleys are of almost equal widths. Statistics on those widths can be computed using a technique called *Euclidean Distance Transform*, EDT [9,26,30,35,12]. Given a binary image, the EDT computes the Euclidean distance from each pixel p to the pixel of opposite value that is closest to p. Two linear-time algorithms are known for the EDT [9,21]. An algorithm by Liang et al. [28] computes a threshold at which the average width of ridges is closest to that of valleys based on binary search and Euclidean distance transform. What happens if only constant working space is available?

4.1   Ohtsu's Thresholding Algorithm

The Ohtsu's thresholding algorithm is described as follows. Suppose we have L intensity levels. Let h_i be the number of pixels with intensity level i. Given a threshold T, we have two clusters, C_0 and C_1 with C_0 for intensity levels $0, 1, \ldots, T-1$ and C_1 for $T, T+1, \ldots, L-1$. If the average intensity levels in C_0 and C_1 are μ_0 and μ_1, respectively, then the intercluster-distance $\delta(T)$ between C_0 and C_1 is defined by

$$\delta(T) = \frac{(\mu_0(T) - \mu_1(T))^2}{|C_0||C_1|}, \tag{1}$$

where

$$|C_0| = \sum_{i=0}^{T-1} h_i, \ |C_1| = \sum_{i=T}^{L-1} h_i,$$

$$\mu_0(T) = (\sum_{i=0}^{T-1} ih_i)/|C_0|, \text{and } \mu_1(T) = (\sum_{i=T}^{L-1} ih_i)/|C_1|.$$

Observation 1. *[34] Let N be the number of pixels in a given image and L be the number of intensity levels. Given such an image, we can find in $O(N+L)$ time using $O(L)$ space in addition to the image array an optimal threshold that maximizes the intercluster distance.*

We can find an optimal threshold using binary search. A key is to decide whether a given threshold T is greater than an optimal threshold. For that purpose we need to calculate the average intensity levels for two classes. First of all we can easily compute the size $|C_0|$ and $|C_1|$ since it suffices to count the number of pixels in the class C_0. It is done in $O(N)$ time by scanning all the pixels. Then, we evaluate the sums $\sum_{i=0}^{T-1} ih_i$ just by taking the sum of all intensity levels that is less than T, which is again done in $O(N)$ time. Hence, one step of the binary search is done in $O(N)$ time. Since we need $O(\log L)$ iterations, the total time required is $O(N \log L)$.

Observation 2. *Let N be the number of pixels in a given image and L be the number of intensity levels. Given such an image, we can find in $O(N \log L)$ time using only constant working space in addition to the image array an optimal threshold that maximizes the intercluster distance.*

Note that the binary search described above works only if each pixel has an integral intensity level. If pixels have real values then it is impossible to find the middle value in each iteration of the binary search. What can we do in this case? Of course, randomization is one possible way, but is there any deterministic way?

One way is to use the median intensity level instead of one maximizing the intercluster distance. What is the median intensity level? It is the median of all intensity levels in a given intensity image. The assumption that each pixel has some real value as its intensity level implies that the number of intensity levels, L, is equal to the number of pixels, N. That is, we have $L = N$. How can we compute the median of N such values using only constant working space? Fortunately, there is an efficient algorithm [31]:

In the literature [31] the authors first present an efficient randomized algorithm for selection, which looks quite efficient in practice.

Observation 3. *[31] The k-th smallest from a list of n elements residing in a read-only memory can be found using $O(1)$ indexing operations and $O(n \log n)$ comparisons on the average.*

They extend the result above further into the following observation:

Observation 4. *[31] The k-th smallest from a list of n elements residing in a read-only memory can be found using $O(1)$ indices and $O(n \log \log n)$ comparisons on the average, if all the permutations of the given input are equally likely.*

A key observation for their deterministic algorithm for selection is the following:

Observation 5. *[31] The k-th smallest from a list of n elements residing in a read-only memory can be found using $O(in^{1+1/i})$ comparisons and $O(i)$ indices in the worst case, where i is any fixed value (parameter) such that $1 < i \leq \sqrt{\log n / \log \log n}$.*

Using this observation, they obtain the following result.

Observation 6. *[31] Given a read-only array of size n and a positive small constant ϵ, there is an algorithm which finds the median of the n elements in $O(n^{1+\epsilon})$ time using $O(1/\epsilon)$ working space.*

An important idea behind their algorithm is a *controlled recursion*. Recursion is, of course, one of the most powerful algorithmic techniques, but recursion on problems of size n may have $O(\log n)$ depth in the worst case, which requires that much working space. In our case we must be careful so that the recursion depth does not exceed some constant. In the above observation, the parameter i specifies the largest possible depth. The larger the value i is the faster the algorithm becomes, but at the same time it requires larger working space.

A number of related results are known [17,18,19,20,22,23,24,25,31,32,33,37].

5 In-Place Algorithm for Rotated Image Restoration

Demand for high-performance scanners is growing as we are moving toward paper-less society. There are a number of problems to be resolved in the current scanner technology. One of such problems is correction of rotated documents. An efficient in-place algorithm is presented in [1,2], which assumes that rotation angle is detected by some hardware.

Once the rotation angle is obtained, it is easy to rotate the image if sufficient working space is provided. Suppose input intensity values are stored in a two-dimensional array $a[.,.]$ and another array $b[.,.]$ of the same size is available. Then, at each lattice point (pixel) in the rotated coordinate system we compute an intensity value using appropriate interpolation (linear or cubic) using intensity values around the lattice point (pixel) in the input array and then store the computed interpolation value at the corresponding element in the array $b[\ ]$. More precisely, for each pixel (x, y) in the rotated image we use $2d \times 2d$ pixels around the corresponding point in the input image for interpolation. The set of pixels is denoted by $N_d(x, y)$. The window $N_d(x, y)$ for interpolation is defined by

$$N_d(x,y) = \{(x', y') \in G_{wh}^{\#} \mid$$
$$\lfloor x \rfloor - d + 1 \le x' \le \lfloor x \rfloor + d,$$
$$\lfloor y \rfloor - d + 1 \le y' \le \lfloor y \rfloor + d\}.$$

Finally, we output intensity values stored in the array $b[\ ]$.

This method, however, requires too much working storage. Is it possible to implement the interpolations without using any extra working storage?

A space-efficient algorithm [1,2] is presented for correcting rotation of a document without using any extra working storage. A simple way of doing this is to compute an interpolation value at each pixel in the rotated coordinate system and store the computed value somewhere in the input array $a[\ ]$ near the point in the original coordinate system. Once we store an interpolation value at some element of the array, the original intensity value at the element is lost and it is replaced by the interpolation value. Thus, if the neighborhood of the pixel in the rotated coordinate system includes interpolated values then the interpolation at that point is not correct or reliable. One of the key observations is that there is an easily-computable condition to determine whether interpolation at a given pixel is reliable or not, that is, whether any interpolated value is included in the neighborhood or not. Using the condition, we first classify pixels in the rotated coordinate system into reliable and unreliable ones. In the first phase we compute interpolation at each unreliable pixel and keep the interpolation value in a queue, which consists of array elements outside the rotated subimage. Then, in the second phase we compute interpolation at every pixel (x, y) in the rotated coordinate system and store the computed value at the (x, y)-element in the array. Finally, in the third phase for each unreliable pixel (x, y) we move its interpolation value stored in the queue back to the (x, y)-element in the array.

5.1   Input Image and Rotated Subimages

The input image G consists of $h \times w$ pixels. Each pixel (x, y) is associated with an intensity level. The set of all those pixels (or lattice points in the xy-coordinate system) is denoted by $G_{wh}^{\#}$ and its bounding rectangle by G_{wh}.

The rotated subimage R consists of $H \times W$ pixels, which form a set $R_{WH}^{\#}$ of pixels (or lattice points in the XY-coordinate system). An intensity level at each pixel (X, Y) is calculated by interpolation using intensity levels in the neighborhood.

We have two coordinate systems, one for the original input and the other for the rotated document. They are denoted by xy and XY, respectively. The rectangle corresponding to the input image is denoted by G_{wh} where w and h are horizontal and vertical dimensions of the rectangle, respectively. By $G_{wh}^{\#}$ we denote a set of lattice points in the rectangle. More precisely, they are defined by

$$G_{wh} = \{(x, y) \mid 0 \leq x < w \text{ and } 0 \leq y < h\}, \text{ and}$$
$$G_{wh}^{\#} = \{(x, y) \mid x = 0, 1, \ldots, w - 1, \text{ and } y = 0, 1, \ldots, h - 1\}.$$

We implicitly assume that intensity values are stored at array elements corresponding to lattice points in the set $G_{wh}^{\#}$. Now, we have another rectangle, which is a bounding box of a rotated image. We denote it by R_{WH}, where W and H are width and height of the rectangle, respectively. The set of lattice points in R_{WH} is denoted by $R_{WH}^{\#}$. More precise definitions are given by

$$R_{WH} = \{(X, Y) \mid 0 \leq X < W \text{ and } 0 \leq Y < H\}, \text{ and}$$
$$R_{WH}^{\#} = \{(X, Y) \mid X = 0, 1, \ldots, W - 1, \text{ and } Y = 0, 1, \ldots, H - 1\}.$$

Figure 2 illustrates two rectangles, G_{wh} as $ABCD$ and R_{WH} as $PQRS$.

5.2   Output Image and Location Function

An interpolation value calculated at a pixel $(X, Y) \in R_{WH}^{\#}$ in a rotated subimage is stored (or overwritten) at some pixel $s(X, Y) \in G_{wh}^{\#}$ in the original input image. The function $s(\ )$ determining the location is referred to as a *location function*. A simple function is $s(X, Y) = (X, Y)$ which maps a pixel (X, Y) in $R_{WH}^{\#}$ to a pixel (X, Y) in $G_{wh}^{\#}$. We may use different location functions, but this simple function seems best for row-major and column-major raster scans. So, we implicitly fix the function.

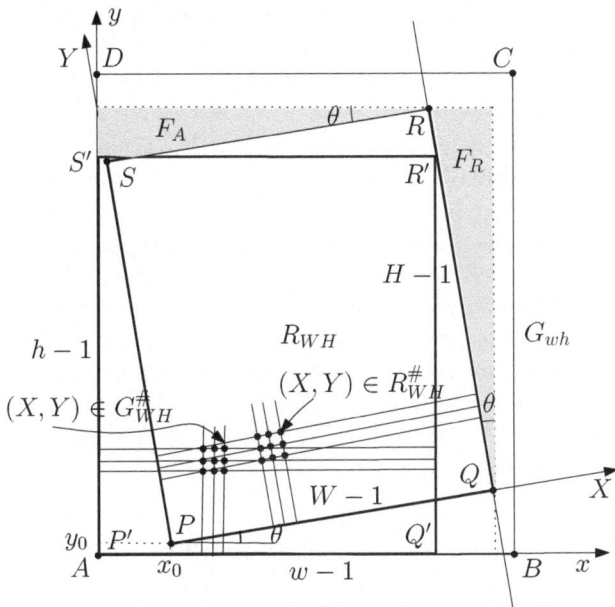

Fig. 2. Two rectangles G_{wh} and R_{WH}

5.3   Correspondence between Two Coordinate Systems

Let (x_0, y_0) be the xy-coordinates of the lower left corner of a rotated document (more exactly, the lower left corner of the bounding box of the rotated subimage). Now, a pixel (X, Y) in $R_{WH}^{\#}$ is a point (x, y) in the rectangle G_{wh} with

$$x = x_0 + X\cos\theta - Y\sin\theta, \text{ and}$$
$$y = y_0 + X\sin\theta + Y\cos\theta.$$

The corresponding point (x, y) defined above is denoted by $p(X, Y)$.

5.4   Basic Interpolation Algorithm

The following is a basic algorithm for interpolation with a scan order σ and location function $s(\ )$.

Basic interpolation algorithm
Phase 1:Scan rotated subimage
for each $(X, Y) \in R_{WH}^{\#}$ in a scan order σ do
  · Calculate a location $p(X, Y) = (x, y)$ in the xy-coordinate system.
  · Execute interpolation at (x, y) using intensity levels in the window $N_d(x, y)$.
  · Store the interpolation value at a pixel $s(X, Y) \in G_{wh}^{\#}$.
Phase 2: Clear the margin
for each $(x, y) \in G_{wh}^{\#}$ do
  if no interpolation value is stored at (x, y)
    then the intensity level at (x, y) is set to *white*.

The basic algorithm above is simple and efficient. Unfortunately, it may lead to incorrect interpolations since when we calculate an interpolation value at some pixel we may reuse intensity levels resulting from past interpolations. A more precise description follows:

Suppose we scan pixels in a rotated subimage $R^{\#}_{WH}$ and an interpolation value computed at each point (X, Y) is stored at the pixel specified by the location function $s(X, Y)$. We say interpolation at $(X, Y) \in R^{\#}_{WH}$ is *reliable* if and only if none of the pixels in the window $N_d(x, y)$ keeps interpolation value. Otherwise, the interpolation is *unreliable*. "Unreliable" does not mean that the interpolation value at the point is incorrect. Consider an image with only one intensity level. Then, interpolation does not cause any change in the intensity value anywhere. Otherwise, if we use interpolated values for interpolation, the computed value may be different from the true interpolation value. We use the terminology "*unreliable*" in this sense. A pixel (X, Y) is called *reliable* if interpolation at (X, Y) is reliable and *unreliable* otherwise.

5.5   Lazy Interpolation and Local Reliability Test

An idea to avoid such incorrect interpolation is to find all unreliable pixels and keep their interpolation values somewhere in a region which is not used for output image. In the following algorithm we use a queue to keep such interpolation values.

[Lazy Interpolation]
Q: a queue to keep interpolation values at unreliable pixels.
for each pixel $(X, Y) \in R^{\#}_{WH}$ in a scan order σ do
   if (X, Y) is unreliable
      then push the interpolation value at (X, Y) into the queue Q.
for each pixel $(X, Y) \in R^{\#}_{WH}$ in the order σ do
   if (X, Y) is unreliable
      then pop a value up from the queue Q and
        store the value at the pixel $s(X, Y)$.
      else calculate the interpolation value at (X, Y)
        and store the value at the pixel $s(X, Y) \in G^{\#}_{wh}$.

Here are two problems. One is how to implement the queue. The other is how to check unreliability of a pixel. It should be remarked that both of them must be done without using any extra working storage.

Suppose we scan pixels in a rotated subimage $R^{\#}_{WH}$ according to a scan order σ and interpolation using a window of size d around each point (X, Y) is calculated and stored at an array element $s(X, Y)$ specified by the location function. Now we can define another sequence τ to determine an order of all pixels in $G^{\#}_{wh}$ to receive interpolated values. That is, the function τ is defined so that

$$\tau(s(X, Y)) = \sigma(X, Y)$$

holds for any $(X, Y) \in R_{WH}^{\#}$. Since a rotated subimage is smaller than the original image, some pixels in the original image are not used for output image. That is, there are pixels (x, y) in $G_{wh}^{\#}$ such that there is no (X, Y) in $R_{WH}^{\#}$ with $(x, y) = s(X, Y)$. For such pixels (x, y) we define $\tau(x, y) = WH$. More precisely, τ is a mapping from $G_{wh}^{\#}$ to $\{0, 1, \ldots, WH\}$ such that

$\tau(x, y) = i < WH$ if i-th computed interpolation value is stored at (x, y) in $G_{wh}^{\#}$,

$\tau(x, y) = WH$ if no interpolation value is stored at (x, y).

Then, interpolation at (X, Y) is reliable in the sense defined in the previous section if none of the pixels in its associated window keeps interpolated value, that is,

$$\tau(x, y) \geq \sigma(X, Y) \text{ for each } (x, y) \in N_d(p(X, Y)).$$

This condition is referred to as the reliability condition.

Lemma 1. [Local Reliability Condition] *Assuming a row-major raster order for σ and τ, pixel $(X, Y) \in R_{WH}^{\#}$ is unreliable if and only if*

(1) $x_0 + X \cos\theta - Y \sin\theta - d + 1 < X$ *and* $y_0 + X \sin\theta + Y \cos\theta - d < Y$, *or*

(2) $x_0 + X \cos\theta - Y \sin\theta - d + 1 < W$ *and* $y_0 + X \sin\theta + Y \cos\theta - d + 1 < Y$.

By Lemma 1, a pixel (X, Y) is unreliable if and only if

(1) $Y > -\frac{1 - \cos\theta}{\sin\theta} X + \frac{x_0 - d + 1}{\sin\theta}$ and $Y > \frac{\sin\theta}{1 - \cos\theta} X + \frac{y_0 - d}{1 - \cos\theta}$ or

(2) $Y > \frac{\cos\theta}{\sin\theta} X - \frac{W - x_0 + d - 1}{\sin\theta}$ and $Y > \frac{\sin\theta}{1 - \cos\theta} X + \frac{y_0 - d + 1}{1 - \cos\theta}$.

By L_1, L_2, L_3 and L_4 we denote the four lines associated with the unreliability condition above. They are defined by

$$L_1: Y = -\frac{1 - \cos\theta}{\sin\theta} X + \frac{x_0 - d + 1}{\sin\theta}, \quad L_2: Y = \frac{\sin\theta}{1 - \cos\theta} X + \frac{y_0 - d}{1 - \cos\theta},$$
$$L_3: Y = \frac{\cos\theta}{\sin\theta} X - \frac{W - x_0 + d - 1}{\sin\theta}, \quad L_4: Y = \frac{\sin\theta}{1 - \cos\theta} X + \frac{y_0 - d + 1}{1 - \cos\theta}.$$

Then, a pixel (X, Y) is unreliable if and only if the point (X, Y) is above the two lines L_1 and L_2 or above the two lines L_3 and L_4.

Figures 3 (a) and (b) depict the four lines and the region of unreliable pixels bounded by them for each of the row-major and column-major raster orders.

5.6   Lazy Interpolation for $d = 1$

Now we know how to decide if a pixel is reliable or not each in constant time. If each pixel is reliable, we just perform interpolation. Actually, if the bottom margin y_0 is large enough, then the location $s(X, Y)$ keeping interpolation value is far from a point (X, Y) and thus it does not affect interpolation around the point. Of course, if the window size d is large, then interpolations become more frequently unreliable.

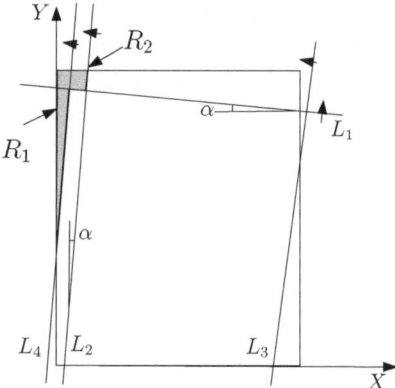

Fig. 3. Regions of unreliable pixels, for row-major raster order

Here is an in-place algorithm for correcting rotation for the case of $d = 1$. A key to the algorithm is the local test on reliability. In the algorithm we scan $R_{WH}^{\#}$ twice. In the first scan, it checks whether (X, Y) is a reliable pixel or not each in constant time. If it is not reliable, we calculate an interpolation value and store it somewhere in $G_{wh}^{\#}$ using a pixel outside the rectangle determining the output image. We call such a region a *refuge*.

In-place algorithm for correcting rotation

Phase 1: For each $(X, Y) \in R_{WH}^{\#}$ check whether a pixel (X, Y) is reliable or not. If it is not, then calculate interpolation there and store the value in the refuge F.

Phase 2: For each $(X, Y) \in R_{WH}^{\#}$ check whether a pixel (X, Y) is reliable or not. If it is not, then update the value at $(X, Y) \in G_{wh}^{\#}$ by the interpolation value stored in the refuge F.

Otherwise calculate interpolation there and store the value at $(X, Y) \in G_{wh}^{\#}$.

The algorithm above works correctly when $d = 1$. The most important is that the total area of refuge available is always greater than the total number of unreliable pixels.

Theorem 1. *The algorithm above correctly computes interpolations for row-major and column-major raster scans with the location function $s(X, Y) = (X, Y)$.*

The above result is based on raster scan, which scans pixels from left to right while going up from the bottom to the top of an image. However, by our experience a rotated raster scan sensitive to rotation angle is more desirable. As an extension or generalization of the raster scan we can consider a *rotated raster scan* in which pixels are enumerated along lines of a given angle. We assume that the angle of those lines is given as a slope a instead of angle and we call the line $y = ax$ the *guide line* for the rotated scan.

We start from the pixel $(0, 0)$. The next pixel or point is either $(0, 1)$ or $(1, 0)$ depending on which is closer to the line $y = ax$ of slope a passing through the origin $(0, 0)$. In this way we output pixels in the increasing order of the vertical distances to the line $y = ax$. Therefore, we can describe the rotated raster scan using a priority queue PQ.

Rotated Raster Scan with Slope a

PQ: priority queue keeping pixels with vertical distances to the line $y = ax$ as keys.
for $x = 0$ to $n - 1$
    Put a pixel $(x, 0)$ into PQ with key $= -ax$.
repeat{
    Extract a pixel (x, y) of the smallest key from PQ.
    Output the pixel (x, y).
    if $(x, y) = (n - 1, n - 1)$ then exit from the loop.
    if $(y < n - 1)$ then put a pixel $(x, y + 1)$ into PQ with key $= y + 1 - ax$.
}

It is easy to see that the algorithm is correct and runs in $O(N \log N)$ time using $O(\sqrt{N})$ working space. Correctness of the algorithm is based on the observation that in each column (of the same x coordinate) pixels are enumerated from bottom to top one at a time. Thus, whenever we output a pixel (x, y), we remove the pixel from the priority queue and insert the pixel just above it, i.e., $(x, y + 1)$ into the priority queue if it is still in the image area G.

A question here is whether we can design a constant-working-space algorithm for rotated scan in a read-only model. Fortunately, the author presented such an algorithm [3]. Surprisingly, it also reduces the time complexity of the algorithm.

Lemma 2. *Given an intensity image consisting of N pixels and a rational slope $a = -q/p$, there is an algorithm for enumerating all pixels in the order determined by the slope which runs in $O(N)$ time using constant extra memory in addition to a read-only memory for the input image.*

It is also shown in the same paper that we can remove the constraint that a given slope must be a rational number. Once we find a rational number approximating the given slope by that of a line passing through two pixels in the given image, we can use that rational number as the slope.

6   Concluding Remarks

We have surveyed recent progress on constant-working-space algorithms especially for image processing. There is a rich source of problems in this direction in image processing and other areas in computer science. The author is currently working on constant-working-space algorithms for geometric problems.

Acknowledgments

This work was partially supported by the Ministry of Education, Science, Sports and Culture, Grant-in-Aid for Scientific Research (B). The author would like to express his sincere thanks to Lilian Buzer, Erik Demaine, Stefan Langerman, Ryuhei Uehara, Mitsuo Motoki, Masashi Kiyomi, and Hiroshi Tanaka for their stimulating discussions.

References

1. Asano, T., Bitou, S., Motoki, M., Usui, N.: In-place algorithm for image rotation. In: Tokuyama, T. (ed.) ISAAC 2007. LNCS, vol. 4835, pp. 704–715. Springer, Heidelberg (2007)
2. Asano, T., Bitou, S., Motoki, M., Usui, N.: Space-efficient algorithm for image rotation. IEICE Transactions on Fundamentals of Electronics, Communications and Computer Sciences (to appear)
3. Asano, T.: Constant-working-space image scan with a given angle. In: Proc. 24th European Workshop on Computational Geometry, pp. 99–102 (March 2008)
4. Asano, T., Tanaka, H.: Constant-working space algorithm for connected components labeling. Technical Report of SIG on Computation, IEICE of Japan (2008)
5. Asano, T., Tanaka, H.: Constant-working-space algorithm for Euclidean distance transform. Technical Report of SIG on Computation, IEICE of Japan (2008)
6. Asano, T., Bose, P., Carmi, P., Maheshwari, A., Shu, C., Smid, M., Wuhrer, S.: Linear-space algorithms for distance preserving embedding. In: Canadian Conference on Computational Geometry, pp. 185–188 (August 2007)
7. Bast, H.: Dimension reduction: A powerful principle for automatically finding concepts in unstructured data. In: Proc. International Workshop on Self-* Properties in Complex Information Systems (SELF-STAR 2004), pp. 113–116 (2004)
8. Bose, P., Maheshwari, A., Morin, P., Morrison, J., Smid, M., Vahrenhold, J.: Space-efficient geometric divide-and-conquer algorithms. Comput. Geom. Theory Appl. 37(3), 209–227 (2007)
9. Breu, H., Gil, J., Kirkpatrick, D., Werman, M.: Linear time Euclidean distance algorithms. IEEE Trans. on Pattern Analysis and Machine Intelligence 17(5), 529–533 (1995)
10. Brönnimann, H., Chan, T.M.: Space-efficient algorithms for computing the convex hull of a simple polygonal line in linear time. 34(2), 75–82 (2006)
11. Bröonnimann, H., Iacono, J., Katajainen, J., Morin, P., Morrison, J., Toussaint, G.T.: Space-efficient planar convex hull algorithms. Theoret. Comput. Sci. 321(1), 25–40 (2004)
12. Chan, T.M.: Faster core-set constructions and data-stream algorithms in fixed dimensions. Comput. Geom. 35(1-2), 20–35 (2006)
13. Chang, F., Chen, C.-J., Lu, C.-J.: A linear-time component-labeling algorithm using contour tracing technique. Comput. Vis. Image Underst. 93(2), 206–220 (2004)
14. Chan, T.M., Chen, E.Y.: Towards in-place geometric algorithms and data structures. In: Proc. 20th Annual ACM Symposium on Computational Geometry, pp. 239–246 (2004)
15. Chen, E.Y., Chan, T.M.: A space-efficient algorithm for segment intersection. In: Proc. 15th Canadian Conference on Computational Geometry, pp. 68–71 (2003)
16. Cox, T., Cox, M.: Multidimensional scaling, 2nd edn. Chapman & Hall CRC, Boca Raton (2001)
17. Dvořak, S., Ďurian, B.: Stable linear time sublinear space merging. The Computer Journal 30(4), 372–375 (1987)

18. Dvořak, S., Ďurian, B.: Unstable linear time O(1) space merging. The Computer Journal 31(3), 279–282 (1988)
19. Frederickson, G.N.: Upper bounds for time-space trade-offs in sorting and selection. Journal of Computer and System Sciences 34, 19–26 (1987)
20. Geffert, V., Katajainen, J., Pasanen, T.: Asymptotically efficient in-place merging. Theoret. Comput. Sci. 237, 159–181 (2000)
21. Hirata, T.: A unified linear-time algorithm for computing distance maps. Information Processing Letters 58(3), 129–133 (1996)
22. Huang, B.-C., Langston, M.A.: Fast stable merging and sorting in constant extra space. The Computer Journal 35(6), 643–650 (1992)
23. Katajainen, J., Pasanen, T.: Stable minimum space partitioning in linear time. BIT 32, 580–585 (1982)
24. Katajainen, J., Pasanen, T.: Sorting multiset stably in minimum space. Acta Informatica 31, 410–421 (1994)
25. Katajainen, J., Pasanen, T., Teuhola, J.: Practical in-place mergesort. Nordic J. Computing 3, 27–40 (1996)
26. Klein, F., Kübler, O.: Euclidean distance transformations and model guided image interpretation. Pattern Recognition Letters 5, 19–20 (1987)
27. Klette, R., Rosenfeld, A.: Digital geometry: Geometric methods for digital picture analysis. Elsevier, Amsterdam (2004)
28. Liang, X., Bishunu, A., Asano, T.: Combinatorial approach to fingerprint binarization and minutiae extraction using Euclidean distance transform. International Journal of Pattern Recognition and Artificial Intelligence 27(7), 1141–1158 (2007)
29. Malgouyresa, R., Moreb, M.: On the computational complexity of reachability in 2D binary images and some basic problems of 2D digital topology. Theoretical Computer Science 283, 67–108 (2002)
30. Miyazawa, M., Zeng, P., Iso, N., Hirata, T.: A systolic algorithm for Euclidean distance transform. Trans. on Pattern Analysis and Machine Intelligence 1(8), 1–26 (2002)
31. Munro, J.I., Raman, V.: Selection from read-only memory and sorting with minimum data movement. Theoretical Computer Science 165, 311–323 (1996)
32. Munro, J.I., Paterson, M.S.: Selection and sorting with limited storage. Theoretical Computer Science 12, 315–323 (1980)
33. Munro, J.I., Raman, V., Salowe, J.S.: Stable in situ sorting and minimum data movement. BIT 30 2, 220–234 (1990)
34. Ohtsu, N.: Discriminant and least squares threshold selection. In: Proc. 4th IJCPR, pp. 592–596 (1978)
35. Paglieroni, D.W.: Distance Transforms. Computer Vision, Graphics and Image Processing: Graphical Models and Image Processing 54, 56–74 (1992)
36. Rosenfeld, A., Pfaltz, J.L.: Sequential operations in digital picture processing. J. ACM 13, 471–494 (1966)
37. Raman, V., Ramnath, S.: Improved upper bounds for time-space tradeoffs for selection with limited storage. Nordic J. of Computing 6(2), 162–180 (1999)
38. Reingold, O.: Undirected st-connectivity in log-space. In: Proc. ACM Symp. on Theory of Computing, pp. 376–385 (2005)
39. Ronse, C., Devijver, P.A.: Connected components in binary images: The detection problem. Wiley, New York (1984)
40. Rosenfeld, A., Kak, A.C.: Digital picture processing, 2nd edn. Academic Press, New York (1978)
41. Suzuki, K., Horiba, I., Sugie, N.: Linear-time connected-component labeling based on sequential local operations. Comput. Vis. Image Underst. 89(1), 1–23 (2003)

Sparse Multiscale Patches
for Image Processing

Paolo Piro, Sandrine Anthoine, Eric Debreuve, and Michel Barlaud

Université de Nice Sophia-Antipolis / CNRS, Sophia-Antipolis, France

Abstract. This paper presents a framework to define an objective measure of the similarity (or dissimilarity) between two images for image processing. The problem is twofold: 1) define a set of features that capture the information contained in the image relevant for the given task and 2) define a similarity measure in this feature space.

In this paper, we propose a feature space as well as a statistical measure on this space. Our feature space is based on a global descriptor of the image in a multiscale transformed domain. After decomposition into a Laplacian pyramid, the coefficients are arranged in intrascale/interscale/interchannel patches which reflect the dependencies between neighboring coefficients in presence of specific structures or textures. At each scale, the probability density function (pdf) of these patches is used as a descriptor of the relevant information. Because of the sparsity of the multiscale transform, the most significant patches, called *Sparse Multiscale Patches (SMP)*, characterize efficiently these pdfs. We propose a statistical measure (the Kullback-Leibler divergence) based on the comparison of these probability density functions. Interestingly, this measure is estimated via the nonparametric, k-th nearest neighbor framework without explicitly building the pdfs.

This framework is applied to a query-by-example image retrieval task. Experiments on two publicly available databases showed the potential of our *SMP* approach. In particular, it performed comparably to a *SIFT*-based retrieval method and two versions of a fuzzy segmentation-based method (the *UFM* and *CLUE* methods), and it exhibited some robustness to different geometric and radiometric deformations of the images.

Keywords: multiscale transform, sparsity, patches, Kullback-Leibler divergence, k-th nearest neighbor.

1 Introduction

1.1 Similarity in Image Processing

Defining an objective measure of the similarity (or dissimilarity) between two images (or parts of them) is a recurrent question in image processing that is dealt with in quite different ways. When dealing with inverse problems such as denoising or deconvolution of images, a similarity measure is needed to evaluate how well the estimate explains the observations. However, for these problems,

F. Nielsen (Ed.): ETVC 2008, LNCS 5416, pp. 284–304, 2009.

efforts have been concentrated in the conditioning of the inverse operator as well as the spatial properties of the estimated images. The measure of fitness to the data has been less studied and is usually a simple euclidean norm in pixel space such as: $d(I_1, I_2) = \sqrt{\sum_{i \in \{pixel\}} |I_1(i) - I_2(i)|^2}$. At the other end of the spectrum, for some applications, the similarity measure is at the core of the problem and has received much more attention. This is the case for applications such as tracking or image retrieval, where the task is to rank the images of a database according to their visual similarity to the given query image. In any case, defining a similarity measure is a two steps process:

1. Define a set of properties that capture the information contained in the image relevant for the given task. This step defines the so-called feature space.
2. Define a similarity measure in the feature space. This measure is often (but not always) a distance.

Number of possibilities have been explored for the feature space itself. Some spaces involve a transform domain (e.g. wavelet transforms), some are based on various descriptors. A variety of descriptors (see [1] for a review) has been proposed in the literature. Local descriptors (e.g. salient points [2]) are based on a subset of the pixels of the image while global descriptors give information about the image as a whole (e.g. color histograms [3]). Local descriptors exploit the information given by a limited of number of points of interest together with their spatial neighborhood. Hence much information in the image is not used in these methods (see [4] for an extensive comparison and performance evaluation of most local descriptors). On the contrary, global descriptors include information of the whole image (e.g. histograms of intensity values). Global descriptors may be defined at the pixel level (e.g. color histograms [3]) and include no notion of spatial correlation or at the patch level including spatial and/or scale correlations. The concept of global patch descriptors is supported by statistical studies on images [5]. Here, we propose a new descriptor of this kind.

The similarity measure can range from simple euclidean norm to more sophisticated measures: robust estimators have been used for optical flow [6,7], Bhattacharya's distance for tracking [8], entropic measure such as entropy, Kullback-Leibler divergence or mutual information for registration [9,10]. A general requirement for the similarity measure is the visual relevance, i.e. a strong correlation with human perception of similarity itself. Research in vision science has already brought some perspectives on how to do so [11]. Nevertheless, designing systems purely based on the perceptual characteristics of the human visual system is a difficult task. Therefore, once meaningful features have been selected, we prefer to employ metrics that have a mathematical foundation and can be easily implemented. For this purpose, several distance metrics have been used to compare feature vectors for various tasks of image processing. The authors of [12] give a variety of such measures and empirically show how the selection of a metric affects the performances of a retrieval system.

In this paper we propose a feature space as well as a statistical measure on this space. Our feature space is based on a global descriptor in a transformed domain that we call *Sparse Multiscale Patches*. The measure we propose on this space is statistical: it compares the probability density function (pdf) of these patches.

1.2 Proposed Feature Space and Measure

We propose a new descriptor based on *Sparse Multiscale Patches*. In short, we integrate using probability distributions the local information brought by the *SMP*. The key aspects of these descriptors are the following:

- A *multiscale* representation of the images;
- Inter/intrascale patches that describe locally the structure of the image at a given scale;
- A *sparse* repartition: most of the energy is concentrated in a few patches.

Note that the occurrence in different parts of an image of similar patches of spatially neighboring pixels has been exploited in image processing [13,14,15]. Here the concept is used for multiscale coefficients as proposed in [16].

The visual content of images is represented by patches of multiresolution coefficients. The extracted feature vectors are viewed as samples from an unknown multidimensional distribution. The multiscale transform of an image being sparse, a reduced number of patches yields a good characterization of the distribution. We estimate the similarity between images by a pseudo-distance (or measure) between these multidimensional probability density functions.

We propose to use the Kullback-Leibler (KL) divergence as a similarity measure that quantifies the closeness between two probability density functions. Such measure has already shown good performances in the context of image retrieval [12]. It has already been used for the simple case of parametrized marginal distributions of wavelet coefficients [17,18], assuming independence of the coefficients. In contrast, we define multidimensional feature vectors (patches), that capture interscale and intrascale dependencies among subband coefficients. These are better adapted to the description of local image structures and texture. In addition, for color images, we take into account the dependencies among the three color channels; hence patches of coefficients are also interchannel. This approach implies to estimate distributions in a high-dimensional statistical space, where fixed size kernel options to estimate distributions or divergences fail. Alternatively, we propose to estimate the KL divergence directly from the samples by using the k-th nearest neighbor (kNN) approach, *i.e.* adapting to the local sample density.

1.3 Organization of the Paper

This paper is organized as follows. In Section 2, we define our feature space which consists of inter/intrascale and interchannel patches of Laplacian pyramid coefficients for color images, called *Sparse Multiscale Patches*. We then define the global similarity on this feature space in Section 3 by combining similarities between the probability density functions of these patches at different scales. The comparison between pdfs is measured by the KL divergence. We also explain how to estimate this quantity. Finally, in the last section we illustrate the use of the proposed measure in a particular application: image retrieval.

2   Feature Space: Sparse Multiscale Patches

Throughout this paper, we will denote the input image by I, the scale of the multiresolution decomposition by j, and the location in the 2D image space by k.

2.1   Multiscale Coefficients: Strengths and Limits

The wavelet transform enjoys several properties that have made it quite successful in signal processing and that are relevant for the definition of similarity between images. Indeed, it provides a sparse representation of images, meaning that it concentrates the informational content of an image into few coefficients of large amplitude while the rest of the coefficients are small. This combined with a fast transform is what makes wavelet thresholding methods so powerful: in fact just identifying large coefficients is sufficient to extract where the information lies in the image. For example, denoising can be done very efficiently by simply thresholding wavelet coefficients as proved in [19]. Such simple coefficient-wise treatments provide results of excellent quality at a reduced computational cost.

In fact, these classical wavelet methods treat each coefficient separately, relying on the fact that they are decorrelated. However, the wavelet coefficients are not independent and these dependencies are the signature of structures present in the image. For example, a discontinuity between smooth regions at point k_0 will give large coefficients at this point at all scales j ($w(\mathrm{I})_{j,k_0}$ large for all j). Classical methods using coefficient-wise treatments may destroy these dependencies between coefficients and hence alter the local structure of images. Therefore models using the dependencies between coefficients have been proposed and used in image enhancement (e.g. [16,20]). In particular, the authors of [16] introduced the concept of patches of wavelet coefficients (which they called "neighborhoods of wavelet coefficient") to represent efficiently fine spatial structures in images.

2.2   Multiscale Patches for Color Images

Following these ideas, we define a feature space based on a sparse descriptor of the image content by a multiresolution decomposition. More precisely, we group the Laplacian pyramid coefficients of the three color channels of the image I into coherent sets called patches. Here the coherence is sought by grouping coefficients linked to a particular scale j and location k in the image.

In fact, the most significant dependencies are seen between a coefficient $w(\mathrm{I})_{j,k}$ and its closest neighbors in space: $w(\mathrm{I})_{j,k\pm(0,1)}, w(\mathrm{I})_{j,k\pm(1,0)}$ and in scale: $w(\mathrm{I})_{j-1,k}$, where $j-1$ represents the scale a step coarser than the scale j. Grouping the closest neighbors in scale and space of the coefficient $w(\mathrm{I})_{j,k}$ in a vector, we obtain the patch $\vec{w}(\mathrm{I})_{j,k}$ (see Fig. 1):

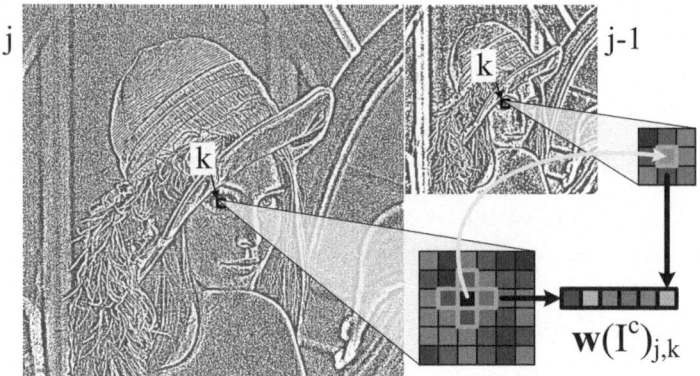

Fig. 1. Building a patch of multiscale coefficients, for a single color channel image

$$\vec{w}(\mathrm{I})_{j,k} = \big(w(\mathrm{I})_{j,k}, w(\mathrm{I})_{j,k\pm(1,0)}, w(\mathrm{I})_{j,k\pm(0,1)}, w(\mathrm{I})_{j-1,k}\big) \qquad (1)$$

which describes the structure of the grayscale image I at scale j and location k. The probability density functions of such patches at each scale j have proved to characterize fine spatial structures in grayscale images [16,21]. Such patches are therefore relevant features for our problem as will be seen in Section 4.3.

We consider color images in the luminance/chrominance space: $\mathrm{I} = (\mathrm{I}^Y, \mathrm{I}^U, \mathrm{I}^V)$. Since the coefficients are correlated through channels, we aggregate in the patch the coefficients of the three channels:

$$\mathbf{w}(\mathrm{I})_{j,k} = \big(\vec{w}(\mathrm{I}^Y)_{j,k}, \vec{w}(\mathrm{I}^U)_{j,k}, \vec{w}(\mathrm{I}^V)_{j,k}\big) \qquad (2)$$

with $\vec{w}(\mathrm{I}^Y)_{j,k}$, $\vec{w}(\mathrm{I}^U)_{j,k}$ and $\vec{w}(\mathrm{I}^V)_{j,k}$ given by Eq.(1).

The low-frequency approximation that results from the Laplacian pyramid is also used to build additional feature vectors. Namely, 3×3 pixel neighborhoods along all three channels are joined together to form patches of dimension 27 (whereas patches from the higher-frequency subbands are of dimension 18, as defined in Eq.(2)). The union of the higher-frequency and low-frequency patches forms our feature space. The patches of this augmented feature space will be denoted by $\mathbf{w}(\mathrm{I})_{j,k}$.

2.3   Multiscale Transform

The coefficients are obtained by a Laplacian pyramid decomposition [22]. Indeed, critically sampled tensor wavelet transforms lack rotation and translation invariance and so would the patches made of such coefficients. Hence we prefer to use the Laplacian pyramid which shares the sparsity and inter/intrascale dependency properties with the wavelet transform while being more robust to rotations. Moreover, the Laplacian pyramid is at the basis of the SVC standard and thus our approach will be compatible with SVC.

Most significant patches ([1/8 1/8 1/8])

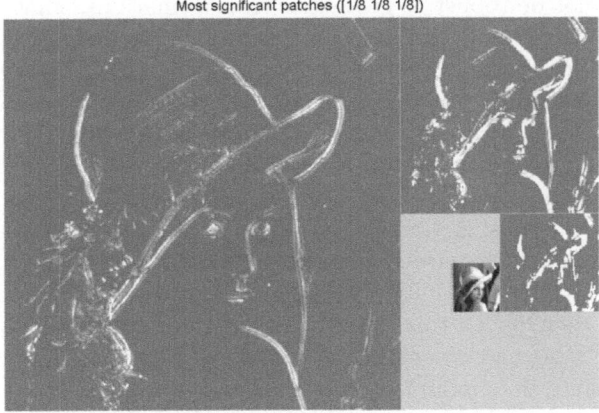

Fig. 2. White indicates the location of patches of largest energy (1/8 of the patches is selected for each subband)

2.4 Sparsity of the Multiscale Patches

As we have seen earlier, multiscale coefficients provide a sparse representation of images by concentrating the information into a few coefficients of large amplitude and this sparsity is exploited on the raw coefficients in thresholding methods. As illustrated in Fig. 2, our experiments show that the patches of multiscale coefficients of large overall energy (sum of the square of all coefficients in a patch) also concentrate the information. Since the total number of patches in an image decomposition is $4/3N$ with N the number of pixels in the image, the number of samples we have in the feature space is quite large as far as measuring a similarity is concerned. The possibility of selecting a small number of patches which represent the whole set well is therefore highly desirable. In practice, we selected a fixed proportion of patches at each scale of the decomposition and proved that the resulting similarity measure (defined in section 3) remains consistent (see [23] for details). This is exploited to speed up our computations.

Note that other selecting procedures may be investigated such as using the energy of the central coefficient, using the sum of absolute differences in the patches or thresholding based on the variance of the patches.

Let us now explain how we define a similarity in this feature space.

3   Similarity Measure

3.1   Definition

Our goal is to define a similarity measure between two images I_1 and I_2 from their feature set i.e. from their respective set of patches $\{\mathbf{w}(I_1)_{j,k}\}_{j,k}$ and $\{\mathbf{w}(I_2)_{j,k}\}_{j,k}$. When images are clearly similar (e.g. different views of the same scene, images containing similar objects...), their patches $\mathbf{w}(I_1)_{j_l,k_l}$ and $\mathbf{w}(I_2)_{j_l,k_l}$ do not necessarily correspond. Hence a measure comparing geometrically corresponding patches would not be robust to geometric transformations. Thus, we propose to compare the pdfs of these patches. Specifically, for an image I, we consider for each scale j the pdf $p_j(\mathrm{I})$ of the set of patches $\{\mathbf{w}(\mathrm{I})_{j,k}\}_k$.

To compare two pdfs, we place ourselves in the framework of Bregman divergences, which allows to generate a class of pseudo-metrics that generalize the classical squared Euclidean distance. These divergences do not necessarily satisfy the triangle inequality nor are symmetric (they are not metrics) but share similar properties. A Bregman divergence is derived from a convex function. For example, the square Euclidean distance stems from the square function $f(x) = x^2$, while the Kullback-Leibler divergence derives from the function $f(x) = x \log x$ [24,25]. In this paper, we use the Kullback-Leibler divergence because it is a Bregman divergence that derives from the Shannon differential entropy (quantifies the amount of information in a random variable through its pdf). The Kullback-Leibler divergence (D_{kl}) is the following quantity [12]:

$$D_{kl}(p_1\|p_2) = \int p_1 \log(p_1/p_2), \tag{3}$$

This divergence has been successfully used for other applications in image processing in the pixel domain   [26,15], as well as for evaluating the similarity between images using the marginal pdf of the wavelet coefficients [17,18]. In this paper, we propose to measure the similarity $S(\mathrm{I}_1, \mathrm{I}_2)$ between two images I_1 and I_2 by summing over scales the divergences between the pdfs $p_j(\mathrm{I}_1)$ and $p_j(\mathrm{I}_2)$:

$$S(\mathrm{I}_1, \mathrm{I}_2) = \sum_j \alpha_j D_{kl}(p_j(\mathrm{I}_1)\|p_j(\mathrm{I}_2)) \tag{4}$$

where α_j is a positive weight that may normalize the contribution of the different scales.

3.2   Limits of the Parametric Approaches to the Estimation

The estimation of the similarity measure S consists of the evaluation of divergences between pdfs $p_j(\mathrm{I}_i)$ of high dimension. This raises two problems. Firstly, estimating the KL divergence, even with a good estimate of the pdfs, is hard because this is an integral in high dimension involving unstable logarithm terms. Secondly, the accurate estimation of a pdf itself is difficult due to the lack of samples in high dimension (curse of dimensionality). The two problems should be embraced together to avoid cumulating both kinds of errors.

A first idea consists in parametrizing the shape of the pdf. The marginal pdf of multiscale coefficients is well modeled by generalized Gaussians. In this case, the KL divergence is an analytic function of the pdf parameters. This technique has been used in [17,18] to compare images on the basis of the marginal pdf of their wavelet coefficients. To our knowledge, the generalized Gaussian model cannot be extended to account for correlations in higher dimension. Mixture of Gaussians on the other hand are efficient multidimensional models accounting for correlations that fit well the pdf of wavelet coefficients patches [21]. However the KL divergence is not an analytic function of the model parameters.

Thus, we propose to make no hypothesis on the pdf at hand. We therefore spare the cost of fitting model parameters but we have to estimate the divergences in this non-parametric context. Conceptually, we combine the Ahmad-Lin approximation of the entropies necessary to compute the divergences with "balloon estimates" of the pdfs using the kNN approach.

3.3 Non-parametric Estimation of the Similarity Measure

The KL divergence can be written as the difference between a cross-entropy H_x and an entropy H (see Eq.(3)):

$$H_x(p_1, p_2) = -\int p_1 \log p_2, \qquad H(p_1) = -\int p_1 \log p_1. \qquad (5)$$

Let us explain how to estimate these terms from an i.i.d sample set $\mathcal{W}^1 = \{\mathbf{w}_1^1, \mathbf{w}_2^1, .., \mathbf{w}_{N_1}^1\}$ of p_1 and an i.i.d sample set $\mathcal{W}^2 = \{\mathbf{w}_1^2, \mathbf{w}_2^2, .., \mathbf{w}_{N_2}^2\}$ of p_2. (The samples are in $\mathbb{R}^d$.)

Assuming we have estimates $\widehat{p_1}$, $\widehat{p_2}$ of the pdfs p_1, p_2, we use the Ahmad-Lin entropy estimators [27]:

$$H_x^{al}(\widehat{p_1}, \widehat{p_2}) = -\tfrac{1}{N_1} \sum_{n=1}^{N_1} \log[\widehat{p_2}(\mathbf{w}_n^1)], \qquad H^{al}(\widehat{p_1}) = -\tfrac{1}{N_1} \sum_{n=1}^{N_1} \log[\widehat{p_1}(\mathbf{w}_n^1)]. \qquad (6)$$

General non-parametric pdf estimators from samples can be written as a sum of kernels K with (possibly varying) bandwidth h (see [28] for a review):

$$\widehat{p_1}(x) = \tfrac{1}{N_1} \sum_{n=1}^{N_1} K_{h(\mathcal{W}^1, x)}(x - \mathbf{w}_n^1). \qquad (7)$$

- Parzen estimators $h(\mathcal{W}^1, x) = h$: the bandwidth is constant. They perform very well with samples in one dimension but become unadapted in high dimension due to the sparsity of the samples: the trade-off between a bandwidth large enough to perform well in low local sample density (which may *oversmooth* the estimator) and a bandwidth small enough to preserve local statistical variability (which may result in an unstable estimator) cannot always be achieved. To cope with this problem, kernel estimators using adaptive bandwidth have been proposed;

- Sample point estimators $h(\mathcal{W}^1, x) = h_{\mathcal{W}^1}(\mathbf{w}_i^1), i \in \{1, N_1\}$: the bandwidth adapts to each sample $\mathbf{w}_i^1$ given the sample set $\mathcal{W}^1$;

- Balloon estimators $h(\mathcal{W}^1, x) = h_{\mathcal{W}^1}(x)$: the bandwidth adapts to the point of estimation x given the sample set $\mathcal{W}^1$.

We use a balloon estimator with a binary kernel and a bandwidth computed in the k-th nearest neighbor (kNN) framework [28]. This is a dual approach to the fixed size kernel methods and was firstly proposed in [29]: the bandwidth adapts to the local sample density by letting the kernel contain exactly k neighbors of x among a given sample set:

$$K_{h_{\mathcal{W}}(x)}(x - \mathbf{w}_n) = \frac{1}{v_d\, \rho_{k,\mathcal{W}}^d(x)}\, \delta\Big[||x - \mathbf{w}_n|| < \rho_{k,\mathcal{W}}(x)\Big] \qquad (8)$$

with v_d the volume of the unit sphere in $\mathbb{R}^d$ and $\rho_{k,\mathcal{W}}(x)$ the distance of x to its k-th nearest neighbor in $\mathcal{W}$. Although this is a biased pdf estimator (it does not integrate to one), it has proved to be efficient for high-dimensional data [28]. Plugging Eq.(8) in Eq.(6), we obtain the following estimators of the (cross-)entropy:

$$H^{\mathrm{knn}}(\widehat{p_1}) = \log[N_1\, v_d] - \log(k) + \frac{d}{N_1} \sum_{n=1}^{N_1} \big(\log[\rho_{k,\mathcal{W}^1}(\mathbf{w}_n^1)]\big), \qquad (9)$$

$$H_x^{\mathrm{knn}}(\widehat{p_1}, \widehat{p_2}) = \log[N_2\, v_d] - \log(k) + \frac{d}{N_1} \sum_{n=1}^{N_1} \big(\log[\rho_{k,\mathcal{W}^2}(\mathbf{w}_n^1)]\big). \qquad (10)$$

As previously stated, these estimates are biased. A correction of the bias has been derived in [30] in a different context. In the non-biased estimators of the (cross)-entropy the digamma function $\psi(k)$ replaces the $\log(k)$ term:

$$H^{\mathrm{knn}}(\widehat{p_1}) = \log[(N_1-1)v_d] - \psi(k) + \frac{d}{N_1} \sum_{n=1}^{N_1} \big(\log[\rho_{k,\mathcal{W}^1}(\mathbf{w}_n^1)]\big), \qquad (11)$$

$$H_x^{\mathrm{knn}}(\widehat{p_1}, \widehat{p_2}) = \log[N_2\, v_d] - \psi(k) + \frac{d}{N_1} \sum_{n=1}^{N_1} \big(\log[\rho_{k,\mathcal{W}^2}(\mathbf{w}_n^1)]\big). \qquad (12)$$

And hence the KL divergence reads:

$$D_{kl}(p_1||p_2) = \log\Big[\tfrac{N_2}{N_1-1}\Big] + \tfrac{d}{N_1} \sum_{n=1}^{N_1} \log[\rho_{k,\mathcal{W}^2}(\mathbf{w}_n^1)] - \tfrac{d}{N_1} \sum_{n=1}^{N_1} \log[\rho_{k,\mathcal{W}^1}(\mathbf{w}_n^1)]. \quad (13)$$

This estimator is valid in any dimension d and robust to the choice of k.

4   Application: Image Retrieval

4.1   Content-Based Image Retrieval

With the rapid growing of general-purpose image collections, performing efficiently a search on such large datasets becomes a more and more critical task. Content-based image retrieval (CBIR) systems tackle this task by analyzing the content of images in order to provide meaningful signatures of them. Automatic search of the target images is made possible by defining a similarity measure on the underlying signature space which has a reduced dimension. As a result, content based image retrieval mainly relies on describing the image content in a relevant way (the feature space) and defining a quantitative measure on this space (the similarity measure): the retrieval task is then accomplished by ranking images in increasing order of the pseudo-distance between their feature vector and the one of a given query image.

As seen in the introduction, a variety of descriptors and similarity measures have been proposed.In this paper, we will compare our *SMP* approach to three different approaches to image retrieval, two of which share the same similarity measure. The first approach is based on *SIFT* descriptors [31], which are considered state-of-the-art amongst local descriptors. Salient points are extracted by detecting the highest coefficients in the wavelet transform of the image and *SIFT* features are then represented by histograms of the gradient orientation in regions of interest. Matching the *SIFT* features obtained in two images allows then to quantify their similarity. The other methods to which we compared ours use a segmentation-based fuzzy logic approach called *UFM* for *Unified Feature Matching* [32]. The descriptors are fuzzy features (called fuzzy sets) reflecting the color, texture, and shape of each segmented region. The *UFM* measure then integrates the fuzzy properties of all the regions to quantify the similarity between two images. Using this measure, the authors proposed two image retrieval algorithms. The first one is a strictly content-based approach (similarly to ours): it consists in ranking the database images based solely on their *UFM* distance to the query. We refer to it as the *UFM* approach. The retrieval accuracy is improved by a second method called *CLUE* : the *UFM* distances between target images themselves are used to obtain a clustering of the data from which the ranking is obtained. Consequently, this method involves additional information compared to strict content-based systems such as our approach.

4.2   Database and Parameter Settings

Databases

Numerical experiments were performed on two different databases. The first one contains small categories and allows to evaluate specific performances of a retrieval system such as its robustness to deformations; while the second database, with larger categories, allows to test global retrieval performances.

One of these databases contains 1,000 images of the Nister Recognition Benchmark collection [33]. The images of size 640x480 pixels are grouped by sets of four images showing the same scene or object. Their content is quite various, from indoor scenes with a single object to outdoor scenes. Images belonging to the same group are related by geometric deformations (rotation, translation, zoom and perspective) as well as radiometric deformations (changes of brightness and contrast). The ground-truth for any query image is clear: exactly the three other images of the same group are relevant.

The *SMP* retrieval method was also tested on a general-purpose image database from COREL that has been widely used for CBIR evaluation purposes. In particular, results presented in [34] can be considered as a reference. We used the same subset of the COREL database as in [34]. It includes 1,000 images of size 384 × 256 or 256 × 384 which are classified in 10 semantic categories (*Africa, Beach, Buildings, Buses, Dinosaurs, Flowers, Elephants, Horses, Food, Mountains*). In some categories, the visual similarity between two given images is not always obvious since the grouping has been made in a semantic sense (e.g. category "Africa").

Parameter settings

To build the patches as defined in section 2.2, the Laplacian pyramid was computed for each channel of the image (in the YUV color space) with a 5-point binomial filter $w_5 = [1\ 4\ 6\ 4\ 1]/16$, which is a computationally efficient approximation of the Gaussian filter classically used to build Laplacian pyramids. Three high-frequency subbands plus the low-frequency approximation were used.

In the following experiments, 1/64 (resp. 1/32, 1/16 and all) of the patches were selected in the first high-frequency (resp. second, third and low-frequency) subband to describe an image (see Section 2.4). At each scale, the KL divergence was estimated in the kNN framework, with $k = 10$. The contributions to the similarity measure from the divergences of all subbands were equally weighted ($\alpha_j = 1$ in Eq.(4)).

Note that the use of the Jensen-Shannon divergence, which is a symmetrized version of the KL divergence, has also been studied. We found that the performances of this symmetric measure are lower than with the KL divergence, and so until further understanding of this phenomenon, we report here only the results with the KL divergence.

4.3   Numerical Experiments

This section presents an experimental analysis of the *SMP* method; the patch-based retrieval algorithm is evaluated in terms of its ability to retrieve similar images in a query-by-example context. Images belonging to the Nister database were used to evaluate the robustness of the method to different geometric transformations. A set of artificially-degraded images of this database was also used to evaluate the retrieval performances with respect to radiometric deformations (JPEG2000 compression noise). The global retrieval performances on the Nister database were evaluated by ROC (Receiver Operating Characteristic) curves and our method was compared to a reference *SIFT*-based retrieval algorithm. For the COREL database, the global retrieval performances were evaluated by precision curves and our method was compared with the fuzzy, segmentation-based *UFM* approach. Note that for all the following experiments, the given distance between images is S (Eq. (4)), hence the smaller the given distance is the more similar the two considered images are.

Robustness to geometric deformations

The robustness of a retrieval system to geometric deformations is its ability to find relevant images in spite of some transformations of the query, such as

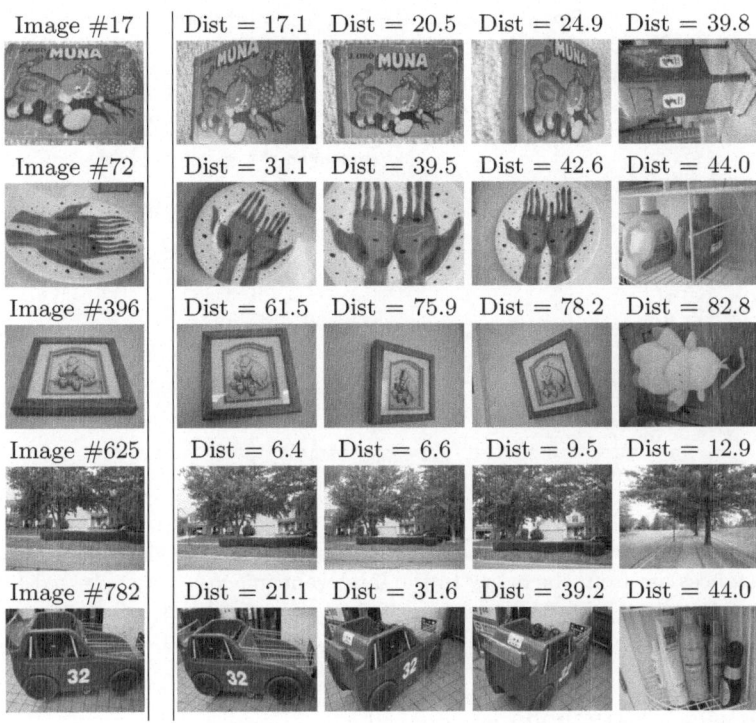

Fig. 3. Retrieval results for 5 images of the Nister database. For each row, left to right: query image; first 4 ranked images of the database (excluding the query). For each retrieved image, the distance to the query is also shown (smaller distances meaning more similar).

changes of viewpoint, rotations, zoom. This is an important requirement in image retrieval, e.g. for finding a given object in different images independently of the viewpoint. Because of its structure, the Nister database allows to evaluate the robustness of the proposed method to geometric deformations. Indeed, the database is composed of groups of four images containing the same object or scene under different viewpoints and/or lightening conditions.

Examples of retrieval for five query images taken from the database are presented in Fig. 3. In this figure, each row displays the retrieval result for the query image shown in the leftmost column. From the second column on, one can see the first 4 retrieved images ranked in increasing order of their distance to the query. Hence the second leftmost image is the most similar one, excluding the query image which is always ranked first with a distance of zero. The first retrieved images are generally relevant for the query, in spite of rotations (row 2), changes of viewpoint (rows 1, 3, 5) and zooms (rows 2, 4). This shows that the proposed descriptors and similarity measure are robust in terms of geometric deformations for the retrieval problem.

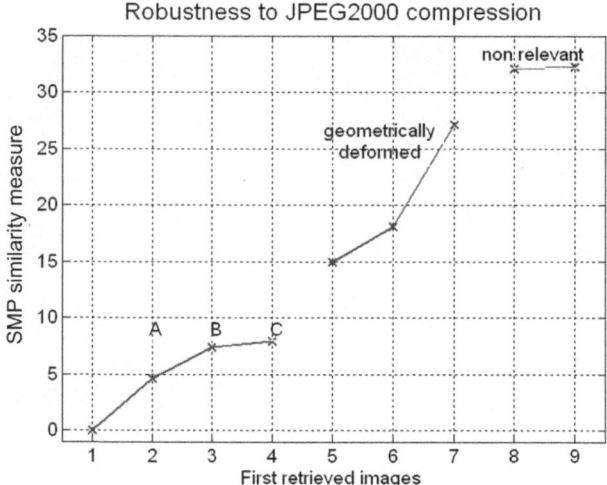

Fig. 4. Evaluation of the robustness to JPEG compression for one query image. Displayed distances are from the query to the 6 relevant images - 3 compressed (A, B, C) and 3 geometrically transformed versions of the query - and to the first 2 non-relevant images. PSNR of the compressed versions: A: 31.8dB, B: 29.7dB and C: 29.3dB.

Robustness to JPEG2000 compression

Another important requirement for content-based retrieval systems is the robustness to radiometric deformations. Transmission on heterogeneous networks requires compression. This process induces a loss of quality that can be significant especially in critical transmission conditions. A retrieval system is expected to be robust to compression quality. To test the proposed method on this specific point, groups of images from the Nister database were expanded. Namely, three highly-compressed versions of one image were added to each group. They were obtained by setting three different quality levels of JPEG2000 compression.

Queries were launched on this dataset with both original and compressed images. An example of the results is shown in Fig. 4, where a non-compressed image is used as a query. The distance from the three compressed versions to the query image being quite small, the system ranked them first and before any geometrically deformed version of the query. This behavior is general and still holds when compressed images are used as queries, confirming the reliability of the proposed similarity measure in terms of its robustness to compression. Moreover, the distance to the query increases as the compression level increases. This is shown in Fig. 4, where images A, B, C are compressed versions of the query image in decreasing order of quality, the PSNR being respectively of 31.8, 29.7 and 29.3 dB.

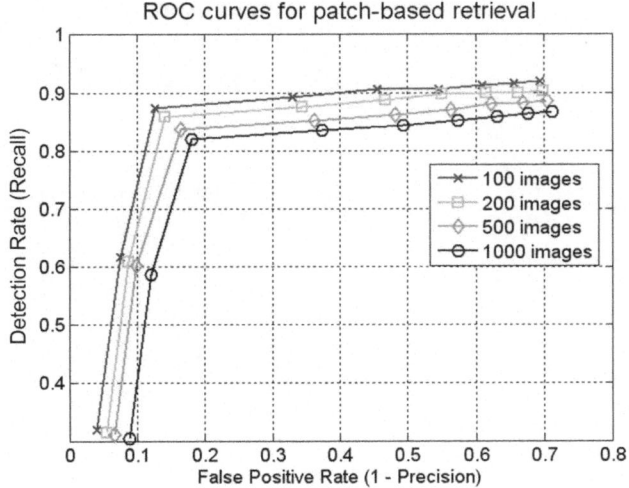

Fig. 5. Retrieval performance of the *SMP* method for different subset sizes of the Nister database; the ROC curves were obtained for cut-off values ranging from 1 to 9

Image retrieval performances (I): ROC curves and comparison with a *SIFT*-based method

The overall performances of the *SMP* retrieval method were evaluated by analyzing retrieval results on the Nister dataset; namely, each of the 1,000 images was used as a query and the similarity measure to all other images was computed. The same experiment was conducted by using a state-of-the-art retrieval method based on (local) *SIFT* descriptors [35]. For this method, the similarity measure is defined as the number of points of interest that can be matched between two images. The results of both methods were quantitatively compared by means of ROC curves. These are *recall* versus $1 - precision$ curves[1] averaged over all queries. The larger the precision and recall values, the better the retrieval performances (this corresponds to the top left side of the plot of an ROC curve).

The results of our *SMP* retrieval method are shown in Fig. 5 for different subset sizes of the database. Namely, average results on the first 100, 200 or 500 images are compared to those on the whole dataset (1000 images). Although the probability of retrieval errors increases with the size of the database, global performance is still satisfactory for a larger dataset. In any case, the best trade-off between precision and recall was reached when we retrieved three images, i.e. when the cut-off value matches exactly the number of relevant images; as a result, there is a high probability that the retrieved images are all and only the relevant ones.

---

[1] *Recall* or *positive rate* $= \frac{D}{R}$,   *1-precision* or *false positive rate* $= 1 - \frac{D}{C}$, with $R=\#\{relevant\ images\ for\ a\ given\ query\}$, $C=\#\{desired\ number\ of\ retrieved\ images\}$ or *cut-off*, $D=\#\{correctly\ detected\ images\}$.

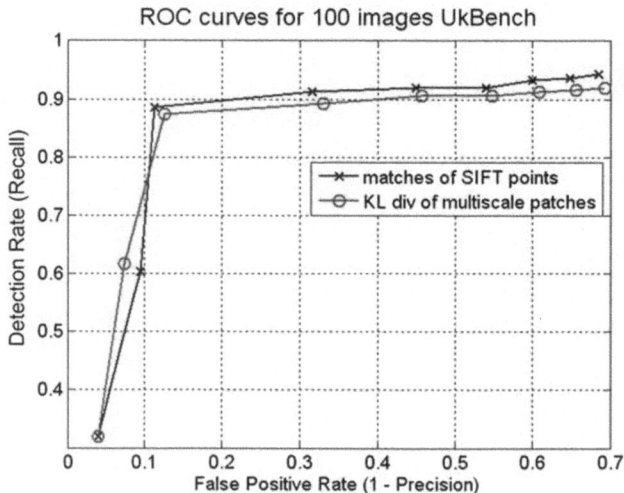

Fig. 6. Comparison of the retrieval performances of the *SMP* approach and the *SIFT*-based algorithm; the ROC curves were obtained for cut-off values going from 1 to 9

Finally, the results for our *SMP* and the *SIFT*-based approach are shown in Fig. 6. The latter were obtained by running a publicly available Matlab implementation of the *SIFT* algorithm [35]. Because of the long processing time of the SIFT implementation (4.8 s on average for each comparison between two images), performing a query with each image of the database could not be done in a reasonable time. In consequence, a comparison was made by querying a subset of 100 images. In light of the ROC curves, the performances of our *SMP* method and the *SIFT*-based algorithm are comparable for this experiment.

Image retrieval performances (II): precision curve and comparison with the *UFM* method

The *SMP* retrieval method was also tested on a subset of the COREL database and compared to the *UFM* and *CLUE* methods [34]. This database is made of a small number of categories (10) containing a large number of images per category (100). Hence, ROC curves are not adapted to evaluate the global performances of a retrieval system in this case. Instead, we used the *Average Precision* to evaluate the retrieval performances for each category (the precision values for a cut-off equal to 100 were averaged over all images of the category) as in [34].

Examples of our retrieval results are shown in Fig. 7 and the *Average Precision* is given for each category in Fig. 8 (dark blue bars). The results of the *UFM* and *CLUE* approaches are also displayed in this latter figure for comparison. Fig. 7 illustrates the fact that the most of time, the first four retrieved images belong to the query's category (row 1, 4, and 5). This figure also illustrates well the difficulties encountered in this task: since the categories are quite large and diverse, images belonging to different categories may have very similar visual properties

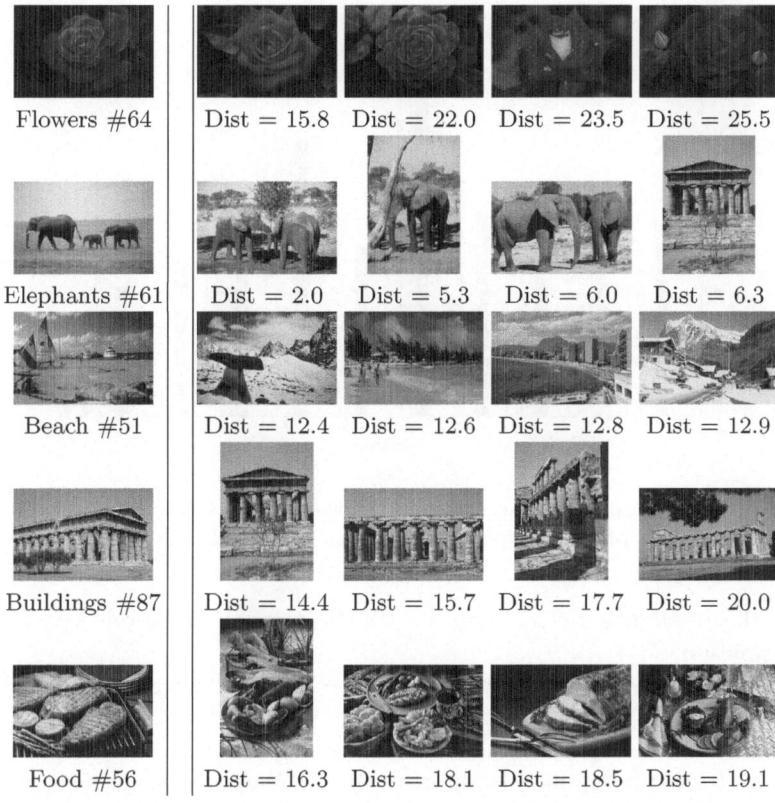

Fig. 7. Retrieval results for 5 images of the COREL database. For each row, left to right: query image; first 4 ranked images of the database (excluding the query image). For each retrieved image, the *SMP* similarity measure to the query is also shown.

that are picked by our method. For example, the elephant and building (row 2 of Fig. 7) have dominating vertical structures and same dominant colors. Likewise, images belonging the "mountains" or "beaches" are freqently mismatched (row 3 of Fig. 7). These retrieval errors are common to all methods comparing images solely on the basis of the image content (i.e. introducing no semantics) and explain the fluctuation of the results displayed in Fig. 8 for all three methods. Our method compares well with the two established methods displayed here: it is more accurate than *UFM* (gray bars) for six categories out of ten; the accuracy is also better than or comparable to *CLUE* (white bars) for five categories out of ten. On average, our method performs better than the *UFM* approach and slightly less well than the *CLUE* one. As pointed out in Section 4.1, the *SMP* and *UFM* approaches are strictly content-based approaches. The *CLUE* method, while performing better, uses additional image distances and is therefore much more time-consuming. Thus, the performances of our method seem quite promising for three reasons:

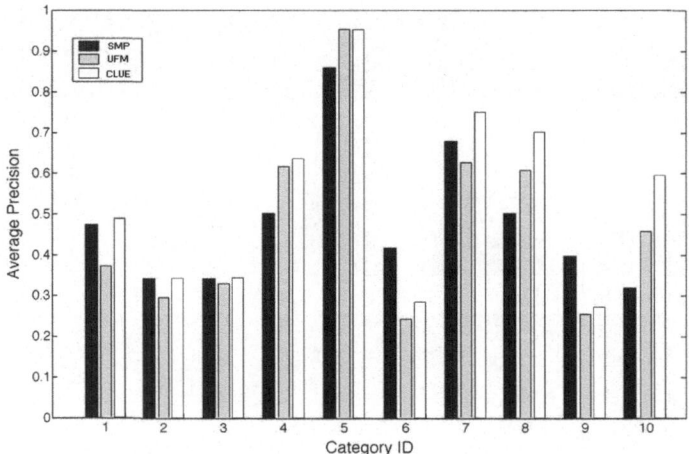

Fig. 8. Average Precision for each category of the COREL database. Dark blue bars: *SMP* approach; gray bars: *UFM* approach; white bars: *CLUE* approach.

- It performs slightly better than the *UFM* approach which relies on the same information.
- The results are not far from those of the more advanced *CLUE* approach which relies on more information.
- A similar clustering processing as the one applied with the *UFM* measure in *CLUE* may be applied to improve the *SMP* approach.

In conclusion, in its current state of development, the proposed *SMP* measure does not outperform the state-of-the-art methods selected as benchmark here. However, it does bring a novel approach to tackle the problem of image retrieval.

4.4   Computational Speed-Up(s)

The evaluation of our *SMP* similarity requires the computation of several KL divergences in a non-parametric framework. Since this is a time-consuming task, we propose two ways to speed-up the computations. The first one is based on a GPU implementation of the algorithm, the second on a preselection of the relevant images in the database.

GPU implementation

When computing the similarity between two images with the *SMP* approach, most of the time is devoted to the search of the k-th nearest neighbors in the evaluation of the KL divergences. Indeed, finding a k-th nearest neighbor requires to compute and sort distances between features (here the patches). The "brute force" algorithm has a complexity of order $O(N^2)$ for N samples in the feature set. Smarter algorithms with a lower complexity (typically of order $O(N \log N)$)

such as the KD-tree-based (ANN) algorithm [36] have been designed. Nevertheless, in practice, the computation time of a similarity between two images with the *SMP* approach remains large even with this low-complexity algorithm: on average 2.2s on a Pentium 4 3.4 GHz (2GB of DDR memory) with the ANN algorithm.

To speed up the computation time, we developed a parallel implementation of the kNN search on a Graphic Processing Unit (GPU) [37] using CUDA. This implementation is based on a brute force approach since recursive algorithms (the preferred strategy when using trees such as in ANN) are not parallelizable. It was implemented on an NVIDIA GeForce 8800 GTX card with 768 MB of memory. The computation time for one similarity measure between two images required 0.2s on average (i.e., 10 times less than with the CPU implementation of ANN).

As of today, the brute force algorithm parallelized on GPU is by far the fastest implementation of our method. Developing smart algorithms (such as the KD-tree one), which may not be parallelizable but have a very low complexity, is a topic of active research, as is the development of GPU for computational purposes. Hence both types of methods should be kept in mind for efficient implementations in the near future.

Preselection of the relevant images

The computational speed can be improved by splitting the retrieval task into two steps:

1. Only the low frequency contribution to the similarity measure defined in Eq. (4) is computed for all images in the database. This "partial" similarity measure produces a first ranking of the database images from which the first n images are selected for the next step.
2. The complete similarity measure is computed between the query and the n selected images.

This procedure saves computation time as it computes the whole similarity measure only for a reduced number of images (computing only part of it for images that are unlikely to be relevant to the query). The smaller the size of the preselected subset, the greater the improvement in terms of computation time. For example, when a query on the Nister database is processed following the described two-step procedure with a selected subset of 50 images, the average computation time per image drops from 0.2s to about 0.06s with the GPU implementation (and with similar retrieval performances). It is clear however that the number of preselected images cannot be arbitrarily small without seriously affecting retrieval performances. It should be large enough compared to the number of images in the database as well as the number of relevant images for the query.

5   Conclusion

In this paper, we proposed a new image similarity framework based on high-dimensional probability distributions of patches of multiscale coefficients which we call *Sparse Multiscale Patches*. Feature sets are represented by these patches of subband coefficients that take into account intrascale, interscale and interchannel dependencies. The similarity between two images was defined as a linear combination of the "closeness" between the distributions of their features at each scale measured by the Kullback-Leibler divergence. The Kullback-Leibler divergences are estimated in a non-parametric framework, via a kNN approach. The proposed similarity measure seems to be stable when selecting a reduced number of patches, proving that a few significant patches are enough to represent the image features. This is a consequence of the sparsity of the multiscale transform.

We applied this framework to image retrieval. The proposed approach takes advantage of the properties of its global multiscale descriptors. In particular, it is robust to JPEG2000 compression (i.e. it matches the visual similarity between images with different amounts of blur or compression noise). Retrieval experiments were conducted on two publicly available datasets of real world images (Nister Recognition Benchmark and the COREL database) to evaluate the average performances of the method. In particular, the Nister dataset was used to benchmark the robustness to several geometric image deformations, such as change of viewpoint, rotation and zoom. Our results showed the reliability of the *SMP* approach with respect to these deformations. In addition, although our method is new, its performances tested on two databases are very close to those of several established retrieval methods: a reference retrieval method based on (local) *SIFT* descriptors and two versions of a fuzzy, segmentation-based *UFM* approach: *UFM* and *CLUE* . This indicates that the *SMP* approach adapts to quite different retrieval tasks, from the object level (on the Nister database) to the level of general categories (on the COREL database). Finally, our Sparse Multiscale Patches approach follows the same multiscale philosophy as the new compression standard SVC [38]. This presumes nearly straightforward use of low-level bitstream components in a foreseen extension of this method to video retrieval.

References

1. Deselaers, T., Keysers, D., Ney, H.: Features for image retrieval: An experimental comparison. Information Retrieval 11, 77–107 (2008)
2. Loupias, E., Sebe, N., Bres, S., Jolion, J.M.: Wavelet-based salient points for image retrieval. In: ICIP, vol. 2, pp. 518–521 (2000)
3. Swain, M., Ballard, D.: Color indexing. IJCV 7, 11–32 (1991)
4. Mikolajczyk, K., Schmid, C.: A performance evaluation of local descriptors. IEEE Trans. Pattern Anal. Mach. Intell. 27, 1615–1630 (2005)
5. Huang, J., Mumford, D.: Statistics of natural images and models. In: CVPR, Fort Collins, CO, USA, vol. 1, pp. 541–547 (1999)

6. Black, M., Anandan, P.: A framework for the robust estimation of optical flow. In: ICCV, Berlin, Germany, pp. 231–236 (1993)
7. Black, M.J., Anandan, P.: The robust estimation of multiple motions: parametric and piecewise-smooth flow fields. CVIU 63, 75–104 (1996)
8. Comaniciu, D., Ramesh, V., Meer, P.: Real-time tracking of non-rigid objects using mean shift. In: CVPR, vol. 2, pp. 142–149 (2000)
9. Viola, P., Wells, I., Wainwright, M.: Alignment by maximization of mutual information. IJCV 24, 137–154 (1997)
10. Bansal, R., Staib, L.H., Chen, Z., Rangarajan, A., Knisely, J., Nath, R., Duncan, J.S.: Entropy-based, multiple-portal-to-3dct registration for prostate radiotherapy using iteratively estimated segmentation. In: Taylor, C., Colchester, A. (eds.) MICCAI 1999. LNCS, vol. 1679, pp. 567–578. Springer, Heidelberg (1999)
11. Marques, O., Mayron, L.M., Borba, G.B., Gamba, H.R.: On the potential of incorporating knowledge of human visual attention into cbir systems. In: ICME, pp. 773–776 (2006)
12. Puzicha, J., Rubner, Y., Tomasi, C., Buhmann, J.M.: Empirical evaluation of dissimilarity measures for color and texture. In: ICCV, pp. 1165–1172 (1999)
13. Buades, A., Coll, B., Morel, J.M.: A review of image denoising algorithms, with a new one. Multiscale Modeling and Simulation 4, 490–530 (2005)
14. Awate, S.P., Whitaker, R.T.: Unsupervised, information-theoretic, adaptive image filtering for image restoration. IEEE Trans. on PAMI 28, 364–376 (2006)
15. Angelino, C.V., Debreuve, E., Barlaud, M.: Image restoration using a knn-variant of the mean-shift. In: ICIP, San Diego, USA (2008)
16. Portilla, J., Strela, V., Wainwright, M., Simoncelli, E.P.: Image denoising using a scale mixture of Gaussians in the wavelet domain. TIP 12, 1338–1351 (2003)
17. Do, M., Vetterli, M.: Wavelet based texture retrieval using generalized Gaussian density and Kullback-Leibler distance. TIP 11, 146–158 (2002)
18. Wang, Z., Wu, G., Sheikh, H.R., Simoncelli, E.P., Yang, E.H., Bovik, A.C.: Quality-aware images. TIP 15, 1680–1689 (2006)
19. Donoho, D.L., Johnstone, I.M.: Ideal spatial adaptation by wavelet shrinkage. Biometrika 81, 425–455 (1994)
20. Romberg, J.K., Choi, H., Baraniuk, R.G.: Bayesian tree-structured image modeling using wavelet-domain hidden markov models. TIP 10, 1056–1068 (2001)
21. Pierpaoli, E., Anthoine, S., Huffenberger, K., Daubechies, I.: Reconstructing sunyaev-zeldovich clusters in future cmb experiments. Mon. Not. Roy. Astron. Soc. 359, 261–271 (2005)
22. Burt, P.J., Adelson, E.H.: The Laplacian pyramid as a compact image code. IEEE Trans. Communications 31, 532–540 (1983)
23. Piro, P., Anthoine, S., Debreuve, E., Barlaud, M.: Image retrieval via kullback-leibler divergence of patches of multiscale coefficients in the knn framework. In: CBMI, London, UK (2008)
24. Nielsen, F., Boissonnat, J.D., Nock, R.: On bregman voronoi diagrams. In: SODA, pp. 746–755 (2007)
25. Nielsen, F., Nock, R.: On the smallest enclosing information disk. Inf. Process. Lett. 105, 93–97 (2008)
26. Boltz, S., Debreuve, E., Barlaud, M.: High-dimensional kullback-leibler distance for region-of-interest tracking: Application to combining a soft geometric constraint with radiometry. In: CVPR, Minneapolis, USA (2007)
27. Ahmad, I., Lin, P.E.: A nonparametric estimation of the entropy for absolutely continuous distributions. IEEE Trans. Inform. Theory 22, 372–375 (1976)

28. Terrell, G.R., Scott, D.W.: Variable kernel density estimation. The Annals of Statistics 20, 1236–1265 (1992)
29. Loftsgaarden, D., Quesenberry, C.: A nonparametric estimate of a multivariate density function. AMS 36, 1049–1051 (1965)
30. Goria, M., Leonenko, N., Mergel, V., Novi Inverardi, P.: A new class of random vector entropy estimators and its applications in testing statistical hypotheses. J. Nonparametr. Stat. 17, 277–298 (2005)
31. Lowe, D.: Distinctive image features from scale-invariant keypoints. In: IJCV, vol. 20, pp. 91–110 (2003)
32. Chen, Y., Wang, J.Z.: A region-based fuzzy feature matching approach to content-based image retrieval. TIP 24, 1252–1267 (2003)
33. Nistér, D., Stewénius, H.: Scalable recognition with a vocabulary tree. In: CVPR, vol. 2, pp. 2161–2168 (2006)
34. Chen, Y., Wang, J.Z., Krovetz, R.: Clue: Cluster-based retrieval of images by unsupervised learning. TIP 14, 1187–1201 (2005)
35. Lowe, D.: Sift keypoint detector, http://www.cs.ubc.ca/~lowe/keypoints/
36. Arya, S., Mount, D.M., Netanyahu, N.S., Silverman, R., Wu, A.Y.: An optimal algorithm for approximate nearest neighbor searching fixed dimensions. J. ACM 45, 891–923 (1998)
37. Garcia, V., Debreuve, E., Barlaud, M.: Fast k nearest neighbor search using GPU. In: CVPR Workshop on Computer Vision on GPU (2008)
38. ITU-T, JTC1, I.: Scalable video coding - joint draft (April 6, 2006)

Recent Advances in Large Scale Image Search

Herve Jegou, Matthijs Douze, and Cordelia Schmid

INRIA, LJK
firstname.lastname@inria.fr

Abstract. This paper introduces recent methods for large scale image search. State-of-the-art methods build on the bag-of-features image representation. We first analyze bag-of-features in the framework of approximate nearest neighbor search. This shows the sub-optimality of such a representation for matching descriptors and leads us to derive a more precise representation based on 1) Hamming embedding (HE) and 2) weak geometric consistency constraints (WGC). HE provides binary signatures that refine the matching based on visual words. WGC filters matching descriptors that are not consistent in terms of angle and scale. HE and WGC are integrated within an inverted file and are efficiently exploited for all images, even in the case of very large datasets. Experiments performed on a dataset of one million of images show a significant improvement due to the binary signature and the weak geometric consistency constraints, as well as their efficiency. Estimation of the full geometric transformation, i.e., a re-ranking step on a short list of images, is complementary to our weak geometric consistency constraints and allows to further improve the accuracy.

1 Introduction

We address the problem of searching for similar images in a large set of images. Similar images are defined as images of the same object or scene viewed under different imaging conditions, cf. Fig. 11 for examples. Many previous approaches have addressed the problem of matching such transformed images [1,2,3,4,5]. They are in most cases based on local invariant descriptors, and either match descriptors between individual images or search for similar descriptors in an efficient indexing structure. Various approximate nearest neighbor search algorithms such as kd-tree [1] or sparse coding with an overcomplete basis set [6] allow for fast search in small datasets. The problem with these approaches is that all individual descriptors need to be compared to and stored.

In order to deal with large image datasets, Sivic and Zisserman [4] introduced the bag-of-features (BOF) image representation in the context of image search. Descriptors are quantized into visual words with the k-means algorithm. An image is then represented by the frequency histogram of visual words obtained by assigning each descriptor of the image to the closest visual word. Fast access to the frequency vectors is obtained by an inverted file system. Note that this approach is an approximation to the direct matching of individual descriptors and

F. Nielsen (Ed.): ETVC 2008, LNCS 5416, pp. 305–326, 2009.

somewhat decreases the performance. It compares favorably in terms of memory usage against other approximate nearest neighbor search algorithms, such as the popular Euclidean locality sensitive hashing (LSH) [7,8]. LSH typically requires 100–500 bytes per descriptor to index, which is not tractable, as a one million image dataset typically produces up to 2 billion local descriptors.

Some recent extensions of the BOF approach speed up the assignment of individual descriptors to visual words [5,9] or the search for frequency vectors [10,11]. Others improve the discriminative power of the visual words [12], in which case the entire dataset has to be known in advance. It is also possible to increase the performance by regularizing the neighborhood structure [10] or using multiple assignment of descriptors to visual words [10,13] at the cost of reduced efficiency. Finally, post-processing with spatial verification, a re-occurring technique in computer vision [1], improves the retrieval performance. Such a post-processing is evaluated in [9].

In this paper we present an approach complementary to those mentioned above. We make the distance between visual word frequency vectors more significant by using a more informative representation. Firstly, we apply a Hamming embedding (HE) to the descriptors by adding binary signatures which refine the visual words. The idea of using short binary codes was recently proposed in [14], where they are used to compact global GIST descriptors [15]. Secondly, we integrate weak geometric consistency (WGC) within the inverted file system which penalizes the descriptors that are not consistent in terms of angle and scale. We also use a-priori knowledge on the transformations for further verification. This contribution can be viewed as an answer to the question stated in [9] of how to integrate geometrical information in the index for very large datasets.

This paper is organized as follows. The interpretation of a BOF representation as an image voting system is given in Section 2. Our contributions, HE and WGC, are described in sections 3 and 4. Complexity issues of our approach in the context of an inverted file system are discussed in Section 5. Finally, Section 6 presents the experimental results.

2   Voting Interpretation of Bag-of-Features

In this section, we show how image search based on BOF can be interpreted as a voting system which matches individual descriptors with an approximate nearest neighbor (NN) search. We then evaluate BOF from this perspective. The main notations used in this paper are summarized in Fig. 1.

2.1   Voting Approach

Given a query image represented by its local descriptors $y_{i'}$ and a set of database images j, $1 \leq i \leq n$, represented by its local descriptors $x_{i,j}$, a voting system can be summarized as follows:

n	number of images in the dataset
d	dimension of the local descriptors
m_j	number of local descriptors describing the image j of the dataset
m'	number of local descriptors describing the query
k	number of centroids (=visual words) defining the quantizer
$x_{i,j}$	i^{th} descriptor of image j
$y_{i'}$	i'^{th} descriptor of the query image
$q(.)$	quantizer function: $q(x_{i,j})$ is the quantized index associated with $x_{i,j}$
s_j^*	final score associated with dataset image j
$\delta_{x,y}$	Kronecker delta function: $\begin{cases} 1 & \text{if } x = y, \\ 0 & \text{otherwise.} \end{cases}$
$f(.,.)$	descriptor matching function, see (1)
$h(.,.)$	Hamming distance (8)

Fig. 1. Notations

1. Dataset images scores s_j are initialized to 0.
2. For each query image descriptor $y_{i'}$ and for each descriptor $x_{i,j}$ of the dataset, increase the score s_j of the corresponding image by

$$s_j := s_j + f(x_{i,j}, y_{i'}), \tag{1}$$

where f is a matching function that reflects the similarity between descriptors $x_{i,j}$ and $y_{i'}$. For a matching system based on ε-search or $k-$NN, $f(.,.)$ is defined as

$$f_\varepsilon(x,y) = \begin{cases} 1 & \text{if } d(x,y) < \varepsilon \\ 0 & \text{otherwise} \end{cases} \qquad f_{k\text{-NN}}(x,y) = \begin{cases} 1 & \text{if } x \text{ is a } k\text{-NN of } y \\ 0 & \text{otherwise} \end{cases} \tag{2}$$

where $d(.,.)$ is a distance (or dissimilarity measure) defined on the descriptor space. SIFT descriptors are typically compared using the Euclidean distance.
3. The image score $s_j^* = g_j(s_j)$ used for ranking is obtained from the final s_j by applying a post-processing function g_j. It can formally be written as

$$s_j^* = g_j \left(\sum_{i'=1..m'} \sum_{i=1..m_j} f(x_{i,j}, y_{i'}) \right). \tag{3}$$

The simplest choice for g_j is the identity, which leads to $s_j^* = s_j$. In this case the score reflects the number of matches between the query and each database image. Note that this score counts possible multiple matches of a descriptor. Another popular choice is to take into account the number of image descriptors, for example $s_j^* = s_j/m_j$. The score then reflects the rate of descriptors that match.

2.2   Bag-of-Features: Voting and Approximate NN Interpretation

Bag-of-features (BOF) image search uses descriptor quantization. A quantizer q is formally a function

$$q : \mathbb{R}^d \rightarrow [1, k]$$
$$x \mapsto q(x) \tag{4}$$

that maps a descriptor $x \in \mathbb{R}^d$ to an integer index. The quantizer q is often obtained by performing k-means clustering on a learning set. The resulting centroids are also referred to as *visual words*. The quantizer $q(x)$ is then the index of the centroid closest to the descriptor x. Intuitively, two descriptors x and y which are close in descriptor space satisfy $q(x) = q(y)$ with a high probability. The matching function f_q defined as

$$f_q(x, y) = \delta_{q(x),q(y)}, \tag{5}$$

allows the efficient comparison of the descriptors based on their quantized index. Injecting this matching function in (3) and normalizing the score by the number of descriptors of both the query image and the dataset image j, we obtain

$$s_j^* = \frac{1}{m_j \, m'} \sum_{i'=1..m'} \sum_{i=1..m_j} \delta_{q(x_{i,j}),q(y_{i'})} = \sum_{l=1..k} \frac{m_l'}{m'} \frac{m_{l,j}}{m_j}, \tag{6}$$

where m_l' and $m_{l,j}$ denote the numbers of descriptors, for the query and the dataset image j, respectively, that are assigned to the visual word l. In this equation, the normalizing value m' does not affect the ordering of the dataset images. Note that these scores correspond to the inner product between two BOF vectors. They are computed very efficiently using an inverted file, which exploits the sparsity of the BOF, i.e., the fact that $\delta_{q(x_{i,j}),q(y_{i'})} = 0$ for most of the (i, j, i') tuples.

At this point, these scores do not take into account the *tf-idf* weighting scheme (see [4] for details), which weights the visual words according to their frequency: rare visual words are assumed to be more discriminative and are assigned higher weights. In this case the matching function f can be defined as

$$f_{\text{tf-idf}}(x, y) = (\text{tf-idf}\,(q(y)))^2 \, \delta_{q(x),q(y)}, \tag{7}$$

such that the *tf-idf* weight associated with the visual word considered is applied to both the query and the dataset image in the BOF inner product. Using this new matching function, the image scores s_j become identical to the BOF similarity measure used in [4]. This voting scheme normalizes the number of votes by the number of descriptors (L_1 normalization). In what follows, we will use the L_2 normalization instead. For large vocabularies, the L_2 norm of a BOF is very close to the square root of the L_1 norm. In the context of a voting system, the division of the score by the L_2 norm is very similar to $s_j^* = s_j/\sqrt{m_j}$, which is a compromise between measuring the number and the rate of descriptor matches.

2.3   Weakness of Quantization-Based Approaches

Image search based on BOF combines the advantages of local features and of efficient image comparison using inverted files. However, the quantizer reduces significantly the discriminative power of the local descriptors. Two descriptors are assumed to match if they are assigned the same quantization index, i.e., if they lie in the same Voronoi cell. Choosing the number of centroids k is a compromise between the quantization noise and the descriptor noise.

Fig. 2(b) shows that a low value of k leads to large Voronoi cells: the probability that a noisy version of a descriptor belongs to the correct cell is high. However, this also reduces the discriminative power of the descriptor: different descriptors lie in the same cell. Conversely, a high value of k provides good precision for the descriptor, but the probability that a noisy version of the descriptor is assigned to the same cell is lower, as illustrated in Fig. 2(a).

Fig. 3 shows the impact of this trade-off when matching real images. The matches obtained by a BOF between two similar images are analyzed. A coarse clustering clearly leads to many bad matches, as shown in Fig. 3(a). We can observe that many of the corresponding regions are quite different. Using a larger codebook, many bad matches are removed (see Fig. 3(b)), but at the same time many correct matches are also removed.

From a more quantitative point of view, have measured the quality of the approximate nearest neighbor search performed by BOF in terms of the trade-off between

- the average recall for the ground truth nearest neighbor
- and the average rate of vectors that match in the dataset.

Clearly, a good approximate nearest neighbor search algorithm is expected to make the nearest neighbor vote with high probability, and at the same time arbitrary vectors vote with low probability. In BOF, the trade-off between these two quantities is managed by the number k of clusters.

For the evaluation, we have used the approximate nearest neighbor evaluation set available at [16]. It has been generated using the affine covariant features program of [17]. A one million vector set to be searched and a test query set of 10000 vectors are provided. All these vectors have been extracted from the INRIA Holidays image dataset described in Section 6.

One can see in Fig. 4 that the performance of BOF as an approximate nearest neighbor search algorithm is of reasonable accuracy: for $k = 1000$, the NN recall is of 45% and the proportion of the dataset points which are retrieved is of 0.1%. One key advantage of BOF is that its memory usage is much lower than concurrent approximate nearest neighbor search algorithms. For instance, with 20 hash functions the memory usage of LSH [7] is of 160 bytes per descriptors compared to about 4 bytes for BOF. In next section, we will comment on the other curves of Fig. 4, which provide a much better performance than standard BOF.

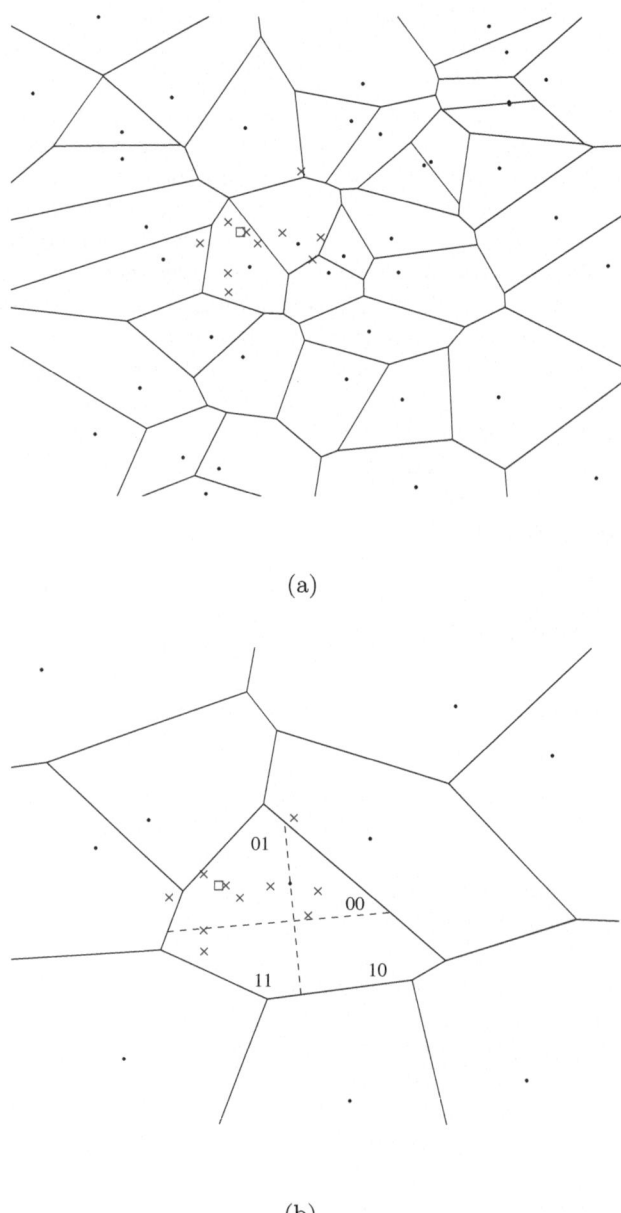

(a)

(b)

Fig. 2. Illustration of k-means clustering and our binary signature. (a) Fine clustering. (b) Low k and binary signature: the similarity search within a Voronoi cell is based on the Hamming distance. Legend: $\cdot$=centroid, □=descriptor, ×=noisy versions of this descriptor.

(a)

(b)

(c)

Fig. 3. (a) Coarse clustering ($k = 20000$), (b) Fine clustering ($k = 200000$), (c) Coarse clustering with Hamming Embedding ($k = 20000$, $h_t = 24$)

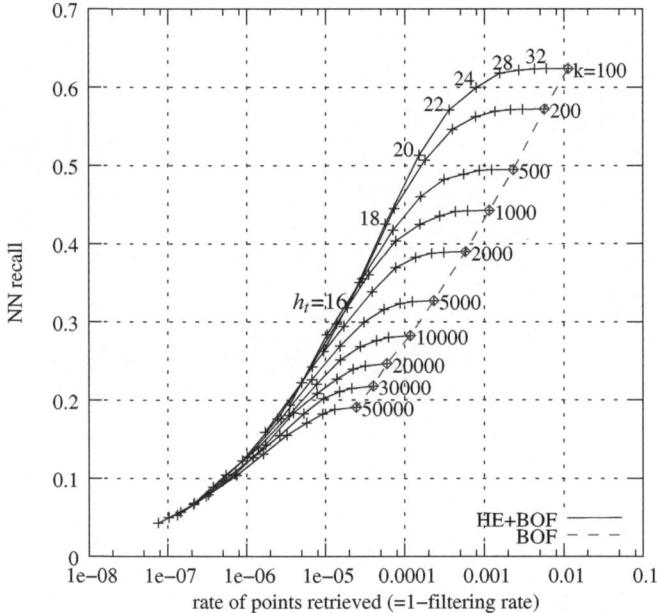

Fig. 4. Approximate nearest neighbor search accuracy of BOF (dashed) and Hamming Embedding (plain) for different numbers of clusters k and Hamming thresholds h_t

3   Hamming Embedding of Local Image Descriptors

In this section, we present an approach which combines the advantages of a coarse quantizer (low number of centroids k) with those of a fine quantizer (high k). It consists in refining the quantized index $q(x_i)$ with a d_b-dimensional binary signature $b(x_i) = (b_1(x_i), \ldots, b_{d_b}(x_i))$ that encodes the localization of the descriptor within the Voronoi cell, see Fig. 2(b). It is designed so that the Hamming distance

$$h(b(x), b(y)) = \sum_{1 \le i \le d_b} 1 - \delta_{b_i(x),b_i(y)} \tag{8}$$

between two descriptors x and y lying in the same cell reflects the Euclidean distance $d(x, y)$. The mapping from the Euclidean space into the Hamming space, referred to as Hamming Embedding (HE), should ensure that the Hamming distance h between a descriptor and its NNs in the Euclidean space is small.

Note that this significantly different from the Euclidean version of LSH (E2LSH) [7,8], which produces several hash keys per descriptor. In contrast, HE implicitly defines a single partitioning of the feature space and uses the Hamming metric between signatures in the embedded space.

We propose in the following a binary signature generation procedure. We distinguish between 1) the *off-line* learning procedure, which is performed on a learning dataset and generates a set of fixed values, and 2) the binary signature computation itself. The offline procedure is performed as follows:

1. **Random matrix generation:** A $d_b \times d$ orthogonal projection matrix P is generated. We randomly draw a matrix of Gaussian values and apply a QR factorization to it. The first d_b rows of the orthogonal matrix obtained by this decomposition form the matrix P.
2. **Descriptor projection and assignment:** A large set of descriptors x_i from an independent dataset is projected using P. These descriptors $(z_{i1}, ..., z_{id_b})$ are assigned to their closest centroid $q(x_i)$.
3. **Median values of projected descriptors:** For each centroid l and each projected component $h = 1, \ldots, d_b$, we compute the median value $\tau_{l,h}$ of the set $\{z_{ih} | q(x_i) = l\}$ that corresponds to the descriptors assigned to the cell l.

The fixed projection matrix P and $k \times d_b$ median values $\tau_{h,l}$ are used to perform the HE of a given descriptor x by:

1. **Assigning** x to its closest centroid, resulting in $q(x)$.
2. **Projecting** x using P, which produces a vector $z = Px = (z_1, \ldots, z_{d_b})$.
3. **Computing the signature** $b(x) = (b_1(x), \ldots, b_{d_b}(x))$ as

$$
b_i(x) = \begin{cases} 1 & \text{if } z_i > \tau_{q(x),i}, \\ 0 & \text{otherwise.} \end{cases} \tag{9}
$$

At this point, a descriptor is represented by $q(x)$ and $b(x)$. We can now define the HE matching function as

$$
f_{\text{HE}}(x, y) = \begin{cases} \text{tf-idf}(q(x)) & \text{if } q(x) = q(y) \text{ and } h\left(b(x), b(y)\right) \leq h_t \\ 0 & \text{otherwise} \end{cases} \tag{10}
$$

where h is the Hamming distance defined in Eqn. 8 and h_t is a fixed Hamming threshold such that $0 \leq h_t \leq d_b$. It has to be sufficiently high to ensure that the Euclidean NNs of x match, and sufficiently low to filter many points that lie in a distant region of the Voronoi cell. Fig. 5 and 6 depict this compromise. These plots have been generated by analyzing a set of 1000 descriptors assigned to the same centroid. Given a descriptor x we compare the rate of descriptors that are retrieved by the matching function to the rate of 5-NN that are retrieved.

Fig. 5 shows that the choice of an appropriate threshold h_t (here between 20 and 28) ensures that most of the cell's descriptors are filtered and that the descriptor's NNs are preserved with a high probability. For instance, setting $h_t = 22$ filters about 97% of the descriptors while preserving 53% of the 5-NN. A higher value $h_t = 28$ keeps 94% of the 5-NN and filters 77% of the cell descriptors. Fig. 6 represents this trade-off for different binary signature lengths. Clearly, the longer the binary signature d_b, the better the HE filtering quality. In the following, we have fixed $d_b = 64$, which is a good compromise between HE accuracy and memory usage (8 bytes per signature).

The comparison with standard BOF shows that the approximate nearest neighbor search performed by BOF+HE is much better. This is qualitatively

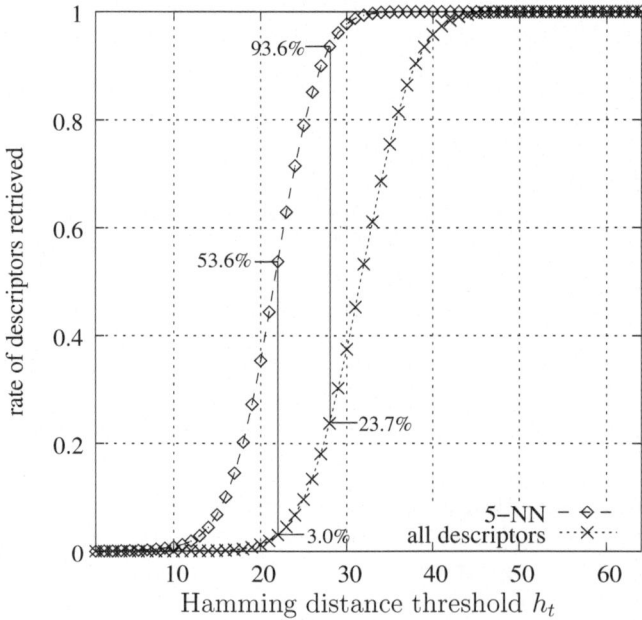

Fig. 5. HE: filtering effect on the descriptors within a cell and on the 5 NNs: trade-off between the rate of cell descriptors and the rate of NN that are retrieved for $d_b = 64$

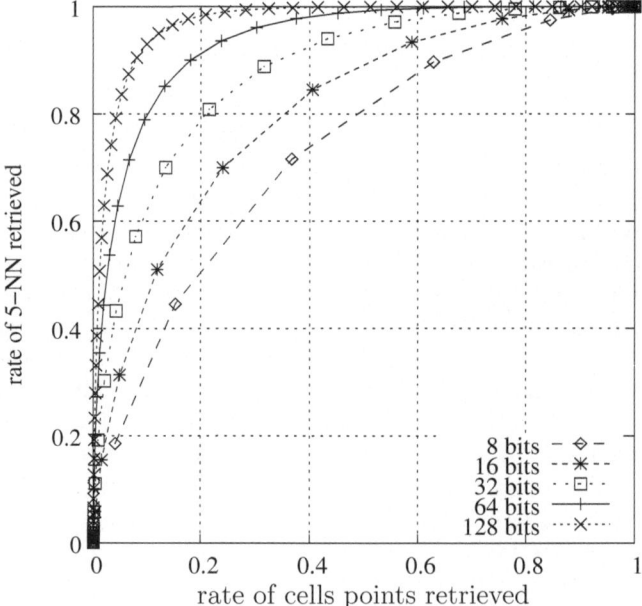

Fig. 6. HE: filtering effect on the descriptors within a cell and on the 5 NNs: impact of the number of bits d_b of the binary signature length

shown in Fig. 3-(c), where one can observe that the bad matches have been removed without removing the correct ones. This is confirmed by the quantitative evaluation of Fig. 4. Using HE for the same number of vectors that are retrieved increases the probability that the NN is among these voting vectors.

4   Large-Scale Geometric Consistency

BOF based image search ranks the database images without exploiting geometric information. Accuracy may be improved by adding a *re-ranking* stage [9] that computes a geometric transformation between the query and a shortlist of dataset images returned by the BOF search. To obtain an efficient and robust estimation of this transformation, the model is often kept as simple as possible [1,9]. In [1] an affine 2D transformation is estimated in two stages. First, a Hough scheme estimates a transformation with 4 degrees of freedom. Each pair of matching regions generates a set of parameters that "vote" in a 4D histogram. In a second stage, the sets of matches from the largest bins are used to estimate a finer 2D affine transform. In [9] further efficiency is obtained by a simplified parameter estimation and an approximate local descriptor matching scheme.

Despite these optimizations, existing geometric matching algorithms are costly and cannot reasonably be applied to more than a few hundred images. In this section, we propose to exploit weak, i.e., partial, geometrical information without explicitly estimating a transformation mapping the points from an image to another. The method is integrated into the inverted file and can efficiently be applied to all images. Our weak geometric consistency constraints refine the voting score and make the description more discriminant. Note that a *re-ranking* stage [9] can, in addition, be applied on a shortlist to estimate the full geometric transformation. It is complementary to the weak consistency constraints (see Section 6).

4.1   Variations of Geometrical Characteristics: Analysis

In order to obtain orientation and scale invariance, region of interest detectors extract the dominant orientation of the region [1] and its characteristic scale [18]. This extraction is performed independently for each interest point. When an image undergoes a rotation or scale change, these quantities are consistently modified for all points, see Fig 7 for an illustration in case of image rotations. It shows the difference of the dominant orientations for individual matching regions. We can observe that only the incorrect matches are not consistent with the global image rotation. This is confirmed by the histograms over the angle differences which illustrate the additional filtering effect of the weak geometric consistency constraints explained in next subsection. For two images having a different geometrical layout, the histogram of orientation differences is uniformly distributed.

Similarly, the characteristic scales of interest points are consistently scaled between two images of the same scene or object, as shown by Fig. 8.

Fig. 7. Orientation consistency. *Top-left:* Query image and its interest points. *Top-right:* two images of the same location viewed under different image rotations. The slices in the right top images show for each matched interest point the difference between the *estimated dominant orientations* of the query image and the image itself. Matches are obtained with our approach HE. *Bottom-right:* Histogram of the differences between the *dominant orientations* of matching points. The peak clearly corresponds to the global angle variation.

4.2 Weak Geometrical Consistency

The key idea of our method is to verify the consistency of the angle and scale parameters for the set of matching descriptors of a given image. We build upon and extend the BOF formalism of (1) by using *several* scores s_j per image. For a given image j, the entity s_j then represents the histogram of the angle and scale differences, obtained from angle and scale parameters of the interest regions of corresponding descriptors. Although these two parameters are not sufficient to map the points from one image to another, they can be used to improve the image ranking produced by the inverted file. This is obtained by modifying the update step of (1) as follows:

$$s_j(\delta_a, \delta_s) := s_j(\delta_a, \delta_s) + f(x_{i,j}, y_{i'}), \tag{11}$$

Fig. 8. Scale consistency for two pairs of matching images. *Top two rows:* The matched interest point regions. *Bottom:* The corresponding histograms of the log-scale difference between the characteristic scales of matched points. The peak clearly corresponds to the scale change between the images.

where δ_a and δ_s are the quantized angle and log-scale differences between the interest regions. The image score becomes

$$s_j^* = g\left(\max_{(\delta_a,\delta_s)} s_j(\delta_a,\delta_s)\right). \tag{12}$$

The motivation behind the scores of (12) is to use angle and scale information to reduce the scores of the images for which the points are not transformed by consistent angles and scales. Conversely, a set of points consistently transformed will accumulate its votes in the same histogram bin, resulting in a high score.

Experimentally, the quantities δ_a and δ_s have the desirable property of being largely independent: computing separate histograms for angle and scale is as precise as computing the full 2D histogram of (11). In this case two histograms s_j^a and s_j^s are separately updated by

$$\begin{aligned} s_j^a(\delta_a) &:= s_j^a(\delta_a) + f(x_{i,j}, y_{i'}), \\ s_j^s(\delta_s) &:= s_j^s(\delta_s) + f(x_{i,j}, y_{i'}). \end{aligned} \tag{13}$$

The two histograms can be seen as marginal probabilities of the 2D histogram. Therefore, the final score

$$s_j^* = g\left(\min\left(\max_{\delta_a} s_j^a(\delta_a),\ \max_{\delta_s} s_j^s(\delta_s)\right)\right) \tag{14}$$

is a reasonable estimate of the maximum of (12). This approximation will be used in the following. It significantly reduces the memory and CPU requirements. In practice, the histograms are smoothed by a moving average to reduce the angle and log-scale quantization artifacts. Note that the translation could be theoretically included in WGC. However, for a large number of images, the number of parameters should be in fewer than 2 dimensions, otherwise the memory and CPU costs of obtaining the scores would not be tractable.

4.3   Injecting a Priori Knowledge

Fig. 9(a) shows that the repartition of the angle difference δ_a is different for matching and non-matching image pairs. As a matching image pair also includes incorrectly matched points, this suggests that the probability mass function of angle difference for the matching points follows a highly non-uniform repartition. This is due to the higher frequency of horizontal and vertical gradients in photos and to the human tendency to shoot either in "portrait" or "landscape" mode. A similar bias is observed for δ_s: image pairs with the same scale ($\delta_s = 0$) are more frequent.

The orientation and scale priors are used to weight the entries of our histograms before extracting their maxima. We have designed two different orientation priors: "same orientation" for image datasets known to be shot with the same orientation and "$\pi/2$ rotation" for more general bases, see Fig. 9(b). It is augmented with a fixed quantity to enable the retrieval of shots with rare orientations.

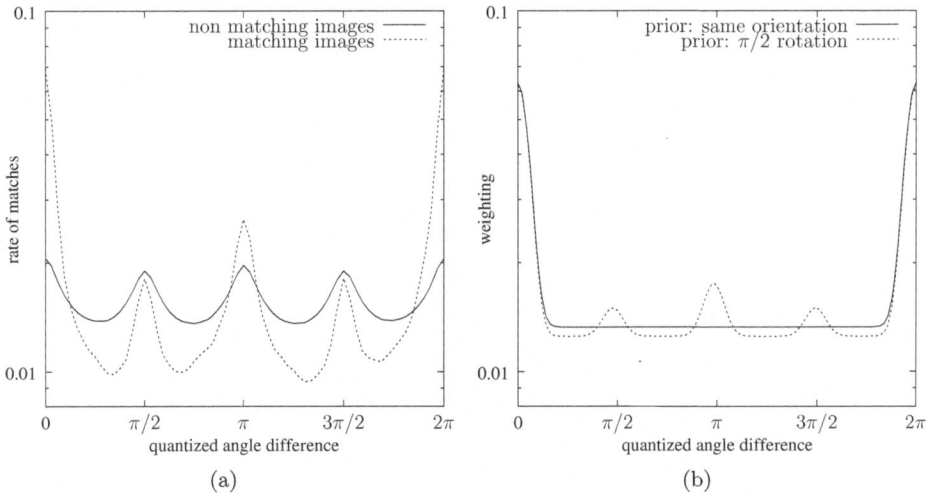

Fig. 9. (a): histogram of δ_a values accumulated over all query images of the Holidays dataset; (b): weighting function applied in the g_j computation

5   Complexity

Both HE and WGC are integrated in the inverted file. This structure is usually implemented as an array that associates a list of entries with each visual word. Each entry contains a database image identifier and the number of descriptors of this image assigned to this visual word. The tf-idf weights and the BOF vector norms can be stored separately. The search consists in iterating over the entries corresponding to the visual words in the query image and in updating the scores accordingly.

An alternative implementation consists in storing one entry per descriptor in the inverted list corresponding to a visual word instead of one entry per image. This is almost equivalent for very large vocabularies, because in this case multiple occurrences of a visual word on an image are rare, i.e., it is not necessary to store the number of occurrences. In our experiments, the overall memory usage was not noticeably changed by this implementation. This implementation is required by HE and WGC, because additional information is stored per local descriptor.

HE impact on the complexity: For each inverted file entry, we compute the Hamming distance between the signature of the query and that of the database entry. This is done efficiently with a binary `xor` operation. Entries with a distance above h_t are rejected, which avoids the update of image scores for these entries. Note that this occurs for a fair rate of entries, as shown in Fig. 5.

WGC impact on the complexity: WGC modifies the score update by applying (13) instead of (1). Hence, two bins are updated, instead of one for a standard inverted file. The score aggregation as well as histogram smoothing

Table 1. Inverted file memory usage and query time per image for a quad-core

image id		21 bits
orientation		6 bits
log-scale		5 bits
binary signature		64 bits
total	WGC	4 bytes
	HE	11 bytes
	WGC+HE	12 bytes

Table 2. Query time per image for a quad-core (Flickr1M dataset)

	$k = 20000$	$k = 200000$
compute descriptors	0.88 s	
quantization + binary signature	0.36 s	0.60 s
search, baseline	2.74 s	0.62 s
search, WGC	10.19 s	2.11 s
search, HE	1.16 s	0.20 s
search, HE+WGC	1.82 s	0.65 s

have negligible computing costs. With the tested parameters, see Table 1, the memory usage of the histogram scores is 128 floating point values per image, which is small compared with the inverted lists.

Runtime: All experiments were carried out on 2.6 GHz quad-core computers. As the new inverted file contains more information, we carefully designed the size of the entries to fit a maximum 12 bytes per point, as shown in Table 1.

Table 2 summarizes the average query time for a one million image dataset. We observe that the binary signature of HE has a negligible computational cost. Due to the high rate of zero components of the BOF for a visual vocabulary of $k = 200000$, the search is faster. Surprisingly, HE reduces the inverted file query time. This is because the Hamming distance computation and thresholding is cheaper than updating the scores. WGC reduces the speed, mostly because the histograms do not fit in cache memory and their memory access pattern is almost random. Most interestingly the search time of HE + WGC is comparable to the inverted file baseline. Note that for $k = 200000$ visual words, the assignment uses a fast approximate nearest neighbor search, i.e., the computation is not ten times slower than for $k = 20000$, which here uses exhaustive search.

6   Experiments

We perform our experiments on two annotated datasets: our own *Holidays* dataset, see Fig. 11, and the Oxford5k dataset. To evaluate large scale image search we also introduce a distractor dataset downloaded from Flickr. For evaluation we use mean average precision (mAP) [9], i.e., for each query image we obtain a precision/recall curve, compute its average precision and then take the

Table 3. Datasets used in our experiments

Dataset	#images	#queries	#descriptors
Holidays	1,491	500	4,455,091
Oxford5k	5,062	55	4,977,153
Flickr60k	67,714	N/A	140,211,550
Flickr1M	1,000,000	N/A	2,072,739,475

Table 4. Results for *Holidays* and *Oxford* datasets. mAP scores for the baseline, HE, WGC and HE+WGC. Angle prior: same orientation for *Oxford*, $0, \pi/2, \pi$ and $3\pi/2$ rotations for *Holidays*. Vocabularies are generated on the independent Flickr60K dataset.

	Parameters		Holidays		Oxford	
	HE: h_t	WGC	$k = 20000$	$k = 200000$	$k = 20000$	$k = 200000$
baseline			0.4463	0.5488	0.3854	0.3950
HE	20		0.7268	0.7093	0.4798	0.4503
HE	22		0.7181	0.7074	0.4892	0.4571
HE	24		0.6947	0.7115	0.4906	0.4585
HE	26		0.6649	0.6879	0.4794	0.4624
WGC		no prior	0.5996	0.6116	0.3749	0.3833
WGC		with prior	0.6446	0.6859	0.4375	0.4602
HE+WGC	20	with prior	0.7391	0.7328	0.5442	0.5096
HE+WGC	22	with prior	0.7463	0.7382	0.5472	0.5217
HE+WGC	24	with prior	0.7507	0.7439	0.5397	0.5252
HE+WGC	26	with prior	0.7383	0.7404	0.5253	0.5275

mean value over the set of queries. Descriptors are obtained by the Hessian-Affine detector and the SIFT descriptor, using the software of [17] with the default parameters. Clustering is performed with k-means on the independent Flickr60k dataset. The number of clusters is specified for each experiment.

6.1   Datasets

In the following we present the different datasets used in our experiments, see Table 3 for an overview.

Holidays. We have collected a new dataset which mainly contains personal holiday photos. The remaining ones were taken on purpose to test the robustness to various transformations: rotations, viewpoint and illumination changes, blurring, etc. The dataset includes a very large variety of scene types (natural, man-made, water and fire effects, etc) and images are of high resolution. The dataset contains 500 image groups, each of which represents a distinct scene.

The first image of each group is the query image and the correct retrieval results are the other images of the group. The dataset is available at [16].

Oxford5k. We also used the Oxford dataset first used in [9]. The images represent Oxford buildings. All the dataset images are in "upright" orientation because they are displayed on the web.

Flickr60k and **Flickr1M.** We have retrieved arbitrary images from Flickr and built two distinct sets: Flickr60k is used to learn the quantization centroids and the HE parameters (median values). For these tasks we have used respectively 5M and 140M descriptors. Flickr1M are distractor images for large scale image search. Compared to *Holidays*, the Flickr datasets are slightly biased, because they include low-resolution images and more photos of humans.

Impact of the clustering learning set. Learning the visual vocabulary on a distinct dataset shows more accurately the behavior of the search in very large image datasets, for which 1) query descriptors represent a negligible part of the total number of descriptors, and 2) the number of visual words represents a negligible fraction of the total number of descriptors. This is confirmed by comparing our results on Oxford to the ones of [9], where clustering is performed on the evaluation set. In our case, i.e., for a distinct visual vocabulary, the improvement between a small and large k is significantly reduced when compared to [9], see first row of Table 4.

6.2   Evaluation of HE and WGC

INRIA Holidays and Oxford building datasets: Table 4 compares the proposed methods with the standard BOF baseline. We can observe that both HE and WGC result in significant improvements. Most importantly, the combination of the two further increases the performance.

Large scale experiments: Fig. 10 shows an evaluation of the different approaches for large datasets, i.e., we combined the Holidays dataset with a varying number of images from the 1M Flickr dataset. We clearly see that the gain of the variant WGC + HE is very significant. In the case of WGC + HE the corresponding curves degrade less rapidly when the number of images in the database increases.

Results for various queries are presented in Fig. 11. The third and fourth rows show that some images from the *Flickr1M* dataset artificially decrease the results in terms of mAP given in Fig. 10, as *false* false positive, marked by FP(?), are some images which are actually relevant to the query image. We can observe in the two first rows that HE and WGC improve the quality of the ranking significantly for these queries. Here again, some false false positives (not displayed here) are interleaved with the correct returned images.

Table 5 measures the improvement of the ranking. It gives the rate of true positives that are in a shortlist of 100 images. For a dataset of one million images, the baseline only returns 31% of the true positives, against 62% for HE+WGC.

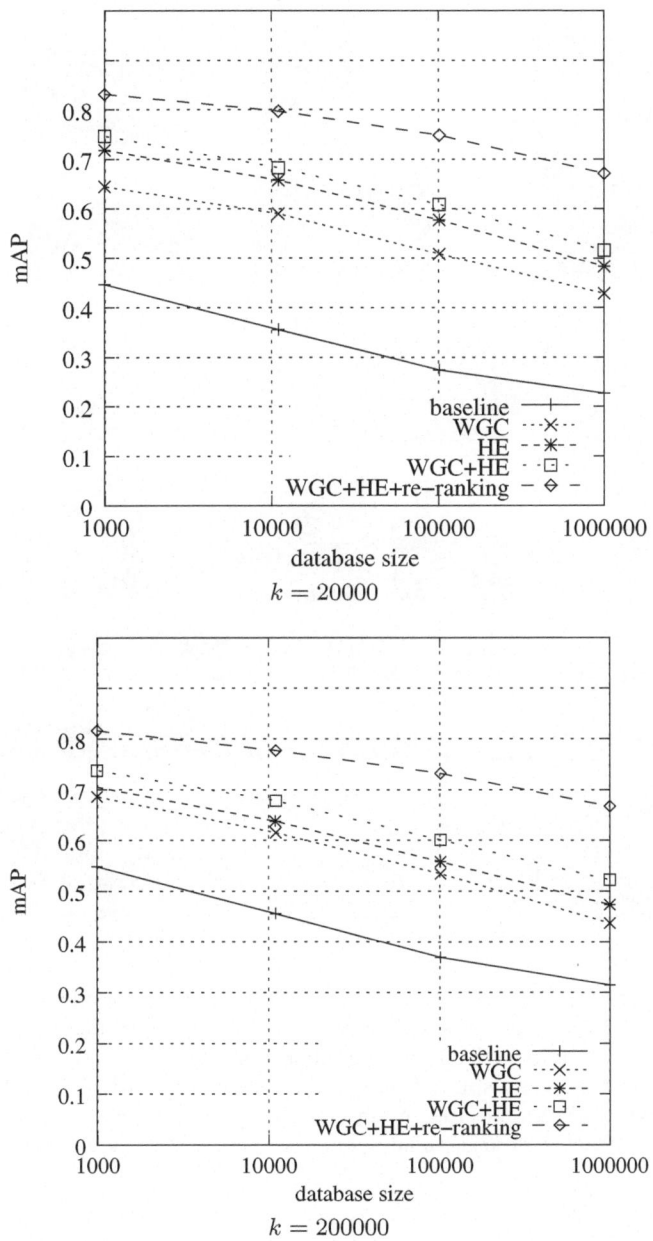

Fig. 10. Performance of the image search as a function of the dataset size for BOF, WGC, HE ($h_t = 22$), WGC+HE, and WGC+HE+re-ranking with a full geometrical verification (shortlist of 100 images). The dataset is *Holidays* with a varying number of distractors from *Flickr1M*.

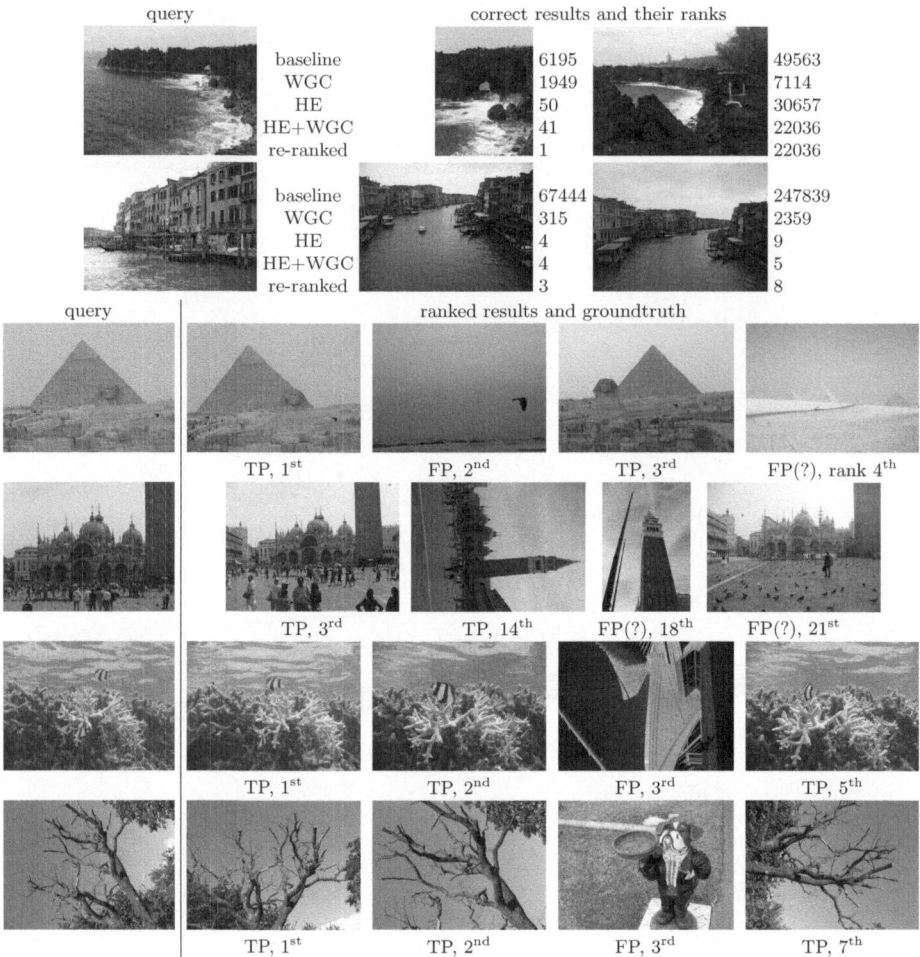

Fig. 11. Queries from the *Holidays* dataset and some corresponding results for *Holidays*+1M distractors from Flickr1M. Rows 1 and 2: how the different methods rank the true matches. Below: example results labeled as true positives (TP) or false positives (FP). Note that the displayed images are interleaved with TPs and FPs. As the *Holidays* dataset includes pictures of popular tourist attractions, casual matches were found in the distractor dataset. They count as false positives and are marked with FP(?).

This reflects the quality of the shortlist that will be considered in a re-ranking stage.

Re-ranking: The re-ranking is based on the estimation of an affine transformation with our implementation of [1]. Fig. 10 also shows the results obtained with

Table 5. *Holidays dataset + Flickr1M:* Rate of true positives as a function of the dataset size for a shortlist of 100 images, $k = 200000$

dataset size	991	10991	100991	1000991
BOF	0.673	0.557	0.431	0.306
WGC+HE	0.855	0.789	0.708	0.618

a shortlist of 100 images. We can observe further improvement, which confirms the complementary of this step with WGC.

7 Conclusion

This paper has introduced two ways of improving a standard bag-of-features representation. The first one is based on a Hamming embedding which provides binary signatures that refine visual words. It results in a similarity measure for descriptors assigned to the same visual word. The second is a method that enforces weak geometric consistency constraints and uses a priori knowledge on the geometrical transformation. These constraints are integrated within the inverted file and are used for all the dataset images. Both these methods improve the performance significantly, especially for large datasets. Interestingly, our modifications do not result in an increase of the runtime.

References

1. Lowe, D.: Distinctive image features from scale-invariant keypoints. IJCV 60, 91–110 (2004)
2. Mikolajczyk, K., Schmid, C.: Scale and affine invariant interest point detectors. IJCV 60, 63–86 (2004)
3. Matas, J., Chum, O., Martin, U., Pajdla, T.: Robust wide baseline stereo from maximally stable extremal regions. In: BMVC, pp. 384–393 (2002)
4. Sivic, J., Zisserman, A.: Video Google: A text retrieval approach to object matching in videos. In: ICCV, pp. 1470–1477 (2003)
5. Nistér, D., Stewénius, H.: Scalable recognition with a vocabulary tree. In: CVPR, pp. 2161–2168 (2006)
6. Omercevic, D., Drbohlav, O., Leonardis, A.: High-dimensional feature matching: employing the concept of meaningful nearest neighbors. In: ICCV (2007)
7. Datar, M., Immorlica, N., Indyk, P., Mirrokni, V.: Locality-sensitive hashing scheme based on p-stable distributions. In: Proceedings of the Symposium on Computational Geometry, pp. 253–262 (2004)
8. Shakhnarovich, G., Darrell, T., Indyk, P.: 3. In: Nearest-Neighbor Methods in Learning and Vision: Theory and Practice. MIT Press, Cambridge (2006)
9. Philbin, J., Chum, O., Isard, M.A., Zisserman, J.S.: Object retrieval with large vocabularies and fast spatial matching. In: CVPR (2007)
10. Jegou, H., Harzallah, H., Schmid, C.: A contextual dissimilarity measure for accurate and efficient image search. In: CVPR (2007)

11. Fraundorfer, F., Stewenius, H., Nister, D.: A binning scheme for fast hard drive based image search. In: CVPR (2007)
12. Schindler, G., Brown, M., Szeliski, R.: City-scale location recognition. In: CVPR (2007)
13. Philbin, J., Chum, O., Isard, M., Sivic, J., Zisserman, A.: Lost in quantization: Improving particular object retrieval in large scale image databases. In: CVPR (2008)
14. Torralba, A., Fergus, R., Weiss, Y.: Small codes and large databases for recognition. In: CVPR (2008)
15. Oliva, A., Torralba, A.: Modeling the shape of the scene: a holistic representation of the spatial envelope. IJCV 42, 145–175 (2001)
16. Jegou, H., Douze, M.: INRIA Holidays dataset (2008),
    http://lear.inrialpes.fr/people/jegou/data.php
17. Mikolajczyk, K.: Binaries for affine covariant region descriptors (2007),
    http://www.robots.ox.ac.uk/~vgg/research/affine/
18. Lindeberg, T.: Feature detection with automatic scale selection. IJCV 30, 77–116 (1998)

Information Theoretic Methods for Diffusion-Weighted MRI Analysis*

Angelos Barmpoutis and Baba C. Vemuri

Department of Computer Information Science & Engineering
University of Florida, Gainesville FL 32611, USA
{abarmpou,vemuri}@cise.ufl.edu

Abstract. Concepts from Information Theory have been used quite widely in Image Processing, Computer Vision and Medical Image Analysis for several decades now. Most widely used concepts are that of KL-divergence, minimum description length (MDL), etc. These concepts have been popularly employed for image registration, segmentation, classification etc. In this chapter we review several methods, mostly developed by our group at the Center for Vision, Graphics & Medical Imaging in the University of Florida, that glean concepts from Information Theory and apply them to achieve analysis of Diffusion-Weighted Magnetic Resonance (DW-MRI) data.

This relatively new MRI modality allows one to non-invasively infer axonal connectivity patterns in the central nervous system. The focus of this chapter is to review automated image analysis techniques that allow us to automatically segment the region of interest in the DWMRI image wherein one might want to track the axonal pathways and also methods to reconstruct complex local tissue geometries containing axonal fiber crossings. Implementation results illustrating the algorithm application to real DW-MRI data sets are depicted to demonstrate the effectiveness of the methods reviewed.

1 Introduction

Modern technological developments in image acquisition techniques have made it possible to capture images from various medical image modalities in high resolution. Magnetic Resonance Imaging (MRI) allows capturing of high contrast images of the soft human tissues. More specifically, Diffusion-Weighted MRI (DW-MRI) is the only non-invasive method for capturing the diffusivity of molecules of water in human tissue. The local diffusion properties usually change in different parts of the tissue being imaged due to changes encountered in anisotropy to water diffusion and these variations in anisotropy result in variations in signal attenuation which are captured in the acquired signal. By analyzing the local diffusion characteristics one can obtain information about the connectivity patterns prevalent say in the brain or the spinal cord, which motivates the development of appropriate methods for processing these datasets.

---

* The research was in part funded by the grant NIH EB007082.

F. Nielsen (Ed.): ETVC 2008, LNCS 5416, pp. 327–346, 2009.

The acquired DW-MRI signal is attenuated at locations of higher diffusivity and can be observed if they are along the direction of the diffusion sensitizing magnetic gradient. This attenuation is popularly approximated by the Stejkal-Tanner equation [1] as follows:

$$S/S_0 = e^{-bd(\mathbf{g})} \tag{1}$$

where S is the signal acquired by applying diffusion-weighting magnetic gradient field with direction $\mathbf{g}$ and (a weighting) b-value b, S_0 is the signal acquired without diffusion-weighting, and $d(\mathbf{g})$ is the so called diffusivity function. In the original form of the signal attenuation equation (by Stejskal and Tanner [1]) the diffusivity function was approximated by a constant $d(\mathbf{g}) = d$ representing the mean diffusivity. The advances in imaging techniques however made it possible to acquire several diffusion-weighted MR images S_i by applying different diffusion gradient directions $\mathbf{g}_i$. This allowed for the approximation of the diffusivity function with a second-order tensor $d(\mathbf{g}) = \mathbf{g}^T \mathbf{D} \mathbf{g}$, where $\mathbf{D}$ is a 3×3 symmetric and positive-definite matrix – see Basser et al., [2], for pioneering research in this direction.

The relation between the diffusion-weighted signal attenuation (eq. 1) and the diffusion propagator equation is given by the following Fourier integral expression

$$P(\mathbf{r}) = \int S(\mathbf{q})/S_0 e^{-2\pi i \mathbf{q}^T \mathbf{r}} d\mathbf{q} \tag{2}$$

where $\mathbf{q}$ is the reciprocal space vector, $S(\mathbf{q})$ is the DW-MRI signal value associated with vector $\mathbf{q}$, S_0 the zero gradient signal and $\mathbf{r}$ is the displacement vector [3]. Note that the direction of vector $\mathbf{q}$ in Eq. 2 is the same with that of $\mathbf{g}$ in Eq. 1 and that b is related to the magnitude of $\mathbf{q}$ with the expression $b = 4\pi q^2 t$, where t is the effective diffusion time.

By using the tensorial approximation of the diffusivity function, the Fourier transform in Eq. 2 can be computed analytically and is given by,

$$P(\mathbf{r}) = \frac{1}{\sqrt{(2\pi)^3 |2t\mathbf{D}|}} e^{-\frac{1}{4t} \mathbf{r}^T \mathbf{D}^{-1} \mathbf{r}}. \tag{3}$$

The orientation $\mathbf{r}$ that maximizes the displacement probability $P(\mathbf{r})$ corresponds to the orientation of maximum water molecule diffusion. In the diffusion tensor model case, it can be easily seen that Eq. 3 is maximized when the quantity $\mathbf{r}^T \mathbf{D} \mathbf{r}$ is also maximized, i.e. for vectors $\mathbf{r}$ which are parallel to the primary eigen-vector of matrix $\mathbf{D}$. Therefore, by computing the primary eigen-vector of $\mathbf{D}$ using the method of spectral decomposition one can easily estimate the orientation of maximum diffusion, which is one of the advantages of diffusion tensor imaging. Furthermore, by following the primary eigen-vectors one can trace the underlying fiber paths in the neural tissue [4]. This procedure is known as fiber tracking and it is a tool for obtaining information and analyzing the brain connectivity.

The estimation of a smooth field of diffusion tensors and its segmentation can be performed by using an information theoretic approach first introduced in literature by Wang et al., [5] and reviewed in Sec. 2. Other methods include the geometric approach using the Riemannian metric of the space of positive-definite matrices [6,7,8,9], tensor spline regularization [10], the log-Euclidean framework [11] and the Geodesic-loxodromes method [12] for tensor interpolation.

The diffusion tensor model can be extended for cases of complex fiber structures, such as fiber crossings, using the multi-compartmental model also known as the mixture model given by:

$$S(\mathbf{q})/S_0 = \sum_i^N w_i S_i(\mathbf{q}) \tag{4}$$

where w_i are unknown mixing weights [13]. The drawback in this discrete mixture model is that its difficult to select a priori, the number N of mixing compartments. This problem can however be solved by using the continuous mixture model as was first proposed in Jian et al., [14] and later in Kumar et al., [15,16], both of which can be expressed in the following unified de-convolution framework introduced in Jian and Vemuri [17],

$$S(\mathbf{q})/S_0 = \int f(X)K(\mathbf{q}|X)dX. \tag{5}$$

In Eq. 5 the signal response is parametrized using a kernel function $K(\mathbf{q}|X)$, where X is a set of parameters, $f(X)$ is a properly chosen mixing density function over the domain of X, and the integration is with respect to X.

In Sec. 3 we study two different versions of Eq. 5: a) setting X to be the diffusion tensor $\mathbf{D}$ and $f(\mathbf{D})$ to be a mixing density function on the space of 3×3 symmetric and positive-definite matrices [14], and b) setting X to be a 3-dimensional unit vector μ representing the orientation of maximum signal response and $f(\mu)$ to be a mixing density over the space of unit vectors (i.e. over the unit sphere) [15].

Other methods for multi-fiber reconstructions include higher-order tensor models [18,19], and their equivalent spherical tensor expansion [20], diffusion orientation transform for computing the displacement probability profiles from given diffusivity profiles [21], the estimation of orientation distribution function in q-ball imaging [22,23,24], spherical de-convolution [25,26,27,28], diffusion spectrum magnetic resonance imaging [29]. Recently, Jian and Vemuri [17] developed the unified de-convolution framework (Eq. 5) for multi-fiber reconstruction within a voxel from diffusion weighted MRI and posed several of the existing methods in this framework that facilitated easy comparison and showed superior performance of their continuous mixture of Wisharts model [14].

The performance of methods reviewed in this chapter are demonstrated using synthetic and real diffusion-weighted MRI data. The goal of applying various information theoretic concepts to analyze the real data is to unravel the underlying fiber geometry making explicit the connectivity patterns in various regions of the neural tissue. From a clinical point of view, to date, several methods for analyzing the diffusivity have been used in monitoring encephalopathy, sclerosis, ischemia and other brain disorders [30,31]. We hope that some of the methods reviewed here will be of use in analyzing these neurological disorders in the near future. The rest of the chapter is organized as follows. In Sec. 2 we review the information theoretic method from [5] for regularizing and segmenting diffusion tensor fields. Information geometric methods for multi-fiber reconstruction are reviewed in Sec. 3. Each section is accompanied by an experimental results subsection demonstrating the performance of the presented methods. Finally in Sec. 4 we conclude.

2 Information Theoretic Methods for Processing DTI

In this section we review an information theoretic dissimilarity measure for the space of positive definite-matrices. A dissimilarity measure between tensors is needed in several tensor-valued image analysis methods, such as in regularization, interpolation and segmentation of tensor fields.

2.1 An Information Theoretic Dissimilarity Measure

It is well known that Brownian motion of the water molecules in the soft tissue is a Gaussian process, and therefore it is known that the diffusion propagator is given by the Gaussian probability expressed in Eq. 3. The diffusion tensor is defined as the covariance matrix in this probability density function; hence a natural dissimilarity measure between diffusion tensors can be defined by employing a divergence between the corresponding Gaussian probabilities. Wang and Vemuri defined a dissimilarity measure between two given tensors $\mathbf{D}_1$ and $\mathbf{D}_2$ by using the J-divergence as follows

$$d(\mathbf{D}_1, \mathbf{D}_2) = \sqrt{J(P(\mathbf{q}|\mathbf{D}_1), P(\mathbf{q}|\mathbf{D}_2))} = \sqrt{\frac{KL(P_1, P_2) + KL(P_2, P_1)}{2}} \quad (6)$$

where $P_1 = P(\mathbf{q}|\mathbf{D}_1)$, $P_2 = P(\mathbf{q}|\mathbf{D}_2)$ and KL is the well known KL-divergence [32] given by $KL(p_1, p_2) = \int p_1(\mathbf{q}) log(\frac{p_1(\mathbf{q})}{p_2(\mathbf{q})}) d\mathbf{q}$. By substituting $P(\mathbf{q}|\mathbf{D}_1)$ and $P(\mathbf{q}|\mathbf{D}_2))$ in Eq. 6 by the Gaussian probability in Eq. 3, the following closed form can be derived

$$d(\mathbf{D}_1, \mathbf{D}_2) = \frac{1}{2} \sqrt{trace(\mathbf{D}_1^{-1}\mathbf{D}_2 + \mathbf{D}_2^{-1}\mathbf{D}_1) - 2n} \quad (7)$$

where n is the dimension of the matrix, i.e. in the diffusion tensor case $n = 3$. The proof of Eq. 7 was first published in [5]. A useful property of the dissimilarity measure defined above is the invariance to affine transformations. In other words, $d(\mathbf{D}_1, \mathbf{D}_2) = d(\mathbf{A}\mathbf{D}_1\mathbf{A}^T, \mathbf{A}\mathbf{D}_2\mathbf{A}^T)$ where $\mathbf{A}$ is an affine transformation matrix.

The dissimilarity measure given by Eq. 7 cannot be considered as a distance between tensors since it fails to satisfy the triangle inequality. However, it can be shown that for infinitesimally close tensors $\mathbf{D}_1$ and $\mathbf{D}_2$, Eq. 7 approximates the squared Riemannian geodesic distance between them (which was used in

[6]). Therefore, in this case we can say that Eq. 7 approximates the Rao distance (which is also the Riemannian distance) between the two nearby Gaussian distributions $P_1(\mathbf{q})$ and $P_2(\mathbf{q})$.

The above dissimilarity measure can be employed for defining the average tensor $\mathbf{D}_\mu$ in a tensor field as the minimizer of $\int d^2(\mathbf{D}_\mu, \mathbf{D}(\mathbf{x}))d\mathbf{x}$, i.e. $\mathbf{D}_\mu$ is the tensor representing the mean of the elements of the field. Here the vector $\mathbf{x}$ denotes the lattice index in the tensor field. By substituting Eq. 7 into the above integral, it was shown in [5] that the average tensor is given by

$$\mathbf{D}_\mu = \sqrt{\mathbf{B}^{-1}} \sqrt{\sqrt{\mathbf{B}} \mathbf{A} \sqrt{\mathbf{B}}} \sqrt{\mathbf{B}^{-1}} \tag{8}$$

where $\mathbf{A} = \int_R \mathbf{D}(\mathbf{x})d\mathbf{x}$ and $\mathbf{B} = \int_R \mathbf{D}^{-1}(\mathbf{x})d\mathbf{x}$

Here we note that Eq. 8 is valid also for computing the average tensor $\mathbf{D}_\mu$ defined as the mid-point in the geodesic between two tensors $\mathbf{D}_1$ and $\mathbf{D}_2$ using the Riemmanian metric of $\mathcal{P}_n$ [6,7,9] and setting $\mathbf{A} = \mathbf{D}_1$ and $\mathbf{B} = \mathbf{D}_2^{-1}$. The symbol $\mathcal{P}_n$ denotes the space of $n \times n$ symmetric positive-definite matrices. However, in the Riemmanian framework there is no analytic formula for computing the average of more than two tensors (e.g. tensor field), and an iterative optimization method has been used instead, which significantly increases the execution time of the diffusion tensor processing algorithms.

In the next section, we review how the formulas presented here can be employed in a level-set framework for segmenting diffusion tensor fields.

2.2   Application to DTI Segmentation

The segmentation of a DTI field can be performed by minimizing the following Mumford-Shah energy function

$$E(\mathbf{D}, C) = E_{dist} + E_{reg} + E_{arc} = \alpha \int_\Omega d^2(\mathbf{D}(\mathbf{x}), \mathbf{D}_0(\mathbf{x}))d\mathbf{x} + \int_{\Omega/C} \nabla \mathbf{D}(\mathbf{x})d\mathbf{x} + \beta|C| \tag{9}$$

where $\mathbf{D}_0(\mathbf{x})$ is the given noisy tensor field, $\mathbf{D}(\mathbf{x})$ is the approximated (fitted) tensor field, Ω is the domain of the field (i.e. $\Re^2$ or $\Re^3$ for 2D or 3D fields respectively), C is the boundary between the segmented regions, and α and β are constant factors. The first term in Eq. 9 measures the dissimilarity between the fitted tensor field and the original noisy field, the second term measures the variation (or the lack of smoothness) within the segmented regions, and the last term measures the arc length of the segmentation curve C.

In the case that the fitted field $\mathbf{D}(\mathbf{x})$ is chosen to be a piecewise constant model, the second term in Eq. 9 becomes $E_{reg} = 0$, while the first term is given by

$$E_{dist} = \sum_{\mathbf{x} \in R} d^2(\mathbf{D}_1, \mathbf{D}_0(\mathbf{x})) + \sum_{\mathbf{x} \in R^c} d^2(\mathbf{D}_2, \mathbf{D}_0(\mathbf{x})) \tag{10}$$

where $\mathbf{D}_1$ is the mean tensor in the region R enclosed by the curve C and $\mathbf{D}_2$ is the mean tensor in the region R^c outside the segmentation curve. Note that since the given tensor field is on a discrete lattice, the integral of Eq. 9 has been replaced by a summation in Eq. 10.

Instead of the piecewise constant model used above, a piecewise continuous model may be chosen to approximate the tensor field. In this case the dissimilarity term in Eq. 9 is given by the following expression

$$E_{dist} = \alpha \sum_{\mathbf{x} \in R} d^2(\mathbf{D}(\mathbf{x}), \mathbf{D}_0(\mathbf{x})) + \alpha \sum_{\mathbf{x} \in R^c} d^2(\mathbf{D}(\mathbf{x}), \mathbf{D}_0(\mathbf{x})) \qquad (11)$$

and the second term in Eq. 9 becomes

$$E_{reg} = \sum_{(\mathbf{x},\mathbf{y}) \in R, \mathbf{y} \in N_{\mathbf{x}}} d^2(\mathbf{D}(\mathbf{x}), \mathbf{D}(\mathbf{y})) + \sum_{(\mathbf{x},\mathbf{y}) \in R^c, \mathbf{y} \in N_{\mathbf{x}}} d^2(\mathbf{D}(\mathbf{x}), \mathbf{D}(\mathbf{y})). \qquad (12)$$

where each term measures the lack of smoothness within the segmented regions and $N_{\mathbf{x}}$ is a neighborhood centered at location $\mathbf{x}$.

In both piecewise constant and piecewise continuous models, the distance function $d(,)$ can be set to the dissimilarity measure defined in Eq. 7 since the latter approximates the geodesic distance between two nearby elements in the space $\mathcal{P}_n$ of positive definite matrices. Furthermore, the simple closed-form expression of Eq. 7 and 8 make it possible to produce analytic update formulas for minimizing the variational principle, which is one of the main advantages of this information theoretic dissimilarity measure over the $\mathcal{P}_n$ Riemannian metric.

The curve evolution equations for the above segmentation framework are reported along with their derivations in [5]. There in also lies a detailed discussion about the implementation of the algorithm and the numerical techniques used to solve the flow equations. The above methods are demonstrated in the next section using simulated synthetic and real diffusion-weighted MR data sets.

2.3   Experimental Results

In this section we present experimental results obtained by applying the DTI segmentation method reviewed earlier to synthetic and real DW-MRI data sets. The synthetic tensor field (shown in Fig. 1) is of size 32×32 and consists of the following regions: (1) a ring with principal eigenvectors tangent to circles centered in the lower left corner of the image; (2) two triangular regions with horizontal principal eigenvectors; and (3) two triangular regions with vertical principal eigenvectors. All three regions have distinct piecewise constant fractional anisotropy. Figure 1 (upper left plate) shows a plot of the primary eigenvectors.

We applied the piecewise continuous DTI segmentation method presented in Sec. 2.2 for segmenting the circular region in the synthetic data set. The challenge in segmenting this data set is due to the smooth transitions between the regions, especially at the locations shown in the upper central plate of Fig. 1. In the method we used the values $\alpha = -2.5$ (advection) and the $\beta = 0.01$ (smoothing). The segmentation boundaries were initialized as shown in the lower left plate of the same figure. After the execution of the method the boundaries converged

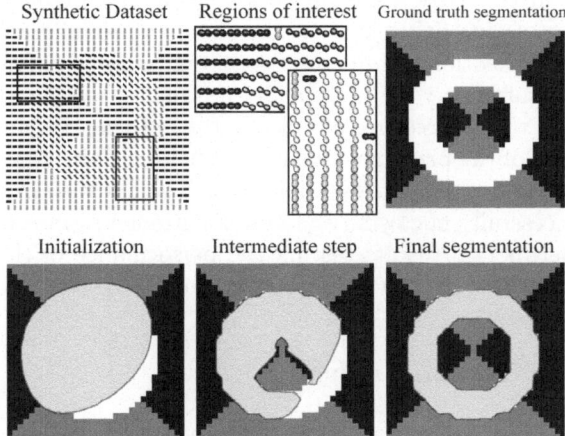

Fig. 1. Application of the piecewise continuous DTI segmentation method in a synthetic dataset

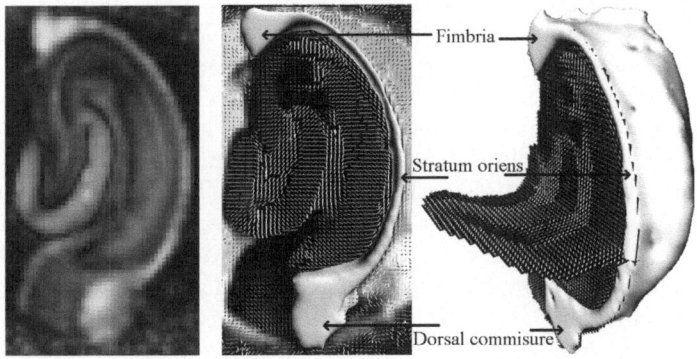

Fig. 2. Segmentation of the fimbria-stratum oriens-dorsal commisure region in a real rat hippocampus dataset. Left: Fractional anisotropy, Center and Right: 2D and 3D view of the segmented region.

as shown in the lower right plate, accurately segmenting the ring region. This demonstrates the effectiveness of the presented method.

Finally, in order to illustrate the performance of the segmentation framework on real data sets, we applied the method to a DTI data set from an excised rat hippocampus (shown in Fig. 2). The original DW-MRI data set contained 22 images acquired using a pulsed gradient spin echo pulse sequence, with 21 different diffusion gradients and approximate b value of 1250 s/mm^2. From this data set we estimated a DTI field using the variational formulation proposed in [33,34]. Then, we segmented the hippocampal region that consists of fimbria, stratum oriens and dorsal commisure using the method reviewed in this section.

The tensor field in this region is smoothly varying and highly anisotropic. For the segmentation of this field we used the same value for α as before, but we increased the regularization parameter $\beta = 2.0$ in order to enforce smoothing of the segmentation curve and therefore avoid producing results with 'bumps' and other artifacts due to the presence of noise in the data set. Figure 2 shows, in 2D and 3D views, part of the principal eigenvector field and the segmentation result. By observing the figures we can see that smooth segmentation boundaries have been created successfully enclosing the aforementioned hippocampal regions.

For more experimental results testing the performance of the method under various noise conditions the reader is referred to [5].

3   Multi-fiber Reconstruction

In the information theoretic framework discussed in the previous section, a second order tensor (Diffusion Tensor) was employed to approximate the diffusivity function in the Stejskal-Tanner model of DW-MRI attenuation (Eq. 1). However, the second-order tensorial approximation fails to represent complex local geometries of the tissue, such as fiber crossings [21,4]. Several methods have been proposed for multi-fiber reconstruction, and they can be categorized into model-free and model-based methods as was mentioned in Sec. 1. Jian and Vemuri [17] have shown that many of the model-based methods can be regarded as special cases of the unified framework formulation presented by them and given by Eq. 5.

In this section we discuss two special cases in this unified framework by setting the mixing density $f(X)$ in Eq. 5 to be (a) a mixture of Wishart distributions, and (b) a mixture of von Mises-Fisher distributions. The motivation for studying these two methods is that the first one approximates the DW-MRI signal attenuation by using statistics on the space of diffusion tensors while the second one solves the same problem by following a more general approach for approximating any function on a spherical domain.

3.1   The Mixture of Wisharts Model

The Wishart distribution of positive-definite matrices is a generalization of the gamma distribution (to non-integer degrees of freedom) and of the chi-square distribution (to multiple dimensions) and its probability density function [35] in the case of (3×3) matrices is given by

$$f_w(\mathbf{D}|\mathbf{\Sigma}, p) = \frac{|\mathbf{D}|^{p-2} exp(-trace(\mathbf{\Sigma}^{-1}\mathbf{D}))}{2^{2p}|\mathbf{\Sigma}|^p \Gamma_3(p)} \tag{13}$$

where $\mathbf{D}$ is the matrix-valued random variable, $\mathbf{\Sigma}$ is the scale parameter (both $\mathbf{D}$ and $\mathbf{\Sigma}$ are positive definite matrices), and p is a scalar that controls the shape of the distribution.

The DW-MRI signal attenuation model of discrete mixture of Gaussians can be extended to a continuous mixture model in this unified framework [14] given by 5 and setting the parameter vector X to be a 3×3 positive-definite matrix $\mathbf{D}$, the mixing density $f(X)$ to be the Wishart distribution (Eq. 13) and the signal Kernel $K(\mathbf{q}|X)$ to be the Stejskal-Tanner model (Eq. 1). After these substitutions, we obtain a continuous mixture model that is given by

$$S/S_0 = \int f_w(\mathbf{D}) e^{-b\mathbf{g}^T \mathbf{D} \mathbf{g}} d\mathbf{D} = \int f_w(\mathbf{D}) e^{-trace(\mathbf{BD})} d\mathbf{D} \qquad (14)$$

where $\mathbf{B}$ is a 3×3 matrix defined as $b\mathbf{g}\mathbf{g}^T$ and the integration is over the space of positive-definite matrices. Note that the exponent in the right side of Eq. 14 is written in the equivalent form of the trace of $\mathbf{BD}$. In this form, Eq. 14 can be seen as the Laplace transform (in the case of matrices) of the Wishart distribution [14]. This Laplace transform integral can be computed analytically as it has been shown in [14], giving the following expression

$$S/S_0 = |\mathbf{I} + \mathbf{B\Sigma}|^{-p} = |1 + b\mathbf{g}^T \mathbf{\Sigma} \mathbf{g}|^{-p}. \qquad (15)$$

Equation 15 is a novel model for the DW-MRI signal attenuation distinct from the commonly used Eq. 1. The latter was however shown to be a limiting case of Eq. 15 by setting $\mathbf{\Sigma} = \mathbf{D}/p$ and $p \to \infty$. Thus, the model in equation 15 is a generalization of the 35 year old and popular Stejskal-Tanner model for MR signal decay. Another interesting observation is that it is also a generalization of the multi-compartmental (bi-Gaussian etc.) models [22] popular in literature.

The obtained model is still incapable of approximating complex local geometries of the tissue due to the fact that the mixing density was limited to the case of a single Wishart distribution. This problem can be solved by setting the mixing density to be a mixture of N Wishart distributions. Note however that, we still have a continuous approximation and not a discrete approximation. In this case, Eq. 14 becomes

$$S/S_0 = \int \sum_{i=1}^{N} w_i f_w(\mathbf{D}|\mathbf{\Sigma}_i, p) e^{-b\mathbf{g}^T \mathbf{D} \mathbf{g}} d\mathbf{D} = \sum_{i=1}^{N} w_i |1 + b\mathbf{g}^T \mathbf{\Sigma}_i \mathbf{g}|^{-p} \qquad (16)$$

where w_i are the mixing weights and $\mathbf{\Sigma}_i$ are the corresponding scaling parameters of the Wishart distributions. For simplicity the shape parameter p was taken to be the same in all mixing components.

Here we should note that although Eq. 16 can be seen as a discrete mixture of functions in the form $|1 + b\mathbf{g}^T \mathbf{\Sigma}_i \mathbf{g}|^{-p}$, it was derived as a continuous mixture of signal attenuations modeled by the Stejskal-Tanner Eq. 1. Hence, the number of mixing components N should not be interpreted as the number of underlying distinct fiber populations but as the resolution of the mixing density $f(\mathbf{D})$. Theoretically, any distribution of positive-definite matrices can be arbitrarily approximated by taking an appropriately large number N in the mixture of Wisharts.

The set of the positive-definite matrices $\mathbf{\Sigma}_i$ must be constructed in such a way that the full space of 3×3 positive-definite matrices is appropriately sampled. However, the space of symmetric positive-definite matrices is a 6-dimensional

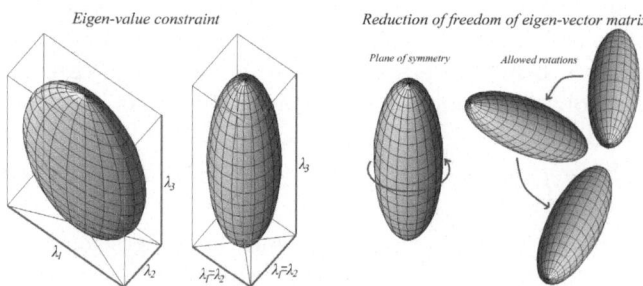

Fig. 3. Illustration of the dimensionality reduction of 3×3 symmetric positive-definite matrices, shown here as Gaussian ellipsoids. Left: We assume the two smallest eigenvalues λ_1 and λ_2 to be equal due to the cylindrical geometry of fibers. Right: Reduction of the space of rotations due to symmetry.

space, hence it cannot be efficiently sampled by a computationally feasible manner. In order to overcome this issue, further assumptions about the fiber geometry must be made in order to reduce the above space to those matrices Σ_i which are practically meaningful in our particular application.

If we express the matrix Σ using the spectral decomposition as $\mathbf{v}\Lambda\mathbf{v}^T$ (where $\mathbf{v}$ is an orthogonal eigen-vector matrix and Λ is a diagonal matrix of eigenvalues), 3 out of the 6 degrees of freedom are in the three eigenvalues λ_1, λ_2, λ_3 and the other 3 degrees are in the orthogonal eigen-vector matrix. By considering the approximately cylindrical geometry of the fibers, we can reduce our solution to those matrices Σ whose two smallest eigen-values are equal [14], i.e. elimination of 1 degree of freedom. Furthermore, due to the rotational symmetry of those matrices along the plane defined by the two smallest eigenvectors, the dimensionality of the orthogonal eigen-vector matrices is reduced to 2 [14], i.e. elimination of 1 additional degree of freedom. The above assumptions (illustrated in Fig. 3) produce a 4-dimensional space whose sampling is practically more feasible and is employed in the experiments presented in Sec. 3.4.

In the next section, we review another special case of the unified deconvolution framework, by using the von Mises-Fisher distribution instead of the Wishart.

3.2   The Mixture of Von Mises-Fisher Model

The von Mises-Fisher (vMF) distribution is the special case in 3 dimensions of the von Mises distribution of unit vectors. The vMF distribution is the analogous of the Gaussian distribution on the space of 3-dimensional unit vectors and it has the following probability density function

$$f_{vMF}(\mathbf{x}|\mu, \kappa) = \frac{\kappa}{4\pi sinh\kappa}e^{\kappa\mu^T\mathbf{x}} \tag{17}$$

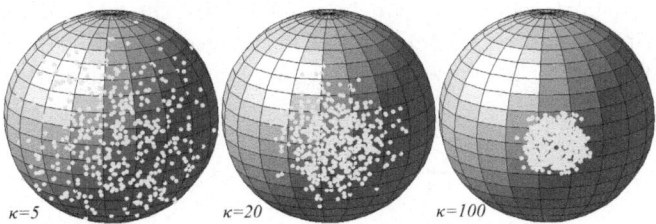

Fig. 4. Samples drawn from von Mises-Fisher distributions using different concentrations κ

where $\mathbf{x}$ and μ are unit vectors, μ is the center of the distribution and κ is a positive scalar that controls the concentration of the probability. Figure 4 shows examples of the von Mises-Fisher distribution for different concentration values.

In the area of diffusion-weighted MR imaging, the vMF distribution has been used by McGraw et al. [36,37] for approximating orientation distribution functions (ODF) and more recently mixtures of hyperspherical vMF have been used for high angular resolution DW-MRI approximation [38]. Here we should note that the magnitude of the DW-MR signal as well as the estimated ODF, the displacement probability and the diffusivity function are all antipodally symmetric, i.e. $f(x) = f(-x)$. Since the vMF distribution function is not antipodally symmetric, a symmetrised vMF expression was employed in a mixture of vMF distributions [36] in order to model the ODF at each voxel of a DW-MRI data set as shown in the following equation.

$$\sum_{i=1}^{N} w_i \left[f_{vMF}(\mathbf{x}|\mu_i, \kappa_i) + f_{vMF}(-\mathbf{x}|\mu_i, \kappa_i) \right] / 2 \tag{18}$$

where w_i are the unknown mixing weights, which are non-negative and sum up to 1 in order the obtained mixture of vMFs (Eq. 18) to be also a probability density function. N is the number components and is assumed to be predefined, which is the main drawback of this model.

The above discrete mixture of vMFs can be extended using a continuous mixture of vMFs [15] by following similar reasoning with the formulation of the continuous mixture of Wisarts distributions, discussed in the previous section. In general, a continuous mixture of vMFs can be used to approximate any spherical function. The diffusion-weighted MR measurements when acquired over a single sphere of the $\mathbf{q}$-space, i.e. with constant b-value and varying diffusion gradient orientation $\mathbf{g}_i$, can be approximated by a spherical function model such as the continuous mixture of vMFs given by the expression

$$S/S_0 = \int f(\mu) \left[f_{vMF}(\mathbf{g}|\mu, 1) + f_{vMF}(-\mathbf{g}|\mu, 1) \right] d\mu = \int f(\mu) \frac{cosh(\mu^T \mathbf{g})}{4\pi sinh(1)} d\mu \tag{19}$$

where $f(\mu)$ is a mixing probability density function and the integration is over the unit sphere, i.e. the space of unit vectors μ. Since $f(\mu)$ is also a probability in the space of unit vectors, it can be modeled by the vMF density function (Eq. 17), or in the more general case by a mixture of vMFs. In this case, the MR signal attenuation is expressed by the following continuous mixture model

$$S/S_0 = \int \sum_{i=1}^{N} w_i f_{vMF}(\mu|\mathbf{v}_i, \kappa) \frac{cosh(\mu^T \mathbf{g})}{4\pi sinh(1)} d\mu \qquad (20)$$

where N is the resolution of the mixing density, i.e. the number of unit vectors $\mathbf{v}_i$ spanning the unit hemi-sphere. Note that the same concentration parameter κ was used in all the components of the mixture for simplicity.

By substituting Eq. 17 into Eq. 20 and taking the summation out of the integral, we obtain a sum of integrals in the form of Laplace transforms. These integrals can be computed analytically, as it was shown in [16,15] obtaining finally the model

$$S/S_0 = \sum_{i=1}^{N} \frac{w_i \kappa}{4\pi sinh(1) sinh(\kappa)} \left[\frac{sinh(\| \kappa \mathbf{v}_i - \mathbf{g} \|)}{\| \kappa \mathbf{v}_i - \mathbf{g} \|} + \frac{sinh(\| \kappa \mathbf{v}_i + \mathbf{g} \|)}{\| \kappa \mathbf{v}_i + \mathbf{g} \|} \right]. \qquad (21)$$

Theoretically, any spherical function $S(\mathbf{g})$ can be arbitrarily accurately approximated by Eq. 21 by using an appropriately large number N for the resolution of mixing density. As it was pointed out also in Sec. 3.1, although Eq. 21 is expressed in the form of a discrete mixture, the approximation is still a continuous mixture of symmetrized vMF distributions since it was derived from Eq. 20.

3.3   Estimation from DW-MRI Data

In this section, we study methods for fitting to DW-MRI data a mixture model such as the mixture of Wisharts or the mixture of von Mises-Fisher distributions discussed in Sec. 3.1 and 3.2 respectively. In both cases, the goal of the fitting procedure is to estimate the unknown mixing weights w_i such that the squared distance between the given data and the model is minimized.

Having acquired a set of M diffusion-weighted MR images, the goal is to fit either one of the mixture models described in the previous sections. At each voxel of the acquired images a spherical function modeled by the selected mixture model is fitted to the data by minimizing the following sum of squares energy

$$E(w_1, ..., w_N) = \sum_{j=1}^{M} \left(S_j/S_0 - \sum_{i=1}^{N} w_i S(b, \mathbf{g}_j|\mathbf{X}_i) \right)^2 \qquad (22)$$

where S_j are the M acquired diffusion-weighted images associated with b-value b and magnetic gradient direction $\mathbf{g}_j$, and S_0 is the acquired image without diffusion weighting. The expression $\sum_{i=1}^{N} w_i S(b, \mathbf{g}_j|\mathbf{X}_i)$ is the general form of Eq. 16 and Eq. 21 for the case of the mixture of Wisharts and the mixture of von

Mises-Fisher respectively, where $\mathbf{X}_i$ denotes the parameters of each model, i.e. Σ_i and $\mathbf{v}_i$ respectively. The energy function is minimized with respect to the unknown mixing weights w_i, $i = 1...N$.

Equation 22 can be rewritten in the form of an over determined linear system $\mathbf{Aw} = \mathbf{b}$, where $\mathbf{A}$ is an $M \times N$ matrix whose elements are $A_{j,i} = S(b, \mathbf{g}_j | \mathbf{X}_i)$, $\mathbf{w}$ is a N-dimensional vector of unknowns w_i, and $\mathbf{b}$ is a N-dimensional vector whose elements are the acquired signal attenuations $b_j = S_j / S_0$. This over determined linear system can be solved in a least square sense, whose solution will correspond to the solution obtained by minimizing Eq. 22. In the case of the mixture of Wisharts model, the elements of matrix $\mathbf{A}$ are given by

$$A_{j,i} = |1 + b\mathbf{g}_j^T \Sigma_i \mathbf{g}_j|^{-p} \tag{23}$$

while in the case of the mixture of von Mises-Fisher model, the elements are

$$A_{j,i} = \frac{\kappa}{4\pi sinh(1)sinh(\kappa)} \left[\frac{sinh(\| \kappa\mathbf{v}_i - \mathbf{g}_j \|)}{\| \kappa\mathbf{v}_i - \mathbf{g}_j \|} + \frac{sinh(\| \kappa\mathbf{v}_i + \mathbf{g}_j \|)}{\| \kappa\mathbf{v}_i + \mathbf{g}_j \|} \right]. \tag{24}$$

Different methods for solving the obtained linear system have been compared extensively by Jian and Vemuri in [39]. According to the results presented in [39] the best results are obtained by using the NNLS algorithm. Here, we should note that theoretically the weights w_i are non negative and they sum up to 1, since they were introduced as the mixing components in a probability distribution function (see Sec. 3.1 and 3.2). However, due to inaccuracies in measuring the signal attenuation ratio S_j / S_0, the sum of the estimated weights may not be 1, although each w_i is greater than or equal to zero. In this case the weights can be normalized by dividing the vector $\mathbf{w}$ as well as the vector $\mathbf{b}$ with the normalizing factor Σw_i.

After having fitted the mixture model to the data, the reconstructed signal $S(\mathbf{g})$ at each voxel can be plotted as a spherical function, i.e. over the space of unit vectors $\mathbf{g}$. However, in order to understand the estimated diffusivity pattern which corresponds to the underlying fiber structure, the displacement probability function $P(\mathbf{r})$ must be computed, whose peaks corresponds to the orientation of distinct fiber distributions. The displacement probability can be estimated by evaluating the Fourier integral given by Eq. 2.

In both mixture model cases this integral cannot be evaluated analytically. In the case of the mixture of Wisharts the integral can be approximated by $\Sigma w_i P_i(\mathbf{r})$, where $P_i(\mathbf{r})$ is given by Eq. 3. The error introduced by this approximation decreases with increasing parameter values for p in the Wishart distribution and becomes zero when $p \to \infty$. Jian et al. [14] have used the value $p = 2$ based on the analogy between Eq. 15 and the Debye-Porod law of diffraction [40] for porous media, and it has been shown that the accuracy of the approximated displacement probability in estimating fiber orientations is higher than that of other existing techniques.

In the case of the mixture of von Mises-Fisher distributions, the Fourier integral cannot be computed analytically either, and no approximation formula has been reported to date. An efficient way to estimate the displacement probability from this model is to use the general method presented in [41] for approximating the probability from a set of DW-MR acquired images. In our particular case of the von Mises-Fisher model, the recovered signal attenuation can be computed from the approximated mixture model by evaluating Eq. 21 for a large set of unit vectors $\mathbf{g}_i$. The set of vectors can be constructed by tessellating the icosahedron on the unit hemi-sphere. After having computed the $S_i = S(\mathbf{g}_i)/S_0$ the set of S_i can be considered as a new high angular resolution DW-MR data set and used by the algorithm in [41] for estimating the displacement probability as a 4th-order Cartesian tensor.

Finally, after having estimated the displacement probability $P(\mathbf{r})$ it can be plotted as a spherical function over displacement vectors $\mathbf{r}$ of same magnitude. The orientations $\mathbf{r}$ that correspond to the peaks of the probability function can be computed by following the maxima of this spherical function. In order to compute all the peaks of the possibly multi-lobed displacement probability, the gradient ascent is initialized in multiple different orientations $\mathbf{r}$. The obtained orientations of maximum water molecule displacement probability can be further used by a fiber tracking method for computing complicated fiber structures such as crossing and splaying fibers [42,43].

In the next section several examples of multi-fiber reconstruction from synthetic as well as real diffusion-weighted MR data are shown. A table of comparison between the discussed mixture models is also presented and it is supported by quantitative experimental results.

3.4   Experimental Results

In this section we present experimental results obtained by applying the multi-fiber reconstruction methods presented previously, using synthetic and real DW-MRI datasets. The synthetic data set was produced by simulating the signal response on a fiber of cylindrical geometry using the realistic model in [44].

First, we compared the basis derived from the MoW and MovMF models (Eq. 23 and 24 respectively) with the simulated signal response, in order to demonstrate the ability of the basis derived from the MoW model in approximating the true DW-MRI signal. In this experiment we first defined a fiber orientation $\mathbf{v}$ and simulated the DW-MRI signal for various diffusion magnetic gradient directions $\mathbf{g}_i$. Then, we evaluated the basis functions given by Eq. 23 and Eq. 24 respectively for various $\mathbf{g}_i$. The primary eigenvector of $\boldsymbol{\Sigma}$ in Eq. 23 was taken to be parallel to the fiber orientation $\mathbf{v}$, and we used the parameters $p = 2$ and $\kappa = 10$ for the MoW and MovMF models respectively. The plots of the three functions are shown in Fig. 5.

By observing Fig. 5 we can see that the MoW model better approximates the simulated DW-MRI signal in comparison to the MovMF model-based approximation. Therefore, a single fiber response can be approximated by employing only one basis in the MoW model (i.e. only one non-zero w_i in Eq. 16), while on the other hand an appropriate mixture of the MovMF basis must be employed (i.e. several non-zero w_i in Eq. 17). This experimentally validates the MoW model as a better suited approximation over the MovMF model which

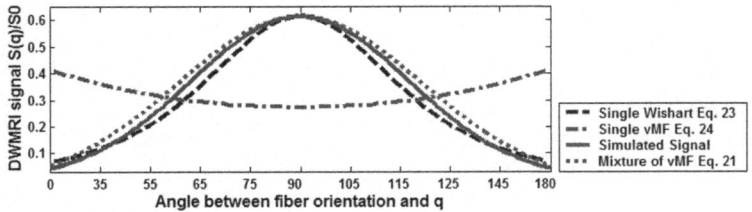

Fig. 5. Plots of the DW-MRI signal response for a single fiber when using the MoW and MovMF basis function-based models respectively

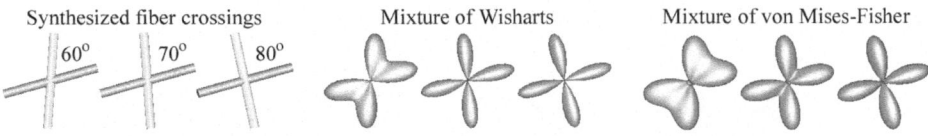

Fig. 6. Multi-fiber reconstruction example. Left: orientations of the synthetic fiber crossings. Center and Right: The corresponding displacement probabilities estimated by the MoW and the MovMF models.

is simply a general set of basis for approximating spherical functions but not necessarily well suited to represent the MR-signal decay. As an interesting side, note that the MovMF model has been also used in approximating facial apparent bidirectional reflectance distribution functions [16], which are also spherical functions.

In order to demonstrate the ability of the methods in resolving fiber orientations in the presence of fiber crossings, we simulated the DW-MRI signal [44] for the cases where two fibers are crossing each other and form an angle of 60°, 70° and 80° degrees respectively (shown in the left plate of Fig. 6). The simulated signal, consisting of 81 measurements (at each crossing location) corresponding to different gradient directions, was approximated by the MoW and MovMF methods. The estimated displacement probabilities for the two methods are shown in the central and right plates of Fig. 6 respectively. In the MoW case the resulting spherical function plots have sharper lobes than those in the MovMF model. The sharpness of the plots in the MoW model is due to the ability of the model to better approximate the true DW-MRI signal and the existence of an analytic form for approximating the displacement probability, which improves the accuracy of computation. A detailed comparison of the accuracy of each method in estimating fiber orientations can be found in [15].

Further, we applied the methods to a real data set from an excised perfusion-fixed rat brain. The DW-MRI data set was acquired using a pulsed gradient spin echo pulse sequence with 32 diffusion gradients and $b \simeq 1250 \ s/mm^2$. The region of interest depicted in Fig. 7 contains intersecting fibers from cingulum

S_0 image   Mixture of Wisharts   Mixture of von Mises-Fisher   Comparison

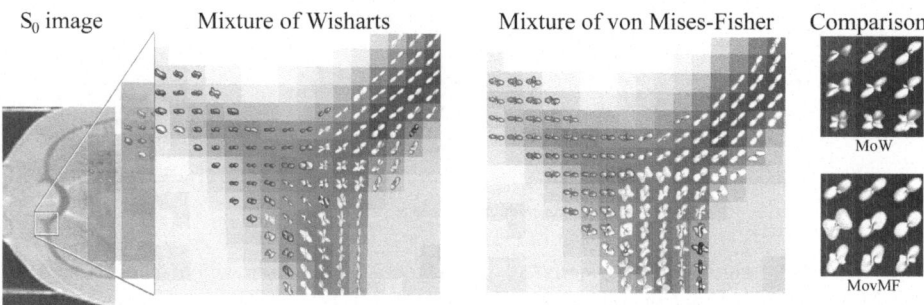

Fig. 7. Application of the MoW and MovMF methods to a rat brain data set. The depicted ROI shows fibers from the cingulum and corpus callosum crossing over.

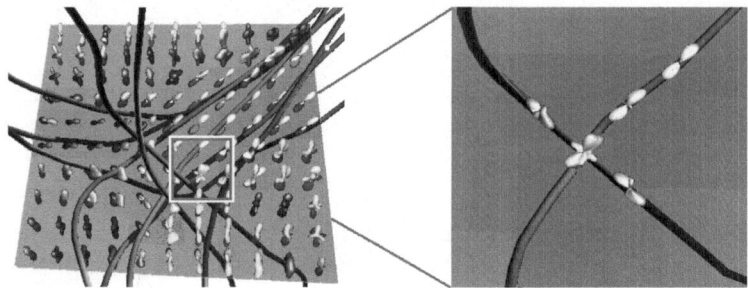

Fig. 8. Fiber tracking example by following the intra-voxel fiber orientations estimated by the MoW method

and corpus callosum. By observing the computed displacement probabilities, as anticipated, we can see that both methods estimated crossings at voxels located in the center of this region.

After having estimated the water molecule displacement probabilities as shown in Fig. 7, one can perform fiber tracking by applying a fiber tracking method to the field of probabilities [4,43]. Figure 8 shows some of the estimated fibers from the cingulum and the corpus callosum crossing over. A fiber crossing is more clearly depicted in the right plate of the same figure, with the estimated displacement probability plots superimposed.

Finally we present in Table 1 a summary of the properties of the two methods studied in this section. First, the MoW model was defined (in Eq. 14) as a continuous mixture of Gaussians, where each Gaussian is in the form of the DW-MRI signal attenuation defined in Eq. 1. This produces a model (in Eq. 23) which is natural for DW-MRI, while on the other hand, the MovMF model is a general basis (Eq. 24) for approximating any spherical function. Furthermore, the basis (Eq. 23) derived in the MoW model, approximates closely the true DW-MRI signal response obtained by using the realistic simulation model in [44]. However, as it was expected, the basis (Eq. 23) derived in the MovMF case

Table 1. Properties of the two models discussed in Sec. 3.1 and 3.2 [14,15]

	Wishart model	von Mises-Fisher model
Model specialized in:	DW-MRI	spherical functions
Integration space:	$\mathcal{P}_n$	S_2
Pre-defined shape parameter:	p	κ
The space of mixing densities:	not spanned completely	spanned uniformly
Signal attenuation is modeled:	very accurately	poorly

fails to approximate the signal response since it is a general spherical function basis and not specifically tailored to approximate the MR signal response from single fibers.

4   Conclusions

In this chapter we reviewed several information theoretic methods for DTI and DW-MRI processing and analysis. In the case of DTI, we reviewed an information theoretic dissimilarity measure between two tensors and then employed it in a tensor field segmentation framework. The main advantages of this dissimilarity measure over other existing metrics is that it has an analytic form and it also approximates the Riemannian geodesic distance between two nearby tensors [5]. Additionally, unlike most other non-Euclidean measures, it provides a closed form expression for computing the mean tensor of a set of tensors and hence is very useful as a computationally efficient tensor interpolation technique.

Furthermore, we studied two methods for multi-fiber reconstruction by modeling the DW-MRI signal as a continuous mixture of basis. In the first method the mixing density was set to be mixture of Wishart distributions, while the von Mises-Fisher distribution of unit vectors was employed in the other method. The mixture of Wisharts model is a natural choice for modeling the MR signal response in the presence of multiple fibers in a voxel since this model constitutes a continuous mixture of responses from single fibers. In contrast, the continuous mixture of vMFs is a natural choice for expressing any multi-lobed spherical functions which may or may not necessarily have anything to do with MR signal responses obtained in the presence of multiple fibers in a voxel. For more details on the mixture of Wishart's and the mixture of vMFs model we refer the reader to [14,39,17] and [15] respectively.

Acknowledgments

Authors thank Drs. Paul R. Carney and Thomas H. Mareci respectively for providing the rat brain data set and Drs. T. M. Shepherd and Evren Özarslan respectively for providing the rat hippocampus data set.

References

1. Stejskal, E.O., Tanner, J.E.: Spin diffusion measurements: spin echoes in the presence of a time-dependent field gradient. J. Chem. Phys. 42(1), 288–292 (1965)
2. Basser, P., Mattiello, J., Lebihan, D.: Estimation of the Effective Self-Diffusion Tensor from the NMR Spin Echo. J. Magn. Reson. B 103, 247–254 (1994)
3. Callaghan, P.T.: Principles of Nuclear Magnetic Resonance Microscopy. Clarendon Press, Oxford (1991)
4. Basser, P.J., Pajevic, S., Pierpaoli, C., Duda, J., Aldroubi, A.: In vivo fiber tractography using dt-mri data. Magnetic Resonance in Medicine 44(4), 625–632 (2000)
5. Wang, Z., Vemuri, B.C.: DTI segmentation using an information theoretic tensor dissimilarity measure. IEEE Transactions on Medical Imaging 24(10), 1267–1277 (2005)
6. Lenglet, C., Rousson, M., Deriche, R., Faugeras, O.: Statistics on the manifold of Multivariate Normal Distributions: Theory and Applications to Diffusion Tensor MRI processing. J. Math. Imaging Vis. 25, 423–444 (2006)
7. Pennec, X., Fillard, P., Ayache, N.: A Riemannian framework for tensor computing. International Journal of Computer Vision 65 (2005)
8. Pennec, X.: Probabilities and statistics on Riemannian manifolds: basic tools for geometric measurements. In: IEEE Workshop on Nonlinear Signal and Image Processing (1999)
9. Fletcher, P., Joshi, S.: Principal geodesic analysis on symmetric spaces: Statistics of diffusion tensors. In: Proc. of CVAMIA, pp. 87–98 (2004)
10. Barmpoutis, A., Vemuri, B., Shepherd, T., Forder, J.: Tensor splines for interpolation and approximation of DT-MRI with applications to segmentation of isolated rat hippocampi. IEEE Transactions on Medical Imaging 26(11), 1537–1546 (2007)
11. Arsigny, V., Fillard, P., Pennec, X., Ayache, N.: Fast and Simple Calculus on Tensors in the Log-Euclidean Framework. In: Duncan, J.S., Gerig, G. (eds.) MICCAI 2005. LNCS, vol. 3749, pp. 259–267. Springer, Heidelberg (2005)
12. Kindlmann, G., Estepar, R., Niethammer, M., Haker, S., Westin, C.F.: Geodesic-loxodromes for diffusion tensor interpolation and difference measurement. In: Ayache, N., Ourselin, S., Maeder, A. (eds.) MICCAI 2007, Part I. LNCS, vol. 4791, pp. 1–9. Springer, Heidelberg (2007)
13. Tuch, D.S., Reese, T.G., Wiegell, M.R., Wedeen, V.J.: Diffusion MRI of complex neural architecture. Neuron (40), 885–895 (2003)
14. Jian, B., Vemuri, B.C., Özarslan, E., Carney, P.R., Mareci, T.H.: A novel tensor distribution model for the diffusion-weighted MR signal. NeuroImage 37(1), 164–176 (2007)
15. Kumar, R., Barmpoutis, A., Vemuri, B.C., Carney, P.R., Mareci, T.H.: Multi-fiber reconstruction from DW-MRI using a continuous mixture of von mises-fisher distributions. In: IEEE Computer Society Conference on Computer Vision and Pattern Recognition CVPR Workshops 2008, pp. 1–8 (June 2008)
16. Barmpoutis, A., Kumar, R., Vemuri, B.C., Banerjee, A.: Beyond the Lambertian assumption: A generative model for apparent BRDF fields of faces using anti-symmetric tensor splines. In: IEEE Conference on Computer Vision and Pattern Recognition, CVPR 2008, pp. 1–6 (June 2008)
17. Jian, B., Vemuri, B.C.: A unified computational framework for deconvolution to reconstruct multiple fibers from diffusion weighted MRI. TMI 26(11), 1464–1471 (2007)

18. Ozarslan, E., Mareci, T.H.: Generalized diffusion tensor imaging and analytical relationships between DTI and HARDI. MRM 50(5), 955–965 (2003)
19. Barmpoutis, A., Jian, B., Vemuri, B.C., Shepherd, T.M.: Symmetric positive 4th order tensors & their estimation from diffusion weighted MRI. In: Karssemeijer, N., Lelieveldt, B. (eds.) IPMI 2007. LNCS, vol. 4584, pp. 308–319. Springer, Heidelberg (2007)
20. Frank, L.R.: Characterization of anisotropy in high angular resolution diffusion-weighted MRI. Magn. Reson. Med. 47(6), 1083–1099 (2002)
21. Özarslan, E., Shepherd, T.M., Vemuri, B.C., Blackband, S.J., Mareci, T.H.: Resolution of complex tissue microarchitecture using the diffusion orientation transform (DOT). NeuroImage (2006)
22. Tuch, D.S.: Q-ball imaging. Magn. Reson. Med. 52(6), 1358–1372 (2004)
23. Descoteaux, M., Angelino, E., Fitzgibbons, S., Deriche, R.: Regularized, fast and robust analytical q-ball imaging. MRM 58(3), 497–510 (2007)
24. Wassermann, D., Descoteaux, M., Deriche, R.: Diffusion maps clustering for magnetic resonance q-ball imaging segmentation. Journal of Biomedical Imaging 8(3), 1–12 (2008)
25. Tournier, J.D., Calamante, F., Gadian, D.G., Connelly, A.: Direct estimation of the fiber orientation density function from DW-MRI data using spherical deconvolution. NeuroImage 23(3), 1176–1185 (2004)
26. Tournier, J.D., Calamante, F., Connelly, A.: Robust determination of the fibre orientation distribution in diffusion MRI: non-negativity constrained super-resolved spherical deconvolution
27. Tournier, J.D., Yeh, C.H., Calamante, F., Cho, K.H., Connelly, A., Lin, C.P.: Resolving crossing fibres using constrained spherical deconvolution: Validation using diffusion-weighted imaging phantom data. NeuroImage 42(2), 617–625 (2008)
28. Alexander, D.C.: Maximum entropy spherical deconvolution for diffusion MRI. Inf. Process Med. Imaging, 76–87 (2005)
29. Wedeen, V., Wang, R.P., Schmahmann, J.D., Benner, T., Tseng, W.Y., Dai, G., Pandya, D.N., Hagmann, P., D'Arceuil, H., de Crespigny, A.J.: Diffusion spectrum magnetic resonance imaging (dsi) tractography of crossing fibers. Neuroimage 41(4), 1267–1277 (2008)
30. Hasan, K.M., Gupta, R.K., Santos, R.M., Wolinsky, J.S., Narayana, P.A.: Diffusion tensor fractional anisotropy of the normal-appearing seven segments of the corpus callosum in healthy adults and relapsing-remitting multiple sclerosis patients. Journal of Magnetic Resonance Imaging 21(6), 735–743 (2005)
31. van Gelderen, P., de Vleeschouwer, M.H.M., DesPres, D., Pekar, J., van Zijl, P.C.M., Moonen, C.T.W.: Water diffusion and acute stroke. Magnetic Resonance in Medicine 31(2), 154–163 (1994)
32. Cover, T.M., Thomas, J.A.: Elements of Information Theory. John Wiley and Sons Inc., Chichester (2001)
33. Wang, Z., Vemuri, B., Chen, Y., Mareci, T.: A constrained variational principle for direct estimation and smoothing of the diffusion tensor field from DWI. In: Taylor, C.J., Noble, J.A. (eds.) IPMI 2003. LNCS, vol. 2732, pp. 660–671. Springer, Heidelberg (2003)
34. Wang, Z., Vemuri, B., Chen, Y., Mareci, T.: A Constrained Variational Principle for Direct Estimation and Smoothing of the Diffusion Tensor Field from complex DWI. TMI 23(8), 930–939 (2004)
35. Letac, G., Massam, H.: Quadratic and inverse regressions for Wishart distributions. Ann. Stat. 2(26), 573–595 (1998)

36. McGraw, T., Vemuri, B.C., Yezierski, R., Mareci, T.: Von Mises-Fisher mixture model of the diffusion ODF. In: ISBI, pp. 65–68 (2006)
37. McGraw, T., Vemuri, B.C., Yezierski, R., Mareci, T.: Segmentation of high angular resolution diffusion MRI modeled as a field of von Mises-Fisher mixtures. In: Leonardis, A., Bischof, H., Pinz, A. (eds.) ECCV 2006. LNCS, vol. 3953, pp. 463–475. Springer, Heidelberg (2006)
38. Bhalerao, A., Westin, C.F.
39. Jian, B., Vemuri, B.C.: Multi-fiber reconstruction from diffusion MRI using mixture of Wisharts and sparse deconvolution. In: Karssemeijer, N., Lelieveldt, B. (eds.) IPMI 2007. LNCS, vol. 4584, pp. 384–395. Springer, Heidelberg (2007)
40. Sen, P., Hürlimann, M., de Swiet, T.: Debye–Porod law of diffraction for diffusion in porous media. Phys. Rev. 51(1), 601–604 (1995)
41. Barmpoutis, A., Vemuri, B.C., Forder, J.R.: Fast displacement probability profile approximation from hardi using 4th-order tensors. In: Proceedings of ISBI 2008: IEEE International Symposium on Biomedical Imaging, May 14-17, 2008, pp. 911–914 (2008)
42. Barmpoutis, A., Vemuri, B.C., Howland, D., Forder, J.R.: Extracting tractosemas from a displacement probability field for tractography in DW-MRI. In: Metaxas, D., Axel, L., Fichtinger, G., Székely, G. (eds.) MICCAI 2008, Part I. LNCS, vol. 5241, pp. 9–16. Springer, Heidelberg (2008)
43. Deriche, R., Descoteaux, M.: Splitting tracking through crossing fibers: Multidirectional q-ball tracking. In: ISBI, pp. 756–759 (2007)
44. Söderman, O., Jönsson, B.: Restricted diffusion in cylindrical geometry. J. Magn. Reson. A (117), 94–97 (1995)

Statistical Computing on Manifolds: From Riemannian Geometry to Computational Anatomy

Xavier Pennec

INRIA Sophia Antipolis - Asclepios Team, 2004 Rte des Lucioles BP 93
06902 Sophia Antipolis Cedex, France

Abstract. Computational anatomy is an emerging discipline that aims at analyzing and modeling the individual anatomy of organs and their biological variability across a population. The goal is not only to model the normal variations among a population, but also discover morphological differences between normal and pathological populations, and possibly to detect, model and classify the pathologies from structural abnormalities. Applications are very important both in neuroscience, to minimize the influence of the anatomical variability in functional group analysis, and in medical imaging, to better drive the adaptation of generic models of the anatomy (atlas) into patient-specific data (personalization).

However, understanding and modeling the shape of organs is made difficult by the absence of physical models for comparing different subjects, the complexity of shapes, and the high number of degrees of freedom implied. Moreover, the geometric nature of the anatomical features usually extracted raises the need for statistics and computational methods on objects that do not belong to standard Euclidean spaces. We investigate in this chapter the Riemannian metric as a basis for developing generic algorithms to compute on manifolds. We show that few computational tools derived from this structure can be used in practice as the atoms to build more complex generic algorithms such as mean computation, Mahalanobis distance, interpolation, filtering and anisotropic diffusion on fields of geometric features. This computational framework is illustrated with the joint estimation and anisotropic smoothing of diffusion tensor images and with the modeling of the brain variability from sulcal lines.

1 Introduction

1.1 Computational Anatomy

Anatomy is the science that studies the structure and the relationship in space of different organs and tissues in living systems. Since the 1980ies, an ever growing number of imaging modalities allows observing both the anatomy and the function *in vivo* and *in situ* at many spatial scales (from cells to the whole body) and at multiple time scales: milliseconds (e.g. beating heart), years (growth or aging), or even ages (evolution of species). Moreover, the non-invasive aspect

F. Nielsen (Ed.): ETVC 2008, LNCS 5416, pp. 347–386, 2009.

allows repeating the observations on multiple subjects. This has a strong impact on the goals of the anatomy which are changing from the description of a *representative individual* to the description of the structure and organization of organs at the *population level*. This led in the last 10 to 20 years to the gradual evolution of *descriptive atlases* into interactive and *generative models*, allowing the simulation of new observations. Typical examples are given for the brain by the MNI 305 [45] and ICBM 152 [97] templates that are the basis of the Brain Web MRI simulation engine [30]. In the orthopedic domain, one may cite the "bone morphing" method [55,125] that allows to simulate the shape of bones.

The combination of these new observation means and of the computerized methods is at the heart of computational anatomy, an emerging discipline at the interface of geometry, statistics and image analysis which aims at developing algorithms to model and analyze the biological shape of tissues and organs. The goal is to estimate representative organ anatomies across diseases, populations, species or ages, to model the organ development across time (growth or aging), to establish their variability, and to correlate this variability information with other functional, genetic or structural information (e.g. fiber bundles extracted from diffusion tensor images). From an applicative point of view, a first objective is to understand and to model how life is functioning at the population level, for instance by classifying pathologies from structural deviations (taxonomy) and by integrating individual measures at the population level (spatial normalization) to relate anatomy and function. A second application objective is to provide better quantitative and objective measures to detect, understand and correct dysfunctions at the individual level in order to help therapy planning (before), control (during) and follow-up (after).

The method is generally to map some generic (atlas-based) knowledge to patients-specific data through atlas-patient registration. In the case of observations of the same subject, many geometrical and physically based registration methods were proposed to faithfully model and recover the deformations. However, in the case of different subjects, the absence of physical models relating the anatomies leads to a reliance on statistics to learn the geometrical relationship from many observations. This is usually done by identifying anatomically representative geometric features (points, tensors, curves, surfaces, volume transformations), and then modeling their statistical distribution across the population, for instance via a mean shape and covariance structure analysis after a group-wise matching. In the case of the brain, one can rely on a hierarchy of structural models:

- Anatomical or functional landmarks like the AC and PC points [133,22];
- Curves like crest lines [132] or sulcal lines [93,88,50];
- Surfaces like the cortical surface or sulcal ribbons [135,3,141];
- images seen as 3D functions, which lead to voxel-based morphometry (VBM) [11];
- Rigid, multi-affine or diffeomorphic transformations [137,101,5], leading to Tensor-based morphometry (TBM).

To exemplify the methodology of computational anatomy, we will detail in Section 6.2 a method to estimate the variability of the cortex shape which relies on sulcal lines manually delineated within MRI brain images of many subjects. A first problem is to define what is the mean and the variance of a set of lines. In this case, the mean line is computed by optimization, and we chose a very simple variability model based on the covariance matrix of the corresponding points in each subject at each point of the mean line. In order to use this model in other applications (for instance to better guide the deformation of a brain template to a specific patient image), a second problem is to extrapolate the covariance information from the lines to the whole brain surface and volume. Indeed, positive definite symmetric matrices only constitute a convex cone in the vector space of symmetric matrices. Thus, convex operations like the mean are stable, but more general algorithms involving partial differential equations (PDEs) or gradient descent inevitably lead to negative eigenvalues which are not physically acceptable. Designing well behaved algorithms to work on covariance matrices also turns out to be crucial for the second application that will be described in Section 6.1: the processing of diffusion tensor images (DTI), a new type of MRI modality that reveals in vivo the anatomical architecture of the brain connections.

Actually, these examples are typical of the difficulty of computing statistics on geometric features. The underlying reason is that these features most often belong to curved manifolds rather than to Euclidean spaces. Thus, one cannot simply use the classical linear statistics and one needs to develop a more general theory on which consistent algorithms could be designed.

1.2 Statistical Analysis on Manifolds

Statistical computing on simple manifolds like the 3D sphere or a flat torus (for instance an image with opposite boundary points identified) might seems easy as we can see the geometrical properties (e.g. invariance by rotation or translation) and imagine tricks to alleviate the different problems. For instance, the average of points on a sphere is located inside the sphere and not on its surface, but unless the distribution is perfectly symmetric, one can always project the mean point on the sphere surface. However, when it comes to slightly more complex manifolds like the space of positive definite matrices or the space of rigid-body motions (rotations and translations), without even thinking to infinite dimensional manifolds like spaces of curves, surfaces or diffeomorphisms, computational tricks are much more difficult to find and have to be determined on a case by case basis.

Statistical analysis on manifolds is a relatively new domain at the confluent of several mathematical and application domains. Its goal is to statistically study geometric object living in differential manifolds. Directional statistics [21,74,82,95] provide a first approach to statistics on manifold. As the manifolds considered here are spheres and projective spaces, the tools developed were mostly *extrinsic*, i.e. relying on the embedding of the manifold in the ambient Euclidean space. More complex objects are obtained when we consider the "shape" of a set of k points, i.e. the part that remains invariant under the action of a given group of transformations (usually rigid body ones or similarities). Statistics on shape spaces [78,36,86,130] raised the need for intrinsic tools. However, the link between the tools developed, the metric used and the space structure was not always very clear.

Another mathematical approach was provided by the study of stochastic processes on Lie groups. For instance, [64] derived central limit theorems on different families of groups and semi-groups with specific algebraic properties. Since then, several authors in the area of stochastic differential geometry and stochastic calculus on manifolds proposed results related to mean values [75,81,44,4,122,31].

In the area of numerical methods for dynamic systems and partial differential equations, quite a few interesting numerical methods were developed to preserve the geometric properties of the flow of a differential equation such as symplectic integrator for Hamiltonian systems, symmetric integrators for reversible systems and optimization methods on Lie groups and manifolds [67,69]. In particular, several Newton iteration schemes relying on different structures were proposed to optimize a function on a matrix Lie group or on Riemannian manifolds [110,92,33]. From the applied mathematics and computer science point of view, people get interested in computing and optimizing on specific manifolds, like rotations and rigid body transformations [118,65,112,62,104], Stiefel and Grassmann manifolds [42].

Over the last years, several groups attempted to federate some of the above approaches in a general statistical and computing framework, with different objectives in mind. For instance, the aim of the theory of statistical manifolds [2,109] is to provide a Riemannian structure to the space of parameters of statistical distribution. This evolved into the more general theory of information geometry [72,76]. Seen from the point of view of statistics on manifolds rather than manifolds of statistical parameters, a few authors characterized the performances of some statistical parametric estimators in manifolds like the bias and the mean square error. For instance, [70] considered extrinsic statistics, based on the Euclidean distance of the embedding space, while [109] considered the intrinsic Riemannian distance, and refined the Cramer-Rao lower bound using bounds on the sectional curvature of the manifold. In [17,18,19], the authors focused on the asymptotic consistency properties of the extrinsic and intrinsic means and variances for large sample sizes, and were able to propose a central limit theorem for flat manifolds.

In view of computer vision and medical image analysis applications, our concern in [113,114] was quite different: we aimed at developing computational tools that can consistently deal with geometric features, or that provide at least good approximations. As we often have few measurements, we were interested in small sample sizes rather than large one, and we preferred to obtain approximations rather than bounds on the quality of the estimation. Thus, a special interest was to develop Taylor expansions with respect to the variance, in order to evaluate the quality of the computations with respect to the curvature of the manifold.

In [109,17,18,19] as well as in our work, the chosen framework is the one of geodesically complete Riemannian manifolds, which appears to be powerful enough to support an interesting theory. To ensure a maximal consistency, we chose to rely only on intrinsic properties of the Riemannian manifold, thus excluding methods based on the embedding of the manifold in an ambient Euclidean space.

1.3 Chapter Organization

We summarize in Section 2 the mathematical bases that are needed to deal with finite dimensional manifolds. Then, we show in Section 3 that a consistent set of statistical tools, including mean and covariance matrix analysis, can be developed based on the choice of a Riemannian metric. This algorithmic framework to compute on manifolds is then extended in Section 4 to process fields of geometric features (manifold-valued image). In particular, we show that one can perform interpolation, filtering, isotropic and anisotropic regularization and restoration of missing data (extrapolation or in-painting) on manifold valued images by using generalized weighted means and partial differential equations (PDEs). Finally, the methodology is exemplified in Section 6 with two example applications: the joint estimation and smoothing of diffusion tensor fields from diffusion weighted images, and the modeling of the variability of the brain from a data-set of precisely delineated sulcal lines, where covariance matrices are used to describe the anatomical variability of points in the brain.

2 A Riemannian Computing Framework

The goal of this section is to establish the mathematical bases that will allow to build a simple but consistent statistical computing framework on manifolds. We describe a few computational tools (namely the Riemannian Exp and Log maps) derived from a chosen Riemannian metric on a given manifold. The implementation of these atomic tools will then constitute the basis to build more complex generic algorithms in Section 3 4. The interested reader may refer to [34] for a more complete but still affordable presentation of Riemannian geometry and to [131, chap. 9] and [84,59] for more details.

2.1 The Riemannian Structure

In the geometric framework, one has to separate the topological and differential properties of the manifold from the geometric and metric ones. The first ones determine the local structure of a manifold $\mathcal{M}$ by specifying neighboring points and tangent vectors, which allows us to differentiate smooth functions on the manifold. This also allows us to define continuous paths on the manifold and to classify them by the number of loops they are doing around "holes" in the manifold. However, within each of these homotopy classes, there is no tool to choose something like the "straightest path". To obtain such a notion, we need to add a geometric structure, called a connection, which allows to compare neighboring tangent spaces. Indeed, differentiating a path on a manifold gives tangent vectors belonging at each point to a different tangent vector space. In order to compute the second order derivative (the acceleration of the path), we need a way to map the tangent space at a point to the tangent space at any neighboring point. This is the goal of a connection $\nabla_X Y$, which specifies how the vector field $Y(p)$ is derived in the direction of the vector field $X(p)$. Such a connection operator also describes how a vector is transported from a tangent space to another along a given curve and specifies the local parallel transport. However, there is usually no global parallelism. As a matter of facts, transporting the same vector along two different curves arriving at the same point might lead to different ending vectors: this is easily seen on the sphere where traveling from north pole to the equator, then along the equator for 90 degrees and back to North pole turns any tangent vector by 90 degrees. This defect of global parallelism is the sign of curvature. By looking for curves that remains locally parallel to themselves (i.e. such that $\nabla_{\dot\gamma}\dot\gamma = 0$), one defines the equivalent of "straight lines" in the manifold: geodesics. One should notice that there exists many different choices of connections on a given manifold which lead to different geodesics.

Geodesics by themselves do not quantify how far away from each other two points are. For that purpose, we need an additional structure: a distance. By restricting to distances which are compatible with the differential structure, we enter into the realm of Riemannian geometry. A *Riemannian metric* is defined by a continuous collection of scalar products $\langle\,.\,|\,.\,\rangle_p$ (or equivalently norms $\|.\|_p$) on each tangent space $T_p\mathcal{M}$ at point p of the manifold. Thus, if we consider a curve on the manifold, we can compute at each point its instantaneous speed vector (this operation only involves the differential structure) and its norm to obtain the instantaneous speed (the Riemannian metric is needed for this operation). To compute the length of the curve, this value is integrated as usual along the curve. The distance between two points of a connected Riemannian manifold is the minimum length among the curves joining these points. The curves realizing this minimum are called metric geodesics. The fundamental theorem of Riemannian geometry states that on any Riemannian manifold there is a unique (torsion-free) connection which is compatible with the metric, called the Levi-Civita (or metric) connection. For that choice of connection, shortest path are geodesics ("straight lines"). In the following, we only consider the Levi-Civita connection. Moreover, we assume that the manifold is geodesically complete, i.e. that all geodesics can be indefinitely extended. This means that the manifold has neither boundary nor any singular point that we can reach in a finite time. As an important consequence, the Hopf-Rinow-De Rham theorem states that there always exists at least one minimizing geodesic between any two points of the manifold (i.e. whose length is the distance between the two points).

2.2   Exponential Charts

The calculus of variations shows that geodesics are the solutions of a system of second order differential equations depending on the connection (thus on the

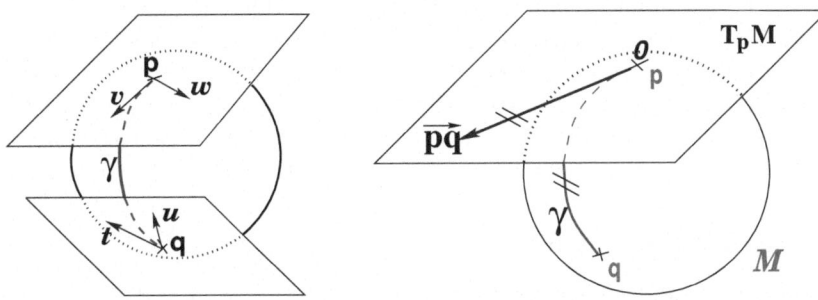

Fig. 1. Left: The tangent planes at points p and q of the sphere $\mathcal{S}_2$ are different: the vectors v and w of $T_p\mathcal{M}$ cannot be compared to the vectors t and u of $T_q\mathcal{M}$. Thus, it is natural to define the scalar product on each tangent plane. **Right:** The geodesics starting at p are straight lines in the exponential map and the distance along them is conserved.

metric)[1]. Let p be a point of the manifold that we consider as a local reference and $\boldsymbol{v}$ a vector of the tangent space $T_p\mathcal{M}$ at that point. From the theory of second order differential equations, we know that there exists one and only one geodesic $\gamma_{(p,v)}(t)$ starting from that point with this tangent vector. This allows to wrap the tangent space onto the manifold, or equivalently to develop the manifold in the tangent space along the geodesics (think of rolling a sphere along its tangent plane at a given point), by mapping to each vector $\boldsymbol{v} \in T_p\mathcal{M}$ the point q of the manifold that is reached after a unit time by the geodesic $\gamma_{(p,v)}(t)$ starting at p with tangent vector $\vec{v}$. This mapping $\mathrm{Exp}_p(\boldsymbol{v}) = \gamma_{(p,v)}(1)$ is called the *exponential map* at point p. Straight lines going through 0 in the tangent space are transformed into geodesics going through point p on the manifold and distances along these lines are conserved (Fig. 1).

The exponential map is defined in the whole tangent space $T_p\mathcal{M}$ (since the manifold is geodesically complete) but it is generally one-to-one only locally around 0 in the tangent space (i.e. around p in the manifold). In the sequel, we denote by $\vec{pq} = \mathrm{Log}_p(q)$ the inverse of the exponential map: this is the smallest vector (in norm) such that $q = \mathrm{Exp}_p(\vec{pq})$. If we look for the maximal definition domain, we find out that it is an open and star-shaped domain which boundary is called the *tangential cut-locus* C_p. The image of C_p by the exponential map is the cut locus $\mathcal{C}_p$ of point p. This is (the closure of) the set of points where several minimizing geodesics starting from p meet. On the sphere $\mathcal{S}_2(1)$ for instance, the cut locus of a point p is its antipodal point and the tangential cut locus is the circle of radius π.

The exponential and log maps within this domain realizes a chart (a local parameterization of the manifold) called *the exponential chart at point p*. It

---

[1] The Christoffel symbols $\varGamma_{ab}^c$ determine the connection in a local coordinate system through $\nabla_{\partial_a}\partial_b = \sum_c \varGamma_{ab}^c.\partial_c$. The Levi-Civita connection is determined from the metric tensor $g_{ab}(p) = \langle\, \partial_a \mid \partial_b \,\rangle_p$ and its inverse g^{cd} by $\varGamma_{ab}^c = \frac{1}{2}\sum_d g^{cd}(\partial_a g_{db} + \partial_b g_{da} - \partial_c g_{ab})$.

covers all the manifold except the cut locus of the reference point p, which has a null measure. In this chart, geodesics starting from p are straight lines, and the distance from the reference point are conserved. This chart is somehow the "most linear" chart of the manifold with respect to the reference point p. The set of all the exponential charts at each point of the manifold realize an atlas which allows working very easily on the manifold, as we will see in the following.

2.3   Practical Implementation

The exponential and logarithmic maps (from now on Exp and Log maps) are obviously different for each manifold and for each metric. Thus they have to be determined and implemented on a case by case basis. Examples of closed form expressions for rotations and rigid body transformations can be found for the left invariant metric in [120], and for covariance matrices (positive definite symmetric matrices, so called tensors in medical image analysis) in [117,8] and Section 5. It has to be noticed that the equation of the geodesics are only needed for the sake of computational efficiency: geodesics are curves minimizing the distance but also the Riemannian energy (the integral of the squared speed) between two points. Thus computing $\overrightarrow{pq} = \log_p(q)$ may be posed as an optimal control problem [77,1], and computing $\mathrm{Exp}_p(v)$ as a numerical integration problem (see e.g. [69,67]). This opens the way to statistical computing in more complex spaces than the one we considered up to now, like curves [100,83,147], surfaces, and diffeomorphic transformations. For instance, the large deformation diffeomorphic metric mapping (LDDMM) method proposed for inter-subject image registration in computational anatomy [15,101,102,73] finds the geodesic in the joint intensity and deformation space by minimizing the Riemannian length of the deformation for a given right-invariant metric on a diffeomorphism group. Through the so called EPDiff equation (Euler-Poincaré equation for diffeomorphisms), this optimization framework has been recently rephrased in an exponential/logarithm framework similar to the one developed here [103]. Despite the infinite number of dimensions, simple statistics like the mean and the principal component analysis of a (finite) set of samples may still be computed [140,40]. Exponential charts constitute very powerful atomic functions in terms of implementation on which we will be able to express practically all the geometric operations: the implementation of Log_p and Exp_q is the basis of programming on Riemannian manifolds, as we will see in the following.

In a Euclidean space, the exponential charts are nothing but one orthonormal coordinates system translated at each point: we have in this case $\overrightarrow{pq} = \mathrm{Log}_p(q) = q - p$ and $\mathrm{Exp}_p(v) = p + v$. This example is more than a simple coincidence. In fact, most of the usual operations using additions and subtractions may be reinterpreted in a Riemannian framework using the notion of *bi-point*, an antecedent of vector introduced during the 19th Century. Indeed, vectors are defined as equivalent classes of bi-points in a Euclidean space. This is possible because we have a canonical way (the translation) to compare what happens at two different points. In a Riemannian manifold, we can still compare things locally (by parallel transportation), but not any more globally. This means that

Table 1. Re-interpretation of standard operations in a Riemannian manifold

	Euclidean space	Riemannian manifold
Subtraction	$\overrightarrow{pq} = q - p$	$\overrightarrow{pq} = \mathrm{Log}_p(q)$
Addition	$p = q + \boldsymbol{v}$	$q = \mathrm{Exp}_p(\boldsymbol{v})$
Distance	$\mathrm{dist}(p, q) = \|q - p\|$	$\mathrm{dist}(p, q) = \|\overrightarrow{pq}\|_p$
Mean value (implicit)	$\sum_i (p_i - \bar{p}) = 0$	$\sum_i \overrightarrow{\bar{p}p_i} = 0$
Gradient descent	$p_{t+\varepsilon} = p_t - \varepsilon \overrightarrow{\nabla C(p_t)}$	$p_{t+\varepsilon} = \mathrm{Exp}_{p_t}(-\varepsilon \overrightarrow{\nabla C(p_t)})$
Geodesic interpolation	$p(t) = p_0 + t\, \overrightarrow{p_0 p_1}$	$p(t) = \mathrm{Exp}_{p_0}(t\, \overrightarrow{p_0 p_1})$

each "vector" has to remember at which point of the manifold it is attached, which comes back to a bi-point.

A second way to see the vector $\overrightarrow{pq}$ is as a vector of the tangent space at point p. Such a vector may be identified to a point on the manifold using the geodesic starting at p with tangent vector $\overrightarrow{pq}$, i.e. using the exponential map $q = \mathrm{Exp}_p(\overrightarrow{pq})$. Conversely, the logarithmic map may be used to map almost any bi-point (p, q) into a vector $\overrightarrow{pq} = \mathrm{Log}_p(q)$ of $T_p\mathcal{M}$. This reinterpretation of addition and subtraction using logarithmic and exponential maps is very powerful to generalize algorithms working on vector spaces to algorithms on Riemannian manifolds, as illustrated in Table 1 and the in following sections.

3   Simple Statistics on Riemannian Manifolds

The Riemannian metric induces an infinitesimal volume element on each tangent space, and thus a reference measure $d\mathcal{M}(p)$ on the manifold that can be used to measure random elements on the manifold (generalization of random variables). Without entering into the details of measure theory, such an element is characterized by its probability measure $dP(p)$. Its probability density function (pdf) is the function ρ such that $dP(p) = \rho(p)d\mathcal{M}(p)$, if it exists. The induced measure $d\mathcal{M}$ actually represents the notion of *uniformity* according to the chosen Riemannian metric. This automatic derivation of the uniform measure from the metric gives a rather elegant solution to the Bertrand paradox for geometric probabilities [123,79]. This paradox proposes three equally acceptable ways to compute the probability that the length of a "random chord" on a circle is greater than the side of an inscribed equilateral triangle, which lead to a probability of $1/2$, $1/3$ and $1/4$. All methods are correct but actually rely on different uniform measures. The canonical definition of the uniform measure by the Riemannian metric prevents such a paradox to appear in our Riemannian setting.

With the probability measure dP of a random element, we can integrate any function $f(p)$ from the manifold to any vector space, thus defining the expected value of this function $\mathbf{E}[f] = \int_{\mathcal{M}} f(p).dP(p)$. This notion of expectation corresponds to the one we defined on real random variables and vectors. However, we cannot directly extend it to define the mean value of the distribution since we generally cannot integrate manifold-valued functions. Thus, one cannot define the mean or expected "value" of a random manifold element that way.

3.1 First Statistical Moment: The Mean

As one cannot define the mean or expected "value" of a random manifold element using a weighted sum or an integral as usual, several alternative definitions based on properties on the usual mean were proposed (see [122] and [114, Sec. 4.3] for a review). The most interesting ones for general geodesically complete Riemannian manifolds were proposed by Fréchet, Karcher and Emery.

One solution is to rely on a distance-based variational formulation: the Fréchet [57,58] (resp. Karcher [75]) expected features minimize globally (resp. locally) the variance:

$$\sigma^2(q) = \int_{\mathcal{M}} \text{dist}(p,q)^2 \, dP(p) = \frac{1}{n} \sum_{i=1}^{n} \text{dist}(p_i, q)^2,$$

written respectively in the continuous and discrete forms. One can generalize the variance to a dispersion at order α by changing the L_2 with an α-norm: $\sigma_\alpha(p) = (\int \text{dist}(p,q)^\alpha dP(p))^{1/\alpha}$. The minimizers are called the central Karcher values at order α. For instance, the median is obtained for $\alpha = 1$ and the modes for $\alpha = 0$, exactly like in the vector case. It is worth noticing that the median and the modes are not unique in general in a vector space, and that even the mean may not exists (e.g. for heavy tailed distribution). In Riemannian manifolds, the existence and uniqueness of all central Karcher values is generally not ensured as they are obtained through a minimization procedure. However, [75] and [80] were able to established existence and uniqueness theorems for distributions with a compact and small enough support. These theorems were then extended in [31] to distributions with non-compact support in a very specific class of manifolds that includes the Hadamard manifolds[2] whose curvature is bounded from below. This does not include rigid body transformations, but this includes the manifold of tensors. For a finite number of discrete samples at a finite distance of each other (which is the practical case in statistics) a mean value always exists (the variance is finite everywhere in a complete space so there exists a minimizer). and it is unique as soon as the distribution is sufficiently peaked.

Emery [44] proposed to use the *exponential barycenters*, i.e. the points at which the mean is null in the local exponential chart : $\int_M \overrightarrow{xy} \, dP(y) = 0$. If the support of the distribution is included in a *strongly convex open set*[3], he showed that the exponential barycenters were the critical points of the variance. They are thus a superset of the Riemannian centers of mass that include themselves the Fréchet means. Showing that these two notions continue to be essentially equivalent for distributions with a larger support is more difficult in the presence of a cut locus.

---

[2] Simply connected and complete manifolds with non-positive sectional curvature.
[3] Here, strongly convex means that for every two points there is a unique minimizing geodesic joining them that depend in a C^∞ of the two points.

Indeed, the distance is continuous but not differentiable at cut locus points where several minimizing geodesic meets. For instance, the distance from a point of the sphere to its antipodal point is maximal although the directional derivatives of the distance at this points are non zero in all directions. Thus, although the variance is continuous, it might not be differentiable everywhere. We showed in [113,114] that it is actually differentiable at all points where the variance is finite and where the cut locus has a null mass for the considered probability measure[4]. In that case, its gradient is:

$$\nabla \sigma^2(q) = -2 \int \overrightarrow{qp} \, dP(p) = \frac{-2}{n} \sum_{i=1}^{n} \overrightarrow{qp_i}$$

respectively in the continuous (probabilistic) and discrete (statistical) formulations.

When we have a positive mass on the cut-locus, the right hand side of this equation is obviously not defined: the variance is continuous but can have a sharp extremum (most probably a maximum).

Thus, the extrema of the Riemannian variance are exponential barycenters or points with $P(C(y)) > 0$: apart from the specific problems with masses on the cut-locus, we have the implicit characterization of Karcher mean points as exponential barycenters which was presented in Table 1. Similar results have been derived independently in [109], where it is assumed that the probability is dominated by the Riemannian measure (which explicitly excludes point-mass distributions and the case $P(C(y)) > 0$), and in [17,18] for simply connected Riemannian manifolds with non-positive curvature. Our proof extends this result to any kind of manifold. Basically, the characterization of the Riemannian center of mass is the same as in Euclidean spaces if the curvature of manifold is non-positive (and bounded from below), in which case there is no cut-locus. If the sectional curvature becomes positive, a cut locus may appear, and a non-zero probability on this cut-locus induces some discontinuities in the first derivative of the variance. This corresponds to something like a Dirac measure on the second order derivative, which is an additional difficulty to compute the exact Hessian matrix of the variance on these manifolds. In practice, the gradient is well defined for discrete samples as soon as there is no sample lying exactly on the cut-locus of the current test point. Of course, perturbing the point position solves the problem (locally), but this might turn out to be a problem for designing certain certified computational algorithmic procedure if the same point is not perturbed exactly the same at different times.

Picard [122] realized a good synthesis of most of these notions of mean value and show that the definition of a "barycenter" (i.e. a mean value) is linked to a connector, which determines itself a connection, and thus possibly a metric. An interesting property brought by this formulation is that the distance between

---

[4] Notice that this is always the case when the random element has a density with respect to the Riemannian measure, but this does unfortunately not include the discrete (statistical) formulation where the probability measure is the sum of point masses at sample locations.

two barycenters (with different definitions) is of the order of $O(\sigma_x)$. Thus, for sufficiently concentrated random points, all these values are close.

3.2   A Newton Algorithm to Compute the Mean

To effectively compute the mean value, we proposed in [111,112] a Gauss-Newton gradient descent algorithm on rotations and rigid-body motions. This algorithm was readily extended to general Riemannian manifolds in [113,114] by approximating the variance using a Taylor expansion in a normal coordinate system: for a vector field $v \in T_q\mathcal{M}$, we have

$$\sigma^2(\mathrm{Exp}_q(v)) = \sigma^2(q) + \left\langle \overrightarrow{\nabla\sigma^2}(q) \mid v \right\rangle_q + \tfrac{1}{2}\mathrm{Hess}\,\sigma^2(v,v) + O(\|v\|_q^2)$$

The gradient of the variance being a vector field, the second order derivative (the Hessian) is obtained using the connection. However, we know that the gradient is not continuous at the cut locus. To circumscribe this problem, one can split the integral into one part that does not take into account the cut locus, which gives us a perfect positive definite matrix (2 times the identity), and one part that account for the cut locus, which can be expressed using integrals of Jacobi fields [75]. For a toy example on the circle, see also [114]. Deliberately neglecting this second term gives us a perfectly concave "second order approximation" with the following Gauss-Newton iterative scheme:

$$\bar{p}^{t+1} = \mathrm{Exp}_{\bar{p}^t}\left(\frac{1}{n}\sum_{i=1}^{n}\overrightarrow{\bar{p}^t p_i}\right).$$

This algorithm essentially alternates the computation of the barycenter in the exponential chart centered at the current estimation of the mean value, and a re-centering step of the chart at the point of the manifold that corresponds to the computed barycenter (geodesic marching step). In practice, we found that this algorithm was very efficient and typically converges in 5 to 10 iterations to the numerical accuracy of the machine for rotations, rigid body transformations and positive definite symmetric matrices. Notice that it converges toward the real mean in a single step in a vector space. One can actually show that the convergence of this type of Newton iteration is locally quadratic around non degenerated critical points [110,92,33].

3.3   Covariance Matrix and Principal Geodesic Analysis

Once the mean point is determined, using the exponential chart at the mean point is particularly interesting as the random feature is represented by a random vector with null mean in a star-shaped domain. However, one important difference with the Euclidean case is that the reference measure is not the Lebesgue one but the pull-back of the Riemannian measure $d\mathcal{M}$ by the Exponential map at the mean point. With this representation, there is no difficulty to define the covariance matrix (respectively continuous and discrete forms):

$$\Sigma = \int \overrightarrow{pq}.\overrightarrow{pq}^{\mathrm{T}} \, dP(q) = \frac{1}{n} \sum_{i=1}^{n} \overrightarrow{pq_i}.\overrightarrow{pq_i}^{\mathrm{T}}$$

and potentially higher order moments. This covariance matrix can then be used to defined the Mahalanobis distance between a random and a deterministic feature that basically weights the distance between the deterministic feature and the mean feature using the inverse of the covariance matrix: $\mu_{(\bar{p},\Sigma)}(q) = \overrightarrow{pq}^{\mathrm{T}} \Sigma^{(-1)} \overrightarrow{pq}$. Interestingly, the expected Mahalanobis distance of a random element with itself is independent of the distribution and is equal to the dimension of the manifold, as in the vector case. This statistical distance can be used as a basis to generalize some statistical tests such as the Mahalanobis D^2 test [114].

To analyze the results of a set of measurements in a Euclidean space, one often performs a principal component analysis (PCA). A generalization to Riemannian manifolds called Principal Geodesic Analysis (PGA) was proposed in [54] to analyze shapes based on the medial axis representations (M-reps). The basic idea is to find a low dimensional sub-manifold generated by some geodesic subspaces that best explain the measurements (i.e. such that the squared Riemannian distance from the measurements to that sub-manifold is minimized). Another point of view is to assume that the measurements are generated by a low dimensional Gaussian model. Estimating the model parameters amounts to a covariance analysis in order to find the k-dimensional subspace that best explains the variance. In a Euclidean space, these two definitions correspond thanks to Pythagoras's theorem. However, in the Riemannian setting, geodesic subspaces are generally not orthogonal due to the curvature. Thus, the two notions differ: while the Riemannian covariance analysis can easily be performed in the tangent space of the mean, finding Riemannian sub-manifolds turns out to become an almost intractable problem. As a matter of fact, the solution retained by [54] was finally to rely on the covariance analysis.

When the distribution is unimodal and sufficiently peaked, we believe that covariance analysis is anyway much better suited. However, for many problems, the goal is rather to find a sub-manifold on which measurements are more or less uniformly distributed. This is the case for instance for features sampled on a surface or points sampled along a trajectory (time sequences). While the one dimensional case can be tackled by regression [32], the problem for higher dimensional sub-manifolds remains quite open. Some solutions may come from manifold embedding techniques as exemplified for instance in [24].

3.4   Gaussian and χ^2 Law

Several generalizations of the Gaussian distribution to Riemannian manifolds have already be proposed so far. In the stochastic calculus community, one usually consider the heat kernel $\rho(p, q, t)$, which is the transition density of the Brownian motion [64,43,66]. This is the smallest positive fundamental solution to the heat equation $\frac{\partial f}{\partial t} - \Delta f = 0$, where Δ is the Laplace-Beltrami operator (i.e. the standard Laplacian with corrections for the Riemannian metric). On compact manifolds, an explicit basis of the heat kernel is given by the spectrum of the manifold-Laplacian (eigenvalues λ_i with associated eigenfunctions f_i solutions of $\Delta f = \lambda f$). However, the explicit computation of this spectrum is impossible but in very few cases [59].

To obtain tractable formulas, several alternative distributions have been proposed in directional statistics [21,74,82,95,96], in particular the wrapped Gaussian distributions. The basic idea is to take the image by the exponential of a Gaussian distribution on the tangent space centered at the mean value (see e.g. [96] for the circular and spherical case). It is easy to see that the wrapped Gaussian distribution tends toward the mass distribution if the variance goes to zero. In the circular case, one can also show that is tends toward the uniform distribution for a large variance. This definition was extended in [109] by considering non-centered Gaussian distributions on the tangent spaces of the manifold in order to tackle the asymptotic properties of estimators. In this case, the mean value is generally not any more simply linked to the Gaussian parameters. In view of a computational theory, the main problem is that the pdf of the wrapped distributions can only be expressed if there is a particularly simple geometrical shape of the cut-locus. For instance, considering an anisotropic covariance on the n-dimensional sphere leads to very complex calculations.

Instead of keeping a Gaussian pdf in some tangent space, we propose in [114,113,111] a new variational approach which is consistent with the previous definitions of the mean and covariance. The property that we took as axiom is that the Gaussian distribution maximizes the entropy among all distributions when we know the mean and the covariance matrix. In the Riemannian setting, we defined the intrinsic entropy as the expectation of the logarithm of the intrinsic pdf:

$$\mathbf{H}[\rho] = - \int_{\mathcal{M}} \log(\rho(p))\, \rho(p)\, d\mathcal{M}(p) = - \int_{\mathcal{M}} \log(\rho(p))\, dP(p)$$

Our definition of the entropy is consistent with the measure inherited from the Riemannian metric since the pdf that maximizes the entropy when we only know that the result is in a compact set $\mathcal{U}$ is the uniform density in this set: $p_{\mathcal{U}}(p) = \mathbb{I}_{\mathcal{U}}(p) / \int_{\mathcal{U}} d\mathcal{M}(p)$.

The intrinsic pdf maximizing this entropy knowing the mean $\bar{x}$ and the covariance matrix Σ is a Gaussian distribution on the exponential chart centered at the mean point and truncated at the cut locus (if there is one)[5] [114]:

$$N_{(\bar{p},\Gamma)}(q) = k \, \exp\left(-\frac{1}{2} \overrightarrow{pq}^{\mathrm{T}} \, \Gamma \, \overrightarrow{pq} \right).$$

However, the relation between the concentration matrix (the "metric" Γ used in the exponential of the probability density function) and the covariance matrix

---

[5] The definition domain of the exponential map at the mean point has to be symmetric to obtain this result. This is the case in particular for symmetric spaces, i.e. Riemannian spaces which metric are invariant under some symmetry.

Σ is more complex than the simple inversion of the vectorial case, as it has to be corrected for the curvature of the manifold. Using a Taylor expansion of the Riemannian measure, one can obtain computationally tractable approximations for any manifold in case of small variances: Let $r = \mathrm{i}(\mathcal{M}, \bar{x})$ be the injectivity radius at the mean point, i.e. the shortest distance to the cut-locus (by convention $r = +\infty$ if there is no cut-locus). Assuming a finite variance for any concentration matrix Γ, we have the following Taylor expansions:

$$k = \frac{1 + O(\sigma^3) + \epsilon\,(\sigma/r)}{\sqrt{(2\pi)^n\,\det(\Sigma)}} \qquad \text{and} \qquad \Gamma = \Sigma^{(-1)} - \frac{1}{3}\mathrm{Ric} + O(\sigma) + \epsilon\,(\sigma/r)$$

Here, $\epsilon(x)$ is a function that is a $O(x^k)$ for any positive k (more precisely, this is a function such that $\forall k \in \mathbb{R}^+,\ \lim_{0+} x^{-k}\,\epsilon(x) = 0$).

This family of distributions ranges from the point-mass distribution (for $\Gamma = \infty$) to the uniform measure (i.e. uniform density for compact manifolds) for a null concentration matrix. For some theoretical reasons (including the non-differentiability of the pdf at the cut locus), this is probably not be the best generalization of the Gaussian. However, from a practical point of view, it provides effective and computationally tractable approximations for any manifold in case of small variances that we were not able to obtain from the other definitions.

Based on this generalized Gaussian, we investigated in [114,113,111] a generalization of the χ^2 law to manifolds by considering the Mahalanobis distance of a Gaussian random feature. In the same conditions as for the Gaussian, one can show that is has the same density as in the vectorial case up to an order 3 in σ. This opens the way to the generalization of many other statistical tests, as we may expect similarly simple approximations for sufficiently centered distributions.

3.5   A Link between Extrinsic and Robust Statistics

From a practical point of view, many of the efficient methods proposed to work on geometric data in real applications actually use tools which rely on an extrinsic distance in a carefully chosen embedding space rather than on the intrinsic Riemannian distance. The goal of this section is to investigate some bridges between extrinsic and intrinsic approaches.

The main tool that we use here is the the notion of statistical robustness, as defined in [71,126] i.e. the property of an estimator to be insensitive to small departures from the statistical model assumptions. In particular, outliers (events that are not modeled) most often lie in the tail of the distribution and robust statistics aim at reducing their influence. What is interesting is that we can often see an extrinsic distance on a manifold as a robust version of the Riemannian distance, as we shall see below on specific examples.

Let us considered more specifically M-estimators [126] of the distance d_ϕ $(p, q) = \phi((\mathrm{dist}(p, q))$ with $\phi(0) = 0$ and ϕ' decreasing monotonically from $\phi'(0) = 1$ while remaining non negatives. These conditions ensure that d_ϕ remains a distance which is equivalent to the Riemannian one for small distances, while giving less weight to points that are far away by tempering their distance. Thus, outliers that lie in the tail of the distribution have much less influence on the results of the estimation, hence the robustness. One can show [63] that using such a ϕ-function amounts to replace in the computation of the mean the tangent vector $\overrightarrow{pq}$ by the vector:

$$\psi(\overrightarrow{pq}) = \frac{\phi(\|\overrightarrow{pq}\|_p)}{\|\overrightarrow{pq}\|_p}\overrightarrow{pq} = \frac{\phi(\text{dist}(p,q))}{\text{dist}(p,q)}\overrightarrow{pq} = \overrightarrow{pq} + O(\|\overrightarrow{pq}\|^2)$$

This mapping constitute a connector in the sense of [122] (a smooth mapping that replaces the Euclidean difference $q - p)^6$, exactly in the way we used the logarithmic map of the Riemannian metric. Thus, we could think of defining mean values, higher order moments and other statistical operations by replacing everywhere the Riemannian logarithmic and exponential map with their ϕ-equivalent.

For instance, one can verify that $\|\psi(\overrightarrow{pq})\|_p = d_\phi(p,q)$. This show that the ϕ-variance of a random point $\sigma_\phi^2(p) = \mathbf{E}\left[d_\phi^2(\boldsymbol{q},p)\right] = \int_{\mathcal{M}} \|\psi(\overrightarrow{pq})\|_p^2 dP(q)$ is properly defined. Likewise, one can define the ϕ-covariance $\Sigma_\phi(p) = \mathbf{E}\left[\psi(\overrightarrow{pq}).\psi(\overrightarrow{pq})^t\right]$, which trace is still equal to the ϕ-variance. This ϕ-variance can be differentiated at the points where the cut-locus has a null probability measure (because the ϕ-distance is dominated by the Riemannian distance), and we obtain:

$$\nabla\sigma_\phi^2(p) = -2\int_{\mathcal{M}} \phi'(\|\overrightarrow{pq}\|_p)\,\psi(\overrightarrow{pq})\,dP(q).$$

This formula is interesting as it shows the divergence of the different notions of mean: the ϕ-center of mass is a weighted barycenter both in the Riemannian and in the ϕ exponential charts, but it is generally different from the (unweighted) ϕ-exponential barycenter. The different notions of means are not any more subsets of each other: although the extrinsic mean is a robust estimator of the mean, the consistency of the distance minimization and the exponential-based algorithms is broken. From a numerical point of view, using an efficient and robust estimator might be an interesting feature, but we need to control the quality of this estimation to establish the domain in which the estimations are numerically consistent. Let us illustrate this with unit vectors and 3D rotations.

Euclidean metric induces on the sphere $\mathcal{S}_{n-1}$ a rotationally invariant Riemannian metric for which geodesics are great circles, and the distance between two unit vectors u and v is the angle $\theta = d(u,v) = \arccos(u^t.v)$. The Euclidean metric $d_E(u,v) = \|u-v\|$ can be considered as a ϕ estimator with $\phi(\theta) = 2\sin(\theta/2)$. With the help of a Lagrange multiplier, one easily computes that the extrinsic Euclidean mean is the renormalized Euclidean mean $\bar{u} = \int u\,dP(u)/\|\int u\,dP(u)\|$, which is thus a robust estimator of the Riemannian mean.

---

[6] Formally, a connector is a smooth mapping from $\mathcal{M} \times \mathcal{M}$ to $T\mathcal{M}$ that maps a bi-point (p,q) in the manifold to a vector in the tangent space $T_p\mathcal{M}$. The mapping should zero at $q = p$ and its differential at that point should be the identity. This ensures that it is locally consistent with the Riemannian Log map.

For directions, a quite used encoding is the tensor $u.u^t$, which may be seen as an immersion of the projective space $\mathcal{P}_{n-1}$ into the vector space of $n \times n$ matrices ($\mathbb{R}^{n^2}$). With this embedding, the squared extrinsic Euclidean distance (renormalized to be consistent with the previous ones) is $d^2(u, v) = \frac{1}{2}\|u.u^t - v.v^t\|^2 = 1 - (u^t v)^2 = \sin^2(\theta)$. This is also a robust distance with $\phi(\theta) = \sin(\theta)$ (for $\theta \leq \pi$). In the tensor space, the encoding of a random direction is the random tensor $T_u = \mathbf{E}\,[\,u.u^t\,]$. One should notice that the mean direction is represented by the tensor $\bar{u}.\bar{u}^t$ which is closest to T_u in the Euclidean sense: this is the eigenvector(s) of T_u corresponding to the largest eigenvalue. One can also show that the ϕ-covariance of the direction is given directly by the restriction of the tensor to the hyperplane orthogonal to the first eigenvector [63]. Thus, the random tensor encodes not only for a robust estimation of the Riemannian mean but also for (an approximation) of the second order moments.

Simulations were run on a large number of cases to measure the relative accuracy of the vector and tensor estimations with respect to the Riemannian mean. Up to a variance of 20 degrees, the three methods have a similar accuracy and results are almost not distinguishable. Between 20 and 40 degrees of variance, the tensor estimation becomes different from the two others while keeping a comparable global accuracy. After 40 degrees, the accuracy of the tensor mean highly degrades; the vector mean becomes different from the Riemannian means while keeping for a while a similar accuracy.

A very similar analysis can be done with 3D rotations: one can also model two well known extrinsic methods to compute the mean as ϕ-connectors. The first method is to represent rotations using unit quaternions, and to compute the renormalized Euclidean mean on the sphere of unit quaternions. As rotation quaternions are defined up to their signs, one theoretically needs to iterate this process and to re-orient the unit quaternions at each step in the hemisphere chosen to represent the mean in order to converge. This method amounts to consider the ϕ-distance $d_{quat}(\theta) = 4\sin(\theta/4)$. The second method is to average the rotation matrices directly in the 3×3 matrix space. Then, the mean is "renormalized" by looking for the rotation matrix which is closest to this result in the Euclidean matrix distance (Froebenius) sense. This can be easily realized using a SVD decomposition on the mean matrix. This method amounts to consider the ϕ-distance $d_{mat}(\theta) = 2\sin(\theta/2)$. Simulation experiments were performed for the two extrinsic methods by [41] in a registration context, and later on for the mean with the three methods by [62]. Like for unit directions/orientations, estimation results were similar up to 40 degrees of variance in the input rotations.

These experiments showed that efficient extrinsic approximations can be designed and used in practice, at the cost of potential inconsistencies between several notions of the mean that might be used in different algorithms (next Section will develop many algorithms based on the mean). However, the intrinsic Riemannian theory may be used as a central tool to compare different extrinsic metrics, to establish the quality of the resulting approximations and to control the limits of their validity.

4   Computing with Manifold-Valued Images

The previous section showed how to derive from the atomic Exp and Log maps many important statistical notions, like the mean, covariance and Principal Component Analysis (PCA). We now turn to the generalization of some image processing algorithms like interpolation, diffusion and restoration of missing data (extrapolation) to manifold-valued images. We show that most interpolation and filtering methods can be reformulated using weighted means. The linear and non-linear diffusion schemes can be adapted to Manifolds through PDEs, provided that we take into account the variations of the metric. For details, we refer the reader to [117].

4.1   Interpolation and Filtering as Weighted Means

One of the important operations in geometric data processing is to interpolate values between known measurements. In 3D image processing, (tri-) linear interpolation is often used thanks to its very low computational load and comparatively much better results than nearest neighbor interpolation. Other popular methods include the cubic and, more generally, spline interpolations [134,99]. The standard way to interpolate on a regular lattice is to make a linear combination of samples f_k at integer (lattice) coordinates $k \in \mathbb{Z}^d$: $f(x) = \sum_k w(x-k) f_k$. A typical example is the sinus cardinal interpolation where the convolution kernel has an infinite support. With the nearest-neighbor, linear (or tri-linear in 3D), and higher order spline interpolations, the kernel is piecewise polynomial, and has a compact support [134,99]. With normalized weights, this interpolation can be seen as a weighted mean. Thus, it can be generalized in the manifold framework as an optimization problem: the interpolated value $p(x)$ on our feature manifold is the point that minimizes $C(p(x)) = \sum_{i=1}^{n} w_i(x) \operatorname{dist}^2(p_i, p(x))$. This can easily be solved using the iterative Gauss-Newton scheme proposed for the Karcher mean. The linear interpolation is interesting and can be written explicitly since it is a simple geodesic walking scheme: $p(t) = \operatorname{Exp}_{p_0}(t\overrightarrow{p_0 p_1}) = \operatorname{Exp}_{p_1}((1-t)\overrightarrow{p_1 p_0})$.

Many other operators can be rephrased as weighted means. For instance approximations and convolutions like Gaussian filtering can be viewed as the average of the neighboring values weighted by a (Gaussian) function of their spatial distance. For instance, $\hat{F}(x) = \int_{\mathbb{R}^n} K(u) F(x+u) \, du$ is the minimizer of $C(\hat{F}) = \int_{\mathbb{R}^n} K(u) \operatorname{dist}^2(F(x+u), \hat{F}(x)) \, du$. In this formulation the kernel can be a discrete measure, for instance if samples are defined on the points of a grid. In a Riemannian manifold, this minimization problem is still valid, but instead of a closed-form solution, we have once again a Gauss-Newton iterative gradient descent algorithm to reach the filtered value:

$$\hat{p}^{t+1}(x) = \int_{\mathbb{R}^n} K(u) \operatorname{Log}_{\hat{p}^t(x)}(p(x+u)) \, du.$$

We can also use anisotropic and non-stationary kernels $K(x, u)$. For instance, it can be modulated by the norm of the derivative of the field in the direction u.

We should notice that for a manifold-value field $p(x)$, the directional derivatives $\partial_u p(x)$ is a tangent vector of $T_{p(x)}\mathcal{M}$ which can be practically approximated using finite "differences" in the exponential chart: $\partial_u p(x) \simeq \mathrm{Log}_{p(x)}(p(x+u)) + O(\|u\|^2)$. However, to measure the norm of this vector, we have to use the Riemannian metric at that point: $\|\partial_u p\|_p$.

4.2   Harmonic Diffusion

An alternative to kernel filtering is to consider a regularization criterion that penalizes the spatial variations of the field. A measure of variation is the spatial gradient (the linear form that maps to any spatial direction u the directional derivative $\partial_u p(x)$), which can be robustly computed as the matrix that best approximates the directional derivatives in the neighborhood (e.g. 6, 18 or 26 connectivity in 3D). The simplest criterion based on the gradient is the Harmonic energy

$$Reg(p) = \frac{1}{2}\int_{\Omega}\|\nabla p(x)\|_{p(x)}^2 \ dx = \frac{1}{2}\sum_{i=1}^{d}\int_{\Omega}\|\partial_{x_i}p(x)\|_{p(x)}^2 \ dx.$$

The Euler-Lagrange equation of this Harmonic regularization criterion with Neumann boundary conditions is as usual $\nabla Reg(p)(x) = -\Delta p(x)$. However, the Laplace-Beltrami operator on the manifold $\Delta p(x)$ is the sum of the usual flat Euclidean second order directional derivatives $\partial_{x_i}^2 p(x)$ in a locally orthogonal system and an additional term due to the curvature of the manifold that distorts the ortho-normality of this coordinate system in the neighborhood. To practically compute this operator, we proposed in [117] an efficient and general scheme based on the observation that the Christoffel symbols and their derivatives along the geodesics vanish at the origin of the exponential chart. This means that the correction for the curvature is in fact already included: by computing the standard Laplacian *in that specific map*, one gets the directional Laplace-Beltrami operator for free: $\Delta_u p = \mathrm{Log}_{p(x)}(p(x+u)) + \mathrm{Log}_{p(x)}(p(x-u)) + O(\|u\|^4)$. Averaging over all the directions in a spatial neighborhood $\mathcal{V}$ finally gives a robust and efficient estimation scheme:

$$\Delta p(x) \propto \sum_{u\in\mathcal{V}}\frac{1}{\|u\|^2}\mathrm{Log}_{p(x)}(p(x+u))$$

A very simple scheme to perform Harmonic diffusion is to use a first order geodesic gradient descent. At each iteration and at each point x, one walks a little bit along the geodesic which start at the current point with the opposite of the gradient of the regularization criterion $p^{t+1}(x) = \mathrm{Exp}_{p^t(x)}(-\varepsilon\Delta p^t(x))$.

4.3   Anisotropic Diffusion

In order to filter within homogeneous regions but not across their boundaries, an idea is to penalize the smoothing in the directions where the derivatives are important [121,61]. This can be realized directly in the discrete implementation of the Laplacian by weighting the directional Laplacian with a decreasing function of the norm $\|\partial_u p\|_p$ of the gradient in that direction. For instance, we used $\Delta_u p = \sum_u c(\|\partial_u p\|_p) \Delta_u p$ with $c(x) = \exp(-x^2/\kappa^2)$ in [117]. As the convergence of this scheme is not guaranteed (anisotropic regularization "forces" may not derive from a well-posed energy), the problem may be reformulated as the optimization of a ϕ-function of the Riemannian norm of the spatial gradient (a kind of robust M-estimator): $Reg_\phi(p) = \frac{1}{2} \int_\Omega \phi(\|\nabla p(x)\|_{p(x)}) \, dx$. By choosing an adequate ϕ-function, one can give to the regularization an isotropic or anisotropic behavior [12]. The main difference with a classical Euclidean calculation is that we have to take the curvature into account by using the Laplace-Beltrami operator, and by measuring the length of directional derivatives using the Riemannian metric at the right point [47]. Using $\Psi(x) = \phi'(x)/x$, we get:

$$\nabla Reg_\phi(p) = -\Psi(\|\nabla p\|_p)\Delta p - \sum_{i=1}^d \partial_{x_i} \Psi(\|\nabla p\|_p)\partial_{x_i} p.$$

4.4 Diffusion-Based Interpolation and Extrapolation

The pure diffusion reduces the noise in the data but also the amount of information. Moreover, the total diffusion time that controls the amount of smoothing is difficult to estimate. At an infinite diffusion time, the field will be completely homogeneous. Thus, it is more interesting to consider the data as noisy observations and the regularization as a prior on the spatial regularity of the field. Usually, one assumes a Gaussian noise independent at each position, which leads to a least-squares criterion through a maximum likelihood approach. For a dense data field $q(x)$, the similarity criterion that is added to the regularization criterion is simply $Sim(p) = \int_\Omega \text{dist}^2(p(x), q(x)) \, dx$. The only difference here is that it uses the Riemannian distance. It simply adds a linear (geodesic) spring $\nabla_p \text{dist}^2(p, q) = -2 \overrightarrow{pq}$ to the global gradient to prevent the regularization from pulling to far away from the original data.

For sparse measures, using directly the maximum likelihood on the observed data leads to deal with Dirac (mass) distributions in the derivatives, which is a problem for the numerical implementation. One solution is to consider the Dirac distribution as the limit of the Gaussian function G_σ when σ goes to zero, which leads to the regularized derivative [117]:

$$\nabla Sim(x) = -2 \sum_{i=1}^n G_\sigma(x - x_i) \overrightarrow{p(x)p_i}.$$

5   The Example of Covariance Matrices

Positive definite symmetric matrices, called tensors in medical image analysis, are used for instance to encode the covariance matrix of the Brownian motion (diffusion) of water in Diffusion Tensor Imaging (DTI) [13,87], to encode the joint variability at different places (Green function) in shape analysis (see [51,50,52]), and in image analysis to guide the segmentation, grouping and motion analysis [98,144,23,145]. They are also appearing in many other application domains. For instance, they are a common tool in numerical analysis to locally drive the size of the adaptive meshes in order to optimize the cost of solving PDEs in 3D [106]. In the formation of echo-Doppler or radar images, Teoplitz Hermitian positive definite matrices uniquely characterized circular complex random processes with a null mean [107].

The main computational problem is that the tensor space is a manifold that is not a vector space with the usual additive structure. As the positive definiteness constraint delimits a convex half-cone in the vector space of symmetric matrices, convex operations (like the mean) are stable in this space but problems arise with more complex operations. For instance, there is inevitably a point in the image where the time step is not small enough when smoothing fields of tensors with gradient descents, and this results into negative eigenvalues. Even when a spectral decomposition is performed to smooth independently the rotation (eigenvectors basis trihedron) and eigenvalues [138,27], there is a continuity problem around equal eigenvalues.

To answer that problem, it was proposed concurrently by several authors in the context of Diffusion Tensor Images (DTI) to endow the space of tensors with a Riemannian metric invariant by any change of the underlying space coordinates, i.e. invariant under the action of affine transformations of covariance matrices. This led to the distance $\mathrm{dist}^2(\Sigma, \Lambda) = \mathrm{Tr}\left(\log(\Sigma^{-1/2}\Lambda\Sigma^{-1/2})^2\right)$ where exp and log stand for the matrix logarithm.

This metric leads to a very regular Hadamard manifold structure (a hyperbolic-like space without cut-locus) which simplifies the computations. Tensors with null and infinite eigenvalues are both at an infinite distance of any positive definite symmetric matrix: the cone of positive definite symmetric matrices is changed into a space of "constant" (homogeneous) non-scalar curvature without boundaries. Moreover, there is one and only one geodesic joining any two tensors, the mean of a set of tensors is uniquely defined, and we can even define globally consistent orthonormal coordinate systems of tangent spaces. Thus, the structure we obtain is very close to a vector space, except that the space is curved. The invariant metric has been independently proposed in [53] for the analysis of principal modes of sets of diffusion tensors; in [105] for its mathematical properties which were exploited in [14] for a new anisotropic DTI index; and in [117] where we were not interested by the metric per-se, but rather as the basis for building the complete computational framework on manifold-valued images that we presented in last section. By looking for a suitable metric on the space of Gaussian distributions for the segmentation of diffusion tensor images, [89] also end-up with the same metric. It is interesting to see that completely different approaches, relying on invariance requirements on the one hand, and relying on an information measure to evaluate the distance between distributions on the other hand, lead to the same metric on the tensor space. The metric has been also previously introduced in statistics as the Fisher information metric to model the geometry of the multivariate normal family [25,129,26] and is considered as a well known result

in other branches of mathematics [16]. In computer vision, it was rediscovered
to deal with covariance matrices [56]. An implicit form was introduced in [69] for
developing flows and dynamic systems on the space of symmetric matrices. The
corresponding integrator (which corresponds to a geodesic walking with this Riemannian metric) was used for the anisotropic regularization of diffusion tensor
images in [28] and [20].

5.1   The One-Parameter Family of Affine-Invariant Metrics

One can question about the uniqueness of this type of Riemannian metric. We
have shown in [116] that there is actually a one-parameter family of such affine-
invariant Riemannian metrics on tensors that all share the same connection. This
is the affine invariant connection on homogeneous spaces of [108] which is used
in many theorems on symmetric spaces in many differential geometry textbooks
[85,68,60].

The basic idea is to define a group action, here the linear group GL_n, and
to provide the space Sym_n^+ of positive definite symmetric matrices (tensors)
with a invariant Riemannian metric with respect to it. Here, the group action
$A \star \Sigma = A\Sigma A^{\mathrm{T}}$ corresponds to the standard action of the affine group on the
covariance matrix of random variables in $\mathbb{R}^n$, hence the name of the metric.
When the group is sufficiently large to transport one point onto any other, the
manifold is said homogeneous and we can also use the group to transport the
metric from one point (called the origin) to any other point. The constraint is
that the metric at the origin should be invariant by transformations that leave
the origin unchanged (the isotropy group of that point).

In the case of tensors, the identity is left unchanged by rotations, so that the
metric at that point should be rotationally invariant. All such dot products on
symmetric matrices are given (up to a constant global multiplicative factor) by:

$$\langle\, V \mid W \,\rangle_{\mathrm{Id}} = \mathrm{Tr}(V\,W) + \beta\,\mathrm{Tr}(V)\,\mathrm{Tr}(W) \quad \text{with} \quad \beta > -1/n$$

where n is the dimension of the space (the inequality ensures the positiveness).
This metric at the identity can then be transported at any point by the group
action using the (symmetric or any other) square root $\Sigma^{1/2}$ considered as a group
element:

$$
\begin{aligned}
\langle\, V \mid W \,\rangle_\Sigma &= \left\langle\, \Sigma^{-1/2}V\Sigma^{-1/2} \mid \Sigma^{-1/2}W\Sigma^{-1/2} \,\right\rangle_{\mathrm{Id}} \\
&= \mathrm{Tr}\left(V\Sigma^{-1}W\Sigma^{-1}\right) + \beta\,\mathrm{Tr}\left(V\Sigma^{-1}\right)\,\mathrm{Tr}\left(W\Sigma^{-1}\right)
\end{aligned}
$$

The Riemannian distance is obtained by integration, or more easily by the norm
of the initial tangent vector of the geodesic joining the two points:

$$
\begin{aligned}
\mathrm{dist}^2(\Sigma, \Lambda) &= \|\log_\Sigma(\Lambda)\|_\Sigma^2 = \|\Sigma^{-1/2}\log_\Sigma(\Lambda)\Sigma^{-1/2}\|_{\mathrm{Id}}^2 \\
&= \mathrm{Tr}\left(\log(\Sigma^{-1/2}\Lambda\Sigma^{-1/2})^2\right) + \beta\mathrm{Tr}\left(\log(\Sigma^{-1/2}\Lambda\Sigma^{-1/2})\right)^2
\end{aligned}
$$

It is worth noticing that tensors with null eigenvalues are at an infinite distance
of any regular tensor, as are tensors with infinite eigenvalues: the original cone of

positive definite symmetric matrices, a linear manifold with a flat but incomplete metric (there is a boundary at a finite distance) has been changed into a regular and complete (but curved) manifold with an infinite development in each of its $n(n+1)/2$ directions.

For $\beta = -1/(n+1)$, we have the metric that [91] proposed by embedding the space of tensors of dimension n into the space of $n+1$ square matrices using homogeneous coordinates (this allows them to seamlessly take into account an additional position that represent the mean of the Gaussian distribution), and by quotienting out $n+1$ dimensional rotations. The same trick could be used to embed the space in higher dimensional spaces (square matrices of dimension $n+p+1$, in which case one would obtain the invariant metric with $\beta = -1/(n+p+1)$). Interestingly, $-1/\beta = n+1$ is the first authorized integer to obtain a proper metric!

In fact, one can show that all the metrics of this affine-invariant family have the same Levy-Civita connection $\nabla_V W = \nabla_W V = -1/2(V\Sigma^{-1}W + W\Sigma^{-1}V)$ [129]. This means that they share the same geodesics and the Riemannian Exp and Log maps at each point:

$$\mathrm{Exp}_\Sigma(W) = \Sigma^{1/2} \exp\left(\Sigma^{-1/2}W\Sigma^{-1/2}\right)\Sigma^{1/2}$$
$$\mathrm{Log}_\Sigma(\Lambda) = \Sigma^{1/2} \log\left(\Sigma^{-1/2}\Lambda\Sigma^{-1/2}\right)\Sigma^{1/2}$$

However, one should be careful that the orthonormal bases are different for each metric which means that distances along the geodesics are different.

From the connection, one can compute the curvature tensor of the manifold [129] $R(X,Y,V,W) = 1/4\mathrm{Tr}(Y\Sigma^{-1}X\Sigma^{-1}V\Sigma^{-1}W - X\Sigma^{-1}Y\Sigma^{-1}V\Sigma^{-1}W)$. From this tensor, one gets the sectional curvature and see that it is non positive and bounded from below (by -1/2). Thus, it is Hadamard manifold, i.e. a kind of hyperbolic space in which we have for instance the existence and uniqueness of the mean. There is also no cut-locus, which simplifies the computations.

5.2 Log-Euclidean Metrics

By trying to put a Lie group structure on the space of tensors, Vincent Arsigny observed that the matrix exponential was a diffeomorphism from the space of symmetric matrices to the tensor space. This well-known fact in mathematics was apparently never used to transport all the operations defined in the vector space of symmetric matrices to the tensor space, thus providing the tensor space with a commutative Lie group structure and even with a vector space structure [9,8]. For instance, the composition (the log-product) is defined by $\Sigma_1 \diamond \Sigma_2 = \exp(\log(\Sigma_1) + \log(\Sigma_2))$. The Euclidean metric on symmetric matrices is transformed into a bi-invariant Riemannian metric on the tensor manifold (i.e. a metric which is invariant by both left and right compositions in the Lie group). As geodesics are straight lines in the space of symmetric matrices, the expression of the Exp, Log and distance maps for the Log-Euclidean metric is easily determined:

$$\mathrm{Exp}_\Sigma(W) = \exp(\log(\Sigma) + \partial_W \log(\Sigma))$$
$$\mathrm{Log}_\Sigma(\Lambda) = D\exp(\log(\Sigma))\,(\log(\Lambda) - \log(\Sigma))$$
$$\mathrm{dist}^2_{LE}(\Sigma_1, \Sigma_2) = \mathrm{Tr}\left((\log(\Sigma_1) - \log(\Sigma_2))^2\right)$$

These formulas look more complex than for the affine invariant metric because they involve the differential of the matrix exponential and logarithm in order to transport tangent vectors from one space to another [119]. However, they are in fact nothing but the transport of the addition and subtraction through the exponential of symmetric matrices. In practice, the log-Euclidean framework consist in taking the logarithm of the tensor data, computing like usual in the Euclidean space of symmetric matrices, and coming back at the end to the tensor space using the exponential [9,7].

From a theoretical point of view, geodesics through the identity are the same as for affine-invariant metrics, but this is not true any more in general at other points of the tensor manifold [8]. The affine-invariant and log-Euclidean means are also identical if the mean commutes with all the data. When they are not equal, one can show that the log-Euclidean mean is slightly more anisotropic [8]. A careful comparison of both metrics in practical applications [7,9] showed that there was very few differences on the results (of the order of 1%) on real DTI images, but that the log-Euclidean computations where 4 to 10 times faster. Thus, for this specific type of application, the log-Euclidean framework seems to be best suited. For other types of applications, like adaptive re-meshing [106], the anisotropy of the tensors can be much larger, which may lead to larger differences. In any case, initializing the iterative optimizations of affine-invariant algorithms with the log-Euclidean result drastically speeds-up the convergence.

5.3   Other Families of Metrics

Other families of metrics were also proposed to work with positive definite symmetric matrices, especially in view of processing diffusion tensor images. For instance, [143] proposed to parameterize tensors by their Cholesky decomposition $\Sigma = LL^\mathrm{T}$ where L is upper triangular with positive diagonal entries. Taking the standard flat Euclidean metric on the (positive) upper diagonal matrices leads to straight line geodesics in that space which are then transported to the tensor space as for the log-Euclidean framework. This lead to tensor space structure which is obviously flat, but where the null eigenvalues are at a finite distance, like in the Euclidean case.

Other square roots might be used to define other metrics on tensors as $\Sigma = (LR)(LR)^\mathrm{T}$ is also a valid decomposition for any rotation R. For instance, the symmetric square root $U\Lambda^{1/2}U^\mathrm{T}$ lead to a well defined metric on tensors which has similar properties as the Cholesky metric above, yet having different geodesics. The fact that the rotation R can be freely chosen to compute the square root recently led Dryden to propose a new metric in [35] which basically measure the shortest distance between all the square roots $L_1 R_1$ of Σ_1 and $L_2 R_2$

of Σ_2. The minimal distance is realized by the Procrustes match of the square roots:

$$\text{dist}(\Sigma_1, \Sigma_2) = \min_{R \in O(n)} \|L_2 - L_1 R\|$$

and the optimal rotation $\hat{R} = UV^{\text{T}}$ is obtained thanks to the singular value decomposition of $L_2^{\text{T}} L_1 = USV^{\text{T}}$. This metric is in fact the standard Kendall metric on the reflection size-and-shape space of $n + 1$ points in dimension n [35,37,130], which geometry is well known. For instance, the minimal geodesic joining Σ_1 to Σ_2 is given by

$$\Sigma(t) = \left((1 - t)L_1 + tL_2\hat{R} \right) \left((1 - t)L_1 + tL_2\hat{R} \right)^{\text{T}}$$

From the equation of the geodesics, one can derive the Riemannian exp and log map and proceed with the general computing framework. However, one must be careful that this space is not complete and has singularities when the matrix Σ has rank $n - 2$, i.e. when 2 eigenvalues are going to zero [86].

In [142], Wang and Vemuri proposed to use the square root of the J-divergence (the symmetrized Kullback Leibler divergence) as a "distance"[7] on the tensor space:

$$\text{dist}_J^2(\Sigma_1, \Sigma_2) = \text{Tr}\left(\Sigma_1 \Sigma_2^{(-1)} + \Sigma_2 \Sigma_1^{(-1)} \right) - 2n$$

This J-distance has interesting properties: it is affine invariant, and the Fréchet mean value of a set of tensors Σ_i has a closed form solution:

$$\bar{\Sigma} = B^{-1/2} \left(B^{1/2} A B^{1/2} \right)^{1/2} A^{-1/2}$$

with $A = \sum_i \Sigma_i$ and $B = \sum_i \Sigma_i^{(-1)}$. However, this is not a Riemannian distance as a Taylor expansion

$$\text{dist}_J^2(\Sigma, \Sigma + \epsilon V) = \frac{\epsilon^2}{2} \text{Tr}(\Sigma^{(-1)} V \Sigma^{(-1)} V) + O(\epsilon^3)$$

indicates that the underlying infinitesimal dot product is the usual affine invariant metric $\langle V \mid W \rangle = 1/2\text{Tr}\Sigma^{(-1)} V \Sigma^{(-1)} W$. In fact, this metric might well be an extrinsic metric, like the one we investigated in Section 3.5 for unit vectors and rotations, and it would be interesting to determine what is the embedding space.

6   Applications in Computational Anatomy

Now that we have seen the generic statistical computing framework on Riemannian manifolds and families of Riemannian metrics that can be designed on the tensor manifold, let us turn to two important applications in medical image analysis and computational anatomy: diffusion tensor imaging, which provides unique in vivo information about the structure of the white matter fibers in the brain, and the estimation of the variability of the cortex among subjects.

---

[7] Quotation marks indicate here that the triangular inequality might not be verified.

6.1   Diffusion Tensor Imaging

Diffusion tensor Imaging (DTI) is a unique tool to assess in vivo oriented structures within tissues via the directional measure of water diffusion. Fiber tracking
is the application targeted by most researchers in order to investigate non inva-
sively the anatomical-functional architecture of the brain. Most of the current
applications are currently in neuroscience, with high signal-to-noise ratios (SNR)
images on healthy subjects rather. DTI might also prove to be an interesting
quantification tool for medical diagnosis [124,127]. However, using such a modality in a clinical environment is difficult: data often have to be acquired quickly
because the patient cannot stay in a static position for too long due to pathologies. As this prevents the acquisition of multiple images for averaging, this results
in a limited number of encoding gradients and low SNR images. The estimation
of the diffusion tensor field from diffusion weighted images (DWI) being noise-
sensitive, clinical DTI is often not suitable for fiber tracking. Thus, one need
to regularize the tensor field without blurring the transitions between distinct
fiber tracts, which delimit anatomical and functional brain regions. Smoothing
independently each DWI before estimating the tensor results in a smoother tensor field but it also blurs the transitions between homogeneous regions, as this
information is not accessible by taking each DWI individually. Consequently, one
would like to perform an anisotropic regularization of the tensor field itself.

Most of the methods developed so far actually estimate the tensor field in
a first phase with a simple algebraic method (see below) and then spatially
regularize some of the geometric features of the tensor field. We believe that
a better idea is to consider a prior on the spatial regularity when estimating
the tensor field itself so that the estimation could remain statistically optimal
with respect to the DWI noise model and could keep the maximum amount of
information from the original data. We designed in [48,49] a maximum likelihood
(ML) criterion for the estimation of tensors fields from DWI with the MRI
specific Rician noise (the amplitude of a complex Gaussian signal), and extended
it to a maximum a posteriori (MAP) criterion by considering a spatial prior on
the tensor field regularity. This results into an algorithm that jointly (rather
than sequentially) performs the estimation and the regularization of the tensor
field.

The Stejskal-Tanner diffusion equation [13] relates the diffusion tensor D to
each noise-free DWI:

$$S_i = S_0 \exp(-b\, g_i^T D g_i)$$

where S_i is the original DWI corresponding to the encoding gradient g_i, S_0
the base image with a null gradient, and b the diffusion factor. By taking the
logarithm of this equation, one obtain a linear system. Solving that system in
a least square (LS) sense leads to the minimization of a quadratic criterion,
which is easily performed using algebraic methods (see e.g. [146]). Doing this
implicitly assumes a log-Gaussian noise on the images, which is justify only
for high SNRs. Very few works did consider non log-Gaussian noise because it
requires optimization techniques on tensors which are very difficult to control
with the standard Euclidean framework. With the log-Euclidean framework,

such an optimization is not difficult (one could also restate everything within the affine-invariant framework but calculations are slightly more complex). For instance, in the case of a Gaussian noise on the DWIs, the tensor $D = \exp(L)$ is parameterized by its logarithm L, an unconstrained symmetric matrix. The criterion to optimize is $Sim_G(L) = \sum(\hat{S}_i - S_i(\exp(L)))^2$, and the gradient is

$$\nabla Sim_G(L) = 2b \sum (\hat{S}_i - S_i).\partial_L S_i \qquad \text{with} \qquad \partial_L S_i = S_i \, \partial_{g_i.g_i^t} \exp(L)$$

For low SNRs, we have to take into account the real nature of the noise in MRI, which is Gaussian in the complex domain (the k-space). [143] proposed an estimation criterion on the complex DWI signal that is adapted to that noise, with a computationally grounded optimization framework based on the Cholesky decomposition. However, one usually only have access to the amplitude of the signal complex signal in clinical images: in that case, the noise is thus Rician. One can show that such a noise induces a signal-dependent bias of the order of $\sigma^2/2S$ on the DWI signal [128]. The signal being systematically larger than what it ought to be, the tensors will be under-estimated. To take explicitly the nature of this noise into account, we should optimize the log-likelihood of the signal corrupted by a Rician noise. This leads to a more complex criterion that above, but its gradient is very similar to the Gaussian case above: $\nabla Sim_R(L) = -1/\sigma^2 \sum(S_i - \alpha\hat{S}_i)\partial_L S$, except that we have a correcting factor $\alpha = I_0'/I_0(\hat{S}_i S_i/\sigma^2)$ depending on the signal and the noise variance (I_0 and I_0' are computable Bessel functions). The noise variance can easily be estimated on the background of the image (outside the head) where there is no signal.

For the spatial regularity, we proposed in [48,49] to use a Markovian prior $p(\Sigma(x + dx)|\Sigma(x)) \propto \exp(-\|\nabla\Sigma(x)^{\mathsf{T}}.dx\|_{\Sigma(x)}/\lambda)$, and to account for discontinuities using a redescending M-estimator (a so-called ϕ-functional). In the log-Euclidean framework, the tensor field $\Sigma(x)$ is parameterized by its logarithm $L(x)$, and the log of the prior is simply: $\mathrm{Reg}(L) = \int_\Omega \phi(\|\nabla L\|)$. In our experiments, we use $\phi(s) = 2\sqrt{1 + s^2/\kappa^2} - 2$. The ϕ-function preserves the edges of the tensor field while smoothing homogeneous regions. To include this regularization as an a-priori into the ML optimization process, we simply need to compute its gradient $\nabla\mathrm{Reg}(L) = -\psi(\|\nabla L\|)\Delta L - \sum_i \partial_i (\psi(\|\nabla L\|)).\partial_i L$ where $\psi(s) = \phi'(s)/s$. Directional derivatives, gradient and Laplacian were estimated with a finite differences scheme like with scalar images (see [48,49] for details).

Experiments on synthetic data with contours and a Rician noise showed that the gradient descent technique was correctly removing the negative eigenvalues that did appear in the standard (Euclidean log-Gaussian) estimation technique. ML and MAP (with regularization) methods with a Gaussian noise model were underestimating the volume of tensors even more than the standard log-Gaussian method (30% instead of 20%), while Rician ML and MAP methods were estimating it within 5%. More interestingly, the methods were tested on two clinical datasets of low and medium quality: a brain image with a very low SNR (Fig. 2), and an experimental acquisition of a tumor in the spinal chord, both with 7 gradient directions (Fig. 3). This last type of acquisition is currently actively investigated in clinical research (e.g. [46]). It is difficult to perform because

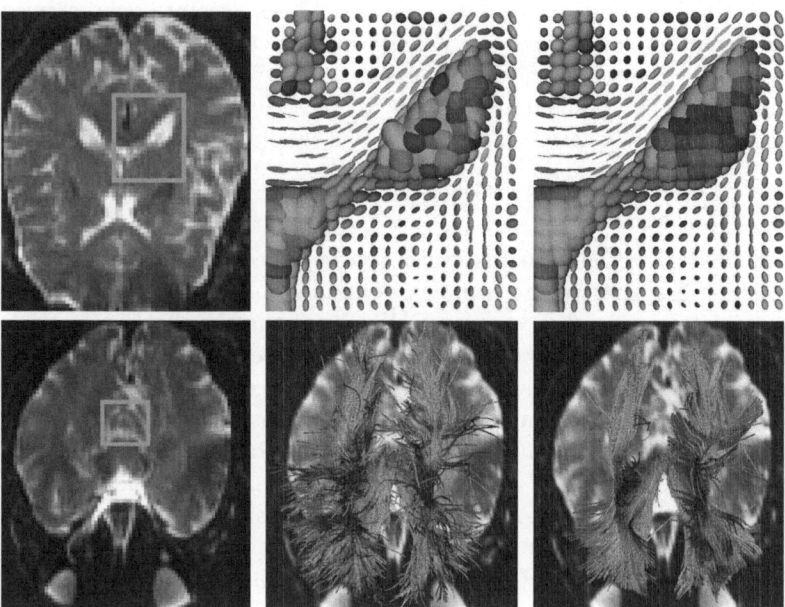

Fig. 2. Tensor field estimation of a brain (top row) and improvement of the fiber tracking (bottom row). Top Left: A slice of the b_0 image. **Top Middle:** The classic log-Gaussian estimation on the ROI. The color codes for the principal direction of tensors: **red:** left-right, **green:** anterior-posterior, **blue:** inferior-superior. Missing tensors in the splenium region are non-positive. **Top Right:** The MAP estimation of the same region. **Bottom row, Left:** ROI where the tracking is initiated. **Bottom row, middle:** The cortico-spinal tract reconstructed after a classic estimation. **Bottom row, Right:** Same tract reconstructed after our MAP estimation. Rendering is obtained using the MedINRIA software developed by P. Fillard and N. Toussaint.

Fig. 3.   Tensor field estimation of the spinal chord. Left: A slice of the b_0 image with the ROI squared in green. **Middle:** Classic **log-Gaussian ML** tensor estimation. There are many missing (non-positive) tensors around and in the spinal cord. **Right: Rician MAP** tensor estimation: tensors are all positive and the field is much more regular while preserving discontinuities. Original DWI are courtesy of D. Ducreux, MD. Rendering is obtained using the MedINRIA software (http://www.inria.fr/sophia/asclepios/software/MedINRIA/).

the position is uncomfortable due to the tumor and the coil cannot be perfectly adapted to the body as it is for the head. The images are consequently much noisier than for the brain.

Like for synthetic data, using gradient descent techniques removed all the negative eigenvalues of the standard method. To evaluate the impact of the noise model on the tensor reconstruction in the brain, we computed the mean apparent diffusion coefficient (ADC), fractional anisotropy (FA) and volume of the diffusion tensors in the ventricles (high but anisotropic diffusion), and in the corpus callosum (lower diffusion with high anisotropy) [49]. Using the Rician noise model increase the tensor volume and the ADC by about 10% in isotropic regions and by 1 to 2% in anisotropic regions without modifying the FA. In the spinal chord, using the Rician noise model also lead to an increase of the tensors of about 30% in volume. This corresponds to the correction of the shrinking effect with Gaussian and Log-Gaussian noises. Adding some spatial regularization (MAP methods) systematically decreases the FA. However, this effect is much lower for anisotropic regions and minimized with the Rician noise model: 3% only in the corpus callosum (versus 11% with log-Gaussian), and 15% in the ventricles (versus 30% with log-Gaussian). Thus, it seems that these measurements are more reproducible with the MAP Rician reconstruction.

The tractography results in a much smoother and longer fibers with less dispersion for the MAP Rician model. The overall number of reconstructed fibers is also much larger. The smoothness of the tensor field indeed leads to more regular and longer fibers: tracts that were stopped due to the noise are now fully reconstructed. A careful quantitative evaluation and validation of the whole framework however remains to be done. In particular, it would be necessary to evaluate the reproducibility across acquisitions and scanners, for instance using repeated scans of the same subject, as well as evaluations of physical phantoms.

6.2 Learning Brain Variability from Sulcal Lines

A second interesting application is the statistical modeling of the brain variability in a given population of 3D images [51,50]. In such a process, the identification of corresponding points among each individual anatomy (structural homologies) allows us to encode the brain variability by covariance matrices. The reason why we should not simplify these tensors into simpler scalar values is that there are evidences that structural variations are larger along certain preferred directions [136]. Thus the metrics on covariance matrices presented in Section 5 and the statical computing framework developed in earlier Sections are once again needed.

In the brain, a certain number of sulcal landmarks consistently appear in all normal individuals and allow a consistent subdivision of the cortex into major lobes and gyri [94]. Moreover, sulcal lines are low dimensional structures easily identified by neuroscientists. In the framework of the associated team program between Epidaure/Asclepios at INRIA and LONI at UCLA[8], we use a data-set

---

[8] http://www-sop.inria.fr/epidaure/Collaborations/UCLA/atlas.html

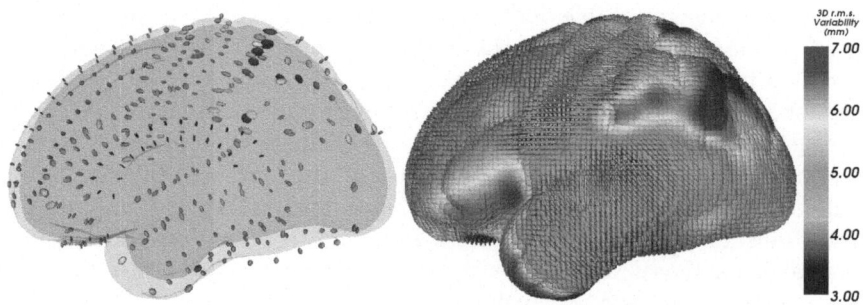

Fig. 4. Variability tensor extrapolation. Left: The 366 tensors retained for our model. Right: Result of the extrapolation. Each point of this average brain shape contains a variability tensor.

of sulcal lines manually delineated in 98 subjects by expert neuroanatomists according to a precise protocol[9]. We used the 72 sulcal curves that consistently appear in all normal subjects (abusively called *sulci* in the sequel).

To find the corresponding points between the 98 instances of each of the 72 sulci, we alternatively computed the matches that minimize the distance between the mean curve and the instances, and re-estimated the mean curve from the updated matches. As a result, we obtain for each point of each mean sulcal curve the set of corresponding anatomical positions in each subject. The number of tensor needed to represent the variability information along each sulcus was then adjusted by picking only a few tensors alors the mean line and linearly interpolating in-between them. The optimal subset of tensors is determined by optimizing the distance between interpolated and measured tensors along the line so that the error does not exceed a prescribed value. In this process, the distance and interpolation between covariance matrices was performed using the affine-invariant metric. Interestingly, selecting only 366 variability tensors was sufficient to encode the variability of the 72 sulci without a significant loss of accuracy. The result is a sparse field of tensors, that can naturally be extrapolated to the whole space using the framework described in Section 4.4 (Fig. 4). This dense map of tensors was shown to be in good agreement with previous published results: the highly specialized and lateralized areas such as the planum parietale and the temporo-parietal areas consistently shows the highest amount of variability. The lowest amount of variability is consistently found in phylogenetically older areas (e.g. orbitofrontal cortex) and primary cortices that myelinate earliest during development (e.g., primary somatosensory and auditory cortex). However, our variability map give more than the amount of variability since we can extract from the tensors the spatial directions where the variability is the greatest at every single anatomical position. We refer the reader to [51,50] for a more detailed explanation of the method and for the neuroscience interpretation of these results.

---

[9] http://www.loni.ucla.edu/~khayashi/Public/medial_surface/

7   Challenges

We have shown in this chapter that the choice of a Riemannian metric and the implementation of a few tools derived from it, namely the Exp and Log maps, provides the bases for building a consistent algorithmic framework to compute on manifolds. In particular, we can compute consistent statistics, perform interpolation, filtering, isotropic and anisotropic regularization and restoration of missing data. Last but not least, powerful computational models of the anatomy could be built thanks to this Riemannian computing framework.

There are however many challenges opened both from the theoretical and application point of views. For instance, the Riemannian approach that we presented here is not perfectly consistent with the structure of Lie groups as soon as they are not compact nor Abelian, which is already the case for rigid body transformations. In that case, there is generally no left and right invariant metric, and most of the operations that we defined (e.g. the mean) with either the left or the right invariant metric are not consistent with inversion. To find an alternative to the Riemannian structure for Lie groups, we investigate with V. Arsigny the idea on relying on one-parameter subgroups instead of geodesics. Preliminary results indicate that this may provide an interesting structure [6,5]. For instance, one can design bi-invariant means that are fully compatible with the group structure [10]. They are define though fixed point equations which are very similar to the Riemannian ones. However, these equations do not derive from a well posed metric. It would be interesting to see what part of the statistical computing framework still holds if we replace the distance by a simple positive or negative energy. This probably amounts to considering the connection as the basic structure of the manifold instead of the Riemannian metric.

Another key problem is to extend our statistical computing framework to infinite dimensional manifolds such as surfaces and diffeomorphism groups. From a theoretical point of view, we known how to provide the diffeomorphism group with left or right invariant Riemannian metrics that are sufficiently smooth to compute the geodesics by optimization [15,101,102,73]. Through the so called EPDiff equation (Euler-Poincarré equation for diffeomorphisms), this optimization framework has been recently rephrased in an exponential/logarithm framework similar to the one developed here [103]. Thus, the basic algorithmic tools are the same, except that optimizing each time to compute the exponential and the logarithm has a deep impact on the computational times. However, one difficulty is that the infinite number of dimensions forbids the use of many tools like the probability density functions! Thus, even if simple statistics like the mean and the principal component analysis of a finite set of samples may still be computed [140,40], one should be very careful about ML-like statistical estimation in these spaces: there is always a finite number of data for an infinite number of parameters. In particular, there are infinitely many left- or right-invariant metrics on diffeomorphisms, and learning the optimal metric is an ill-posed problem. Estimations need to be regularized with prior models or performed within finite dimensional families of metrics whose assumptions are suited for the problem at hand. An interesting track for that is to establish specific models of the Green's function based on the mixture of smoothly varying local and long-distance inter-action convolution kernels. If we only consider the local kernel, the Riemannian elasticity [119,115] could be an interesting family of metrics allowing to measure statistically the properties of the virtual underlying material. Moreover, it was recently shown that such a criterion was consistently separating monozygotic twins from others, which suggest that such deformation-based measures could be anatomically meaningful [90].

Last but not least, surfaces are an important source of anatomical structires in computational anatomy, and one need to design efficient methods and metrics to capture their statistical properties. It would also be useful to fuse the informa-tion coming from image deformations and from surfaces in a single framework. Courants (generalization of distributions) provide consistent mathematical tools for discrete and continuous surfaces [29]. A diffeomorphic registration algorithm of surfaces based on that notion was proposed for instance in [139]. The tools were then drastically improved in [40,39,38] to provide the basis of a compu-tationally efficient statistical computing framework on curves and surfaces. We expect very interesting advances in this direction in the coming years.

From a computational anatomy standpoint, the huge number of degrees of free-dom involved in the estimation of the anatomical variability will require to aggre-gate information coming from many different sources in order to improve the sta-tistical power. As there is no gold standard, we should also be careful that many biases may be hidden in the results. Thus, methods to compare and fuse statistical information coming from many different anatomical features will need to be devel-oped in order to confirm anatomical findings. For the brain variability, one could for instance add to the sulci other cortical landmarks like sulcal ribbons and gyri, the surface of internal structures like the ventricles, the hippocampus or the corpus callosum, or fiber pathways mapped from DTI. These sources of information are individually providing a partial and biased view of the whole variability. Thus, we expect to observe a good agreement in some areas, and complementary measures in other areas. This will most probably lead in a near future to new anatomical findings and more robust medical image analysis applications.

References

1. Allassonnière, S., Trouvé, A., Younes, L.: Geodesic shooting and diffeomorphic matching via textured meshes. In: Rangarajan, A., Vemuri, B.C., Yuille, A.L. (eds.) EMMCVPR 2005. LNCS, vol. 3757, pp. 365–381. Springer, Heidelberg (2005)
2. Amari, S.-i.: Differential-geometric methods in Statistics, 2nd corr. edn. Lecture Notes in Statistics, vol. 28. Springer, Heidelberg (1990)
3. Andrade, A., Kherif, F., Mangin, J.-F., Worsley, K., Paradis, A.-L., Simon, O., Dehaene, S., Poline, J.-B.: Detection of fMRI activation using cortical surface mapping. Human Brain Mapping 12, 79–93 (2001)
4. Arnaudon, M.: Barycentres convexes et approximations des martingales continues dans les variétés. In: Yor, M., Azema, J., Meyer, P.A. (eds.) Séminaire de prob-abilités XXIX. Lect. Notes in Math., vol. 1613, pp. 70–85. Springer, Heidelberg (1995)

5. Arsigny, V., Commowick, O., Pennec, X., Ayache, N.: A log-Euclidean framework for statistics on diffeomorphisms. In: Larsen, R., Nielsen, M., Sporring, J. (eds.) MICCAI 2006. LNCS, vol. 4190, pp. 924–931. Springer, Heidelberg (2006)
6. Arsigny, V., Commowick, O., Pennec, X., Ayache, N.: A log-Euclidean polyaffine framework for locally rigid or affine registration. In: Pluim, J.P.W., Likar, B., Gerritsen, F.A. (eds.) WBIR 2006. LNCS, vol. 4057, pp. 120–127. Springer, Heidelberg (2006)
7. Arsigny, V., Fillard, P., Pennec, X., Ayache, N.: Fast and simple calculus on tensors in the log-Euclidean framework. In: Duncan, J.S., Gerig, G. (eds.) MICCAI 2005. LNCS, vol. 3749, pp. 115–122. Springer, Heidelberg (2005)
8. Arsigny, V., Fillard, P., Pennec, X., Ayache, N.: Geometric means in a novel vector space structure on symmetric positive-definite matrices. SIAM Journal on Matrix Analysis and Applications 29(1), 328–347 (2006)
9. Arsigny, V., Fillard, P., Pennec, X., Ayache, N.: Log-Euclidean metrics for fast and simple calculus on diffusion tensors. Magnetic Resonance in Medicine 56(2), 411–421 (2006)
10. Arsigny, V., Pennec, X., Ayache, N.: Bi-invariant means in lie groups. application to left-invariant polyaffine transformations. Research report rr-5885, INRIA Sophia-Antipolis (April 2006)
11. Ashburner, J., Friston, K.J.: Voxel-based morphometry - the methods. NeuroImage 11(6), 805–821 (2000)
12. Aubert, G., Kornprobst, P.: Mathematical problems in image processing - Partial differential equations and the calculus of variations. Applied Mathematical Sciences, vol. 147. Springer, Heidelberg (2001)
13. Basser, P.J., Mattiello, J., Le Bihan, D.: MR diffusion tensor spectroscopy and imaging. Biophysical Journal 66, 259–267 (1994)
14. Batchelor, P., Moakher, M., Atkinson, D., Calamante, F., Connelly, A.: A rigorous framework for diffusion tensor calculus. Magnetic Resonance in Medicine 53, 221–225 (2005)
15. Beg, M.F., Miller, M.I., Trouvé, A., Younes, L.: Computing large deformation metric mappings via geodesic flows of diffeomorphisms. Int. Journal of Computer Vision 61(2), 139–157 (2005)
16. Bhatia, R.: On the exponential metric increasing property. Linear Algebra and its Applications 375, 211–220 (2003)
17. Bhattacharya, R., Patrangenaru, V.: Nonparametric estimation of location and dispersion on Riemannian manifolds. Journal of Statistical Planning and Inference 108, 23–36 (2002)
18. Bhattacharya, R., Patrangenaru, V.: Large sample theory of intrinsic and extrinsic sample means on manifolds, I. Annals of Statistics 31(1), 1–29 (2003)
19. Bhattacharya, R., Patrangenaru, V.: Large sample theory of intrinsic and extrinsic sample means on manifolds, II. Annals of Statistics 33(3), 1225–1259 (2005)
20. Bierkens, G.N.J.C.: Geometric methods in diffusion tensor regularization. Master's thesis, Technishe Universiteit Eindhoven, Dept. of Math. and Comp. Sci. (2004)
21. Bingham, C.: An antipodally symmetric distribution on the sphere. Annals of Statistics 2(6), 1201–1225 (1974)
22. Bookstein, F.L.: The Measurement of Biological Shape and Shape Change. Lecture Notes in Biomathematics, vol. 24. Springer, Heidelberg (1978)

23. Brox, T., Weickert, J., Burgeth, B., Mrázek, P.: Nonlinear structure tensors. Image and Vision Computing 24(1), 41–55 (2006)
24. Brun, A.: Manifolds in Image Science and Visualization. PhD thesis, Linköping University, Linköping Studies in Science and Technology Dissertions No. 1157 (2007)
25. Burbea, J., Rao, C.R.: Entropy differential metric, distance and divergence measures in probability spaces: a unified approach. Journal of Multivariate Analysis 12, 575–596 (1982)
26. Calvo, M., Oller, J.M.: An explicit solution of information geodesic equations for the multivariate normal model. Statistics and Decisions 9, 119–138 (1991)
27. Chefd'hotel, C., Tschumperlé, D., Deriche, R., Faugeras, O.: Constrained flows of matrix-valued functions: Application to diffusion tensor regularization. In: Heyden, A., Sparr, G., Nielsen, M., Johansen, P. (eds.) ECCV 2002. LNCS, vol. 2350, pp. 251–265. Springer, Heidelberg (2002)
28. Chefd'hotel, C., Tschumperlé, D., Deriche, R., Faugeras, O.: Regularizing flows for constrained matrix-valued images. J. Math. Imaging and Vision 20(1-2), 147–162 (2004)
29. Cohen-Steiner, D., Morvan, J.M.: Restricted delaunay triangulations and normal cycle. In: Proceedings of the nineteenth annual symposium on Computational geometry, pp. 312–321 (2003)
30. Collins, D.L., Zijdenbos, A.P., Kollokian, V., Sled, J.G., Kabani, N.J., Holmes, C.J., Evans, A.C.: Design and construction of a realistic digital brain phantom. IEEE Transactions on Medical Imaging 17(3), 463–468 (1998)
31. Darling, R.W.R.: Martingales on non-compact manifolds: maximal inequalities and prescribed limits. Annales de l'institut Poincaré - Probabilités et Statistiques 32(4), 431–454 (1996)
32. Davis, B., Fletcher, P.T., Bullitt, E., Joshi, S.: Population shape regression from random design data. In: Proc. of ICCV 2007 (2007)
33. Dedieu, J.-P., Malajovich, G., Priouret, P.: Newton method on Riemannian manifolds: Covariant alpha-theory. IMA Journal of Numerical Analysis 23, 395–419 (2003)
34. do Carmo, M.: Riemannian Geometry. Mathematics. Birkhäuser, Boston (1992)
35. Dryden, I.L., Koloydenko, A., Zhou, D.: Non-euclidean statistics for covariance matrices with application to diffusion tensor imaging (submitted, 2008)
36. Dryden, I.L., Mardia, K.V.: Theoretical and distributional aspects of shape analysis. In: Probability Measures on Groups, X (Oberwolfach, 1990), pp. 95–116. Plenum, New York (1991)
37. Dryden, I.L., Mardia, K.V.: Statistical Shape Analysis. John Wiley, Chichester (1998)
38. Durrleman, S., Pennec, X., Trouvé, A., Ayache, N.: A forward model to build unbiased atlases from curves and surfaces. In: Pennec, X., Joshi, S. (eds.) Proc. of the International Workshop on the Mathematical Foundations of Computational Anatomy (MFCA 2008) (September 2008)
39. Durrleman, S., Pennec, X., Trouvé, A., Ayache, N.: Sparse approximation of currents for statistics on curves and surfaces. In: Metaxas, D., Axel, L., Fichtinger, G., Székely, G. (eds.) MICCAI 2008, Part II. LNCS, vol. 5242. Springer, Heidelberg (2008)
40. Durrleman, S., Pennec, X., Trouvé, A., Thompson, P., Ayache, N.: Inferring brain variability from diffeomorphic deformations of currents: an integrative approach. Medical Image Analysis 12(5), 626–637 (2008)

41. Fisher, R.B., Eggert, D.W., Lorusso, A.: Estimating 3d rigid body transformations: A comparison of four major algorithms. Machine Vision Applications, Special Issue on Performance Characterisitics of Vision Algorithms 9(5/6), 272–290 (1997)
42. Edelman, A., Arias, T., Smith, S.T.: The geometry of algorithms with orthogonality constraints. SIAM Journal of Matrix Analysis and Applications 20(2), 303–353 (1998)
43. Emery, M.: Stochastic Calculus in Manifolds. Springer, Berlin (1989)
44. Emery, M., Mokobodzki, G.: Sur le barycentre d'une probabilité dans une variété. In: Yor, M., Azema, J., Meyer, P.A. (eds.) Séminaire de probabilités XXV. Lect. Notes in Math., vol. 1485, pp. 220–233. Springer, Heidelberg (1991)
45. Evans, A.C., Collins, D.L., Mills, S.R., Brown, E.D., Kelly, R.L., Peters, T.M.: 3D statistical neuroanatomical models from 305 MRI volumes. In: Proc. IEEE-Nuclear Science Symposium and Medical Imaging Conference, pp. 1813–1817 (1993)
46. Facon, D., Ozanne, A., Fillard, P., Lepeintre, J.-F., Tournoux-Facon, C., Ducreux, D.: MR diffusion tensor imaging and fiber tracking in spinal cord compression. American Journal of Neuroradiology (AJNR) 26, 1587–1594 (2005)
47. Fillard, P., Arsigny, V., Ayache, N., Pennec, X.: A Riemannian framework for the processing of tensor-valued images. In: Fogh Olsen, O., Florack, L.M.J., Kuijper, A. (eds.) DSSCV 2005. LNCS, vol. 3753, pp. 112–123. Springer, Heidelberg (2005)
48. Fillard, P., Arsigny, V., Pennec, X., Ayache, N.: Clinical DT-MRI estimation, smoothing and fiber tracking with log-Euclidean metrics. In: Proceedings of the IEEE International Symposium on Biomedical Imaging (ISBI 2006), Crystal Gateway Marriott, Arlington, Virginia, USA, pp. 786–789 (April 2006)
49. Fillard, P., Arsigny, V., Pennec, X., Ayache, N.: Clinical DT-MRI estimation, smoothing and fiber tracking with log-Euclidean metrics. IEEE Transactions on Medical Imaging 26(11), 1472–1482 (2007)
50. Fillard, P., Arsigny, V., Pennec, X., Hayashi, K.M., Thompson, P.M., Ayache, N.: Measuring brain variability by extrapolating sparse tensor fields measured on sulcal lines. Neuroimage 34(2), 639–650 (2007)
51. Fillard, P., Arsigny, V., Pennec, X., Thompson, P.M., Ayache, N.: Extrapolation of sparse tensor fields: Application to the modeling of brain variability. In: Christensen, G.E., Sonka, M. (eds.) IPMI 2005. LNCS, vol. 3565, pp. 27–38. Springer, Heidelberg (2005)
52. Fillard, P., Pennec, X., Thompson, P.M., Ayache, N.: Evaluating brain anatomical correlations via canonical correlation analysis of sulcal lines. NeuroImage (accepted for publication, 2008)
53. Fletcher, P.T., Joshi, S. C.: Principal geodesic analysis on symmetric spaces: Statistics of diffusion tensors. In: Sonka, M., Kakadiaris, I.A., Kybic, J. (eds.) CVAMIA/MMBIA 2004. LNCS, vol. 3117, pp. 87–98. Springer, Heidelberg (2004)
54. Fletcher, P.T., Joshi, S., Lu, C., Pizer, S.: Gaussian distributions on Lie groups and their application to statistical shape analysis. In: Taylor, C.J., Noble, J.A. (eds.) IPMI 2003. LNCS, vol. 2732, pp. 450–462. Springer, Heidelberg (2003)
55. Fleute, M., Lavallée, S.: Building a complete surface model from sparse data using statistical shape models: Application to computer assisted knee surgery. In: Wells, W.M., Colchester, A.C.F., Delp, S.L. (eds.) MICCAI 1998. LNCS, vol. 1496, pp. 879–887. Springer, Heidelberg (1998)

56. Förstner, W., Moonen, B.: A metric for covariance matrices. In: Krumm, F., Schwarze, V.S. (eds.). Qua vadis geodesia..? Festschrift for Erik W. Grafarend on the occasion of his 60th birthday, number 1999.6 in Tech. Report of the Dpt of Geodesy and Geoinformatics, pp. 113–128. Stuttgart University (1999)

57. Fréchet, M.: L'intégrale abstraite d'une fonction abstraite d'une variable abstraite et son application à la moyenne d'un élément aléatoire de nature quelconque. Revue Scientifique, pp. 483–512 (1944)

58. Fréchet, M.: Les éléments aléatoires de nature quelconque dans un espace distancié. Annales de l'Institut Henri Poincaré 10, 215–310 (1948)

59. Gallot, S., Hulin, D., Lafontaine, J.: Riemannian Geometry, 2nd edn. Springer, Heidelberg (1993)

60. Gamkrelidze, R.V. (ed.): Geometry I. Encyclopaedia of Mathematical Sciences, vol. 28. Springer, Heidelberg (1991)

61. Gerig, G., Kikinis, R., Kübler, O., Jolesz, F.A.: Nonlinear anisotropic filtering of MRI data. IEEE Transactions on Medical Imaging 11(2), 221–232 (1992)

62. Gramkow, C.: On averaging rotations. International Journal of Computer Vision 42(1-2), 7–16 (2001)

63. Granger, S., Pennec, X.: Statistiques exactes et approchées sur les normales aléatoires. Research report RR-4533, INRIA (2002)

64. Grenander, U.: Probabilities on Algebraic Structures. Wiley, Chichester (1963)

65. Grenander, U., Miller, M.I., Srivastava, A.: Hilbert-schmidt lower bounds for estimators on matrix Lie groups for ATR. IEEE Transations on Pattern Analysis and Machine Intelligence (PAMI) 20(8), 790–802 (1998)

66. Grigor'yan, A.: Heat kernels on weighted manifolds and applications. In: Jorgenson, J., Walling, L. (eds.) The Ubiquitous Heat Kernel. Contemporary Mathematics, vol. 398, pp. 91–190. AMS (2006)

67. Hairer, E., Lubich, C., Wanner, G.: Geometric numerical integration: structure preserving algorithm for ordinary differential equations. Springer series in computational mathematics, vol. 31. Springer, Heidelberg (2002)

68. Helgason, S.: Differential Geometry, Lie groups, and Symmetric Spaces. Academic Press, London (1978)

69. Helmke, U., Moore, J.B.: Optimization and Dynamical Systems. Communication and Control Engineering Series. Springer, Heidelberg (1994)

70. Hendricks, H.: A Cramer-Rao type lower bound for estimators with values in a manifold. Journal of Multivariate Analysis 38, 245–261 (1991)

71. Huber, P.: Robust Statistics. John Wiley, New York (1981)

72. Amari, S.-i., Nagaoka, H.: Methods of Information Geometry. Translations of Mathematical Monographs. American Mathematical Society (2000)

73. Joshi, S.C., Miller, M.I.: Landmark matching via large deformation diffeomorphisms. IEEE Trans. Image Processing 9(8), 1357–1370 (2000)

74. Jupp, P.E., Mardia, K.V.: A unified view of the theory of directional statistics, 1975-1988. International Statistical Review 57(3), 261–294 (1989)

75. Karcher, H.: Riemannian center of mass and mollifier smoothing. Communications in Pure and Applied Mathematics 30, 509–541 (1977)

76. Kass, R.E., Vos, P.W.: Geometric Foundations of Asymptotic Inference. Wiley series in Probability and Statistics. John Wiley & Sons, Chichester (1997)

77. Kaya, C.Y., Noakes, J.L.: Geodesics and an optimal control algorithm. In: Proceedings of the 36th IEEE Conference on Decision and Control, San Diego, CA, U.S.A, pp. 4918–4919 (1997)

78. Kendall, D.G.: A survey of the statistical theory of shape (with discussion). Statistical Science 4, 87–120 (1989)

79. Kendall, M.G., Moran, P.A.P.: Geometrical probability. Griffin's statistical monographs and courses, vol. 10. Charles Griffin & Co. Ltd. (1963)

80. Kendall, W.S.: Probability, convexity, and harmonic maps with small image I: uniqueness and fine existence. Proc. London Math. Soc. 61(2), 371–406 (1990)

81. Kendall, W.S.: Convexity and the hemisphere. Journal of the London Mathematical Society 43(2), 567–576 (1991)

82. Kent, J.T.: The art of Statistical Science. In: Mardia, K.V. (ed.) New Directions in Shape Analysis, ch. 10, pp. 115–127. John Wiley & Sons, Chichester (1992)

83. Klassen, E., Srivastava, A., Mio, W., Joshi, S.: Analysis of planar shapes using geodesic path on shape spaces. IEEE Trans. on PAMI 26(3), 372–383 (2004)

84. Klingenberg, W.: Riemannian Geometry. Walter de Gruyter, Berlin (1982)

85. Kobayashi, S., Nomizu, K.: Foundations of differential geometry. Interscience tracts in pure and applied mathematics, vol. 15. John Wiley & Sons, Chichester (1969)

86. Le, H., Kendall, D.G.: The Riemannian structure of Euclidean shape space: a novel environment for statistics. Annals of Statistics 21, 1225–1271 (1993)

87. Le Bihan, D., Mangin, J.-F., Poupon, C., Clark, C.A., Pappata, S., Molko, N., Chabriat, H.: Diffusion tensor imaging: Concepts and applications. Journal Magnetic Resonance Imaging 13(4), 534–546 (2001)

88. Le Goualher, G., Procyk, E., Collins, D., Venugopal, R., Barillot, C., Evans, A.: Automated extraction and variability analysis of sulcal neuroanatomy. IEEE Transactions on Medical Imaging 18(3), 206–217 (1999)

89. Lenglet, C., Rousson, M., Deriche, R., Faugeras, O.: Statistics on the manifold of multivariate normal distributions: Theory and application to diffusion tensor MRI processing. Journal of Mathematical Imaging and Vision 25(3), 423–444 (2006)

90. Lepore, N., Brun, C., Chou, Y.-Y., Lee, A.D., Barysheva, M., Pennec, X., McMahon, K., Meredith, M., de Zubicaray, G.I., Wright, M.J., Toga, A.W., Thompson, P.M.: Best individual template selection from deformation tensor minimization. In: Proc. of the 2008 IEEE Int. Symp. on Biomedical Imaging: From Nano to Macro (ISBI 2008), Paris, France, May 14-17, pp. 460–463 (2008)

91. Lovrić, M., Min-Oo, M.: Multivariate normal distributions parametrized as a Riemannian symmetric space. Journal of Multivariate Analysis 74(1), 36–48 (2000)

92. Mahony, R., Manton, R.: The geometry of the Newton method on non-compact Lie groups. Journal of Global Optimization 23, 309–327 (2002)

93. Mangin, J.-F., Riviere, D., Cachia, A., Duchesnay, E., Cointepas, Y., Papadopoulos-Orfanos, D., Collins, D.L., Evans, A.C., Régis, J.: Object-based morphometry of the cerebral cortex. IEEE Transactions on Medical Imaging 23(8), 968–982 (2004)

94. Mangin, J.-F., Rivière, D., Cachia, A., Duchesnay, E., Cointepas, Y., Papadopoulos-Orfanos, D., Scifo, P., Ochiai, T., Brunelle, F., Régis, J.: A framework to study the cortical folding patterns. NeuroImage 23(suppl. 1), 129 (2004)

95. Mardia, K.V.: Directional statistics and shape analysis. Journal of applied Statistics 26, 949–957 (1999)

96. Mardia, K.V., Jupp, P.E.: Directional statistics. Wiley, Chichester (2000)

97. Mazziotta, J., et al.: A probabilistic atlas and reference system for the human brain: International consortium for brain mapping (ICBM). Philos. Trans. R Soc. Lond B Biol. Sci. 356, 1293–1322 (2001)

98. Medioni, G., Lee, M.-S., Tang, C.-K.: A Computational Framework for Segmentation and Grouping. Elsevier, Amsterdam (2000)

99. Meijering, E.: A chronology of interpolation: From ancient astronomy to modern signal and image processing. Proceedings of the IEEE 90(3), 319–342 (2002)

100. Michor, P.W., Mumford, D.: Riemannian geometries on spaces of plane curves. J. Eur. Math. Soc (JEMS) 8, 1–48 (2006)
101. Miller, M.I., Trouvé, A., Younes, L.: On the metrics and Euler-Lagrange equations of computational anatomy. Annual Re-view of Biomedical Engineering, 375–405 (2003)
102. Miller, M.I., Younes, L.: Group actions, homeomorphisms, and matching: A general framework. International Journal of Computer Vision 41(1/2), 61–84 (2001)
103. Miller, M.I., Trouvé, A., Younes, L.: Geodesic shooting for computational anatomy. Journal of Mathematical Imaging and Vision (2006)
104. Moakher, M.: Means and averaging in the group of rotations. SIAM Journal of Matrix Analysis and Applications 24(1), 1–16 (2002)
105. Moakher, M.: A differential geometric approach to the geometric mean of symmetric positive-definite matrices. SIAM Journal of Matrix Analysis and Applications 26(3), 735–747 (2005)
106. Mohammadi, B., Borouchaki, H., George, P.L.: Delaunay mesh generation governed by metric specifications. Part II: applications. Finite Elements in Analysis and Design, 85–109 (1997)
107. Moran, B., Suvorova, S., Howard, S.: Sensor management for radar: a tutorial. In: Advances in Sensing with Security Applications, Il Ciocco, Italy, July 17–30. NATO Advanced Study Institute (2005)
108. Nomizu, K.: Invariant affine connections on homogeneous spaces. American J. of Math. 76, 33–65 (1954)
109. Oller, J.M., Corcuera, J.M.: Intrinsic analysis of statistical estimation. Annals of Statistics 23(5), 1562–1581 (1995)
110. Owren, B., Welfert, B.: The Newton iteration on Lie groups. BIT Numerical Mathematics 40(1), 121–145 (2000)
111. Pennec, X.: L'incertitude dans les problèmes de reconnaissance et de recalage – Applications en imagerie médicale et biologie moléculaire. Thèse de sciences (Ph.D. thesis), Ecole Polytechnique, Palaiseau (France) (December 1996)
112. Pennec, X.: Computing the mean of geometric features - application to the mean rotation. Research Report RR-3371, INRIA (March 1998)
113. Pennec, X.: Probabilities and statistics on Riemannian manifolds: Basic tools for geometric measurements. In: Cetin, A.E., Akarun, L., Ertuzun, A., Gurcan, M.N., Yardimci, Y. (eds.) Proc. of Nonlinear Signal and Image Processing (NSIP 1999), Antalya, Turkey, June 20-23, vol. 1, pp. 194–198. IEEE-EURASIP (1999)
114. Pennec, X.: Intrinsic statistics on Riemannian manifolds: Basic tools for geometric measurements. Journal of Mathematical Imaging and Vision 25(1), 127–154 (2006); a preliminary appeared as INRIA RR-5093 (January 2004)
115. Pennec, X.: Left-invariant Riemannian elasticity: a distance on shape diffeomorphisms? In: Pennec, X., Joshi, S. (eds.) Proc. of the International Workshop on the Mathematical Foundations of Computational Anatomy (MFCA 2006), pp. 1–13 (2006)
116. Pennec, X.: Statistical Computing on Manifolds for Computational Anatomy. Habilitation à diriger des recherches, Université Nice Sophia-Antipolis (December 2006)
117. Pennec, X., Fillard, P., Ayache, N.: A Riemannian framework for tensor computing. International Journal of Computer Vision 66(1), 41–66 (2006); a preliminary version appeared as INRIA Research Report 5255 (July 2004)

118. Pennec, X., Guttmann, C.R.G., Thirion, J.-P.: Feature-based registration of medical images: Estimation and validation of the pose accuracy. In: Wells, W.M., Colchester, A.C.F., Delp, S.L. (eds.) MICCAI 1998. LNCS, vol. 1496, pp. 1107–1114. Springer, Heidelberg (1998)

119. Pennec, X., Stefanescu, R., Arsigny, V., Fillard, P., Ayache, N.: Riemannian elasticity: A statistical regularization framework for non-linear registration. In: Duncan, J.S., Gerig, G. (eds.) MICCAI 2005. LNCS, vol. 3750, pp. 943–950. Springer, Heidelberg (2005)

120. Pennec, X., Thirion, J.-P.: A framework for uncertainty and validation of 3D registration methods based on points and frames. Int. Journal of Computer Vision 25(3), 203–229 (1997)

121. Perona, P., Malik, J.: Scale-space and edge detection using anisotropic diffusion. IEEE Trans. Pattern Analysis and Machine Intelligence (PAMI) 12(7), 629–639 (1990)

122. Picard, J.: Barycentres et martingales sur une variété. Annales de l'institut Poincaré - Probabilités et Statistiques 30(4), 647–702 (1994)

123. Poincaré, H.: Calcul des probabilités, 2nd edn., Paris (1912)

124. Provenzale, J.M., Mukundan, S., Barboriak, D.P.: Diffusion-weighted and perfusion MR imaging for brain tumor characterization and assessment of treatment response. Radiology 239(3), 632–649 (2006)

125. Rajamani, K.T., Joshi, S.C., Styner, M.A.: Bone model morphing for enhanced surgical visualization. In: IEEE (ed.) Proc. of IEEE Symp. on Biomedical Imaging: Nano to Macro (ISBI) 2004, vol. 2, pp. 1255–1258 (2004)

126. Rousseeuw, P.J., Leroy, A.M.: Robust Regression and Outliers Detection. Wiley series in prob. and math. stat. J. Wiley and Sons, Chichester (1987)

127. Rovaris, M., Gass, A., Bammer, R., Hickman, S.J., Ciccarelli, O., Miller, D.H., Filippi, M.: Diffusion MRI in multiple sclerosis. Neurology 65, 1526–1532 (2005)

128. Sijbers, J., den Dekker, A.J., Scheunders, P., Van Dyck, D.: Maximum likelihood estimation of Rician distribution parameters. TMI 17(3) (June 1998)

129. Skovgaard, L.T.: A Riemannian geometry of the multivariate normal model. Scand. J. Statistics 11, 211–223 (1984)

130. Small, C.G.: The Statistical Theory of Shapes. Springer series in statistics. Springer, Heidelberg (1996)

131. Spivak, M.: Differential Geometry, 2nd edn., vol. 1. Publish or Perish, Inc. (1979)

132. Subsol, G., Thirion, J.-P., Ayache, N.: A scheme for automatically building 3D morphometric anatomical atlases: application to a skull atlas. Medical Image Analysis 2(1), 37–60 (1998)

133. Talairach, J., Tournoux, P.: Co-Planar Stereotaxic Atlas of the Human Brain: 3-dimensional Proportional System: an Approach to Cerebral Imaging. Thieme Medical Publishers, New York (1988)

134. Thévenaz, P., Blu, T., Unser, M.: Interpolation revisited. IEEE Transactions on Medical Imaging 19(7), 739–758 (2000)

135. Thompson, P.M., MacDonald, D., Mega, M.S., Holmes, C.J., Evans, A.C., Toga, A.W.: Detection and mapping of abnormal brain structure with a probabilistic atlas of cortical surfaces. Journal of Computer Assisted Tomography 21(4), 567–581 (1977)

136. Thompson, P.M., Mega, M.S., Woods, R.P., Zoumalan, C.I., Lindshield, C.J., Blanton, R.E., Moussai, J., Holmes, C.J., Cummings, J.L., Toga, A.W.: Cortical change in alzheimer's disease detected with a disease-specific population-based brain atlas. Cerebral Cortex 11(1), 1–16 (2001)

137. Trouvé, A.: Diffeomorphisms groups and pattern matching in image analysis. International Journal of Computer Vision 28(3), 213–221 (1998)
138. Tschumperlé, D.: PDE-Based Regularization of Multivalued Images and Applications. PhD thesis, University of Nice-Sophia Antipolis (December 2002)
139. Vaillant, M., Glaunès, J.: Surface matching via currents. In: Christensen, G.E., Sonka, M. (eds.) IPMI 2005. LNCS, vol. 3565, pp. 381–392. Springer, Heidelberg (2005)
140. Vaillant, M., Miller, M.I., Younes, L., Trouvé, A.: Statistics on diffeomorphisms via tangent space representations. NeuroImage 23(supp. 1), S161–S169 (2004)
141. Vaillant, M., Qiu, A., Glaunès, J., Miller, M.: Diffeomorphic metric surface mapping in subregion of the superior temporal gyrus. NeuroImage 34(3), 1149–1159 (2007)
142. Wang, Z., Vemuri, B.C.: DTI segmentation using an information theoretic tensor dissimilarity measure. IEEE Trans. on Medical Imaging 24(10), 1267–1277 (2005)
143. Wang, Z., Vemuri, B.C., Chen, Y., Mareci, T.: A constrained variational principle for direct estimation and smoothing of the diffusion tensor field from complex DWI. IEEE Trans. on Medical Imaging (2004)
144. Weickert, J., Brox, T.: Diffusion and regularization of vector- and matrix-valued images. In: Nashed, M.Z., Scherzer, O. (eds.) Inverse Problems, Image Analysis, and Medical Imaging, Providence. Contemporary Mathematics, vol. 313, pp. 251–268. AMS (2002)
145. Weickert, J., Hagen, H. (eds.): Visualization and Processing of Tensor Fields. Mathematics and Visualization. Springer, Heidelberg (2006)
146. Westin, C.F., Maier, S.E., Mamata, H., Nabavi, A., Jolesz, F.A., Kikinis, R.: Processing and visualization for diffusion tensor MRI. Medical Image Analysis 6(2), 93–108 (2002)
147. Younes, L.: Computable elastic distances between shapes. SIAM Journal on Applied Mathematics 58(2), 565–586 (1998)

Author Index